To discover something about the limits
and potentialities of human nature,
to see how this universal nature
is molded by varying cultures,
and especially to learn something
about those nonrational cultural responses
which appear to the naïve view
to possess almost the automatic character
of "instinctive" reactions—
this is no mere academic query.
The fate of our Western civilization
and perhaps of civilization in general
may hang upon humanity's gaining some orderly
and systematic insight into the nonrational
and irrational factors in human behavior.

Clyde Kluckhohn

GENERAL EDITOR

Thomas Weaver UNIVERSITY OF ARIZONA

SECTION EDITORS

Gerald D. Berreman University of California at Berkeley
THE SOCIAL RESPONSIBILITY OF THE ANTHROPOLOGIST
ANTHROPOLOGY AND THE THIRD WORLD

Arthur J. Rubel University of Notre Dame
THE MYTH OF THE MELTING POT

Harriet J. Kupferer University of North Carolina
THE MYTH OF THE MELTING POT

Hermann K. Bleibtreu University of Arizona
RACE AND RACISM

John Meaney University of Arizona
RACE AND RACISM

Seymour Parker University of Utah
POVERTY AND CULTURE

John Singleton University of Pittsburgh
SCHOOLING: COPING WITH EDUCATION IN A MODERN SOCIETY

Bernard J. Siegel Stanford University
VIOLENCE

Michael H. Crawford University of Kansas
OUR TROUBLED ENVIRONMENT

Art Gallaher, Jr. University of Kentucky
INTERVENTION: CHANGING THE SYSTEM

To See Ourselves

Anthropology
and Modern
Social Issues

SCOTT, FORESMAN AND COMPANY GLENVIEW, ILLINOIS LONDON

To George Vlach

Acknowledgments

The idea behind this book originated in discussions with George Vlach, Program Director in charge of the Social Sciences at Scott, Foresman. Always a gentleman and a diplomat, he gave freely of his publishing experience in encouraging us in the preparation of this book. He has been an inspiration, and we have learned a great deal from him. To the measure we invested our affection and friendship in George, we have been diminished by his death. This book is dedicated to his memory.

Others have helped prepare this book. First, of course, we must thank the various section editors for their cooperation, expertise, and patience. We are also grateful for the expert help of two editors from Scott, Foresman, Isabel Grossner and Sybil Sosin. Secretarial assistance, without which we would have been helpless, was provided by Cynthia Murrieta, Billie Brewer, and Beverly Modory of the Bureau of Ethnic Research at the University of Arizona. Finally, we would like to thank Brenn Lea Pearson, Lucille Lesiak, and Sandra Ann Smith of Scott, Foresman, who worked behind the scenes to produce this book.

We wish to thank the authors and publishers who gave us permission to use their material in this book.

Picture Credits

Cover and section-opening photos courtesy of Jerry N. Uelsmann.

Page 322: The Bettmann Archive (top); The Bettmann Archive (middle); Lee Lockwood/Black Star (bottom).

Sources for Introductory Quotes

Half-title: Clyde Kluckhohn, "Common Humanity and Diverse Cultures," in *The Meaning of the Social Sciences*, Daniel Lerner, ed. (New York: Meridian Books, 1959), pp. 280–281.

Toward an Anthropological Statement of Relevance: R. D. Laing, *The Politics of Experience* (New York: Ballantine Books, 1967), pp. 189–190, 61–62.

The Social Responsibility of the Anthropologist: Robert Redfield, *The Primitive World and Its Transformations* (Ithaca, N.Y.: Cornell University Press, 1953), p. 141; Ernest Becker, *The Lost Science of Man* (New York: George Braziller, Inc., 1971), p. xi; Alvin Gouldner, "Anti-Minotaur: The Myth of a Value-Free Sociology," in *The New Sociology*, I. Horowitz, ed. (New York: Oxford University Press, 1964), p. 216.

The Myth of the Melting Pot: Franz Boas, *Race, Language and Culture* (New York: The Macmillan Company 1940), p. 17; Ruth Benedict, *An Anthropologist at Work*, Margaret Mead, ed. (Boston: Houghton Mifflin Company, 1959), p. 360; Ad Hoc Committee to Evaluate the Controversy Concerning Anthropological Activities in Relation to Thailand, "Report to the Executive Board of the American Anthropological Association," September 27, 1971.

Anthropology and the Third World: Fred G. Burke, "The Meaning of Montreal," *Africa Today* 16 (October–December 1969): 8; Jean-Paul Sartre, "Preface to *The Wretched of the Earth*" by Frantz Fanon (New York: Grove Press, Inc., 1966), p. 12; Claude Lévi-Strauss, "How I Became an Anthropologist," in *Tristes Tropiques* (New York: Atheneum Publishers, 1964), p. 64.

Race and Racism: George A. Dorsey, "Race and Civilization," in *Whither Mankind: A Panorama of Modern Civilization*, Charles A. Beard, ed. (New York: Longmans, Green and Company, 1928), p. 254; Paul R. Ehrlich and Richard W. Holm, "A Biological View of Race," in *The Concept of Race*, Ashley Montagu, ed. (New York: The Free Press, 1964), p. 175;

Eugene Rabinowitch, "Jensen vs. Lewontin: A Comment," *Bulletin of the Atomic Scientists* 26 (May 1970): 25.

Poverty and Culture: Herbert J. Gans, "Culture and Class in the Study of Poverty: An Approach to Anti-Poverty Research," in *On Understanding Poverty*, Daniel Moynihan, ed. (New York: Basic Books, Inc., 1968), p. 205; Hylan Lewis, "Culture, Class and the Behavior of Low-Income Families," in *Culture, Class and Poverty* (Washington, D.C.: Cross-Tell, 1967), pp. 38–39; Lee Rainwater, *Behind Ghetto Walls* (Chicago: Aldine Publishing Company, 1967), p. 403.

Schooling: Coping with Education in a Modern Society: Margaret Mead, "Our Educational Emphases in Primitive Perspective," *American Journal of Sociology* 48 (May 1943): 634; Albert Einstein, *The World as I See It* (New York: The Philosophical Library, 1949), p. 22.

Violence: Margaret Mead, ed., *Cultural Patterns and Technological Change* (New York: The New American Library Inc., 1955), preface.

Our Troubled Environment: Richard M. Nixon, "State of the Union Message," *Time*, February 2, 1970, p. 56; René Dumont and Bernard Rosier, *The Hungry Future*, trans. Rosamund Linell and R. B. Sutcliffe (New York: Praeger Publishers, Inc., 1969), p. 73; La Monte Cole, "Paul Revere of Ecology," *Time*, February 2, 1970, p. 59.

Intervention: Changing the System: Robert Oppenheimer, "Prospects in the Arts and Sciences," *Perspectives USA* 11 (Spring 1955): 10–11.

Contents

Toward an Anthropological Statement of
Relevance   1
Thomas Weaver

**1 THE SOCIAL RESPONSIBILITY OF
THE ANTHROPOLOGIST   5**

The Social Responsibility of the
Anthropologist   8
Gerald D. Berreman

On Politics   10
C. Wright Mills

On Ethics and Anthropology   19
Joseph G. Jorgensen

Adventures in Culture Change   26
Allan R. Holmberg

Appendix to the Preface of 1944   31
Cora Du Bois

Human Life vs. Science   32
Donald K. Grayson

A Case for Intervention in the Field   33
Bernard Gallin

Freedom and Responsibility in Research:
The "Springdale" Case   39
William Foote Whyte

"Freedom and Responsibility in Research":
Comments   42
Arthur Vidich and Joseph Bensman

Resolutions   43
*Executive Board of the American
Anthropological Association*

Principles of Professional Responsibility   46
American Anthropological Association

Ethics Report Criticized   49
Anthony Leeds

Resolution Issues   50
Stephen P. Dunn

Scientists as Spies   51
Franz Boas

Council Meeting, December 30, 4:45 P.M.   52
American Anthropological Association

Letter to the Student Mobilization
Committee   53
Eric R. Wolf and Joseph Jorgensen

Statement   54
*Executive Board of the American
Anthropological Association*

Letter to the Executive Board   54
*Committee on Ethics of the American
Anthropological Association*

The Need to Popularize Basic Concepts   55
Omer C. Stewart

Contemporary Anthropology and Moral
Accountability   58
Gerald D. Berreman

**2 THE MYTH OF THE MELTING
POT   63**

The Myth of the Melting Pot   66
Arthur J. Rubel and Harriet J. Kupferer

The Doctrine of the Ghost Dance   68
James Mooney

Psychodynamic Inventory of the Negro
Personality   76
Abram Kardiner and Lionel Ovesey

History and Current Status of the Houma
Indians   84
Ann Fischer

The Pecan Shellers' Strike in San Antonio   91
Harold Arthur Shapiro

The Alianza Movement: Catalyst for Social
Change in New Mexico   96
Frances L. Swadesh

The Consequences of a Myth   103
Harriet J. Kupferer and Arthur J. Rubel

3 ANTHROPOLOGY AND THE THIRD WORLD 109

Anthropology and the Third World 112
Gerald D. Berreman

Functionalism, Realpolitik, and Anthropology in Underdeveloped Areas 113
Robert A. Manners

Conservative Thought in Applied Anthropology: A Critique 126
Guillermo Bonfil Batalla

Custer Died for Your Sins 130
Vine Deloria, Jr.

The Life and Death of Project Camelot 138
Irving Louis Horowitz

The Established Order: Do Not Fold, Spindle, or Mutilate 148
Marshall Sahlins

Academic Colonialism: Not So Innocent Abroad 152
Gerald D. Berreman

World Revolution and the Science of Man 156
Kathleen Gough

No Longer at Ease: Confrontation at the 12th Annual African Studies Association Metting at Montreal 165
Herchelle Sullivan Challenor

The Montreal Affair: Revolution or Racism 171
Pierre L. van den Berghe

Africa, America, and the Africanists 173
Immanuel Wallerstein

The Problem 174
Satish Saberwall

Anthropology and Moral Accountability 178
Gerald D. Berreman

4 RACE AND RACISM 181

Race and Racism 184
Hermann K. Bleibtreu and John Meaney

Racial Differences in Behavior 188
James N. Spuhler and Gardner Lindzey

The Concept of Race and the Taxonomy of Mankind 192
Jean Hiernaux

The Multiple Bases of Human Adaptability and Achievement: A Species Point of View 199
Benson E. Ginsburg and William S. Laughlin

Behavior-Genetic Analysis and Its Biosocial Consequences 209
Jerry Hirsch

A Tract for the Times: Some Sociobiological Aspects of Science, Race, and Racism 218
Benjamin Pasamanick

Racial Differences in Behavior: Cultural and Evolutionary Considerations 224
Hermann K. Bleibtreu and John Meaney

5 POVERTY AND CULTURE 229

Poverty and Culture 232
Seymour Parker

The Culture of Poverty 234
Oscar Lewis

Men and Jobs 240
Elliot Liebow

Social-Psychological Dimensions of Ojibwa Acculturation 245
Bernard J. James

The Culture of Poverty: An Adjustive Dimension 253
Seymour Parker and Robert J. Kleiner

Another Look at Lower-Class Black Culture 260
Ulf Hannerz

Culture and Class in the Study of Poverty: An Approach to Anti-Poverty Research 265
Herbert J. Gans

Poverty: An Altering View 271
Seymour Parker

6 SCHOOLING: COPING WITH EDUCATION IN A MODERN SOCIETY 275

Schooling: Coping with Education in a Modern Society 278
John Singleton

The School as a Small Society 280
Bud B. Khleif

Ceremony, Rites, and Economy in the Student System of an American High School 285
Jacquetta Hill Burnett

White Rites versus Indian Rights 290
A. D. Fisher

The Enemies of the People 294
Rosalie H. Wax and Murray L. Wax

Early Childhood Intervention: The Social Science Base of Institutional Racism 299
Stephen S. Baratz and Joan C. Baratz

Studying Education in the Ghetto 310
Carol Talbert

The Role of Village Schools in the Process of Cultural and Economic Modernization 315
Manning Nash

The Futility of Schooling in Latin America 320
Ivan Illich

The Educational Uses of Anthropology 326
John Singleton

7 VIOLENCE 331

Violence 334
Bernard J. Siegel

Gusii Sex Offenses: A Study in Social Control 336
Robert A. LeVine

Death as a Way of Life: The Increasing Resort to Homicide in a Maya Indian Community 346
June Nash

Cleavage and Internal Conflict: An Example from India 355
Alan R. Beals

The Game of Black and White at Hunters Point 361
Arthur E. Hippler

Conflict and Society 370
Asen Balikci

Violence and Social Change 379
Bernard J. Siegel

8 OUR TROUBLED ENVIRONMENT 383

Our Troubled Environment 386
Michael H. Crawford

The End 389
Isaac Asimov

Crowding 395
Estie Stoll

The Experience of Living in Cities 400
Stanley Milgram

The Causes of Pollution 407
Barry Commoner, Michael Corr, and Paul J. Stamler

Lessons from a "Primitive" People 416
James V. Neel

The Genetic Implications of Population Control 423
Carl Jay Bajema

Some Environmental Problems for Physical Anthropologists 429
Michael H. Crawford

9 INTERVENTION: CHANGING THE SYSTEM 433

Intervention: Changing the System 436
Art Gallaher, Jr.

The Strategy of the Fox Project 438
Fred Gearing

Human Problems of U.S. Enterprise in Latin America 442
William F. Whyte and Allan R. Holmberg

Strategies and Tactics of Planned Organizational Change: Case Examples on the Modernization Process of Traditional Societies 450
Garth N. Jones

Steel Axes for Stone-Age Australians 459
Lauriston Sharp

The Research and Development Approach to the Study of Change 464
Allan R. Holmberg

Revitalization Processes 470
Anthony F. C. Wallace

On Changing the System 475
Art Gallaher, Jr.

Index 479

To See Ourselves: Anthropology and Modern Social Issues

Garden.
Cat at bird.
Shoo off nasty cat, and catch bird.
How elusive she is,
and I am turning into a cat myself.
Stop.
Cat is a cat
is a bird is a nonbird
of ineffably frail space suddenly spreading
in parabolic grace of authority.
How foolish to worry, to try to save her.
Perhaps the cat was trying to save her.
Let be.
Cat and bird.
Begriff.
The truth I am trying to grasp
is the grasp that is trying to grasp it. . . .

If I could turn you on,
if I could drive you out of your wretched mind,
if I could tell you
I would let you know.

R. D. Laing

The theoretical and descriptive idiom
of much research in social science
adopts a stance of apparent "objective" neutrality.
But we have seen
how deceptive this can be.
The choice of syntax and vocabulary
is a political act
that defines and circumscribes the manner
in which "facts" are to be experienced.
Indeed, in a sense
it goes further
and even creates the facts that are studied.

The "data" (given) of research
are not so much given
as taken
out of a constantly elusive matrix of happenings.
We should speak of capta
rather than data.
The quantitatively interchangeable grist
that goes into the mills
of reliability studies and rating scales
is the expression
of a processing that we do on reality,
not the expression
of the processes of reality.

R. D. Laing

Thomas Weaver

Toward an Anthropological Statement of Relevance

In recent years, the social and ethical standards of various American institutions have been called into question. Americans in general, and students in particular, have been demanding answers to a variety of questions regarding our society and the relation of various institutions to the people with whom they deal. Among other things, they have pointed out the disparity between action and statement in the behavioral sciences. What, they want to know, have anthropologists been doing for a hundred years?

It is common knowledge that anthropologists have developed general ideas about the operations of societies and the integration of various facets of society, and have provided descriptions of the ways of life of peoples in faraway lands. But students want to know how this knowledge relates to the poverty, injustice, and inequality they see all around them. Hence, our purpose in compiling this reader is to discuss the contributions of anthropology to contemporary social issues. Anthropology is not relevant simply because it holds up a "mirror for man," thus forcing him to solve his own problems by looking at the problems of people in other societies. Instead, anthropology can and should address itself to the questions being raised by young people. Furthermore, anthropology does not present itself as *the* solution to these problems, nor as an infallible authority. Instead, it is one potential contribution toward achieving an intermediate working solution.

How the Anthropologist Thinks

Looking at social problems is a unique activity for the academically based and theoretically oriented discipline of anthropology. Except on rare occasions, this discipline has not been directly or primarily concerned with social problems or social issues. Most anthropologists believe that the behavioral sciences—especially anthropology—have not acquired the level of knowledge, the data, or the theoretical framework necessary to identify precise societal or cultural mechanisms, and thus cannot be used to predict the outcomes of social policies. For this reason, most anthropologists have not become directly involved in changing societies.

The subspecialty of anthropology that comes closest to involvement in social change is applied anthropology. But applied anthropologists, too, have been reticent agents of change. They provide "basic research" for use by agents of change and do not control the uses to which their data and conclusions are put. Their commitment to basic research and to a value-free approach—in other words, to "pure" science—has led them to feel that they do not know or cannot identify the precise button to press in order to get an appropriate cultural response.

That the distinction made by anthropologists between pure and applied science is a spurious one has been clearly pointed out by William Bevan:

To be preoccupied with the primacy of pure, as contrasted to applied, science is to reify a specious distinction, for science is, in its most fundamental sense, only an approach to solving problems—an approach based on logic tempered by experience— and its goals may be both specific and general, concrete and abstract, practical and theoretical, and immediate and long-range. Indeed, history has taught that fundamental knowledge often emerges in the course of attempting to solve practical problems.[1]

Furthermore, in recent years, activist anthropologists have pointed out that others do not have this so-called requisite knowledge either. Social-welfare workers, politicians, architects, community-development experts, teachers, lawyers, economists, community psychiatrists, vocational-rehabilitation counselors, and others have been busy "running the system" and, in the process, making decisions that have long-range effects on peoples and cultures. If anthropologists lack specific knowledge, so do these other people; and the special "nonrelevant" expertise and background acquired by the academic anthropologist should not disqualify him from becoming involved in political procedures that affect the lives of himself, his family, and his fellow citizens.

The major problem in considering anthropology a "pure" science is brought out in a report in *Science*,[2] which lauded Japan's great economic progress, citing U.S. Department of Commerce figures comparing the growth rates of advanced nations in five industries. Although there were many other factors involved, research and development have played an important part in this advance. Unlike the United States and other Western countries, Japan invests very little in "basic" research; instead, its scientists focus on narrow, practical problems, such as process improvements and production problems. Its phenomenal growth, then, may be attributed to emphasizing research on processual problems rather than concentrating on basic, long-range research.

One could assume, based on this analogy, that one of the problems anthropology faces as an applied behavioral science is that it has been concentrating too much on how the whole system operates rather than on such problems as welfare, politics, poverty, and health. The problem, however, cannot be blamed entirely on the applied scientist, for "social-engineering institutions" are not focusing on the "production" problems standing in the way of the final desired social product and, further, are employing applied social engineers only as "basic research staff." Furthermore, most anthropologists do not want to become involved in the application of research results. The problem is additionally complicated by the commitment of behavioral scientists to academia and their unavailability for staffing applied institutes.

Until recent times, anthropologists have generally studied primitive and peasant societies, rather than modern societies. The concepts of cultural holism and cultural relativity and the attempt at "scientific objectivity" have kept anthropologists from making value judgments whenever they have found social problems. Thus, they have been able to accept—without imposing their own private system of values—many bizarre practices. Since everything has been viewed as culturally relative and as serving some presumed "function" in the society—as somehow supporting or integrating certain necessary values that help the society perpetuate itself through time as a viable entity—anthropologists have not been critical of what their subjects have done to each other, even if, for example, they have been waging war. Where they have been critical, or when they have expressed criticism, it has always been in defense of the natives they have been studying. Hence, anthropologists have often been accused of helping perpetuate societies in abject poverty or other dire circumstances for the sole purpose of maintaining a "laboratory" for selfish "scientific" interests. Recently, anthropologists have come under much criticism for this from "natives" who object to "being studied" (see Vine Deloria, "Custer Died for Your Sins," in the section "Anthropology and the Third World").

The anthropologist who depends on the types and results of research done in the past is limited in

[1]William Bevan, "The Welfare of Science in an Era of Change," *Science* 176 (June 2, 1972): 990.
[2]Philip M. Boffey, "Japan: Industrial Research Struggles to Close the 'Gap,'" *Science* 167 (January 16, 1970): 264–267.

what he can say about social problems. The old approach, for example, would allow him to excuse the separation of races in the South and their unequal access to such resources as education and housing by trotting out "cultural relativism," or by making a "functional" analysis of the place of racism in American society. Furtunately, anthropologists are moving away from this approach. The items we have chosen for this volume demonstrate some of the recent concerns and research approaches of contemporary anthropology.

Anthropologists Look at Social Issues

The major social issues confronting society today are easy to identify. They are overpopulation, pollution, juvenile delinquency, crime, political and educational overcontrol, violence, poverty, and war. Other problems include the uneven distribution of resources among classes, racism and prejudice, the generation gap, and the ethical responsibility of institutions.

What does the anthropologist—in his professional role—have to say about these issues? And what bases in anthropological research and practice do his statements have? In other words, what is the anthropological point of view on social issues?

In the first section, Gerald Berreman presents the major concern of this volume, the issue of the anthropologist's responsibility to his constituencies—the people he studies, his students, and the public. There has been an increasing demand for accountability from anthropologists for the work they do and the uses to which their work is put. Berreman has selected items which emphasize that anthropologists and other behavioral scientists can no longer excuse how their work is used by claiming that it is value-free research practiced by "nonpolitical" scientists. Anthropology, by its very existence and by the nature of the data it produces, is a political activity. The American Anthropological Association, by its existence, is a political force. Failure to take a position—or the assumption of a neutral position by failing to face basic ethical problems—is a political action. The contributions in this section range from discussions of ethics and politics, through the results of studies of primitive and modern peasant groups, to the discussions—and arguments—taking place in the American Anthropological Association on political and ethical issues.

"The Myth of the Melting Pot" discusses the attempts of members of ethnic groups in the United States to attain an economically and socially viable way of life. The major point in this section, compiled by Arthur Rubel and Harriet Kupferer, is that the immigrant and original inhabitants of the United States have been pressured to assimilate or acculturate into the mainstream culture. The articles in this section clearly demonstrate not only the pathos of the process but also the certainty of its failure. In discussing the myth of the melting pot, Rubel and Kupferer state one of the themes of the book: "The ideal holds out promises; the real demonstrates that promises are not kept."

Berreman turns our attention in the third section to the plight of Third World peoples—the peoples of the developing nations—especially the role of anthropology in the internal politics and development of Third World communities. Inevitably, the views held of the United States by these "studied" countries are reflected in their reaction to and beliefs about American anthropologists. The anthropologist has been naïve in believing that his involvement in "value-free research" and activities related solely to academic and scholarly goals would free him from the onus of the activities of his own culture. However, recent events, such as the scandal over Project Camelot, have clearly demonstrated that the anthropologist must take responsibility for his country's actions.

Returning to the theme of the Rubel and Kupferer section, Hermann Bleibtreu and John Meaney discuss racism as "a social pathology without scientific meaning" and describe how racism has become part of the social fabric and heritage of Western civilization. This section, which explains the meaning of *race* and demonstrates the fallacy of racist philosophy, shows the necessity of disseminating anthropological knowledge to the American public. The information and arguments presented are all the more important in light of recent discussions on the relationship between race, ethnicity, and intelligence renewed by behavioral scientists who oppose the view presented by Bleibtreu and Meaney.

In the fifth section, Seymour Parker provides an overview of how the work of anthropologists can lead to a better understanding of the uses of science in modern society. He focuses on the concept of "culture of poverty" and its relationship to those minority groups termed "disadvantaged," and asks if poverty constitutes a culture that is passed on in the socialization process or if it is a secondary adaptation to frustrations in achieving primary cultural goals similar to those of more advantaged groups. Anthropologists have been in the forefront of efforts to answer this question, as is evident from the contributions of Oscar Lewis, Elliot Liebow, Ulf Hannerz, and Bernard James. The anthropologist has also looked to other disciplines—to psychiatry (Robert Kleiner) and sociology (Herbert Gans)—in his attempt to understand the values of ethnic subcultures. These contributions highlight a major problem in the use of social science analysis and its effects on its subjects—that people and their problems can be dismissed by labeling them.

John Singleton's section looks at the ethnography of educational activities and emphasizes the differences between ideology and practice, especially as they affect persons of different ethnic or subcultural backgrounds. The anthropological study of schools demonstrates that schools reflect the same norms and biases found in the total society. Singleton describes how educational institutions are socializing agents, filling the roles needed to keep society functioning, and sorting devices, indicating which people will reap the rewards of our class system. At the same time, the schools reinforce the lower social status of some ethnic and subcultural groups. The selections chosen by Singleton focus on the ethnography of white American, Latin American, and Canadian and American Indian school systems, as well as on the education of American blacks. The central theme is that education must be studied as a social institution and a social problem, with major emphasis on how the schools fail, rather than on how the students fail.

Another area studied by anthropologists that can be of value in understanding some of the problems facing modern society is violence. As Bernard Siegel vividly begins his section, "The history of civilization is among other things a history of violence." By looking at how other societies handle the problem of violence and aggression, and by determining the part it plays in the total cultural picture, we can understand the psychological problems that create and are caused by violence and aggression in our own society, and the difficulties we have accepting and handling that violence. In selections concerned with sex offenses, homicide, internal dissension and conflict, violence between ethnic groups and representatives of established political orders, and violence and aggression in small-scale societies, Siegel provides a cogent picture of how societies deal with ambiguous social goals and conflicting values and norms. He indicates that inequities in a social system can result in inordinate rates of violence and aggression—that violence is an adaptive process—and helps us understand it by comparing violence to nonviolence, just as we can understand change by relating it to stasis.

Michael Crawford—whose section borrows freely from the other behavioral and physical sciences—assesses the physical environment that man lives in and the problems of overpopulation, pollution, and aggression (a theme previously discussed by Siegel). As he shows, overpopulation, pollution, and aggression are intricately interwoven. We are using up our limited natural resources, and our use of them is hastening the pollution of our environment; if this rate of consumption and pollution continues, we may make it impossible for man to exist on the earth. After selections on such issues as the possible genetic consequences of failure to control population increase and the development in urban man of screening devices to avoid information overload, Crawford suggests areas in which the work of cultural and biological anthropologists is essential.

The final section, prepared by Art Gallaher, Jr., summarizes the goals of this book. Gallaher discusses the problems posed by intervention in the established way of life of any people, whether part cultures or whole nation-states. He emphasizes the need to consider other peoples' views and social goals. That intervening in the practical affairs of any society involves many pitfalls and few successes is demonstrated in the selections on the Fox Indians, Latin America, the Third World (previously covered by Berreman), Australian aborigines, and the Vicoseños of Peru, the last mentioned being one of the most famous case studies in applied anthropology. Guidelines are provided for planned intervention in societies. As Gallaher states:

Our concern is not to provide a formula for success; no such formulas are known. But we can gain, from anthropological insight, some understanding which should enable us to make more enlightened judgments about intervention designed to change the system.

1 The Social Responsibility of the Anthropologist

Gerald D. Berreman
The Social Responsibility of the Anthropologist

C. Wright Mills
On Politics

Joseph G. Jorgensen
On Ethics and Anthropology

Allan R. Holmberg
Adventures in Culture Change

Cora Du Bois
Appendix to the Preface of 1944

Donald K. Grayson
Human Life vs. Science

Bernard Gallin
A Case for Intervention in the Field

William Foote Whyte
**Freedom and Responsibility in Research:
The "Springdale" Case**

Arthur Vidich and Joseph Bensman
"Freedom and Responsibility in Research": Comments

Executive Board of the American Anthropological Association
Resolutions

American Anthropological Association
Principles of Professional Responsibility

Anthony Leeds
Ethics Report Criticized

Stephen P. Dunn
Resolution Issues

Franz Boas
Scientists as Spies

American Anthropological Association
Council Meeting, December 30, 4:45 P.M.

Eric R. Wolf and Joseph Jorgensen
Letter to the Student Mobilization Committee

Executive Board of the American Anthropological Association
Statement

Committee on Ethics of the American Anthropological Association
Letter to the Executive Board

Omer C. Stewart
The Need to Popularize Basic Concepts

Gerald D. Berreman
Contemporary Anthropology and Moral Accountability

I have placed myself squarely on the side of mankind, and have not shamed to wish mankind well.   Robert Redfield

I don't see how it can be denied that the science of man is, historically and by its very nature, a utopian science. . . .

But this does not mean that a utopian stance by the science of man is unrealistic or unseemly. On the contrary, we must believe more strongly than ever in the "instrumental utopianism" which stems from 2,500 years of Western thought: that we must become as rational and critical as possible in our social arrangements and that we must continue to design, rework, and uphold an ideal vision for the masses of men.

As consummate realists, let us continue to work and richly to dream, lest the militarists and other bureaucrats bend our best ideas to their age-old practical nightmares.   Ernest Becker

If today we concern ourselves exclusively with the technical proficiency of our students and reject all responsibility for their moral sense, or lack of it, then we may someday be compelled to accept responsibility for having trained a generation willing to serve in a future Auschwitz.   Alvin Gouldner

Gerald D. Berreman

The Social Responsibility of the Anthropologist

Social responsibility and professional ethics have become major issues in anthropology. In 1970, the American Anthropological Association was locked in controversy, two members of its Committee on Ethics having resigned less than two years after the committee was formed, after they were rebuked for speaking out against clandestine activities by anthropologists in connection with the war in Southeast Asia. Two of four candidates for the presidency of the Association withdrew from the election in which such clandestine research was a major issue, in a successful attempt to insure that the more liberal candidate (the editor of this section, Gerald D. Berreman, a member of the Committee on Ethics) would be defeated by his senior, more conservative opponent. Yet at the meeting where the outcome of the election was announced, the membership overwhelmingly endorsed the recommendations of the Committee on Ethics. The following year, an ad hoc committee was formed, under the chairmanship of Dr. Margaret Mead, to look into the entire issue of anthropological research and consultation in Southeast Asia and the findings of the Committee on Ethics. The resultant report, sharply critical of the Committee on Ethics, was resoundingly rejected by vote of the membership when it was presented at the 1971 annual meeting of the Association. A Committee on Potentially Harmful Research was then established, with the purpose of serving as a focus for inquiry into the effects of, and safeguards sur-

rounding, anthropological work among relatively powerless peoples. At the same meeting, the results of the election of incoming members of the Executive Board of the Association reflected the trend toward a more liberal stance and greater concern with political, social, and ethical issues in the profession.

Clearly, anthropologists are concerned with social issues, but are divided. The division is along political lines which tend to correspond to generational ones. The reverberations will be felt for many years, for the demand that anthropological research be relevant and socially responsible is increasing. The age structure of the Association and the mortality of its members virtually assure that these demands will win out in the end.

This trend, and the issues which underlie it, are not unique in anthropology. They are part of the intellectual climate of the 1960s and '70s; part of the reaction to the Southeast-Asian War, to neocolonialism, and to America's failure to overcome internal problems of racism and poverty. In the academic world, the trend has been reflected in the proliferation of concerned scholars' organizations, radical caucuses, opposition candidates, and counterconventions in many professional associations—all reflecting a demand for social responsibility, moral accountability, social relevance, and political effectiveness. There has been a Radical Caucus at the American Anthropological Association meetings for several consecutive years, culminating in the nomination in 1970, for the first time, of a presidential candidate outside of the official slate (a response to the growing concern for responsibility and relevance), and the formation in 1972 of the Anthropologists for Radical Political Action. There was a counterconvention at the meetings of the American Sociological Association in 1969, and a meeting of the Concerned Asian Scholars concurrent with and counter to that of the Association for Asian Studies in 1970 and 1971. The African Studies Association virtually split in 1970 over the demands of black and radical members for reorganization and redirection (see the section on "Anthropology and the Third World"). Staughton Lynd was a radical opposition candidate for the presidency of the American Historical Association in 1969. In 1968 the conservative Modern Languages Association elected Louis Kampf its second vice-president (thus slating him for the presidency in 1970), the result of a trend toward radical change in the Association. In each instance, these were unprecedented developments, but they were hardly surprising to anyone familiar with the changing temper and concerns of young intellectuals.

Simultaneously, various new publications have appeared: the *Bulletin of the Committee of Concerned Asian Scholars, The Insurgent Sociologist, Critical Anthropology,* Theodore Roszak's book, *The Dissenting Academy, Reinventing Anthropology* edited by Dell Hymes, the series of "countertexts" being published by Random House, the occasional publications of such groups as the North American Congress on Latin America, the Radical Education Project, the Africa Research Group, the Committee of Returned Volunteers, the Student Mobilization Committee, and the publications of radical research groups such as the Bay Area Institute in San Francisco and the Pacific Studies Center in Palo Alto. And there are many others.

The traditional view that one is accountable only to himself and his sponsors for his research, its goals, methods, funding, reporting, and consequences is dying. Anthropologists, like other social scientists, will increasingly be held accountable to those among whom they work, to their colleagues, to their students, and to the public. As in other professions, they will doubtless be called to account by their professional association when they transgress canons of professional ethics and responsibility, for such transgressions reflect on all and jeopardize all. Above all, and more effectively than in any other way, they will be held accountable by their own consciences, sensitized by the experiences of their forebears and fellows—some of which are described in the articles in this section—

and reminded by the admonitions of those they study, those they teach, and those they work with. Consequently, they may be expected to act so as only rarely to invite the criticism of their fellows. Or so it is to be hoped.

The plea for disinterested social science, for value-free research, and hence for a nonpolitical profession and a nonpolitical professional association will be increasingly recognized for the siren song it is. Anthropology, by the very fact that it is a science of man, has political impact. An anthropological association is by its very existence a political force, as the history of the American Anthropological Association demonstrates, and as its Resolutions (some reprinted in this section) make clear. Those who claim otherwise confuse tranquillity and consensus with political neutrality; worse, they confuse support of the status quo with political neutrality. When one does research or consults in support of, or in harmony with, established institutions, established authority, and established customs, the impact of one's work is likely to be inconspicuous. This may be mistaken for neutrality. When one works in ways or on problems which discomfit established authority, question established institutions, challenge accepted values, or contravene established customs, the results are conspicuous. It is then that cries of politicization are likely to be heard. It is then that admonitions about failure to maintain scientific objectivity are likely to be made. But support of any status quo is as political as a challenge to it. The choice *not* to study a particular issue or *not* to question a particular institution or value is as much a value choice as a decision *to* study or question it. Quietly taking money from a questionable source for a research project is as much a political act as publicly refusing to do so.

Those who equate controversy, challenge, and change with the unscientific and political, while equating consensus and support of the status quo with objectivity, scholarship, and science, are like occupants of a boat floating rapidly downstream toward an unseen waterfall, who shout at those in another boat energetically rowing against the current, "Don't row, it is dangerous to move in these waters, there are waterfalls around here. You ought to stand still like we are!" One acts like the boatmen, whether one recognizes it or not; better to move knowingly and purposefully than to delude oneself into the false calm of false neutrality. The impending waterfall, in the above analogy, is the reaction of the rest of the world to "value-free" anthropology and its consequences.

The selections presented in the following section of

this book illustrate issues of responsibility and ethics which confront the anthropologist in his or her professional work—issues which are coming to occupy a central place in his or her thinking, teaching, research, and applied work. The issues are difficult, without simple or agreed-upon solutions. Every year brings fresh perspectives, new awareness, new problems, and new efforts to grapple with them. Many of these selections are excerpts from ongoing debates; most raise more questions than they answer; all represent a science struggling with its conscience.

C. Wright Mills

On Politics

C. Wright Mills was the foremost advocate and exemplar of a social science relevant to the social and political issues of the post-World War II era. He was passionately committed to their solution through the exercise of informed intellect and hard work. He literally died from the tremendous exertions of uncompromising adherence to that commitment. He defined the "sociological imagination" as the capacity to see the relationship between problems facing individuals and the issues facing society, and the use of that insight to formulate solutions. That concept, and his persuasive advocacy of it, has inspired a generation of social scientists; his book by that title is a modern classic. In this chapter from that book, claims to ethical neutrality in social science are identified as moral bankruptcy; the political role of the social scientist is defined as "the politics of truth," which is both obligatory and inescapable for the genuine scientist. This selection comprises a brilliant definition and advocacy of the role of social science in a democratic society.

There is no necessity for working social scientists to allow the political meaning of their work to be shaped by the "accidents" of its setting, or its use to be determined by the purposes of other men. It is quite within their powers to discuss its meanings and decide upon its uses as matters of their own policy. To a considerable, and largely untested, extent, they can influence or even determine these policies. Such determination requires that they make explicit judgments, as well as decisions upon theory, method, and fact. As matters of policy, these judgments are the proper concern of the individual scholar as well as of the fraternity. Yet is it not evident that implicit moral and political judgments have much more influence than explicit discussions of personal and professional policy? Only by making these influences matters of debated policy can men become fully aware of them, and so try to control their effects upon the work of social science and upon its political meaning.

There is no way in which any social scientist can avoid assuming choices of value and implying them in his work as a whole. Problems, like issues and troubles, concern threats to expected values, and cannot be clearly formulated without acknowledgment of those values. Increasingly, research is used, and social scientists are used, for bureaucratic and ideological purposes. This being so, as individuals and as professionals, students of man and society face such questions as: whether they are aware of the uses and values of their work, whether these may be subject to their own control, whether they want to seek to control them. How they answer these questions, or fail to answer them, and how they use or fail to use the answers in their work and in their professional lives determine their answer to the final question: whether in their work as social scientists they are (a) morally autonomous, (b) subject to the morality of other men, or (c) morally adrift. The catchwords with which these problems have been carried along—often, I am certain, with good intentions—are no longer good enough.

Social scientists must now really confront these quite fateful questions. In this chapter I am going to suggest some of the things it seems necessary to consider in any answer to them, and also to set forth the kind of answer I have come, in the last few years, to believe reasonable.

1

The social scientist at work is not suddenly confronted with the need to choose values. He is already working on the basis of certain values. The values that these disciplines now embody have been selected from the values created in Western society; elsewhere social science is an import. Of course some do talk as if the values they have selected "transcend" Western or any other society; others speak of their standards as if they were "immanent" within some existing society, as a sort of unrealized potential. But surely it will now be widely agreed that the values inherent in the traditions of social science are neither transcendent nor immanent. They are simply values proclaimed by many and within limits practiced in small circles. What a man calls moral judgment is merely his desire to generalize, and so make available for others, those values he has come to choose.

Three overriding political ideals seem to me inherent in the traditions of social science, and certainly involved in its intellectual promise. The first of these is simply the value of truth, of fact. The very enterprise of social science, as it determines fact, takes on political meaning. In a world of widely communicated nonsense, any statement of fact is of political and moral significance. All social scientists, by the fact of their existence, are involved in the struggle between enlightenment and obscurantism. In such a world as ours, to practice social science is, first of all, to practice the politics of truth.

But the politics of truth is not an adequate statement of the values that guide our enterprise. The truth of our findings, the accuracy of our investigations—when they are seen in their social setting—may or may not be relevant to human affairs. Whether they are, and how they are, is in itself the second value, which in brief, is the value of the role of reason in human affairs. Along with that goes a third value—human freedom, in all the ambiguity of its meaning. Both freedom and reason, I have already argued, are central to the civilization of the Western world; both are readily proclaimed as ideals. But in any given application, as criteria and as goals, they lead to much disagreement. That is why it is one of our intellectual tasks, as social scientists, to clarify the ideal of freedom and the ideal of reason.

If human reason is to play a larger and more explicit role in the making of history, social scientists must surely be among its major carriers. For in their work they represent the use of reason in the understanding of human affairs; that is what they are about. If they wish to work and thus to act in a consciously chosen way, they must first locate themselves within the intellectual life and the social-historical structure of their times. Within the social domains of intelligence, they must locate themselves; and they must relate these domains, in turn, to the structure of historical society. This is not the place to do such work. Here I want only briefly to distinguish three political roles in terms of which the social scientist as a man of reason may conceive of himself.

Much social science, perhaps especially sociology, contains the theme of the philosopher-king. From August Comte to Karl Mannheim, one finds the plea for and the attempted justification of greater power for "the man of knowledge." In a more specific statement the enthronement of reason means, of course, the enthronement of "the man of reason." This one idea of the role of reason in human affairs has done much to cause social scientists to keep very general indeed their acceptance of reason as a social value. They have wished to avoid the foolishness of such an idea when it is considered alongside the facts of power. The idea also goes against the grain of many versions of democracy, for it involves an aristocracy, even if an aristocracy of talent rather than of birth or wealth. But the rather foolish idea that he should become a philosopher-king is only one idea of the public role that the social scientist may attempt to enact.

The quality of politics depends very much upon the intellectual qualities of those who are engaged in it. Were the "philosopher" king, I should be tempted to leave his kingdom; but when kings are without any "philosophy," are they not incapable of responsible rule?

The second, and now the most usual role, is to

become an advisor to the king. The bureaucratic uses which I have described are a current embodiment of this. The individual social scientist tends to become involved in those many trends of modern society that make the individual a part of a functionally rational bureaucracy, and to sink into his specialized slot in such a way as not to be explicitly concerned with the structure of post-modern society. In this role, we have seen, social science itself often tends to become a functionally rational machine; the individual social scientist tends to lose his moral autonomy and his substantive rationality, and the role of reason in human affairs tends to become merely a refinement of techniques for administrative and manipulative uses.

But that is the role of advisor to kings in one of its worst forms; this role need not, I believe, assume the shape and meaning of the bureaucratic style. It is a difficult role to fulfill in such a way as to retain moral and intellectual integrity, and hence, freedom to work on the tasks of social science. It is easy for consultants to imagine themselves philosophers and their clients enlightened rulers. But even should they be philosophers, those they serve may not be enlightenable. That is one reason I am so impressed by the loyalty of some consultants to the unenlightened despots they serve. It is a loyalty that seems strained neither by despotic incompetence nor by dogmatic silliness.

I do not assert that the role of advisor cannot be performed well; in fact I know that it can, and that there are men who are doing it. Were there more such men the political and intellectual tasks of those social scientists who elect the third role would become much less burdensome, for it overlaps this one.

The third way in which the social scientist may attempt to realize the value of reason and its role in human affairs is also well known, and sometimes even practiced. It is to remain independent, to do one's own work, to select one's own problems, but to direct this work *at* kings as well as *to* "publics." Such a conception prompts us to imagine social science as a sort of public intelligence apparatus, concerned with public issues and private troubles and with the structural trends of our time underlying them both—and to imagine individual social scientists as rational members of a self-controlled association, which we call the social sciences.

In taking up such a role, which I shall explain more fully in a moment, we are trying to *act* upon the value of reason; in assuming that we may not be altogether ineffective, we are assuming a theory of history-making: we are assuming that "man" is free and that by his rational endeavors he can influence the course of history. I am not now concerned to debate the *values* of freedom and reason, but only to discuss under what theory of history they may be realizable.

2

Men are free to make history, but some men are much freer than others. Such freedom requires access to the means of decisions and of power by which history may now be made. It is not always so made; in the following, I am speaking only of the contemporary period in which the means of history-making power have become so enlarged and so centralized. It is with reference to this period that I am contending that if men do not make history, they tend increasingly to become the utensils of history-makers and also the mere objects of history-making.

How large a role any explicit decisions do play in the making of history is itself an historical problem. It depends very much upon the means of power that are available at any given time in any given society. In some societies, the innumerable actions of innumerable men modify their milieux, and so gradually modify the structure itself. These modifications are the course of history; history is drift, although in total "men make it." Thus, innumerable entrepreneurs and innumerable consumers, by ten thousand decisions per minute, may shape and re-shape the free-market economy. Perhaps this was the chief kind of limitation Marx had in mind when he wrote, in *The 18th Brumaire:* "Men make their own history, but they do not make it just as they please; they do not make it under circumstances chosen by themselves. . . ."

Fate, or "inevitability," has to do with events in history that are beyond the control of any circle or group of men having three characteristics: (1) compact enough to be identifiable, (2) powerful enough to decide with consequence, and (3) in a position to foresee these consequences and so to be held accountable for them. Events, according to this conception, are the summary and unintended results of innumerable decisions of innumerable men. Each of their decisions is minute in consequence and subject to cancellation or reinforcement by other such decisions. There is no link between any one man's intention and the summary result of the innumerable decisions. Events are beyond human decisions: History is made behind men's backs.

So conceived, fate is not a universal fact; it is not inherent in the nature of history or in the nature of man. Fate is a feature of an historically specific kind of social structure. In a society in which the ultimate weapon is the rifle; in which the typical economic unit is the family-farm and the small shop; in which the national-state does not yet exist or is merely a distant framework; in which communication is by word-of-mouth, handbill, pulpit—in *such* a society, history is indeed fate.

But consider now, the major clue to our condition: Is it not, in a word, the enormous enlargement and the decisive centralization of all the means of power and decision, which is to say—all the means of history-making? In modern industrial society, the facilities of economic production are developed and centralized—as peasants and artisans are replaced by private corporations and government industries. In the modern nation-state, the means of violence and of political administration undergo similar developments—as kings control nobles, and self-equipped knights are replaced by standing armies and now by fearful military machines. The *post-modern* climax of all three developments—in economics, in politics, and in violence—is now occurring most dramatically in the United States and the USSR. In our time, international as well as national means of history-making are being centralized. Is it not thus clear that the scope and the chance for conscious human agency in history-making is just now uniquely available? Elites of power in charge of these means do now make history—to be sure, "under circumstances not of their own choosing"—but compared to other men and other epochs, these circumstances themselves certainly do not appear to be overwhelming.

Surely this is the paradox of our immediate situation: The facts about the newer means of history-making are a signal that men are not necessarily in the grip of fate, that men *can* now make history. But this fact is made ironic by the further fact that just now those ideologies which offer men the hope of making history have declined and are collapsing in the Western societies. That collapse is also the collapse of the expectations of The Enlightenment, that reason and freedom would come to prevail as paramount forces in human history. And behind it there is also the intellectual and political default of the intellectual community.

Where is the intelligentsia that is carrying on the big discourse of the Western world *and* whose work as intellectuals is influential among parties and publics and relevant to the great decisions of our time? Where are the mass media open to such men? Who among those who are in charge of the two-party state and its ferocious military machines are alert to what goes on in the world of knowledge and reason and sensibility? Why is the free intellect so divorced from decisions of power? Why does there now prevail among men of power such a higher and irresponsible ignorance?

In the United States today, intellectuals, artists, ministers, scholars, and scientists are fighting a cold war in which they echo and elaborate the confusions of officialdoms. They neither raise demands on the powerful for alternative policies, nor set forth such alternatives before publics. They do not try to put responsible content into the politics of the United States; they help to empty politics and to keep it empty. What must be called the Christian default of the clergy is as much a part of this sorry moral condition as is the capture of scientists by nationalist Science-Machines. The journalistic lie, become routine, is part of it too; and so is much of the pretentious triviality that passes for social science.

3

I do not expect (nor does my present argument as a whole require) that this view be accepted by all social scientists. What I want most to say here is that, having accepted the values of reason and freedom, it is a prime task of any social scientist to determine the limits of freedom and the limits of the role of reason in history.

In assuming the third role, the social scientist does not see himself as some autonomous being standing "outside society." In common with most other people, he *does* feel that he stands outside the major history-making decisions of this period; at the same time he knows that he is among those who take many of the consequences of these decisions. That is one major reason why to the extent that he is aware of what he is doing, he becomes an explicitly political man. No one is "outside society"; the question is where each stands within it.

The social scientist usually lives in circumstances of middling class and status and power. By his activities in these milieux, he is often in no better position than the ordinary individual to solve structural problems, for their solution can never be merely intellectual or merely private. Their proper statement cannot be confined to the milieux open to the will of social scientists; neither can their solutions, which means, of course, that they are problems of social and political and economic power. But the social scientist is not only an "ordinary man." It is his very task intellectually to transcend the milieux in which he happens to live, and this he does when he considers the economic order of nineteenth-century England or the status hierarchy of twentieth-century America, the military institutions of Imperial Rome, or the political structure of the Soviet Union.

In so far as the values of freedom and reason concern him, one of his themes for study has to do with the objective chances available for given types of men within given types of social structure to become free and rational as individuals. Another of his themes has to do with what chances, if any, men of different positions in differing types of society have, first, by their reason and experience, to transcend their everyday milieux, and second, by virtue of their power, to act with consequence for the structure of their society and their periods. These are the problems of the role of reason in history.

In considering them, it is easy to see that in modern societies, some men have the power to act with much structural relevance and are quite aware of the consequences of their actions; others have such power but are not aware of its effective scope; and there are many who cannot transcend their everyday milieux by their awareness of structure or effect structural change by any means of action available to them.

Then, as social scientists, we locate ourselves. By the nature of our work, we are aware of social structure and somewhat aware of the historical mechanics of its movement. But clearly we do not have access to the major means of power which now exist and with which these mechanics can now be influenced. We do, however, have one often fragile "means of power," and it is this which pro-

vides a clue to our political role and to the political meaning of our work.

It is, I think, the political task of the social scientist who accepts the ideals of freedom and reason, to address his work to each of the other three types of men I have classified in terms of power and knowledge.

To those with power and with awareness of it, he imputes varying measures of responsibility for such structural consequences as he finds by his work to be decisively influenced by their decisions and their lack of decisions.

To those whose actions have such consequences, but who do not seem to be aware of them, he directs whatever he has found out about those consequences. He attempts to educate and then, again, he imputes responsibility.

To those who are regularly without such power and whose awareness is confined to their everyday milieux, he reveals by his work the meaning of structural trends and decisions for these milieux, the ways in which personal troubles are connected with public issues; in the course of these efforts, he states what he has found out concerning the actions of the more powerful. These are his major educational tasks, and they are his major public tasks when he speaks to any larger audience. Let us now examine some of the problems and tasks set by this third role.

4

Regardless of the scope of his awareness, the social scientist is usually a professor, and this occupational fact very much determines what he is able to do. As a professor, he addresses students, and on occasion, by speeches and by writings, publics of larger scale and more strategic position. In discussing what his public role may be, let us stick close to these simple facts of power, or if you like, to the facts of his powerlessness.

In so far as he is concerned with liberal, that is to say liberating, education, his public role has two goals: What he ought to do for the individual is to turn personal troubles and concerns into social issues and problems open to reason—his aim is to help the individual become a self-educating man, who only then would be reasonable and free. What he ought to do for the society is to combat all those forces which are destroying genuine publics and creating a mass society—or put as a positive goal, his aim is to help build and to strengthen self-cultivating publics. Only then might society be reasonable and free.

These are very large goals, and I must explain them in a slightly indirect way. We are concerned with skills and with values. Among "skills," however, some are more and some are less relevant to the tasks of liberation. I do not believe that skills and values can be so easily separated as in our search for "neutral skills" we often assume. It is a matter of degree, with skills at one extreme and values at the other. But in the middle ranges of this scale, there are what I shall call sensibilities, and it is these which should interest us most. To train someone to operate a lathe or to read and write is in large part a training of skill; to help someone decide what he really wants out of his life, or to debate with him Stoic, Christian, and Humanist ways of living, is a cultivation or an education of values.

Alongside skill and value, we ought to put sensibility, which includes them both, and more besides: it includes a sort of therapy in the ancient sense of clarifying one's knowledge of self. It includes the cultivation of all those skills of controversy with oneself that we call thinking, and which, when engaged in with others, we call debate. An educator must begin with what interests the individual most deeply, even if it seems altogether trivial and cheap. He must proceed in such a way and with such materials as to enable the student to gain increasingly rational insight into these concerns, and into others he will acquire in the process of his education. And the educator must try to develop men and women who can and who will by themselves continue what he has begun: the end product of any liberating education is simply the self-educating, self-cultivating man and woman; in short, the free and rational individual.

A society in which such individuals are ascendant is, by one major meaning of the word, democratic. Such a society may also be defined as one in which genuine publics rather than masses prevail. By this, I mean the following:

Whether or not they are aware of them, men in a mass society are gripped by personal troubles which they are not able to turn into social issues. They do not understand the interplay of these personal troubles of their milieux with problems of social structure. The knowledgeable man in a genuine public, on the other hand, is able to do just that. He understands that what he thinks and feels to be personal troubles are very often also problems shared by others, and more importantly, not capable of solution by any one individual but only by modifications of the structure of the groups in which he lives and sometimes the structure of the entire society. Men in masses have troubles, but they are not usually aware of their true meaning and source; men in publics confront issues, and they usually come to be aware of their public terms.

It is the political task of the social scientist—as of any liberal educator—continually to translate personal troubles into public issues, and public issues into the terms of their human meaning for a variety of individuals. It is his task to display in his work—and, as an educator, in his life as well—this kind of sociological imagination. And it is his purpose to cultivate such habits of mind among the men and women who are publicly exposed to him. To secure these ends is to secure reason and individuality, and to make these the predominant values of a democratic society.

You may now be saying to yourself, "Well, here it comes. He is going to set up an ideal so high that in terms of it everything must seem low." That I might be thought to be doing so testifies to the lack of seriousness with which the word democracy is now taken, and to the indifference of many observers to the drift away from any plain meaning of the word. Democracy is, of course, a complicated idea about which there is much legitimate disagreement. But surely it is not so complicated or ambiguous that it may no longer be used by people who wish to reason together.

What I mean by democracy as an ideal I have already tried to indicate. In essence, democracy implies that those vitally affected by any decision men make have an effective voice in that decision. This, in turn, means that all power to make such decisions be publicly legitimated and that the makers of such decisions be held publicly accountable. None of these three points can prevail, it seems to me, unless there are dominant within a society the kinds of publics and the kinds of individuals I have described. Certain further conditions will presently become evident.

The social structure of the United States is not an altogether democratic one. Let us take that as a point of minimum agreement. I do not know of any society which is altogether democratic—that remains an ideal. The United States today I should say is generally democratic mainly in form and in the rhetoric of expectation. In substance and in practice it is very often nondemocratic, and in many institutional areas it is quite clearly so. The corporate economy is run neither as a set of town meetings nor as a set of powers responsible to those whom their activities affect very seriously. The military machines and increasingly the political state are in the same condition. I do not wish to give the impression that I am optimistic about the chances that many social scientists can or will perform a democratic public role, or—even if many of them do so—about the chances that this would necessarily result in a rehabilitation of publics. I am merely outlining one role that seems to me to be open and is, in fact, practiced by some social scientists. It happens also to be a role that is in line with both liberal and socialist views of the role of reason in human affairs.[1]

My point is that the political role of social science—what that role may be, how it is enacted, and how effectively—this is relevant to the extent to which democracy prevails.

If we take up the third role of reason, the autonomous role, we are trying to act in a democratic manner in a society that is not altogether democratic. But we are acting as if we were in a fully democratic society, and by doing so, we are attempting to remove the "as if." We are trying to make the society more democratic. Such a role, I contend, is the only role by which we may as social scientists attempt to do this. At least I do not know of any other way by which we might try to help build a democratic polity. And because of this, the problem of the social sciences as a prime carrier of reason in human affairs is in fact a major problem of democracy today.

5

What are the chances of success? Given the political structure within which we must now act, I do not believe it is very likely that social scientists will become effective carriers of reason. For men of knowledge to enact this strategic role, certain conditions must be present. Men make their own history, Marx said, but they do not make it under conditions of their own choice. Well then, what are the conditions *we* require to play this role effectively? What are required are parties and

movements and publics having two characteristics: (1) within them ideas and alternatives of social life are truly debated, and (2) they have a chance really to influence decisions of structural consequence. Only if such organizations existed, could we become realistic and hopeful about the role of reason in human affairs which I have been trying to outline. Such a situation, by the way, I should consider one major requirement for any fully democratic society.

In such a polity social scientists in their political roles would probably "speak for" and "against" a variety of movements and strata and interests, rather than merely address an often vague, and—I fear—dwindling, public. Their ideas, in short, would compete, and this competition (as a process as well as in its result at any given time) would be politically relevant. If we take the idea of democracy seriously, if we take the democratic role of reason in human affairs seriously, our engagement in such a competition will in no way distress us. Surely we cannot suppose that all definitions of social reality, much less all statements of political ways and means, much less all suggestions of goals, would result in some undebatable, unified doctrine.[2]

_____

[1] In passing, I should like to remind the reader that, quite apart from its present bureaucratic context and use, the style of abstracted empiricism (and the methodological inhibition it sustains) is not well suited for the democratic political role I am describing. Those who practice this style as their sole activity, who conceive of it as the "real work of social science," and who live in its ethos, cannot perform a liberating educational role. This role requires that individuals and publics be given confidence in their own capacities to reason, and by individual criticism, study, and practice, to enlarge its scope and improve its quality. It requires that they be encouraged, in George Orwell's phrase, to "get outside the whale," or in the wonderful American phrase, "to become their own men." To tell them that they can "really" know social reality only by depending upon a necessarily bureaucratic kind of research is to place a taboo, in the name of Science, upon their efforts to become independent men and substantive thinkers. It is to undermine the confidence of the individual craftsman in his own ability to know reality. It is, in effect, to encourage men to fix their social beliefs by reference to the authority of an alien apparatus, and it is, of course, in line with, and is reinforced by, the whole bureaucratization of reason in our time. The industrialization of academic life and the fragmentation of the problems of social science cannot result in a liberating educational role for social scientists. For what these schools of thought take apart they tend to keep apart, in very tiny pieces about which they claim to be very certain. But all they could thus be certain of are abstracted fragments, and it is precisely the job of liberal education, *and* the political role of social science, *and* its intellectual promise, to enable men to transcend such fragmented and abstracted milieux: to become aware of historical structures and of their own place within them.

[2] The idea of such a monopoly in the sphere of social ideas is

In the absence of such parties and movements and publics, we live in a society that is democratic mainly in its legal forms and its formal expectations. We ought not to minimize the enormous value and the considerable opportunity these circumstances make available. We should learn their value from the fact of their absence in the Soviet world, and from the kind of struggle the intellectuals of that world are up against. We should also learn that whereas there many intellectuals are physically crushed, here many morally crush themselves. That democracy in the United States is so largely formal does not mean that we can dodge the conclusion that if reason is to play any free part in a democratic making of history, one of its chief carriers must surely be the social sciences. The absence of democratic parties and movements and publics does not mean that social scientists as educators ought not to try to make their educational institutions a framework within which such a liberating public of individuals might exist, at least in its beginnings, and one in which their discussions might be encouraged and sustained. Nor does it mean that they should not try to cultivate such publics in their less academic roles.

To do so of course, is to risk "trouble"; or what is more serious, to face a quite deadly indifference. It requires that we deliberately present controversial theories and facts, and actively encourage controversy. In the absence of political debate that is wide and open and informed, people can get into touch neither with the effective realities of their world nor with the realities of themselves. Nowadays especially, it seems to me, the role I have been describing requires no less than the presentation of conflicting definitions of reality itself. What is usually termed "propaganda," especially of a nationalist sort, consists not only of opinions on a variety of topics and issues. It is the promulgation, as Paul Kecskemeti once noted, of official definitions of reality.

Our public life now often rests upon such official definitions, as well as upon myths and lies and crackbrained notions. When many policies—debated and undebated—are based on inadequate and misleading definitions of reality, then those who are out to define reality more adequately are bound to be upsetting influences. That is why publics of the sort I have described, as well as men of individuality, are, by their very existence in such a society, radical. Yet such is the role of

mind, of study, of intellect, of reason, of ideas: to define reality adequately and in a publicly relevant way. The educational and the political role of social science in a democracy is to help cultivate and sustain publics and individuals that are able to develop, to live with, and to act upon adequate definitions of personal and social realities.

The role of reason I have been outlining neither means nor requires that one hit the pavement, take the next plane to the scene of the current crisis, run for Congress, buy a newspaper plant, go among the poor, set up a soap box. Such actions are often admirable, and I can readily imagine occasions when I should personally find it impossible not to want to do them myself. But for the social scientist to take them to be his normal activities is merely to abdicate his role, and to display by his action a disbelief in the promise of social science and in the role of reason in human affairs. This role requires only that the social scientist get on with the work of social science and that he avoid furthering the bureaucratization of reason and of discourse.

Not every social scientist accepts all the views I happen to hold on these issues, and it is not my wish that he should. My point is that one of his tasks is to determine his own views of the nature of historical change and the place, if any, of free and reasonable men within it. Only then can he come to know his own intellectual and political role within the societies he is studying, and in doing so find out just what he does think of the values of freedom and of reason which are so deeply a part of the tradition and the promise of social science.

If individual men and small groups of men are not free to act with historical consequence, and at the same time are not reasonable enough to see those consequences; if the structure of modern societies, or of any one of them, is now such that history is indeed blind drift and cannot be made otherwise with the means at hand and the knowledge that may be acquired—then the only autonomous role of social science is to chronicle and to understand; the idea of the responsibility of the

one of the authoritarian notions which lie under the view of "The Method" of the science-makers as administrators of reason, and which is so thinly disguised in the "sacred values" of grand theorists. More obviously it is embodied in the technocratic slogans [analyzed by Mills in a previous chapter].

powerful is foolish; and the values of freedom and of reason are realizable only in the exceptional milieux of certain favored private lives.

But that is a lot of "ifs." And although there is ample room for disagreement over degrees of freedom and scales of consequence, I do not believe that there is sufficient evidence to necessitate abandoning the values of freedom and reason as they might now orient the work of social science.

Attempts to avoid such troublesome issues as I have been discussing are nowadays widely defended by the slogan that social science is "not out to save the world." Sometimes this is the disclaimer of a modest scholar; sometimes it is the cynical contempt of a specialist for all issues of larger concern; sometimes it is the disillusionment of youthful expectations; often it is the pose of men who seek to borrow the prestige of The Scientist, imagined as a pure and disembodied intellect. But sometimes it is based upon a considered judgment of the facts of power.

Because of such facts, I do not believe that social science will "save the world" although I see nothing at all wrong with "trying to save the world"—a phrase which I take here to mean the avoidance of war and the rearrangement of human affairs in accordance with the ideals of human freedom and reason. Such knowledge as I have leads me to embrace rather pessimistic estimates of the chances. But even if that is where we now stand, still we must ask: If there *are* any ways out of the crises of our period by means of intellect, is it up to the social scientist to state them? What we represent—although this is not always apparent—is man become aware of mankind. It is on the level of human awareness that virtually all solutions to the great problems must now lie.

To *appeal* to the powerful, on the basis of any knowledge we now have, is utopian in the foolish sense of that term. Our relations with them are more likely to be only such relations as they find useful, which is to say that we become technicians accepting their problems and aims, or ideologists promoting their prestige and authority. To be more than that, so far as our political role is concerned, we must first of all reconsider the nature of our collective endeavor as social scientists. It is not at all utopian for one social scientist to appeal to his colleagues to undertake such a reconsideration. Any social scientist who is aware of what he is about must confront the major moral dilemma I have implied in this chapter—the difference between what men are interested in and what is to men's interest.

If we take the simple democratic view that *what men are interested in* is all that concerns us, then we are accepting the values that have been inculcated, often accidentally and often deliberately by vested interests. These values are often the only ones men have had any chance to develop. They are unconsciously acquired habits rather than choices.

If we take the dogmatic view that *what is to men's interests,* whether they are interested in it or not, is all that need concern us morally, then we run the risk of violating democratic values. We may become manipulators or coercers, or both, rather than persuaders within a society in which men are trying to reason together and in which the value of reason is held in high esteem.

What I am suggesting is that by addressing ourselves to issues and to troubles, and formulating them as problems of social science, we stand the best chance, I believe the only chance, to make reason democratically relevant to human affairs in a free society, and so realize the classic values that underlie the promise of our studies.

Joseph G. Jorgensen

On Ethics and Anthropology

Anthropologists have probably always felt some sentimental attachment to those among whom they have worked. Rarely, however, have their responsibilities to those people been addressed directly. This essay, prepared originally as part of its author's participation in the Committee on Ethics of the American Anthropological Association, in 1969, explicitly sets forth the ethical issues confronting anthropologists in their relationships with those they study. It forthrightly calls for the establishment of a code of ethics to guard against misuse of the anthropologist's role in those relationships. This is a position which, as later selections make clear, is highly controversial—regarded by some as infringing on their freedom of research. Inevitably, such a code was adopted, and this essay was an important contribution to it.

There is a need for discussion of ethical problems in anthropological research and for the drafting of a voluntary code of professional ethical conduct to articulate the values anthropologists should share. Furthermore, though a voluntary code would be an excellent beginning, I do not believe it will be sufficient; consequently, I think that ethics committees should be established by the various local and national anthropological associations. Agreement upon, and enforcement of, ethical standards for the profession would permit ethical scholars to conduct research without causing suspicion or fear among their hosts and help a researcher decide whether he should tackle research projects in which, for instance, free and voluntary consent cannot be accommodated with the integrity of the research.

The need for some such development is evident and real. It is my impression that in our graduate and undergraduate programs we seldom raise the many obvious ethical issues of which every anthropologist who has engaged in primary research is well aware. Seldom, if ever, are the more subtle ethical issues raised by anthropologists, either for the benefit of their fellow professionals or for their students.

Briefly, issues of ethical concern for anthropologists arise in their relations with the people they study, their professional relations with one another, their relations with the institutions and foundations that support them, their relations with the governments of the nations in which they conduct their research, and their relations with their own governments. Each of these relationships has many dimensions, and I do not wish to explore all of them here. *I shall explore those relationships that seem the most important to me: the relations between anthropologists and the people they study.* Many of the suggestions I shall make here will be found impossible to follow: some will be considered too stringent and some will be considered unnecessary, depending on the context. Others will seem more appropriate to our personal moral codes or life-styles than to a professional ethical code.

I shall raise many more problems than I can answer adequately. Nevertheless, all of the problems I shall discuss are relevant to current anthropological research, and all, I think, should be considered by anthropologists and prospective anthropologists, if not all social scientists. I ask each anthropologist to think seriously about the nature of his research and its potential harmful effects. Each anthropologist must consider the advisability of conducting research or using research results in ways that can bring harm to the subjects of the research. . . .

The Ethical Issues

Let us now explore several topics of ethical concern to us when we deal as anthropologists with human subjects. I shall discuss the right to private personality and the nature of privacy, consent, and confidentiality, . . . the consequences of research reports and the damage "truth" may do, the validity of anthropological research reports, and the effects of the researcher on the host community. All of these topics are intertwined, but I have attempted to separate them for ease of presentation.

From "On Ethics and Anthropology" by Joseph G. Jorgensen from *Current Anthropology*, Vol. 12 (June, 1971). Reprinted by permission of The University of Chicago Press.

Right to Private Personality

Generally, we think of ourselves as studying social behavior which is not trivial and about which our informants are usually protective. They may be protective because their deepest interests are involved. The Eastern Pueblo Indian, for instance, may protect his information about myth and ritual because he treasures it as absolutely inviolable, critical to his well-being and to the well-being of his community, and because he is honoring a public trust to safeguard the information. Informants may be protective because they do not know to what uses their information will be put. The squatter in a *barriada* in Lima, or a *callampa* in Santiago, for instance, may protect information about the source and amount of his income or about his political attitudes because he does not know or is not sure for what ends his revelations may be used. Informants may also be protective for other reasons. For instance, a Campa "big man" may be offended because you spoke to his younger and less influential brother before you spoke to him, lowering his status and prestige in his own community, and because of your blunder may keep his information from you. Or the "big man" may consider the anthropologist a threat to his position and withhold information in order to preserve it.

Each of these situations points to the right of the individual to private personality. Ruebhausen and Brim have called this right a "moral imperative" of our times, though in the United States and elsewhere it has not reached the status of a law. Indeed, except in a few special cases the claim to private personality is not recognized by the law, and dissemination of news, law enforcement, and effective government constitute constant challenges to this claim. Recently in the United States even the Fifth Amendment guarantee that an individual need not bear witness against himself (self-incrimination) has been challenged as unnecessary.

We all sense that we need to share some information and withhold other information. We communicate some things in order to get feedback, or to cleanse consciences, or to test what we believe, and so forth. Yet other things we wish to withhold. Some facts we cannot face, so we repress them; others we know, but prefer not to know or to discuss; still other facts, ideas, situations, and so forth we think we know, but are not sure we understand. In any case most of us prefer to choose for ourselves the time and circumstances under which, and the extent to which, the facts about our lives, our attitudes, beliefs, behavior, and opinions are to be shared with or withheld from others.

In the United States the law does not accord the anthropologist a privileged status in regard to the information he collects. Like the press, we have no legal right to claim confidential information. Our information can be subpoenaed. If we recognize our own claim to privacy and if we imagine the sticky situation that could result were some of our private information divulged to the press, to those who make laws, or to those who enforce the law, we realize that we bear a heavy responsibility to the subjects of our research. In the face of a subpoena—at home or abroad—we may find ourselves powerless to protect the information we collect.

The law aside, if an informant unwittingly or unwillingly divulges information which would bring him personal anguish if it were broadcast, we anthropologists should be very clear in our thinking before we publish that information.

Each person's claim to private personality, the anthropologist's desire to collect nontrivial information about which people are protective, the lack of legal safeguards for confidential information collected by anthropologists, and the community's need to know raise major ethical problems for the anthropologist.

Consent and Confidentiality

The claim to private personality and the community's need to know create many problems for the anthropologist. Our situation is unlike that of the priest, the lawyer, or the physician, whose help is *requested by the client* and whose right to privileged communication is deemed necessary (by law, in the United States) if he is to serve his clients. In contrast, as anthropologists we *ask for the help* of our subjects and we *offer* confidentiality as an *inducement* to informants for their cooperation. As I see it, the conditions of our verbal contracts place a twofold responsibility on us as anthropologists; we are bound by the informant's claim to the right of privacy and by the commitment we made as an inducement to gain cooperation. We are *ethically* bound to honor that commitment.

I also think that the assumption of ethical obligations entails an assertion of a *right* to fulfill those obligations. In practice, however, our right as anthropologists to fulfill those obligations is not so clear-cut. Others—for instance government bureaus, law enforcement agencies, or the editors of our professional journals—may be reluctant to grant that right and they may advance diverse notions about what is ethical in a particular situation.

Before I can deal with the ethical questions of privacy and confidentiality, or questions about the conditions under which information is used, I must deal with the ethical question of consent, or the question of the conditions under which information is obtained.

Consent. It seems sufficiently simple and obvious to say that the anthropologist should obtain from subjects consent to invade their privacy. The anthropologist should apprise his subjects of the intentions of his research and of the uses to which the information will be put. It also seems obvious that consent should always be obtained for the purposes mentioned by the anthropologist and not for other purposes. Thus, if we have apprised our informants of our intentions beforehand, they know at least something of the risks involved in giving information. In the following paragraphs, however, I will show how these "simple and obvious" principles can be wittingly and unwittingly violated and why we should be extraordinarily sensitive to the consequences of violating them.

Because our research is usually conducted among illiterate or semiliterate people who have scant knowledge of the uses to which data can be put, we are doubly obligated to spell out our intentions and not to exploit their naiveté. The extent to which we must explain our intentions will vary with the problems we address and the knowledge possessed by the host population. Our host populations, in particular, will vary greatly in their understandings of the implications of the ways in which research conducted among them could damage their own interests. I am not suggesting that it will be easy to apprise them of everything they ought to know, nor to make them immediately understand all that they ought to know. The anthropologist himself is often naive about the implications of his own research.

This seems to me a problem that the researcher will find quite difficult in some situations and much less so in others. Taking a simple situation first, the student of kinship semantics may convey his intentions best by simply telling people that he wants to study how they are related to one another and the words they use to refer to and to address their relatives. They need not be told that the researcher intends to construct a set of rules to account for their terminological system. If some informants become interested in the research as it progresses, or if the researcher's goals change while he is in the field, informants will often intuit some things the researcher intends to do but has not spelled out. Other changes in goals they will not intuit. If they ask questions about the new goals— for instance, if some of the informants become concerned about why the researcher is collecting genealogical information and linking terms to individuals and their attributes—they should most certainly be told why. If the answer is that you want to correlate practices of inheritance and succession with birth order, lineality, etc., it is in their interest to know such things. Indeed, the ethical thing to do is to explain that your interests are broadening before you are asked.

The researcher is not free to think that because he has received consent to collect information on one topic he is free to collect and use information on other topics. Implied consent often overlaps with concealed coercion. It is a special problem in anthropology because the researcher is usually in the host community for several months, his research goals are seldom very clearly formulated, and he may become privy, through observations and familiarity alone, to information that his informants would prefer he did not have. Just a little reflection will bring the point home to us: if we use this information we can hurt people in ways we cannot anticipate in advance nor compensate for afterwards.

The dimensions of implied consent should be evaluated by each researcher in each research context. Is it, for instance, appropriate to publish information on sorcery and witchcraft among reservation Indians or slum-dwellers if your informants fear sorcery and witchcraft, and would not, if questioned early in your residence in the field, freely give any information about sorcerers and witches (though they freely gave information about their household budgets and several other topics), fearing that harm might come to them from law agencies or witches or their cohorts if such information were broadcast? It is my own experience, and that of others, that after lengthy association with a researcher an informant begins to offer tidbits of information about his beliefs in sorcery in order to explain recent events—assuming, perhaps, that both the informant and the researcher understand this kind of information and its relevance in explaining certain phenomena. The informant does not provide the information because he is directly questioned nor does he assume that it will be published. Indeed, he does not offer it at all until he begins to regard the researcher as an "old shoe," i.e., someone who has been around so long and who is so well-worn that secret information need no longer be treated as secret. . . .

My point thus far is that consent should be requested for the research ends that are anticipated. This does not mean that the informant must be told all the details of the methodology involved in the analysis, nor every relationship that is determined in the course of the research. On the other hand, the researcher should not assume that consent to the use of some information implies consent to the use of all, nor that he is free to use information collected at the expense of his informant's naiveté.

A reverse dimension of the preceding problem is created by the anthropologist as the naive informant. I think it is unethical and irresponsible for the anthropologist to pass on to people of power and influence privileged information that is not openly published (or could not be published), and made available to all in the conduct of free and open inquiry, especially when the uses to which these people will put the data are not known. For example, I can imagine a patriotic American anthropologist, funded by the National Science Foundation or the National Institutes of Health to conduct research on family organization among the Ibo of Nigeria, being "debriefed" by the CIA. The CIA might offer the anthropologist a carrot, say $100.00 a day plus expenses to visit the Agency, appeal to his patriotism, flatter him by requesting his information about Ibo political elites and political agitators—or other topics on which the anthropologist may have some information, but which he did not intend to publish, may not fully understand, had not gained consent to publish, or could not publish without bringing harm to his unwitting informants—and he might, in turn, give this information to his inquisitors. All the good intentions in the world aside, by what right can this man disclose such information, and what, possibly, will the CIA do with it? Will they apologetically terrorize a few Ibos in the name of United States security?

Moving from consent and implied consent to concealed coercion and deceit in anthropological research raises still other ethical questions. Concealed coercion will no doubt become more and more prevalent as we anthropologists have more and more contact with agencies in the welfare establishment and as the welfare establishment grows to service the people we traditionally study. For instance, the Land and Operations Director at an Indian reservation in the United States may be required to give information to the anthropologist about land use and land development because he is a public employee. But he may be covertly coerced to give other information— personal information about himself, such as his extramarital philandering or his political preferences, or information on the private lives of his coworkers—that he would prefer not to expose. He fears repercussions to his job and position in the Bureau if he does not comply. The researcher may also coerce, in a concealed fashion, Indians living on the land to yield information about their use of the land that they would prefer not to give. For instance, they may indicate whether they worked it when, according to tribal law, they should not have, or whether they diverted irrigation water in violation of state law. Like the Land and Operations Director, the Indians may supply information because they too fear what would happen if they did not.

It seems to me that concealed coercion is as unethical a way to get information as is taking advantage of the naiveté of an informant. Neither, however, is as unethical as outright deceit. The anthropologist may verbally deceive his informants, assume a masquerade or a disguised role, or conduct covert and clandestine research. Deceit in research compromises the researcher, the sponsor for whom the deceit is conducted, and the subjects of the fraud. Although the espionage agent (competence aside) may masquerade as he collects intelligence information on the attitudes and opinions of, say, Cuban peasants and bourgeoisie, it does not follow that the anthropologist should do the same. Although neither journalist nor anthropologist has the right to privileged information, and although journalists, especially muckraking journalists, masquerade as they pursue information for public exposure, the anthropologist is not thereby obliged to follow suit. I accept the premise that anthropologists, by the very nature of their dedication to free and open inquiry and the pursuit of truth, cannot condone deceit in research. If the anthropologist seeks truth, exposes falsehood, feels an ethical obligation to others of his profession not to compromise them or make their own legitimate research suspect, and feels he has a right and a duty to honor the obligations he has made to his informants in requesting their help in giving him information about which they were protective, he cannot assume a masquerade at all. I contend that the ethical anthropologist, if he has trustworthy and valid information about a deceiver—say an espionage agent using an anthropological cover, or a political scientist who is "keeping his ear to the ground" for some foreign or domestic government agency— is obligated to expose him, although this is possible only if the anthropologist's own goals are sufficiently understood in the community in which he is working. At the very least, exposure of imposters will make our informants aware that their privacy is being invaded by deceitful means and that they may be giving information they would prefer not to give, to people they would prefer not to give it to, for ends they do not understand. . . .

Wherever and however masquerade is practiced, the anthropologist is violating his obligations to his hosts. His acts can be damaging to his colleagues, to his students, and because of his influence on the subject, to the situation he studies. If the anthropologist perpetrates a fraud and misleads his informants, he can blunder in situations he only pretends to understand, no matter how sympathetic he is. If he does not understand the situation, he can hurt people by violating customs, causing dissension in the society, or publishing misunderstood and damaging information. . . .

Deceitful research is liable to damage the reputation of anthropology and close off promising areas of legitimate investigation. Squatter settlements in Santiago or even whole nations, such as India or Chile, could be closed to study because of the repercussions from, or policies enacted in response to, deceitful research. When this possibility is coupled with the more important ethical problem of the deceitful invasion of privacy, it seems wholly within the bounds of ethics for an anthropologist to challenge the integrity of another's work. I feel that I, as a committee of one, should expose researchers involved in clandestine or disguised research, especially in politically sensitive areas. I would hope that others would do the same and that the various anthropological associations would condone exposure and, depending on the context of the research and the use of the data, censure.

It is naive to argue that if the subjects of the research are illiterate they will not read or learn about what we write. In part because we try to reach wider audiences, research results are popularized in lay magazines and books. The illiterate, semiliterate, and literate people I have studied are intensely interested in my researches among them. Can any anthropologist say that the people he studies are not interested in what he is doing and do not desire to learn what is written about them?

The confidence the public has in anthropology will be partially determined, perhaps, by the anthropologist's attitude towards consent and confidentiality. If we do not want to generate great suspicion of our intentions, we should safeguard ourselves through an ethical code which we take seriously and act upon in appropriate situations.

At this point I should mention again that gadgets, substances, and techniques exist today which can be used in ways that directly challenge individual freedom. These devices may interfere not only with an individual's liberty to choose what he wishes to disclose or withhold about himself, but when, to whom, and the extent to which his disclosures are to be made. Miniaturized microphones, tape recorders, and cameras, directional microphones, and infrared photography can be used in anthropological research. The miniaturized tape recorder, for instance, can be used to record conversations that the participants do not know are being recorded, and a miniaturized camera can be used simultaneously to correlate the faces of the participants with their conversations. In some future situations it is even conceivable that one-way mirrors, polygraph machines, hypnosis, behavior-controlling drugs, and trick questionnaires could be used by anthropologists, alone or in collaboration with other students of behavior, to collect information. Finally, though this is not intended to exhaust the available means and techniques, the computer, with its enormous capacity for the storage and retrieval of information about people, can be used for many—some of them illicit —purposes.

It is my opinion that these devices and techniques should be used only if consent for their use is received from the subject and only if the data are used for the purposes specified by the researcher. One cannot, in the name of academic freedom or scientific research, probe beyond the bounds of decent inquiry. We have no right to violate the privacy of human lives with these forms of deceit. . . .

Let me summarize my position on consent in research. I think consent should be gained before and during the course of research. As goals change in the course of fieldwork, consent for new inquiry should be obtained. Consent applies only to the purposes specified, not to other purposes. The individuals being studied should be allowed to choose for themselves the time and circumstances under which, and the extent to which, their attitudes, beliefs, behavior, opinions, and personal histories, including jobs, income, and information on scores of other topics, are to be shared with, or withheld from, others.

It follows that I think it is unethical for an anthropologist to disguise his identity in order to enter a private domain, to lie about the character of the research he is conducting, or to allow the data he has collected to be used for purposes he does not understand but which he has reason to believe can cause harm to his informants.

Confidentiality. In the simplest terms, we must protect the identity of individual informants once we promise confidentiality. In such situations, responses should be treated as if they were anonymous, since we have an obligation not to reveal any information which could identify or implicate an individual.

Because the law does not accord an anthropologist's information privileged status, we should exercise all safeguards necessary to protect our informants. For instance, if names are left on interview pages, individuals can be exposed if and when the data are subpoenaed. Codes should be devised to replace names for informants' records, and these should be used until identification is no longer necessary, when the code numbers should be destroyed. In extreme cases it may be wise to keep records under lock and key and to destroy records that could be used for harmful purposes, or, if subpoenaed, would violate the anthropologist's obligations to his informants.

If data are stored, either for longitudinal studies or because someone may want the raw data in the future, consent should be obtained to store the data and for all future uses of it.

In the past, anthropologists have seldom been subpoenaed. But at present the subjects (i.e., the people we study, not necessarily the topics we pursue) of our worldwide research are increasingly threatening to the stability of local governments and world power blocks. I suspect that our data, whether intentionally politically sensitive or not, are increasingly subject to subpoena. We should take precautions, then, to preserve anonymity and, if necessary, destroy records. . . .

There will be cases in which our research findings cannot be applied towards our research goals and others in which the information cannot be communicated, once sworn to confidentiality. We should always think our research proposals through before we embark on them. Confidentiality may not be desired or necessary in some situations, and, if not, we should have the presence of mind to inform our subjects, when we request their help, that we cannot guarantee anonymity and do not wish to guarantee confidentiality. I have already pointed out that leaders, especially of small groups, can be identified rather easily. In complexly organized societies, ranking bureaucrats can be identified, as can elected officials and prominent evangelists.

Though this is very difficult, perhaps we could explain to our informants, in some situations, that we cannot promise confidentiality for some of the behavior we will report on. This would make explicit our claim that we have a right to study social behavior in certain situations in a nonconfidential way.

In the United States and Canada, at least, we anthropologists could perhaps study publicly accountable behavior in nonconfidential ways. We would attempt to maintain the anonymity of our public informants, but recognize that we cannot guarantee it. Let it be clear, however, that I am talking about the *public* behavior of elected and appointed public officials, businessmen, professors, physicians, and all other civilians who perform jobs for which they are publicly accountable. I do not mean that we can study and publish other aspects of personal behavior without the consent of our subjects, lest we succumb to the ethically indefensible practices of concealed coercion or implied consent. If we take seriously the contention that we anthropologists have special skills and special knowledge about human behavior and that we also have special responsibilities to seek out the truth, we should perhaps consider as one of these responsibilities the task of furthering public accountability in complex societies.

Can the Truth Hurt?

In suggesting that we have a special responsibility to make known the public behavior of publicly accountable people, I recognize that the anthropologist who is a citizen of the United States cannot easily do this in, say, Bolivia without causing problems for himself and probably for all other anthropologists. However, an anthropologist can do this in his own country, if he is willing to pay the consequences and has the consent of his subjects. Nevertheless, we may fear what the truth, if published, will do to our informants, even if consent to publish it has been obtained. If the public considers the behavior described immoral, our report may eventually damage our informants. For instance, a report on alcohol-related criminal offenses among American Indians may prompt Congress to cut funds for Indian family welfare, from the Bureau of Indian Affairs budget, or it may firm up prejudice and provide rationalization for bigotry towards Indians, or both.

It seems to me that we can publish the truth as we understand it, assuming that truth makes men freer or more autonomous (but not assuming that "science must advance"), or we can avoid the kinds of research subjects that will lead us into these painful problems. For instance, if we feel we should assess, analyze, and publish our data on the behavior of the revolutionary leaders in the squatter settlements of Santiago, and if we also have reason to believe that we cannot assure the anonymity of the leaders nor the confidentiality of our data, and that our published and unpublished information can bring physical and political harm to them, then we should not undertake the research. It does not seem ethical to me to waste time and someone else's money publishing watered-down results or results known to be half-truths.

If we decide to go ahead with, for example, the "alcohol-related criminality" research among American Indians, we will have to anticipate the probable misuses of our reports. If we do have special knowledge of social behavior and special responsibilities to present the truth, we should

not have great difficulty in anticipating and averting misuses of our reports. When we tell the truth as we understand it, we should make all efforts that seem reasonable to deny weapons to potential misusers. Should we, for instance, demonstrate that reservation Indian youths drink and commit crimes at a rate which is 500 percent greater than urban and rural white youths, and that reservation Indian adults also have a high rate of alcohol-related criminal convictions, these data could easily be used to show that the crime problem stems from the Indian race or the Indian home. Because only reservation Indians are under constant supervision of the Bureau of Indian Affairs, these data could also be used to show that the alcohol-related crime rate of the American Indian is a product of Bureau management (or lack of management) of funds allocated to Indian families. We should anticipate these misuses, say, by describing the contexts in which Indians live, drink, and commit crimes. We must connect Indian life on reservations, their lack of access to strategic resources and power, and their meager expectations for a better life, and suggest that these are the causes of their alcohol-related criminality (though in time the alcohol-related criminality affects the economic and political predicament of the Indian and the two become causal-effects of one another). Race, family history, and the Bureau of Indian Affairs did not "cause" the problem.

I feel, then, that we can avoid misuse only if we pursue answers to "why" questions. If we establish as an explanandum (an empirical generalization or statement of fact to be explained), that Indians drink a lot and also commit crimes while under the influence of alcohol, anyone can ask "why?" Even if the explanation offered is that the Indian is very lazy and has a red skin, there is no way to know whether the explanation (assertion) is correct unless we test it. We have no inductive or deductive laws from which we can infer or deduce an explanation for our explanandum. We can merely ask a new "why" question about the empirical generalization we have just established to "explain" the empirical generalization that preceded and prompted it. We cannot terminate a series of "why" questions with an appeal to laws, as can be done in the conceptual scheme of natural science.

We must, then, anticipate the harmful "explanations" that will be offered for our research findings.

As we conduct more primary research in the slums of developed and underdeveloped nations, what we have to say will become increasingly fateful in the lives of individuals and groups. It behooves us not only to report our findings accurately, but also to be sensitive to the way these findings are used. . . .

The Effect of the Researcher on the Host Community

A final point, entailing the questions of consent, confidentiality, and validity, is the effect a researcher may have on the community in which he works. Whether a person is honest or deceitful about his purposes, he will have some effect on the community he studies. He will, after all, change the composition, if not the life-style, of the community somewhat. His effect depends, of course, on where he is and what he is doing. In some communities he may represent one more mouth to feed, or a source of amusement, or a source of fear, or the big spender and big provider his informants have been waiting for, and so on. The behavior of the host population may well be modified in ways we do not understand, especially if we have no prior knowledge of its behavior, when we work in its midst.

The fraud, deceiver, or masquerader, in particular, does not know what "data" he brings to the situation he studies and how his hosts respond to his presence and his assumed manner. He does not know how and in what ways he affects a situation by his own fraudulent interaction. I do not know how to exercise controls over the effects introduced by the fraudulent observer. I have more confidence that I can ferret out the influence of the honest observer, one who makes his intents and purposes known and who gains consent to conduct his study, than I can that of the sham.

Examples of the unintended consequences of deceitful research are manifold. A particularly poignant one comes from the sociology of deviance. Ball cites the experience of a Ph.D. candidate who deceived the members of an urban gang and joined them with the intention of studying their organization and behavior. He cleared himself with the local police before doing so, thus obligating himself to that law enforcement agency. The gang leaders proposed an ill-conceived robbery soon after the student joined the gang. He did not want to lose his dissertation study group, so he offered a few revisions in the plans. They soon asked him to become the leader. . . .

Allan R. Holmberg
Adventures in Culture Change

The Siriono of eastern Bolivia were studied in 1941 by Allan Holmberg in one of the most difficult and harrowing research undertakings in the anthropological literature. This moving excerpt reflects the author's misgivings about the consequences of that research on the precarious life of the people whose lives he had so briefly but fatefully entered. Holmberg subsequently became one of the foremost researchers on planned and directed culture change, having headed a major study in the Vicos valley of Peru where, as landlord of the valley, he was in a position to control the changes experienced by its inhabitants as they moved toward the economic independence he planned for them. This

raised important ethical issues again. In this context, the last sentences of this selection take on added significance: "When I contemplate what I did, I am not infrequently filled with strong feelings of guilt. Maybe they should have been left as they were."

Today there are few aboriginal cultures of the world which have not been profoundly affected by the influences of Western society. Especially the

Holmberg, Allan R. "Adventures in Culture Change" from *Method and Perspective in Anthropology* edited by Robert F. Spencer. University of Minnesota Press, Mpls. © 1954 U. of M. Reprinted by permission of the University of Minnesota Press.

effects of the modern technological revolution have been deeply felt in the most remote corners of the world. Because of this, modern anthropologists, concerned with problems of culture change, have been afforded (or they have sought) few opportunities to observe at first hand situations in which there has previously been little or no contact between an isolated aboriginal group and representatives of the Western world. Here it is proposed to discuss an instance in which just such an opportunity arose.

During the course of an ethnological investigation among the Siriono Indians of eastern Bolivia in 1941–42 I, in company with a Bolivian companion and a number of semi-acculturated Siriono, encountered in August of 1942, after wandering some fifteen days through the swamp jungles southeast of the village El Carmen, a band of Siriono who had had so little contact with the outside world that about the only items of Western technology found among them were two machetes worn to the size of pocket knives. Having devoted several months previously to a study of the native language and culture at a Bolivian Government Indian School called Casarabe—situated about thirty miles east of Trinidad, capital of the Department of the Beni—and having adjusted myself to the semi-nomadic conditions of forest life, I followed these Indians around for a while, finally settling with them on the banks of the Rio Blanco at a site which we founded and named Tibaera, the Indian word for a palm tree which grew in great abundance there. It was while I was in residence at Tibaera, from October 1942 to April 1943, that I was presented with favorable opportunities to initiate a number of "experiments" in culture change which brief subsequent visits to the area enabled me to check on from time to time. This paper, therefore, is devoted to a consideration of a few of the changes introduced at that time and of some of the effects resulting therefrom.

Under aboriginal conditions, the Siriono are a semi-nomadic people who, in terms of technology at least, may be classified among the most handicapped peoples of the world. They live with a bare minimum of what the late Professor Malinowski called "material apparatus." In fact, the most effective tools with which they wrest but a meager living from their environment consist of a cumbersome bow and arrow and a crude digging stick, the former being used exclusively by men and the latter principally by women. While they practice agriculture—small amounts of maize, manioc, camotes, and tobacco are planted in natural clearings in the forest—they live principally by hunting, fishing, and collecting. Having neither stone nor steel tools—little stone is found in the environment—they are unable to clear any large amounts of land for agriculture; and because they occupy a relatively harsh environment, much of which is inundated for about four or five months of the rainy season, from December to May, the major problem with which they have to contend is that of supplying sufficient food for survival. Since the solution of this problem is impeded in part, at least, by a technological insufficiency, the setting struck me as an excellent one in which to initiate technological change and observe its effect on the native economy and other aspects of culture.

It should be made clear at the outset, however, that on first contact with this band of Siriono I was in no position to assume the role of an innovator. We were traveling as light as possible at the time, and besides, my central problem required that I make observations on the native culture as it functioned under aboriginal conditions. Thus it was only after such observations had been made and the band had voluntarily returned with us to Tibaera (we had previously established ourselves there with remnants of another group of Siriono who had escaped from bondage several months before) that I was able to initiate what attempts I made at innovation. It should be stated for the record, however, that my Bolivian companion and I had taken with us a few basic items of Western technology upon which our own survival depended. These included a rifle and shotgun, a number of machetes, fishhooks, hammocks, mosquito nets, several changes of clothing, and a few aluminum cooking utensils. In addition, I carried a camera, notebooks, and a few common remedies such as quinine, aspirin, and injections of emetine hydrochloride. The only supplies of food we carried with us were salt, sugar, and coffee. Unfortunately our supplies of sugar and salt were accidentally lost during the first few days of our trip so that about all we had to remind us of our former diet during a sojourn of about a month was coffee, of which we had taken an abundant supply and for which the Indians had not yet acquired an appetite.

I mention these matters in passing to indicate

that at the time of first contact and for about two months thereafter our influence on the band was minimal, for we needed what supplies we possessed to take care of ourselves. Nevertheless, the desire on the part of the Indians for a superior technology was immediately felt. We had been with the band for little more than a few minutes before we were bombarded with requests for tools, especially machetes. These we did not have, but I had brought with me several boxes of cotton thread, which were distributed to the Indians by way of compensation. It was at this time that the idea of future experiment first presented itself to me.

Shortly after returning to Tibaera, therefore (I had established by this time that the Siriono under aboriginal conditions do face a life of extreme impoverishment), I made a journey of several days down the Rio Blanco by canoe in quest of some basic items of technology to introduce. Limited by matters of budget, however, as is so often the case in field work, I was only able to afford to purchase a few machetes and axes together with a small supply of such seeds as rice and watermelon, which the Siriono did not then plant under aboriginal conditions. These, together with trade goods and food, I brought back with me to Tibaera. The machetes and axes, of which I had only six each, I presented to members of the band who I thought were the most influential and with whom I had had greatest contact. They were distributed in this manner because I felt that my own residence among the Siriono depended on maintaining rapport with at least the persons of most prestige in the group, particularly the chief and some of his immediate kinsmen. In order to temper the disappointment (in some cases, hostility) of those who did not receive tools, I made gifts to them of such trade goods as beads, necklaces, cloth, thread, pocket knives, and salt. Since it was not yet the season for agriculture, the seeds were withheld for future planting.

The introduction of these few tools alone represented a drastic change in the technological system of the people who received them; they progressed overnight from a technology of the pre-Stone Age to one of the Iron Age. As might be expected, of course, repercussions of this change were immediately apparent, especially on the economic life. Whereas formerly, for example, a person spent as much as half a day in extracting a palm cabbage, a Siriono staple, with a digging stick, he could remove more than a half dozen in a similar period with an axe. For the people possessing tools, therefore, the production of palm heart ceased to be a serious economic problem. To take another example, the Siriono are extremely fond of wild honey, the only sweet they possess. They seldom become satiated with it, however, for lack of an efficient means of extracting it. Wild bees generally build their hives in dead, hollow trees still standing in the forest, and in order to extract the honey the hole through which the bees enter the hive must be enlarged sufficiently to permit the entrance of the hand. Under aboriginal conditions firebrands and digging sticks are employed for this purpose, but often an entire day of labor is rewarded by only a few handfuls of honey. Actually, by aboriginal methods but a small proportion of the exploitable wild honey is removed from the environment each year. By using an axe, however, a hive of wild honey could be removed—and much more efficiently—in less than an hour's time. Since the introduction of axes corresponded with the season for gathering wild honey, the production of this food also increased enormously.

The same may be said with respect to most economic activities. Wild fruits were more easily harvested, the inaccessible ones by cutting down the trees; wood for bows and arrows and house-building was more readily extracted; slain animals were more rapidly cut up; mobility through swamp and jungle was greatly increased; wooden utensils and tools were better and more rapidly constructed. In short, the productive capacity of the families receiving tools more than doubled at once.

With respect to the social effects of these innovations, only a few remarks can be made. In general, the economic benefits were not enjoyed by all members of the band. Native ideas of personal property and patterns of food distribution were, at first at least, rigidly adhered to. Among the Siriono feelings of food deprivation are extremely high, and they are reluctant to share products outside the extended family. Actually, the machetes and axes were jealously guarded and the fruits of their production confined principally to the families who possessed them. Because of this, complaints were bitter, and demands for tools—demands which I could not fulfill—were constant.

Another consequence of the limited introduction of more efficient tools was a noticeable rise in in-group hostility. One of the first effects of the increased production of wild honey, for example, was an increase in the supply of native beer and in the number and duration of drinking bouts. This in turn led to a more frequent expression of aggression, since drinking feasts are the principal occasions when both verbal and physical aggression are expressed among the men. Under aboriginal conditions these drinking feasts seldom lead to long-lasting hostilities because the supply of native beer is limited by the arduous labor involved in the extraction of honey. But with improved techniques it was possible to hold these feasts with greater frequency and greater intensity. On one occasion, in fact—and this was a direct result of the increased production of native beer—the aggressions expressed at a drinking bout of considerable intensity resulted in such a strong hostility among the members of two extended families that the unity of the band itself was threatened. Needless to say, this was an effect which I had not anticipated at the time the tools were introduced.

Perhaps the most significant consequence of the introduction of steel tools, however, was that it paved the way for an expansion of agriculture—and hence an ensuring of the food supply—hitherto unknown among the Siriono. Attempts to improve agricultural methods and to introduce new plants met with a variety of responses. I had originally suggested to the men who received steel tools that they might most fruitfully employ them to intensify agriculture. But since it was the dry season, the best one for hunting and fishing, 3 of the men were away from camp so much of the time that little heed was paid to my advice. With another 3, however, I was able to establish workable relations. These were Eantándu, a chief, and two of his brothers-in-law, Enía and Mbíku. Changes in agriculture were initiated largely through them. The pattern followed was that of disrupting as little as possible native agricultural practices, such as that of each man planting for himself, and of fitting the changes as nearly as possible into the existing culture pattern. The procedure consisted first in convincing each of the men to clear a sizable plot of good land for himself. When this was done and the brush was thoroughly dried, the plots were burned over. Then shortly after the first rains came in late November each man was encouraged to seed his land with maize, manioc, and other native products. For lack of better tools, this was done largely with the digging stick; however, the methods of planting were considerably improved. In addition, each man was asked to reserve a piece of land for dry rice farming, which my Bolivian companion and I introduced at Tibaera. Finally, Eantándu alone was encouraged to seed a small patch of watermelon.

All of the agricultural labor connected with the experiment was performed by the men themselves or by their wives. But not voluntarily, nor without reward. Often during the course of the work, I or my Bolivian companion had to supply the families with meat, which we could obtain only by hunting and fishing ourselves, sometimes at night; otherwise they would have spent almost all of their days in the forest, and our attempts would doubtless have failed. Then too, some such encouragement was necessary because of a logical suspicion on the part of the Siriono that we intended to profit by the results of their labor, as had been the case in all previous instances of contact with whites.

Since the season was favorable and the land was new, the crops thrived far beyond expectations. After being weeded and hoed a number of times (again largely with digging sticks), the resulting harvest was—to the Siriono at least—prodigious. Suddenly Eantándu, Enía, and Mbíku found themselves with more food than they had ever possessed before at one time in their lives. From this small patch alone, Eantándu harvested more than a hundred watermelons. These he ate in such quantity that on two occasions he became violently ill with indigestion. During a week or so of harvest, Eantándu, Enía, and Mbíku laid away what might normally be regarded as a six months' supply of rice and maize. Others, planting by aboriginal methods, had harvested much smaller yields of maize for themselves, supplies which were almost exhausted by the time I left the band a month later. During this month Eantándu, Enía, and Mbíku had only occasionally shared the results of their bountiful harvest and then only begrudgingly in exchange for meat or other products they happened to be in need of at the moment. Everyone, however, had managed at least to taste rice and watermelons and to acquire seeds which they were reserving for later planting. Two years later the Siriono to a man were growing these crops on the banks of Lago Huachi, some twenty miles east of Tibaera. In the meantime they had acquired more steel tools through trade with the whites, and the nomadic pattern of life had been greatly reduced.

Hand in hand with experiments in agriculture, attempts were made to introduce some domestic animals. These were made through one man alone, Chief Eantándu. Under aboriginal conditions the Siriono possess no domestic animals, not even the dog. This is not surprising; their semi-nomadic pattern of life is hardly consistent with animal husbandry. Even the dog would be of little use to them in hunting in a tangled jungle where the meat supply is mostly shot in trees and where it is not sufficient to feed even themselves, to say nothing of others. Moreover, the Siriono responded with great fear to the dog. Since the footprint of a dog is very similar to that of a jaguar, the two animals were equated under one term (*yákwa*) and the suspicions and fears of one were generalized to include the other. Consequently Eantándu expressed grave doubts as to the utility of the dog, which I attempted to introduce. Actually his suspicions were well founded. Even though well trained in some types of hunting, the dog proved to be a burden to him. He scared more game away than he hunted; he robbed food from camp; he frightened women and children; he even bit a child or two. In short, he was not adaptable to the existing culture pattern. This was brought home to me on many occasions but especially once when I was absent from camp for about five days. I returned to find the dog almost dead of starvation. Consequently, on leaving the Siriono, I left the mongrel with my Bolivian companion, and on my visit of a couple of years later found that the Indians were still doing nicely without the animal.

Attempts to introduce domestic fowl were somewhat more successful. Returning from a trip down the river, I brought with me several roosters and a number of hens which I had planned to use as a provision for meat and eggs for myself and as an experiment in culture change among the Siriono. With this latter idea in mind, I presented a pair of hens and a rooster to Eantándu with an explanation of the benefits he might expect providing he took proper care of his brood. In this case it was not even necessary for him to feed and water the chickens since there was plenty of food around camp in the form of insects, rotten wild fruits, grubs, and worms, and the supply of water in the river was unlimited. In spite of this, the first attempt failed. Within three days after receiving the fowls, Eantándu, feeling the pinch of bad luck in hunting,

butchered them. He explained to me that his wives—he had two at this time—had urged him to do so because his children were hungry. Needless to say, I gave him no more at the moment.

Meanwhile I had a number of hens setting myself which, within the expected time, hatched out more than twenty chicks. While they were growing to maturity—we had constructed a rude chicken house of bamboo to shelter the brood—Eantándu began to regret his previous lack of foresight and asked me if I would give him a few more hens and a rooster to begin the experiment anew. This I agreed to do, but only after he had constructed a chicken house and after he had promised to take good care of his chickens. On this occasion the experiment produced different results. Within five months his flock had grown to the size of my own, and he was able to enjoy the fruits of their production whenever pickings in the forest were slim. Up to this time, however, his good fortune had been shared with no one.

After leaving Tibaera in April 1943, I did not see Eantándu again for more than two years. During the interim one of his wives had been killed by a falling tree, and the band had undergone numerous unpleasant encounters with whites. The pattern of chicken-raising, however, still persisted with Eantándu and had by this time diffused to three or four of his kinsmen as well.

Another item of Western technology which served as the basis for experiment while I was living among the Siriono was the shotgun. Although no attempt was made by me to introduce the use of firearms to the Indians generally, this weapon did serve as a means of confirming a hypothesis as to the relation between prestige and hunting in Siriono society. While living with the Indians in the forest and at Tibaera, I was daily impressed, of course, by the importance of hunting and food-producing activities. I had also observed that the men who hunted the most game were generally the most respected. But in no way were these observations more neatly confirmed than in an experimental situation which arose while living at Tibaera. Among the Indians living there was a young man named Enía, who was regarded by everyone as a poor hunter. Part of the reason for this was that he had resided on a Bolivian *estancia* at an age when he would normally have been acquiring the techniques of hunting with the bow and arrow had he been living under aboriginal conditions. As an adult he rejoined his band and married the sister of the chief. But he had never been able to develop his skill in hunting, although he made every effort to do so. Actually, when I first knew him, he was very unhappy about his lack of hunting ability, for he was being constantly insulted at drinking feasts and was almost daily ridiculed by his wife for returning from the forest empty-handed. Once he had possessed two wives, one of whom he lost. His brother-in-law, the chief, made no bones about telling me (and Enía) that he was not much good.

This situation struck me as an excellent one in which to introduce a more efficient technology. Having firearms myself, I began to take Enía with me on the hunt and gradually taught him the use of the shotgun, which he soon learned to manipulate very well by himself. As a result of this, his meat production jumped enormously and his prestige began to rise. In addition to this he was one of the participants in the successful agricultural experiment, so that when I left the band he was enjoying exceptionally high status, as exemplified by the fact that he had acquired a second wife and was insulting others at drinking feasts instead of being insulted by them. When I left the band, taking the shotgun with me, I feared for the status of Enía, but on a visit by plane to Lago Huachi, on the banks of which remnants of his band of Siriono were camping a couple of years later, I found that he had again latched himself onto "white" civilization and was working on a plantation of wild rubber, apparently doing quite well. What has happened to him since, I do not know.

After the war, however, the working of wild rubber became a losing game. The plantation probably fell into disrepair. In any case, the Indians left. Recent letters indicate that they are now living with my former Bolivian companion, Silva—by whom they are probably being exploited—about halfway between the missions of Guarayos and the village of El Carmen. For the most part they abandoned their old way of life, shifting from a largely nomadic to a largely settled existence based on agriculture. Today I am frequently disturbed by the fact that I had a hand in initiating some of the changes which probably ultimately overwhelmed them and over which neither I nor they had control. Indeed, when I contemplate what I did, I am not infrequently filled with strong feelings of guilt. Maybe they should have been left as they were.

Cora Du Bois

Appendix to the Preface of 1944

This brief appendix to a classic social-psychological study, The People of Alor, *carried out on an island in what is now Indonesia, is a stark reminder of the fact that research is never without consequences, many of them unanticipated. The anthropologist cannot escape the fact that his work entails meddling in the lives of others, and he cannot escape its human and moral consequences.*

In the fifteen years that have elapsed since this first preface was written I have not returned to Alor. In that interim World War II swept over the area. In July, 1942, four months after the Dutch forces capitulated in Java, the Japanese garrisoned the island. The Dutch, having foreseen several years in advance the possibility of a Japanese invasion, are rumored to have had standing orders for the evacuation of their personnel from the outer islands of Indonesia. In any event, the Japanese took possession of Alor without opposition. . . .

After the war I received a letter from a young

Reprinted by permission of the publishers from *People of Alor: A Social-Psychological Study of an East Indian Island* by Cora Du Bois, Cambridge, Mass.: Harvard University Press, Copyright 1944 by the University of Minnesota; 1960, 1972 by Cora Du Bois.

controleur who was sent to Alor during the Dutch interregnum before Indonesia achieved independence. It was a jovial, almost a flippant, letter. I don't remember his name, but he offered me every hospitality if I wished to return and asked me for a copy of this book. He told me quite casually the story of Atimelang and the house called Hamerika. The Japanese had used it as a patrol station, for the Japanese, like the Dutch, sent small groups of troops to crisscross the island at irregular intervals to maintain order and prevent uprisings. Word reached the Japanese command in Kalabahi that the village leaders of Atimelang were claiming that Hamerika would win the war. This could have been nothing but the most innocent fantasy to my friends in Atimelang since they had never even heard of the United States prior to my arrival. But to the Japanese, suffering from all the nervous apprehensions of any occupying power in a strange and therefore threatening environment, such talk could mean only rebellion. As the Dutch, years before, had sent a punitive expedition to the area after the murder of the radjah, as they had later imprisoned Malelaka because he had visions of the arrival of "good beings" (nala kang), so the Japanese sent troops to arrest five of my friends in Atimelang. I am not sure who all of them were from the young controleur's letter, but apparently Thomas, Malelaka, and the Chief of Dikimpe were among them. In Kalabahi they were publicly decapitated as a warning to the populace.

There is no end to the intricate chain of responsibility and guilt that the pursuit of even the most arcane social research involves. "No man is an island."

Donald K. Grayson

Human Life vs. Science

This letter to the editor juxtaposes the definition of people as objects of study and people as subjects for humane action. While the two definitions need not be incompatible, they are frequently used as though they were. It is perhaps the test of a viable social science that curiosity never take precedence over humanity.

The April 1969 issue of the *Newsletter* seems to spell out, for those who are interested, the true state of American anthropology. In the short note, "'Stone Age' Group Encountered," the Smithsonian Institution Center for Short-lived Phenomena reports the discovery of a "non-agricultural hunting and gathering band" in southeastern Surinam—a highly significant and very welcome addition to the anthropological realm.

But the reader is also told that "these bands will soon be decimated by disease from this contact." We are now faced with a clear dilemma: which is more important—human life, or, the scientific pursuit of anthropology? Being an anthropologist, the author of this article, as a representative of the Smithsonian Institution, seeks to ensure that these people will indeed be short lived. Instead of pleading that anthropologists, as humans, mobilize all the economic and political resources at their command to provide proper medical treatment for the Akuri and their neighbors, we see a request for anthropological help in the study of a people which we are to let die.

I cannot help but be reminded of the [World War II] Nazi physician dissecting live persons in the interest of his science. Luckily, the Nazi doctor is no longer permitted to perform his atrocities, and I suggest that anthropologists, too, should realize that it is far more important to save life than to record its passing.

It is immoral and inhuman to take "support

"Human Life vs. Science" by Donald K. Grayson. Reproduced by permission of the American Anthropological Association from *Newsletter*, Vol. 10, No. 6, (1969).

funds" for this anthropological study when these funds could be used to provide medical help for the Akuri people. I suggest that we make known to William Crocker, Priscilla Reining, as well as to all those who feel otherwise, that the objective study of anthropology has no right to exist when it denies the right of existence to the living. And, by making no attempt to help the Akuri, by cheerfully taking funds which could be spent for medical aid,

we are denying this right.

I hope that the attitude which spawned the requests in the Smithsonian's note will itself be short lived. If the Institution's Center for Short-lived Phenomena is to be characterized by such attitudes, then I also hope that it will soon qualify as one of those phenomena which it purports to study. Right now, however, our concern must be for the Akuri.

Bernard Gallin

A Case for Intervention in the Field

In this essay an anthropologist finds himself confronted with demands on his person as a result both of his relationships in the community where he lives and works and of his special role and capabilities. Those demands will have specific and telling consequences in the community. His scientific desire to be a "neutral observer" thus conflicts with his human desire to be a friend and benefactor. He tells clearly why and how the human role prevailed and, incidentally, how it enhanced his scientific understanding.

I

The question of the field anthropologist's participation or intervention in the affairs of the people he is studying has often been discussed. In the past (with the exception of James Spillius), this question has been considered only in terms of the field worker who has a choice in the matter of intervention. The pros and cons in the discussions of this question have in fact been based on the assumption that there is always a free choice for the anthropologist in such field situations.

But one must also consider the situation in which the anthropologist does not have a free choice of action. Although we like to feel that the anthropologist in the field can maintain his principles in such matters, it is not always the case. Rather the field worker may have the role of interventionist or participant thrust upon him by the community.

Should he refuse to assume such a role—on the grounds that he wishes to remain neutral and objective—his position in the village could become virtually untenable and so result in the necessary termination of his research work.

In this paper I will attempt to show: (1) a situation in which the anthropologist may not have a choice in the question of intervention and (2) what may be gained through intervention.

II

Recently I spent fifteen months carrying on field research in a small Taiwanese agricultural village where I was thrust into just such a situation. I had little choice but to intervene by lending my help, and it is this case study which I will discuss here.

Hsin Hsing village is an agricultural village on the west-central coastal plain of Taiwan. Its people emigrated from the mainland's southeastern coastal province of Fukien about 150 years ago. As villages go in the area, it is relatively small having a population of somewhat over 600 people.

The village families have about nine different family names, of which four names comprise about 80 percent of the village population. But even families having the same surname are not neces-

"A Case for Intervention in the Field" by Bernard Gallin from *Human Organization* (Vol. 18, No. 3, 1959). Reproduced by the permission of the Society for Applied Anthropology and the author.

sarily related. While a highly segmented family village is not unusual for this area of Taiwan, it is in sharp contrast with the clan villages which are so commonly found in the southeastern provinces of the Chinese mainland.

Like most of the villages in the area, Hsin Hsing grows rice as its main crop, although other crops such as vegetables and wheat in the winter—the third crop of the year—are also grown. Wet rice usually comprises the first two crops of the year in the area. The key factor which determines whether or not rice and other water-demanding crops will successfully be grown is irrigation water and its availability at the right time and place in large enough quantities.

Water is so crucial in the area that at various times it has been the root of violence. It was in such an incident of violence over the water problem that I became actively involved in village affairs.

III

Early in the spring of 1958, a Hsin Hsing villager, Li Fan, and his elderly father, were severely beaten while tending their fields. They were beaten by two men from the next village of Ta Yu. The reason for the beating was that Li Fan, in order to water his crop, had taken water from a public irrigation ditch which was considered to be carrying, at the time, privately owned water rather than public water. The men claimed that the water which Li Fan had taken out of the ditch was from the co-operative pumping station of which Li Fan was not a member. As the two men were beating Li Fan senseless with an iron hoe, his father tried to come to his aid and so was also beaten.

This cooperative pumping station pumps water from a nearby river to the members' fields. The pumping station is located in the larger and wealthier neighboring village of Ta Yu. Most of its members are from Ta Yu village although there are several members from other nearby villages, including a few from Hsin Hsing. Because the great majority of the pumping station members are Ta Yu villagers, these members have the controlling hand while members from other villages have little if any voice in the cooperative's policy making. The large size of the organization caused the Ta Yu members to feel that they had little to fear from outsiders. The attitude with which the cooperative had apparently unofficially agreed was that if any

of its members caught an outsider taking the cooperative's water, it would be desirable to beat the individual as an example to others. In such a case the association would fully back whoever did the beating in case any trouble should ensue. Before the beating of Li Fan and his father there were several other such beatings which went unchallenged.

When Li Fan and his father were carried back from the fields after having been beaten, the word quickly spread through Hsin Hsing village. The villagers were at once incensed at this brutal act and felt that the guilty ones should be duly punished. The police had immediately been notified and also a doctor was called to treat the men's severe wounds. But until the doctor or police arrived, I was called in to administer first aid—mainly to stop the bleeding. At the same time some of the villagers present asked me to take pictures of the main victim in his bloody condition. I had neither reason nor desire to refuse either request.

Already, without any sign of just how much I would soon become involved in this case, I was now involved at least to the point of having seen the victims, administered first aid, photographed Li Fan and heard the first-hand story of what had happened from two teen-aged boys who had witnessed the beating.

The two police officers, who soon came on their bicycles from the local police station, were also angry at this new violence and recorded the stories of the two victims and the witnesses. Later, however, when the police wished to arrest the two Ta Yu villagers, the latter insisted that they had not started the fight, but had only fought back in self-defense, and had in fact themselves been beaten by Li Fan and his father. Such a situation, under the law meant that the two men would not necessarily be held by the police, especially since a wealthy and influential man in the area—who was a friend of the Ta Yu pumping station cooperative—had acted as guarantor for the two men. The men were therefore released and they immediately pressed charges against Li and his father. The latter act was done with the greatest haste and efficiency. This was made possible because of the wealthy Ta Yu landlord and other leaders who are important persons in the cooperative and influential in the area and the local district office and so know how to handle such matters.

Although the police saw for themselves and later

testified that the two Ta Yu men were not hurt in the fight, the two men were nevertheless able to purchase false affidavits of injury from a notorious doctor in a nearby market town.

On the other hand, the Hsin Hsing villagers faced problems. They did not have anyone who could help write up an accurately detailed letter of accusation required under Chinese law. When the letter was finally written it was submitted through the local police which meant that it had to go up through a long series of channels before it finally reached the courts.

Several days went by and nothing seemed to happen in this case. When the Hsin Hsing villagers—mainly the few relatives and close friends of Li Fan and his father—went to ask the police what was happening they were told that such things take time and that perhaps it would be better if they tried to settle the case with the Ta Yu villagers through mediation.

About this time, the Ta Yu villagers, who were in the pumping station cooperative and who represented the two assailants, made overtures to mediate. But the basis for their mediation was that, since both sides were hurt in the fight, they should forget the whole matter instead of pressing further and going to court. To this there was of course no agreement.

The Hsin Hsing villagers were in an awkward position. Although most of them would have liked to help Li Fan and his father to win satisfaction and compensation for their injuries and to teach their assailants a lesson, they could do little.

One of the main problems was that they had no one who would or could act as their leader. The villagers were in an unorganized grumbling group, which did not know what to do or how to go about handling the case. This was unlike the assailants in the other village, who not only had a large powerful pumping station organization to support them, but also had the wealthy and influential village landlord—who was a key figure in the cooperative, besides being an influential and powerful man in the area—to act in their behalf. On the other hand, Hsin Hsing village no longer has capable and interested village landlords who can lead them in times of trouble. This may well be a general problem in those villages where the land reform has at least indirectly caused the downfall in wealth and prestige of the former landlords.

Possibly if Hsin Hsing was a clan village, Li Fan and his father, as part of such a clan, could have received more active support from the village as a whole. A clan village's organization and leadership, which is based on family relationships, would undoubtedly have been much more highly structured than this small segmented family village with its highly divisive units. To make the matter even worse, Li Fan and his father are from one of the smallest family groups which made it all the more difficult for the village to marshal and organize its leadership, since there is no formal organization to handle such matters.

Another problem was that many of the villagers who were at first much aroused by the beating of their fellow villager, later cooled off considerably when they began to realize that many of the Ta Yu villagers taking an active part on that side were their own relatives on the maternal side or through marriage. Thus to actively participate in this case meant that they would be fighting against their own relatives—with whom it had always been considered so important to maintain good social relations. The result was that, although these people still wanted to help Li Fan and their own village in this case, they could not help in an open way but rather had to do it in secret. Included in this group of the village population was the village mayor and several others who might otherwise have been organizers in Li Fan's behalf. Therefore on the Hsin Hsing side there was a complete vacuum with regard to organized leadership, so that the village, for want of someone who could or would lead, did little except talk about the case.

Not very long after the day of the beating of Li Fan and his father, the story of the incident had spread through the whole area. People were talking about the case so much that winning of the case by Hsin Hsing now became almost more a matter of face than anything else. Hsin Hsing villagers began to express fears that if these two Ta Yu villagers were to go unpunished, it would mean that anyone could and probably would beat Hsin Hsing villagers or their children just for fun. No one would respect their rights or face anymore if they did nothing about this case.

To make matters even worse, some Ta Yu villagers mentioned to Hsin Hsing villagers that if Hsin Hsing village could not get satisfaction in this case—considering the fact that there was an obviously powerful American living in their village—then Hsin Hsing was not worth anything.

This demonstrated clearly to the villagers that face would be completely lost by the village as a whole if they could do nothing. But most of all, it meant that my very presence in the village would be a contributing factor to their loss of face.

As some days passed without anything being accomplished in the matter, some villagers, who could openly show concern in the case (i.e., several relatives of Li Fan and his father and also some of their close friends in the village), came to me for advice on how to handle the matter. One of the main problems now was that the villagers not only did not know how to go about getting an honorable and fair settlement, but did not even know just what they wanted to happen or how they wanted this matter to be settled. While everyone wanted to punish the guilty parties in the beating, they realized that their demands had to be reasonable if they wanted a settlement and also if they expected to be able to go on living as friendly neighbors with Ta Yu village. The latter was a most important factor.

All these problems in determining the kind of solution desired were further complicated by the lack of leadership to help the villagers formulate their ideas and desires. The affair was at a standstill.

IV

It was at this point that villagers began more and more to call upon me for advice and general aid. At the beginning I attempted to avoid being involved in the affair, feeling that as an anthropologist it was not my place nor my purpose to take an active stand on the issue—especially with regard to giving advice which could conceivably direct the action taken by the Hsin Hsing villagers.

Finally, one evening the matter of my involvement came to a head. One of the Hsin Hsing villagers, somewhat drunk at the time, came into my house to talk. (It was very common for villagers to come into our home in the evening or any time they had leisure just to make conversation.) The conversation almost immediately turned to the beating. Undoubtedly because of his state, the drunken man was quite outspoken as to the role he, and the village generally, felt that I should play in this affair. After all, they considered me as one of them, and, as such, it was my duty to act as somewhat of a leader in the situation since there was no one else who would assume the position in this case. If I would not help in this way it would mean that I was letting them down by not assuming this responsibility toward the village. He made it evident that, in a sense, I was considered the patriarch of the village in the absence of anyone else who would, in this particular matter, assume the position with the accompanying responsibilities.

All this was related to me by the drunk in no uncertain words. His forthrightness in the matter was, of course, excusable because of his drunken state. But, in the meantime, he had been able to state the village's case to me—letting me know exactly where they thought I should stand in this matter. It is even possible that the drunken Chen was actually sent to see me, after being encouraged by some of the village men, to state the village case. Had a sober person come to the house to speak to me in such a manner, it would have been felt by the village to have been an inexcusable departure from courtesy toward a respected person of the village. No one, unless drunk, would do such a thing.

Drunken Chen had achieved his purpose because, by his direct conversation, I was made to realize that, if I was to maintain my position and my good relations in the village, it was necessary for me to show more than an interest in the case. When I took the bait and asked him what he suggested, he quickly answered that the village men should be called to a meeting in my house so that they could decide what action to take. No sooner had I agreed to this than was Chen on his way to call the villagers. Within twenty minutes the majority of the village men, including the mayor and other influential men of the village, were assembled in the room. Apparently they were on ready call for the supposedly unexpected meeting.

During the course of the meeting, it became evident that the villagers did not know what they should do in this case. Their main hope was to settle the matter through the process of mediation rather than having to take the case through the courts. They feared that having to go to court would be expensive and take a great deal of time before settlement. But perhaps more important, they felt that, because they were a small and poor village which was up against a large village and pumping station association with relatively large amounts of money and influence at their disposal, the whole thing would be of no avail. They had always held the idea that the poor man without influence could do nothing against the rich and influential. The latter two elements, money and influence, were to them what constituted power; and to attempt to do anything without this power was useless. For them even the law is subject to influence by the individuals who hold the power. This belief was undoubtedly reinforced during the period of Japanese rule.

At the same time Ta Yu was a neighboring village in which many Hsin Hsing villagers had relatives. They felt that it was necessary to avoid doing anything which would contribute to future antagonism if they were to continue to live with Ta Yu and their relatives in a peaceful way.

After several of the men had expressed their feelings, all looked to me to ask what next. "Considering all these factors how do we obtain satisfaction and save face?" The villagers had demonstrated that they themselves in general knew what they wanted done but had to have someone to spell out the situation as it was and the possible alternative actions. For this they looked to me, making me realize that, in lieu of a real village leader, they were asking me to be one or, rather, were actually dropping the leadership into my lap.

There was no alternative for me but to try to help and to do it in such a way as to make them realize what they themselves wanted to do. I therefore summed up the situation—as they had described it—and presented the possible alternatives of action which were (1) to mediate, (2) to go to court, or (3) to drop the matter. It immediately became evident that they preferred first to try again to mediate the problem. But if this did not work out satisfactorily then the case would have to go to court, although they very much doubted that anything could be gained from a court trial.

The villagers thus felt that they had benefited from what they considered to be my leadership in that they now knew what had to be done. In actuality, all I had done was to help them summarize their own thoughts and ideas—by putting some order into the confusion.

A few days after the meeting at my home, the Ta Yu side again approached the village—this time through the mayor—asking if perhaps, they could again try to mediate the case. One of the influential men of the area had offered to be mediator at his home, which was in another village about two miles down the road. The mayor and other Hsin Hsing villagers directly concerned asked a Mr. Huang, a Hsin Hsing villager—who through his education

had obtained a good job with the Taiwan Sugar Company and now lived near town—to be one of the people to represent Hsin Hsing village. It turned out that Mr. Huang would go along only if I agreed also to take part in the mediation meeting.

Again I could not very well refuse and so went along to the mediation meeting. I actually took no active part in the proceedings; it was mainly my presence which was desired. Nothing came of the meeting since the mediator suggested that the Ta Yu side pay Li Fan and his father only a small amount of money as compensation for their injuries.

This occasion turned out to be the only opportunity that I had during my entire stay in the village to witness such a mediation meeting. I was able to observe the manner in which the mediation meeting was carried out, who took part, the formalities of courtesy which were observed, and generally the way in which the mediator conducted the meeting and the respect that each side had for this individual as the mediator.

The role of the mediator is a very respected one. And even in this case where he was considered to be biased in favor of the Ta Yu village side and showed it in the way he tried to mediate, still the Hsin Hsing villagers felt that it would be disrespectful to the mediator to leave too soon. They felt that by leaving too quickly the mediator would lose face and this was to be avoided.

After several such attempts at mediation, the case was finally called up for investigation in the courts. The court procedure followed was for the accused and the accusers, with their witnesses, to appear in a special investigation court—the purpose of which was to investigate the charges, hear the charges and witnesses and then to decide if the court should indict the accused. This investigating court is somewhat similar to a grand jury.

The form of the investigation is highly formalized. Since neither the accused nor the accuser may have his lawyer present at the time, the only thing the investigators can go by in making their inquiry is the original letter of accusation. On the basis of the information furnished in this statement it is up to the investigator to get at all the facts in the case.

Unfortunately, the letter of accusation sent in by the Hsin Hsing side and the questions asked of the witnesses according to the accusation were such that the investigator felt there was not enough evidence for an indictment to send the case to court since each side insisted that they had been beaten. Instead he suggested that the two parties involved mediate their differences. Unfortunately he did not know many facts in the case, including the fact that mediation had already failed, and that the local police could be called to testify that the Ta Yu men had not been beaten.

When the Hsin Hsing villagers came out of this private hearing they were completely stunned and insisted that only I could now do something, since otherwise it was all over and would mean that they had lost to the more powerful and influential side.

Upon their insistence, I paid a personal visit to the investigator, making my visit merely in the form of an inquiry on how the investigation and court system operated. During the course of our conversation, in which the Li Fan case was used as an example, I mentioned several facts in the case of which the investigator was unaware. Upon hearing these he noted that this threw an entirely different light on the case and was grounds for another investigation. The investigation was held immediately and an indictment was brought forth. Several weeks later the case came to court and Li Fan and his father were awarded an amount of money large enough to cover doctor and hospital bills.

V

Although I had actually done little to help in the case until the very end (the time of the investigation of which few knew about), the villagers felt that I was the one to be thanked for the results.

Their thanks were in the form of a much greater intimacy than I had ever been able to achieve before. Li Fan—who had seemed potentially an excellent informant but who in the past always seemed to be too busy—now made it his business to be available whenever I had any questions. This was also true of several other good informants. My participation thus turned out to be a great advantage for me in conducting the remainder of my research.

Besides my participation in the case helping to establish my own position in the village, to the point where there were few things which I could not ask about or take part in, I also had the opportunity to see and learn about a great many things which I otherwise might never have known existed.

I was able to learn how important it is to a village to have the leadership of an influential person—usually someone in the landlord class. It was mostly because of the fact that Hsin Hsing village does not have a landlord active in village affairs that I had the leadership thrust upon me. Along with this it became evident to me, through my participation in the case, that the villagers felt that one had to have money, influence, and power in order to be able to win such a case or to get anything done. They believed that there was no justice for the poor. This idea was something which had been very much built up during the period of Japanese rule, when the Japanese were only willing to deal with the villages through their rich landlords.

From my involvement, I was able to see in actual operation a mediation session and, more valuable, to learn how relied upon is the system of mediation in Taiwan, on both the local and governmental levels, for the solution of all kinds of problems.

With regard to the social structure, my involvement made it necessary for some of the villagers concerned to explain to me why many villagers had to give Li Fan help in secrecy for fear of antagonizing their relatives in Ta Yu village. Thus they had to make it appear that they were maintaining a neutral position. On the other hand, I was able to learn how villagers, who were caught up in the problem of dual loyalties (to their own village and to their relatives in the other village), were actually forced into the position of telling their Ta Yu village relatives what new action was being planned in Hsin Hsing. When I took an active part in the case, it immediately became necessary to inform me why some villagers could not be trusted with the plans for the case.

VI

My intervention in the village situation which I have described will undoubtedly be considered by some to be unscientific and not part of the role of the anthropologist in the field. But the little help I did offer—and it should be noted that I did so only upon being urged by the villagers—greatly enhanced my understanding of village life and therefore furthered my scientific endeavor. Beyond this, my intervention for their benefit (which is what the villagers took it to be and that is what is important) relieved me of the feeling that I had come to live in this village only to take—in terms of knowledge and understanding of the life of these people—and not to give anything in return. I was in a situation of being given the opportunity to do something in return for those who were doing so much for me by their cooperation. To refuse to help would have seemed to me immoral.

For me the question of whether or not the anthropologist in the field has a moral or ethical right to refuse to intervene in the villagers' lives, even when the villagers are requesting such intervention and expect to receive it, is a most important one. But this question is for each field researcher to decide for himself according to his own feelings and, most important, according to the particular situation.

Had I not been more or less forced into the position of intervening—in other words had I been given an easy chance to refuse to help, and had I done so—I would understand far less today about the people I had come to study. I also would have had to come away with a heavy feeling of guilt.

William Foote Whyte

Freedom and Responsibility in Research: The "Springdale" Case

"Springdale," a town in upstate New York, was studied by a team of social scientists, two of whom, Arthur Vidich and Joseph Bensman, published a book on the town entitled Small Town in Mass Society. *Though pseudonyms were used for all persons and places, they were easily identifiable to the townspeople, who took offense at the book. A controversy ensued between the authors and various other social scientists, including senior members of the research project. Part of that controversy appeared in the pages of* Human Organization, *the journal of the Society for Applied Anthropology, from which these extracts are taken. Matters of confidentiality, of obligation to a project versus that to one's own research, obligations to host people versus those to science, all are raised. Another matter, more widely recognized now than when Vidich and Bensman raised it, is the difference between the way social scientists deal with relatively powerless people and with those who have power. The trouble they encountered was not so much in what they reported— most anthropologists are as culpable as they or more so—but about whom they reported it. They reported about literate, articulate pillars of an American town rather than about the poor, the marginal, the inarticulate, the nonliterate, or the remote. Should a different set of rules apply to the former than to the latter? This is an issue which is raised again in the section on "Anthropology and the Third World," and it is expressed in the currently widespread discussion of the role of anthropology in researching elite institutions in American society.*

A small upstate New York village has now been immortalized in anthropological literature under the name of "Springdale." The local newspaper reports that the experience has not been entirely a pleasing one. We pass on this account:

The people of the Village [Springdale] waited quite awhile to get even with Art Vidich, who wrote a Peyton Place-*type book about their town recently.*

The featured float of the annual Fourth of July parade followed an authentic copy of the jacket of the book, Small Town in Mass Society, *done large-scale by Mrs. Beverly Robinson. Following the book cover came residents of [Springdale] riding masked in cars labeled with the fictitious names given them in the book.*

But the pay-off was the final scene, a manure-

"Freedom and Responsibility in Research: The 'Springdale' Case" by William Foote Whyte. Reproduced by the permission of the Society for Applied Anthropology and the author from Vol. 17, No. 2, 1958 *Human Organization*.

spreader filled with very rich barnyard fertilizer, over which was bending an effigy of "The Author."

The account suggests that a good time was had by all—on this particular occasion. Nevertheless, local observers report that the disturbance caused by the book in the village has not been entirely compensated for by even such a ceremony carried out in the best anthropological traditions. The book and its aftermath raise some serious questions which, so far as we know, have never been publicly discussed. We feel that it is high time that these issues be raised:

1. What obligation does the author of a community study have to the people of the community he studies, particularly when it comes to publication of his findings?
2. When the author is a member of a research team, what obligations does he have to the project director? And what obligations does the project director have to him?

Vidich spent two and a half years living in "Springdale" as field director of a Cornell project carried out in the Department of Child Development and Family Relations. The project was directed by Urie Bronfenbrenner, a social psychologist. As a result of this research experience, Vidich published several articles, but the official report in book form regarding the project did not materialize during his tenure at Cornell and is only getting into print at this writing. Some time after he left Cornell, Vidich began work on a book of his own, in collaboration with Joseph Bensman, who had had no previous association with the project.

The Vidich manuscript gave rise to considerable controversy between the author and the Springdale project director. In presenting the issues which arose between them, we are indebted to both Bronfenbrenner and Vidich for allowing us to examine their correspondence (from late 1955 to 1958) regarding the manuscript.

The points of controversy were essentially these:

1. Should individuals be identified in the book?
2. If individuals were identified, what—if anything—should be done to avoid damage to them?
3. Did Vidich have a right to use—or should he be allowed to use—project data which he did not gather himself? Who "owns" project data?

Before Vidich came onto the scene, Springdale people had been assured, when their collaboration was sought, that no individuals would be identified in printed reports. While all of the Vidich characters are given fictitious names, they can easily be identified within Springdale. The author argues that, when there is only one mayor and a small number of village and town officials and school board members, it is impossible to discuss the dynamics of the community without identifying individuals. He further argues that what he has reported in the book is "public knowledge" within Springdale. Even if this be true, is there a difference between "public knowledge" which circulated from mouth to mouth in the village and the same stories which appear in print?

In addition to his objections regarding the anonymity pledge, Bronfenbrenner claimed that certain individuals were described in ways which could be damaging to them. On this he submitted a long bill of particulars. One example (p. 97):

One member of invisible government, in agreement with the principal's educational policy, has remarked that "He's a little too inhuman—has never got into anything in the town. He's good for Springdale until he gets things straightened out. Then we'll have to get rid of him."

Bronfenbrenner took the position that Vidich had no right to—and should not be allowed to—use project data beyond that which he personally had gathered. When Vidich wrote that, while he did not agree with Bronfenbrenner's reasoning, "wherever possible I will delete the material you consider objectionable," Bronfenbrenner responded by writing that, in this case, he would not object to having other project data used in this book. However, a comparison of the book with Bronfenbrenner's written objections indicates that, in most cases, changes were not made.

Beyond the specific questions raised by Bronfenbrenner, there is the more amorphous question of the "tone" of a book describing a community. Vidich speaks throughout of the "invisible government." (For this reason, the characters in his book rode with masks in the Fourth of July celebration.) The words themselves suggest an illegitimate form of activity, a conspiracy to gain and hold power. While Vidich himself says in a footnote that this is not true, the use of such a phrase, and the tone of his treatment, presents the behavior in that light, and so it has been interpreted in Springdale.

The Springdale experience also raises a general problem regarding the relations of a staff member to the project director in a team project, especially when there is a long period between the initiation of the study and the publication of major research reports. The junior member of such a staff must naturally think about establishing his own professional reputation, which he can do primarily through publication. An article or two will help, but a book would help even more. Is he to be a co-author on a book which represents a major report of the study? In that case, he may have to wait some time for the appearance of the book, and, in the meantime, he has little in the way of credentials to offer as he seeks new teaching and research jobs. Furthermore, when his name does finally appear on such a book, many people naturally assume that the book is largely the creation of the project director. A junior member may feel that he does not, in this way, get adequate recognition. The project director, on the other hand, already owns an established academic reputation and so does not feel a strong compulsion to rush into print with the findings of the project. Furthermore, he has other involvements on the campus of his university, which is not true of the field director.

Is there some way in which the project director can promote opportunities so that the junior staff members win their own reputations—without encouraging each man to go off in a completely independent direction? It was hoped in the Springdale project that this could be accomplished. Experience so far indicates that the results have not met the expectations on either side of the controversy.

We will let the author have the next-to-last word on the controversy. Replying in the *Ithaca Journal* to a statement made by Bronfenbrenner, Vidich writes:

Strictly speaking, I take the position that in the in-terests of the pursuit of scientific truth, no one, including research organizations, has a right to lay claims of ownership of research data.

That is a violation of the entire spirit of disinterested research.

Asked whether he was aware that there would be a reaction in Springdale, Vidich replied:

I was aware that there would be a reaction in the town when the book was published. While writing the book, however, it did not occur to us to anticipate what these reactions might be, nor did it occur to us to use such anticipations of reactions as a basis for selecting the data or carrying out the analysis.

One can't gear social science writing to the expected reactions of any audience, and, if one does, the writing quickly degenerates into dishonesty, all objectivity in the sense that one can speak of objectivity in the social sciences is lost.

We do not have any firm answers to the various problems raised by this case, but we are quite convinced that the Vidich answer will not serve. He seems to take the position that he has a responsibility only to science. Has the researcher no responsibility to the people whom he studies? We are not prepared to state what the nature of this responsibility should be, but we find it strange indeed to hear a researcher argue that he assumes no responsibility at all.

We suggest that this is a field in which we all need to reflect upon our own experiences in an effort to clarify the responsibilities we should be prepared to assume. The editor would be glad to hear from our members on any of the points raised here. Perhaps in this way, to borrow a phrase from the motto of Cornell University, we shall arrive at a better understanding of "freedom and responsibility" in field research.

Arthur Vidich and Joseph Bensman

"Freedom and Responsibility in Research": Comments

[The editor's] implication that publication in general is related only to career opportunism and that, specifically, this was our motive, is an extraordinarily limited perspective. In our case, we would feel that there are a large number of factors bearing on the writing of a book. All of these cannot be taken up in a brief reply such as this and, especially, they cannot be treated within the range of possibilities suggested by the editorial. We had thought that our Springdale material offered us an opportunity to define some problems central to basic anthropological and sociological theory, in a way which would lead to some understanding of the development of contemporary society. In doing our work, we believe that these problems were worthy of inquiry and analysis, in and of themselves. We are gratified that almost all reviewers of *Small Town in Mass Society* have granted that we selected important problems and that we made some progress in stating and analysing them. . . .

The particular fates of Vidich, Bensman, the project, the department, Cornell University, Springdale, etc. are of much less significance than the problems which the editorial raises for the future of scientific investigation in western society. Not that the Springdale example presents a new problem; on the contrary, negative reactions by organizations, individuals, and interest groups have been characteristic for the Lynds' study of Middletown, West's study of Plainville, Warner's study of Yankee City, Selznick's study of the T.V.A., Hunter's study of Community Power, and Whyte's study of Street Corner Society. In the latter case, Doc still suffers from the recognition he received in the book.

Historically, this problem has not appeared, or has appeared to a much lesser extent, in the anthropology of non-western society. This is because primitive populations have been less concerned, aware, and vocal in their response to the anthropological description of their societies. The life history, studies of native politics and organizations, etc., all invade the native's "privacy," subject his inner life to exposure, and strip him of the magic on which his existence rests. Because it was possible to do this with native society, sociologists and anthropologists have learned a great deal about social life which they could apply to western society. Now that so many primitives have become westernized and are aware of the implications of anthropological research, they, too, resent the invasion of privacy and descriptions of the inner structure of their society.

There is an interesting parallel between the license taken by anthropologists and that taken by sociologists who have studied crime, minority groups, caste groups, factory workers, prostitutes, psychopathic personalities, hoboes, taxi-dancers, beggars, marginal workers, slum dwellers, and other voiceless, powerless, unrespected, and disreputable groups. Negative reaction to community and organizational research is only heard when results describe articulate, powerful, and respected individuals and organizations. We believe there would have been no objection to our study if it had been limited solely to the shack people.

We think all of the community and organizational studies mentioned above made important contributions. The problem is: *At what price should a contribution be made?*

One of the principal ideas of our book is that the public atmosphere of an organization or a community tends to be optimistic, positive, and geared to the public relations image of the community or the organization. The public mentality veils the dynamics and functional determinants of the group being studied. Any attempt in social analysis at presenting other than public relations rends the veil and must necessarily cause resentment. Moreover, any organization tends to represent a balance of divergent interests held in some kind of equilibrium by the power status of the parties involved. A simple description of these factors, no matter how stated, will offend some of the groups in question.

"Freedom and Responsibility in Research: Comments" by Arthur Vidich and Joseph Bensman. Reproduced by the permission of the Society for Applied Anthropology and the author from Vol. 17, No. 4, 1959 *Human Organization*.

The only way to avoid such problems is not to deal with articulate groups who will publicly resist the attention which research gives to them, or to deal with the problems in such a way that they are inoffensive. Research of this type becomes banal, irrespective of its technical and methodological virtuosity.

Executive Board of the American Anthropological Association
Resolutions

Anthropologists have a long and honorable tradition of speaking out collectively on public issues related to their professional concerns, broadly defined. Here we present a selection from among numerous resolutions passed by the Association over the years, beginning in 1945, pertaining to a variety of public and professional issues. The selection is designed to indicate the scope and variety of the concerns which were enshrined in resolutions of the Association, rather than to evaluate their importance. Hence, many significant ones have inevitably been omitted. Those dated 1970 were among an unprecedented outpouring of seventeen resolutions passed at a single meeting of the Association (and later ratified by mail ballot)—an indication of the increasing concern with public issues among the membership of the Association.

Be it resolved: That the American Anthropological Association, constituted of scientists interested in the study of human nature and society, recognizes the responsibility of anthropologists to study the effects of the discovery of the use of atomic energy, and to participate actively with other scientists in efforts to make appropriate social inventions to guard against the dangers, and utilize the promise, inherent in atomic use.[1] [1946]

Resolution on Indian Affairs. Sol Tax moved that the Council adopt the following resolution:

"Whereas: it appears to us that in the past two years the United States government policy with respect to the American Indians, their cultures, and their integration into the general community has undergone a radical change of direction; and

"Whereas: the change occurred without adequate public discussion; and

"Whereas: we believe that great and irremediable harm and injustice may result;

"Therefore be it resolved: That the American Anthropological Association recommend to the President of the United States and to the Secretary of the Interior that there be created immediately an independent commission of qualified nongovernment persons, distinguished in public service, to determine the nature of present policy in the Bureau of Indian Affairs and its probable consequences; to state for the American people what our goals should be in the light of humanitarian and scientific principles, and to make appropriate recommendations for legislative and administrative action to implement these goals."[2] [1952]

Be it resolved that: The American Anthropological Association repudiates statements now appearing in the United States that Negroes are biologically and in innate mental ability inferior to whites and reaffirms the fact that there is no scientifically established evidence to justify the exclusion of any race from the rights guaranteed by the Constitution of the United States. The basic principles of equality of opportunity and equality before

[1] "Resolutions of the Executive Board of the American Anthropological Association." Reproduced by permission of the American Anthropological Association from *American Anthropologist*, Vol. 48, No. 2, 1946.

[2] "Resolutions of the Executive Board of the American Anthropological Association." Reproduced by permission of the American Anthropological Association from *American Anthropologist*, Vol. 54, No. 2, 1952.

the law are compatible with all that is known about human biology. All races possess the abilities needed to participate fully in the democratic way of life and in modern, technological civilization.[3] [1962]

Margaret Mead moved the following Resolution on the Use of Anthropology:

Whereas as anthropologists we recognize that mankind, a single interconnected biological species, is now threatened with the possibility of extinction through the methods and preparations of modern warfare—nuclear, biological and chemical, and

Whereas we recognize that in the past not only civilizations but entire species have perished, and that mankind is now faced with an entirely new problem of survival, and that it is of utmost importance to end the present armament race, and

Whereas mankind must now learn to live with the continuing possibility of total destruction, which provides mankind's first opportunity to develop ways of maintaining world-wide order within which to preserve and develop the works of man and the human species itself, and

Whereas we recognize that at this crossroads it is urgently necessary that the full resources of our science, of related human sciences, and of the whole scientific community be brought to bear on the easing of the immediate crisis and the development of social institutions which will enable all peoples to live and work, however great their differences,

Be it therefore resolved,

(1) That to this task we devote our scientific resources as anthropologists, in cooperation with
   a. Other American associations in the human sciences,
   b. The American Association for the Advancement of Science, as representing the whole scientific community,
   c. Our colleagues in other parts of the world, and
   d. International scientific organizations.

(2) That we call upon our governmental bodies —federal, state, and local—to make fuller use of anthropology and other human sciences in pursuit of our stated national policy of the search for disarmament and the search for peace, and

(3) That individual anthropologists seek appropriate opportunities within their professional competences to develop with colleagues in other disciplines ways and means to ensure the survival and well-being of our species.[4] [1967]

Reaffirming our 1961 resolution, we condemn the use of napalm, chemical defoliants, harmful gases, bombing, the torture and killing of prisoners of war and political prisoners, and the intentional or deliberate policies of genocide or forced transportation of populations for the purpose of terminating their cultural and/or genetic heritages by anyone anywhere.

These methods of warfare deeply offend human nature. We ask that all governments put an end to their use at once and proceed as rapidly as possible to a peaceful settlement of the war in Vietnam.[4] [1967]

Resolution 2. (Dell Hymes and George M. Foster)

Whereas the participation in research and teaching of persons of diverse backgrounds is essential to objectivity and relevance in anthropology,

And whereas knowledge of significant aspects of communities and groups is often accessible only to persons with roots in those communities and groups,

And whereas persons with roots in other than the white middle-class sector of American society can make invaluable contributions to knowledge of all sectors of contemporary life,

And whereas few persons from other than the white middle-class sector now enter anthropology in the United States and achieve professional recognition,

Therefore,

Be it resolved that the American Anthropological Association urges vigorous recruitment of students of Black, Chicano, American Indian, Asian, and other such backgrounds into anthropology in universities and colleges, and vigorous efforts to hire and facilitate the careers of such persons in the profession.[5] [1970]

Resolution 5. (Samuel L. Stanley)

Whereas the American Anthropological

---

[3] "Resolutions of the Executive Board of the American Anthropological Association." Reproduced by permission of the American Anthropological Association from *American Anthropologist*, Vol. 64, No. 3, 1962.

[4] "Resolutions of the Executive Board of the American Anthropological Association." Reproduced by permission of the American Anthropological Association from *American Anthropologist*, Vol. 69, No. 3–4, 1967.

Association has officially gone on record as expressing its concern for the welfare of American Indians in the context of their relationships to the United States Government,

And whereas as anthropologists, we are aware of the manner in which, over the centuries, the traditional rights to land have been systematically stripped from American Indian societies, usually with disastrous economic, social, and psychological effects,

And whereas the Native people (Aleut, Eskimo, and Indian) of Alaska will soon have their rights to the land area of that State extinguished by Congressional action,

And whereas never again will the United States have an opportunity to deal justly in extinguishing the title of the aboriginal owners of such a large extent of territory,

And whereas it behooves the Federal Government to protect the rights and equities of the Native citizens of Alaska against the desires of powerful interest groups who wish to benefit from the land and its products,

And whereas the United States Government faces a unique opportunity in its defense of Alaskan Natives' rights to provide for their economic development and thereby forestall any future dependence on public support,

Therefore,

Be it resolved that the American Anthropological Association urges the United States Congress to legislate a settlement which will appear just and equitable to all future generations and which will include: (1) fair monetary compensation for all the property rights being taken, and for previous exploitation of the land and its resources; (2) title to an adequate land base for the future, taking into account the probable increase in size of the Native population of Alaska; and (3) provision for continued economic support of these communities by granting them an equitable proportion of the revenues which its new owners take from their land in the future.[5] [1970]

Resolution 6. (F. T. Cloak, Jr.)

Whereas an advisory report to the President of the United States has proposed that the U.S. should adopt a national policy requiring the supplying of quantities of weapons and military equipment to Latin American nations, the stated purpose of this proposed policy being to "strengthen internal security" and "cope with the forces of subversion,"

And whereas such phrases as "strengthen internal security" and "cope with the forces of subversion" are frequently used to mask suppression by force or threat of force of legitimate struggles for social, political, and economic change on the part of citizens of the countries in question,

Therefore,

Be it resolved that the American Anthropological Association demand that the United States Congress investigate the use to which U.S. weapons and military equipment are put by each of the several Latin American governments, and that in each case where a Latin American government has frequently or repeatedly used or threatened to use such weapons and equipment against its own citizens, the Congress prohibit the further supplying of weapons or military equipment or parts or supplies thereof to that government.[5] [1970]

Resolution 9. (Joan Mencher)

Be it resolved that the AAA go on record against discrimination based on sex.[5] [1970]

Resolution 12. (Joan Mencher)

Be it resolved that in cases of proven discrimination the Association develop sanctions and put the strength of its authority behind legal actions resulting from such cases.[5] [1970]

Resolution 13. (Karen Sacks)

Resolved that members of the AAA shall not engage in any secret or classified research.[5] [1970]

Resolution 14. (Karen Sacks)

Resolved that fieldworkers shall not divulge any information orally or in writing, solicited by government officials, foundations, or corporation representatives about the people they study that compromises and/or endangers their well-being and cultural integrity.[5] [1970]

[5] "Statement of the Executive Board of the American Anthropological Association." Reproduced by permission of the American Anthropological Association from *Newsletter*, Vol. 11, No. 6, 1970.

American Anthropological Association

Principles of Professional Responsibility

In 1965 the Executive Board of the American Anthropological Association expressed concern over United States military support of research in insurgency and counterinsurgency in other nations, growing out of the ill-fated Project Camelot in Latin America (see selections by Horowitz and Sahlins in "Anthropology and the Third World"). Consequently, an ad hoc committee was appointed to look into problems of research and ethics in anthropology. The end result was a "Statement of Problems of Anthropological Research and Ethics" adopted by the Fellows of the Association in 1967. Thereafter, in 1968, a Committee on Ethics was appointed which prepared a draft report published in the Association's Newsletter in April 1969. This report proposed an elected, standing Committee on Ethics, and it set forth a draft of a code of ethics for the Association. Although the report was tabled, the standing Committee was elected and, in November 1970, its own draft code, retitled "Statement of Professional Responsibility," was published, revising and expanding on the previous one. This document is reproduced here. It sets forth clearly the major ethical issues confronting American anthropologists in their research, teaching, and public service. It was the focus of heated debate, but was adopted, for the demand for accountability and responsibility in research had become irresistible as instances to the contrary reached public and professional notice and resulted in impairment of future research opportunities and infringement on the autonomy of peoples studied.

Preamble

Anthropologists work in many parts of the world in close personal association with the peoples and situations they study. Their professional situation is, therefore, uniquely varied and complex. They are involved with their discipline, their colleagues, their students, their sponsors, their subjects, their own and host governments, the particular individuals and groups with whom they do their field work, other populations and interest groups in the nations within which they work, and the study of processes and issues affecting general human welfare. In a field of such complex involvements, misunderstandings, conflicts, and the necessity to make choices among conflicting values are bound to arise and to generate ethical dilemmas. It is a prime responsibility of anthropologists to anticipate these and to plan to resolve them in such a way as to [do] damage neither to those whom they study nor, in so far as possible, to their scholarly community. Where these conditions cannot be met, the anthropologist would be well-advised not to pursue the particular piece of research.

The following principles are deemed fundamental to the anthropologist's responsible, ethical pursuit of his profession.

1. Relations with Those Studied

In research, an anthropologist's paramount responsibility is to those he studies. When there is a conflict of interest, these individuals must come first. The anthropologist must do everything within his power to protect their physical, social, and psychological welfare and to honor their dignity and privacy.

a. Where research involves the acquisition of material and information transferred on the assumption of trust between persons, it is axiomatic that the rights, interests, and sensitivities of those studied must be safeguarded.

b. The aims of the investigation should be communicated as well as possible to the informant.

c. Informants have a right to remain anonymous. This right should be respected both where it has been promised explicitly and where no clear understanding to the contrary has been reached. These strictures apply to the collection of data by means of cameras, tape recorders, and other data-gathering devices, as well as to data collected in face-to-face interviews or in participant observation. Those being studied should understand the capacities of such devices; they should be free to reject them if they wish; and if they

"AAA: Principles of Professional Responsibility." Reproduced by permission of the American Anthropological Association from *Newsletter*, Vol. 11, No. 9, (1970).

accept them, the results obtained should be consonant with the informant's right to welfare, dignity, and privacy.

d. There should be no exploitation of individual informants for personal gain. Fair return should be given them for all services.

e. There is an obligation to reflect on the foreseeable repercussions of research and publication on the general population being studied.

f. The anticipated consequences of research should be communicated as fully as possible to the individuals and groups likely to be affected.

g. In accordance with the Association's general position on clandestine and secret research, no reports should be provided to sponsors that are not also available to the general public and, where practicable, to the population studied.

h. Every effort should be exerted to cooperate with members of the host society in the planning and execution of research projects.

i All of the above points should be acted upon in full recognition of the social and cultural pluralism of host societies and the consequent plurality of values, interests, and demands in those societies. This diversity complicates choice-making in research, but ignoring it leads to irresponsible decisions.

2. Responsibility to the Public

The anthropologist is also responsible to the public—all presumed consumers of his professional efforts. To them he owes a commitment to candor and to truth in the dissemination of his research results and in the statement of his opinions as a student of man.

a. He should not communicate his findings secretly to some and withhold them from others.

b. He should not knowingly falsify or color his findings.

c. In providing professional opinions, he is responsible not only for their content but also for integrity in explaining both these opinions and their bases.

d. As people who devote their professional lives to understanding man, anthropologists bear a positive responsibility to speak out publicly, both individually and collectively, on what they know and what they believe as a result of their professional expertise gained in the study of human beings. That is, they bear a professional responsibility to contribute to an "adequate definition of reality" upon which public opinion and public policy may be based.

e. In public discourse, the anthropologist should be honest about his qualifications and cognizant of the limitations of anthropological expertise.

3. Responsibility to the Discipline

An anthropologist bears responsibility for the good reputation of his discipline and its practitioners.

a. He should undertake no secret research or any research whose results cannot be freely derived and publicly reported.

b. He should avoid even the appearance of engaging in clandestine research, by fully and freely disclosing the aims and sponsorship of all his research.

c. He should attempt to maintain a level of integrity and rapport in the field such that by his behavior and example he will not jeopardize future research there. The responsibility is not to analyze and report so as to offend no one, but to conduct research in a way consistent with a commitment to honesty, open inquiry, clear communication of sponsorship and research aims, and concern for the welfare and privacy of informants.

4. Responsibility to Students

In relations with students an anthropologist should be candid, fair, nonexploitative, and committed to their welfare and academic progress.

As Robert Leckachman has suggested, honesty is the essential quality of a good teacher, neutrality is not. Beyond honest teaching, the anthropologist as a teacher has ethical responsibilities in selection, instruction in ethics, career counseling, academic supervision, evaluation, compensation, and placement.

a. He should select students in such a way as to preclude discrimination on the basis of sex, race, ethnic group, social class, and other categories of people indistinguishable by their intellectual potential.

b. He should alert students to the ethical problems of research and discourage them from participating in projects employing questionable ethical standards. This should include providing them with information and discussions to protect them from unethical pressures and enticements emanating from possible sponsors, as well as helping them to find acceptable alternatives (see point i below).

c. He should be receptive and seriously responsive to students' interests, opinions, and desires in all aspects of their academic work and relationships.

d. He should realistically counsel students regarding career opportunities.

e. He should conscientiously supervise, encourage, and support students in their anthropological and other academic endeavors.

f. He should inform students of what is expected of them in their course of study. He should be fair in the evaluation of their performance. He should communicate evaluations to the students concerned.

g. He should acknowledge in print the student assistance he uses in his own publications, give appropriate credit (including coauthorship) when student research is used in publication, encourage and assist in publication of worthy student papers, and compensate students justly for the use of their time, energy, and intelligence in research and teaching.

h. He should energetically assist students in securing legitimate research support and the necessary permissions to pursue research.

i. He should energetically assist students in securing professional employment upon completion of their studies.

j. He should strive to improve both our techniques of teaching and our techniques for evaluating the effectiveness of our methods of teaching.

5. Responsibility to Sponsors

In his relations with sponsors of research, an anthropologist should be honest about his qualifications, capabilities, and aims. He thus faces the obligation, prior to entering any commitment for research, to reflect sincerely upon the purposes of his sponsors in terms of their past behavior. He should be especially careful not to promise or imply acceptance of conditions contrary to his professional ethics or competing commitments. This requires that he require of the sponsor full disclosure of the sources of funds, personnel, aims of the institution and the research project, disposition of research results. He must retain the right to make all ethical decisions in his research. He should enter into no secret agreement with the sponsor regarding the research, results, or reports.

6. Responsibilities to One's Own Government and to Host Governments

In his relation with his own government and with host governments, the research anthropologist should be honest and candid. He should demand assurance that he will not be required to compromise his professional responsibilities and ethics as a condition of his permission to pursue the research. Specifically, no secret research, no secret reports, or debriefings of any kind should be agreed to or given. If these matters are clearly understood in advance, serious complications and misunderstandings can generally be avoided.

Epilogue

In the final analysis, anthropological research is a human undertaking, dependent upon choices for which the individual bears ethical as well as scientific responsibility. That responsibility is a human, not superhuman responsibility. To err is human, to forgive humane. This statement of principles of professional responsibility is not designed to punish, but to provide guidelines which can minimize the occasions upon which there is a need to forgive. When an anthropologist, by his actions, jeopardizes peoples studied, professional colleagues, students, or others, or if he otherwise betrays his professional commitments, his colleagues may legitimately inquire into the propriety of those actions, and take such measures as lie within the legitimate powers of their Association as the membership of theAssociation deems appropriate.

Anthony Leeds

Ethics Report Criticized

The two draft codes of the Committee on Ethics, and in fact the very existence of such a committee, have been hotly debated in the American Anthropological Association. Here are two views, the first a negative response to the 1969 "Report of the Committee on Ethics" (similar in content to the previous selection); the second a rebuttal to such critics (but not to this specific letter). These are brief, cogent expositions of the opposing viewpoints.

I am deeply disturbed by the "Report of the Ethics Committee" published in the current *Newsletter,* so much so that I hope most of its major recommendations will be rejected by the membership of the Association. I find it personally most distressing that this feeling has arisen because as person and citizen, I agree with the values set forth by the Committee members and, indeed, have participated with several of the members (e.g., Aberle, Adams, and Wolf) in a number of battles and with pretty much the same viewpoints.

The Report builds in as assumption an absolutistic and unitary value system, on one hand, and the conception that there is an intrinsic connection between the science of anthropology and a particular value position, the one they set forth and they, and I, as citizens, participate in. There is no clear evidence that there is a definable *logical* connection between this particular value system and the thought structure of anthropology, let alone between the former and any particular social system. Philosophers—students of ethics, logicians, and others—have as yet been unable to make any such assertion and anthropologists have fared no better. Moreover, it is quite plain that not all anthropologists—anthropologists of equivalent competence as anthropologists—share this value system.

These built-in assumptions have a series of most unfortunate, and even pernicious, consequences which are manifest in the Report and which, I believe, lead the proponents into ethical and moral contradiction.

First, they propose to set forth *an* ethical system as *the* ethical system. Second, they propose to codify *in detail* ethical standards. Third, they propose to set up a registration system for research projects as a way to create *bonae fides* of legitimacy of the researcher and his project, on one hand, and deny the same, i.e., exert pressure against, those they judge to be illegitimate. Fourth, they propose to apply sanctions.

In other words, what is happening here is the definition of a community of the elect, the designation of a Right Ideology, the delimitation of Right Behavior, and specification of sanctions.

In effect, it is attempting to legislate a socio-ideological system. As such it is strangely—for persons who purport to be protecting the rights of individuals and groups—a document of our times. It is analogous to the attempts in the U.S. in recent years to register subversives and legislatively to define areas of subversion; to define Right Ideology for Americans and to exclude others as aliens, alienateds, subversives, aberrants, and so on; to force conformity by direct and indirect sanctions, e.g., in the school prayer issue (note!—students who do *not* want to pray are said not to have to—yet it has been the recognition of all interested in freedom of person and civil liberties that such a situation involves both compulsion and sanction—as does the freedom of the researcher *not* to register).

We *know* that all attempts to legislate morality fail—whether the morality of "honest business" or the morality of the New Left or the morality of the Drug Users, or what-have-you. They will fail here, too. Those who wish to engage in the "subversive" activities that the Ethics Committee wishes to control will continue to do so, in secret, under various covers, just as all those controlled by legislative fiat or marijuana control bills or HUACs or whatnot continue their activities.

The report of the Committee—to me, as citizen and person, to me as one-time Conscientious Objector and member of the American Civil

"Ethics Report Criticized" by Anthony Leeds. Reproduced by permission of the American Anthropological Association from *Newsletter,* Vol. 10. No. 6, 1969.

Liberties Union—is a striking and pernicious failure, especially coming from anthropologists. They have produced a document which is highly ethnocentric, completely swept up in the temper of the times, a product of the same sort of forces that they purport to be fighting by setting up the procedures advocated. It is authoritarian and sets forth the right of one body—even if it *is* a majority of the profession—to impose its values on the rest. What is most striking is the implicit abandonment of reason, enlightenment, and feeling, applied with reference to the materials of our field and with respect to the issues they feel at stake, to lead colleagues and students to the ethical standards or vision they feel correct in favor of a system of constraint, sanction, repression, and conformity. I know as well as they do the dangers which they are attempting to deal with; I am threatened as much as they by the closure of field sites (as is threatening in the case of India), the hostility of our studied peoples, the messing up of field sites, but I think that scientific inquiry itself, anthropology in particular, freedom of exploration and variation, are much more threatened by the proposed abandonment of persuasion and reason in favor of the imposition of codified regulation. I think members of the Committee have gotten themselves into ethical contradictions in terms of their own value system.

I oppose the entire organization as proposed.

Stephen P. Dunn

Resolution Issues

Several letters have appeared in the *Newsletter* recently taking issue with various resolutions submitted to the membership . . . .

The major issues raised are as follows:

1. The right of a majority to commit the Association. (". . . I am protesting a system of operating which can put the authority of a whole membership behind any opinion which might be approved by a majority of only one vote."—Alice M Brues, May 1970 *Newsletter*) This is a phony issue. The fact that a certain position has been adopted or a certain person elected, by the voters of my district or my country, does not obligate me to support that position or that person, as a matter of principle, if I do not wish to do so, and no one with the slightest grasp of democratic procedure would assume that it did.

2. The issue of compulsion. ("I recognize the right of my colleagues to tell me what they think I *should* or *should not*, *ought* or *ought not*, do. I do not recognize that right to issue directives as to what *I shall* or *shall not*, do."—Robert W Ehrich, May 1970 *Newsletter*)

Another phony issue. Other professional associations (for example, the AMA, the Bar Association and, I believe, the various engineering societies) have codes of conduct by which their members must abide, or face expulsion and loss of good standing in their professions. The concrete provisions of these codes are a proper subject for debate, and are in fact vigorously debated, but to my knowledge no one questions the intrinsic propriety of having such a code. I see no legitimate objection to a code of professional conduct for anthropologists, *provided* that it is democratically adopted after full and adequately informed discussion. After all, some form and degree of compulsion is a prerequisite for any kind of organized human life—as anthropologists should know better than anyone else.

3. The proper role of the Association. ". . . the Association should be a professional and not a political body. . ."—Ehrich. "The Association is

"Resolution Issues" by Stephen P. Dunn. Reproduced by permission of the American Anthropological Association from *Newsletter*, Vol. 11, No. 7, (September, 1970).

an academic association and not a political one..."—Brues. This is a genuine issue which has been misstated. The statements quoted imply two things: first, that, philosophically, politics is one thing and what we do professionally is quite another; and, second, that, empirically, our professional activities have no political effect. I think it can be demonstrated that the second implication is factually false. If it were true, it would confirm what we hear from many of our more gifted younger colleagues and prospective colleagues— that anthropology is an irrelevant, ivory-tower game, and hence not worth bothering with. As for

the first implication: if carried to its logical conclusion, it would commit the Association (following the logic of Ehrich and Brues) to the philosophical position involved in "value-free social science"—a position which many competent social scientists find untenable and which creates serious intellectual difficulties for those who hold it.

An attitude such as Ehrich and Brues would have us adopt would be appropriate to a philatelic society, a bowling team or an amateur glee club, but certainly not to a body of people professionally concerned with the "study of man."

Franz Boas

Scientists as Spies

"On December 30, 1919, at the Cambridge meeting of the American Anthropological Association, the man who for two decades had dominated American anthropology was censured, stripped of his membership in the Association's governing Council, threatened with expulsion from the Association itself, pressured into resigning from the National Research Council, and then denied even the courtesy of public explanation by the expunging of his letter of resignation from the Association's minutes."[1] The cause for this action was a letter to the editor of The Nation, *reproduced here together with the initial resolution of censure.*

Sir: In his war address to Congress, President Wilson dwelt at great length on the theory that only autocracies maintain spies; that these are not needed in democracies. At the time that the President made this statement, the Government of the United States had in its employ spies of unknown number. I am not concerned here with the familiar discrepancies between the President's words and the actual facts, although we may perhaps have to accept his statement as meaning correctly that we live under an autocracy; that our democracy is a fiction. The point against which I wish to enter

a vigorous protest is that a number of men who follow science as their profession, men whom I refuse to designate any longer as scientists, have prostituted science by using it as a cover for their activities as spies.

A soldier whose business is murder as a fine art, a diplomat whose calling is based on deception and secretiveness, a politician whose very life consists in compromises with his conscience, a business man whose aim is personal profit within the limits allowed by a lenient law—such may be excused if they set patriotic devotion above common everyday decency and perform services as spies. They merely accept the code of morality to which modern society still conforms. Not so the scientist. The very essence of his life is the service of truth. We all know scientists who in private life do not come up to the standard of truthfulness, but who, nevertheless, would not consciously falsify the results of their researches. It is bad

From "Correspondence: Scientists as Spies" by Franz Boas from *The Nation* (Vol. 109, 1919). Copyright 1919 by *The Nation*. Reprinted by permission of *The Nation*.
[1] George W. Stocking, Jr., *Race, Culture and Evolution* (New York: The Free Press, 1968), p. 273.

enough if we have to put up with these, because they reveal a lack of strength of character that is liable to distort the results of their work. A person, however, who uses science as a cover for political spying, who demeans himself to pose before a foreign government as an investigator and asks for assistance in his alleged researches in order to carry on, under this cloak, his political machinations, prostitutes science in an unpardonable way and forfeits the right to be classed as a scientist.

By accident, incontrovertible proof has come to my hands that at least four men who carry on anthropological work, while employed as government agents, introduced themselves to foreign governments as representatives of scientific institutions in the United States, and as sent out for the purpose of carrying on scientific researches. They have not only shaken the belief in the truthfulness of science, but they have also done the greatest possible disservice to scientific inquiry. In consequence of their acts every nation will look with distrust upon the visiting foreign investigator who wants to do honest work, suspecting sinister designs. Such action has raised a new barrier against the development of international friendly cooperation.

American Anthropological Association

Council Meeting, December 30, 4:45 P.M.

Resolutions received from the Anthropological Society of Washington were read and on motion accepted and placed on file.

The following resolution was moved by Neil M. Judd:

"*Resolved*: That the expression of opinion by Dr. Franz Boas contained in an open letter to the editor of *The Nation* under date of October 16, 1919, and published in the issue of that weekly for December 20, 1919, is unjustified and does not represent the opinion of the American Anthropological Association. Be it further resolved:

"That a copy of this resolution be forwarded to the Executive Board of the National Research Council and such other scientific associations as may have taken action on this matter."

Yes: Judd, Hyde, Hooton, Kidder, Wilder, Farabee, Spinden, Hagar, Wardle, Lothrop, Saville, Fewkes, MacCurdy, Gates, Guernsey, Guthe, Gordon, Dixon, Hodge, Morley.

No: Speck, Spier, Kroeber, Peabody, Sullivan, Lowie, Nelson, Parsons, Tozzer, Goddard.

Not voting: Willoughby, Wissler (presiding).

"Council Meeting, Dec. 30, 4:45 P.M." Reproduced by permission of the American Anthropological Association from *American Anthropologist*, Vol. 22, No. 1, (1920).

Eric R. Wolf and Joseph Jorgensen

Letter to the Student Mobilization Committee

The grave issues of ethics and responsibility in the profession which Boas raised in his letter were not pursued and did not even engage the serious attention of his colleagues in their eagerness to protect the image of the Association and the sensibilities of those implicated. And fifty years later, when the Committee on Ethics came into possession of documents pertaining to the involvement of anthropologists and others in U.S. government sponsored counterinsurgency activities in Thailand, the drama was reenacted. Two members of the Committee (one of them its chairman), who publicly deplored these activities and sought to pursue the matter privately within the Committee, were rebuked by the Executive Board of the Association which sought to keep the issue of counterinsurgency in Thailand from engaging the attention of the Association. The two resigned their Committee membership and wrote a stinging account of the incident in the New York Review of Books *("Anthropologists on the Warpath" by Joseph Jorgensen and Eric Wolf). Their original statement and the rebuke are reproduced here, together with the disputed statement of the Committee on Ethics pertaining to the same issue and the same documents. This statement was submitted to the Executive Board before the rebuke, but was published five months afterwards.*

The efforts to maintain harmony within the Association by overlooking the concerns expressed by the Committee on Ethics and its erstwhile members were doomed by the temper of the times, of which resentment of the war in Southeast Asia and demands for social responsibility within the profession were crucial ingredients. The issue of clandestine research had, in fact, become a major focus of attention in the Association.

March 30th, 1970

The undersigned members of the Ethics Committee of the American Anthropological Association have had occasion to see xeroxed copies of the following documents:

1. Minutes of the Jason Summer Study, Institute for Defense Analysis, Falmouth Intermediate School, Falmouth, Mass., June 20th-July 6th, 1967;
2. A proposal to the Advanced Research Projects Agency, Pittsburgh, Pa., entitled "Counter-Insurgency in Thailand: The Impact of Economic, Social, and Political Action Programs," American Institutes for Research, Dec. 1967;
3. Trip Report for a visit to Amphoe Nong Han, Changwad Udon, May 28th-June 6th, 1969;
4. Agenda for an Advisory Panel, American Institutes for Research meeting, June 30th-July 4th, 1969;
5. Amendment to a Contract between the United States of America, represented by the Agency for International Development, and the Regents of the University of California, to facilitate advice and assistance on the part of the academic community for the Academic Advisory Council for Thailand, Sept. 1st, 1968;
6. Minutes of the Academic Advisory Council for Thailand, Oct. 19th, 1968-July 24th, 1969.

Since these documents contradict in spirit and in letter the resolutions of the American Anthropological Association concerning clandestine and secret research, we feel that they raise the most serious issues for the scientific integrity of our profession. We shall therefore call the attention of the American Anthropological Association to these most serious matters.

Eric R. Wolf
Professor of Anthropology
Chairman, Ethics Comm.,
AAA

Joseph Jorgensen
Associate Prof. of
Anthropology

"The Thailand Issue and the Ethics Committee: A Reply to the AAA Executive Board" by Eric R. Wolf and Joseph Jorgensen. Reproduced by permission of the American Anthropological Association from *Newsletter*, Vol. 11, No. 9, 1970.

Executive Board of the American Anthropological Association

Statement

In view of recent public discussion of the activities of members of the Association who have research interests in Thailand, occasioned by a recent news release of the Student Mobilization Committee and by subsequent public statements, the Executive Board unequivocally reaffirms the 1967 Statement on Problems of Anthropological Research and Ethics, notes recent ratification by the Council of Resolutions 13 and 14 offered at the New Orleans Meeting and affirms that:

(1) Actions by anthropologists in Thailand or elsewhere which contravene the above statement of ethics are a breach of the ethical standards of the Association.

(2) Evidence so far available, on either side of this issue, is incomplete and not adequately verified; hence, no evaluation of the Thai issue is possible at this time.

(3) Current discussion confirms the necessity and desirability of a viable Committee on Ethics of the American Anthropological Association.

(4) The Chairman (Wolf) and a member (Jorgensen) of the Ethics Committee, in communicating on this matter outside the Ethics Committee, went beyond the mandate of the Executive Board to that Committee and were speaking as individuals and not on behalf of the Committee or the Association.

The Board instructs the Ethics Committee to limit itself to its specific charge, narrowly interpreted, namely to present to the Board recommendations on its future role and functions, and to fulfill this charge without further collection of case materials or by any quasi-investigative activities.

The Board explicitly instructs the members of the Ethics Committee to refrain from public statements in the name of that Committee and to make clear in individual statements that they do not speak for the Committee or the Association.

Committee on Ethics of the American Anthropological Association

Letter to the Executive Board

Chicago, Illinois
May 2, 1970

To: The President, President-elect, and Members of the Executive Board of the American Anthropological Association

From: The Committee on Ethics of the American Anthropological Association

Our examination of the documents available to us pertaining to consultation, research, and related activities in Thailand convinces us that anthropologists are being used in large programs of counterinsurgency whose effects should be of grave concern to the Association. Those programs comprise efforts at the manipulation of people on a giant scale and intertwine straightforward anthropological research with overt and covert counterinsurgency activities in such a way as to threaten the future of anthropological research in Southeast Asia and in other parts of the world.

"Statement of the Executive Board of the AAA." Reproduced by permission of the American Anthropological Association from *Bulletins of AAA*, Annual Report, 1969.

"Letter to the Executive Board" by Gerald D. Berreman and others. Reproduced by permission of the American Anthropological Association from *Newsletter*, Vol. 11, No. 9, 1970.

Although involvement by anthropologists seems to range between acceptance of the goals of counterinsurgency activities and rejection of them, the orientations of individual anthropologists are not our concern. On the other hand, the effects of their participation concern us deeply. They generate conflicts between the ethical standards of the Association as expressed in the "Statement of Problems of Anthropological Research and Ethics," of 1967, and the personal ethics of individual anthropologists. They polarize members of the Association, threatening a deep and lasting division within it. They downgrade the credibility of social science and social scientists. Such participation also entails direct and fateful intervention in the lives of the people of Southeast Asia.

Signed by the members of the Committee:

Gerald D. Berreman William A. Shack
Norman A. Chance Wayne Suttles
Joseph S. Jorgensen Terence S. Turner
Eric R. Wolf

Omer C. Stewart

The Need to Popularize Basic Concepts

Most anthropologists are teachers. We therefore close with a paper pointing up the responsibility of the anthropologist to inform his students and the public of some of the basic, yet crucial and practical things we know about man and society. Social science in general and anthropology in particular do have things to say that are relevant to public issues and their resolution. Many of the problems we see in our society and elsewhere originate, or remain unresolved, from ignorance—ignorance not of obscure social facts and processes, but of relatively simple aspects of social existence which have been identified, analyzed, understood, and amply demonstrated by anthropologists. Stewart makes a strong case for the need to convey this knowledge to a broader public in order to increase the use of reason in human affairs.

I wish to present some basic anthropological concepts which have relevance in international affairs. If these points seem too obvious to warrant discussion, let me assure you that they are not accepted by vast numbers of people.

Human beings are a unique section of the animal kingdom because they have culture. Culture provides the tools to utilize the natural environment and to communicate with one another in ways not available to other animals. We must conclude that human behavior is of a different order from the behavior of other animals. Although all human beings show their relationship to other animals in the physical inheritance of bodily forms and the inheritance of patterns for animal physiological functions, the only known hereditary behavior patterns are the ability to cry, suckle, grasp, etc. If humanity inherits other animal behavior patterns, these become so obscured by the infinite number of learned behavior patterns that possible innate patterns are not established. There persist, of course, the needs for food, shelter, companionship, care of infants, sex, etc., to keep the species in existence. These needs are so completely controlled by human rules and customs, however, that we seldom think of them as part of our animal nature.

Culture is behavior and ideas learned and transmitted from generation to generation; as learned behavior, it predetermines or modifies such a large part of human behavior that we can work on the assumption that all adult human behavior is learned.

War is a part of culture, and as such it is a learned

From "The Need to Popularize Basic Concepts" by Omer C. Stewart from *Current Anthropology*, Vol. 5, No. 5 (Dec. 1964). Reprinted by permission of The University of Chicago Press.

cultural complex which can be changed or abandoned. I am constantly surprised at the small number of people who accept this point of view and who are willing to base their ideas concerning the possibility of learning peace upon such propositions. The belief that international warfare must be part of world culture because it is "natural for nations to fight as they always have," is the popular view. The idea that, since war is inevitable, it would be folly not to be prepared for war is a conclusion based upon the proposition that "war is natural." The U.S. Congress and the administrative branch of the government appear to act on the assumption that the world will be "naturally" subjected to World War III. Seldom do the molders of world opinion indicate that they understand that warfare, like cannibalism, is a culture pattern subject to the same learning process as other aspects of culture.

One of the corollaries to the proposition that culture is learned behavior is the proposition that cultural differences result from the accidents of history, usually identified as the presence or absence of materials or environmental conditions. The acceptance of this point of view encourages the acceptance of diversity in various aspects of culture because it equalizes the origin and method of development of culture. Furthermore the concept of culture removes the basis for preserving ancient beliefs that are said to be divinely revealed.

There are numerous other corollaries to the proposition that human behavior is learned that could be germane to a discussion of world affairs by anthropologists. However, these points are probably sufficient to serve as examples for the next suggestion I wish to make.

I am encouraged to put forward these elementary ideas because of the reaction of the members of the American Anthropological Association in general and the anthropologists of the vicinity of Denver, Colorado, in particular to the invitation of the Wenner-Gren Foundation to participate in a series of conferences on "Anthropology and World Affairs." Only 46 professional anthropologists responded to the first invitation to consider the problem of world survival and the theories of "deterrent strategy." Philosopher Robert Paul Wolfe's analysis of the 46 papers, sent as the participants' initial statements on "deterrent strategy," causes me further concern. 13 (more than one-fourth) of the respondents "insisted that anthro-

pology and anthropologists should have nothing to do with" theories of the use or non-use of atomic bombs in world affairs. Furthermore, the reaction of several of the 20 additional anthropologists at the conference showed that many members of our profession believe it improper and unwise for us to be concerned with finding ways to avoid an atomic world war.

Is this evidence that a large portion of anthropologists feel they should labor exclusively in archaeological trenches to throw light upon the Paleolithic, or in ivory towers sorting kinship terms, and ignore the insights offered by their training which might help solve the great problems of our times? Anthropologists should *all* be teachers as well as scientists, and teachers of broad scope whose subject is not only man and his past, but man and his outcome. We are the scholars most concerned with culture, with learned behavior. It is our duty as anthropologists, as scientists, and as human beings, to teach everyone, by all possible means, the basic precepts of culture and the universal role of culture.

If the leaders, opinion-molders, and decision-makers of the world were persuaded and convinced that war is learned behavior and that mankind can learn to live without war, the chances for the survival of human life would be improved. The alternative is that those who believe war is inevitable because it is natural and innate will continue to devote themselves to preparations for war. Since the vast majority of people of the world seem to believe behavior is inherited and that war is natural and inevitable, we are faced with a tremendous task of enlightenment. As the discoverers of culture and as the experts in the scientific study of culture and its relationship to race, religion, nationality, war, etc., we anthropologists cannot avoid our responsibility, to the scientific community and to mankind. It is our duty to popularize those basic propositions we have discovered; without them people in all areas of the world may make grave errors.

To strengthen the argument that anthropologists should be concerned with current national and international affairs, I will cite more evidence of misconceptions which continue to exist and interfere with congenial national and international relations. Currently the most spectacular national phenomenon in the United States is the irrational intensity with which citizens in the southern states try to preserve special privilege to Caucasians and to deny legal equality to Negro citizens. This phenomenon flows from expressed or implied convictions that bad character traits are genetically linked to kinky hair and that such traits cannot be changed by education. Both the size of the population which accepts such fallacies and the intensity of the desire to maintain the positions of privilege rationalized by the fallacies, are truly shocking. The impact of anthropology in the southeastern section of the United States has been small indeed. With few anthropologists in the southern states, the profession has little direct influence, but limited number is no longer an excuse in the northern and western states. Yet in a dozen states in the north and west, antimiscegenation laws continue to remind us that innate inferiority is assumed to be inherited with darker skin pigmentation. Our national immigration laws, based as they are on the assumption that some peoples are genetically unfit to be freely admitted to American citizenship, are further evidence of the pervasiveness of the notion of inheritance of group behavior.

The myth that only white Christians can be trusted to keep treaty commitments or can be expected to respect basic human rights reduces American support for the United Nations and hinders all efforts to negotiate and compromise international disputes. The mistrust of all who have a strange appearance (particularly those with dark skin) pervades American traditions and persists because it is predicated on the belief in the innate inferiority of colored people. One outcome of this is that with the increase in the numbers of United Nations members with predominantly colored populations, support for that international body decreases in the United States.

There is probably no anthropologist who would deny that total disarmament of all nations would be desirable, if the peace of the world could be insured. Anthropologists desire the survival of the species *Homo sapiens* and the continued growth and diffusion of civilization. Anthropologists see dangers to humanity resulting from unjustified fear of strange-appearing peoples and unusual customs. These fears grow out of ignorance and misinformation. As scientists and teachers we must attempt to dispel ignorance, disseminate information and knowledge, and improve the chances for human survival in every way possible.

We should accept our civic responsibilities as have fellow scientists in other fields. At its 100th Anniversary Program, the National Academy of Sciences honored Dr. Linus Pauling, "the only man to win both the Nobel Peace Prize and the Nobel Prize" for scientific achievement; he suggested that the nation would be better served by spending money for research on molecular structure than by sending a man to the moon.

Another report from the meeting might give us even greater encouragement:

The most memorable event of the final Academy session on the nature of the scientific enterprise was the lecture by Robert Oppenheimer. On the difficult matter of how and when scientists should speak on "common and public questions," Oppenheimer said:

"If I doubt whether professionally we have special qualification on these common questions, I doubt even more that our professional practices should disqualify us, or that we should lose interest and heart in preoccupations which have ennobled and purified men throughout history, and for which the world has great need today."

Oppenheimer, perhaps the American scientist who has paid the highest price for his role in increasing the light from the tower, received the greatest ovation of the three-day session: a moving recognition by his colleagues of a quality of character even rarer than first-order scientific achievement.[1]

The National Academy of Sciences thus invites us to do our utmost to ease international tensions and to help prepare the populations of the world for rational evaluation of all problems. The anthropological point of view of the primacy of culture in human affairs could be an immeasurable force for reason, objectivity, and tolerance in intergroup relations. General acceptance of the basic principles I have outlined might change the world climate of opinion toward human behavior in a manner comparable to the shifts in physical science that resulted from the acceptance of Einstein's theory that $E = MC^2$.

[1] "Meeting reports—National Academy of Sciences: 100th Anniversary Program," *Science* 142 (1963): 561–563.

Gerald D. Berreman

Contemporary Anthropology and Moral Accountability

As we have seen, anthropologists find themselves deeply and personally involved in the very substance of their science. Working among and studying their fellow human beings, they form opinions about their subjects which grow out of their own culturally conditioned understanding and beliefs, as well as out of their scientific formulations. The topics they choose to study, the interpretations they make, the conclusions they draw—even the decision to become anthropologists and then to work in a particular society or on a particular problem—are not simply scientific decisions. They are a consequence of all of the anthropologist's social experience. Yet he lays claim to being a scientist, governed in his work by the precepts of science, for he seeks verifiable truth based on specifiable evidence. He sees no inherent contradiction between his humanistic subject and his scientific method, although he may place greater emphasis on one or the other. Certain dilemmas and disagreements based on differing values and priorities are to be expected, and some of these have been the subject of this section.

Simply by being in a society he or she is studying, the anthropologist affects that society. By importing alien customs and novel equipment, he affects it even more. By importing opinions and values which are inevitably conveyed, he increases the effect. And, by being in a position to communicate findings and responses directly or indirectly to persons of authority or influence, the anthropologist may indeed drastically affect those he studies. These consequences may be planned or unintentional; inevitable, inadvertent, or even undetected. On the other hand, in some situations an anthropologist may feel humanly bound to intervene even though, as a scientist, he might wish to be a neutral factor in the situations he studies. The wish is futile, but it presents most anthropologists with agonizing decisions and troubling second thoughts.

Characteristic of the anthropologist's study of man has been his preference to study people and situations markedly different from his own. Often they are people whose lives and welfare are heavily influenced by his own countrymen. Not infrequently, some of his countrymen have a direct vested interest in the research, deriving from administrative responsibility or from economic, political, or social exploitation.

All these facts create ethical or moral problems for the anthropologist, and problems in defining standards of professional responsibility. These problems have long been recognized but, in recent years—and especially with the emergence into full citizenship, into nationhood, and into national and international economic, political, and social viability of peoples previously powerless and regarded primarily as subjects for study—the problems have become more acute, more clearly stated, and more widely recognized. The demand for their resolution has been more uncompromisingly demanded within and without the profession. Contributing to that trend is the fact that anthropologists have increasingly come to define American and European societies as proper subjects for study, and so have begun to turn their attention not only to alien peoples and to the deprived and marginal segments of their own societies, but to dominant groups, powerful institutions, and routine aspects of life. The people they study are increasingly vocal, critical, and in a position to be heard. They raise issues of research ethics which went unnoticed when the subjects of study were alien, nonliterate, or powerless.

The most pressing sources of criticism directed toward anthropology and its works are its own practitioners, their relentlessly inquiring students, and their uncompromising informants. The context of anthropology today is war in Southeast Asia, universal nuclear terror, international economic exploitation and political domination, racism, deep political division, and ethnic and generational conflict. In America the minorities, the young, and the intellectuals are demanding an end to hypocrisy in our national life and our international policies. In this context, the demand that scientists, including anthropologists, have high ethical standards, accept professional responsibility, and feel personally accountable has become urgent. It is combined with the demand that scientific research be involved with the important practical issues facing mankind. The demand cannot be, and is not being, ignored. It is concurred in by many of whom it is made. In anthropology, as in the society at large, increasing numbers of people are beginning to believe that "if you are not part of the solution, you are part of the problem." The ivory tower is fast becoming a relic.

I set forth my own position on the subject in my presidential address to the Southwestern Anthropological Association in March 1967.[1] Some of the points made then bear repetition here:

The notion that contemporary world events are irrelevant to the professional concerns of anthropologists was laid neatly to rest at the 1966 meeting of the American Anthropological Association when Dr. Michael Harner rose to challenge the ruling of the president-elect that a resolution condemning the United States' role in the war in Vietnam was out of order because it did not "advance the science of anthropology," or "further the professional interests of anthropologists." Dr. Harner suggested that "genocide is not in the professional interests of anthropologists." With that, the chair was voted down.

The dogma that public issues are beyond the interests or competence of those who study and teach about man comprises myopic and sterile professionalism, and a fear of commitment which is both irresponsible and irrelevant. Its result is to dehumanize "the most humanist of the sciences," as Eric Wolf has called our discipline; to betray utterly the opportunity and obligation which he has claimed for anthropology, namely: "the creation of an image of man that will be adequate to the experience of our time."

That neutrality in science is illusory is a point which has been made often and well.

The famous anthropologist, Franz Boas, was alert to startlingly similar problems in the uses of anthropology and anthropologists during World War I, and deplored them publicly. "A number of men who follow science as their profession [including 'at least four men who carry on anthropological work'] . . . have prostituted science by using it as a cover for their activities as spies," he wrote in 1919.

If science has no responsibility, scientists do. Scientists are people. They cannot escape values in the choices they make nor in the consequences of their acts.

If anthropologists choose to collect their data and make their analyses without regard to their use—leaving that choice to others—they may believe that they are adhering to the most rigorous scientific canons. But to say nothing is not to be neutral. To say *nothing* is as much a significant act as to say *something*. Douglas Dowd noted that "the alternatives are not 'neutrality' and 'advocacy.' To be uncommitted is not to be neutral, but to be committed—consciously or not—to the *status quo;* it is, in C. Wright Mills' phrase, 'to celebrate the present.'"

Silence permits others in the society who are less reticent, perhaps less scrupulous, almost certainly less informed, to make their own use of scientific findings. It leaves to politicians and journalists, to entrepreneurs, scoundrels, and madmen, as well as to statesmen and benefactors—but especially to the powerful—the interpretation and manipulation of matters about which they frequently know little, and of whose implications they know less, and nearly always far less than those who collected the material or made the analyses. It is therefore wishful thinking of the most elemental sort to assume that anthropological work can be put before the public without context or interpretation, there to be judged freely and intelligently on its merits without prejudice or manipulation, and to be acted upon accordingly. To assume *that* is to contribute to misuse born of ignorance or worse. Scientists cannot divorce themselves from the consequences of their scientific acts any more than they can from those of any of their other acts as human beings. This is a fact of existence in human society and it is a tenet of democracy.

Science—even social science—has finally arrived in our society. The rewards to be obtained for supplying social science data and social science interpretations of the right kinds and in the right places are generous. The intellectual today can join the hired myth-makers and apologists of Madison Avenue and Washington. On campus he can be the paid consultant or the academic entrepreneur and grantsman. As Irving Howe has remarked, "for once, the carrots are real." In this context, the prevalence of social scientists whose eyes are on the main chance rather than on the condition of man should not be surprising. This is the context within which we find social scientists whose "ideology of non-involvement in the social effects of scientific research," Sidney Willhelm noted, simply frees them from social responsibility, creating an "unaccountable scientific aristocracy," closely allied to the governmental, military, and corporate elites who buy their services and validate their heady status. As Noam Chomsky has

[1] Published in *Current Anthropology,* Vol. 9 (1968), pp. 391–396, under the title, "Is Anthropology Alive? Social Responsibility in Social Anthropology." Excerpted and revised with the permission of *Current Anthropology.*

written, "The problems with which research is concerned are those posed by the Pentagon or the great corporations, not, say, by the revolutionaries of Northeast Brazil or by SNCC [the Student Nonviolent Coordinating Committee]. Nor am I aware of a research project devoted to the problem of how poorly armed guerillas might more effectively resist a brutal and devastating military technology." Yet such alternative problems would be likely to interest at least some social scientists.

The rationale which supports this scientific unaccountability among moral men is the myth of a value-free social science. This myth has been exposed to all but its most avid beneficiaries and the most credulous in its audience, as we have seen in this section. Yet it still serves to maintain a whole segment of the profession—or at least to sustain the symbiotic relationship between that segment of social scientists and the corporate foundations and governmental agencies who buy its findings, using them only as and if they see fit. It was Alexander Leighton who said that administrators use the findings of social scientists as a drunk uses a lamp post—for support rather than illumination. It is not important what social scientists say so much as how what they say is used. That depends upon how amenable it is to use and *that* is where the myth of freedom from values is crucial, and where the social responsibility of the social scientist lies.

The myth of value-freedom in physical science disappeared in the atomic cloud. In social science it is fading, as we have seen, in the dust of Camelot, the blood of Vietnam, and the duplicity of the CIA.

Today, if scientific truth is to be understood and acted upon, those who discover and know it must forcefully announce not only their knowledge, but its implications and consequences. As Winetrout says in the closing paragraph of his essay honoring the courageous Mills: "In our present-day world, it is not enough to be scholarly; one must be concerned and angry enough to shout. It is not enough to understand the world; one must seek to change it."

No doubt, the world will change; no doubt, the social scientist's knowledge will contribute to that change. His responsibility is to see that this knowledge is used for humane changes. Simply, scientists must be responsible for what they do.

Thirty years ago, Robert Lynd maintained that "either the social sciences know more than do . . . *de facto* leaders of the culture as to what the findings of research mean, as to the options the institutional system presents, as to what human personalities want,

why they want them, and how desirable changes can be effected, *or* the vast current industry of social science is an empty façade." To repeat Kathleen Gough's question, "Who is to evaluate and suggest guidelines for human society, if not those who study it?"

Our positive responsibility as scientists is to present what we know and what inferences we draw from our knowledge as clearly, thoughtfully, and responsibly as we can. This is a value position with practical and humane consequences. We have already heard from C. Wright Mills. In another work, he decried the "divorce of knowledge from power," and wrote:

As a type of social man, the intellectual does not have any one political direction, but the work of any man of knowledge, if he is the genuine article, does have a distinct kind of political relevance: His politics, in the first instance, are the politics of truth, for his job is the maintenance of an adequate definition of reality. In so far as he is politically adroit, the main tenet of his politics is to find out as much of the truth as he can, and to tell it to the right people, at the right time, and in the right way. Or, stated negatively: to deny publicly what he knows to be false, whenever it appears in the assertions of no matter whom; and whether it be a direct lie or a lie by omission, whether it be by virtue of official secret or an honest error. The intellectual ought to be the moral conscience of his society, at least with reference to the value of truth, for in the defining instance, that is his politics. And he ought also to be a man absorbed in the attempt to know what is real and what is unreal.[2]

I know of no statement which speaks to the responsibility of social scientists in our time as cogently as that one.

Douglas Dowd identifies the focal point of opposition by the young and by intellectuals in the word *hypocrisy*—hypocrisy in American deeds versus American words. This is where we as scientists and as teachers have a major responsibility: to speak the truth; to provide "an adequate definition of reality." Candor is a major precondition for trust and for rational action, and this is what is lacking or threatened in our society—in foreign policy, in race relations, in poverty programs, in support of scholarship and research, in university administration, in virtually every sphere of our national life.

[2] "On Knowledge and Power," in *Power, Politics and People,* I. Horowitz, ed. (New York: Ballantine Books, 1964), p. 611.

The reaction of many anthropologists is to say and do nothing about the problems of the day; to retreat into research, administration, or teaching. Lulled by activity into a sense of purpose, accomplishment, and virtue, they hope that things will somehow work out. Do we need Edmund Burke to remind us that "the only thing necessary for the triumph of evil is for good men [and, I might add, informed men] to do nothing"?

Anthropologists have not lacked outspoken champions of truth—truth about race, about poverty, about professional ethics, about the heavy hands of government and private capital in formulating research, about war, and especially about the war in Indo-China. Probably anthropologists have more of them in proportion to their numbers than any other academic discipline and any other profession. But we need to emphasize and value these contributions in order to counteract the powerful and irresponsible professionalism which belittles or condemns these humane endeavors in favor of the mindless and trivial successes obtained under the illusion of freedom from responsibility for one's self and one's work.

In a world where anything scientists learn is likely to be put to immediate and effective use for ends beyond their control and antithetical to their values, anthropologists must choose their research undertakings with an eye to their implications. They must demand the right to have a hand or at least a say in the use of what they do as a condition for doing it.

We anthropologists must seek to apply our knowledge and skills to real problems, defined by us and not simply accepted from the sources which provide our funds. We must ask questions which address the problems of our time rather than merely those which minimize or obscure them. Nor does the incompleteness of our knowledge disqualify us scientifically, rationally, or morally from asserting what we know. Mills pointed out 20 years ago that "if one half of the relevant knowledge which we now possess were really put into the service of the ideals which leaders mouth, these ideals could be realized in short order." Gouldner has followed logically with the statement: "The issue . . . is not whether we know enough; the real questions are whether we have the courage to say and use what we know." This is why we must not be timid in asserting ourselves individually and collectively wherever we can. This is why our professional association should not now be chary to express views on matters of public policy just as we have not been in the past (as you have seen in the Resolutions) and just as other such groups express views on such matters. For students of human behavior to decline comment on human behavior is irresponsibility in a democracy, no matter how controversial the issues.

2 The Myth of the Melting Pot

Arthur J. Rubel and Harriet J. Kupferer
The Myth of the Melting Pot

James Mooney
The Doctrine of the Ghost Dance

Abram Kardiner and Lionel Ovesey
Psychodynamic Inventory of the Negro Personality

Ann Fischer
History and Current Status of the Houma Indians

Harold Arthur Shapiro
The Pecan Shellers' Strike in San Antonio

Frances L. Swadesh
The Alianza Movement:
Catalyst for Social Change in New Mexico

Harriet J. Kupferer and Arthur J. Rubel
The Consequences of a Myth

As long as we insist on a stratification in racial layers, we shall pay the penalty in the form of interracial struggle. Will it be better for us to continue as we have been doing, or shall we try to recognize the conditions that lead us to the fundamental antagonisms that trouble us?   Franz Boas

For what America needs is no mere shifting of different groups up and down on a ladder; America needs the help of all her citizens to ensure human dignity to all Americans.   Ruth Benedict

News of atrocities perpetrated by the United States and its allies [in Indochina] produces deep psychic disturbances among many people, because the incidents stem in part from racist attitudes which stain our social fabric and at the same time contravene our most revered ideals and cherished views of ourselves.   Ad Hoc Committee to Evaluate the Controversy Concerning Anthropological Activities in Relation to Thailand

Arthur J. Rubel and Harriet J. Kupferer

The Myth of the Melting Pot

Anthropologists have always been concerned with the processes by which members of a society learn to behave in a manner considered appropriate. Moreover, they have always tried to discover the nature of the relationship between a group's way of life—its culture—and the personality traits of members of that group. In the United States, more so than in other countries, anthropologists have been especially interested in the effects that changes in the larger environment have on both cultural systems and the personalities of the people who bear those cultures. This interest is no coincidence, for two of the most characteristic phenomena of our nation's brief social history have been in-migration of diverse ethnic groups and their movement westward. These phenomena have caused a continuous confrontation between the cultures of diverse groups living as neighbors in the new land.

Such confrontations began more than two centuries ago, when the Scots-English and Irish culture-bearers arrived in the original thirteen colonies and were brought face-to-face with the several cultures of the native American Indians. Confrontations became more frequent as more cultural groups came to America. The colonists imported black slaves, and brought with them the various cultures of western Africa. Then, as the settlers moved westward, they encountered culturally different Indian groups, as, for example, the Sioux, Navajo, and Hopi. In the middle of the nineteenth century began the expansion of English-speaking Americans into the Southwest, which had long been home to the Spanish-speaking heirs to land grants dating back to the sixteenth century. Finally, the nineteenth and twentieth centuries have seen immigrant groups from all over the globe pour into the United States and come into contact with those groups that came both before and after them.

In each instance, the bearers of one set of cultural values, norms, and behavior took stock of the culture of the others and borrowed a few—but not all—items. These meetings of people with distinctive ways of life led to the creation of the popular American theme—that from them emerged a homogenized national society characterized by a single set of shared cultural values, normative expectations, and behavior. The United States is a melting-pot nation, the theme relates; a nation of immigrants, it proudly proclaims. Thus it contributes to the expectation that each person living in the United States—whether immigrant newcomer or one whose ancestors were here before the arrival of the *Mayflower*—would, in fact, assimilate to a uniform way of life, and that, if he did not conform and shed nonuniform ways of thought or behavior, his children would. Moreover, it holds this passage into the cultural "mainstream" to be not only inevitable, but right and proper.

The social and economic pressures to assimilate, some subtle, others blatant, which are and customarily have been exerted on all ethnic segments of our complex society, may be regarded as little short of coercive. Cultural distinctiveness is abhorred. Indeed, in this nation of immigrants, to be called a foreigner is ignominious, and any trait suggestive of foreignness—language, clothing, forms of kinship—is to be erased.

In the face of such arrogant demands to assimilate, members of some of our ethnic minorities have struggled to accommodate themselves in one of two ways to the superordinate society. Either they tried to become culturally indistinguishable from those exemplars presented to them as models of appropriateness, or they changed their traditional styles of life enough to reduce the above-mentioned social pressures to tolerable levels. Thus, persons of Scots-English background and most immigrants from Germany and Scandinavia have discarded their traditions so as to become indistinguishable from what is represented to us as *the* American way of life.

Other groups have made efforts to retain as much of their original cultural heritage as possible. Among these are the Hassidic Jews, the Amish, and such American Indian tribes as the Hopi and Navajo. Still other groups have given up most of their unique cultural characteristics—e.g., language, distinctive clothing, patterns of family relationships—while retaining one or several other traits—such as traditional food preparations, religious rites, or holding dear one day of symbolic importance to them alone. Many of the poorer Italians, Greek Orthodox, and Irish fit into this category.

The decisions made by groups as to which features of the traditional way of life were to be erased or changed, or even if the attempt were to be made to accommodate themselves to the prescriptions of the majority, have exacted many tolls. Dissension has torn asunder the Norwegian immigrant communities in the midwest and has appeared in the chicano neighborhoods in Texas.[1] Moreover, as Joshua Fishman has detailed in *Language Loyalty in the United States,* similar schisms have rent the central and eastern European communities in our country during the first half of this century; and many anthropologists have recorded in telling fashion the schisms which occurred in American Indian communities as a consequence of pressures to assimilate.

Each of the readings in this section comments on the close relationship between the simple fact of being culturally different and the attainment of an economically viable standard of living. In each there is reference to some of the historical forces which contributed to the contemporary relationship between the majority group and the respective minorities. Explicitly or implicitly, the authors have made unmistakably clear that one cannot comprehend either the personality characteristics or the self-image distinctive of each group unless one understands how that group has been historically perceived and related to by the dominant society.

It is profoundly tragic that broken promises and outright skulduggery should appear so consistently in the recorded history of the majority's relationship to three of the groups represented in our selections: the Sioux, the Houma, and the chicanos.[2] The history of the blacks in America is another such episode—African culture traits have been completely suppressed—but this has been too often documented to need repeating here.

The social history of minority-majority group relations in the United States demonstrates clearly the emotional, social, and economic costs which attend the expectation of our nation of immigrants that all segments will and should "melt" into congeries of uniform values, language, behavior, and, even, hopes for the future. The costs are highest for a group that chooses not to melt, for, as the articles in this section suggest, the less similar a group to the middle-class exemplars of the larger society, the more its members will suffer both economically and socially.

[1] See Einar Haugen, *The Norwegian Language in America,* 2nd ed. (Bloomington: Indiana University Press, 1969); and Arthur J. Rubel, *Across the Tracks* (Austin: University of Texas Press, 1966).

[2] See the useful history of the federal government's Indian legislation, compiled by James Officer, "The American Indian and Federal Policy," in *The American Indian in Urban Society,* J. O. Waddell and O. M. Watson, ed. (Boston: Little, Brown and Company, 1971), pp. 8–75.

James Mooney

The Doctrine of the Ghost Dance

When the federal government repressed the Sioux Ghost-dance religion it did so because it did not understand that this religion was an attempt by the Sioux to accommodate themselves to the expectations of the dominant white society without giving up all vestiges of their traditional way of life.

Mooney's account of the government's punitive effort to eradicate the Ghost-dance religion shows how varied may be the forms by which societies, such as the Sioux, organize their cultures to meet stresses generated by external as well as internal sources. Furthermore, it demonstrates clearly how a different and more intelligent understanding of a dramatic and emotion-laden phenomenon can be arrived at by adopting an anthropological holistic view of circumstances relevant to such an event, as did the author, instead of fastening one's attention on what are only surface manifestations of the profound sociocultural problems caused by one society's efforts to adapt better to the demands of another, upon which it has become dependent.

Finally, Mooney may well have been the first American anthropologist called upon to examine and explain a conflict between culturally distinctive segments of our society. Unfortunately, his help was not requested until the misinterpretation of the motives and goals of the Ghost-dance religion had already caused grave damage.

You must not fight.
Do no harm to anyone.
Do right always.—Wovoka.

The great underlying principle of the Ghost-dance doctrine is that the time will come when the whole Indian race, living and dead, will be reunited upon a regenerated earth, to live a life of aboriginal happiness, forever free from death, disease, and misery. On this foundation each tribe has built a structure from its own mythology, and each apostle and believer has filled in the details according to his own mental capacity or ideas of happiness, with such additions as come to him from the trance. Some changes, also, have undoubtedly resulted from the transmission of the doctrine through the imperfect medium of the sign language. The dif-ferences of interpretation are precisely such as we find in Christianity, with its hundreds of sects and innumerable shades of individual opinion. The white race, being alien and secondary and hardly real, has no part in this scheme of aboriginal regeneration, and will be left behind with the other things of earth that have served their temporary purpose, or else will cease entirely to exist.

All this is to be brought about by an overruling spiritual power that needs no assistance from human creatures; and though certain medicine-men were disposed to anticipate the Indian millennium by preaching resistance to the further encroachments of the whites, such teachings form no part of the true doctrine, and it was only where chronic dissatisfaction was aggravated by recent grievances, as among the Sioux, that the movement assumed a hostile expression. On the contrary, all believers were exhorted to make themselves worthy of the predicted happiness by discarding all things warlike and practicing honesty, peace, and good will, not only among themselves, but also toward the whites, so long as they were together. Some apostles have even thought that all race distinctions are to be obliterated, and that the whites are to participate with the Indians in the coming felicity; but it seems unquestionable that this is equally contrary to the doctrine as originally preached. . . .

On returning to the Cheyenne and Arapaho in Oklahoma, after my visit to Wovoka in January, 1892, I was at once sought by my friends of both tribes, anxious to hear the report of my journey and see the sacred things that I had brought back from the messiah. The Arapaho especially, who are of more spiritual nature than any of the other tribes, showed a deep interest and followed intently every detail of the narrative. As soon as the news of my return was spread abroad, men and women, in groups and singly, would come to me, and after grasping my hand would repeat a long and earnest prayer, sometimes aloud, sometimes with the lips silently moving, and frequently with tears rolling

From James Mooney, "The Ghost Dance Religion and the Sioux Outbreak of 1890." *Fourteenth Annual Report of the Bureau of American Ethnology,* Part 2, 1896.

down the cheeks, and the whole body trembling violently from stress of emotion. Often before the prayer was ended the condition of the devotee bordered on the hysterical, very little less than in the Ghost dance itself. The substance of the prayer was usually an appeal to the messiah to hasten the coming of the promised happiness, with a petition that, as the speaker himself was unable to make the long journey, he might, by grasping the hand of one who had seen and talked with the messiah face to face, be enabled in his trance visions to catch a glimpse of the coming glory. During all this performance the bystanders awaiting their turn kept reverent silence. In a short time it became very embarrassing, but until the story had been told over and over again there was no way of escape without wounding their feelings. . . .

As I had always shown a sympathy for their ideas and feelings, and had now accomplished a long journey to the messiah himself at the cost of considerable difficulty and hardship, the Indians were at last fully satisfied that I was really desirous of learning the truth concerning their new religion. A few days after my visit to Left Hand, several of the delegates who had been sent out in the preceding August came down to see me, headed by Black Short Nose, a Cheyenne. After preliminary greetings, he stated that the Cheyenne and Arapaho were now convinced that I would tell the truth about their religion, and as they loved their religion and were anxious to have the whites know that it was all good and contained nothing bad or hostile they would now give me the message which the messiah himself had given to them, that I might take it back to show to Washington. He then took from a beaded pouch and gave to me a letter, which proved to be the message or statement of the doctrine delivered by Wovoka to the Cheyenne and Arapaho delegates, of whom Black Short Nose was one, on the occasion of their last visit to Nevada, in August, 1891, and written down on the spot, in broken English, by one of the Arapaho delegates, Casper Edson, a young man who had acquired some English education by several years' attendance at the government Indian school at Carlisle, Pennsylvania. On the reverse page of the paper was a duplicate in somewhat better English, written out by a daughter of Black Short Nose, a school girl, as dictated by her father on his return. These letters contained the message to be delivered to the two tribes, and as is expressly stated in the text were not

intended to be seen by a white man. The daughter of Black Short Nose had attempted to erase this clause before her father brought the letter down to me, but the lines were still plainly visible. It is the genuine official statement of the Ghost-dance doctrine as given by the messiah himself to his disciples. . . .

The Messiah Letter (free Rendering)

When you get home you must make a dance to continue five days. Dance four successive nights, and the last night keep up the dance until the morning of the fifth day, when all must bathe in the river and then disperse to their homes. You must all do in the same way.

I, Jack Wilson, love you all, and my heart is full of gladness for the gifts you have brought me. When you get home I shall give you a good cloud [rain?] which will make you feel good. I give you a good spirit and give you all good paint. I want you to come again in three months, some from each tribe there [the Indian Territory].

There will be a good deal of snow this year and some rain. In the fall there will be such a rain as I have never given you before.

Grandfather [a universal title of reverence among Indians and here meaning the messiah] says, when your friends die you must not cry. You must not hurt anybody or do harm to anyone. You must not fight. Do right always. It will give you satisfaction in life. . . .

Do not tell the white people about this. Jesus is now upon the earth. He appears like a cloud. The dead are all alive again. I do not know when they will be here; maybe this fall or in the spring. When the time comes there will be no more sickness and everyone will be young again.

Do not refuse to work for the whites and do not make any trouble with them until you leave them. When the earth shakes [at the coming of the new world] do not be afraid. It will not hurt you.

I want you to dance every six weeks. Make a feast at the dance and have food that everybody may eat. Then bathe in the water. That is all. You will receive good words again from me some time. Do not tell lies.

Every organized religion has a system of ethics, a system of mythology, and a system of ritual observance. . . . The feasting enjoined is a part of every Indian ceremonial gathering, religious, political, or social. The dance is to continue four successive nights, in accord with the regular Indian system, in which *four* is the sacred number, as *three* is in Christianity. . . .

The mythology of the doctrine is only briefly indicated, but the principal articles are given. The dead are all arisen and the spirit hosts are advancing and have already arrived at the boundaries of this earth, led forward by the regenerator in shape of cloud-like indistinctness. The spirit captain of the dead is always represented under this shadowy semblance. The great change will be ushered in by a trembling of the earth, at which the faithful are exhorted to feel no alarm. The hope held out is the same that has inspired the Christian for nineteen centuries—a happy immortality in perpetual youth. As to fixing a date, the messiah is as cautious as his predecessor in prophecy, who declares that "no man knoweth the time, not even the angels of God.". . .

The moral code inculcated is as pure and comprehensive in its simplicity. . . . *"Do no harm to any one. Do right always."* Could anything be more simple, and yet more exact and exacting? It inculcates honesty—*"Do not tell lies."* It preaches good will—*"Do no harm to any one."* It forbids the extravagant mourning customs formerly common among the tribes—*"When your friends die, you must not cry,"* which is interpreted by the prairie tribes as forbidding the killing of horses, the burning of tipis and destruction of property, the cutting off of the hair and the gashing of the body with knives, all of which were formerly the sickening rule at every death until forbidden by the new doctrine. As an Arapaho said to me when his little boy died, "I shall not shoot any ponies, and my wife will not gash her arms. We used to do this when our friends died, because we thought we would never see them again, and it made us feel bad. But now we know we shall all be united again.". . .

It preaches peace with the whites and obedience to authority until the day of deliverance shall come. Above all, it forbids war—*"You must not fight."* It is hardly possible for us to realize the tremendous and radical change which this doctrine works in the whole spirit of savage life. The career of every Indian has been the warpath. His proudest title has been that of warrior. His conversation by day and his dreams by night have been of bloody deeds upon the enemies of his tribe. His highest boast was in the number of his scalp trophies, and his chief delight at home was in the war dance and the scalp dance. The thirst for blood and massacre seemed

inborn in every man, woman, and child of every tribe. Now comes a prophet as a messenger from God to forbid not only war, but all that savors of war—the war dance, the scalp dance, and even the bloody torture of the sun dance—and his teaching is accepted and his words obeyed by four-fifths of all the warlike predatory tribes of the mountains and the great plains. Only those who have known the deadly hatred that once animated Ute, Cheyenne, and Pawnee, one toward another, and are able to contrast it with their present spirit of mutual brotherly love, can know what the Ghost-dance religion has accomplished in bringing the savage into civilization. It is such a revolution as comes but once in the life of a race.

The beliefs held among the various tribes in regard to the final catastrophe are as fairly probable as some held on the same subject by more orthodox authorities. As to the dance itself, with its scenes of intense excitement, spasmodic action, and physical exhaustion even to unconsciousness, such manifestations have always accompanied religious upheavals among primitive peoples, and are not entirely unknown among ourselves. In a country which produces magnetic healers, shakers, trance mediums, and the like, all these things may very easily be paralleled without going far from home. . . .

We may now consider details of the doctrine as held by different tribes, beginning with the Paiute, among whom it originated. The best account of the Paiute belief is contained in a report to the War Department by Captain J. M. Lee, who was sent out in the autumn of 1890 to investigate the temper and fighting strength of the Paiute and other Indians in the vicinity of Fort Bidwell in northeastern California. We give the statement obtained by him from Captain Dick, a Paiute. . . .

All Indians must dance, everywhere, keep on dancing. Pretty soon in next spring Big Man [Great Spirit] come. He bring back all game of every kind. The game be thick everywhere. All dead Indians come back and live again. They all be strong just like young men, be young again. Old blind Indian see again and get young and have fine time. When Old Man [God] comes this way, then all the Indians go to mountains, high up away from whites. Whites can't hurt Indians then. Then while Indians way up high, big flood comes like water and all white people die, get drowned. After that water go way and then nobody but Indians everywhere and game all kinds thick. Then medicine-man tell Indians to send word to all Indians to keep up dancing and the good time will come. Indians who don't dance, who don't believe in this word, will grow little, just about a foot high, and stay that way. Some of them will be turned into wood and be burned in fire. . . .

One of the first and most prominent of those who brought the doctrine to the prairie tribes was Porcupine, a Cheyenne, who crossed the mountains with several companions in the fall of 1889, visited Wovoka, and attended the dance near Walker lake, Nevada. In his report of his experiences, made some months later to a military officer, he states that Wovoka claimed to be Christ himself, who had come back again, many centuries after his first rejection, in pity to teach his children. . . . that both races are to live together as one. We have also the doctrine of healing by touch. Whether or not this is an essential part of the system is questionable, but it is certain that the faithful believe that great physical good comes to them, to their children, and to the sick from the imposition of hands by the priests of the dance, apart from the ability thus conferred to see the things of the spiritual world. . . .

The manner of the final change and the destruction of the whites has been variously interpreted as the doctrine was carried from its original center. East of the mountains it is commonly held that a deep sleep will come on the believers, during which the great catastrophe will be accomplished, and the faithful will awake to immortality on a new earth. The Shoshoni of Wyoming say this sleep will continue four days and nights, and that on the morning of the fifth day all will open their eyes in a new world where both races will dwell together forever. The Cheyenne, Arapaho, Kiowa, and others, of Oklahoma, say that the new earth, with all the resurrected dead from the beginning, and with the buffalo, the elk, and other game upon it, will come from the west and slide over the surface of the present earth, as the right hand might slide over the left. As it approaches, the Indians will be carried upward and alight on it by the aid of the sacred dance feathers which they wear in their hair and which will act as wings to bear them up. They will then become unconscious for four days, and on waking out of their trance will find themselves with their former friends in the midst of all the oldtime surroundings. By Sitting Bull, the Arapaho apostle, it is thought that this new earth as it advances will be preceded by a wall of fire which will drive the whites across the water to their original and proper country, while the Indians will be enabled by means of the sacred feathers to surmount the flames and reach the promised land. When the expulsion of the whites has been accomplished, the fire will be extinguished by a rain continuing twelve days. . . .

Among all the tribes which have accepted the new faith it is held that frequent devout attendance on the dance conduces to ward off disease and restore the sick to health, this applying not only to the actual participants, but also to their children and friends. . . .

Among the powerful and warlike Sioux of the Dakotas, already restless under both old and recent grievances, and more lately brought to the edge of starvation by a reduction of rations, the doctrine speedily assumed a hostile meaning and developed some peculiar features, for which reason it deserves particular notice as concerns this tribe. . . .

Perhaps the best statement of the Sioux version is given by the veteran agent, James McLaughlin, of Standing Rock agency. In an official letter of October 17, 1890, he writes that the Sioux, under the influence of Sitting Bull, were greatly excited over the near approach of a predicted Indian millennium or "return of the ghosts," when the white man would be annihilated and the Indian again supreme, and which the medicine-men had promised was to occur as soon as the grass was green in the spring. They were told that the Great Spirit had sent upon them the dominant race to punish them for their sins, and that their sins were now expiated and the time of deliverance was at hand. Their decimated ranks were to be reinforced by all the Indians who had ever died, and these spirits were already on their way to reinhabit the earth, which had originally belonged to the Indians, and were driving before them, as they advanced, immense herds of buffalo and fine ponies. The Great Spirit, who had so long deserted his red children, was now once more with them and against the whites, and the white man's gunpowder would no longer have power to drive a bullet through the skin of an Indian. The whites themselves would soon be overwhelmed and smothered under a deep landslide, held down by sod and timber, and the few who might escape would become small fishes in the rivers. In order to bring about this happy result, the Indians must believe and organize the Ghost dance....

When the time was near at hand, they must assemble at certain places of rendezvous and prepare for the final abandonment of all earthly things by stripping off their clothing. In accordance with the general idea of a return to aboriginal habits, the believers, as far as possible, discarded white man's dress and utensils. Those who could procure buckskin—which is now very scarce in the Sioux country—resumed buckskin dress, while the dancers put on "ghost shirts" made of cloth, but cut and ornamented in Indian fashion. No metal of any kind was allowed in the dance, no knives, and not even the earrings or belts of imitation silver which form such an important part of prairie Indian costume.... No weapon of any kind was allowed to be carried in the Ghost dance by any tribe, north or south, a fact which effectually disposes of the assertion that this was another variety of war dance. At certain of the Sioux dances, however, sacred arrows and a sacred bow, with other things, were tied on the tree in the center of the circle....

The most noted thing connected with the Ghost dance among the Sioux is the "ghost shirt" which was worn by all adherents of the doctrine—men, women, and children alike. During the dance it was worn as an outside garment, but was said to be worn at other times under the ordinary dress. Although the shape, fringing, and feather adornment were practically the same in every case, considerable variation existed in regard to the painting, the designs on some being very simple, while the others were fairly covered with representations of sun, moon, stars, the sacred things of their mythology, and the visions of the trance. The feathers attached to the garment were always those of the eagle, and the thread used in the sewing was always the old-time sinew. In some cases the fringe or other portions were painted with the sacred red paint of the messiah. The shirt was firmly believed to be impenetrable to bullets or weapons of any sort. When one of the women shot in the Wounded Knee massacre was approached as she lay in the church and told that she must let them remove her ghost shirt in order the better to get at her wound, she replied: "Yes; take it off. They told me a bullet would not go through. Now I don't want it any more."

The protective idea in connection with the ghost shirt does not seem to be aboriginal. The Indian warrior habitually went into battle naked above the waist. His protecting "medicine" was a feather, a tiny bag of some sacred powder, the claw of an animal, the head of a bird, or some other small object which could be readily twisted into his hair or hidden between the covers of his shield without attracting attention. Its virtue depended entirely on the ceremony of the consecration and not on size or texture. The war paint had the same magic power of protection....

It may be remarked here that, under present conditions, when the various tribes are isolated upon widely separated reservations, the Ghost dance could never have become so widespread, and would probably have died out within a year of its inception, had it not been for the efficient aid it received from the returned pupils of various eastern government schools, who conducted the sacred correspondence for their friends at the different agencies, acted as interpreters for the delegates to the messiah, and in various ways assumed the leadership and conduct of the dance.

In the fall of 1889, at a council held at Pine Ridge by Red Cloud, Young Man Afraid, Little Wound, American Horse, and other Sioux chiefs, a delegation was appointed to visit the western agencies to learn more about the new messiah.... They started on their journey to the west, and soon began to write from Wyoming, Utah, and beyond the mountains, confirming all that had been said of the advent of a redeemer. They were gone all winter, and their return in the spring of 1890 aroused an intense excitement among the Sioux, who had been anxiously awaiting their report. All the delegates agreed that there was a man near the base of the Sierras who said that he was the son of God, who had once been killed by the whites, and who bore on his body the scars of the crucifixion. He had now returned to punish the whites for their wickedness, especially for their injustice toward the Indians. With the coming of the next spring (1891) he would wipe the whites from the face of the earth, and would then resurrect all the dead Indians, bring back the buffalo and other game, and restore the supremacy of the aboriginal race. He was now the God of the Indians, and they must pray to him and call him "father," and prepare for his awful coming.

The delegates made their report at Pine Ridge in April, 1890.... Good Thunder and two others [were] arrested and imprisoned. They were held in confinement two days, but refused to talk when questioned.... Soon afterward Kicking Bear returned from a visit to the northern Arapaho in Wyoming with the news that those Indians were already dancing, and could see and talk with their dead relatives in the trance. This excitement which the agent had thought to smother by the arrest of the leaders broke out again with added strength. Red Cloud himself, the great chief of the Ogalala, declared his adhesion to the new doctrine and said his people must do as the messiah had commanded. Another council was called on White Clay creek, a few miles from Pine Ridge agency, and the Ghost dance was formally inaugurated among the Sioux, the recent delegates acting as priests and leaders of the ceremony.

Wonderful things were said of the messiah by the returned delegates. It is useless to assert that these men, who had been selected by the chiefs of their tribe to investigate and report upon the truth or falsity of the messiah rumors, were all liars, and that all the Cheyenne, Arapaho, and other delegates who reported equally wonderful things were liars likewise. They were simply laboring under some strange psychologic influence as yet unexplained.

We now come to the Sioux outbreak of 1890, but before going into the history of this short but costly war it is appropriate to state briefly the causes of the outbreak. These causes are fully set forth by competent authorities—civilian, military, missionary, and Indian. They may be summarized as (1) unrest of the conservative element under the decay of the old life, (2) repeated neglect of promises made by the government, and (3) hunger.

The Sioux are the largest and strongest tribe within the United States. In spite of wars, removals, and diminished food supply since the advent of the white man, they still number nearly 26,000. Millions of buffalo to furnish unlimited food supply, thousands of horses, and hundreds of miles of free range made the Sioux, up to the year 1868, the richest and most prosperous, the proudest and, withal, perhaps, the wildest of all the tribes of the plains.

In that year, in pursuance of a policy inaugurated for bringing all the plains tribes under the direct control of the government, a treaty was negotiated with the Sioux living west of the Missouri by which they renounced their claims to a great part of their territory and had "set apart for their *absolute and undisturbed use and occupation*"—so the treaty states—a reservation which embraced all of the

present state of South Dakota west of Missouri river.... At the same time agents were appointed and agencies established for them; annuities and rations, cows, physicians, farmers, teachers, and other good things were promised them, and they agreed to allow railroad routes to be surveyed and built and military posts to be established in their territory and neighborhood. At one stroke they were reduced from a free nation to dependent wards of the government. It was stipulated also that they should be allowed to hunt within their old range, outside the limits of the reservation, so long as the buffalo abounded—a proviso which, to the Indians, must have meant forever.

The reservation thus established was an immense one, and would have been ample for all the Sioux while being gradually educated toward civilization, could the buffalo have remained and the white man kept away. But the times were changing. The building of the railroads brought into the plains swarms of hunters and emigrants, who began to exterminate the buffalo at such a rate that in a few years the Sioux, with all the other hunting tribes of the plains, realized that their food supply was rapidly going. Then gold was discovered in the Black hills, within the reservation, and at once thousands of miners and other thousands of lawless desperadoes rushed into the country in defiance of the protests of the Indians and the pledges of the government, and the Sioux saw their last remaining hunting ground taken from them. The result was the Custer war and massacre, and a new agreement in 1876 by which the Sioux were shorn of one-third of their guaranteed reservation, and this led to deep and widespread dissatisfaction throughout the tribe. The conservatives brooded over the past and planned opposition to further changes which they felt themselves unable to meet. The progressives felt that the white man's promises meant nothing.

On this point Commissioner Morgan says, in his statement of the causes of the outbreak:

Prior to the agreement of 1876 buffalo and deer were the main support of the Sioux. Food, tents, bedding were the direct outcome of hunting, and with furs and pelts as articles of barter or exchange it was easy for the Sioux to procure whatever constituted for them the necessaries, the comforts, or even the luxuries of life. Within eight years from the agreement of 1876 the buffalo had gone and the Sioux had left to them

alkali land and government rations. It is hard to over-
estimate the magnitude of the calamity, as they viewed
it, which happened to these people by the sudden dis-
appearance of the buffalo and the large diminution in
the numbers of deer and other wild animals. Suddenly,
almost without warning, they were expected at once
and without previous training to settle down to the
pursuits of agriculture in a land largely unfitted for
such use. The freedom of the chase was to be ex-
changed for the idleness of the camp. The boundless
range was to be abandoned for the circumscribed
reservation, and abundance of plenty to be supplanted
by limited and decreasing government subsistence and
supplies. Under these circumstances it is not in human
nature not to be discontented and restless, even tur-
bulent and violent.

The white population in the Black hills had rapidly increased, and it had become desirable to open communication between eastern and western Dakota. To accomplish this, it was proposed to cut out the heart of the Sioux reservation, and in 1882, only six years after the Black hills had been seized, the Sioux were called on to surrender more territory. A commission was sent out to treat with them, but the price offered—only about 8 cents per acre—was so palpably unjust, that friends of the Indians interposed and succeeded in defeating the measure in Congress. Another agreement was prepared, but experience had made the Indians suspicious, and it was not until a third commission went out, under the chairmanship of General Crook, known to the Indians as a brave soldier and an honorable man, that the Sioux consented to treat. The result, after much effort on the part of the commission and determined opposition by the conservatives, was another agreement, in 1889, by which the Sioux surrendered one-half (about 11,000,000 acres) of their remaining territory, and the great reservation was cut up into five smaller ones, the northern and southern reservations being separated by a strip 60 miles wide.

Then came a swift accumulation of miseries. Dakota is an arid country with thin soil and short seasons. Although well adapted to grazing it is not suited to agriculture, as is sufficiently proven by the fact that the white settlers in that and the adjoining state of Nebraska have several times been obliged to call for state or federal assistance on account of failure of crops. As General Miles points out in his official report, thousands of white settlers

after years of successive failures had given up the struggle and left the country, but the Indians, confined to reservations, were unable to emigrate, and were also as a rule unable to find employment, as the whites might, by which they could earn a subsistence. The buffalo was gone. They must depend on their cattle, their crops, and government rations issued in return for the lands they had surrendered. If these failed, they must starve. The highest official authorities concur in the statement that all of these did fail, and that the Indians were driven to outbreak by starvation.

Sullenness and gloom, amounting almost to despair, settled down on the Sioux, especially among the wilder portion. "The people said their children were all dying from the face of the earth, and they might as well be killed at once." Then came another entire failure of crops in 1890, and an unexpected reduction of rations, and the Indians were brought face to face with starvation. They had been expressly and repeatedly told by the commission that their rations would not be affected by their signing the treaty, but immediately on the consummation of the agreement Congress cut down their beef rations by 2,000,000 pounds at Rosebud, 1,000,000 at Pine Ridge, and in less proportion at other agencies....

The Ghost dance itself, in the form which it assumed among the Sioux, was only a symptom of the real causes of dissatisfaction.... That it was not the cause of the outbreak is sufficiently proved by the fact that there was no serious trouble, excepting on the occasion of the attempt to arrest Sitting Bull, on any other of the Sioux reservations, and none at all among any of the other Ghost-dancing tribes from the Missouri to the Sierras, although the doctrine and the dance were held by nearly every tribe within that area and are still held by the more important.

Notwithstanding the lack of violence associated with the Ghost dance, Indian Agents, police, and the army all directed forceful efforts to prohibit the religious ceremony of the Ghost dance. For example, on the Rosebud reservation Agent Wright, then in charge, went out to the Indians and told them the dance must be stopped, which was accordingly done. He expressly states that no violence was contemplated by the Indians, and that no arms were carried in the dance, but that he forbade it on account of its physical and mental effect on the participants and its tendency to draw them from their homes. In some way a rumor got among the Indians at this time that troops had arrived on the reservation to attack them, and in an incredibly short time every Indian had left the neighborhood of the agency and was making preparations to meet the enemy. It was with some difficulty that Agent Wright was able to convince them that the report was false and persuade them to return to their homes. Soon afterward circumstances obliged him to be temporarily absent, leaving affairs in the meantime in charge of a special agent. The Indians took advantage of his absence to renew the Ghost dance and soon defied control. The agent states, however, that no Indians left the agency until the arrival of the troops, when the leaders immediately departed for Pine Ridge, together with 1,800 of their followers.

On October 9 Kicking Bear of Cheyenne River agency, the chief high priest of the Ghost dance among the Sioux, went to Standing Rock by invitation of Sitting Bull and inaugurated the dance on that reservation at Sitting Bull's camp on Grand river. The dance had begun on Cheyenne river about the middle of September, chiefly at the camps of Hump and Big Foot. On learning of Kicking Bear's arrival, Agent McLaughlin sent a force of police, including two officers, to arrest him and put him off the reservation, but they returned without executing the order, both officers being in a dazed condition and fearing the power of Kicking Bear's "medicine." Sitting Bull, however, had promised that his visitors would go back to their own reservation, which they did a day or two later, but he declared his intention to continue the dance, as they had received a direct message from the spirit world through Kicking Bear that they must do so to live. He promised that he would suspend the dance until he could come and talk the matter over with the agent, but this promise he failed to keep. Considering Sitting Bull the leader and instigator of the excitement on the reservation, McLaughlin again advised his removal, and that of several other mischief makers, and their confinement in some military prison at a distance.

The two centers of excitement were now at Standing Rock reservation, where Sitting Bull was the open and declared leader, and at Pine Ridge, where Red Cloud was a firm believer in the new doctrine, although perhaps not an instigator of direct opposition to authority. At Rosebud the movement had been smothered for the time by the prompt action of Agent Wright, as already described. At the first-named reservation McLaughlin met the emergency with bravery and ability reinforced by twenty years of experience in dealing with Indians, and, while recommending the removal of Sitting Bull, expressed confidence in his own ability to allay the excitement and suppress the dance. At Pine Ridge, however, where the crisis demanded a man of most positive character Gallagher had resigned and had been succeeded in October by D. F. Royer, a person described as "destitute of any of those qualities by which he could justly lay claim to the position—experience, force of character, courage, and sound judgment." This appears in every letter and telegram sent out by him during his short incumbency, and is sufficiently evidenced in the name by which the Sioux soon came to know him, Lakota Kokopa-Koshkala, "Young-man-afraid-of-Indians." Before he had been in charge a week, he had so far lost control of his Indians as to allow a half dozen of them to release and carry off a prisoner named Little, whom the police had arrested and brought to the agency. On October 12 he reported that more than half of his 6,000 Indians were dancing, and that they were entirely beyond the control of the police, and suggested that it would be necessary to call out the military.

About the same time Agent Palmer at Cheyenne River reported to the Department that Big Foot's band (afterward engaged at Wounded Knee) was very much excited over the coming of the messiah, and could not be kept by the police from dancing. In reply, both agents were instructed to use every prudent measure to stop the dance and were told that military assistance would be furnished if immediate need should arise. A few days later, the agent at Cheyenne River had a talk with the dancers, and so far convinced them of the falsity of their hopes that he was able to report that the excitement was dying out, but recommended the removal of Hump, as a leader of the disaffection.

On the last day of October, Short Bull, one of those who had been to see the messiah, made an address to a large gathering of Indians near Pine Ridge, in which he said that as the whites were interfering so much in the religious affairs of the Indians he would advance the time for the great change and make it nearer, even within the next month. He urged them all to gather in one place and prepare for the coming messiah, and told them they must dance even though troops should surround them, as the guns of the soldiers would be rendered harmless and the white race itself would soon be annihilated.

As the local agents had declared the situation beyond their control, the War Department was at last called on and responded. . . .

Abram Kardiner and Lionel Ovesey

Psychodynamic Inventory of the Negro Personality

This examination by Kardiner and Ovesey of the mark made on the American black by the oppressiveness of racial discrimination represents yet another indication of the scarring effects of a sociocultural system unable to accommodate itself to the ethnic diversity of its component segments. In the case of the American black, the changes imposed on a racially and culturally distinct people were accompanied by an extraordinary unwillingness to afford them an opportunity to participate fully in the institutions of the dominant white society.

Although Kardiner and Ovesey's analysis of personality traits of the American black is based on a small sample—twenty-five cases in all—it has not, to our knowledge, been successfully refuted (see, for example, "The Game of Black and White at Hunters Point," by Arthur E. Hippler, in the section, "Violence"; also see Robert Coles' article, "When I Draw the Lord He'll Be a Real Big Man," in Confrontation: Psychology and the Problems of Today, *ed. Michael Wertheimer, Scott, Foresman, 1970); nor has it been replaced by an alternative. The plausible association, which Kardiner and Ovesey postulate in this article, between a society in which caste (based on racial characteristics) is institutionalized, despite its philosophical unacceptability, and the low personal esteem characteristics of members of the subordinated case should help us understand the importance to young blacks of the "Black is Beautiful" theme.*

It is a consistent feature of human personality that it tends to become organized about the main problems of adaptation, and this main problem tends to polarize all other aspects of adaptation toward itself. This central problem of Negro adaptation is oriented toward the discrimination he suffers and the consequences of this discrimination for the self-referential aspects of his social orientation. In simple words, it means that his self-esteem suffers (which is self-referential) because he is constantly receiving an unpleasant image of himself from the behavior of others to him. This is the subjective impact of social discrimination, and it sounds as though its effects ought to be localized and limited in influence. This is not the case. It seems to be an ever-present and unrelieved irritant. Its influence is not alone due to the fact that it is painful in its intensity, but also because the individual, in order to maintain internal balance and to protect himself from being overwhelmed by it, must initiate restitutive maneuvers in order to keep functioning—all quite automatic and unconscious. In addition to maintaining an internal balance, the individual must continue to maintain a social façade and some kind of adaptation to the offending stimuli so that he can preserve some social effectiveness. All of this requires a constant preoccupation, notwithstanding the fact that these adaptational processes all take place on a low order of awareness. The following is a diagram of a typical parallelogram of forces:

From "Psychodynamic Inventory of the Negro Personality" by Abram Kardiner and Lionel Ovesey from *The Mark of Oppression: Explorations in the Personality of the American Negro.* Reprinted by permission of Lucy Kroll Agency.

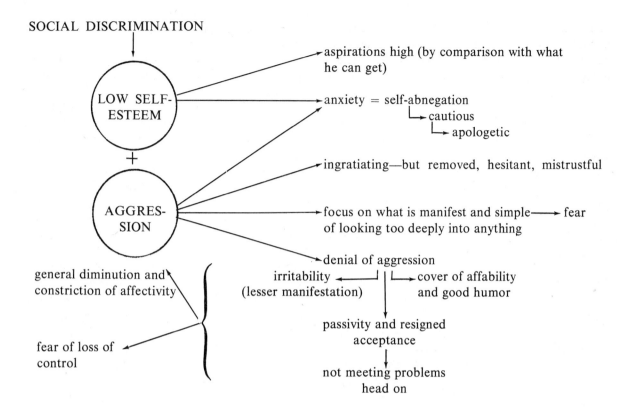

SOCIAL DISCRIMINATION

LOW SELF-ESTEEM
+
AGGRES-SION

aspirations high (by comparison with what he can get)

anxiety = self-abnegation
↳ cautious
↳ apologetic

ingratiating—but removed, hesitant, mistrustful

focus on what is manifest and simple ⟶ fear of looking too deeply into anything

denial of aggression

general diminution and constriction of affectivity

irritability (lesser manifestation)

cover of affability and good humor

fear of loss of control

passivity and resigned acceptance

not meeting problems head on

In the center of this adaptational scheme stand the low self-esteem (the self-referential part) and the aggression (the reactive part). The rest are maneuvers with these main constellations, to prevent their manifestation, to deny them and the sources from which they come, to make things look different from what they are, to replace aggressive activity which would be socially disastrous with more acceptable ingratiation and passivity. Keeping this system going means, however, being constantly ill at ease, mistrustful, and lacking in confidence. The entire system prevents the affectivity of the individual that might otherwise be available from asserting itself.

This is the adaptational range that is prescribed by the caste situation. This is, however, only a skeletal outline. Many types of elaboration are possible, particularly along projective or compensatory lines. For example, the low self-esteem can be projected as follows:

Low self-esteem = self-contempt → idealization of the white →
hostility to whites
frantic efforts
to be white = unattainable
introjected white ideal →
self-hatred → projected on to other Negroes = hatred of Negroes.

The low self-esteem can also mobilize compensations in several forms: (1) apathy, (2) hedonism, (3) living for the moment, (4) criminality.

The disposition of aggression is similarly susceptible to elaboration. The conspicuous feature of rage lies in the fact that it is an emotion that primes the organism for motor expression. Hate is an attenuated form of rage, and is the emotion toward those who inspire fear and rage. The difficult problem for those who are constantly subject to frustration is how to contain this emotion and prevent its motor expression. The chief motive for the latter is to avoid setting in motion retaliatory aggression.

The most immediate effect of rage is, therefore, to set up a fear of its consequences. Fear and rage become almost interchangeable. When the manifestations of rage are continually suppressed, ultimately the individual may cease to be aware of the emotion. In some subjects the *only* manifestation of rage may be fear.

The techniques for disposing of rage are varied. The simplest disposition is to suppress it and replace it with another emotional attitude—submission or compliance. The greater the rage, the more abject the submission. Thus, scraping and bowing, compliance and ingratiation may actually be indicators of suppressed rage and sustained hatred. Rage can be kept under control but replaced with an attenuated but sustained feeling—resentment. It may be kept under control, but ineffectively, and show itself in irritability. It may be kept under sustained control for long periods, and then become explosive. Rage may show itself in subtle forms of ingratiation for purposes of exploitation. It may finally be denied altogether (by an automatic process) and replaced by an entirely different kind of expression, like laughter, gaiety, or flippancy.

Rage may ricochet back on its author, as it does in some types of pain-dependent behavior (masochism). This is only likely to happen when rage is directed toward an object that is loved; the rage is then accompanied by strong guilt feelings. In this case the only manifestation of rage may be depression.

The tensions caused by suppressed or repressed aggression often express themselves through psychosomatic channels. Headaches of the migrainous variety are often the expression of rage which is completely repressed. These are usually not accompanied by amorphous anxiety—though the latter may be the sole vehicle for this aggression. Hypertension is another psychosomatic expression of the same, but predominantly suppressive, process.

In the case histories, we found all these varieties of the expression and control of rage. All kinds of combinations are possible. The two commonest end products of sustained attempts to contain and control aggression were low self-esteem and depression. These are merely the results of the continuous failure of a form of self-assertion.

The adaptational scheme we have charted above takes in the impact of discrimination but does not account for the integrative systems due to other conditions operative in the process of growth. This division is purely arbitrary for actually both series run concomitantly. There is no time in the life of the Negro that he is not actively in contact with the caste situation. The other personality traits derive, however, from the disturbances in his family life. This source gives rise to the following constellations: the affectivity range, the capacity for idealization and ideal formation, the traits derived from reactions to discipline, and conscience mechanisms. In these categories there is some difference as we proceed from the lower- to the upper-

class Negro. Let us take up the lower-class Negro first.

Affectivity range means the range of emotional potential. In appraising the role of emotion in personal and social adaptation, we have both quantitative and qualitative features to take into account. The total adaptation of the individual will depend on how much and what kind of emotion he has in a given situation. Emotion in man's adaptation tends to operate on a mass action principle. That is, the predominance of one emotion tends to stifle all others.

Emotion has the function of orientation toward objects in the outer world that can be the source of frustration or gratifications. The individual responds to a frustrating object with the emergency emotions of fear and rage, and their derivatives of hate, suspicion, distrust, apprehensive anticipation, and the like. These functions are self-preservative in intent and gear the organism for defensive action. The feeling toward objects which are the source of gratifications is the wish to be near, to perpetuate the influence of, to love, to desire, to have anticipations of continued gratifications, to trust, to have confidence, to cooperate with.

We must stress the point from this inventory that the emotions most conducive to social cohesion are those that pertain to the categories of love, trust, and confidence. All creatures are natively endowed with the capacity for fear and rage. The positively toned feelings of love, trust, and confidence, however, must largely be cultivated by experience. Hence, when we refer to the affectivity potential of an individual, we do not mean the emergency functions of fear and rage. We mean rather the capacity for cooperative and affectionate relatedness to others.

None of these emotions functions in isolation; they have a continuous adaptive interplay during the entire process of growth and living. What counts in the individual are the types of emotional response that become habitual and automatic. These fixed patterns of emotion are not only adaptive, in the sense that they are reaction types to actual situations; they also play a dominant role in shaping anticipations and to a degree, therefore, influence how events will shape up. For example, a person trained to be suspicious will shape the actual events of his life in such a way that his suspicions appear warranted.

The emotions play a decisive role in determining

the sociability (peaceful cooperation with others) of the individual through the development of conscience mechanisms and the formation of ideals. The desire on the part of the child to be loved and protected is the dominant incentive for the child to be obedient to his protectors. He needs this because he is helpless himself. The child thus becomes socialized in order to continue the boons of love and protection. He learns to anticipate the requirements for these returns by internalizing them and making them automatic. He also learns the methods of escaping blame and of devising techniques for reinstatement. Thus, the fear of punishment and the withdrawal of love exert a powerful restraining influence against antisocial behavior. The reward for conformity is a sense of pride in the social recognition of "good" behavior, while the fear of detection and punishment leads to guilty fear and either an anticipation of punishments or self-punishment.

However, in order for these positive emotional feelings and the functions of conscience to be instituted, certain behavior by the parents toward the child is required. Thus, we cannot expect the child to develop affection and dependence on the parent who is not constant in his care, who does not love in return for obedience, whose punishments are either disproportionate, or have no relation to the offense. In this instance, conformity is of no adaptive value at all. A child who is constantly abused by the parent cannot be expected to have pleasant anticipations or to idealize the parent or wish to be like him. A child exposed to this kind of behavior from the parent will not love, trust, or cooperate. It can take flight from the hostile environment and try to seek another more friendly one. Or it can stay and hate the parent, and suppress all the hostile feeling.

On the institutional side, the family structure of the lower-class Negro is the same as the white. However, in the actual process of living, the vicissitudes of the lower-class family are greater and its stability much less. This is where the broken family, through early death of parents, abandonment, or divorce, takes a heavy toll on the opportunities for developing strong affective ties to the parents. First, the needs for dependency are frustrated. This makes the mother a frustrating object, rather than one the child can depend on. This does not mean that it is the intention of the mothers to neglect or mistreat their children. Quite the contrary, the

intention is the usual one, and many lower-class Negro mothers have strong maternal feelings, are exceedingly protective, and try to be good providers. This is not, however, what one hears from the subjects. They tell chiefly the story of frustration and of arbitrary discipline by mothers. Not infrequently there is also the constant story of beating and cursing as disciplinary reinforcements. The rivalry situation between siblings in the lower classes is greatly enhanced by the general scarcity in which they live. This situation, of course, is greatly magnified when the child is given to some other relative for custody, as a consequence of a broken home. These children fare worse than any of the others. They are the ones who, because of mistreatment, decide at the age of 10 or 12 to run away and shift for themselves. In these children, some of whom we studied, the premature independence hardly works to the advantage of the personality in the long run. They become shrewd and adjustable, but at the cost of complete mistrust in everyone.

The result of the continuous frustrations in childhood is to create a personality devoid of confidence in human relations, of an eternal vigilance and distrust of others. This is a purely defensive maneuver which purports to protect the individual against the repeatedly traumatic effects of disappointment and frustration. He must operate on the assumption that the world is hostile. The self-referential aspect of this is contained in the formula "I am not a lovable creature." This, together with the same idea drawn from the caste situation, leads to a reinforcement of the basic destruction of self-esteem.

Thus, many of the efforts of the lower-class Negro at emotional relatedness are canceled out by the inner mistrust in others, the conviction that no one can love him for his own sake, that he is not lovable. Under these conditions, not much real social relatedness is possible. It is, however, very significant that the lower-class Negro is an inveterate "joiner" in one kind of social voluntary organization or another, of clubs and cliques with high-sounding names and with much ritualism in initiation rites. In these organizations, which have a very short life span, there is continuous discord, jockeying for position and prestige, and insistence that each member must have his own way. In other words, through these clubs and associations, the Negro tries to compensate for his lack of relatedness. But for the greater part, he fails. The intrapsychic mistrust and need for dominance destroy the effectiveness of these compensatory efforts. This is a noteworthy feature of Negro life, because the social organizations are supposed to facilitate cooperative endeavor and to give the members the satisfaction of belonging to something, to diminish their isolation. This end is not accomplished because most of the energy of these "associations" is taken up with overcoming mutual distrust and very little energy goes into the mutual supportive aspects of the organization.

Closely related to the question of the affectivity potential is the capacity for idealization. This trait is a general human characteristic, and is rooted in the biological make-up of man. It is the most powerful vehicle for the transmission of culture. During his helpless state man must place his trust in the parent who is his support. If this support and affection aid the individual in his adjustment, the natural tendency is to magnify the powers of the parent to magical proportions. This projection of magical attributes on the parent is the most powerful implement the parent has in enforcing discipline, because the threat of withdrawal of this support creates anxiety in the child. It follows, therefore, that the idealized parent is the satisfying parent whose authority is less enforced than it is delegated, and the acquiescence to discipline is a method the child has for perpetuating those boons he has already enjoyed in the past and hence expects to enjoy in the future.

The formation of ideals to pursue is a corollary of the idealization of the parent. It is easy to identify oneself with the idealized parent if the expectations from him have been realized. If these expectations are frustrated, then there may develop a reactive ideal or the opposite to the one experienced. This is generally a rare phenomenon, where a mistreated child becomes an ideal parent by living the opposite of what he has experienced. It does indeed happen. But it is far from the rule. The commonest outcome of this situation is that despite the hatred to the parent, the child takes on and identifies himself with the hated and frustrating attributes and becomes the replica of the frustrating parent. Here one must draw the line between an activating ideal and the unconscious identification. The activating ideal may be "I will be a provident parent"; the unconscious identification, however, may be with the frustrating parent.

In some instances, the mistreated child when it becomes the parent is actuated by the idea: "Why should I give you what I never had myself?" These are the cases in which the frustrated dependency cravings interfere with the protective parental role.

The question of Negro-ideal formation is hardly limited to the parental role. The "ideal" answers the question: "Whom do I want to be like?" This is where the Negro encounters a great deal of difficulty. The parent is a member of a despised and discriminated-against group. Hence, this ideal is already spoiled because it carries with it a guarantee of external and reflected hatred. No one can embrace such an ideal. Furthermore, until very recently the Negro has had no real culture heroes (like Joe Louis and Jackie Robinson) with whom he could identify. It is therefore quite natural that the Negro ideal should be *white*. However, accepting the white ideal is a recipe for perpetual self-hatred, frustration, and for tying one's life to unattainable goals. It is a formula for living life on the delusional basis of "as if." The acceptance of the white ideal has acted on the Negro as a slow but cumulative and fatal psychological poison. Its disastrous effects were due to the fact that the more completely he accepted the white ideal, the greater his intrapsychic discomfort had to become. For he could never become *white*. He had, therefore, to settle for the delusion of whiteness through an affectation of white attributes or those that most closely resembled them. This also means the destruction of such native traits as are susceptible of change (kinky hair, etc.). In its most regressive form, this ideal becomes the frantic wish to be reborn white. . . . Pride in oneself could not, therefore, be vested in attributes one had, but in attributes one aspired to have, that is to say, on borrowed ideals. This maneuver, calculated as a restitutive one, ends by being destructive of self-esteem.

The reactions to discipline and the dynamics of conscience mechanisms are closely interrelated, and these in turn are related to the general affectivity potential and ideal formation.

In general, there are several factors operating on the parental side of the induction of disciplines which differ from the situation among whites. The Negro parent has no authority in the social world in which he lives. It is, therefore, a strong temptation for the Negro parent to tend to be authoritative in the only place where he can exercise it, namely in his own home. Hence, we get repeated stories of children being subjected to disciplines that are both arbitrary, instantaneous, and inconsistent, depending often on whim, and at the same time without the ability to offer the child the appropriate rewards for obedience and conformity. Children recognize these rewards chiefly in terms of need satisfactions. These the parent, more often than not, cannot implement. They often fail on the sheer subsistence level. Such a parent cannot have much delegated authority or inspire much dependence. Hence, the authority of the parent is destroyed. A second factor occurs especially in those cases where the mother works. She has no time to be the careful and provident mother. After a day's work, during which time the child often shifts for itself, she is inclined to be tired and irritable which accounts for much of her impatience and insistence on immediate and unqualified obedience.

As between mother and father, many factors conspire to make the mother the chief object of such dependency as is possible under the circumstances. The male as provider and protector definitely suffers disparagement. The mother's objective—since she has so little time—is to make the child as little nuisance as possible. This makes her both an object to be feared and at the same time the only one that can be relied upon.

In passing, we must mention here the place of street life for the Negro child and adolescent. In many ways this street life is no different from corresponding street life in lower-class whites. The crowded home is not a happy place for the growing child, especially when parents are so often away. Since the family does not implement its disciplines with appropriate rewards, the children tend to get their ideals and pattern their amusements on the opportunities of the street, with its values, its heroism, its ideals, and its factionalism. They differ from corresponding white groups in the quantity of the savagery of their mutual aggression, in which the boys get seriously hurt and in some instances killed. Part of this street life pattern is the result of sheer boredom and the irrelevancy of education. Hence, they cannot be attentive at school or get the feeling that they are engaged in a meaningful and ego-enhancing activity. Many of these high school boys have been to bed with women the age of their female teachers and the disciplines and obligations of school life make no sense to them. In consequence, school is treated as a meaningless routine.

The street, on the other hand, offers adventure, struggle for dominance, mock and real hostilities. It is, in other words, a better training for life—according to their sights—than education. Delinquency among adolescents runs high for very good reasons.

In this general setting we can evaluate the effects of the socializing disciplines.

We have seen but little evidence of rigid anal training in childhood. There is no serious contest of will between parent and child over this aspect of socialization. It is largely neglected, and in those who came from the South, there was little emphasis on order, neatness, or systematization. Hence, in this group we would not expect much adventitious use of the anal zone for elaborate constellations about expulsion and retention. If there are any compulsive traits in the Negroes of this group, they do not derive from this source.

A more important aspect of socializing discipline is in the sexual domain. Here the picture is very confused. In the lower classes, the sex morality taught is of the Victorian variety. However, there is but little effort made to implement it. There is, on the whole, much less anxiety introduced into sexual disciplines than is the case with the white middle classes. The result is actually more sexual freedom among lower-class Negro children than among whites. And it is by no means unusual for boys and girls to be inducted into sexual activity quite early (7 to 13). It is therefore highly unlikely that potency troubles in both males and females of this group derive from anxieties introduced into the picture by parental threats. In those cases observed these difficulties usually arose from another source. They came from the confusion in the sociosexual roles of male and female. The male derives these difficulties from his inability to assume the effective masculine role according to white ideals, as against the dominant position of the female, first in the dominant mother and later in the dominant wife. The economic independence of the female plays havoc with the conventional male-female roles, and this in turn, influences the potency of the males. In the case of the female, her sociosexual role is reversed. She is dominant, and rebels against the passive and dependent role. Thus, the sexuality of the Negro in the lower classes is confused by the sexual significance of the social role.

Contrary to expectations, the sexual drive of the adult Negro is relatively in abeyance. We saw no evidence of the sex-craved and abandoned Negro. This playing down of sex is the result of the socio-economic hardship and the confusion in the sexual roles.

What kind of conscience mechanisms can be integrated under these conditions? This situation is, if anything, more complex than in the white. Basically, the tonicity of the conscience mechanisms depend on the ability of the parent to act as provider of satisfactions. Hence, in the lower-class Negro, we cannot expect strong internalized conscience. If we add to this the disastrous effects of the caste system, then the lower-class Negro, in his hatred for the white, is robbed of any incentive for developing a strong conscience. However, the effects of the caste system are such that they inspire a great deal of fear. Therefore, antisocial tendencies would be held in rigid check by fear of detection. In fact, we can say that conscience in the lower-class Negro is held in tow by his general vigilance over his hatred and aggression, and that the fear of detection of his aggression and antisocial tendencies are both governed by the same control mechanisms. The great danger for the lower-class Negro is that these control devices may occasionally and impulsively be overwhelmed—a factor that is of enormous concern to every lower-class Negro.

This group of constellations sets up in the Negro a strong need for compensatory activities, to help establish some semblance of internal harmony. These compensatory activities have the function of (a) bolstering self-esteem, (b) narcotizing the individual against traumatic impact, (c) disparaging the other fellow, (d) getting magical aid for status improvement.

Among the activities for bolstering self-esteem are flashy and flamboyant dressing, especially in the male, and the denial of Negro attributes, such as doing away with kinky hair.

Narcotizing the individual against traumatic influences is effected largely through alcohol and drugs. In these activities, the males predominate. Alcoholic psychoses in Negroes occur with twice the frequency that they do in whites. Narcotics have a wide use among Negroes, but their high cost makes alcohol much more available.

Disparaging the other fellow is widespread among urban Negroes. It is of a vindictive and vituperative kind and derives largely from the status strivings. The street corner and candy store are favorite places for malicious gossip.

In the domain of magical aid to self-esteem, gambling takes a high place. This takes the form of card playing but more often of participation in the numbers racket. Here everyone has a chance at beating fate, of being the favored one, if only for a day. The lure of this tantalizing game must be very high, judging from the vast fortune spent annually by the bulk of the Negro population.

In addition to these, there are occasional outlets, chiefly by males, which stem from their inability to plan or have any confidence in a future. Since the general tendency is to live from day to day, explosive spending when they have money is not infrequent. An occasional illusion of plenty and luxury can thus be created, even if to do so means to mortgage one's energy for months ahead to pay for the luxury.

This psychological picture is to some extent changed in the middle and upper classes. Here the family organization corresponds more closely to the middle-class white group. The emphasis shifts from subsistence problems to status problems. There is also a shift from female to male dominance in the family. The chief conflict area is that concerned with status. In general, the benefits derived from better parental care, better induction of affectivity, better ideal formation, and more tonic conscience mechanisms are to a large extent canceled out by the enormous increase in status conflict caused by the caste situation.

In appraising the adaptation of the middle- and upper-class Negro, we encountered a good deal of difficulty in differentiating the real from the apparent. For example, the affectivity potential is much better in this group than in the lower class. But against this we must discount the fact that the representations of better affectivity rest largely on a formal basis. Their marriages are more stable; they induct affectivity more appropriately, etc. But these features are due largely to the fact that the upper- and middle-class Negroes strive hardest to live and feel like the whites. They are more conventional, have more rigid sex mores, set more store by "respectability" than do lower-class Negroes. They know what the "right" feelings are for a given situation and they try very hard to have them. But whether they do or not depends on the quantity of the conflicts they have on the issues of skin color and status strivings, all of which tend to detract from the freedom of feeling.

In the specific integrative areas this group approximates the white. Parental care is good in the same sense and with the same incompatibilities as with whites. The affectivity potential is apparently higher than in lower-class Negroes and they have more capacity for relatedness. They have a high capacity for idealization, but what is idealized is white and not Negro. Here again the ideal formation in the Negro has two layers. The natural figure to idealize is the provident parent; but he is a disparaged figure. Introjecting this object means to hate it to the accompaniment of perpetual guilt. The substitution of a white object as the source of the ideal does not solve the problem. It, too, is hated and likewise must give rise to guilt. The Negro cannot win in either case. As one upper-class Negro observed: "The only thing black that I like is myself." Their ideal formation is of a high order, but founders on the rock of unattainable ideals. The fact that these ideals are relatively more capable of achievement than in the lower classes renders the conflict sharper. Thus, they tend to drive themselves harder, make greater demands on themselves for accomplishment, and are obligated to refuse the compensatory activities open to lower-class Negroes. This greatly augments the internal self-hatred and makes it more difficult to accept the Negro status. I could love myself "if" is all the more tantalizing because they can almost make the grade, but for skin color. They are therefore more vulnerable to depressed self-esteem than the lower class.

The need to conform to white standards of middle-class respectability gives the upper classes a harder time with their control of aggression. And this in turn has a constricting effect on all their affectivity.

In view of the good parental care, one would expect that their tendencies to passivity would be accentuated. But this is countered by the strong pressure against any form of passivity or subordination especially to other Negroes—since they cannot avoid subordination to the white. This constellation would be very valuable to follow through in Negro homosexuals. . . . The conflict about passivity in the males [is] enormous.

The points where the intrapsychic conflicts are sharpened for the middle- and upper-class Negro, then, are in the disposition and compensations for lowered self-esteem, the disposition of aggression, and in the uncompromising acceptance of white ideals.

The self-hatred of this group takes the usual form of projection on both white and on Negroes lower than themselves. However, they have more guilt about their Negro hatred than is the case with lower classes. To the whites, the formula is hatred + control = disguise; to the Negro the formula is hatred + guilt = anxiety of retaliation. Thus, every middle- and upper-class Negro has increased competitiveness with whites, but his psychological task is merely one of control and concealment. The hatred to the Negro has a way of ricocheting back on its source. Every Negro who is higher than lower class has a sense of guilt to other Negroes because he considers success a betrayal of his group and a piece of aggression against them. Hence, he has frequently what might be called a "success phobia," and occasionally cannot enjoy the fruits of his achievements.

In his acceptance of white ideals, the Negro often overshoots the mark. He overdoes the sex mores so that the incidence of frigidity in the women is very high. In his acceptance of the white man's cleanliness obsession, the Negro ends by identifying himself with feces, and becomes extraordinarily clean and meticulous. However, the obstructions to the accomplishments of white ideals lead to increase in aggression, anxiety, depression of self-esteem, and self-hatred. This compels him to push harder against the social barriers, to drive himself harder, and ends with more frustration and more self-hatred. This vicious circle never ends.

Thus, as we stated above, it is difficult to appraise the advantages and disadvantages of the upper classes as regards their intrapsychic effects. The shift from female to male orientation at least saves this group from the confusion of social and sexual roles. It is one of male dominance and clear definition of sexual role. However, they overdo the rigidity of sexual restrictions, and this affects the female more than the male. The marriages are more stable, but the importance of conventionality is very high; hence the impression remains that as an average the marriages are not more happy. Affectivity is better; but its betterment is largely on the formal side.

Ann Fischer

History and Current Status of the Houma Indians

The Houma Indians of Louisiana are a self-designated "Indian" group, members of which reside in geographically remote and economically impoverished enclaves. Like other "Indian" groups of the rural South, the Houma have, with equivocation, sought to melt into the larger society, at the same time retaining an identity that separates them socially from both white and black castes.

Much of the land on which Houma subsistence agriculture was dependent has been taken—by means both fair and foul—by petroleum companies, fur-trapping interests, and the federal government; the remainder has been subjected to uncontrolled pollution. Houma have responded to these crises by reaching out for aid to anthropologists, sympathetic lawyers, and missionaries in a variety of efforts to gain a measure of the protection and status accorded the white citizenry of Louisiana.

Brewton Berry, in *Almost White*, reports that there are some 200 groups of "racial orphans" in the United States. Among these, those who have some claim to Indian ancestry are known as *so-called Indians*. This term is apt for a people of tenuous racial status and mixed ancestry. When racial identification is necessary, they emphasize their Indian blood.

So-called Indians stand in contrast to Mulatto groups, since the latter consider themselves to be midway between white and Negro. On the other hand, Indian groups living in Louisiana have consistently fought against identification with Negroes, hoping by their resistance to avoid the disadvantages of the southern caste system. As a result of this resistance, whites, Indians, and Negroes agree that the Indian groups are generally more deprived than Negroes.

The Houma, a group of so-called Indians of Louisiana, live in scattered settlements isolated from the Negro settlements of the same area. The scattered settlement pattern is partially the result of migration, undertaken to escape the problems created by lack of racial identity, since the racial status of these people varies from parish to parish.

Negro settlements are easily distinguishable from those of the Houma. Negroes work in and usually live surrounded by the cane fields in identical unpainted houses in rows perpendicular to the road. Indians live in houses, often run-down, along the levees in the typical line villages of the bayou country. In many parts of this region white and Indian houses may be mixed in the line villages, due to the movement of the whites down the line. Negro and Indian housing, on the other hand, is never mixed in the situations which I have observed. Many Indians know no Negroes, and when they compare themselves to any other group it is usually to the white French.

There is much evidence that the Houma think of themselves as Indians. In many homes there are collections of items about U.S. Indians from old newspapers. Houma search through papers for news of Indians, and on reading about the Chicago Conference for Indians being organized in 1961, one group collected money and sent representatives to the conference on the basis of these newspaper reports. Church gatherings provide occasional contacts with the recognized Choctaws on the reservation at Philadelphia, Mississippi. The Choctaw apparently acknowledge the affinity of the Houma with their own group.

The whites of the region know virtually nothing of the Houma. The local derogatory term for the Indians—Sabines—is heard in the community, but many whites would be unable to identify a member of the group, and most have never met one of them. The Houma feel that they have a reputation for sexual immorality in the surrounding white community. They reject this judgment of the whites, pointing out, probably accurately, that the same sexual patterns are common in white and Indian groups. Generally, the Houma feel that the whites resent any visible Indian economic successes. Aside from the matter of sexual conduct, whites, in

From "History and Current Status of the Houma Indians" by Ann Fischer from *The American Indian Today*, edited by Stuart Levine and Nancy O. Lurie. Reprinted by permission of Everett/Edwards, Inc.

my experience, complain little about Indian character traits, though they assume that their poverty is due largely to lack of industry and education. Some whites who have lived in the area throughout their lives will say that the Indians were charmingly innocent and friendly before they learned from experience that exploitation often followed the apparent kindliness of strangers.

The Houma have only a few surnames. Some of these, such as Billiot, belong almost exclusively to Indians. Others, such as Naquin, are also found among descendants of the Acadians who occupy territory slightly upstream from the Houma. These characteristic family names enable the surrounding whites to identify them; they could not do so by physical features alone. Indians look like the white population of this area in part because single male hunters and trappers of many nationalities and races have repeatedly come into the area. Some of these have established both long-term and more transient affectional ties with women of all three local groups, Indian, Negro, and white. Therefore, identity within the framework of the rigid caste system of the South is not only a problem for the Houma, but for much of the surrounding population.

There is great variation in physical type among the Indians as well as among other local French-speaking people. Hair varies from almost kinky to straight; its color varies from reddish blonde to black; eyes may be blue although they are usually brown; skin color varies from brown to very white. F. G. Speck, an anthropologist who visited the Houma in 1938, reported on their physical character to the Bureau of Indian Affairs as follows: "In my judgment, as based upon comparisons with Indians of the southeastern tribes over a number of years, I should rate the Houma as a people possessing Indian blood and cultural characters to a degree about equal to that of the Creek, Choctaw, Catawbe, and Seminoles." A special investigator from the Bureau of Indian Affairs pronounced the Houma to be too mixed to be considered Indian by the Bureau. However, aid was given to the Chitimacha, who are simply a localized group of the people who now call themselves the Houma Indians.

In the summer of 1960 I lived among the Houma, studying their herbal medicines and collecting genealogies. Since then I have been in fairly constant contact with groups living along Bayous Terrebonne and Pointe au Chênes, and, to a lesser extent, with a group on Isle de Jean Charles. The Houma live in other places as well, along many bayous which divide like the fingers on a hand to flow into the Gulf of Mexico at the southern end of Louisiana. From the Mississippi west to Morgan City their shrimp boats and muskrat traps are found throughout the swamps and brackish bays separating the Gulf from dry land.

Approximately 2,000 people identify themselves primarily with the Houma. The small groups are widely separated by swampland, but genealogical relationships and names unite them psychologically.

History

There is only fragmentary documentation of the history of the Houma. They evidently originally lived to the east of the Mississippi, and moved, by way of New Orleans, steadily southwestward from the time of French and Spanish settlement of Louisiana. Many accounts report that they are extinct. Ruth Underhill says, in a report to the Bureau of Indian Affairs, and I agree, that "It is the opinion of the writer that Houma has become a generic name for a number of Muskogian remnants which mixed and concentrated in southern Louisiana." Evidence from the language indicates that the Houma dialect belonged to the Muskogian family. A few numbers can be recalled by some present-day informants, who also recognize a linguistic connection with the Choctaw. Today, the Indians are French-speaking. . . .

The history of the economic exploitation of the Houma, which results partially from the rich natural resources of their environment, is so clouded by rumor and passage of time that fact and fancy have been woven into a tale in which truth and fiction are inseparable. For our purposes the tale is most appropriately told from the Indian point of view. . . .

The Houma have been the victims of a long series of ecological and economic changes in their homeland. Beneath their homes lies one of the richest natural gas and petroleum fields in the United States. The development of this field has changed the face of the land, altered the economy, and brought in outsiders. Exploitation of the wildlife resources of the area on which they live, the age-old complaint of Indians against whites, goes on apace.

The oil on the land has led to increasing agitation among the Indians to reclaim the land they feel is rightfully theirs. Various legal procedures, formerly unintelligible to them, have lost the Houma their land titles. The tax sale was the legal device which allowed companies and politicians to acquire swamp lands when they became valuable....

My presence in the area had tended to spread hope among the Houma for recovering their land. Even though I have often indicated the practical impossibility of this task, my willingness to listen to the accounts of the land problems and to investigate them has resulted in renewed hope.

Even before the development of the oil field, land was a problem for the Houma. The land on which the Indians now trap was once public land. Public lands in Louisiana in other places were originally established on land which the Indians claimed and to which the whites disputed their titles. Doubtless the land of the Houma was such a case. From the courthouse records Ruth Underhill concluded that the swamp-land was purchased by private individuals from the levee district of Atchafalaya in 1895. In 1924 the owners noted the high price of furs and decided to charge for trapping permits. The land was suddenly offered for sale or lease in the local papers. The illiterate Indians were faced with incoming trapping companies who bought up or leased these tracts and negotiated with the Indians for the rights to trap muskrat on the land. Indians had to work for the companies, starve, or trap illicitly in the more inaccessible regions. Annually Indians were required to sign leases indicating that they had no claim to these lands. The fur companies owned the local stores to which the Indians sold furs and from which they received credit. The credit system led to further losses of other lands to which the Indians had sounder claims.

Over the years the trapping and land companies, with legal advice and technical maneuvering, have acquired titles to a considerable acreage. One method used has been to put up fences on Indian lands as an indication of ownership. Where these fences have gone unprotested fairly solid claims have been established by the companies.

While most of my summary is based on the Indian view of the matter, legal efforts have disclosed elements of truth in the Indians' stories of exploitation. The truth of all of their claims is difficult to ascertain, however.

Trapping companies have meant lowered returns on furs for the individual trapper. And, since the Second World War, other things have worked to depress the trapping industry. In an attempt to raise nutria on a farm at McIlhenny Island, these animals were accidentally released into the swamps. Nutria now thrive in the swamps and fill the traps in place of the desired muskrats. There is no important market for nutria in the United States, although with assistance it is possible that one could be developed. Nutria can be sold only as dog food at present; it is not profitable for the trapper to collect it.

Rice was formerly raised as a crop in the area. Some of the older Indians can remember this period. Diversion of fresh water from the region has made this impossible.

Oil from the off-shore oil fields has polluted some of the oyster beds. Damages can be and have been collected in some cases, since oyster beds are considered to be privately owned. But the Indians, who work on but usually do not own the oyster beds, have not benefitted from these reimbursements.

Sportsmen find ready access to Indian fishing and hunting grounds by means of roads built to develop the oil fields. In spite of legal protection against fishing for profit, many sportsmen fill large deep freezes with their catches, depleting the quantity available to those who are dependent on these resources for a livelihood. Indians, many of whom cannot swim, are afraid of the waters of the open Gulf. They confine their shrimping to the bays which are also most accessible to sportsmen. The white French work in the more distant shrimping grounds and have managed to maintain a higher productivity.

The economic difficulties encountered by the Houma have been aggravated by their lack of education. The history of Indian education in Terrebonne Parish is a history of bitterness and hate. From the beginning, Indians have been denied entrance to white schools in Terrebonne Parish on the basis that an Indian is equivalent to a Negro....

From the beginning, Indians would not attend Negro schools and were denied access to white schools. Until about 1937, Indians had no schools at all. At that time, church groups began to take an interest in them. Missionaries offered education, and as a result many formerly Catholic Indians became Baptists or Methodists. But today, much of the adult population is actually illiterate, and, most of the remainder is functionally so. Most Indians over 40 years of age sign documents with an "X." Their inability to read what they are signing adds to their already well-founded suspicions that they are being duped.

Eventually, schools were built exclusively for the Indians in Terrebonne Parish by LaFourche Parish, which adjoins Terrebonne. This deviousness enabled the local Terrebonne Parish government to avoid recognizing the Indians as a distinct group, somewhat in the manner in which the U.S. Government avoids recognizing Red China. Bayou Pointe au Chênes divides Terrebonne from LaFourche, and Indians live on both sides of this bayou. In LaFourche, an Indian is considered to be white, and may attend the white schools. Until 1964 LaFourche Parish operated two schools for Indians, one on Bayou Pointe au Chênes and one on Bayou Terrebonne, in return for certain considerations from Terrebonne Parish. In 1964 one of these was closed. These schools were elementary schools; until about 1957, after a child graduated from the eighth grade, no further schooling was available to him unless he chose to drive 30 miles into LaFourche to attend high school or left Terrebonne Parish for more distant New Orleans private or public schools. Very few Indians managed this difficult arrangement, and few were able to finish high school.

A few years after the Supreme Court decision directed schools to integrate with all deliberate speed, Terrebonne Parish established a high school exclusively for the Indians. Beginning in 1957, a year of high school was added each year until in 1961 Indians in Terrebonne Parish were able to graduate from high school.

During the first year of operation the high school enrolled about 14 students. This number increased over time to around 30 in 1963. At first the Houma from Pointe au Chênes, Terrebonne Bayou, and Isle de Jean Charles disliked the idea of the Indian high school, feeling that it was one more step in the direction of continued segregation. Up to the present, very few of these Indians have attended this school, preferring to go to LaFourche to the white high school, to join the armed forces for a high school education, or to go away to live with relatives and get their diplomas in areas where they are accepted as whites. The Indians who have attended the Indian high school are mostly from Grande Caillou or Bayou Dularge, both too distant from LaFourche for daily commuting.

Difficulties in getting an education and economic pressure combine to encourage children to drop out of school early. They provide additional economic assistance for parents as soon as they are physically able. Indian girls usually manage to finish elementary school, and if they are able students or if their parents are ambitious for them, they attempt to continue for a few years in high school. Boys generally begin dropping out of school at about the third grade. They attend less regularly during the shrimping season when they are needed to work with their fathers. . . .

Needless to say, no Indian school is accredited by the Southern Regional Educational Association. Parents and teachers seldom meet and have little respect for each other. Complaints on both sides may be well founded.

The Houma as a group are distinguished by law in only one sense: Indians may marry on either side of the Negro-white caste line with no objections from authorities. In the last generation or two, marriages to Negroes have meant that the Indian partner lives among the Negroes and the children of the union identify themselves as Negro. One woman interviewed in Charity Hospital, New Orleans, was the child of an Indian mother. Her mother, after bearing her, married a Negro. The Indian child grew up with Negro siblings and now identifies herself as a Negro. She is very loath to discuss any matters relating to her Indian relatives. Most marriages with whites have occurred between Houma girls and white boys from the vicinity. If the children of mixed marriages have surnames which do not identify them as Indian, and if they move into the town of Houma, the children pass into the white school system unnoticed, or at least unchallenged.

Marriages occur when Houma boys meet white girls from other parts of the country during their tours of duty in the Armed Forces. None of these partners live in the Indian communities. It can be said that the people who remain in the community for life marry within it. Out-marriage usually means departure. The exceptions to this are two marriages between Indian men and white women who came to the Houma as missionaries. These married pairs resided in Indian communities for some time, but one pair has now left, and the second has reached the point where the son must be sent away to school. It seems possible that this pair also will leave in the not too distant future.

There are only a few routes of escape from the community, and these mostly present themselves during adolescence. For the girls, the chief method of escape involves going away to school, meeting white boys, and marrying them. For boys, going into the Armed Services seems to be the easiest way to learn a trade other than that of their fathers, and they leave the community by this means.

The traditional occupations of fishing, hunting, and trapping are territorial in nature; the territory must be maintained and exploited or it will fall to other hands. The territorial nature of the occupations of the Houma has forced them to remain in a region which deprives them of other opportunities, and in which a century of prejudice works to their disadvantage.

Identification with Indian-ness follows the cycle indicated above. During adolescence, when there is the best opportunity to escape from their deprived condition, a number of patterns of activity are evident. Parents with adolescent children become concerned with the problem only in cases where there has been some outside contact through missionaries or jobs on boats or oil rigs which carry the men to the outside world. Where the parents have followed traditional patterns of life, the extra impetus needed to overcome the difficulties is not present. Parents who have had a glimpse of the economic contrast between themselves and the rest of the world often become militantly interested in obtaining equal rights for their children. Once the crisis is past, and the children have either succeeded or failed in escaping the cycle of poverty and deprivation, the parents' interest in working for Indian rights disappears, and they return to their life within the in-grown Indian community.

Another factor in escape seems to be the birth order of children in the household. Younger sons may more easily leave home than elder sons. Elder sons have at times contributed to the education of their younger brothers. Men do not like to go alone shrimping or fishing. Accidents occur, and if the men are alone they may drown. After the father has initiated one son as his helper, he is much more willing to allow the others to leave home.

The individual nature of the effort made to solve various problems among the Houma is in part responsible for the failure to find a solution for the social problems of the whole group. The oil on the land, like the pot of gold at the end of the rainbow, glitters in the eyes of many people and distorts their vision completely. For if a Houma profits from the lease of land to the oil companies, his neighbors will often suspect him of profiting at their expense. Proof of title depends largely on having birth, death, and legitimate marriage records of one's ancestors. Many Indians, if they married legally, married in churches where records have been destroyed by fire or other loss. Whole volumes of land records are reported missing from State record offices. If an individual succeeds in substantiating his own claims to property it seems unfair to others who do not have the proper documents. Yet, if all are to benefit, profits will be smaller for the individuals concerned. Under such circumstances, suspicions directed at neighbors lead Indians to refuse to sign papers drawn up to help them by lawyers because they distrust the motives of their neighbors who are working with the lawyers. This is a force that pulls the Houma apart psychologically and adds to their problems of identity.

Many lawyers and "lease hounds" hold signatures of Indians whom they presumably represent. Some Indians sign these papers easily, and readily sign up with more than one representative. Others will not sign with any of them. Eventually, this kind of behavior becomes unprofitable for the legal representatives, since they must fight even for their rights to represent certain of the people who have signed up to be represented by them. Lawyers' visions of profits fade into nothingness in the confusion.

In spite of the fact that Swanton reported that Bob Verret was the chief of the Houma, it seems unlikely that the Houma have ever had a very strong central authority among them which might act as a rallying point for action to overcome their social condition.... This lack of central authority may be the historical result of the diverse nature of the tribal origins of the group.

The Houma at Pointe au Chênes and Isle de Jean Charles may have had more cohesiveness up to about twelve years ago when the first road was built into their territory. Before that time all contact with the outside world was by boat....

The development of the standard of living at Pointe au Chênes in the last five years during which I have visited there has been startling. The road has made the important difference, but it is not the only difference. What might be called a model Indian family lived at Pointe au Chênes. The father spent time in France during the Second World War, and sent his daughter to college to become a school teacher when he returned. He built a house with modern accoutrements, and as his children married they followed his example. This family served as a model for other young people who learned something about how modern standards of living might be obtained by going into debt.

Throughout the history of the Houma there have always been some individuals who have been actively working for their own social betterment, seeking help from the outside when completely frustrated by the local white community. One man wrote repeatedly to the Indian Bureau just prior to World War II. He and a few other Indians still cherish letters from the Bureau and from anthropologists sent to investigate the situation. Speck evidently visited the Houma under this stimulus. He attempted to revitalize local crafts and for a time succeeded in getting a few craftsmen to produce baskets. He is still remembered by those who had contact with him.

One Houma man is particularly active in seeking outside contacts. He has dreams similar to those found in other North American groups. One of his dreams involved a huge flag waving over the shore line with an Indian Chief's head in the position where the field of stars should be.

When I came to the Houma, the middle-aged people were most interested in soliciting my help for them. Once they were convinced that I was not an investigator sent to arrest illegal medical practitioners, they quickly told me about their problems. I wanted to learn about the local remedies, but the Houma were interested only in gaining help with their land claims. For every ounce of knowledge I painfully acquired about herbal medicines, I received pounds of volunteered information on land frauds. After they had made many appeals to my sense of justice, I agreed to contact the Association for American Indian Affairs, naively stating that this was as far as I intended to go. This small effort resulted in finding legal help for the Houma in New Orleans. John P. Nelson was the attorney, and he too fell under the spell of the Indians and has never completely given up their cause, although the hopelessness of the legal task gradually dampens all enthusiasm. These efforts gained the confidence of many Indians, while at the same time they increased the suspicions of others. Old interests in the Indian case were revived; leasehounds re-entered the area, thinking legal action could be expected momentarily, and new lists of signatures were acquired by all of those waiting to reap the rewards of years of sporadic effort.

In New Orleans a committee was formed under the auspices of the Association for American Indian Affairs. The committee generally agreed that the school problems could be solved, but the Indians, on their part, while complaining about their educational lot, gave no indication that they were willing to face the discomforts certain to attend an attempt to integrate the schools. So long as this was so, it appeared that there was very little the committee could do without financial help for work on the land problem. After a year of meetings, with no foreseeable way to obtain financial aid, the committee subsided into inactivity.

A year later the efforts to help the Houma suddenly jogged to new life by the appearance at Pointe au Chênes mission of a new and enthusiastic missionary, who was unfamiliar with the difficulties in the case. Like other outsiders who had come before him, he could not believe that there would be any objection to the Indian children attending the white schools. He felt, as had others, that the Indians were simply imagining that such deep prejudices against them existed. Buoyed up by his confidence and enthusiasm five children went with him to register for the white high school. The Registrar, seeing nothing out of the way in their appearance, began the registration process. When asked what school they attended last year, the Indians gave the name of the Indian school. At this point the Registrar telephoned the Superintendent of Schools, following which he informed the Indians that they would not be able to register.

Previous to this the Indians did not feel actively rejected by the whites and had been able to maintain their self-respect. The rebuff they received in response to their attempt to register set them apart as inferiors in their own eyes. They were a group in a way that had not seemed possible previously. All were eager to retaliate, although some felt the slight much less than did others. Letters from my Houma friends told of this event, and requested that I come to Pointe au Chênes to meet the new missionary and hear the story. Indian informants felt certain that if the opportunity were offered, Indians would be willing to attempt to integrate the white schools.

In New Orleans John Nelson agreed to take the school case without fee if the court costs could be met from some source. These costs were more than adequately subscribed by an appeal to personal friends for contributions. More than fifty Indian children signed as plaintiffs through their parents on Bayou Terrebonne, Bayou Pointe au Chênes, and Isle de Jean Charles. About ten months later, after numerous delays arranged by the opposition, the case was heard by a Federal judge. Indians developed a new pride in themselves which they expressed to me as the case progressed.

That year the judge delayed his decision until after school started in the fall. After school had already been in session for two weeks, Indians in the eleventh and twelfth grades were legally admitted to the white high school. None of the plaintiffs were in either of these grades. Indian children living many miles from the area where the suit originated were surprised to learn that they had received this new privilege.

The judge made his decision at night. The following morning teachers in the Indian High school announced to eleventh and twelfth grade children that they would be able to choose which high school they would attend. They were asked which they would choose publicly, and unanimously they chose to remain in the Indian school. Rumors spread among the children that outsiders were trying to force them into the white schools.

Mr. Nelson waited until the weekend after the decision was handed down to visit the Houma. Learning that children on Grande Caillou were eligible to enter school, he visited a leader there. This leader urged the most intelligent of the school children to reconsider and to help Indians take this important step. Two of the children went through a personal struggle, deciding first one way on the advice of the leader then another when their friends urged them to remain with their own group. Finally, it seemed unwise for the leader to attempt to urge them further. He decided instead to prepare the way for a large shift to the white schools in the following year.

In October the judge lowered the entrance requirement for entrance into the white schools to the tenth grade. But it was too late. An Indian boy among the plaintiffs who would have been in the tenth grade had attempted to register at the white school at the beginning of school. When rejected, he became quite angry and decided to quit school entirely and go to work instead with his father on a shrimp boat. All in all, the first year of integrated schools was singularly unintegrated.

Word of the entire history of the effort to enter the white schools quickly spread up and down Grande Caillou and Bayou Dularge through Indians from the areas where the integration effort had originated. One of them visited these regions for the first time and informed the people of what had been done, urging them to cooperate. By fall in 1964, Indians along all bayous were eager to join in the desegregation movement. The judge moved the requirement for entering the white schools down to the seventh grade level, the Civil Rights Bill had been passed by Congress, and the legal opposition to Indian entrance into the schools began to disappear. The Terrebonne School Board closed the Indian elementary school on Bayou Terrebonne, and the 24 children attending that school were admitted to the white elementary schools nearest their homes. Most of the Indian students eligible elected to enter the white schools. In all, in the fall of 1964, some 60 Indian children were admitted to six previously all-white schools.

During the year when the school problems seemed certain to be resolved, Indian minds returned to the question of the oil land. A strange messiah appeared upon the scene, and Indians were learning about him by messengers from relatives living to the east along Bayou LaFourche at Golden Meadow. Radio and television, as well as limousines bearing loud speakers, assaulted Indian ears with messages of new land grant evidence discovered in Washington. Already loyal Indian supporters of this messiah, who was introduced into the group in a manner unknown to me, had developed a following for him among their close friends and relatives. . . . This stranger, with his green Cadillac, his plastic deerslayer's jacket, and his Navajo string tie was a leasehound in a new guise. He had his own view of the rainbow's pot which could more than match that of the Indians for irrationality, but he has done a remarkable job of getting Indians to come to him and accept him as their representative. The sad part of it is that the long-time funding needed to carry on a difficult five-year legal investigation with the decided risk that all will be lost in the end is not available to him or to anyone else connected with the case.

Conclusion

A group which has been so frustrated and deprived as the Houma, in which internal organization is lacking, must usually get help from the outside. The Indians recognize this and have never ceased their efforts to reach possible outside sources of aid. Only when the goals óf the Houma are in some accord with the goals of these outsiders is it possible for the Houma to succeed. Insofar as the Houma appeal is of interest to me as an anthropologist or as representative of a people deprived of a right I believe in, that of equal educational opportunity, I will acquiesce in being of service to them. Insofar as Mr. Nelson sees them as an interesting legal case, or as a group deprived of equal opportunity before the law, he will help them. Insofar as the leasehound sees in them an opportunity to get rich he will help them. But none of us behaves as a Houma himself would in support of his own cause. Even the Houma themselves do not behave in a manner in accord with some group ideal, for Houma group cohesiveness is based on ramifying kinship ties rather than on central group ties. Kin ties are often unsuitable for acting in relationship to the non-kin institutions of the larger society. Kin ties are of varying strength, in part depending upon the genealogical distance from the individuals with whom you are concerned in interaction. Group ties are of a single strength for all members of the group from the point of view of any one member.

To succeed in any venture, people so deprived need more help than a few sympathetic individuals representing the outside world can give them. For funds, I had to appeal to a group of friends who feel as I feel about the values of education. There had to be a movement in the outside world and the passage of the Civil Rights Bill or our meager efforts would have come up against a much larger opposition in the immediate and prejudiced white community. The leasehound would need powerful friends with financial resources sufficient to overcome the resistance among the land companies and other contesting title holders to succeed in winning the land. This power is not at present in evidence, and an individual here and there chipping away at the work which the problem requires will probably have little effect. The pot of gold at the end of the rainbow remains there, however, and it is certain that it will never go unsought. Eventually, the external conditions necessary to the solution to this problem, too, may be found, by which time perhaps there will be 3,000 or more descendants of [the Houma] to share in the pot.

Harold Arthur Shapiro

The Pecan Shellers' Strike in San Antonio

An issue too many people have ignored for too long is the relationship between employment policies and the cultural and economic characteristics of the ethnic group that comprises the labor force. Wage levels, working conditions, and labor-management disputes have often been viewed as produced by only economic considerations. However, there is now a heavy accumulation of evidence indicating that the attitudes of bias or low esteem on the part of members of the majority society toward its cultural and racial minorities are correlated with the working conditions of the latter.

In the article that follows, Harold Arthur Shapiro describes a strike by workers in the pecan industry of San Antonio, Texas, which seemed to have resulted from infamously low wage scales and notoriously bad working conditions. However, as Shapiro shows, those standards were inextricably related to the low social status of the still unassimilated chicanos of that city, the ethnic segment from which the pecan industry drew its labor force.

San Antonio has been the center of the pecan-shelling industry for more than fifty years. G. A. Duerler, candy-maker and soft-drink concocter, pioneered the way in the closing years of the 19th century. Soon he was shelling more meats than he

From "The Pecan Shellers of San Antonio, Texas," by Harold A. Shapiro, (*Southwestern*) *Social Science Quarterly*, 32 (March, 1952), pp. 229–244.

needed for his delicacies, and the excess was disposed of in national markets.

Initially the shelling process was performed by hand, but the introduction and development of machinery proceeded rapidly among all of the major operators. The mechanization of plants in St. Louis and in other cities progressed even during the Great Depression era. In San Antonio, however, the trend toward more modern production methods was reversed; for a vast army of migratory agricultural laborers and thousands of immigrants gravitated to San Antonio, the "capital of the Mexico that lies within the United States." They were unskilled, illiterate Mexican peasants, unaccustomed to urban life and to the American standard of living. They welcomed the opportunity for employment at any price.

Quick to perceive a competitive advantage over their machine-minded rivals, San Antonio's entrepreneurs, under the leadership of the Southern Pecan Shelling Company, inverted the technological process. Machines were displaced by men. Thousands of Mexican peons were hired at amazingly low piece-work rates....

A corollary of the hand-shelling technique was the contracting system. Under this procedure Southern and other large concerns bought the nuts from farmers and dealers and transferred them to "independent" contractors. The latter directly employed crackers and pickers to process the pecans, and reconveyed them to the companies. The contractors were to all intents and purposes employees of the big operators, who controlled the supply of nuts and set the prices for shelling, but the polite fiction was maintained that the contractors were private entrepreneurs—in business for themselves....

Home-shelling was a doubly convenient procedure since the pecan industry was concentrated on the West Side of the city, an area of four square miles wherein fully two-thirds of the community's Mexican inhabitants resided. The section was and is one of the most extensive slum areas found anywhere in the United States. The only vital substances that ever thrived in the area are the germs of tuberculosis and infant diarrhea. Thousands of human beings living in decrepit wooden shacks or in crowded corrals breathlessly shelled pecans in a race with starvation. In these homes, which lacked toilets and running water and which rented for as little as fifty cents a week, pecans were shelled and

picked for the fastidious tables of northern and eastern gourmets....

Fluctuations in the level of employment make it difficult to measure the size of the working force. The only reasonably accurate record is provided by the city health authorities who administered the requisite health examinations and issued permits to the pecan workers. At one time (1938) over 12,000 individuals employed in 110 different plants were registered. If the shellers without health cards are added to those legally working, their numbers would undoubtedly total 15,000 or more....

Wages were unbelievably low. The owner of the Southern Company testified at a Regional Labor Board[1] hearing in 1934 that his employees were paid three cents per pound for small pieces and five cents per pound for halves and that the usual worker could shell eight pounds in an eight hour day. At that rate the average sheller earned less than $2.00 per week.

Another report, this one by an NRA investigator,[2] on the wages of 1,030 employees of 14 San Antonio contractors disclosed average earnings during December, 1934, of $1.29 per week for 34.8 hours of work. Pickers and cleaners averaged three and five cents per hour, respectively. Some operators paid as little as two cents per pound in 1933–34. The rates went up the next year to five cents for pieces and six cents for halves but dropped to three and four cents the following season. From 1936 to 1938 the five and six cent scale generally prevailed....

It may be difficult for an outside observer to understand how the shellers and their families managed to survive, but it was no mystery to the president of the Southern Company. He explained to government officials that five cents per day was sufficient to support the Mexican pecan shellers because they ate a good many pecans while they worked. Since no limit was set on the amount they could eat, money incomes could be used for any

[1] The Regional Labor Board was an arm of the National Labor Relations Board, which was established to ensure employees of a company or an industry the right and opportunity to freely form trade unions and to elect union representatives, who could bargain for them collectively with their employers.—Ed.

[2] The NRA, or National Recovery Administration, was the executive arm of the National Industrial Recovery Act, which was designed in 1933 to combat unemployment in industry by shortening the work day, increasing wages, and eliminating unfair trade and pricing practices.—Ed.

additional wants that the shellers might wish to satisfy.

Another of the Company's officers spoke in a different vein. He claimed that if the shellers made 75 cents by three o'clock, they would go home, for they did not care to make much money. They were satisfied to earn little, and besides, they had a nice warm place to work and could visit with their friends while they earned.

In 1938 two government analysts probed into the details of the shellers' lives in an effort to understand how they actually lived. Five hundred and twelve Mexican pecan workers and their families were interviewed. Four out of every ten of them had been working "in pecans" for at least eight years. Median yearly income was $251 for a family of 4.6 persons; only 2 percent of the families had incomes of $900 or more. The mean weekly income reported by individuals in pecan work was $2.73; for all jobs reported by the shellers' families, the mean income was $3.01 for a 51–hour week. The average family studied had two wage earners with a total income of 69 cents per day.

Seventy-seven percent of the pecan workers paid rental for their houses at an average rental of $4.49 per month. Over 5 percent of the "renters" paid no rent at all; they lived with relatives or in deserted or makeshift shacks. An additional 8 percent paid from one to two dollars rent per month.

Nine percent of the shellers had flush toilets; 39 percent had old-fashioned pit privies; evidently the others possessed no toilet facilities or shared communal privies with their neighbors. Only 25 percent illuminated their dwellings electrically; the rest used kerosene lamps.

Of the shellers interviewed 17 percent were born in San Antonio; 50 percent came to the city between 1911 and 1930. Hence most of them were long-standing residents of the community. . . .

As primitive as their existence was, however, most of the workers succeeded in surviving the darkest days of the 1930s. The Southern Pecan Shelling Company also managed to weather the depression. In a two year period its net realization exceeded $500,000—not too disheartening a return for an enterprise with a very nominal capital outlay for plant and equipment. During the same years workers who shelled the pecans for the Company continued to be a public charge. WPA relief,[3] church aid, and private charity bridged the gap between their slender earnings and starvation.

At that time, when the national government through the NIRA[4] was attempting to stabilize the pecan industry and to raise wages, two rival labor unions competed for the patronage of the shellers. One, *El Nogal*, a truly independent union, claimed a membership of nearly 4,000 between 1933 and 1936. It tried to extract dues of five cents a month from the members, but the secretary conceded that half of them did not pay. The other, the Pecan Shelling Workers' Union of San Antonio, was financially supported by the President of the Southern Company. It was practically a one man affair conducted by Magdaleno Rodriguez, who was characterized by an NRA representative as a "fugitive from justice, a citizen of Mexico and a labor agitator who betrays his workers." . . .

After the abortive attempt under the NRA to boost the earnings of the pecan shellers, little or no attention was directed to their lowly state by government representatives. Piece rates ranged from three to eight cents per pound and the living conditions of the shellers varied from miserable to increasingly miserable.

Both "independent" unions were singularly ineffective; a docile labor force became still more passive. But apparently their docility was only a surface manifestation, for on February 1, 1938, at the peak of the season, thousands of shellers left their work tables in protest over a one cent per pound reduction in rates.

San Antonio has never witnessed an industrial dispute of like magnitude. Fully half of all of the pecan workers, scattered among 130 plants in the western portion of the city, "hit the pavement" (unpaved dirt roads would be more accurate in this case). More than 1,000 pickets were arrested during the course of the strike on charges ranging from "blocking the sidewalks" to "disturbing the peace" and "congregating in unlawful assemblies." Within the first two weeks tear gas was used at least a half-dozen times to disperse the throngs that milled about the shelleries.

From the outset the city officials, Mayor Quin, Police Commissioner Wright, and Chief of Police Kilday, fought the pickets with all weapons, legal

---

[3]The WPA, or Work Projects Administration, was created by President Roosevelt to initiate and operate projects intended to improve the general well-being of the public and, by so doing, to provide employment to needy, unemployed persons.—Ed.

[4]NIRA: National Industrial Recovery Act. See footnote 2.—Ed.

and otherwise. An obscure city ordinance of doubtful constitutionality was invoked to prevent the pickets from carrying signs:

. . . it shall be unlawful for any person to carry . . . through any public street . . . any advertising sign, until said sign shall first have been submitted to the City Marshal, and a permit given for said carrying.

A "City Marshal" had to approve of all signs carried by pickets—but there was no "City Marshal" in San Antonio at that time. The office had been eliminated many years before. . . .

The Bexar County sheriff tendered a less unique interpretation of the law. He held that picketing was legal and announced that strikers would be unmolested as long as they created no disturbance. Thus peaceful picketing of a few shelling plants outside of the city limits continued. . . .

Throughout the 37–day dispute Chief Kilday insisted that no strike existed. When Donald Henderson of the United Cannery, Agricultural, Packing and Allied Workers Union (Ucapawa) arrived in San Antonio, the Chief stated: "He is an intruder down here that hasn't 600 or 700 followers in the pecan industry. You call it a strike; I call it a disturbance out of Washington, D.C." Actually, when Henderson came to the city, he took the strike leadership away from fiery Emma Tenayuca, San Antonio's most renowned Communist, and turned it over to Beasley, whose political sympathies were unknown in San Antonio. . . .

But Chief Kilday was adamant. He continued his strike suppression activities to prevent, as he put it, a "communistic revolution" among the pecan shellers. "I branded the leadership as communistic and I still think so." When a union attorney queried Kilday as to his authority to judge the leadership, the Chief pontifically exclaimed: "It is my duty to interfere with revolution, and communism is revolution."

Dr. Edwin Elliott, regional director of the National Labor Relations Board, also interposed objection to police actions. Again Kilday argued that "if the strike was won under its present leadership, 25,000 workers on the West Side would fall into the Communist Party." Dr. Elliott suggested that it was not Kilday's function to keep 25,000 people out of the Communist Party, but the Chief averred that he would make it his function.

The crusade proceeded. Based on his definition: "A Communist is a person who believes in living in

a community on the government and tearing down all religion," Kilday packed "his" jail in a manner remindful of the "Black Hole of Calcutta." At one time almost 250 men were confined in a jail section with a normal capacity of 60 persons.

Five prominent women of the community inspected the Kilday domain in an effort to determine precisely the conditions under which the pecan shellers were held. It was discovered that the shellers were not allowed the privilege of using the runway between the cells as were burglars, drunks, and pickpockets. Eight to 18 men were kept night and day in cells built to accommodate four persons. Female prisoners were packed in like fashion. As many as 33 women were confined to a cell designed for six people. Prostitutes and pecan shellers resided in the same cell. And although 90 percent of the prostitutes suffered from infectious venereal diseases, all cellmates shared a common toilet and the lone drinking cup.

The inquisitorial methods of the police department were greeted with general approbation by the "respectable" element of San Antonio. The Mexican Chamber of Commerce, the Lulac (League of United Latin-American Citizens), and Archbishop Drossaerts refused to support the strike under Henderson's leadership. The Archbishop commended the police for their actions against "communistic influences," but somewhat paradoxically he also called upon employers to raise wages, because he said, low wages breed communism. At a lower level in the hierarchy Reverend John Lopez had a different solution for the problems of the pecan shellers. He urged them to return to the principles of the church, for the church was a friend of the working masses. Not to be outdone, the members of the San Antonio Ministers' Association, in their demand for a prompt settlement of the strike, insisted that "all Communistic, Fascist, or any un-American elements not be parties of the settlement." They neglected to define their terms, however.

The newspapers also joined the chorus. The *San Antonio Express* editorialized:

To all appearances, outside influences were mainly responsible for the strike. Paid agents from the Committee for Industrial Organization, and Communist agitators before them, convinced the pecan shellers that they were being treated unfairly . . .

Chief of Police Kilday—knowing the CIO—did

well to take firm action to prevent serious disorders.

No one will begrudge the pecan shellers a better living wage, if that be possible without destroying the industry."[5]

Government investigators were less sympathetic with Kilday's machinations. The State Industrial Commission, ordered by Governor Allred to conduct public hearings in San Antonio, reported unanimously that police interference with peaceful assembly and picketing was without justification. Dr. Elliott, NLRB observer at the hearings, concluded that "there has been a misuse of police authority in handling the strike." The Governor himself took exception to some of the acts charged against the police of San Antonio: refusing to permit strikers to congregate peacefully on vacant lots hired by them for that purpose; grabbing union buttons from the strikers and trampling them underfoot; and forcing people to become "scabs" [strike breakers] under threat of deportation.

But the forces of "law and order" prevailed. Even the soup kitchens set up to provide free food for the strikers were ordered closed because they allegedly violated the city health ordinances.

The shellers finally sought to put "the law" to work for themselves; they prayed for a temporary restraining injunction to enjoin police interference with peaceful picketing. . . .

The Judge conceded that:

There can be no doubt about the right of the strikers to cease work and also to attempt peaceably to persuade other workers to cease their work and to also attempt to dissuade other persons from entering into the employ of their former employers.

With the undoubted right of the strikers to peacefully picket firmly established, the justice proceeded to explain to the pecan shellers why they did not possess this right after all.

The assembling in one place of a large number of pickets incensed by a spirit of resentment to grievances, whether real or imaginary, tends to produce disorder and become a menace to the public peace, as well as an interference with orderly traffic and use of the streets by others, and I cannot think that the Legislature has transcended its rightful powers or violated any natural, constitutional or other lawful rights in enacting or authorizing the enactment of such preventative measures.[6]

In effect, then, the judge said that although there was no doubt about the right of the shellers to picket, there was also no doubt about their not having that right. . . .

Finally on March 9th, after 37 days of strife, the opposing forces consented to submit their cases to a board of arbitration. Local Union No. 172 of Ucapawa was recognized as agent for all employees in the industry for purposes of arbitration. The board . . . rendered its decision on April 13th. . . .

Contracts were duly consummated with all major operators. When the contracts expired, new agreements were negotiated with 13 operators who normally employed some 8,000 workers; even Southern Pecan Company fell into line. The new contracts, signed in the fall of 1938, provided for a closed shop, a check-off system, grievance machinery, and piece rates of seven and eight cents per pound. The wage scale was to apply only if the industry could obtain an exemption from the minimum wage rates set by the Fair Labor Standards Act which had recently been passed by the federal Congress. Otherwise, of course, the statutory minimum of 25 cents per hour would prevail.

The union joined the Southern Pecan Shelling Company and the other operators in maintaining that pecan shelling involved the processing of an agricultural product; that San Antonio and all of Texas were within the area of production for pecans; hence exempt from the provisions of the minimum wage law.

When its plea was rejected, the Southern Company petitioned for a learning period of three months during which time 2,500 to 3,000 workers were to be trained to operate its newly installed machine-shelling equipment. In lieu of the statutory 25 cents per hour the Company offered to pay 15 cents per hour to the learners while they absorbed the intricacies of machine production. Southern claimed that the learning period was necessary because "there is no labor available, trained, skilled or experienced for machine operations. The entire processing operation must be learned.". . .

The Wage and Hour Division of the U.S. Department of Labor conducted public hearings in San Antonio before acting on the Company's application. Except for one other employer, representa-

[5]*San Antonio Express*, March 11, 1938.
[6]*Manuel Martinez et al. v. Owen W. Kilday, et al.* (1938), files of the District Court, San Antonio, Texas.

tives of the industry were unanimously opposed to the "learning period." E. M. Funston of St. Louis, Southern's largest competitor, testified that a beginner did not require more than a week to become an efficient sheller or picker. A Chicago operator, representing an association of 21 houses, agreed. A Texas sheller insisted that he could break in and develop a new worker in two days, while an agent of the manufacturer who installed the machines at the Southern Company argued that an experienced hand-picker would reach average proficiency the same day that he commenced work with the new machines. . . .

[One] employer took a different approach.

The Mexicans don't want much money . . . Compared to those shanties they live in, the pecan shelleries are fine. They are glad to have a warm place to sit in the winter. They can be warm while they're shelling pecans, they can talk to their friends while they're working, their kids come in after school and play because it's better than going home. If they get hungry they can eat pecans.

If they put the 25 cent minimum wage law over on us, all these Mexicans will be replaced by white girls. The Mexicans have no business here anyway. They flock into San Antonio with their kind, and they cause labor troubles or go on relief at the expense of the taxpayer.

Despite their contentions the larger operators at least were forced to pay their workers the legal minimum wage. . . .

The effect of the minimum wage law on the pecan industry in San Antonio is readily apparent. The earnings of those who continued in employment doubled and in some cases tripled. However, approximately 5,000 of the less skillful shellers lost their jobs almost immediately and 5,000 more were let out within the next few years. They were either replaced by machines, as described above, or they left the industry along with the "straggler enterprises" which were forced out of existence by the increase in production costs. Two labor economists observed in this regard that in the entire United States the only major group of workers displaced as a direct result of the minimum wage law was in the pecan-shelling industry.

Thus, regardless of humanitarian or other justification for the statutory setting of minimum employment standards, thousands of individuals in San Antonio became "unemployable" as a result. It was a boon to the younger, more vigorous and productive of the pecan workers. One wage earner in a family could earn as much as two or three had done before. But the old and the feeble, most of whom were unable to speak English and many of whom were excluded from public assistance because of their alien citizenship, were removed from the employed labor force. Few employers found them "productive" enough to warrant paying them the legal minimum wage.

Frances L. Swadesh

The Alianza Movement: Catalyst for Social Change in New Mexico

In this selection, Swadesh examines a militant protest movement formed by chicanos to regain control over lands which they or their forefathers have lost to Anglo ranchers, the federal government, or speculative realtors. In her anthropological analysis of this movement—the Alianza—Swadesh concludes that it is best understood as a social movement to obtain basic civil rights and should not be considered an adaptive process similar to the Ghost-dance religion among the Sioux. To that conclusion another anthropologist, Nancy Gonzalez, takes hearty, although ambiguous, exception (The Spanish-Americans of New Mexico, Albuquerque: University of New Mexico Press, 1967, p. 183).

Whether we consider the Alianza a social revolutionary movement or not, its activities and goals demonstrate most cogently those difficulties which inhere in a conclusion that the United States is a melting-pot nation. If it were, indeed, a melting pot, there would be no occasion for chicanos as chicanos to engage in conflict with the dominant Anglo society.

A series of dramatic incidents, set in the spectacular surroundings of some tiny mountain communities of northern New Mexico, have made familiar to countless people in the United States, Mexico, and other countries such terms as "Tierra Amarilla," "Canjilon," "Coyote," "The Alianza," and "Reies Lopez Tijerina."

These terms first burst into front-page headlines on June 5, 1967, when some twenty men entered the Rio Arriba County courthouse at Tierra Amarilla, bent on making a "citizens' arrest" of Alfonso Sanchez, district attorney of New Mexico's first judicial district. Grounds for the attempted arrest were that Sanchez had banned a public meeting at Coyote, where land-grant heirs were gathering for a fresh assertion of their claims to lands granted their ancestors by the governments of Colonial Spain and Mexico. Sanchez had arrested a number of leaders and members of the Alianza (renamed "Confederation of Free City States" but still better known by the original name), which is the main organization of land-grant heirs. He had arrested these people both in Coyote and on the highway, and had seized Alianza records and called Alianza leaders "Communists."

Alfonso Sanchez was not found in the courthouse at Tierra Amarilla, but the wrathful men who sought him held the courthouse for two hours. They shot and wounded a state policeman and a jailor, drove a judge and various county employees into closed rooms, and shot out many of the courthouse windows before they departed. The last men to leave loaded two hostages into a police car and made a spectacular getaway.

That same day, 350 New Mexico Guardsmen, 250 State Policemen, 35 members of the Mounted Patrol, with horses, tanks, and helicopters, mobilized for a historic manhunt. Eventually, thirty people were charged with crimes, including kidnaping, a capital offense. At preliminary hearings on these charges in early 1968, charges were dropped against all but eleven and the kidnaping charge was reduced to "false arrest," a fourth

degree felony.

The accused, however, were not all rounded up for a number of months. The first targets of the manhunt were women, children, and elderly members of the Alianza, who were camped out near Canjilon. They were seized and held overnight at the point of bayonets, under conditions of physical hardship and personal indignity.

News photographs of mothers with babies in their arms, teen-agers, and elderly cripples being herded by the National Guardsmen drew swift intervention by the Human Rights Commission and by the New Mexico Civil Liberties Union. Liberal Anglos became uncomfortably aware that the Spanish-speaking people of their state might have some cause for feeling rebellious.

Behind the sensational headlines of June, 1967, and the even more sensational headlines which have announced subsequent events in northern New Mexico, there is an ongoing process of social change, constantly accelerating, of which the Alianza is the chief catalyst. . . .

Introduction:
Changes Desired by Hispanos

The Alianza was founded to deal with grievances which are widespread and deep-seated among the Hispanos of New Mexico. Specifically, these grievances stem from alleged violations of the Treaty of Guadalupe Hidalgo. Under that treaty, signed in 1848, Hispanos became citizens of the United States, but citizens with special rights acquired through previous governments, such as the right to their grant lands. Historical evidence supports the allegation that citizenship has been only nominal and that deprivation of the grant lands has forced a large percentage of Hispanos into chronic poverty. Economic loss has been accompanied by loss of cultural rights, especially the right to use the Spanish language in the environment of the school and the State Legislature.

The grievances are founded on facts, and many interested observers of the early 1960s conceded that something ought to be done about them. The prevailing opinion about the Alianza in its forma-

From "The Alianza Movement: Catalyst for Social Change in New Mexico," by Frances L. Swadesh, from *Spanish-Speaking People in the United States: Proceedings of the 1968 Annual Spring Meeting of the American Ethnological Society.* Reprinted by permission of the University of Washington Press.

tive years, however, was: "Those people won't get anywhere."

The reason for this septicism was the isolated and rustic character of the Hispano communities. New Mexico's 269,000 Hispanos constitute only 30 percent of the total state population, and are the most isolated and atypical of the more than four million Spanish-speaking people dwelling in five southwestern states. Despite occasional published opinions that the Hispanos are politically the most active of all Spanish-speaking groups and that, in the counties where they constitute a majority, they have "complete control of the power structure," the reverse is more nearly the case.

What passes for "Hispano political activity" is largely the activity of a handful of precinct leaders and henchmen who are deeply involved in the power structure but are far from controlling it. Any small base of power, in a social setting where so many are impoverished and powerless, can be used to control voting and other political behavior with a minimum of promises, bribes, threats, and sanctions. . . .

Control is still maintained, much as in the late nineteenth century, by garbling as much as possible the information which reaches Hispano communities and by taking advantage of the extended kin groups by extending small favors or handing a their key members. This system is today the foundation of precinct politics in Albuquerque, a city of some 300,000, in every precinct with a high percentage of Hispano residents. Leaders and candidates build their influence through their relatives, affines, and compadres and win support of other kin groups by extending small favors or handing a few dollars to key members.

In communities where the tendency for social enclavement is strong, the plea of ethnicity is useful as a last resort. Of many a Hispano incumbent who has proven himself incompetent or worse, the saying goes, "He's a bastard, but he's *our* bastard," since it is assumed that any Anglo in his place would be worse. To satisfy this sentiment, the New Mexico power structure allots certain slots to Hispanos whom they can control.

Along with this system goes widespread factionalism, dividing the smallest as well as the largest communities, mainly into rival kin groups. While this system can decide the vote in counties where the Hispanos constitute a majority, and is important in counties where their united vote can

constitute a balance of power, it provides them with little say on the issues and with very narrow choice in candidates. Political lag will continue in New Mexico, along with its regressive system of taxation upon the backs of the poor, until Hispanos learn to form coalitions around issues of common concern with other ethnic groups.

Schedule of Innovative Changes

The Alianza has existed as a formal organization since 1963, but its organizational roots go back somewhat further:

1. 1959

Reies Tijerina was invited to give his views on the land-grant problem to a meeting of the Abiquiu Corporation of Tierra Amarilla Grant heirs. The meeting was broken up by fighting between factions of the Corporation, some insisting that nonmembers had no right to speak. Tijerina, assisted from time to time by his brothers and other supporters, spent much time during the next five years collecting data on the Spanish and Mexican land grants of the Southwest in the National Archives of Mexico.

2. 1963

Having completed his researches in Mexico, Tijerina returned to New Mexico and promptly founded the Alianza Federal de Mercedes (Federated Alliance of Land Grants), whose first annual convention held during the Labor Day weekend, was attended by some 800 delegates. The Alianza was incorporated under Federal and State laws as a nonprofit, nonpolitical organization. Its constitution, adopted by the convention, represented a new approach to the grievances of the Hispanos.

(a) United action. Most previous efforts to press land grant claims had been initiated on behalf of individuals, families, or factions on a single grant, often in opposition to other heirs. Never before had representatives of many grants united to press their claims.

(b) The common lands. Common, or "ejido," lands constituted the greatest acreage by far of all community land grants. The principle of "ejido" has been no less dynamic in New Mexico than in Post-Revolutionary Mexico, where it continues to serve as the basis for land reform and the establishment of producers' cooperatives. Until the Alianza

raised the issue, however, the very existence of ejido lands in the southwest had been obscured.

A large percentage of the New Mexico ejido lands had been assigned to the Public Domain by the Surveyors General of the period 1854–1880, because they paid no attention to claims other than those made on behalf of individuals. Some of the ejido lands were later opened up for Homestead entry, but a much larger acreage was incorporated into National Forest lands in the early years of the twentieth century.

The heirs were largely unaware of these transactions, due to isolation and the language barrier, and only reacted when fences were erected on these lands, cutting off their access to grazing and firewood. The history of violence in New Mexico is closely linked with the fencing off of ejido lands, from the Lincoln County outbreaks in 1876 to those on the Sangre de Cristo Grant at the Colorado-New Mexico border in 1963.

(c) New legal strategy. Previous to the formation of the Alianza, heirs had repeatedly sought relief through the courts. There, case after case had been lost while the lawyers reaped fortunes. For instance, the lawyer who represented the heirs of the Canyon de San Diego in 1904, managed to get confirmation of 80 percent of the original 110,000 acres, then took half the acreage as his fee. A quiet-title suit on behalf of some Tierra Amarilla heirs undertaken by Alfonso Sanchez shortly before he became district attorney won nothing for the heirs but brought Sanchez into ownership of some Tierra Amarilla real estate.

The Alianza took the position that no competent legal decision on the grant lands could be made below the level of the Supreme Court. Early efforts were made to persuade the Attorney General of the United States and the New Mexico Senators to work for a Congressional bill to investigate the facts. . . .

3. 1964

By the time of its second annual convention, the Alianza claimed a membership of 6,000 land grant heirs from the five states of New Mexico, Colorado, California, Texas, and Utah. Some out-of-state delegates attended the convention, giving New Mexicans the sense of a common cause beyond their individual and community problems.

(a) Contact with Indians. Friendly contact with members of several Indian Pueblos developed following the 1964 convention. The potential for joint efforts with the Pueblos began to be considered, since the documentary basis for both Hispano and Pueblo land claims was the Spanish and Mexican Archives. With this thought in mind, when Taos Pueblo began to press its claim to the Blue Lake area, the Alianza voiced its support. . . .

Having once taken this position, the Alianza has continued to seek further for friendly relations with Indians, and the number of Pueblos represented has risen with each annual convention.

(b) Direct action. Some Alianza members had scant hope that Congressional action would be taken, despite continuing efforts toward the introduction of a bill. Some Tierra Amarilla Grant heirs began posting notices against "trespassers" on what used to be the Tierra Amarilla ejido lands, by which they meant Anglo ranchers who had bought tracts, built ranches, and claimed ownership of these lands. A new "Mano Negra" scare was born.

Ever since 1912, when fencing was begun on the Tierra Amarilla common lands, a vigilante organization called the "Mano Negra" (Black Hand) had intermittently cut fences, slashed livestock, and set fire to barns and haystacks. Lately, it has been rumored that some ranchers have set fire to their own premises so that they could whip up sentiment against the Mano Negra and, by implication, the Alianza, while collecting insurance on the damages.

Hispanos have had to resort to vigilante action whenever they have lost hope of securing justice through the government or the courts. Most Hispanos will not condone vigilante action, neither will they condemn it under certain circumstances.

4. 1966

This was a year of accelerated change for the Alianza. Many of the older members were hesitant about making the changes, but in this year the total membership claimed for the Alianza rose to 20,000. . . .

(a) Self-identity. Over the 1966 Fourth of July weekend, a large delegation of Alianza members marched from Albuquerque to Sante Fe, many camping by the roadside at night and 125 assembling in Santa Fe to seek an audience with Governor Campbell. After a long wait, the delegation was able to present the Governor a petition asking his support for a Congressional bill to investigate their land-grant grievances. On this oc-

casion, the inaction of Senator Montoya was criticized openly for the first time. For many Alianza members, this was their first taste of group demonstrative action.

Although the official purpose of the march fell short of accomplishment, in that no substantial help came from the Governor, its enduring effect on the membership was to change their perception of themselves. Through the public action they had jointly taken, they affirmed their identity as members of "La Raza," or what Reies Tijerina calls "a new breed," the people of New World Hispanic culture with its many increments from indigenous sources.

This broadening and firming-up of group self-identity gave Alianza members pride and tranquil self-confidence to a degree which is uncommon among Hispanos of today. Like members of other groups who are subject to lifelong social discrimination, maddeningly covert when it is not blatantly overt, Hispanos have tended to feel painfully ambivalent about themselves. Questionnaires which they have to fill in our prevalently racist land leave them wondering whether they are "white" or "other nonwhite." The language question is a constant thorn, since few of today's adults have escaped the ordeal of initiation into a school system where the use of English is forced upon pupils who can often barely understand it, let alone speak it. Such situations feed feelings of inadequacy and timidity—and also burning resentment against the dominant Anglos.

(b) Changing role of women. Women, from the start, had been devoted members of the Alianza. The fund-raising dinners they prepared and served were vital supporting activities, yet no women had assumed a public role in the organization until the march to Santa Fe. Since then, their activist role has unfolded, sharpened by the experience of arrest, of the jailing of their husbands for weeks at a time, and of visits by FBI agents. More and more women have taken these events in their stride and have emerged as fluent spokesmen for their organization.

(c) Youth roles. No formal youth group has been formed in the Alianza yet, informally, the teen-age and young adult sons and daughters of active Alianza members have made a place for themselves in the organization. Many of them participated in the July, 1966, march to Santa Fe and an increasing number have participated in subsequent activ-

ities of the organization. In addition to the arrests which followed the Tierra Amarilla uprising, some very young people were charged in the original indictment. Perhaps because of the stresses voluntarily incorporated into their lives, these young people appear more poised and purposeful than is common for their age-group. Despite the police surveillance with which they are surrounded, none of these youth have been mentioned in the records of pick-ups for marihuana and drug use which are constant among youth of their income level. Disorder and brawling at Alianza dances are unknown.

(d) Renewal of community ethic. In October, 1966, convinced that only by direct acts of civil disobedience could they force official attention to the land issue, Alianza members began to spend weekends in a National Forest campground located on ejido land of the San Joaquin del Rio de Chama (or Chama Canyon) Grant. Its area totalled some one-half million acres bestowed upon a group of settlers in 1806. . . . The Carson National Forest was created at this time and included the San Joaquin Grant area.

The heirs to the grant continued to live there, mainly in Canjilon at the northeast corner. For years, they were unaware that their grant had been taken away from them.

The Alianza campers took possession of the campground in the name of the San Joaquin Corporation, whose legal existence as the governing body they proclaimed. They refused to buy the required camping permits, cut a few trees for firewood, and forbade the Forest Rangers to trespass on their grant.

Not all the campers were heirs to this particular grant. Some had come from as far away as California to participate in the "test case." On the other hand, the San Joaquin Corporation was real enough. This corporation had been reactivated under a constitution dated February 9, 1940, and for twenty-seven years had been dedicated to the following goals:

. . . to protect the society which is encompassed by said Corporation against the injustices and tricks of tyrants and despots, of those who insult us and seize our lands; to seek Law and Justice; to initiate lawsuits; to acquire, hold, possess, and distribute through proper legal channels the rights, privileges, tracts of land, wood, water, and minerals which were deeded to, and bequeathed by our ancestors, the heirs and as-

signs of the Grant of the Corporation of San Joaquin del Rio de Chama.

On October 26, the Forest Service proceeded against the Alianza by placing a stop sign at the campground entrance and stationing uniformed personnel there. When the Alianza caravan drove into the campground without stopping, the Rangers followed them and demanded that they pay up or vacate. At this point, the Rangers were seized, their trucks and radios were impounded, and a mock trial was conducted, in which they were charged with violation of the laws of the grant.

Participants in these proceedings who came from nearby communities and had deep-seated personal resentments against the Rangers would have preferred to carry matters much farther, but they were restrained by leading Alianza members. The Forest Service trucks and radios were returned and the Rangers were instructed to depart.

One year later, Reies and Cristobal Tijerina and three others were convicted in Federal Court of having "assaulted" Forest Rangers and of expropriating Government equipment. The verdict is being appealed.

The experience of living together under the community legal code and customary rules of their ancestors, often wistfully recollected by their grandparents, revived among Alianza members a sense of the vitality of their traditional value system. The feeling for solidary relations of the community, reaching beyond the ties of the extended kin group, was expressed by many Alianza members after the San Joaquin experience, and has become crystallized in strong ties of loyalty and affection among the members. . . .

(e) Quest for an alliance with Negroes. While Alianza leaders had, in the past, stated that they did not intend to adopt the militant direct action methods of the Negro movement, their admiration for the organizational strength and effectiveness of this movement had grown with time and experience. Dr. Martin Luther King was invited to be a featured speaker at the 1966 annual convention of the Alianza. When he declined on the grounds of a previous commitment, Stokely Carmichael was invited. Carmichael accepted but was called elsewhere at the last moment.

A young Negro staff member of the local Poverty Program agreed to pinch hit. Despite his hastily prepared speech, delivered in broken Spanish, he was cordially thanked for his expression of Negro sympathy for Hispano aspirations.

Alianza members had hitherto been trying to win the sympathy of people in power for their slogan, "The land is our heritage. Justice our credo." Now they had come to realize that they would not be heard until they had the strength to force a hearing and that, to have this strength, they must seek allies among other subordinated peoples.

5. 1967

The "uprising" at Tierra Amarilla has been described in the opening paragraphs of this report. What remains to be discussed are the innovative changes it produced:

(a) Recognition by other Spanish-speaking groups. Since June, 1967, "Tierra Amarilla" has become a rallying cry as well as a place name. From Denver came Rodolfo "Corky" Gonzales, leader of the Crusade for Justice, to hail the Alianza members for having "had the guts" to take their stand. A few weeks later, Bert Corona, leader of the Los Angeles Mexican-American Political Association ("MAPA"), made a like pilgrimage to Albuquerque. Cesar Chavez, leader of the migrant farm workers of the Southwest, was invited to Albuquerque to address liberal organizations, but took time out to attend a regular meeting of the Alianza. There, after an effusive greeting by the membership and a public embrace with Tijerina, Chavez announced that, if he were a New Mexico resident, he would sure be an Alianza member. He hoped all Hispanos of New Mexico would join, because the issue of the land is crucial to rural Mejicanos and reflects the cruel injustices to which they have been subjected. Chavez predicted no early victories, but spoke soulfully of the road of sacrifice that would have to be travelled by those who are committed to the struggle, sacrifice in atonement for the sins of others. . . .

(b) Partnership with Negroes. The 1967 annual convention of the Alianza was attended by a busload of Mejicano and Negro activists from Los Angeles. The culminating point of the convention was a "Treaty of Peace, Harmony, and Mutual Assistance" jointly signed by the Alianza leaders and leaders of SNCC, CORE, Black Panthers, and other Black Power organizations. The members of the Alianza, with the ringing approval of all present at the convention, thus identified their movement with the objectives of Black Power, no longer on

the basis of temporary and conditional "mutual self-interest," but in the context of "full brotherhood." . . .

6. 1968

(a) Impact on youth. Partly inspired by the "Black Beret" and "Brown Beret" movement of Los Angeles activist Negro and Mejicano youth, the Alianza youth are starting to move out in new directions. In Albuquerque, it will be hard to build unity between "Black and Brown," as the two groups are now identified, because of the record of poor communication between the groups and of clashes between their youth. The coolness is partly the product of conservative trends in the local Negro leadership which, in the future, is likely to be stimulated to new trends or else to be replaced.

On April 22, 1968, students of an Albuquerque junior high school called a strike. Under the slogan, "We want Education, not Contempt," the students charged that the educational curriculum of the school was adequate only for its few Anglo students, no effort being made to compensate for the educational handicaps of the Hispano majority and the Negro minority. Other student demands were an end to hitting the students, punishing them for speaking Spanish on school premises, and displaying prejudice against Hispanos and Negroes. Forty of the students were arrested while marching to recruit students from other junior high and high schools to form a joint delegation to the School Board. Among those charged with "littering," "loitering," and "truancy" were two Tijerina offspring.

An ambitious plan has been written for a free summer workshop for fifty Spanish-speaking youth, to provide them with a background in all the knowledge of the world of today that they will need in order to become effective leaders. . . .

(b) Leadership role of the Alianza. Paradoxical as it may seem, the relatively small Alianza with its widely scattered and largely rural membership occupies a central place in the regionwide united movement of minority groups. As such, the Alianza has become significant on a nationwide scale. The Tierra Amarilla episode so stirred the imagination that the Alianza has become standardbearer for the entire Southwest.

The authentic leadership of the Alianza in the ranks of the poor caused Dr. Martin Luther King to invite Reies Tijerina to the planning conference for the Poor People's March, held shortly before his assassination. King also chose Tijerina to be mobilization director for New Mexico and to be one of three leaders representing Mejicano-Chicano-Hispano demands in Washington.

Predictably, the implementation of these decisions produced hostile editorials in the New Mexico press and anguished wails from some liberals. While the mobilization commanded strong support from poor people and many middle-class liberals, measures to paralyze Tijerina's leadership were promptly taken.

On April 27, Reies and Cristobal Tijerina were arrested and warrants were out for the arrest of eleven other Alianza members on an indictment issued by the Rio Arriba County Grand Jury. The indictment reversed the decisions of the preliminary hearing on the "Tierra Amarilla Uprising" and reinstated the kidnapping and other charges which had been reduced or thrown out of the case by judicial decision. No new evidence was cited. Bond for most of the defendants was set at $24,500.

The national leaders of the Poor People's March expressed their conviction that these arrests were an attack on the March itself. They demanded through the Justice Department's intervention release of the accused by writ of Habeas Corpus.

The State Attorney General and District Attorney Alfonso Sanchez, however, cling to the expressed belief that, once the Alianza leaders are behind bars for a long stay, the Hispanos will once more relapse into apathy. The State Attorney General has taken the position that the Alianza is part of a Communist plot and that elements at the University of New Mexico and in the Poverty Programs are in league with the plot. The State OEO director was dismissed as a result of the allegations, and covert investigations have been made of a number of Community Action programs. It is not known whether the recent firing of several University deans is connected in any way with the State Attorney General's campaign.

(c) Progress. Despite the storm of controversy and accusation which surrounds the Alianza, it is considered a real political force in the upcoming elections. While no direct, overt concessions may be made on issues which the Alianza has raised, behind-the-scenes promises are expected, as in the gubernatorial elections of 1966. Very quietly, action is being taken to soften Hispano grievances and to still the protests. It is said that the Forest

Service has opened grazing facilities to Hispanos to a greater extent than at any time since the 1930's. In addition, projects funded both publicly and privately are centering on the economic problems of the northern counties. Producers' cooperatives have been established in several communities, with promising results. Whether or not these concessions will still Hispano demands remains to be seen.

Summary and Conclusions

The development of the Alianza in less than five years since its foundation in 1963 is notable for the changes in the very process of change itself which can be traced. At the start, the organization had many of the characteristics of a nativistic cult; the charismatic leader, the goal of restoration of socioeconomic forms to a prior state, the search for ethnic identity, and the renewal of the traditional community ethic. Had these been the only characteristics of the organization, the Alianza might have become a revitalization movement according to the definition of Anthony Wallace. . . .

The Alianza, on the other hand, included from its inception innovative changes such as unity of purpose and action on a scale long unfamiliar to Hispanos, the linking of human, ethnic, and political rights with those of property and, finally, the transformation of the action program from a base in traditional vigilantism to active participation in today's major national sweep for social change. . . .

It is in the light of this national perspective that the social changes of which the Alianza is the catalyst should be viewed.

Harriet J. Kupferer and Arthur J. Rubel
The Consequences of a Myth

In our introductory essay, we identified a myth cherished by "Americans" and familiar to all of us, which has helped shape our view of ourselves and our image of American society—the myth of the melting pot. Indeed, other nations—especially European ones—have had their view of us shaped by the same myth.

How myths in general, and the melting-pot myth in particular, come to be institutionalized has been described by Philip J. Gleason.[1] The special conditions of our history that contributed to the rapid enshrinement of the myth of a melting-pot nation attract our attention here. At least two related phenomena play a role. The first settlers, disillusioned with the myths of the Old World, came to the comparative mythlessness of the new, which provided fertile soil for the emergence of the "American Dream" and its constituent idea of the melting pot. Succeeding waves of immigrants added substance to it. These new immigrants, who came from northern Europe eager to advance their fortunes, were culturally related and physically similar to earlier immigrants. Thus, the threats they posed the older residents were minimal. Moreover, as the frontiers moved west, there was free land for the taking—if one overlooked the prior claims of the Indians. With relative ease, the new immigrants gave up the cultural baggage they brought as they merged with the population of the young nation. And so the myth was born and institutionalized.

Soon enshrined as a secular symbol, the myth of the melting pot became entangled in a complex set of institutions and, in addition, developed an emotional dimension, not too different from the symbolic significance of the flag or the national anthem. Symbols are necessary to social life, and no society is without them. Nor could it be, for symbols provide means of group identification and are rally points for sociocultural systems.

However, unlike *symbol*, the word *myth* now connotes falsehood—an untrue story. Scholars have

[1] "The Melting Pot: Symbol of Fusion or Confusion," *American Quarterly* 16 (Spring 1964): 20–46.

noted that the historical truth of a particular myth is irrelevant; and under ordinary conditions that argument is sound. But there are circumstances wherein the veracity of a myth is exceedingly significant. Nowhere is this more true than where myths relate to political and social ideologies. Such is the case with the myth of the melting pot.

To understand why this is so, it is helpful to examine two cultural concepts: *ideal culture* and *real culture.* When anthropologists describe ideal culture, they report what people *say* they do or *say* they believe. Real culture, on the other hand, is what they *actually* do. Schisms between the real and the ideal are almost universal, and ordinarily they are not of much significance. If, for example, people in an arctic village say, "we all trap to survive," but on close examination the ethnographer finds that less than 50 percent actually do trap, the disparity has few negative consequences. But when the gap between the real and ideal is in the realm of political philosophy, or morality, trouble may follow. Most especially is this true in a literate, complex society whose members are educated to think analytically and to question premises. The ideal holds out promises; the real demonstrates that promises are not kept. For this reason, then, the melting-pot myth generates frustration and ultimate anger.

To explain the social effects of this myth, it is useful to know something of the dynamics of culture change. We shall employ two concepts, *acculturation* and *assimilation*, to understand the processes through which an individual may go if he leaves the society of his origin to enter another.

Each individual, from the moment of his birth, is shaped to fit the culture of the society into which he is born. By various means, he is taught the beliefs, behaviors, feelings, and life ways considered proper by his elders. In effect, maturation means that he becomes a participating member of his culture. Why cultures are so diverse and contrasting need not concern us here. It is sufficient to note that all of them are more or less adaptive at a certain time and in specific places. When persons migrate to other places, however, some or most of these learned behaviors may not be totally adaptive in the new situation. For this reason, it may become necessary for an individual to learn to meet the major expectations of the new society. The processes which occur when an individual learns a culture different from his own are called *acculturation.* Usually, the first generation of migrants learns the new life ways imperfectly or selectively. And, of course, it is important to remember that they do not forget or re-

place, except behaviorally, their old cultural repertoire. When their behavior is reasonably consistent with the new norms, acculturation has occurred.

Successful assimilation depends upon some acculturation of the newcomers and their acceptance by already established members of the larger society. An individual or group of individuals are assimilated when they are free to participate without qualifications in the institutions of the adopted society. Assimilation and acculturation are simple enough to understand. However, when they occur they are by no means simple; nor are they painless.

Resistance to acculturation and assimilation is common and comes from several sources. One obvious obstacle to the successful completion of the process lies in the attitude of the larger society, which produces reasons to bar some ethnic groups—regardless of the extent of their acculturation—from full participation in the society. The dominant society defines the ethnic group as less worthy or desirable, and therefore relegates its members to low-status jobs, subtly confines them to certain residential areas, and deprives them of rights. Ultimately, deprivations are rationalized by racial explanations, however farfetched.

On the other hand, some groups self-consciously resist total acculturation or assimilation. In other words, they elect to participate selectively in the new society, most often choosing to participate in political and economic institutions. The extent to which they are permitted to participate depends in large measure on the degree to which the cultural traits they retain conflict with their counterparts in the larger society.

The fact that some segments of our population are not allowed free participation or do not wish to be totally assimilated creates skepticism or bitterness about American claims of egalitarianism. Further skepticism is caused by various other permutations and combinations of acculturative and assimilative processes, including forced culture change. The articles in this section demonstrated some of the types of acculturation and assimilation. With the analytical framework provided by theories of anthropologists, we can better understand the dynamics of these situations and their results.

The Results

One distinctive characteristic of contemporary life in the United States is a vigorous demand by ethnic minority groups that their cultural differences be accorded recognition. Representative of this innovative posture are the Black Panthers, the Crusade for Justice, and the National Indian Youth Council—Black Power, Brown Power, and Red Power. These groups and others with similar orientation contribute to the distinctiveness of our times, not because they represent the special interests of their constituencies—for that is the basis of the American political system—but rather because of the identity of those whose needs they are articulating. These are the minority groups with a long presence in continental America. Two of them had well-established societies in America long before the representatives of the dominant majority group arrived.

If the melting-pot thesis were valid, the special cultural characteristics of these groups would have been lost in the acculturation and assimilation processes to which they have been subject for several centuries. But, clearly, these groups did not lose their ethnic and cultural identities, largely because they were not permitted to do so. The great abyss between the democratic philosophy and the behavior of members of this democratic society functioned not only to set them apart, but to relegate to them the smallest share of material goods and those other goods which feed men's souls—esteem and prestige.

The earliest adjustment to this chasm between philosophy and conduct was an overt acceptance of, sometimes accompanied by efforts to achieve and to conform to, the norms set by the majority. Those efforts went for naught and, as we have just seen, exacted a high price both in individual personality structures and in the effectiveness of the subculture or subsociety to meet the needs of its members. (For examples of some of the effects of this, see the section "Violence.") Today, for a variety of complex reasons, a different type of adjustment is being attempted. With goals still blocked, increasingly large numbers of ethnic minority groups are trying to retain—sometimes to regain and extol—ethnic uniqueness. To oversimplify, groups representing our minority constituencies are saying: "You didn't want us, now we don't want you; but we do want our economic share and we demand the right to be different!"

The Work of an Early Anthropologist

James Mooney's classic account of the Sioux outbreak of 1891 was part of the basis of American anthropology's long tradition of deep interest in, real concern for, and sometimes active intervention in the difficulties brought about by contact between distinctive cultures. As we stated earlier, it is unfortunate that Mooney was commissioned to investigate the relationship between the federal government and the Sioux after the debacle, rather than before it. His report makes clear the fact that the Ghost-dance religion was an attempt by the Sioux and other Indian peoples to adjust to stresses on their traditional society and culture—stresses caused by demands of the white society that the Indian adapt to the way of life of that society without any reasonable and viable means of so doing.

By examining the relationship between traditional Sioux culture, the Ghost-dance religion, and the outbreak of 1890, Mooney was able to demonstrate that the Ghost dance did not *lead to* the outbreak, rather that both were products of the same forces. He not only looked for and found a relationship between what appeared to be superficially disparate phenomena, he also placed his findings in a comparative framework. By comparing the exotic Ghost dance with other, more familiar, religious movements, Mooney contributed to the development of a theory of religious movements and the ways in which they symbolically assist the adjustment of a way of life to changing circumstances. That contribution to theory is clearly visible in the seminal work of Ralph Linton on nativistic movements, and was later refined by A. F. C. Wallace in a paper on "Revitalization Movements,"[2] as well as in his introduction to a new edition of Mooney's study.

Culture and Personality: Of Profound Interest to Anthropology

We are not yet certain that the adjusted needs of a subordinate group in our society are met by the use of symbolic protest. There are, however, some indications that in the past such protest has not been effective. The American black has been and still is the most psychically abused, the most subject to punitive denial of his humanness of all minority groups. He did, however, develop forms of symbolic protest which were uniquely American, but contained unmistaken African elements. Yet, despite the emergence of such symbolic forms as the blues, black humor, and the espousal of Protestantism with a special ethos, the blacks in the study by Kardiner and Ovesey were among the walking wounded. The study makes clear the relationship between individual personality characteristics of American blacks and the sociocultural repression by which they have been victimized. The generation

[2] See the section "Changing the System" for Wallace's "Revitalization Processes."

of American blacks investigated by Kardiner and Ovesey was scarred by oppression.

What then of the current generation of blacks? Unfortunately, the study by Kardiner and Ovesey has not been brought up to date, but scattered information hints that a similar basic personality structure remains characteristic of many blacks today. However, contemporary behavior differs markedly from the accepting passiveness of the past. Today's behavior ranges from quiet but determined efforts to gain a more acceptable status in the total society, to extreme militant "nonnegotiable demands" occasionally accompanied by violence. The reasons for these phenomena are many and complex, and to blame them on group modal personality is gross reductionism. But we can understand some of the current symbolic behavior of blacks with the help of the findings of Kardiner and Ovesey. The phrase *black is beautiful*, Afro hair styles, simulated African modes of dress—all may be regarded as efforts to build a positive self-image, to bolster self-esteem, and to encourage the development of a strong ego structure; in other words, to develop the very traits Kardiner and Ovesey found weak or absent in their sample of an earlier generation. In effect, years of using white models did not profit American blacks either materially or emotionally. For today's young, then, and some of the not-so-young, hair straighteners and skin bleaches are despised as a denial of a people's birthright. Had the clues in *The Mark of Oppression* been utilized in policy making, in education, in the provision of social and health services, and wherever else the lives of black and white intersected, our society might have been spared some of its current agony.

The Results of Marginality

For a long time, social scientists have been concerned with "marginal men"—individuals who do not quite fit. Everett Stonequist has provided us with an excellent definition of the "marginal man":

one who is poised in psychological uncertainty between two (or more) social worlds; reflecting in his soul the discords and harmonies, repulsions and attractions of these worlds, one of which is often "dominant" over the other; within which membership is implicitly if not explicitly based on birth or ancestry . . . and where exclusion removes the individual from a system of group relations.[3]

With some modification, this definition can be applied to entire groups which do not fit neatly into identifiable categories. The Houma Indians, of whom Ann Fischer writes, are just such a group. They are neither white, black, nor "real Indian." Surely, had the melting pot been a reality, groups such as this would never have developed. The Houma invalidate our favorite myth. Moreover, they have no champions. The federal government has not afforded them what little security is to be found in the Bureau of Indian Affairs. The Urban League and the National Association for the Advancement of Colored People have no attraction for them, for the reasons elucidated by Dr. Fischer. The Houma continue to exist as an entity undereducated and over-exploited by self-seeking individuals. If their population is sufficient to support it, and if a leader emerges, they will probably engage in a collective movement to better their lives materially and to demand civility from those who presently withhold it.

The Grievances of the Spanish-Speaking

In many ways, the Spanish-speaking people of the American Southwest have suffered social and cultural marginality similar to that of the Houma Indians. For those populations living away from the border, in the relatively isolated regions of Colorado and New Mexico, the problem has been less severe than for those living in California and along the Mexican border. In the former communities, a long, stable period of settlement and adjustment, undisturbed by outside influences, continued from the late sixteenth to the mid-nineteenth centuries. In the last half of the nineteenth century, their traditional way of life was upset by the arrival of representatives of the Anglo way of life.

An entirely new legal, commercial, and political system confronted them. For the first time, questions of identity were raised: They were the Spanish-speaking American citizens, a group derived from a Hispanic cultural tradition distinct from the cultures of northern Europe in which the new settlers had their roots. Small wonder that the contemporary social movement described in the selection by Swadesh has assumed for itself a title which reflects a time long past—an Alliance of Free City States in which representatives of the majority society are not present.

The situation which characterizes the Spanish-speaking peoples residing along the border between

[3] *The Marginal Man: A Study in Personality and Culture Conflict* (New York: Charles Scribner's Sons, 1937), p. 8.

the United States and Mexico is quite distinct from the one in Colorado and New Mexico. The former have been subjected for more than a century to almost continuous influences both from representatives of the larger Anglo society and from immigrants arriving from central and northern Mexico. Seeking on the one hand an accommodation to the alien ways of the Anglo society of the United States, they are constantly buffeted by Mexican ways carried to them by each wave of new immigrants. The selection by Shapiro describes some aspects of the dialectic interaction between the culture of the Spanish-speaking Americans of south Texas and the impinging Anglo culture and society. These are the chicanos of the border who describe themselves as *neither* American nor Mexican, but who continue to search for a satisfactory way of life on the frontier between two different societies.

An Alternative

This collection of papers has clearly demonstrated that, except for a few, the ideology of the melting pot has been self-deluding for most of the major ethnic groups in the United States. The continued belief in a melting-pot ideology has had tragic consequences for the groups who have not been assimilated. It has left them undereducated and underfed, and has contributed to the high illness and death rates so characteristic of our minorities. Because the myth has persisted so tenaciously, some groups are reacting vehemently in making known their demands. They are creating new symbols around which to rally. Others are clinging to or reviving old symbols to provide continued identity as separate groups. But all deny the reality of the myth and some

now reject it completely. Their activities lend undeniable support to the research findings and consistently articulated concerns and predictions of anthropologists who, from Mooney's time forward, have sought to understand the consequences of contact between groups with distinctive cultures.

What now, then, for these groups and others like them? There is an alternate model available, which anthropologists call *cultural pluralism*. While there is some disagreement among scholars on its precise definition, this model postulates the existence within a nation of smaller units which retain or have developed a culture peculiar to themselves. Some students have referred to these smaller units as *part cultures* or *subcultures*. In a pluralistic society, each of these subcultures would retain or erect various "structures." For example, they may or may not construct self-conscious boundary-maintaining mechanisms— devices to prevent the erosion of the cultural tradition. However, they would all cling to their own value and belief systems and would frequently be bilingual. Furthermore, all would participate effectively in the economic, and often the political, systems of the larger society.

Thus, cultural pluralism resembles the current situation, but guarantees members of the subcultures full and free participation in any or all of the institutions of the larger society. It also guarantees the end of harrassment and pressures to change or conform. The realization of a truly pluralistic society would indeed give substance to the "American dream" of freedom of choice and, at the same time, permit those who so desire to enter the cultural "mainstream."

3 Anthropology and the Third World

Gerald D. Berreman
Anthropology and the Third World

Robert A. Manners
Functionalism, Realpolitik, and Anthropology in Under-developed Areas

Guillermo Bonfil Batalla
Conservative Thought in Applied Anthropology: A Critique

Vine Deloria, Jr.
Custer Died for Your Sins

Irving Louis Horowitz
The Life and Death of Project Camelot

Marshall Sahlins
The Established Order: Do Not Fold, Spindle, or Mutilate

Gerald D. Berreman
Academic Colonialism: Not So Innocent Abroad

Kathleen Gough
World Revolution and the Science of Man

Herchelle Sullivan Challenor
No Longer at Ease: Confrontation at the 12th Annual African Studies Association Meeting at Montreal

Pierre L. van den Berghe
The Montreal Affair: Revolution or Racism?

Immanual Wallerstein
Africa, America, and the Africanists

Satish Saberwal
The Problem

Gerald D. Berreman
Anthropology and Moral Accountability

As scholars we have been sensitive to the processes of change in Africa. We write eloquently and frequently about problems of transition. We devise models and methodologies to identify, measure, and compare aspects of change. It is not the substance of our scholarship, however, which has elicited the violent and bitter hostility of many Africans and Afro-Americans. It is rather the posture of our scholarship that is questioned and resented. And we are not alone in this position, for the scholarly community everywhere is being forced to justify its existence by demonstrating its relevance to the human condition. It is the arrogant rejection and denial of the validity of these demands that increasingly infuriates the young and the Third World.   Fred G. Burke

You who are so liberal and so humane, who have such an exaggerated adoration of culture that it verges on affectation, you pretend to forget that you own colonies and that in them men are massacred in your name.   Jean-Paul Sartre

The reader must imagine to himself the privilege of making contact with primitive societies which were more or less intact and had never before been studied seriously. Just how recently, as luck would have it, the whites had set out to destroy them will be clear from the following story: the Californian tribes had still been quite wild at the time of their extermination, and it happened that one Indian escaped, as if by a miracle, from the holocaust. For years he lived unknown and unobserved only a dozen miles from the great centers of population, and kept himself alive with his bow and the sharp-pointed arrows whose stone heads he carved himself. Gradually there was less and less for him to shoot, and finally he was found, naked and starving, on the outskirts of a city suburb. He ended his days in peace as a college porter in the University of California.   Claude Lévi-Strauss

Gerald D. Berreman
Anthropology and the Third World

Questions of ethics, responsibility, and accountability in anthropology were raised in the section on "The Social Responsibility of the Anthropologist," both theoretically and as they confront the anthropologist in his actual research. In this section we turn our attention to these same questions as they affect the relationships between the anthropologists and the nations and peoples who have traditionally been their subjects of inquiry. These are primarily the peoples of the Third World, of the "underdeveloped" or "developing" nations, as they are often called: those outside of Europe and North America; those of neither the Western European-American political bloc nor the Eastern European bloc; the peoples of Latin America, Africa, the Middle East, South Asia, Southeast Asia, East Asia, and Oceania. Most Third World cultures are not Western; their people are not white; they have experienced colonial exploitation; they contain large peasant populations; and they are largely economically dependent on other nations. They comprise most of the world, both in population and territory.

Ethnic minorities in America and elsewhere have a similar relationship to the Western world and to its anthropologists, for they share with the Third World similar circumstances: cultural difference, relative powerlessness, and economic dependence on the societies which the anthropologists represent. They have, in fact, been referred to as victims of "internal colonialism," in recognition of the parallels between

their experience at the hands of the dominant societies which surround them and the colonial experience of most Third World peoples. In the United States, the most conspicuous internal colonies are blacks, native Americans, and chicanos. Like Third World nations, their powerlessness appears to be diminishing, but their heritage of exploitation is strong, and it deeply influences their relationships with anthropologists.

The context in which anthropologists are being called to account by Third World peoples is the postcolonial and neocolonial world—in which social science is perceived as a product of Western culture which grew out of colonial interests and which served those interests, consciously or not, leaving a legacy of colonialist attitudes and assumptions to many of its practitioners. American anthropologists face the additional problem that America is seen in much of the Third World as an imperialist nation of a new sort. Without explicitly claiming territory, Americans find themselves seeking, extending, and protecting American spheres of influence by political, economic, and military means. Often they find themselves aligned against indigenous populations in support of unpopular governments which could not survive without American support. Often they find themselves aligned on one side of an international dispute in which the American presence is supporting American interests rather than justice or even peace. Not infrequently, power—often military power—is the only basis for the American presence, pride and greed the only discernible motives. Anthropologists and other scholars have found themselves actual or putative accessories before and after such facts. Some have served as advisers to their government, informants about those whose lives that government seeks to influence. And the works of virtually all anthropologists have been appropriated for those purposes. They have been accused, therefore, of being either witting or unwitting agents of empire.

In this context many anthropologists have abandoned the notion that scholarship justifies itself. Many have come to the conclusion that it must be justified in the light of the ends it serves and the consequences it wreaks, especially the consequences for those among whom their research is done and upon whose trust and cooperation its accomplishment entirely depends. The concerns expressed by Holmberg, Du Bois, and Gallin, in the first section of this book ("The Social Responsibility of the Anthropologist"), for the individuals among whom they worked, have been expanded (as in Grayson's letter in the same section), to concern for the consequences for entire populations. The consequences which cause concern are the subtle as well as the readily apparent effects of research, and even of the very decision to conduct research at all in a given context.

The paramount factor that has aroused these concerns is the response to anthropological research of spokesmen from the Third World. The writings in this section bring the issues to the fore by presenting arguments which challenge conventional anthropological research, especially the research of Americans in the Third World and in our own "internal colonies." American research is the focus of these challenges partly because it is mostly Americans who do such research, but more especially because America's power—military, political, and economic—and the interests which that power supports are well known, conspicuous, and widely resented in the Third World. America is perceived in many Third-World nations as the embodiment of a new colonialism, and anyone who works with its explicit or tacit support, be he anthropologist or Peace Corps volunteer, is regarded as an agent of that colonialism.

Robert A. Manners

Functionalism, Realpolitik, and Anthropology in Underdeveloped Areas

The role of the Western anthropologist in neocolonial society is put sharply and critically into focus in this selection. Drawing a parallel, in 1956, between the old colonialism and contemporary aid programs, Manners discussed problems which were not apparent to most of the profession or the public until a decade later. Manners was concerned with the politics of the Western anthropologist's work in the developing nations, the politics of economic aid and planned development, the politics of stability and change, and the politics of cultural pluralism and cultural assimilation. His context, of course, is the vested interests of the Western nations in the Third World and the power and resources they command to maximize those interests. The central dilemma of Western anthropologists working with any program of planned change in a developing nation is that "having identified themselves with the project, they have become identified with the goals of the project." In particular, the American anthropologist is inevitably identified with the goals and methods of his government, especially if its funds support him.

Introduction

Point Four, technical aid, and the facts of "economic cooperation" have added a new and some-

"Functionalism, Realpolitik, and Anthropology in Underdeveloped Areas" by Robert A. Manners from *America Indigena*, Vol. 16 (1956). Copyright © 1956 Instituto Indigenista Interamericano. Reprinted by permission.

what urgent dimension to the old anthropological interest in the phenomena of acculturation and culture change. A number of anthropologists have shifted from the largely theoretical examination of the conditions and consequences of culture contact to endeavors of a programmatic and practical nature. This is not to say, of course, that applied anthropology is itself brand new or that Mr. Truman is the putative father of even the American variety. But it is apparent that the recent efforts of this country and of the United Nations to introduce radical changes in underdeveloped areas through technical assistance, health, education, and a host of other programs have involved even greater numbers of anthropologists than were utilized by the British and others in their colonial activities over the past few decades.

The crucial distinction between most of the older acculturation studies and the recent efforts of anthropologists is that the former had been occupied primarily with description—or even analysis—of the *consequences* of one kind of culture contact or another, while the latter are concerned primarily with *instruction* of administrators and other agents of enforced culture change in the best ways of introducing the new elements with the least difficulty. In her UNESCO handbook on *Cultural Patterns and Technical Change*, Margaret Mead specifies the practical value of anthropological research in assistance programs. The aim of the study which led to the publication of this book, she says, was to discover "the ways in which changed agricultural or industrial practices, new public health procedures, new methods of child and maternal health care, and fundamental education can be introduced so that the culture will be disrupted as little as possible and so that whatever disruption does occur can either be compensated for, or channeled into constructive developments for the future." Therefore, the anthropologists offer their findings for the use of "experts, policy makers, specialists, technicians of all sorts, chiefs of missions and teams, members of ministries of health, education, agriculture, and industrial development in countries actively seeking to guide technological change—all those who are immediately concerned, at any level, with purposive technological change."

Some recent research efforts have attempted to improve the accuracy of prediction in introduced culture change by actual experimentation. In these controlled studies, the new elements are introduced under the watchful guidance of the experimenters who then record the changes in the culture which follow. . . . They thus endeavor to demonstrate the precise effects of the introduction of new technological, educational, and health practices into a "cultural community" whose prior circumstances are well known. The assumption behind these inquiries and behind the employment of anthropological advisers in the many programs of foreign aid now being undertaken is, of course, that detailed knowledge of a culture permits prediction of some of the reactions to and the effects of introduced changes. If one accepts the premise that there is a need for aid and that such aid should be introduced with the least possible disruption of community and individual adjustment and stability, then the anthropologist *seems* fairly well equipped to act as an adviser in these matters.

Malinowski has defended the anthropologist's practical efforts in colonial administration with the assertion that "social engineering is simply the empirical aspect of social theory." It is not my purpose here to question the propriety of the social scientist's functioning in practical matters where his special knowledge may be of use to administrators. But it does not, as Gluckman and others have already pointed out, follow that his understanding offered as advice will necessarily influence the policies of the administrator or that it will actually produce effects which are of benefit to the majority of the people in the contacted community. In fact, it has been suggested that for the colonial situation, at least, the results may be just the opposite—that the anthropologist's professional advice may, if used at all, serve to facilitate the manipulation of the local population in violation of their own immediate interests.

To the degree that contemporary programs of foreign aid are concerned with mass elevation of the standard of living of peoples of underdeveloped areas, the anthropological advisers to these programs may stand on higher ethical eminences than their colonial office colleagues who, in effect, lend their talents and their knowledge to the prosecution of an unhampered exploitation. Unfortunately, however, for the peace of mind of those anthropologists involved in the new assistance endeavors, there has been more than a suggestion that the aims of Point Four and other technical, health, and educational programs are themselves "tainted" by self-interest or nonaltruistic political considerations. For example, in a review of J. E. Bingham's *Shirt-Sleeve Diplomacy*, Clarence R. Decker observes that "...the 'integration' of technical cooperation and political and military strategy all strongly suggest that Point Four is already the stepchild of a revived old-fashioned power diplomacy ... [there is a fear that] *realpolitik* has been reinstated as the sole basis of our diplomacy."

In his speech to Congress on June 24, 1949, President Truman himself observed that one of the chief purposes of "technical assistance [was to] create conditions in which capital investment can be fruitful." Paul Sweezy, taking his lead from Mr. Truman's description, concludes that the object of Point Four "is pretty clearly the encouragement and protection of American foreign investments, not the balanced development of backward countries." Later on, I shall return to this topic, but at the moment it seems proper to suggest that the "goal" of improved living standards is likely, in assistance programs, to be forced to accommodate itself to the practical considerations of economically and politically wise investments. In effect, then, the "global potlach" is encumbered by political and economic strings. I suppose there is nothing intrinsically objectionable about such arrangements. I merely raise the point to suggest that the role of the anthropological adviser to aid programs may in essence be not unlike the role of his colonial office prototype. If aid should in any way be tied to practical economic and political considerations of the aiding countries, it must follow that the anthropologists will play an auxiliary role to that of the administrator and the goals will be set for him by these considerations. Within these limits, as within the limits imposed upon anthropologists in the employ of conventional colonial administrations, the adviser functions largely to predict the possible consequences of policy. He can never determine the policy itself. For if major policies arise out of the deeper necessities of power-political and economic considerations, it is unlikely that they will be deflected or drastically renovated to accommodate to the anthropologist's cautious *caveats*.

This is not to say, of course, that the anthropologist serves no function to the agencies involved in the introduction of culture changes on a worldwide scale. His very employment refutes such a view. Anthropologists can and do inform on many matters involving customs, taboos, social forms, and the like. Unquestionably their advice is often considered in the tactics of introducing new elements into a culture. But where grand strategy inevitably involves the precipitation of conflict and disruption, and where these disturbing potentialities may also be envisaged by the anthropologist, it is hardly likely that his advice on these matters could lead to abandonment of the project itself. Thus, the anthropologist may, for example, suggest that it would be unwise to make a frontal attack on exchange marriage or on polygyny, and the administrators of the program may decide it would be best, therefore, to overlook these practices for the time being. On the other hand, should the anthropologist advise that a landless peasantry could be won over to support a program of agricultural assistance by the gift of individual plots of farm land or by some pattern of collectivization, the realities of the program would probably doom the suggestion as unworkable. The real role of the anthropologist involved in technical and other assistance programs, then, emerges—like that of the colonial office technician—as one of prediction of cultural resistances.

The anthropologist, as professional student of the problems of acculturation and culture change, has acquired a vested interest in this realm of forecasting. Fantastic numbers of books and articles have been written dealing with the phenomena of culture change, with the origins, the reactions, the resistances, and the consequences of cultural innovation. In the examination of these phenomena, writers and researchers have employed a number of concepts, some of which I shall examine in the sections which follow. Among these are the concepts of integration and disintegration, of social organization and disorganization, of rapid and enforced vs. gradual and guided acculturation, of cultural anomie, of dynamic and static cultures, of the strength of custom, of resistance to change, of differential or selective acceptance, of the functional interrelationship of the parts, and so on.

Cultural Integration and Individual Resistance as Factors in Change

The more "highly integrated" cultures have sometimes been compared with a delicate watchlike mechanism. It has been suggested that the sudden introduction of new elements into such a culture acts very much like the dropping of a grain of sand into the delicate works of the watch. The watch runs erratically, or the culture becomes disorganized, anomic. Less delicately balanced cultures, it is said, tend to assimilate change better if the change itself is not too "radical" or too sudden. By and large, however, there is wide agreement among many anthropologists that all changes should be introduced into cultures with extreme care since any change will be likely to have repercussions which may be felt throughout the culture. Since change inevitably implies some degree of disruption—even in societies which are not so "well integrated"—it follows that almost any introduced change may result in "social disorganization." The more "highly integrated" the culture, the more profound the disruptive effects of innovation, and the greater the consequent disorganization.

This is only one of many problems that must be faced by the agents of guided or enforced culture change. Not only is the delicately-balanced cultural mechanism liable to disorganization in change, but the even more delicately-balanced carriers of the culture are likely to sense the disorganizing potential of the change and, therefore, to *resist* it. This type of response is sometimes described as an unwillingness or reluctance to accept innovation. It is suggested that most beliefs, customs, and practices exert a conservatizing influence on culture, that there is a "natural" tendency to react against acceptance of any kind of change. There is a sizable body of data which suggests that cultures are *normally* conservative, that people—anywhere—are suspicious of change, feel at ease in the presence of the customary and uncomfortable when confronted by the new. If this be so, then the anthropological advisers in assistance programs have, on one level, a fairly easy job. They can make the blanket prediction that all change will disorganize, all change will be resisted—and predict themselves out of a job. But obviously the matter is not quite so simple. It appears that some parts of culture are "more resistant to change than others"; that some changes are more or less disruptive of the total culture than others; and that some segments or groups of individuals within a society demonstrate different degrees of resistance to change. In practice, then, the administrator and the anthropologist understand these differences and are prepared to consider them in introducing change.

Understanding and consideration, however, may in themselves have small impact on policy. Since, in their local aspects, assistance programs are ostensibly nonpolitical in character, they must conduct their activities within the framework of an existing sociopolitical structure. Thus, health, education, and technical assistance must be proffered not only with a minimal "disorganizing" effect on the general cultural situation, but these must not be permitted either to alter the social and political *status quo ante*.

Wherever possible, then, aid is channeled through existing political and administrative agencies within the underdeveloped area. Thus, the official disinclination of the assisting agencies to interfere with political and social arrangements lends moral and material support to the groups in political power. In this sense, the technical, educational, hygienic, and other changes which are introduced function to *strengthen* the *status quo*. If they did not they would be resisted by the controlling elements; no group in a position of political dominance is likely to relinquish that position willingly. And the very changes which may be welcomed by the group in power may be resisted by others in the society.

Colonialism and the Ethnographer

In this connection, however, it has been suggested that the patterns of intervention involved in technical assistance differ radically from those practiced during more than 400 years of colonial penetration. The predatory behavior of preassistance times included specific exploitative and control aims. Contact was ordinarily undertaken with the object of procuring raw materials, providing markets, or opening areas for profitable investment of capital. Where expediency demanded at least nominal preservation of preexisting political forms, these were preserved. Where they, or concomitant patterns of social organization, interfered with the primary exploitative aims of the intrusive power, they were modified, revamped, or swept aside. Sometimes, of course, mistakes (acts which slowed up exploitation) were made and new methods had to be explored. Eventually it became apparent that the trained ethnographer, as well as the colonial administrator and the missionary, might be profitably employed in the pursuit of the practical ends. The Netherlands, France, Great Britain, and other colonial powers consulted with and employed anthropologists in the interest of "understanding the native cultures," for "understanding," it was felt, might reduce friction, minimize violations of local customs, beliefs, traditions, and deeply-held values. Then one could get on with the job.

But the goals of the job and the contact itself implied radical changes in preexistent cultural patterns. If, as Tylor has asserted, "The savage is firmly, obstinately conservative," and as Malinowski has more recently affirmed, "... conservatism is the most important trend in a primitive society..." then the intruding culture could expect resistance to the changes which it was "forced" to introduce. But if a way could be found to achieve the desired practical results without at the same time producing profound changes in the old way of life, then the job could proceed with greater smoothness and with fewer resistances. Anthropologists could tell administrators when they might go ahead or where they must go easy; or administrators could be trained so that they would themselves be able to function with anthropological knowhow. However, all parts of a culture, as Malinowski himself insisted and taught, fit together. If you introduce change in any part, contingent changes of varying intensity will make themselves felt throughout the culture.

This posed a dilemma for one of the world's outstanding anthropologists and advisers in problems of colonial administration. If all parts of a culture are interrelated, how does one prevent or even minimize the radiation effects of, let us say, the change from a subsistence economy to a subsistence-plus-cash economy? Or does one, recognizing the interrelationship of the parts, oppose the introduction of this change because it threatens to have disruptive effects on the family structure, marriage, internal political and social relations, the unity of the clan, and so on? To ask the question is to answer it. If it was cash crops—or mines—or mills—or factories that one wanted introduced, they were introduced, no matter the consequences, no matter the plaintive jeremiads of the perceptive ethnographer. Because Malinowski's functional view of culture—which stresses the interrelationship of its parts—cannot be reconciled with his applied anthropological point of view—which

suggests that change may proceed by a process of quarantining those elements which should not be disturbed—he was forced to fabricate an unreal cultural system. Contact produces conflict and disorganization, and true cultural communities cannot, by definition, be improperly integrated or disorganized. Hence cultures in conflict, or cultural communities under contact are in a sense not true cultures. Only those parts of them which involve interrelationships among the native population constitute the true cultural community. The personnel of the contacting culture do not fit into the native organization, and must not, therefore, be reckoned a part of the native culture.

Malinowski apparently refused to apply to the contact situation his awareness of the fact that, while it is perfectly true that cultures cannot be disorganized and remain viable, they are constantly undergoing alterations in the level or kind of their organization without disappearing. True cultural disorganization can at most be but a temporary thing. It must eventuate almost immediately in a new kind of organization or in the death of the culture itself. Exploitative contact appears severely disorganizing only if we assume some arbitrary and utterly unrealistic ideal of organization. If, on the other hand, we consider the changes wrought under this type of contact only an intensified manifestation of an inherent process in culture, we may look upon the result—*ethical considerations aside*—as a new level of organization or as reorganization. New experiences, new problems, and new frustrations on a massive scale accompanied the changes introduced in the African cultures which were Malinowski's chief concern. But those cultures that did not die became reorganized—even though reorganization probably involved more personal hardship, insecurity, and anxieties than had precontact organization. These were still valid cultures, although involved in contact and new forms of conflict, and although there had been serious alterations in the old way of life.

Malinowski's formulations seem to have solved to his satisfaction the seemingly insoluble contradiction between his functionalism and his applied anthropology. He found it possible to admonish the administrator against tampering with the native custom of bride-price or exchange marriage while, at the same time observing that the colonial office had levied a hut or poll tax on the natives which effectively removed the young men to labor-scarce areas. The native culture—i.e., the life in the village—remained integrated, organized, and relatively conflictless. It continued to include bride-price, mother-in-law taboos, and buttered umbilici. The forms of social relations in the native village—having been rescued by the anthropologist—seemed almost the same as they had been before. Because, as Gluckman so clearly points out, Malinowski does not see the contactors and the contacted as part of the same "social field," he can almost assume that a substantial part of the village culture remains the same despite the profound consequences unleashed, let us suppose, by the opening of a new gold field 500 miles away.

In point of fact, however, Malinowski does not quite assume that the culture of the village has been unaffected by the poll tax and the opening of the mine. Such a position would be patently absurd. What he does maintain is that while the contact induces changes in the tribal culture, *description* of the latter should not include reference to the contactors as integral and functioning parts of the native culture. This kind of reasoning, then, justified Malinowski in assuming that important segments of tribal culture might in part be insulated from the consequences of contact—since contact and its agents originate or lie outside of the tribal or village unit. If such a view were accurate, then it would be proper to say that an ethically-oriented and autonomous anthropologist could implement certain practices which would, in effect, maintain the cultural status quo in the face of outside changes. Or, at the very least, the anthropologist and the administrator might insure that novelty be introduced so subtly as scarcely to be noticed or felt. There are, however, at least two basic errors involved in these assumptions. The first of these, as I have already suggested, is the assumption that the tribe itself is the only realistic unit of integrated cultural interaction, even under circumstances of intense contact. Malinowski and others seem, in this case, to be saying that a cultural community cannot include diverse and conflicting ethnic groups. Or, by extension, that when a community becomes internally heterogenous or conflict-ridden it is "disorganized" and hence ceases to be an authentic and integrated cultural community. The second is the assumption, equally invalid, that the anthropologist is either autonomous or policy-significant.

And in this connection Firth remarks that:

"The conditions in which the problems are set for him are not within the discretion of the anthropologist to vary. He cannot change the broad lines of policy—legal, administrative, economic, religious, educational—even though his researches may lead him to think that they are unsuitable to native needs."

American Anthropologists and the "Underdeveloped" American Indian

Some of the errors which flow from these or related assumptions about culture and the role of the anthropologist in introduced culture change are, I believe, expressed in the writings of a number of American ethnologists who have dealt with the problems of our native Indian populations, particularly some of those in the southwest. Among these writers there is evident a strong belief that many aspects of these cultures may—and should—be retained by their bearers. If it were true that these cultures could perpetuate themselves as enclave isolates, free of contact with or dependence upon "outside" forces, then, of course, it would be justifiable—possibly desirable—so to maintain them. But this is no longer feasible. Whether they wish it or not, they have become involved in many ways, in many forms of clear material dependence, with the white culture which has surrounded and even infiltrated their tribal areas. To assert that it would be desirable for the Hopi, or the Navaho, or any other group to hold on to the "old ways" in the face of the assaults upon them which have effectively destroyed the material base which made them possible is to assert a wish which is contrary to reality and to the possibilities of reality.

This position suggests, moreover, that the Indians themselves are wholeheartedly in favor of perpetuation of the old; and this has not been conclusively demonstrated. On the other hand, it would be an equally invalid oversimplification to assert that *all* of the Indians favor the kind of total change which would absorb them completely into white American culture. There are many who fear such an eventuality—with good reason—given the experience of Indians under the conditions of minority discrimination and prejudice which still prevail in most parts of the country. Others, too, would resist absorption because the "old ways" still provide them with subsistence and a sense of security. But the decision to accept or reject no longer lies with them, and their wishes are almost irrelevant. The American Indians, like "under-developed peoples" the world over, have been involved; new needs have been implanted, and the means for gratifying these needs have been revealed to them. In the process of satisfying the new needs they are becoming involved in new forms of economic and social behavior, and these must inevitably affect all other aspects of their culture. To resist these efforts by throwing a magic circle around art, technology, education, and family, etc., and saying, in effect: "Do not touch," is to deny the interrelationship of the parts. The anthropological consultant—whether he be retained by the Bureau of Indian Affairs or the administrators of technical assistance programs in Latin America, Africa, or the Near East—who suggests the feasibility of such a program is, it seems to me, somewhat less than realistic.

But the position I am here presenting is itself open to the accusation of over-simplification unless I qualify it further. I am not, of course, suggesting that when the first trader, trapper, or missionary enters an area and hands out iron pots, iron axes, or Bibles that he causes the economic, social, and ritual organization to crumble and the native language to disappear. I am merely asserting that introduction of these and related elements sets in motion a process or series of processes whose results are felt in other parts of the culture; that these consequences, though not readily predictable in detail, are bound to follow some such radiant pattern; and that no amount of advice, consultation, precaution, or admonition can appreciably frustrate or alter the side-effects of introduced changes. A committee of experts convened by UNESCO has declared their recognition of these consequences as follows: "The effort to extend the benefits of industrialization and technological advances to all peoples must inevitably be accompanied by profound cultural dislocations."

In short, it is the contact and the nature of the contact along with the changes it presents which determine the total cultural effect. It is not the wishes of the contacting group or of those contacted which can make this selective determination. From this it does not necessarily follow that we can predict with accuracy the pattern of cultural radiation or the side-effects of contact even when we know well the details of the contact and the cultural superstructure on which it has impinged. But

it does follow that the anthropologist's advice to "go easy" with the family structure, the religion, the taboos against this or that are of doubtful practical value in the face of the massive dynamism which may be unleashed by the introduction of the iron axe, the bulldozer, insecticides, and work for wages.

The Anthropologist and Altruistic Intervention

This brings us back to the important question: whether programs of intervention in under-developed areas which are altruistically motivated are to any degree handicapped by the necessities which govern contact guided by aims of exploitation and profit. Are not the technical, health, educational, and other agents of assistance programs free to perform their jobs without regard for the interests of the "investors" who support their activities? And would they not, under such circumstances, be in a far better position to observe the cautions and make use of the advice that the anthropologist is prepared to give?

The answer to the first of these questions is exceedingly complex. However, it merits some consideration here, for it suggests that a contact which imports the material, educational, medical, and nutritional impedimenta of advanced Western civilization in a spirit of benevolent selflessness will be followed by results which differ profoundly from those which ensue when these elements are introduced as the baggage of self-interest. To an important degree this may actually be the case; and it would be demonstrably absurd to deny it. On the other hand, it would be equally absurd to overlook the many and growing similarities between the earlier forms of intrusion and those which, like Point Four, appear to have been otherwise motivated. Present political and economic realities, like those of the past, make their own demands. Not only are the areas for technical assistance, educational, and other programs determined by these realities, but the nature and extent of assistance is itself limited by the same imperatives. Speaking of South Asia, Werner Levi notes that: "... United States loans to this region are bound to have strings attached also; at least, I doubt whether loans can be granted in a completely altruistic manner. I think altruism is too much to ask in international relations. If the U.S. even on a governmental basis makes loans, it will tie them in with some sort of political policy. . . ."

It is illuminating also to examine President Truman's inaugural address launching Point Four in January of 1949 and the restatement of the aims of technical assistance enunciated in the message to Congress just five months later. In January, Mr. Truman said: "The old imperialism—exploitation for foreign profit—has no place in our plans." On June 24th of the same year he specified the conditions of assistance in greater detail than he had in the initial statement. And it hardly follows from even a cursory examination of the later statement that the "new" differs very radically from the "old imperialism" with respect at least to its economic aims. For the June message reemphasizes that the main purpose of "technical assistance [is to] create conditions in which capital investment can be fruitful." Mr. Truman also urged that "private sources of funds [in addition to those furnished by such public agencies as the Export-Import Bank and the International Bank for Reconstruction and Development] must be encouraged to provide a major part of the capital required." To make the project even more attractive to investors, Mr. Truman added two additional incentives. The first of these was contained in the proposal that there be "special treaties guaranteeing equal and nondiscriminatory treatment to American capital"; and the second that there be instituted a plan for "government insurance to private investors against the special risks of foreign investment."

But Point Four, it may be protested, is not the only program of aid being extended by this country to underdeveloped areas. Perhaps programs that are under the guidance of the UN, FAO, ILO, UNESCO, WHO, and other agencies of a more-or-less international complexion are not governed by the same considerations as are those which govern American assistance delivered under the MSA or one of its successors. Jacob Viner makes a pertinent observation. The United States, he notes, is participating in its own aid programs and in multinational programs as well ". . . but the bulk of our aid is granted by us directly to the recipient countries." And Eugene Staley in his analysis of the *Future of Underdeveloped Countries* says: "The U.S. share of the subscribed capital of the International Bank is 35 percent. The U.S. has contributed about 60 percent in the first few years of the 'expanded

program' of United Nations technical assistance. The 12 million dollars provided by the U.S. in 1952 for this program and the somewhat smaller amount contributed in 1953 *are but small fractions of the amounts the U.S. has been spending directly in its bilateral* [as opposed to multilateral] *Point Four program"* (emphasis added). Thus, the United States is clearly the most important contributor in both bilateral and multilateral programs of assistance; and our bilateral operations involve far greater sums than are expended in our generous contributions to the UN and related agencies.

If we may judge from the "practical" conditions enunciated to justify the expenditures of Point Four, we may, I believe, assume also that certain practical benefits are expected to follow from investment in *any* assistance program abroad, even when it is part of an "internationally" cooperative endeavor. Earlier I referred to a statement by Clarence Decker regarding the *realpolitik*-al nature of our assistance endeavors. Viner is even more pointed: "As long as strategic and military considerations continue to be important, we cannot surrender to the United Nations, which includes the Iron Curtain countries, 'neutralist' countries, and borderline countries . . . the decision as to how and for what purposes our aid is to be allotted."

Stringfellow Barr finds that under the first years of the United Nations: "American aid . . . was going not where suffering was most acute but where cold war politics directed it . . . our programs of economic aid, technical assistance, or whatever they might at any given moment be called, were doomed to become one facet of our foreign policy . . . any economic aid that could not be fitted into our military policies became either a pittance or an immoral handout."

It is, of course, not my desire in introducing these observations to reflect upon the morality of assistance given with ulterior motives of a practical strategic, military, economic, or political color. For purposes of this discussion it is, it seems to me, only necessary to suggest that the motivation itself governs who gets help as well as what, how and how much will be offered. If this be so, one might logically expect that aid will be withheld from those areas where no advantages are anticipated— no matter how grave the need—and denied to people of governments which refuse to fulfill the "practical" conditions upon which the offer of assistance is predicated. Where such offers are extended by or in the name of the "Western bloc" or by and in the name of the "Soviet bloc" we may be justified in assuming that there is involved more than a tacit assumption of a *quid pro quo*.

Conservatism and Functionalism

Favoring the preservation of "some of the old ways," as I have already suggested, is not only a denial of the basic anthropological conception of the functional interrelationship of a culture's "parts" but is a doctrine of conservatism as well. While there is no question that cultural or any other kind of conservatism is the privilege of any one, anthropologist or not, it should, I must emphasize, be recognized for what it is.

In an article on "The Metaphysics of Conservatism" Gordon K. Lewis observes that the vocabulary of conservatism—the pleas to proceed with caution, to eschew violence to tradition, to cherish the past—offers us, ". . . when all the sound and fury are over . . . nothing much more than the defense of the present order. . . ." If it is the present order which the anthropologist defends when he is concerned over the consequences of change, he should be aware of this. If he opposes the "present order" as inadequate, or unjust, or stifling for any moral or ethical reasons of his own choosing, and is therefore willing to see it supplanted, he must as well be willing to recognize the pervasive after-effects which will follow changes in the "present order." If he wishes strongly to preserve some of the old ways and the old values of a culture, he will find that the means to preservation of the parts may inevitably be preservation of the whole. Thus, the anthropologist's high regard for a religious rite, or for a type of family or clan organization, or for certain systems of cooperative endeavor—however admirable or desirable these may be—could conceivably promote his opposition to a technical assistance program which, by functional radiation, may threaten these cultural forms.

Cultural Relativism and Enforced Culture Change

It is curious to note how many of the anthropologists who espouse the preservation of some of the old ways in terms of their essential "validity" do thereby implicitly abandon the very relativity which they offer in defense of the espousal. Not only is their willingness to accept change and improvement in some *material* conditions a denial—and, I would agree, a most salutary denial—of the doctrine of absolute cultural relativism, but their championing of the parts to be preserved suggests that these parts are to be more highly regarded than those which threaten, under change, to supplant or alter them.

The widespread anthropological resistance to change stems understandably from this non-relativistic evaluation in which many anthropologists are constantly—if resistantly—indulging. They are always running into items and practices which seem well worth preserving. It is therefore inevitable that they should actively advocate such preservation. It would be foolish to deny that there is much "good" in underdeveloped areas which will be replaced as they develop by much that is "bad." But nostalgia and a sincere concern for those cultural devices which seem good and desirable are unlikely to prevail against the profoundly disturbing forces of industrialism and a money economy.

This is not to say that the effects of such involvement need be or will be everywhere the same. They will not. But the dream of perpetual pluralism needs serious recasting in the light of our experience and observation. Much that we may cherish will inevitably be lost. We only hope that the larger gains to humankind will amply compensate for these losses which are adjunct to the course of introduced culture change.

At least a part of the world's cultural pluralism is today the pluralism of inequality, of differentials in wealth and access to the advantages of wealth. Few anthropologists would argue for the preservation of these pluralistic inequities. But even the pluralism which is the product of diverse cultural histories is declining under the impact of increasingly similar forces. Pluralism without gross inequality may add an interest, a zest, and a potential source of perennial enrichment to the future citizens of the world. But the ironical reality appears to be that as the mechanisms for capitalizing these cross-fertilizing potentialities become increasingly effective—that is, as communication and non-evaluative tolerance improve—the differences diminish; and world culture moves at least in the direction of a broad sameness, perhaps, in Browning's poignant phrasing, towards a "common greyness."

Differential Acculturation and Acceptance

Among the ethical and moral biases embraced by some anthropologists engaged in assistance programs is the bias in favor of the assumption, as I have stated earlier, that culture changes are, *per se,* unsettling to the people involved. Because changes in the way of life are upsetting, the beneficiaries of assistance programs are likely to resist them. Thus the go-slow admonition of the anthropologist may be doubly-grounded in the pragmatics of program implementation and a concern for the emotional stability of the people. Here is a curious dilemma on the horns of which many anthropologists might be indefinitely impaled were it not for the fact that the administrators are charged with the responsibility for getting changes introduced, come what anomic consequences may come. If anthropologists were to subscribe rigidly to the related doctrines of relativism and the anomic effects of change they would have to oppose any program of assistance whatsoever. But few anthropologists are even theoretically so committed, and certainly none of those involved in aid programs are practically so committed.

Perhaps this is so because anomie and resistance to change turn out to be neither so dependable nor so widespread as has sometimes been suggested. In practice, anthropologists commonly recognize that there are differentials in the rate and manner of acceptance of change. Sometimes it is said that people will accept change more readily in the material than in the nonmaterial realm; or that differential acculturation may be seen in the greater resistance to changes in the "costumbres" than to changes in other parts of the culture. Or it may be asserted that since no culture is completely static anyway, it might be useful and decent to engage in some judicious and selective manipulation by way of hastening an inherent dynamism. It is deemed far better to exercise scientific and humane guidance over the process than to permit it to proceed whimsically and anarchically to the detriment of the "developing" peoples.

In point of fact, then, cultures do change, and people are not inevitably resistant to change, and virtually all anthropologists would agree. Whether some people are more congenial to change than others, or whether changes are more acceptable in certain parts of culture than in others is still debatable. Speaking of Mexico, Beals says: "In the

main the Mexican Indian does not have sharp rejection patterns to those things which have 'practical' value." Somewhat later he suggests what he may mean by practical value when he states: "You get periods of rejection when they don't take any European culture. These are associated with a period of unpleasant [sic] relationships between Indian and white. When you get . . . more rapid acculturation coming in, it generally marks an improvement in relations. These are cases in which the government tries to do something constructive for the Indian rather than simple exploitation of him."

Two nonanthropological experts in the field of underdeveloped areas concur in Beals' view that cultures do not necessarily resist change . . . even change of a profound nature . . . that entrenched attitudes or values can even be swept aside or replaced. Although they do not concern themselves with the possible costs of rapid and enforced change, they do imply a profound shift in values which sometimes makes change and acceptance of change immediately sequential. Speaking of the prerevolutionary period in Russia, Gerschenkorn says: ". . . how quickly in the last decades of the past century a pattern of life that had been so strongly opposed to industrial values and that tended to consider any nonagricultural economic activity as sinful and unnatural began to give way to very different attitudes." And Lamb notes, for the post revolutionary period, how quickly the Russians have come to know that "The industrial revolution is today a complex entity which can be exported to the backward areas of the world, set up there, and made to run. . . . They have drawn into their industrial society over a hundred peoples living within the borders of the Soviet Union and altered their traditional way of life."

In studying the patterns of resistance and acceptance demonstrated by the peoples of "underdeveloped" areas in the face of directed attempts to change their ways, Charles J. Erasmus finds that "practical" and perceivable advantages speed acceptance. "In agriculture, for example, the introduction of improved plant varieties (higher yielding or more disease-resistant) which result in a greater profit to the farmer has repeatedly resulted in spectacular success stories."

And Ralph Beals, in an article dealing with the people of the Ecuadorian village of Nayon, observes that "Many members of the group have accepted major shifts in the sociocultural system with little difficulty and look forward to additional changes."

As illustrations of the prevailing view that elements of material culture are more readily accepted than the nonmaterial, I quote briefly from Barnett's analysis of innovation. He finds that "new tools, appliances, house and dress style" are more readily adopted than nonmaterial elements because, "on the whole they create fewer, and in many cases not any, social complications." This somewhat over-simplified statement which attributes conservatism in culture to a fear of "social complications" is slightly less mystical—but hardly more analytical or illuminating—than the assumption entertained by Malinowski and others about the "natural" conservatism of primitive and "backward" peoples.

Another and highly sensitive observer, the artist-anthropologist, Covarrubias, suggests not only that change may be acceptable to a people but that it may even be accepted within that most nonmaterial part of their culture, their religion. Of the Balinese, he says: "[they] have been extremely liberal in matters of religion. Every time a new idea was introduced into the island, instead of repudiating it they took it for what it was worth and, if they found it interesting enough, assimilated it into their religion. . . ." On acceptance and conservatism generally, he has this to say: "The Balinese are extremely proud of their traditions, but they are also progressive and unconservative, and when a foreign idea strikes their fancy, they adopt it with great enthusiasm as their own."

In general there appears to be some evidence for the view that in an "unforced" acculturational situation those elements and ideas will be most readily accepted which hold out a promise of benefit to the acceptors. In the forced situation, the same general rule would hold true theoretically but would be largely inoperative in practical terms since *adoption* and not acceptance (implying volition and positive affect) is the purpose. Here again it seems reasonable to insist that the anthropologist, with all of his knowledge of the "delicate balance" of a culture—of what it may accept or reject—can be of small practical value to the administrator confronted with the job of foisting changes on a people "for their own" (or someone else's) sake.

Acceptance and the Local Hierarchy

Few—if any—of the present assistance programs are concerned with peoples in truly primitive, un-differentiated, and homogeneous communities. In terms of social organization, the aid-receiving countries are complex and hierarchically structured. Under these circumstances, introduced changes which benefit certain segments of the community may bring little or no improvement in the condition of others. If aid is extended by or under the aegis of the "Western democracies," it must be offered under the conditions imposed by their traditional and our Constitutional regard for property rights. Forcible expropriation can play no part in programs aimed at economic betterment. The Western nations cannot, as can the nations of the Soviet Bloc, *promise* land confiscation without compensation, followed by redistribution to the landless agricultural workers. In most of the "backward" world redistribution *after legal condemnation and purchase* with adequate compensation to the landlords is admittedly impracticable. This is one of the more serious dilemmas confronting the assistance programs of the West, and it is one which, we may note, gives to the West's Soviet Bloc competitors one of their most powerful propaganda weapons.

Hakim puts his finger on the significance of this fact when he speaks of the enthusiasm with which land redistribution changes would be accepted in agrarian cultures. ". . . The landless agricultural workers and share tenants of underdeveloped countries would not fail to welcome assistance to implement a program of land reform which would give them land and would set them up as independent farmers. In fact, the peasant class has more than once been won over by movements which make precisely such promises [sic]." An aid program which fails to take this kind of step, he adds, is only likely to "leave the majority of the people in poverty." If the aid program cannot include plans for immediate and basic land reforms it will do little good for the anthropologist to protest that there will be cultural resistance to the program or apathy on the part of the landless agriculturalist. He may know, as Linton cogently observes, that the benefits offered will not help those most in need of assistance, that the very social structure of the community must in some respects be altered before the aid will reach those most in need of it. But even if he knows this truth and suggests the consequences of ignoring it, it is hardly likely that the plan can be tailored to meet his objections.

Many colonial peoples and the sharecroppers and tenants who form a large part of the population in even independent "backward" nations know from sad experience that, every time their income increases, so do their taxes and rents. After each advertised economic advance they find themselves with very much the same standard of living they had before they underwent the trouble and uncertainty involved in practicing new techniques.

One also finds that the members of the average peasant community view any attempts to improve their economic condition which originate with their rulers with considerable and not unjustified suspicion. This holds whether the rulers are foreign imperialists or a native upper class. The peasant feels that anything which his rulers offer as a chance to improve his condition is probably more to their advantage than to his own. Since his rulers have always mulcted him in the past, he assumes that they will continue to mulct him in the future. (Linton)

Hakim sees the pattern as a "tendency of the Western powers ... to bolster up existing feudal and reactionary regimes rather than to help the progressive forces in opposition to them." He finds this situation paralleled closely by the programs of the "governments of ... advanced countries [which deal] with colonial and semi-colonial territories." For these "have sought to win over a small minority group or class, strengthen it in its domination over the people, and allow it to reap the benefits of economic development, while the majority of the people remain in poverty and degradation."

In these observations is revealed one of the many distressing but significant parallels between the "old imperialism" and the current assistance programs which are—perhaps not improperly—imbedded in considerations of a power-political nature. Under the old imperialism the agricultural laborer was exploited for the benefit of the imperial investor and his local agents. Under the existing patterns of aid, and without the basic land reforms that would be required to make them significantly different, he may continue to suffer the same kind or degree of exploitation. The very pattern of Western assistance insures the preservation of the socioeconomic *status quo*. To violate the status quo

and the present system of drastic exploitation which prevails so widely in much of the underdeveloped agrarian areas of the world would demand measures which are either financially infeasible or clearly contradictory to our concern for the sanctity of property. Thus, under the old imperialism and under the new assistance programs the picture for the more depressed segments of populations of "backward" areas continues to be a gloomy one. The role of the anthropological adviser must thus remain pretty much what it has been before—namely, that of helping the administrator "to make wise decisions" (Evans-Pritchard) but within the context of a broad policy over which he has no control and which clearly determines the larger cultural consequences of contact. The anthropologist may predict that complex cultures will be divided in their reaction to contact and assistance. Those who benefit may be happy to accept the aid. Those members of the same community who may not benefit may resist. In a certain sense, *this* is a far more dependable and predictable pattern of "resistance to culture change" than the more-frequently-referred-to conflict between acceptance of material and nonmaterial elements.

But what of fairly homogeneous societies which appear illogically to resist the introduction of changes calculated to improve their economic conditions? Isn't this kind of resistance, one is asked, good evidence for the assertion that cultures "normally resist change"? The charge, as Linton says, has often been levelled at "our own reservation Indians." He finds the evidence unconvincing.

Government experts will tell them how to breed cattle or to get better crops by scientific methods, but they will go on as they are. If one follows back the history of the dealings of our Indians with the United States Government, it is easy to understand the reason for such apathy. Tribe after tribe made a real effort to copy white ways when they were placed on reservations. They saw that the old life was ended and did their best to adapt. However, whenever a tribe got a communally-owned cattle herd which could be a valuable source of income, stockmen who wanted the range brought pressure in Washington, and the tribe suddenly found its herd sold and the money "put in trust." If a tribe developed an irrigation project and brought new lands under cultivation, presently an excuse would be found for expropriating this and moving the tribe to a still more submarginal territory. The Indians were frustrated and puzzled by changing government policies, in which the only consistent feature was that they always lost, and settled back into apathy and pauperism.

This kind of historical referrant would, it seems, give us a more satisfactory explanation of some of the forms of "cultural resistance to change" than such an assumption, let us say, as Laura Thompson's thesis of a "logico-aesthetic integration" whose delicate balance might be upset by change. It is, she says, to the preservation of this balance, somehow felt or understood by the people themselves, that they devote their energies when they fight off changes. Linton views the matter differently, tells us that many groups do not resist change but, on the contrary, appear to accept and even welcome it when it promises to bring them benefits.

Theoretical Orientation and Practical Aid

The question may now be asked whether, in view of the apparent differences in theoretical approach to the problem of culture change, certain anthropologists may be of more practical value in assistance programs than others. Is not the anthropologist who is acquainted with the facts of possible past frustrations, or with the different attitudes expressed or felt by the various groups or classes in a society, likely to be more useful to the administrator who is implementing a program already decided upon than the anthropologist who is wary of any change because he sees change itself as a threat to the stability and the balance of a culture? If the analysis made so far is at all valid, the answer must be a pessimistic and virtually unqualified no. To the anthropologist who advises caution and is worried about the effects of any change, the administrator must answer roughly that the ends are calculated to justify the means—and the ends are a complexly woven fabric of "improved living standards" and "practical diplomatic, strategic, political" goals in a time of tension and world crisis. And to the anthropologist who may stress differential class reaction to or desire for change, or who points to the past sins of industrialized nations as a clue to a generalized response of suspicion in the present, the administrator must offer the same answer and proceed in the same way to the same desired ends.

Conclusions

Speaking of the Island of Bali, Covarrubias says: ". . . the power of our civilization to penetrate can no longer be ignored. It would be futile to recommend measures to prevent the relentless march of Westernization; tourists can not be kept out, the needs of trade will not be restricted for sentimental reasons. . . . To advocate the unconditional preservation of their picturesque culture in the midst of modern civilization would be the equivalent of turning Bali into a living museum, putting the entire island into a glass case for the enjoyment of hordes of tourists."

The anthropologists who have assisted colonial administrators, and those who are presently engaged as advisers in uninational or multinational programs of assistance, have not been and are not being charged with the responsibility for stemming the penetration of "our civilization." On the contrary, their job under the old colonialism and under the new assistance programs is one of aiding in the "relentless march of Westernization." They have been asked to advise in order to facilitate that penetration which is, in one form or another, deemed inevitable or necessary. The aims of penetration under modern colonialism were clearly and unequivocally mercenary, and the means to achievement were patterned—in somewhat varying ways, it is true—along lines which seemed most likely to maximize these aims. The aims of contemporary assistance programs are in part altruistic, in part practical in the political as well as the economic sense. The patterns of distribution of current assistance programs reflect the prepotent significance of the political and economic considerations.

The anthropologist under colonialism as well as the anthropologist who assists in the conduct of aid programs advises on areas of cultural sensitivity and suggests which tactics may best insure achievement of the strategic goals of the administrator or the assistance mission. In both cases the grand strategy is imposed from above and the tactics are accommodated to the goals. If the anthropologist feels that he must explain his participation in either type endeavor, he may say that the programs are going forward anyway, and anything he can do to ease the "cultural shock" to the objects of penetration is ethically and morally justifiable. Since most anthropological workers in the colonial and "underdeveloped" vineyards are modest fellows, it may well be that this relatively minor aid is all that they would claim to provide.

But they must then, as Gluckman points out, be prepared to accept the full implications of their "minor" activities. Having identified themselves with the project, they have become identified with the goals of the project. I have tried to suggest what some of the less obvious correlates may be. Far more is involved, it seems to me, than simple easement of the "shock of accommodation." If, by their participation, the applied anthropologists are contributing in *any* measure to the achievement of the goals of colonial or assistance programs, they are contributing to one of the most profound cultural developments of our time. It is in this context, and in the context of the controlling cultural dynamics of which I spoke earlier, that they must evaluate their participation in and their contributions to such programs.

Until that distant day when the cultural interests of a world community may conceivably allow nonpolitical solutions of social and economic problems, these contributions will, I believe, have small influence over patterns of culture change in underdeveloped areas undergoing contact. Perhaps the best that the applied anthropologists—and the rest of us—may do between now and then would be to try to illuminate the very nature of those cultural processes which restrict the part played by the "scientist of man" on behalf of man in "backward" areas.

Guillermo Bonfil Batalla
Conservative Thought in Applied Anthropology: A Critique

In the following article, a Mexican anthropologist pinpoints the conservative and essentially ethnocentric assumptions which underlie much applied anthropology in Latin America—even, or perhaps especially, when carried out by "liberal" North Americans. The term "conservative" in his title refers to maintenance of the status quo: gradualism where change is inevitable, and suppression of overt conflict under any circumstances and at any cost, the last being a condition of the first two. His discussion reflects the deep concern of a social scientist who sees the vital problems of his people intellectualized rather than confronted, treated symptomatically rather than in terms of underlying causes. It is the anguished analysis of one who recognizes the total failure of foreign anthropologists— who have the money, time, and influence to conduct research which might affect policy—to exercise the sociological imagination, that is, to see the relationship between the troubles of living people and the social, economic, and political circumstances which nurture and perpetuate them.

Most of the people in Latin American countries live in an actual state of unrest which frequently manifests itself in outbursts of violence. This is a reflection, without doubt, of a growing demand from large sectors of the population to achieve a rapid and complete satisfaction of their established needs, as well as of the new ones which arise from contact with forms of modern urban life. Even with national and international efforts undertaken to raise the living standards of millions of Latin Americans, our region continues to be one of the poorest in the world. This fact cannot be ignored by those who work applying social science knowledge to the integral development of our countries. Do the social sciences, particularly anthropology, possess the theoretical equipment

"Conservative Thought in Applied Anthropology: A Critique" by Guillermo Bonfil Batalla, translated by Lucy M. Cohen, Ph.D., from *Human Organization* (Vol. 25, No. 2, 1966). Reproduced by the permission of the Society for Applied Anthropology and the authors.

necessary to understand Latin American problems and to propose effective solutions for them? Undoubtedly the social sciences are indeed prepared to contribute their part in such tasks, even though, of course, the contribution of other disciplines is needed.

Now then, the body of theory used in applied anthropology possesses a conservative trend of thought, whose influence is wide and manifest. In my opinion, this current not only prevents the proposal of effective solutions, but it also represents a tendency which goes against the national interests of our countries.

The characterization of this conservative thought in anthropology is a decisive and inevitable task which has been fruitfully undertaken by various investigators. The ideas outlined in this paper are intended only to stimulate the already proposed discussion. I shall attempt to present briefly but not exhaustively some of the fundamental theoretical premises of this conservative tendency. For such purposes I have carefully analyzed a number of studies in applied anthropology, particularly those which refer to problems of nutrition and public health in Latin America. Even though the topic for which I have analyzed bibliography is a very specific one, I believe that the conclusions of this analysis can be validly applied in their essence to other areas in which attempts have been made to apply anthropology....

To speak of the existence of a conservative trend of thought does not necessarily imply that a group of anthropologists shares belief in the complete set of premises which characterizes that tendency; it is rather, that the conservative point of view in the theory of applied anthropology has influenced the thought of many anthropologists to a greater or lesser degree. The central problem, therefore, is not who are the conservative anthropologists, but, what are the conservative ideas of anthropologists.

In broad terms, the conservative trend in applied anthropology may be characterized by accepting the following postulates, not listed in hierarchical order:

First: A heavy psychological emphasis, not only in the selection of problems for study, but in the interpretation of research results. In the selection of topics for study, one need only review the bibliographies, on problems of public health, and the essays which classify anthropological studies on the subject, such as those prepared by Caudill in 1953 and by Polgar in 1962, as evidence that most of them refer to subjects such as ideas and beliefs on health and illness; concepts and rationalizations about nutrition; stereotypes carried by the community about the personnel in charge of sanitation programs; communication problems derived from differences in cultural traditions, and other subjects. The need and value of such studies is unquestionable; but it is more important still to point out the fact that greater attention has been paid to these subjects than to the study of basic causes of public health and malnutrition problems in our countries. In general, the problems studied have secondary importance as causal elements; that is, they are not primary factors in the alarming state of chronic malnutrition and poor health which affects most of the people in Latin America. At least in many cases, the selection of topics responds to a trend which interprets social realities in purely or largely psychological terms. The phenomenon is well known and it has been consistently criticized. It may be sufficiently illustrated with Dr. George Foster's observations:

It appears as if the most important *categories of culture that should be more or less completely understood to carry out successful health and hygiene programs are* local ideas *about health, welfare, illness, their causes and treatment.* [author's italics.]

If field materials are interpreted according to Dr. Foster's proposal, then the basic structure of a society, the low levels of technology, and the inadequate and unjust social organization are factors which take second place in the explanation of the problems that are supposed to be analyzed. The solutions that might be proposed with the above-mentioned study emphasis will not produce the improvement of life conditions, because they do not suggest any alterations in the structures that have determined their existence. In summary, the psychological manifestations of a problem have been taken as its causes.

Second: Another basic postulate of the conservative trend of thought in applied anthropology is the almost axiomatic affirmation that the main function of the anthropologist is to avoid rapid changes, because of the resulting maladjustments and conflicts which frequently produce social and cultural "disorganization." This affirmation implicitly carries with it the idea that all societies present resistance to directed changes; to avoid conflict, anthropologists must try to promote development and general welfare programs which adjust to the local culture, respecting the established social structure, the value systems and the norms of behavior of the population to which programs are directed. Consequently, the anthropologist takes the position of favoring slow and long-term changes, he promotes small and partial reforms, and consequently rejects and condemns radical changes which are the only ones that affect the basic institutional structures of a society. At times this fear of radical change goes to such an extreme that the anthropologist pays little attention to the fundamental processes of social dynamics. Thus, Dr. Richard N. Adams writes:

Basically, there are two different types of cultural changes: the first is a slow, gradual and evolutionary type . . . ; the other is rapid and revolutionary, caused by the efforts of societal members who wish to produce immediate alterations, of far reaching consequences. Applied anthropology can and must focus concern, principally on the first of these types of change.

With such an emphasis, the knowledge proper to the field of applied anthropology is limited and mutilated.

Third: One must now refer to the form in which the concept of cultural relativism is usually handled in applied anthropology. The obvious existence of various value systems, of differing cultural alternatives to satisfy the same needs, frequently leads to a theoretical position that rejects the possibility of pronouncing value judgments in relation to societies and cultures. Edwin Smith points out:

As men and women we may have our opinions about the justice or injustice of certain acts and attitudes, but anthropology as such can pronounce no judgment, for to do so is to invade the province of philosophy and ethics. If anthropology is to judge and guide it must have a conception of what constitutes the perfect society; and since it is debarred from having ideals it cannot judge, cannot guide, and cannot talk about progress.

When the meaning of cultural relativism is taken to such extremes, one enters into a basic contradiction with the very claim of applying anthropological science to the solution of human problems. That is, the *raison d'être* of applied anthropology is denied.

I believe that lack of historical focus is one of the reasons for adopting such a mistaken position. Knowledge of social and cultural history is, in my opinion, an absolute requirement for any attempt to apply anthropology. The study of history gives origin to outlines, patterns, and laws of changes which should be used in the promotion of development programs.

Fourth: The multiple causation theory, according to which all phenomena are a product of countless small and diverse causes, is another common postulate of this trend. C. Wright Mills aptly concludes that according to this position, as long as it is impossible to know all the causes of a phenomenon, the anthropologist must confine himself to the proposal of small modifications of little consequence. On the other hand, this postulate points to the impossibility of enunciating general societal laws; the function of the anthropologist thus reduces itself to the mere description of each particular case. Richard N. Adams is quite clear in this respect when he states:

One thing is to make generalizations in a monograph or article for discussion among colleagues, and it is quite a different matter to make such generalizations when these are to be used as a basis for the action in a specific region and have real effect on the way of life of the people inhabiting such an area. Applied work deals directly with specifics; in opposition to science, it does not formulate generalizations.

Anthropologists who think in this form emphasize the necessity for making careful research in each particular case, because, according to Dr. Foster's assertion, "there are no two groups of population with the same needs." It is an opinion that, on the other hand, increases our employment possibilities. By this path, one unavoidably arrives at a denial of science itself, of which one characteristic and specific function is, precisely, to find regularities in order to establish general laws.

In passing, we shall mention another postulate, very much related to the above-mentioned: Research in applied anthropology is usually undertaken at the community level, and on many occasions, only one sector of the community is studied; so, because according to the multiple causation theory it is impossible to generalize, the results obtained have validity only for the small sector of the population that the anthropologist studies directly.

On the other hand, as Prof. Ricardo Pozas has

pointed out, focus on the community as the unit of study has led, on occasions, to underrating the importance of relations maintained by a community with external influences. That tendency is clearly seen in many monographs with an "Indianist" orientation, which consider indigenous communities as isolated societies; outside the spheres of national society; we believe that, at least in many cases, such a stand is erroneous. Essentially, communities must be understood within a wider framework: at regional, national, and in certain cases, international levels (as in the case of the community of Sudzal, whose basic crop, sisal, is assigned in its totality to the international market). The relevance of such a problem cannot be underestimated, particularly by the growing importance given to community development programs.

According to this conservative trend, the problems of marginal societies with traditional culture have their origin in the very existence of just these kinds of societies. This is, in my opinion, an illogical point of view, a naive one at best, because it is exactly the existence or survival of these groups that needs to be explained. In focusing on the problem, it is completely useless to apply conservative assumptions; it would be better to study similar situations with the aid of some other analytic concepts like the "internal colonialism" proposed by Dr. González Casanova.

Fifth: Almost all the social problems in the so-called underdeveloped countries are related in a direct and fundamental manner with low levels of income. These in turn are the result of a type of social organization that prevents an increase in productivity at the necessary pace, and also conditions an unequal distribution of wealth. Such a fact cannot be reasonably doubted. However, most anthropological investigations connected with development and welfare programs seem to consider level of income as a phenomenon that can be modified only in a slow and long-term manner. Anthropologists who like to call themselves realists and practical frequently attempt to raise levels of living without touching the institutional structures that cause and permit the existence of large numbers of people who grow more impoverished day-by-day. In short, this refers to an "anthropology of poverty": attempts are made to modify but not to eradicate conditions which give rise to poverty.

Sixth: Even though one could still point to other theoretical premises that characterize this conser-vative trend in applied anthropology, I shall mention only one more: the consideration that diffusion is the most important, and for some, the only process which must be brought to play in efforts to promote change in the communities under study. This tendency may possibly be related to the fact that many investigations have been undertaken in connection with international assistance projects, in which, one naturally searches for the best way of applying external aid. In few cases is there an establishment of goals to accelerate the internal dynamics of the societies studied. The problems which preoccupy anthropologists are related with greatest frequency to the action forms needed so that the population receiving the aid program benefits may use it profitably. The intention is a valid one; but by no means may it be considered as a statement of the whole problem.

In summary, we have presented in broad terms the theoretical postulates which characterize the trend of conservative thought within applied anthropology. I must repeat that I do not conceive this trend as a school of thought that has thus far identified its total body of postulates with great clarity. Nevertheless, it is a trend followed to a greater or lesser extent by a number of anthropologists; some only hold implicitly or explicitly to one of the above mentioned postulates, and at times, even reject the rest. Others orient their professional activity closely following the above-outlined model, and separating from it only fortuitously.

Now then, in my opinion, the realities of the countries usually called underdeveloped, like those of Latin America, require that the anthropologist interested in the application of this science separate himself consciously from this conservative trend. The type of applied anthropology required by our countries must begin with premises which are very different from the ones we have singled out. The magnitude of the problem with which we are faced and the scarcity of our resources place us in a situation far different from that of wealthy and highly industrialized nations, like the United States of America. We need to establish hierarchies for our problems; we cannot permit ourselves the luxury of turning our efforts to the acquisition of knowledge about inconsequential aspects of problems. Thus, as we do not believe that our poverty has a psychological origin, nor that it results from the ideas and images peculiar to our cultural tradition, nor that our basic problems can be explained by "deficiencies in channels of communications"; so, we do not believe that studies on these themes will give us the knowledge that we fundamentally need to face our problems.

These are not opportune times to deceive ourselves into thinking that efforts should be limited to the promotion of small changes, shielding ourselves with the fear that radical changes will produce disorganization. On the contrary, we believe that it is the task of the anthropologist to point to the very frequent uselessness of timid development programs, and that it is also his task to demonstrate with scientific rigor the need to carry out radical changes, that is, changes which get to the root of the problems themselves. Sometimes it looks as if those who work along the road of slow evolution intend to achieve only minimal changes, so that the situation continues to be substantially the same; this is, in other words, *to change what is necessary so that things remain the same.* Those who act according to such a point of view may honestly believe that their work is useful and transforming; however, they have in fact aligned themselves with the conservative elements who oppose the structural transformations that cannot be postponed in our countries.

The Latin American anthropologist needs to learn to work well and rapidly. In Mexico there are more than 100,000 localities; I do not believe that any locality wants to be the last studied by anthropologists, so that it may then receive scientifically dosed attention. If we are not capable of generalizing and proposing efficiently and uniformly applied measures, then we must recognize that our discipline is not prepared to respond to the pressing actual needs of our countries.

To state that science is universal is only part of the truth, because science is also an institution and a cumulative tradition, and, after all, a social product; as such, it necessarily reflects in some way the conditions, values, and orientations of the society that produces it. To date, the theory of applied anthropology has been one of the items imported into the underdeveloped countries—an imported item, as many others. We receive from producing countries (such as the United States, England, France, and other European nations) many well-elaborated theoretical postulates, some of them perfectly adjusted to our reality and our needs; but others are infused with a different spirit, foreign to our interest and on occasions, decidedly contrary to them. This is the conservative thought, before which there must arise a dynamic and progressive conception of applied anthropology, whose proposals correspond to the deep and urgent needs of Latin America and the rest of the impoverished and backward areas.

Others before me have discussed these subjects with greater authority and with better documentation, such as Dr. R. A. Manners, when he studied the influence of political interest in foreign aid programs of the United States, or Dr. Max Gluckman, as he critically analyzed the applied anthropology proposed by Malinowski, in the light of British colonial interests. After them, little can be added; however, I have found myself in the need to do so, because in addition to my responsibility and interest as an anthropologist, I have the responsibilities and sentiments of a Latin American.

Vine Deloria, Jr.
Custer Died for Your Sins

American anthropologists have devoted more attention to the Indians of the United States than to any other people. Indeed, the discipline virtually owes its existence in this country to such studies. As a result, the anthropologist is a familiar figure to many American Indians. It has been said, for example, that the average Navajo household comprises a wife, husband, three children, and an anthropologist. Only recently has the response of the native Americans to this situation been communicated to the outside world.

The following selection, later expanded into a book, is the best-known and among the most vehement of these responses. Its author is an American Indian. While he caricatures anthropologists and their wives in a way many would find unjust, and though he overlooks both the sincere and selfless efforts some have made on behalf of the American Indian and the trust and respect many have earned from those among whom they worked, he nevertheless makes important points that have been seconded by many Indians and by a good many anthropologists as well. The similarity of his response to those of Third World peoples on other continents (such as Bonfil Batalla's article on Latin America) will become clearer as you read other selections in this section, especially Challenor on black Africa, and Saberwal on India. Deloria's criticism of the basic assumptions of applied anthropologists is not unlike Bonfil Batalla's of North American anthropologists working in Latin America. This selection also emphasizes the dilemma of all minority peoples and those who deal with them: whether assimilation or the maintenance of their ethnic identity and of cultural pluralism are to be the goals, and how either might least traumatically be achieved. Anthropologists may resent, but they cannot ignore, Deloria's charges.

Into each life, it is said, some rain must fall. Some people have bad horoscopes; others take tips on the stock market. McNamara created the TFX and the Edsel. American politics has George Wallace. But Indians have been cursed above all other people in history. Indians have anthropologists.

Every summer when school is out, a stream of immigrants heads into Indian country. The Oregon Trail was never as heavily populated as Route 66 and Highway 18 in the summertime. From every rock and cranny in the East, *they* emerge, as if responding to some primeval migratory longing, and flock to the reservations. They are the anthropologists—the most prominent members of the scholarly community that infests the land of the free and the homes of the braves. Their origin is a mystery hidden in the historical mists. Indians are certain that all ancient societies of the Near East had anthropologists at one time, because all those societies are now defunct. They are equally certain that Columbus brought anthropologists on his ships when he came to the New World. How else could he have made so many wrong deductions about where he was? While their origins are uncertain, anthropologists can readily be identified on the reservations. Go into any crowd of people.

Pick out a tall, gaunt white man wearing Bermuda shorts, a World War Two Army Air Corps flying jacket, an Australian bush hat and tennis shoes and packing a large knapsack incorrectly strapped on his back. He will invariably have a thin, sexy wife with stringy hair, an IQ of 191 and a vocabulary in which even the prepositions have 11 syllables. And he usually has a camera, tape recorder, telescope, and life jacket all hanging from his elongated frame.

This odd creature comes to Indian reservations to make *observations*. During the winter, these observations will become books by which future anthropologists will be trained, so that they can come out to reservations years from now and verify the observations in more books, summaries of which then appear in the scholarly journals and serve as a catalyst to inspire yet other anthropologists to make the great pilgrimage the following summer. And so on.

The summaries, meanwhile, are condensed. Some condensations are sent to Government agencies as reports justifying the previous summer's research. Others are sent to foundations, in an effort to finance the following summer's expedition West. The reports are spread through the Government agencies and foundations all winter. The only problem is that no one has time to read them. So $5000-a-year secretaries are assigned to decode them. Since these secretaries cannot comprehend complex theories, they reduce the reports to the best slogans possible. The slogans become conference themes in the early spring, when the anthropological expeditions are being planned. They then turn into battle cries of opposing groups of anthropologists who chance to meet on the reservations the following summer.

Each summer there is a new battle cry, which inspires new insights into the nature of the "Indian problem." One summer Indians will be greeted with the joyful cry "Indians are bilingual!" The following summer this great truth will be expanded to "Indians are not only bilingual, they are *bicultural*!" Biculturality creates great problems for the opposing anthropological camp. For two summers, they have been bested in sloganeering and their funds are running low. So the opposing school of thought breaks into the clear faster than Gale

Sayers. "Indians," the losing anthros cry, "are a *folk* people!" The tide of battle turns and a balance, so dearly sought by Mother Nature, is finally achieved. Thus go the anthropological wars, testing whether this school or that school can long endure. The battlefields, unfortunately, are the lives of Indian people.

The anthro is usually devoted to *pure research.* A 1969 thesis restating a proposition of 1773, complete with footnotes to all material published between 1773 and 1969, is pure research. There are, however, anthropologists who are not clever at collecting footnotes. They depend on their field observations and write long, adventurous narratives in which their personal observations are used to verify their suspicions. Their reports, books and articles are called *applied research.* The difference, then, between pure and applied research is primarily one of footnotes. Pure has many footnotes, applied has few footnotes. Relevancy to subject matter is not discussed in polite company.

Anthropologists came to Indian country only after the tribes had agreed to live on reservations and had given up their warlike ways. Had the tribes been given a choice of fighting the cavalry or the anthropologists, there is little doubt as to who they would have chosen. In a crisis situation, men always attack the biggest threat to their existence. A warrior killed in battle could always go to the happy hunting grounds. But where does an Indian laid low by an anthro go? To the library?

The fundamental thesis of the anthropologist is that people are objects for observation. It then follows that people are considered objects for experimentation, for manipulation, and for eventual extinction. The anthropologist thus furnishes the justification for treating Indian people like so many chessmen, available for anyone to play with. The mass production of useless knowledge by anthropologists attempting to capture real Indians in a network of theories has contributed substantially to the invisibility of Indian people today. After all, who can believe in the actual existence of a food-gathering berrypicking, seminomadic, fire-worshiping, high-plains-and-mountain-dwelling, horse-riding, canoe-toting, bead-using, pottery-making, ribbon-coveting, wickiup-sheltered people who began flourishing when Alfred Frump mentioned them in 1803 in *Our Feathered Friends*?

Not even Indians can see themselves as this type of creature—who, to anthropologists, is the "real" Indian. Indian people begin to feel that they are merely shadows of a mythical super-Indian. Many Indians, in fact, have come to parrot the ideas of anthropologists, because it appears that they know everything about Indian communities. Thus, many ideas that pass for Indian thinking are in reality theories originally advanced by anthropologists and echoed by Indian people in an attempt to communicate the real situation. Many anthros reinforce this sense of inadequacy in order to further influence the Indian people.

Since 1955, there have been a number of workshops conducted in Indian country as a device for training "young Indian leaders." Churches, white Indian-interest groups, colleges, and, finally, poverty programs have each gone the workshop route as the most feasible means for introducing new ideas to younger Indians, so as to create leaders. The tragic nature of the workshops is apparent when one examines their history. One core group of anthropologists has institutionalized the workshop and the courses taught in it. Trudging valiantly from workshop to workshop, from state to state, college to college, tribe to tribe, these noble spirits have served as the catalyst for the creation of workshops that are identical in purpose and content and often in the student-body itself.

The anthropological message to young Indians has not varied a jot or a tittle in ten years. It is the same message these anthros learned as fuzzy-cheeked graduate students in the post-War years—Indians are a folk people, whites are an urban people, and never the twain shall meet. Derived from this basic premise are all the other sterling insights: Indians are between two cultures, Indians are bicultural, Indians have lost their identity, and Indians are warriors. These theories, propounded every year with deadening regularity and an overtone of Sinaitic authority, have become a major mental block in the development of young Indian people. For these slogans have come to be excuses for Indian failures. They are crutches by which young Indians have avoided the arduous task of thinking out the implications of the status of Indian people in the modern world.

If there is one single cause that has importance today for Indian people, it is tribalism. Against all odds, Indians have retained title to some 53,000,000 acres of land, worth about three and a half billion dollars. Approximately half of the country's 1,000,000 Indians relate meaningfully to this land, either by living and working on it or by frequently visiting it. If Indians fully recaptured the idea that they are tribes communally in possession of this land, they would realize that they are not truly impoverished. But the creation of modern tribalism has been stifled by a ready acceptance of the Indians-are-a-folk-people premise of the anthropologists. This premise implies a drastic split between folk and urban cultures, in which the folk peoples have two prime characteristics: They dance and they are desperately poor. Creative thought in Indian affairs has not, therefore, come from the younger Indians who have grown up reading and talking to anthropologists. Rather, it has come from the older generation that believes in tribalism—and that the youngsters mistakenly insist has been brainwashed by Government schools.

Because other groups have been spurred on by their younger generations, Indians have come to believe that, through education, a new generation of leaders will arise to solve the pressing contemporary problems. Tribal leaders have been taught to accept this thesis by the scholarly community in its annual invasion of the reservations. Bureau of Indian Affairs educators harp continuously on this theme. Wherever authority raises its head in Indian country, this thesis is its message. The facts prove the opposite, however. Relatively untouched by anthropologists, educators, and scholars are the Apache tribes of the Southwest. The Mescalero, San Carlos, White Mountain, and Jicarilla Apaches have very few young people in college, compared with other tribes. They have even fewer people in the annual workshop orgy during the summers. If ever there was a distinction between folk and urban, this group of Indians characterizes it.

The Apaches see themselves, however, as neither folk nor urban but *tribal*. There is little sense of a lost identity. Apaches could not care less about the anthropological dilemmas that worry other tribes. Instead, they continue to work on massive plans for development that they themselves have created. Tribal identity is assumed, not defined, by these reservation people. Freedom to choose from a wide variety of paths of progress is a characteristic of the Apaches; they don't worry about what type of Indianism is real. Above all, they cannot be ego-fed by abstract theories and, hence, unwittingly manipulated.

With many young people from other tribes, the situation is quite different. Some young Indians attend workshops over and over again. Folk theories pronounced by authoritative anthropologists become opportunities to escape responsibility. If, by definition, the Indian is hopelessly caught between two cultures, why struggle? Why not blame all one's lack of success on this tremendous gulf between two opposing cultures? Workshops have become, therefore, summer retreats for nonthought rather than strategy sessions for leadership. Therein lies the Indian's sin against the anthropologist. Only those anthropologists who appear to boost Indian ego and expound theories dear to the hearts of workshop Indians are invited to teach at workshops. They become human recordings of social confusion and are played and replayed each summer, to the delight of a people who refuse to move on into the real world.

The workshop anthro is thus a unique creature, partially self-created and partially supported by the refusal of Indian young people to consider their problems in their own context. The normal process of maturing has been confused with cultural difference. So maturation is cast aside in favor of cult recitation of great truths that appear to explain the immaturity of young people.

While the anthro is thus, in a sense, the victim of the Indians, he should, nevertheless, recognize the role he has been asked to play and refuse to play it. Instead, the temptation to appear relevant to a generation of young Indians has clouded his sense of proportion. Workshop anthros often ask Indians of tender age to give their authoritative answers to problems that an entire generation of Indians is just now beginning to solve. Where the answer to reservation health problems may be adequate housing in areas where there has never been adequate housing, young Indians are shaped in their thinking processes to consider vague doctrines on the nature of man and his society.

It is preposterous that a teen-aged Indian should become an instant authority, equal in status to the Ph.D. interrogating him. Yet the very human desire is to play that game every summer, for the status acquired in the game is heady. And since answers can be given only in the vocabulary created by the Ph.D., the entire leadership-training process internalizes itself and has no outlet beyond the immediate group. Real problems, superimposed on the ordinary problems of maturing, thus become insoluble burdens that crush people of great leadership potential.

Let us take some specific examples. One workshop discussed the thesis that Indians were in a terrible crisis. They were, in the words of friendly anthro guides, "between two worlds." People between two worlds, the students were told, "drank." For the anthropologist, it was a valid explanation of drinking on the reservation. For the young Indians, it was an authoritative definition of their role as Indians. Real Indians, they began to think, drank; and their task was to become real Indians, for only in that way could they re-create the glories of the past. So they *drank*. I've lost some good friends who drank too much.

Abstract theories create abstract action. Lumping together the variety of tribal problems and seeking the demonic principle at work that is destroying Indian people may be intellectually satisfying, but it does not change the situation. By concentrating on great abstractions, anthropologists have unintentionally removed many young Indians from the world of real problems to the lands of make-believe.

As an example of a real problem, the Pyramid Lake Paiutes and the Gila River Pima and Maricopa are poor because they have been systematically cheated out of their water rights, and on desert reservations, water is the single most important factor in life. No matter how many worlds Indians straddle, the Plains Indians have an inadequate land base that continues to shrink because of land sales. Straddling worlds is irrelevant to straddling small pieces of land and trying to earn a living.

Along the Missouri River, the Sioux used to live in comparative peace and harmony. Although land allotments were small, families were able to achieve a fair standard of living through a combination of gardening and livestock raising and supplemental work. Little cash income was required, because the basic necessities of food, shelter, and community life were provided. After World War Two, anthropologists came to call. They were horrified that the Indians didn't carry on their old customs, such as dancing, feasts, and giveaways. In fact, the people did keep up a substantial number of customs, but they had been transposed into church gatherings, participation in the county fairs, and tribal celebrations, particularly fairs and rodeos. The people did Indian dances. But they didn't do them all the time.

Suddenly, the Sioux were presented with an authority figure who bemoaned the fact that whenever he visited the reservations, the Sioux were not out dancing in the manner of their ancestors. Today, the summers are taken up with one great orgy of dancing and celebrating, as each small community of Indians sponsors a weekend powwow for the people in the surrounding communities. Gone are the little gardens that used to provide fresh vegetables in the summer and canned goods in the winter. Gone are the chickens that provided eggs and Sunday dinners. In the winter, the situation becomes critical for families who spent the summer dancing. While the poverty programs have done much to counteract the situation, few Indians recognize that the condition was artificial from start to finish. The people were innocently led astray, and even the anthropologists did not realize what had happened.

One example: The Oglala Sioux are perhaps the most well known of the Sioux bands. Among their past leaders were Red Cloud, the only Indian who ever defeated the United States in a war, and Crazy Horse, most revered of the Sioux war chiefs. The Oglala were, and perhaps still are, the meanest group of Indians ever assembled. They would take after a cavalry troop just to see if their bowstrings were taut enough. When they had settled on the reservation, the Oglala made a fairly smooth transition to the new life. They had good herds of cattle, they settled along the numerous creeks that cross the reservation, and they created a very strong community spirit. The Episcopalians and the Roman Catholics had the missionary franchise on the reservation and the tribe was pretty evenly split between the two. In the Episcopal Church, at least, the congregations were fairly self-governing and stable.

But over the years, the Oglala Sioux have had a number of problems. Their population has grown faster than their means of support. The Government allowed white farmers to come into the eastern part of the reservation and create a county, with the best farmlands owned or operated by whites. The reservation was allotted—taken out of the collective hands of the tribe and parceled out to individuals—and when ownership became too complicated, control of the land passed out of Indian hands. The Government displaced a number of families during World War Two by taking a part of the reservation for use as a bombing range to train crews for combat. Only last year was this land returned to tribal and individual use.

The tribe became a favorite subject for anthropological study quite early, because of its romantic past. Theories arose attempting to explain the apparent lack of progress of the Oglala Sioux. The true issue—white control of the reservation—was overlooked completely. Instead, every conceivable intangible cultural distinction was used to explain the lack of economic, social, and educational progress of a people who were, to all intents and purposes, absentee landlords because of the Government policy of leasing their lands to whites.

One study advanced the startling proposition that Indians with many cattle were, on the average, better off than Indians without cattle. Cattle Indians, it seems, had more capital and income than did noncattle Indians. Surprise! The study had innumerable charts and graphs that demonstrated this great truth beyond the doubt of a reasonably prudent man. Studies of this type were common but unexciting. They lacked that certain flair of insight so beloved by anthropologists. Then one day a famous anthropologist advanced the theory, probably valid at the time and in the manner in which he advanced it, that the Oglala were "warriors without weapons."

The chase was on. Before the ink had dried on the scholarly journals, anthropologists from every library stack in the nation converged on the Oglala Sioux to test this new theory. Outfitting anthropological expeditions became the number-one industry of the small off-reservation Nebraska towns south of Pine Ridge. Surely, supplying the Third Crusade to the Holy Land was a minor feat compared with the task of keeping the anthropologists at Pine Ridge.

Every conceivable difference between the Oglala Sioux and the folks at Bar Harbor was attributed to the quaint warrior tradition of the Oglala Sioux. From lack of roads to unshined shoes, Sioux problems were generated, so the anthros discovered, by the refusal of the white man to recognize the great desire of the Oglala to go to war. Why expect an Oglala to become a small businessman, when he was only waiting for that wagon train to come around the bend? The very real and human problems of the reservation were considered to be merely by-products of the failure of a warrior people to become domesticated. The fairly respectable thesis of past exploits in war, perhaps romanticized for morale purposes, became a

spiritual force all its own. Some Indians, in a tongue-in-cheek manner for which Indians are justly famous, suggested that a subsidized wagon train be run through the reservation each morning at nine o'clock and the reservation people paid a minimum wage for attacking it.

By outlining this problem, I am not deriding the Sioux. I lived on that reservation for 18 years and know many of the problems from which it suffers. How, I ask, can the Oglala Sioux make any headway in education when their lack of education is ascribed to a desire to go to war? Would not, perhaps, an incredibly low per-capita income, virtually nonexistent housing, extremely inadequate roads, and domination by white farmers and ranchers make some difference? If the little Sioux boy or girl had no breakfast, had to walk miles to a small school, and had no decent clothes nor place to study in a one-room log cabin, should the level of education be comparable with that of Scarsdale High?

What use would roads, houses, schools, businesses, and income be to a people who, everyone expected, would soon depart on the warpath? I would submit that a great deal of the lack of progress at Pine Ridge is occasioned by people who believe they are helping the Oglala when they insist on seeing, in the life of the people of that reservation, only those things they want to see. Real problems and real people become invisible before the great romantic and nonsensical notion that the Sioux yearn for the days of Crazy Horse and Red Cloud and will do nothing until those days return.

The question of the Oglala Sioux is one that plagues every Indian tribe in the nation, if it will closely examine itself. Tribes have been defined; the definition has been completely explored; test scores have been advanced promoting and deriding the thesis; and, finally, the conclusion has been reached: Indians must be redefined in terms that white men will accept, even if that means re-Indianizing them according to the white man's idea of what they were like in the past and should logically become in the future.

What, I ask, would a school board in Moline, Illinois—or Skokie, even—do if the scholarly community tried to reorient its educational system to conform with outmoded ideas of Sweden in the glory days of Gustavus Adolphus? Would they be expected to sing "*Ein' feste Burg*" and charge out of the mists at the Roman Catholics to save the Reformation every morning as school began? Or the Irish—would they submit to a group of Indians coming to Boston and telling them to dress in green and hunt leprechauns?

Consider the implications of theories put forward to solve the problem of poverty among the blacks. Several years ago, the word went forth that black poverty was due to the disintegration of the black family, that the black father no longer had a prominent place in the home. How incredibly shortsighted that thesis was. How typically Anglo-Saxon! How in the world could there have been a black family if people were sold like cattle for 200 years, if there were large plantations that served merely as farms to breed more slaves, if white owners systematically ravaged black women? When did the black family unit ever become integrated? Herein lies a trap into which many Americans have fallen: Once a problem is defined and understood by a significant number of people who have some relation to it, the fallacy goes, the problem ceases to exist. The rest of America had better beware of having quaint mores that attract anthropologists, or it will soon become a victim of the conceptual prison into which blacks and Indians, among others, have been thrown. One day you may find yourself cataloged—perhaps as a credit-card-carrying, turnpike-commuting, condominium-dwelling, fraternity-joining, church-going, sports-watching, time-purchase-buying, television-watching, magazine-subscribing, politically inert transmigrated urbanite who, through the phenomenon of the second car and the shopping center, has become a golf-playing, wife-swapping, etc., etc., etc., suburbanite. Or have you already been characterized—and caricatured—in ways that struck you as absurd? If so, you will understand what has been happening to Indians for a long, long time.

In defense of the anthropologists, it must be recognized that those who do not publish perish. Those who do not bring in a substantial sum of research money soon slide down the scale of university approval. What university is not equally balanced between the actual education of its students and a multitude of small bureaus, projects, institutes, and programs that are designed to harvest grants for the university?

The effect of anthropologists on Indians should be clear. Compilation of useless knowledge for knowledge's sake should be utterly rejected by the Indian people. We should not be objects of observation for those who do nothing to help us. During the critical days of 1954, when the Senate was pushing for termination of all Indian rights, not one scholar, anthropologist, sociologist, historian, or economist came forward to support the tribes against the detrimental policy. Why didn't the academic community march to the side of the tribes? Certainly the past few years have shown how much influence academe can exert when it feels compelled to enlist in a cause. Is Vietnam any more crucial to the moral stance of America than the great debt owed to the Indian tribes?

Perhaps we should suspect the motives of members of the academic community. They have the Indian field well defined and under control. Their concern is not the ultimate policy that will affect the Indian people, but merely the creation of new slogans and doctrines by which they can climb the university totem pole. Reduction of people to statistics for purposes of observation appears to be inconsequential to the anthropologist when compared with the immediate benefits he can derive —the acquisition of further prestige and the chance to appear as the high priest of American society, orienting and manipulating to his heart's desire.

Roger Jourdain, chairman of the Red Lake Chippewa tribe of Minnesota, casually had the anthropologists escorted from his reservation a couple of years ago. This was the tip of the iceberg. If only more Indians had the insight of Jourdain. Why should we continue to provide private zoos for anthropologists? Why should tribes have to compete with scholars for funds, when their scholarly productions are so useless and irrelevant to life?

Several years ago, an anthropologist stated that over a period of some 20 years he had spent, from all sources, close to $10,000,000 studying a tribe of fewer than 1000 people. Imagine what that amount of money would have meant to that group of people had it been invested in buildings and businesses. There would have been no problems to study.

I sometimes think that Indian tribes could improve relations between themselves and the anthropologists by adopting the following policy: Each anthro desiring to study a tribe should be made to apply to the tribal council for permission to do his study. He would be given such permission only if he raised as a contribution to the tribal budget an amount of money equal to the amount he proposed to spend on his study. Anthropologists would thus become productive members of Indian society, instead of ideological vultures.

This proposal was discussed at one time in Indian circles. It blew no small number of anthro minds. Irrational shrieks of "academic freedom" rose like rockets from launching pads. The very idea of putting a tax on useless information was intolerable to the anthropologists we talked with. But the question is very simple. Are the anthros concerned about freedom—or license? Academic freedom certainly does not imply that one group of people has to become chessmen for another group of people. Why should Indian communities be subjected to prying non-Indians any more than other communities? Should any group have a franchise to stick its nose into someone else's business?

I don't think my proposal ever will be accepted. It contradicts the anthropologists' self-image much too strongly. What is more likely is that Indians will continue to allow their communities to be turned inside out until they come to realize the damage that is being done to them. Then they will seal up the reservations and no further knowledge—useless or otherwise—will be created. This may be the best course. Once, at a Congressional hearing, someone asked Alex Chasing Hawk, a council member of the Cheyenne Sioux for 30 years, "Just what do you Indians want?" Alex replied, "A leave-us-alone law."

The primary goal and need of Indians today is not for someone to study us, feel sorry for us, identify with us, or claim descent from Pocahontas to make us feel better. Nor do we need to be classified as semiwhite and have programs made to bleach us further. Nor do we need further studies to see if we are "feasible." We need, instead, a new policy from Congress that acknowledges our intelligence, and our dignity.

In its simplest form, such a policy would give a tribe the amount of money now being spent in the area on Federal schools and other services. With this block grant, the tribe itself would communally establish and run its own schools and hospitals and police and fire departments—and, in time, its own income-producing endeavors, whether in industry or agriculture. The tribe would not be taxed until enough capital had accumulated so that individual Indians were getting fat dividends.

Many tribes are beginning to acquire the skills necessary for this sort of independence, but the odds are long: An Indian district at Pine Ridge was excited recently about the possibility of running its own schools, and a bond issue was put before them that would have made it possible for them to do so. In the meantime, however, anthropologists visiting the community convinced its people that they were culturally unprepared to assume this sort of responsibility; so the tribe voted down the bond issue. Three universities have sent teams to the area to discover why the issue was defeated. The teams are planning to spend more on their studies than the bond issue would have cost.

I would expect an instant rebuttal by the anthros. They will say that my sentiments do not represent the views of all Indians—and they are right, they have brainwashed many of my brothers. But a new day is coming. Until then, it would be wise for anthropologists to climb down from their thrones of authority and pure research and begin helping Indian tribes instead of preying on them. For the wheel of karma grinds slowly, but it does grind fine. And it makes a complete circle.

Irving Louis Horowitz

The Life and Death of Project Camelot

The first major debate in the United States regarding government-sponsored social science research overseas for military and political purposes occurred as a result of Project Camelot, a projected study of insurgency and potential revolution in Latin America, sponsored by the United States Departments of Defense and State. It was terminated before it had hardly begun. This article describes the project and recounts the turbulent debate which surrounded it.

Horowitz views the elimination of the project by government fiat as a threat to freedom of inquiry; on the other hand, he recognizes the dangers inherent in governmentally sponsored research projects that are motivated by political and military interests, especially when they are carried out in other nations. More stringent critics viewed the project itself as a threat to the lives and freedom of those studied, as the selection following this one makes clear. The issues raised by this debate will reverberate among anthropologists for generations to come. They are even now a focus of controversy in the American Anthropological Association, as you saw in the first section, "The Social Responsibility of the Anthropologist."

In June of this year [1965]—in the midst of the crisis over the Dominican Republic—the United States Ambassador to Chile sent an urgent and angry cable to the State Department. Ambassador Ralph Dungan was confronted with a growing outburst of anti-Americanism from Chilean newspapers and intellectuals. Further, left-wing members of the Chilean Senate had accused the United States of espionage.

The anti-American attacks that agitated Dungan had no direct connection with sending US troops to Santo Domingo. Their target was a mysterious and cloudy American research program called Project Camelot.

Dungan wanted to know from the State Department what Project Camelot was all about. Further, whatever Camelot was, he wanted it stopped because it was fast becoming a *cause célèbre* in Chile (as it soon would throughout capitals of Latin America and in Washington) and Dungan had not been told anything about it—even though it was sponsored by the US Army and involved the

tinderbox subjects of counterrevolution and counterinsurgency in Latin America.

Within a few weeks Project Camelot created repercussions from Capitol Hill to the White House. Senator J. William Fulbright, chairman of the Foreign Relations Committee, registered his personal concern about such projects as Camelot because of their "reactionary, backward-looking policy opposed to change. Implicit in Camelot, as in the concept of 'counterinsurgency,' is an assumption that revolutionary movements are dangerous to the interests of the United States and that the United States must be prepared to assist, if not actually to participate in, measures to repress them."

By mid-June the State Department and Defense Department—which had created and funded Camelot—were in open contention over the project and the jurisdiction each department should have over certain foreign policy operations.

On July 8, Project Camelot was killed by Defense Secretary Robert McNamara's office which has a veto power over the military budget. The decision had been made under the President's direction.

On the same day, the director of Camelot's parent body, the Special Operations Research Organization, told a Congressional committee that the research project on revolution and counterinsurgency had taken its name from King Arthur's mythical domain because "It connotes the right sort of things—development of a stable society with peace and justice for all." Whatever Camelot's outcome, there should be no mistaking the deep sincerity behind this appeal for an applied social science pertinent to current policy.

However, Camelot left a horizon of disarray in its wake: an open dispute between State and Defense; fuel for the anti-American fires in Latin America; a cut in US Army research appropriations. In addition, serious and perhaps ominous implications for social science research, bordering on censorship, have been raised by the heated reaction of the executive branch of government.

Global Counterinsurgency

What was Project Camelot? Basically, it was a project for measuring and forecasting the causes of revolutions and insurgency in underdeveloped areas of the world. It also aimed to find ways of eliminating the causes, or coping with the revolutions and insurgencies. Camelot was sponsored by the US Army on a four to six million dollar contract, spaced out over three to four years, with the Special Operations Research Organization (SORO). This agency is nominally under the aegis of American University in Washington, D.C., and does a variety of research for the Army. This includes making analytical surveys of foreign areas; keeping up-to-date information on the military, political, and social complexes of those areas; and maintaining a "rapid response" file for getting immediate information, upon Army request, on any situation deemed militarily important.

Latin America was the first area chosen for concentrated study, but countries on Camelot's four-year list included some in Asia, Africa, and Europe. In a working paper issued on December 5, 1964, at the request of the Office of the Chief of Research and Development, Department of the Army, it was recommended that "comparative historical studies" be made in these countries:

(Latin America) Argentina, Bolivia, Brazil, Colombia, Cuba, Dominican Republic, El Salvador, Guatemala, Mexico, Paraguay, Peru, Venezuela.
　(Middle East) Egypt, Iran, Turkey.
　(Far East) Korea, Indonesia, Malaysia, Thailand.
　(Others) France, Greece, Nigeria.

"Survey research and other field studies" were recommended for Bolivia, Colombia, Ecuador, Paraguay, Peru, Venezuela, Iran, Thailand. Preliminary consideration was also being given to a study of the separatist movement in French Canada. It, too, had a code name: Project Revolt.

In a recruiting letter sent to selected scholars all over the world at the end of 1964, Project Camelot's aims were defined as a study to "make it possible to predict and influence politically significant aspects of social change in the developing nations of the world." This would include devising procedures for "assessing the potential for internal war within national societies" and "identify(ing) with increased degrees of confidence, those actions which a government might take to relieve conditions which are assessed as giving rise to a potential for internal war." The letter further stated: "The US Army has an important mission in the positive and constructive aspects of nation-building in less developed countries as well as a responsibility to assist friendly governments in dealing with active insurgency problems." Such activities by the US Army were described as "insurgency prophylaxis" rather than the "sometimes misleading label of counterinsurgency."

Project Camelot was conceived in late 1963 by a group of high-ranking Army officers connected with the Army Research Office of the Department of Defense. They were concerned about new types of warfare springing up around the world. Revolutions in Cuba and Yemen and insurgency movements in Vietnam and the Congo were a far cry from the battles of World War II and also different from the envisioned—and planned for—apocalypse of nuclear war. For the first time in modern warfare, military establishments were not in a position to use the immense arsenals at their disposal—but were, instead, compelled by force of a geopolitical stalemate to increasingly engage in primitive forms of armed combat. The questions of moment for the Army were: Why can't the "hardware" be used? And what alternatives can social science "software" provide?

A well-known Latin American area specialist, Rex Hopper, was chosen as director of Project Camelot. Hopper was a professor of sociology and chairman of the department at Brooklyn College. He had been to Latin America many times over a thirty-year span on research projects and lecture tours, including some under government sponsorship. He was highly recommended for the position by his professional associates in Washington and elsewhere. Hopper had a long-standing interest in problems of revolution and saw in this multimillion dollar contract the possible realization of a life-long scientific ambition.

The Chilean Debacle

How did this social science research project create a foreign policy furore? And, at another level, how did such high intentions result in so disastrous an outcome?

The answers involve a network spreading from a professor of anthropology at the University of

Pittsburgh, to a professor of sociology at the University of Oslo, and yet a third professor of sociology at the University of Chile in Santiago, Chile. The "showdown" took place in Chile, first within the confines of the university, next on the floor of the Chilean Senate, then in the popular press of Santiago, and finally, behind US embassy walls.

It was ironic that Chile was the scene of wild newspaper tales of spying and academic outrage at scholars being recruited for "spying missions." For the working papers of Project Camelot stipulated as a criterion for study that a country "should show promise of high pay-offs in terms of the kinds of data required." Chile did not meet these requirements—it is not on the preliminary list of nations specified as prospects.

How then did Chile become involved in Project Camelot's affairs? The answer requires consideration of the position of Hugo G. Nutini, assistant professor of anthropology at Pittsburgh, citizen of the United States and former citizen of Chile. His presence in Santiago as a self-identified Camelot representative triggered the climactic chain of events.

Nutini, who inquired about an appointment in Camelot's beginning stages, never was given a regular Camelot appointment. Because he was planning a trip to Chile in April of this year—on other academic business—he was asked to prepare a report concerning possibilities of cooperation from Chilean scholars. In general, it was the kind of survey which has mild results and a modest honorarium attached to it (Nutini was offered $750). But Nutini had an obviously different notion of his role. Despite the limitations and precautions which Rex Hopper placed on his trip, especially Hopper's insistence on its informal nature, Nutini managed to convey the impression of being an official of Project Camelot with the authority to make proposals to prospective Chilean participants. Here was an opportunity to link the country of his birth with the country of his choice.

At about the same time, Johan Galtung, a Norwegian sociologist famous for his research on conflict and conflict resolution in underdeveloped areas, especially in Latin America, entered the picture. Galtung, who was in Chile at the time and associated with the Latin American Faculty of Social Science (FLACSO), received an invitation to participate in a Camelot planning conference scheduled for Washington, D.C., in August 1965. The fee to social scientists attending the conference would be $2,000 for four weeks. Galtung turned down the invitation. He gave several reasons. He could not accept the role of the US Army as a sponsoring agent in a study of counterinsurgency. He could not accept the notion of the Army as an agency of national development; he saw the Army as managing conflict and even promoting conflict. Finally, he could not accept the asymmetry of the project—he found it difficult to understand why there would be studies of counterinsurgency in Latin America, but no studies of "counterintervention" (conditions under which Latin American nations might intervene in the affairs of the United States). Galtung was also deeply concerned about the possibility of European scholars being frozen out of Latin American studies by an inundation of sociologists from the United States. Furthermore, he expressed fears that the scale of Camelot honoraria would completely destroy the social science labor market in Latin America.

Galtung had spoken to others in Oslo, Santiago, and throughout Latin America about the project, and he had shown the memorandum of December 1964 to many of his colleagues.

Soon after Nutini arrived in Santiago, he had a conference with Vice-Chancellor Alvaro Bunster of the University of Chile to discuss the character of Project Camelot. Their second meeting, arranged by the vice-chancellor, was also attended by Professor Eduardo Fuenzalida, a sociologist. After a half-hour of exposition by Nutini, Fuenzalida asked him pointblank to specify the ultimate aims of the project, its sponsors, and its military implications. Before Nutini could reply, Professor Fuenzalida, apparently with some drama, pulled a copy of the December 4 circular letter from his briefcase and read a prepared Spanish translation. Simultaneously, the authorities at FLACSO turned over the matter to their associates in the Chilean Senate and in the left-wing Chilean press.

In Washington, under the political pressures of State Department officials and Congressional reaction, Project Camelot was halted in midstream, or more precisely, before it ever really got under way. When the ambassador's communication reached Washington, there was already considerable official ferment about Project Camelot.

Senators Fulbright, Morse, and McCarthy soon asked for hearings by the Senate Foreign Relations Committee. Only an agreement between Secretary of Defense McNamara and Secretary of State Rusk to settle their differences on future overseas research projects forestalled Senate action. But in the House of Representatives, a hearing was conducted by the Foreign Affairs Committee on July 8. The SORO director, Theodore Vallance, was questioned by committee members on the worth of Camelot and the matter of military intrusion into foreign policy areas.

That morning, even before Vallance was sworn in as a witness—and without his knowledge—the Defense Department issued a terse announcement terminating Project Camelot. President Johnson had decided the issue in favor of the State Department. In a memo to Secretary Rusk on August 5 the President stipulated that "no government sponsorship of foreign area research should be undertaken which in the judgment of the Secretary of State would adversely affect United States foreign relations."

The State Department has recently established machinery to screen and judge all federally-financed research projects overseas. The policy and research consequences of the Presidential directive will be discussed later.

What effect will the cancellation of Camelot have on the continuing rivalry between Defense and State departments for primacy in foreign policy? How will government sponsorship of future social science research be affected? And was Project Camelot a scholarly protective cover for US Army planning—or a legitimate research operation on a valid research subject independent of sponsorship?

Let us begin with a collective self-portrait of Camelot as the social scientists who directed the project perceived it. There seems to be general consensus on seven points.

First, the men who went to work for Camelot felt the need for a large-scale, "big picture" project in social science. They wanted to create a sociology of contemporary relevance which would not suffer from the parochial narrowness of vision to which their own professional backgrounds had generally conditioned them. Most of the men viewed Camelot as a bona fide opportunity to do fundamental research with relatively unlimited funds at their disposal. (No social science project

ever before had up to $6,000,000 available.) Under such optimal conditions, these scholars tended not to look a gift horse in the mouth. As one of them put it, there was no desire to inquire too deeply as to the source of the funds or the ultimate purpose of the project.

Second, most social scientists affiliated with Camelot felt that there was actually more freedom to do fundamental research under military sponsorship than at a university or college. One man noted that during the 1950s there was far more freedom to do fundamental research in the RAND corporation (an Air Force research organization) than on any campus in America. Indeed, once the protective covering of RAND was adopted, it was almost viewed as a society of Platonist elites or "knowers" permitted to search for truth on behalf of the powerful. In a neoplatonic definition of their situation, the Camelot men hoped that their ideas would be taken seriously by the wielders of power (although, conversely, they were convinced that the armed forces would not accept their preliminary recommendations).

Third, many of the Camelot associates felt distinctly uncomfortable with military sponsorship, especially given the present United States military posture. But their reaction to this discomfort was that "the Army has to be educated." This view was sometimes cast in Freudian terms: the Army's bent toward violence ought to be sublimated. Underlying this theme was the notion of the armed forces as an agency for potential social good—the discipline and the order embodied by an army could be channeled into the process of economic and social development in the United States as well as in Latin America.

Fourth, there was a profound conviction in the perfectibility of mankind; particularly in the possibility of the military establishment performing a major role in the general process of growth. They sought to correct the intellectual paternalism and parochialism under which Pentagon generals, State Department diplomats, and Defense Department planners seemed to operate.

Fifth, a major long-range purpose of Camelot, at least for some of its policy-makers, was to prevent another revolutionary holocaust on a grand scale, such as occurred in Cuba. At the very least, there was a shared belief that *Pax Americana* was severely threatened and its future could be bolstered.

Sixth, none of them viewed their role on the project as spying for the United States government, or for anyone else.

Seventh, the men on Project Camelot felt that they made heavy sacrifices for social science. Their personal and professional risks were much higher than those taken by university academics. Government work, while well-compensated, remains professionally marginal. It can be terminated abruptly (as indeed was the case) and its project directors are subject to a public scrutiny not customary behind the walls of ivy.

In the main, there was perhaps a keener desire on the part of the directing members of Camelot not to "sell out" than there is among social scientists with regular academic appointments. This concern with the ethics of social science research seemed to be due largely to daily confrontation of the problems of betrayal, treason, secrecy, and abuse of data, in a critical situation. In contrast, even though a university position may be created by federally-sponsored research, the connection with policy matters is often too remote to cause any *crise de conscience*.

The Insiders Report

Were the men on Camelot critical of any aspects of the project?

Some had doubts from the outset about the character of the work they would be doing, and about the conditions under which it would be done. It was pointed out, for example, that the US Army tends to exercise a far more stringent intellectual control of research findings than does the US Air Force. As evidence for this, it was stated that SORO generally had fewer "free-wheeling" aspects to its research designs than did RAND (the Air Force-supported research organization). One critic inside SORO went so far as to say that he knew of no SORO research which had a "playful" or unregimented quality, such as one finds at RAND (where for example, computers are used to plan invasions but also to play chess). One staff member said that "the self-conscious seriousness gets to you after a while." "It was all grim stuff," said another.

Another line of criticism was that pressures on the "reformers" (as the men engaged in Camelot research spoke of themselves) to come up with ideas were much stronger than the pressures on the military to actually bring off any policy changes recommended. The social scientists were expected to be social reformers, while the military adjutants were expected to be conservative. It was further felt that the relationship between sponsors and researchers was not one of equals, but rather one of superordinate military needs and subordinate academic role. On the other hand, some officials were impressed by the disinterestedness of the military, and thought that far from exercising undue influence, the Army personnel were loath to offer opinions.

Another objection was that if one had to work on policy matters—if research is to have international ramifications—it might better be conducted under conventional State Department sponsorship. "After all," one man said, "they are at least nominally committed to civilian political norms." In other words, there was a considerable reluctance to believe that the Defense Department, despite its superior organization, greater financial affluence, and executive influence, would actually improve upon State Department styles of work, or accept recommendations at variance with Pentagon policies.

There seemed to be few, if any, expressions of disrespect for the intrinsic merit of the work contemplated by Camelot, or of disdain for policy-oriented work in general. The scholars engaged in the Camelot effort used two distinct vocabularies. The various Camelot documents reveal a military vocabulary provided with an array of military justification; often followed (within the same document) by a social science vocabulary offering social science justifications and rationalizations. The dilemma in the Camelot literature from the preliminary report issued in August 1964 until the more advanced document issued in April 1965, is the same: an incomplete amalgamation of the military and sociological vocabularies. (At an early date the project had the code name SPEARPOINT.)

Policy Conflicts Over Camelot

The directors of SORO are concerned that the cancellation of Camelot might mean the end of SORO as well in a wholesale slash of research funds. For while over $1,000,000 was allotted to Camelot each year, the annual budget of SORO, its parent organization, is a good deal less. Although no such action has taken place, SORO's future is being examined. For example, the Senate and House Appropriations Committee blocked a move by the Army to transfer unused Camelot funds to SORO.

However, the end of Project Camelot does not necessarily imply the end of the Special Operations Research Office, nor does it imply an end to research designs which are similar in character to Project Camelot. In fact, the termination of the contract does not even imply an intellectual change of heart on the part of the originating sponsors or key figures of the project.

One of the characteristics of Project Camelot was the number of antagonistic forces it set in motion on grounds of strategy and timing rather than from what may be called considerations of scientific principles.

The State Department grounded its opposition to Camelot on the basis of the ultimate authority it has in the area of foreign affairs. There is no published report showing serious criticism of the projected research itself.

Congressional opposition seemed to be generated by a concern not to rock any foreign alliances, especially in Latin America. Again, there was no statement about the project's scientific or intellectual grounds.

A third group of skeptics, academic social scientists, generally thought that Project Camelot, and studies of the processes of revolution and war in general, were better left in the control of major university centers, and in this way, kept free of direct military supervision.

The Army, creator of the project, did nothing to contradict McNamara's order cancelling Project Camelot. Army influentials did not only feel that they had to execute the Defense Department's orders, but they are traditionally dubious of the value of "software" research to support "hardware" systems.

Let us take a closer look at each of these groups which voiced opposition to Project Camelot. A number of issues did not so much hinge upon, as swim about, Project Camelot. In particular, the "jurisdictional" dispute between Defense and State loomed largest.

State vs. Defense

In substance, the debate between the Defense Department and the State Department is not unlike that between electricians and bricklayers in the construction of a new apartment house. What "union" is responsible for which processes? Less generously, the issue is: who controls what? At the policy level, Camelot was a tool tossed about in a larger power struggle which has been going on in government circles since the end of World War II, when the Defense Department emerged as a competitor for honors as the most powerful bureau of the administrative branch of government.

In some sense, the divisions between Defense and State are outcomes of the rise of ambiguous conflicts such as Korea and Vietnam, in contrast to the more precise and diplomatically controlled "classical" world wars. What are the lines dividing political policy from military posture? Who is the most important representative of the United States abroad: the ambassador or the military attaché in charge of the military mission? When soldiers from foreign lands are sent to the United States for political orientation, should such orientation be within the province of the State Department or of the Defense Department? When undercover activities are conducted, should the direction of such activities belong to military or political authorities? Each of these is a strategic question with little pragmatic or historic precedent. Each of these was entwined in the Project Camelot explosion.

It should be plain therefore that the State Department was not simply responding to the recommendations of Chilean left-wingers in urging the cancellation of Camelot. It merely employed the Chilean hostility to "interventionist" projects as an opportunity to redefine the balance of forces and power with the Defense Department. What is clear from this resistance to such projects is not so much a defense of the sovereignty of the nations where ambassadors are stationed, as it is a contention that conventional political channels are sufficient to yield the information desired or deemed necessary.

Congress

In the main, congressional reaction seems to be that Project Camelot was bad because it rocked the diplomatic boat in a sensitive area. Underlying most congressional criticisms is the plain fact that most congressmen are more sympathetic to State Department control of foreign affairs than they are to Defense Department control. In other words, despite military sponsored world junkets, National Guard and State Guard pressures from the home State, and military training in the backgrounds of many congressmen, the sentiment for political rather than military control is greater. In addition, there is a mounting suspicion in Congress of varying kinds of behavioral science research stemming from hearings into such matters as wiretapping, uses of lie detectors, and truth-in-packaging.

Social Scientists

One reason for the violent response to Project Camelot, especially among Latin American scholars, is its sponsorship by the Department of Defense. The fact is that Latin Americans have become quite accustomed to State Department involvements in the internal affairs of various nations. The Defense Department is a newcomer, a dangerous one, inside the Latin American orbit. The train of thought connected to its activities is in terms of international warfare, spying missions, military manipulations, etc. The State Department, for its part, is often a consultative party to shifts in government, and has played an enormous part in either fending off or bringing about *coups d'état*. This State Department role has by now been accepted and even taken for granted. Not so the Defense Department's role. But it is interesting to conjecture on how matter-of-factly Camelot might have been accepted if it had State Department sponsorship.

Social scientists in the United States have, for the most part, been publicly silent on the matter of Camelot. The reasons for this are not hard to find. First, many "giants of the field" are involved in government contract work in one capacity or another. And few souls are in a position to tamper with the gods. Second, most information on Project Camelot has thus far been of a newspaper variety; and professional men are not in a habit of criticizing colleagues on the basis of such information. Third, many social scientists doubtless see nothing wrong or immoral in the Project Camelot designs. And they are therefore more likely to be either confused or angered at the Latin American response than at the directors of Project Camelot. (At the time of the blowup, Camelot people spoke about the "Chilean mess" rather than the "Camelot mess.")

The directors of Project Camelot did not

"classify" research materials, so that there would be no stigma of secrecy. And they also tried to hire, and even hired away from academic positions, people well known and respected for their independence of mind. The difficulty is that even though the stigma of secrecy was formally erased, it remained in the attitudes of many of the employees and would-be employees of Project Camelot. They unfortunately thought in terms of secrecy, clearance, missions, and the rest of the professional nonsense that so powerfully afflicts the Washington scientific as well as political ambience.

Further, it is apparent that Project Camelot had much greater difficulty hiring a full-time staff of high professional competence, than in getting part-time, summertime, weekend, and sundry assistance. Few established figures in academic life were willing to surrender the advantages of their positions for the risks of the project.

One of the cloudiest aspects to Project Camelot is the role of American University. Its actual supervision of the contract appears to have begun and ended with the 25 percent overhead on those parts of the contract that a university receives on most federal grants. Thus, while there can be no question as to the "concern and disappointment" of President Hurst R. Anderson of the American University over the demise of Project Camelot, the reasons for this regret do not seem to extend beyond the formal and the financial. No official at American University appears to have been willing to make any statement of responsibility, support, chagrin, opposition, or anything else related to the project. The issues are indeed momentous, and must be faced by all universities at which government sponsored research is conducted: the amount of control a university has over contract work; the role of university officials in the distribution of funds from grants; the relationships that ought to be established once a grant is issued. There is also a major question concerning project directors: are they members of the faculty, and if so, do they have necessary teaching responsibilities and opportunities for tenure as do other faculty members.

The difficulty with American University is that it seems to be remarkably unlike other universities in its permissiveness. The Special Operations Research Office received neither guidance nor support from university officials. From the outset, there seems to have been a "gentleman's agreement" not to inquire or interfere in Project Camelot, but simply to serve as some sort of camouflage. If American University were genuinely autonomous it might have been able to lend highly supportive aid to Project Camelot during the crisis months. As it is, American University maintained an official silence which preserved it from more congressional or executive criticism. This points up some serious flaws in its administrative and financial policies.

The relationship of Camelot to SORO represented a similarly muddled organizational picture. The director of Project Camelot was nominally autonomous and in charge of an organization surpassing in size and importance the overall SORO operation. Yet at the critical point the organizational blueprint served to protect SORO and sacrifice what nominally was its limb. That Camelot happened to be a vital organ may have hurt, especially when Congress blocked the transfer of unused Camelot funds to SORO.

Military

Military reaction to the cancellation of Camelot varied. It should be borne in mind that expenditures on Camelot were minimal in the Army's overall budget and most military leaders are skeptical, to begin with, about the worth of social science research. So there was no open protest about the demise of Camelot. Those officers who have a positive attitude toward social science materials, or are themselves trained in the social sciences, were dismayed. Some had hoped to find "software" alternatives to the "hardware systems" approach applied by the Secretary of Defense to every military-political contingency. These officers saw the attack on Camelot as a double attack— on their role as officers and on their professional standards. But the Army was so clearly treading in new waters that it could scarcely jeopardize the entire structure of military research to preserve one project. This very inability or impotence to preserve Camelot—a situation threatening to other governmental contracts with social scientists—no doubt impressed many armed forces officers.

The claim is made by the Camelot staff (and various military aides) that the critics of the project played into the hands of those sections of the military predisposed to veto any social science recommendations. Then why did the military offer

such a huge support to a social science project to begin with? Because $6,000,000 is actually a trifling sum for the Army in an age of multi-billion dollar military establishment. The amount is significantly more important for the social sciences, where such contract awards remain relatively scarce. Thus, there were differing perspectives of the importance of Camelot: an Army view which considered the contract as one of several forms of "software" investment; a social science perception of Project Camelot as the equivalent of the Manhattan Project.

Was Project Camelot Workable?

While most public opposition to Project Camelot focused on its strategy and timing, a considerable amount of private opposition centered on more basic, though theoretical, questions: was Camelot scientifically feasible and ethically correct? No public document or statement contested the possibility that, given the successful completion of the data gathering, Camelot could have, indeed, established basic criteria for measuring the level and potential for internal war in a given nation. Thus, by never challenging the feasibility of the work, the political critics of Project Camelot were providing back-handed compliments to the efficacy of the project.

But much more than political considerations are involved. It is clear that some of the most critical problems presented by Project Camelot are scientific. Although for an extensive analysis of Camelot, the reader would, in fairness, have to be familiar with all of its documents, salient general criticisms can be made without a full reading.

The research design of Camelot was from the outset plagued by ambiguities. It was never quite settled whether the purpose was to study counter-insurgency possibilities, or the revolutionary process. Similarly, it was difficult to determine whether it was to be a study of comparative social structures, a set of case studies of single nations "in depth," or a study of social structure with particular emphasis on the military. In addition, there was a lack of treatment of what indicators were to be used, and whether a given social system in Nation A could be as stable in Nation B.

In one Camelot document there is a general critique of social science for failing to deal with social conflict and social control. While this in itself is admirable, the tenor and context of Camelot's documents make it plain that a "stable society" is considered the norm no less than the desired outcome. The "breakdown of social order" is spoken of accusatively. Stabilizing agencies in developing areas are presumed to be absent. There is no critique of U.S. Army policy in developing areas because the Army is presumed to be a stabilizing agency. The research formulations always assume the legitimacy of Army tasks—"if the US Army is to perform effectively its parts in the U.S. mission of counterinsurgency it must recognize that insurgency represents a breakdown of social order. . . ." But such a proposition has never been doubted—by Army officials or anyone else. The issue is whether such breakdowns are in the nature of the existing system or a product of conspiratorial movements.

The use of hygienic language disguises the anti-revolutionary assumptions under a cloud of powder puff declarations. For example, studies of Paraguay are recommended "because trends in this situation (the Stroessner regime) may also render it unique when analyzed in terms of the transition from 'dictatorship' to political stability." But to speak about changes from dictatorship to stability is an obvious ruse. In this case, it is a tactic to disguise the fact that Paraguay is one of the most vicious, undemocratic (and like most dictatorships, stable) societies in the Western Hemisphere.

These typify the sort of hygienic sociological premises that do not have scientific purposes. They illustrate the confusion of commitments within Project Camelot. Indeed the very absence of emotive words such as revolutionary masses, communism, socialism, and capitalism only serves to intensify the discomfort one must feel on examination of the documents—since the abstract vocabulary disguises, rather than resolves, the problems of international revolution. To have used clearly political rather than military language would not "justify" governmental support. Furthermore, shabby assumptions of academic conventionalism replaced innovative orientations. By adopting a systems approach, the problematic, open-ended aspects of the study of revolutions were largely omitted; and the design of the study became an oppressive curb on the study of the problems inspected.

This points up a critical implication for Camelot (as well as other projects). The importance of the subject being researched does not *per se* determine the importance of the project. A sociology of large-scale relevance and reference is all to the good. It is important that scholars be willing to risk something of their shaky reputations in helping resolve major world social problems. But it is no less urgent that in the process of addressing major problems, the autonomous character of the social science disciplines—their own criteria of worthwhile scholarship—should not be abandoned. Project Camelot lost sight of this "autonomous" social science character.

It never seemed to occur to its personnel to inquire into the desirability for successful revolution. This is just as solid a line of inquiry as the one stressed—the conditions under which revolutionary movements will be able to overthrow a government. Furthermore, they seem not to have thought about inquiring into the role of the United States in these countries. This points up the lack of symmetry. The problem should have been phrased to include the study of "us" as well as "them." It is not possible to make a decent analysis of a situation unless one takes into account the role of all the different people and groups involved in it; and there was no room in the design for such contingency analysis.

In discussing the policy impact on a social science research project, we should not overlook the difference between "contract" work and "grants." Project Camelot commenced with the US Army; that is to say, it was initiated for a practical purpose determined by the client. This differs markedly from the typical academic grant in that its sponsorship had "built-in" ends. The scholar usually *seeks* a grant; in this case the donor, the Army, promoted its own aims. In some measure, the hostility for Project Camelot may be an unconscious reflection of this distinction—a dim feeling that there was something "nonacademic," and certainly not disinterested, about Project Camelot, irrespective of the quality of the scholars associated with it.

The Ethics of Policy Research

The issue of "scientific rights" versus "social myths" is perennial. Some maintain that the scientist ought not penetrate beyond legally or morally sanctioned limits and others argue that such limits cannot exist for science. In treading on the sensitive issue of national sovereignty, Project Camelot reflects the generalized dilemma. In deference to intelligent researchers, in recognition of them as scholars, they should have been invited by Camelot to air their misgivings and qualms about government (and especially Army-sponsored) research— to declare their moral conscience. Instead, they were mistakenly approached as skillful, useful potential employees of a higher body, subject to an authority higher than their scientific calling.

What is central is not the political motives of the sponsor. For social scientists were not being enlisted in an intelligence system for "spying" purposes. But given their professional standing, their great sense of intellectual honor and pride, they could not be "employed" without proper deference for their stature. Professional authority should have prevailed from beginning to end with complete command of the right to thrash out the moral and political dilemmas as researchers saw them. The Army, however respectful and protective of free expression, was "hiring help" and not openly and honestly submitting a problem to the higher professional and scientific authority of social science.

The propriety of the Army to define and delimit all questions, which Camelot should have had a right to examine, was never placed in doubt. This is a tragic precedent; it reflects the arrogance of a consumer of intellectual merchandise. And this relationship of inequality corrupted the lines of authority, and profoundly limited the autonomy of the social scientists involved. It became clear that the social scientist savant was not so much functioning as an applied social scientist as he was supplying information to a powerful client.

The question of who sponsors research is not nearly so decisive as the question of ultimate use of such information. The sponsorship of a project, whether by the United States Army or by the Boy Scouts of America, is by itself neither good nor bad. Sponsorship is good or bad only insofar as the intended outcomes can be predetermined and the parameters of those intended outcomes tailored to the sponsor's expectations. Those social scientists critical of the project never really denied its freedom and independence, but questioned instead the purpose and character of its intended results.

It would be a gross oversimplification, if not an outright error, to assume that the theoretical problems of Project Camelot derive from any reactionary character of the project designers. The director went far and wide to select a group of men for the advisory board, the core planning group, the summer study group, and the various conference groupings, who in fact were more liberal in their orientations than any random sampling of the sociological profession would likely turn up.

However, in nearly every page of the various working papers, there are assertions which clearly derive from American military policy objectives rather than scientific method. The steady assumption that internal warfare is damaging disregards the possibility that a government may not be in a position to take actions either to relieve or improve mass conditions, or that such actions as are contemplated may be more concerned with reducing conflict than with improving conditions. The added statements about the United States Army and its "important mission in the positive and constructive aspects of nation building . . ." assumes the reality of such a function in an utterly unquestioning and unconvincing form. The first rule of the scientific game is not to make assumptions about friends and enemies in such a way as to promote the use of different criteria for the former and the latter.

The story of Project Camelot was not a confrontation of good versus evil. Obviously, not all men behaved with equal fidelity or with equal civility. Some men were weaker than others, some more callous, and some more stupid. But all of this is extrinsic to the heart of the problem of Camelot: What are and are not the legitimate functions of a scientist?

In conclusion, two important points must be clearly kept in mind and clearly apart. First, Project Camelot was intellectually, and from my own perspective, ideologically unsound. However, and more significantly, Camelot was not cancelled because of its faulty intellectual approaches. Instead, its cancellation came as an act of government censorship, and an expression of the contempt for social science so prevalent among those who need it most. Thus it was political expedience, rather than its lack of scientific merit, that led to the demise of Camelot because it threatened to rock State Department relations with Latin America.

Second, giving the State Department the right to screen and approve government-funded social science research projects on other countries, as the President has ordered, is a supreme act of censorship. Among the agencies that grant funds for such research are the National Institutes of Mental Health, the National Science Foundation, the National Aeronautics and Space Agency, and the Office of Education. Why should the State Department have veto power over the scientific pursuits of men and projects funded by these and other agencies in order to satisfy the policy needs—or policy failures—of the moment? President Johnson's directive is a gross violation of the autonomous nature of science.

We must be careful not to allow social science projects with which we may vociferously disagree on political and ideological grounds to be decimated or dismantled by government fiat. Across the ideological divide is a common social science understanding that the contemporary expression of reason in politics today is applied social science, and that the cancellation of Camelot, however pleasing it may be on political grounds to advocates of a civilian solution to Latin American affairs, represents a decisive setback for social science research.

Marshall Sahlins

The Established Order: Do Not Fold, Spindle, or Mutilate

In this selection, Marshall Sahlins voices the grave concerns which most anthropologists shared about Project Camelot—concerns which have arisen again more recently, with the involvement of anthropologists and other social scientists in counterinsurgency activities in Thailand. Although there are serious differences of opinion about the ethics of such involvement, it is clear that those who do research under military or quasi-military sponsorship in foreign nations are playing a dangerous game and can expect little sympathy when they are called to account, and especially when called to account by those whose lives their research affects directly—whose efforts at self-determination their research jeopardizes.

We all know what the right to investigate freely, to think freely, and to write freely means to our field and ourselves, and what the loss of these would mean. I am concerned that our involvement in cold war projects such as Camelot does jeopardize these freedoms. Of course I speak for myself; but the sentiments are not entirely my own. I have had a chance to discuss these matters with colleagues from several universities. Without presuming to represent them, I am trying here to formulate concerns many have expressed.

The following ... constitute grounds for apprehension:

1. The scale and character of government interest in Strategic Social Science. In the nature of things, this is seen only through a glass darkly. We do know the six-million dollars allotted to Camelot was merely for a "feasibility" study (3 and one-half years). An ultimate investment of several times that per annum was contemplated—one ex-Camelot scholar told me the talk was of 50 million a year. Meanwhile *Problem* Camelot goes on, with the aid of some anthropologists, in Africa as well as Latin America, New Guinea as well as Southeast Asia. And on the home front, intelligence agencies erect concealed bases of support: sundry "front" foundations or "pass-throughs" created with covert government funds. These funds dispense "grants" for certain "academic" research and travel. There are grounds to suspect the CIA

Marshall Sahlins, "The Established Order: Do Not Fold, Spindle, or Mutilate." Reprinted from *The Rise and Fall of Project Camelot: Studies in the Relationship Between Social Science and Practical Politics*, edited by Irving Louis Horowitz, by permission of The M.I.T. Press, Cambridge, Massachusetts. Copyright © 1967 by The Massachusetts Institute of Technology.

fronts are camouflaged by names closely approximating those of listed and legitimate private foundations.

2. . . . There is a serious possibility that such tactics will become our tactics. It is already a minimum demand of internal vigilance that everyone investigate the source of funds he is offered for foreign-area research, conferences on field work needs, or the like. I understand that in at least one instance anthropologists have been invited by colleagues to attend a conference subsidized by the Defense Department without however being informed in advance of this sponsorship. Here is an example of the corrosion of integrity that must accompany an enlistment of scholars in a *gendarmerie* relation to the Third World. Subversion of the mutual trust between field worker and informant is the predictable next step. The relativism we hold necessary to ethnography can be replaced by cynicism, and the quest for objective knowledge of other peoples replaced by a probe for their political weaknesses.

3. The State Department announces it will create a board of review for government-sponsored external research, with the aim of blocking investigations not in the nation's best interests. This is a clear threat to free inquiry. I realize the purpose of the broadly worded presidential directive was to prevent repetitions of Camelot. But directives outlive the intentions of those who issue them and ought to reckon with those who implement them; so that directives wrong in principle must be opposed on principle. Nor is the theory of good people administering bad laws a proper philosophy of American democracy.

4. As it is, we cannot get into half the world; as scholars-in-armor we would soon not be on speaking terms with the other half.

I refer to the call to this meeting [of the American Anthropological Association in November 1965]:

Some field work already in progress in various parts of the world, particularly in Latin America, has already suffered adversely, being forced to curtail or even suspend operations. Reports have been received and verified about the investigation and embarrassment by their governments of foreign scholars who have been actively helping United States social scientists. This, in turn, rapidly erodes the resources of goodwill upon which we can draw and militates

against the conduct of adequately staffed and assisted field work.

The New York Times foresaw just this predicament in September 1964, in commenting on the disclosure by a congressional subcommittee of a CIA front foundation: "What evidence," *The Times* asked, "can American professors or field workers present to prove they are not engaged in underground activities when it is known that the CIA is using its money to subsidize existing foundations, or is creating fictitious ones?"

This harassment falls on everyone, just or unjust: independent scholar or academic cold warrior, foreign intellectuals as well as the Americans with whom they work. In some sense it is not our fault. It is not our fault that America appears to many people an interventionist and counterrevolutionary power. And it is not our fault that American agents, whose relations to progressive movements seem instinctively hostile, operate under cover in the Third World. But the least we can do is protect the anthropologist's relation to the Third World, which is a scholarly relation. Field work under contract to the U.S. Army is no way to protect that relation.

Perhaps it was Camelot's greatest irony that it forgot to program itself into the project. As a tactic of fomenting Latin American unrest and anti-North American sentiment, Camelot would be the envy of any Communist conspiracy. We have heard of the self-fulfilling prophecy; here was the self-fulfilling research proposal.

5. Strategic research raises serious issues of classification and clearance. Scientifically, the relevant concerns are the right to freely communicate one's experiences to colleagues at home and abroad and the right to participate in research according to one's merit and promise—without regard to the FBI's understanding of patriotism. Here we should take into account a distinction much favored by the Camelot scientists: that it *is* research, not intelligence. Participating scholars conceived the project to be a fine opportunity to develop knowledge useful, even critical, to social science. It was a chance, too, to advance the frontiers of research technique. The project design of April 1, 1965, indeed opens new vistas on the study of revolution and counterrevolution, such as "operations research techniques, manual and machine simulation, machine content analysis,

and new types of analysis of survey data"—which is perhaps why one friend, an unautomated anthropologist of decided views, suggested that the most heartening thing about Camelot was its intellectual prognosis.

For Project Camelot, the DOD gave assurance that findings would not be classified and clearance would not be necessary. In fact, there are no iron-clad guarantees. The government has the power; in this respect the scholar is in very unequal relation to Defense, State, or the CIA. And what will the ruling be on Project Kula-Ring, Operation Leopard-Skin Chief, and other future scientific investigations of the CIA or DOD? Moreover, it is difficult to conceive that classification would not have eventually occurred in Camelot. A working paper of December 5, 1964, stipulates as the most significant criterion for inclusion in the study the relevance of the country to U.S. foreign policy interests. The program for historic studies (April 1) asks investigators to probe official corruption, the strength of insurgent parties, and the measures taken to cut off external aid to insurgents; to determine the effectiveness of the established government's intelligence service; to give approximate numbers of forces available for counterinsurgency; to say whether the regime fomented foreign wars or "black" coups to suppress internal unrest; to determine whether the government permitted Communist infiltration of itself or radical movements; to name names, note groups, and identify leaders. All sorts of questions such as these were deemed important in the preliminary archival studies. Suppose the answers proved important and informed the field worker's check lists. Can you now suppose these field reports would be published?

(In connection with the assurances about classification, I understand that when Camelot was summarily cancelled the DOD asked participants not to publicly discuss the project, and this request was respected. That the DOD's request was prompted by the international repercussions of Camelot's premature disclosure is better understood as an augury than a mitigating circumstance, and as a reflection on the character of the project.)

6. The idea that Strategic Social Science will liberalize strategy as it advances science seems to me a snare and a delusion.

I form the impression that good and conscientious Camelot scientists thought they might put something over on the Defense Department. They were going to get in some good research, whatever the U.S. Army's objectives. Besides, if somebody's going to do this sort of thing, better it be sensible and humane people. Here was a chance to educate the military to foreign realities, an opportunity to reconstruct American attitudes and policies. And with this hope went the perception that the Defense Department is divisible into "good guys" and "bad guys"; and the former, although a minority, managed to get this "software" research through and ought to be encouraged.

I think this all unnecessarily naive, a failure to analyze the structure of the Establishment, the relation of the sword to the pen, the strengths of the cold-war demonology, and the present foreign-political position of this country. The quixotic scholar enters the agreement in the belief that knowledge breeds power; his military counterpart, in the assurance that power breeds knowledge. The level of innocence is best documented by ethnography, although the point appears also in Camelot documents. I asked a Camelot psychologist who was pleased to expound this distinction between black knights and white knights, what was the content of the progressives' program. He said, in the first place, that enlightened Pentagon officers see the military of Latin America—acting in concert with the U.S. Army—as the best available vehicle for reform: they are organized, efficient, intelligent, and have the social machinery. That is what he said. So help me.

7. The cold-war researcher is potentially a servant of power, placed in a sycophantic relation to the state unbefitting science or citizenship. The scholar sells his services to a military, intelligence, or foreign policy client, who has certain plans for the product. Although formal clearance requirements may be suspended, it is only artless to claim there is no informal selection of academic personnel on the basis of agreement in cold-war principle —if not tactic—or no penalty to outspoken public criticism. Academicians who have demonstrated creative support are at least differentially favored for higher appointments in the existing scheme of things; those who cannot agree run some risk of being shut out, unless they shut up. If this is important research, carried out as it may be under institutional contract, the government agency is in a position to make one's commitment to prevailing policy a condition of professional opportunity and

success. On the other side, one's freedom as a citizen to dissent is constrained, on pain of antagonizing the employers-that-be. This fate can be predicted even for those first engaged by the agency on research of their own choosing, "basic research": they are equally retainers, mortgaged to past and future favors. Clearly, neither science nor democracy can function in such an atmosphere.

The science and government question is delicate, complicated, and perennial. But now that it has come to us, perhaps we can add an understanding of the sociology in it that betrays all good intentions. Even the military or intelligence agency may have good intentions about academic independence; yet informal screening and watchful discretion will go on. For the agreement between cold-war scholar and government bureau is largely self-policing. "Cameloticians" themselves understood the principle and wrote it into their project. In the checklist for case studies appears a section titled "Government Control of Scientific Institutions." It aims to assess the power of the established regime and the loyalties it could command in a crisis. There is a subhead called "Scientists." It asks only this: "What percentage of scientists work for Government and for private organizations? Of those who work for private organizations, such as universities, what percentage supplement their income through Government contracts, extra jobs, consultations?"

8. The scientific status of cold-war research is equivocal. Camelot documents bear out Senator Fulbright's suspicions: "Implicit in Camelot," he said, "as in the concept of 'counterinsurgency' is an assumption that revolutionary movements are dangerous to the interest of the United States and that the United States must be prepared to assist, if not actually to participate in, measures to repress them." Consider this example of "scientific" question from the project design: "Was the Government guilty of excessive toleration of alienated, insurgent, or potentially insurgent groups?"

But most clearly in its characterizations of revolutionary unrest does Camelot reveal its basic valuations. I am not speaking of personal biases or construing anything about motivations. It seems a better—and sufficient—interpretation that what had been for some time a cultural common-law marriage between scientific functionalism and the natural interest of a leading world power in the status quo became under the aegis of Project Camelot an explicit and legitimate union. In any event, revolutionary movements are described in Camelot documents as "antisystem activities," indications of "severe disintegration," varieties of "destabilizing processes," threats to "legitimate control of the means of coercion within the society," facilitated by "administrative errors." Movements for radical change are in Camelot's view a disease, and a society so infected is sick. Here was a program for diagnosing social illness, a study in "epidemiology," called just that by a senior researcher. Another consistently refers to revolutionary movements as "social pathology," though disclaiming in footnote that they are necessarily to be avoided. A third conceives the growth of demands for change as "contagion." "Did the government," he proposes to determine, "couple limited and managed reforms with repressive measures to prevent the contagion and spread of social unrest?" Of course, waiting on call is the doctor, the U.S. Army, fully prepared for its self-appointed "important mission in the positive and constructive aspects of nation-building." The indicated treatment is "insurgency prophylaxis."

If Camelot had been given a title more appropriate to its "scientific" character, it might have been, "The Established Order: Do Not Fold, Spindle or Mutilate." But aside from President Kennedy's fondness for the musical comedy, "Camelot" was apparently for the Army happily symbolic of the knight in shining armor come to slay the dragon of disorder—and so gain half the kingdom. Social scientists, however, might have reflected on the deeper medieval connotation: their recruitment as the scholastics of cold-war theology.

Every citizen has the right to engage in counterinsurgency research and practice. But in my opinion none of us has leave, as scholar or citizen, to so delude himself and others about the scientific legitimacy and disinterested objectivity of this work. Here certain distinctions must be made. Just because the subject of research is intellectually important, it does not mean that the research proposal is important, or even any good. And just because the people involved in a bureaucratic operation are honest and conscientious—as every Camelot scholar I know is—does not mean that what they are engaged in has these qualities. This last sad fact all recent history teaches us.

... I have tried to formulate colleagues' opinions I have heard and which I share. For each and all the reasons stated I object to any further engagement in strategic research by American anthropologists working under contract to defense, foreign policy, or intelligence agencies of the U.S. government. I happen to believe it is no good for the country or the peoples among whom we have lived. I am convinced it is no good for our discipline or our mortal selves. I frame no resolutions, however, because I am undecided on the value of doing so. It would be an advantage to make clear to our government and the world that we are autonomous scientists concerned in our studies with a rational inquiry into man and his works. As against this, tedious debate and discussions of wording would probably not enhance solidarity nor produce a resolution of moral strength. More critical, we have no sanctions and cannot legislate ethics, and perhaps we should not try. For the moment, I favor the principle of letting each man learn to live with himself.

Gerald D. Berreman

Academic Colonialism: Not So Innocent Abroad

This selection puts the issue of anthropology in the Third World into an American perspective; the case in point is, as in Saberwal's article, which appears later in this section, India. It is important to recognize that India is a country whose population, including its academics, is largely sympathetic to the United States. The alarm with which they view free wheeling and free-spending research by Americans in their country is therefore of great significance to our consideration of the role of anthropology in the Third World, for many other nations and peoples of that world are far less sanguine about the aims and consequences of American anthropological research.

In the summer of 1968, American scholars of South Asian studies found their research in India jeopardized by disclosure in the New Delhi Parliament that the University of California's Himalayan Border Countries Project was to be financed for three years in the amount of $282,844 by the United States Department of Defense. This project had been in existence on a modest scale for several years under civilian, nongovernmental sponsorship. It comprised a number of independent, nonsecret investigations into the society, culture, and politics of India's northern border region, to be carried out by scholars from a number of American universities. The region is politically sensitive, and India's response to the Defense Department connection was vigorous; the project died. At the same time, visa applications by all American social science scholars were held up and closely scrutinized. There seem to have been pre-existing doubts about the aims and desirability of all foreign social science research, but the suspicions were exacerbated by the disclosures and resultant political clamor regarding the Himalayan Project. These events followed by less than six months the termination of activities by the Asia Foundation in India, requested by the government of India when it became known that the foundation had been receiving money from the CIA.

In the past year a more sweeping decision has been reported from India that no social science projects supported by United States Government funds will be approved, although it seems that individual scholars will be permitted to work on research fellowships, if their plans and sources of funds are approved by the appropriate Indian Government agencies. This unhappy picture for

American scholars is complemented in the United States by drastic reductions in financial support for research in India—reductions by at least 50 percent in the major sources, which are primarily governmental but unassociated with the defense or intelligence establishments.

The people most sadly affected are the American scholars who regard their work as a legitimate, sympathetic pursuit of knowledge contributing to international understanding, the results of which will be available to all and will serve no single or ulterior interest. These men and women have devoted many years to learning the languages and cultures of South Asia and to acquiring high competence in their various disciplines (notably anthropology, economics, geography, history, linguistics, philosophy, political science, sociology, and related fields). They have, for the most part, earned the respect and friendship of their Indian colleagues. Suddenly all of this is threatened.

It is a bitter but hardly surprising fact of life to these scholars that money for their work has dwindled as the American national administration has become more conservative, as the nation's resources continue to be devoted to the war machine, and as support for social science research has shifted to topics and regions of more immediate strategic interest than those of South Asia. They recognize it as ominous but not remarkable that increasing numbers of their colleagues have been driven to the Defense Department for funds to support research which is for the most part open and as innocuous as any can be these days. Increasingly, that has been the only place where funds could be readily found, or found at all. (The civilian backing of the ill-starred Himalayan Project had dried up when the Defense Department stepped in.)

But if some potential recipients of such funds have been willing to sacrifice long-run research opportunities for short-term financial advantages, many scholars have been aware of the inherent dangers. They have realized that, regardless of their own scientific objectivity, their investigations inevitably have social and political implications for the host nation. No matter how pure the researchers' motives, the research—particularly when supported by the defense or intelligence agencies—may be regarded by local authorities as dangerous or inappropriate, and it is *that* definition which is crucial for the continued opportunity to pursue the studies. The Executive Board of the American Anthropological Association put the matter clearly in a 1967 statement on Problems of Research and Ethics which was adopted by the Fellows of the Association. It said in part:

Anthropologists engaged in research in foreign areas should be especially concerned with the possible effects of their sponsorship and sources of financial support. Although the Department of Defense and other mission-oriented branches of the Government support some basic research in the social sciences, their sponsorship may nevertheless create an extra hazard in the conduct of fieldwork and jeopardize future access to research opportunities in the areas studied.

The concern thus expressed seems justified in light of testimony presented before the Senate Committee on Foreign Relations, May 9, 1968, on "Defense Department Sponsored Foreign Affairs Research." In an introductory statement, John S. Foster, Jr., director of Defense Research and Engineering of the Department of Defense, said of projects sponsored by his department in foreign areas: "We are interested only in those so-called cultural and social factors that have clear relationship to defense activities. Today this spans a great range because the Defense Department shares responsibility for many international activities." He went on to say that the Defense Department seeks "understanding of how to deter war and build a peaceful world. Part of this understanding comes, in turn, from social and behavioral sciences research and foreign area assessments related to any contingency and area in which a substantial American commitment might occur" (see also *The Nation*, July 22, 1968). These statements suggest the reasons why most scholars shy away from Defense Department money and why they find naive at best the belief of some of their colleagues that the source of funds is irrelevant if the research is pure—certainly it is not irrelevant in the nations where they hope to be made welcome.

The reaction in Indian political circles has been what one might expect. In the case of the Himalayan project, for example, the government found itself subject to criticism from every opposition quarter for appearing to permit American defense-oriented research in its sensitive border regions. The leftist *National Herald* said in an irate editorial on August 7, 1968:

The External Affairs Ministry seems to be innocent of many things, and the Education Ministry is not only innocent but ignorant. But someone in authority should have known the implications of such a project as the California University's research on the Himalayan border countries. The university's authorities could not have been innocent or ignorant of what research in the Himalayan border means, and if there was any doubt among others, it should now be dispelled by the report that the project has been partly financed by an agency of the mighty U.S. Defence Department. . . . The Government should have been correctly advised on the Himalayan project . . . [which] should never have been approved by anyone alive to the nation's self-respect and security.

The government reacted quickly; and the compromised research was not undertaken.

The problems are real, they are now widely recognized and, while there are no easy solutions, some attempts at amelioration are in progress. One of the most notable, although it would appear to come too late to help in India, has been the continuing effort by Senators Fulbright, Harris, and others to initiate a National Social Science Foundation to facilitate nonmilitary government sponsorship of nonmilitary projects. The Senate voted recently to cut substantially Defense Department funds for this type of research. Meanwhile, the Committee on South Asia of the Association for Asian Studies is seeking additional nongovernment money to supplement the dwindling sources available for support of American post-doctoral studies in South Asia.

But these are not the gravest problems facing American social scientists in India. A more fundamental and far-reaching threat to their opportunities has only recently come to the shocked attention of many of those whom it will affect. It is the questioning by Indian scholars of the prerogatives foreigners have enjoyed in their research in India. This attitude is familiar in other regions of the world, and it will no doubt increase in intensity everywhere. In India it is found especially among the young, dynamic generation of scholars who had not borne the brunt of political colonialism or the Independence period, but who have experienced the social, economic, and political frustrations of the post-Independence era. Many of them are at least partly foreign-trained, but they have resisted the temptations of the "brain drain," often at

considerable personal sacrifice, in order to participate in the hoped for solution to India's problems. Their questioning of foreign research in India is sharp and uncompromising. Its tone is best suggested by their own term: "academic colonialism." What some would define as the exercise of free and objective inquiry among members of the international community of scholars, they see as a threat to India's scientific and ideological independence, to its self-interest and self-respect. The attitudes underlying this point of view are associated with opposition to political, economic, and cultural colonialism throughout the world, and to a similar exploitation characterized as "internal colonialism" by blacks and other minorities in the United States.

The issue came vividly to my attention during an international seminar at the Indian Institute of Advanced Study in July 1968, shortly before the Himalayan Project reached public notice. An Indian social anthropologist who had received his postgraduate degree in Australia and taught in the United Kingdom before returning to India, gave a paper entitled "Science and *Swaraj*" (self-rule), using in the title a watchword of the Independence movement. He made the point that Indian social science is dominated by foreign money and ideology; that foreigners (especially Americans and Britons) largely determine what research is to be done and how. Extremely little money is available to Indian social scientists; foreign scholars, by comparison, arrive lavishly financed. Therefore, foreigners carry out an overwhelmingly disproportionate amount of such research in India, although the absolute amount is modest indeed. Outside dominance is accomplished by characteristically colonial attitudes of academic superiority and is enhanced in turn by a concession of that superiority on the part of many Indian scholars. Too many of them defer to the prestige of foreign degrees, foreign publications, and foreign ideas, and those who do attract most of the scarce local resources. The Indian anthropologist said in his paper: "The existing system of foreign aid in science . . . upholds the system of foreign dominance in all matters of scientific and professional life and organization. It is nothing but the satellite system, with an added subsidy." He called for the development of an Indian social science, attuned to Indian problems and with Indian standards of relevance, ethics, and excellence, to replace the predominant scientific internationalism that implicitly denigrates indigenous science and scientists. Others have referred directly to the racism inherent in many Western scholars' assessments of Asian scholarship.

In December 1968 the Indian intellectual journal *Seminar* published a symposium of six papers under the title "Academic Colonialism." The authors showed special concern about the potential intelligence activities of foreign academics, or at least the intelligence uses made of their findings. They expressed alarm at the tendency to judge scholarship by foreign standards, with the result that research topics, methods, and analyses relevant to the Indian situation are being ignored. A complementary concern was that overreaction might produce an equally dangerous devaluation of *all* that is foreign in science and scholarship.

The remedies suggested for these ills might disturb foreign scholars even more than the ailments identified. One writer proposed a five-year moratorium on foreign aid for academic needs in India, and an end to foreign experts, advisers, and visiting professors, and perhaps a ban on foreign travel by Indian scholars. In his concluding words, "Academic autarchy is the most appropriate slogan for the present generation of academics." Another contributor suggested, among other things, a panel of Indian experts to screen all research proposed by foreign scholars, to comment on their academic and technical qualifications, on their sources of money, and on the implications of their work for the national interest. He advocated a similar screening for Indian scholars but without a judgment as to projects' desirability, "political or otherwise." And he advocated the founding of a social science archive where copies of all data collected by foreign scholars in India would be deposited. Other authors suggested less drastic measures to protect India's autonomy in social science, without jeopardizing the benefits to be derived from foreign contacts.

The basic motivation for this new assertiveness is not unlike that of black Americans who today call for separatism in order to rebuild a shattered self-esteem and to create institutions responsive to the needs and desires of their own people, long and disastrously excluded from the institutions and rewards of the dominant society. As one contributor to the symposium put it, the political problem for the Indian is whether he will be a cog in someone else's research wheel, or be in a position of control or at least parity through hard bargaining, pitting the double advantage of his expertise and his position as citizen of the host nation against the monetary resources of the foreign researcher. If the conditions of research "are unfavorable to the [Indian] researcher or his and his country's dignity to the slightest degree, the proposal should be rejected forthwith."

The problem of academic colonialism is real both for Indians and for foreign scholars in India. Many of the latter are surprised that it is raised by those with whom they felt they had the greatest rapport. But surprise should not turn to anger or to pessimism. The editor of the *Seminar* symposium indicated in his introductory essay that "the situation demands sober and balanced assessment, accurate perception and definition of reality, aware that our own judgments are the only ultimate basis for public policy." American scholars would do well to heed this statement and its implications. The financial, political, and prestige advantage we have enjoyed for many years are now disappearing along with other, more widely recognized aspects of colonialism. Indian scholars welcome this disappearance, and I believe that thoughtful scholars everywhere should do the same; it signals the end of intellectual subservience. Whatever the future availability and distribution of funds, Americans will never again find unquestioning acquiescence in their research plans. In India, as in most of the rest of the world, they will be questioned: why this research; how will it benefit you; how will it benefit us; what are your qualifications to do it, and what will be our role? If forthright and satisfactory answers are not given, and quickly, the research will simply be banned. The same questions are being asked here at home by the dispensers of funds, and unfortunately the answers they demand of researchers in foreign areas are often precisely antithetical to those demanded by the host nations. Those who provide the money here want control and relevance to their interests; those who permit research in their own lands want control and relevance to *their* interests. The dilemma can be solved in only one way: funds must come from sources acceptable to the host nations, and projects must be designed to coincide with their interests and their standards of scientific and social relevance. Projects will be judged partly in terms of fostering a social environment and an identity consistent with the final disappearance of colonization and the emergence of true equality and reciprocity in a nation's relationships with other nations and other peoples. Approval of research will inevitably depend on nationalistic as well as scientific criteria.

The only hope for continued American academic research abroad (as among our own ethnic minorities) lies in genuine responsiveness to the needs, desires, and demands of the host communities. This means not only conformity to explicit requirements when those are set forth but evidence of full respect for the intellect, judgment, and responsibility of scholars and citizens in the other society. Scholarly respect has too often taken the form of lip service. It has been easy to express collaborative and reciprocal intent, but harder to make certain that Indian colleagues have the opportunity to share in the choice of research topic, in its planning and execution, in the analysis and writing of results. It has been easy to send social science graduate students to India for research, but harder to be sure that Indian students can participate in American-financed research in India or come here for study. It has been easy to give a few university lectures while doing research in India, but harder to bring Indian colleagues here to work and teach. Now these harder tasks must be undertaken, belatedly, if the easier ones are to continue.

Respect for Indian colleagues must now include respect for a kind of academic and scientific nationalism that many scholar-liberals will find hard to swallow—just as their domestic counterparts find hard to swallow the demands of their black or Chicano or other minority colleagues and students that teaching and research be not only relevant to their communities but conducted by members of those communities. The foreign scholar's position of advantage in India may well be replaced, for a time, not with equality but with subordination. Liberalism and tolerance then will have to be replaced by acceptance of and cooperation in what some would regard as a radically nationalistic social science. Collaborative research may well be the only foreign research.

If deference to indigenous values and scientific priorities is the price to be paid for research in newly emancipated societies, it should be remembered that this price has always been exacted by uncolonized societies. It is neither exorbitant nor dishonorable. If American scholars are to be welcomed or even tolerated in the Third World, they must prove that they are not simply well-meaning cultural emissaries or disinterested scientific innocents abroad but that they are aware of the implications of their work for those among whom they work and are prepared to act accordingly. If that is not achieved, Americans face a long period of enforced academic isolationism.

Kathleen Gough
World Revolution and the Science of Man

The next selection became almost at once a classic and controversial advocacy of radical anthropology. Its message, that anthropology has served governments, empires, and capitalistic economic interests, rather than people, is hard to refute. Its plea that anthropology turn around and serve those it has traditionally studied rather than those who rule or exploit them is impossible to ignore, even by those who oppose it. It strikes a responsive cord among peoples of the Third World, among repressed internal minorities, and among all others who are oppressed and excluded in the contemporary world. Since these are the people most anthropologists have studied, their views and their interests have a legitimate and perhaps a paramount claim on the anthropologist's attention. And since these people are increasingly in positions to grant or withhold access to research situations, their opinions are crucial to the future of the discipline.

You, who are so liberal and so humane, who have such an exaggerated adoration of culture that it verges on affectation, you pretend to forget that you own colonies and that in them men are massacred in your name.

—Jean-Paul Sartre, Preface to *The Wretched of the Earth* by Frantz Fanon[1]

Since early 1965, United States military forces have been responsible for exterminating large numbers of people in Vietnam. Both the political circumstances of the Vietnam war and the peculiar weapons used in it make clear that this has been no conflict between nations of comparable strength. It has been an attempt by a great industrial power to impose a native tyranny on a small, preindustrial nation in defiance of international law. By January 1967 about a quarter of a million children had been killed and over a million burned or otherwise maimed for life.[2]

A naive observer might have expected that anthropologists, among whom respect for human life, tolerance of cultural differences, and equal regard for races are axiomatic, would have risen to condemn this slaughter collectively and uncompromisingly. This did not happen. Many anthropologists have signed public protests, and some have taken part in teach-ins. One or two anthropologists who had worked in Vietnam added their voices and wrote up their research,[3] and at least one visited Saigon independently and interviewed American intelligence agents. Significantly, this study was published in liberal and left-wing journals,[4] not in the *American Anthropologist*. It was not until November 1966 that the American Anthropological Association, at its annual business meeting, passed a resolution that condemned "the use of napalm, chemical defoliants, harmful gases, bombing, the torture and killing of political prisoners and prisoners of war, and the intentional or deliberate policies of genocide or forced transportation of populations." It asked that "all governments" put an end to their use at once and "proceed as rapidly as possible to a peaceful settlement of the war in Vietnam."

The Vietnam resolution had, however, a history that illustrates some of the conflicts and strained loyalties among anthropologists. It came from a small number of socialists and left-wing liberals whose views cannot be called representative of the Association at large. Its introduction was opposed by the president-elect and by a majority of the executive board. The chairman felt obliged to judge the resolution "political," and hence out of order, since the Association's stated purpose is "to advance the science of anthropology and to further the professional interests of American anthropologists."[5] A hubbub ensued at the conference in which the resolution was salvaged when one member suddenly proclaimed, "Genocide is not in the professional interests of anthropologists!" This allowed the proponent to cite previous "political" resolutions passed by the anthropologists on such subjects as racial equality, nuclear weapons, and the lives and welfare of aboriginal peoples. A motion to overrule the chair then passed by a narrow margin. Amendments were next introduced that removed an allegation that the United States was infringing international law by using forbidden weapons, and transferred responsibility for the war from the United States government to "all governments." The amended resolution was passed by a large majority, some of whom later said it was the strongest, and others the weakest, that they could hope for. The proceedings showed that under pressure, most anthropologists are willing to put their profession on record as opposed to mass slaughter. But most are evidently unwilling to condemn their own government.

Why this ethical ambiguity among anthropologists, and why their doubts whether the life or death of a Southeast Asian people has anything to do with them, in their professional capacity, at all?

"World Revolution and the Science of Man," by Kathleen Gough from *The Dissenting Academy*, edited by Theodore Roszak. Copyright © 1968 by Random House, Inc. Reprinted by permission of Random House, Inc. and Chatto and Windus Ltd.

[1] Frantz Fanon, *The Wretched of the Earth*, trans. Constance Farrington (New York: Grove Press, 1963), p. 12.

[2] William F. Pepper, "The Destruction of a Culture," *Viet Report*, November–December 1966, and "The Children of Vietnam," *Ramparts*, January 1966. Pepper estimates 60 to 70 percent of the population of South Vietnam to be children under 16. Total civilian casualties in Vietnam since 1961 are estimated at about 2.6 million.

[3] See Gerald Hickey's study of a Mekong delta village, *Village in Vietnam* (New Haven: Yale University Press, 1964).

[4] Marshall Sahlins, "The Destruction of Conscience in Vietnam," *Dissent*, January–February 1966, pp. 36–62. Part of this article was earlier published in the *Nation*.

[5] The resolution appears in *Science* 154 (December 23, 1966): 1525. For reports of the debate see the *New York Times*, November 20, 1966, and "Constitution and By-Laws of the American Anthropological Association," *Fellow Newsletter of the American Anthropological Association*, 7 (1966).

One answer is that there have been too many massacres in the past thirty years for anthropologists, as a profession, to take positions on each of them. If anthropologists discussed and lobbied against every atrocity, they would have no time for research and would not be anthropologists. This is a serious argument, as anyone knows who has tried to carry out his own particular work side by side with action against the war in Vietnam.

Even so, anthropologists do afford time for relatively trivial pursuits. Each of their annual conferences presents several hundred highly specialized papers; and their business meetings are filled with tedious discussions of budget problems and of the numbers of words and pages their journals devote to various kinds of book reviews. Some of this time, surely, could be set aside to discuss issues of national and international significance instead of having these issues crammed into the last ten minutes of the business meeting and the first ten minutes of the cocktail hour. Anthropological journals are full of articles on such very limited subjects as, for example, prescriptive marriage systems, kinship terms, or the Tzental words for "firewood." Such topics are of course legitimate, even fascinating, in their own right or as illustrations of new research methods. However, they bypass the most crucial problems of world society. Cumulatively, they also evade a central question: Who is to evaluate and suggest guidelines for human society, if not those who study it? It is as though the more we study the world's cultures, the less capable we feel of making judgments as citizens; certainly, the less able to speak or act collectively on the basis of our knowledge.

This partial paralysis results, I think, from the way in which, over time, the social settings of anthropologists have affected their research problems, theories, and conceptions of social responsibility.

The roots of modern anthropology can be traced back to the humanist visions of such writers of the Enlightenment as Rousseau and Montesquieu in France, Lord Monboddo in England, and Adam Ferguson in Scotland. These thinkers and others who followed them in the early nineteenth century were concerned to develop a complete science of man which they assumed would automatically result in the enhancement of mankind's welfare and the expansion of human freedom, knowledge,

and power. It was a grand vision, and one we have not entirely lost sight of. As a modern empirical science, however, anthropology came into its own in the last decades of the nineteenth and the early twentieth century. The period was one in which the Western nations were making their final push to bring the preindustrial and preliterate peoples of virtually the entire earth under their political and economic control. Thus modern anthropology, as a university discipline, is a child of Western capitalist imperialism.

Before World War II, fieldwork was almost all done in societies under the domination of the government of the anthropologist's own country; occasionally, under that of a friendly Western power. In the Old World the imperial powers were clearly recognizable and predominantly European. The world of most American anthropologists was, of course, different from that of Europeans, for the primitive peoples chiefly studied by Americans were conquered Indian groups who had been placed on reservations. Nevertheless, there were essential similarities, and in some respects it is justifiable to regard the American Indians, like the Negroes, as colonial people living under varying forms of Western imperialism. In the course of their field studies anthropologists worked out customary relationships with both the conquered peoples they studied and their own imperial governments. Living in close contact with "the natives," anthropologists tended to adopt liberal attitudes toward them and to uphold their interests against the encroachments of their conquerors. At the same time, anthropologists were usually white men, higher in rank than those whom they studied, virtually immune to attack or judgment by their informants, and protected by imperial law. Of necessity, they accepted the imperial framework as given.

Since World War II, a new situation has come about. Today some 2.3 billion people live in "underdeveloped" countries, that is to say, countries outside Europe, North America, Australia, New Zealand, and Japan, that were formerly colonies or spheres of influence of industrial capitalist powers.[6] About 773 million out of these 2.3 billion, or one third, have, through revolution, passed out of the orbit of capitalist imperialism

[6] The figures used here are from *The World Alamanac and Book of Facts* (New York, 1967), and are derived from United Nations estimates.

into the Communist states of China, North Korea, North Vietnam, Mongolia, and Cuba. Because of the Cold War, they have also almost passed out of the purview of American anthropologists, although a few Europeans like Jan Myrdal and Isabel and David Crook have made recent studies. On the other hand, another 49 million, or 2 percent of the total, remain in colonies or former colonies under white governments. Most of these governments are European or of recent European origin, but American capital and influence have penetrated them deeply since World War II. The largest of these colonial states, containing 39 million people, are in southern Africa. Three of them (South Africa, South-West Africa, and Rhodesia) have lost or severed their connection with the mother country. In general, southern African colonial governments are now so represssive that it is difficult for foreign anthropologists to work in these colonies.

Between these extremes live some 1.5 billion people, or 65 percent of the total, in nations that are politically at least nominally independent yet are still within the orbit of Western power and influence. Outside the American Indian reservations, this is the world in which most anthropological studies are made today.

In order to grasp the situation in which most anthropologists carry on their professional work, let us briefly survey the political geography of their world.

About 22 percent, or at least 511 million of the 1.5 billion people who inhabit underdeveloped societies remaining outside either Communist or more-or-less classical colonial control, live in what we may call "client states." The largest of these states (those with populations of over 5 million) are Colombia, Argentina, Peru, Brazil, Ecuador, Chile, Venezuela, the Philippines, South Vietnam, South Korea, Thailand, Taiwan, Malaysia, the Republic of the Congo, Nigeria, Iran, Saudi Arabia, Cameroon, and Turkey. These are nations with indigenous governments which are, however, so constrained by Western military and economic aid, trade, or private investments that they have little autonomy. Many of their governments would collapse if Western aid were withdrawn.

About 318 million people, or 14 percent of the underdeveloped world, live in nations whose governments are beholden to the United States; most of the rest, to Britain or France. Most of the United States-sponsored client states lie in Latin America, the traditional preserve of United States capital, or on the borders of the Communist world, where the United States has established satellite regimes in an effort to prevent the spread of Communism.

Client states are more difficult to identify than old-style colonies, for modern neo-imperialism varies in intensity. It is hard to determine the point at which the government of an underdeveloped nation has surrendered its ability to decide the main directions of its country's policy. My list of client states is therefore tentative. If, as many would, we add Mexico and Pakistan to the list of the United States client states, this brings the population of client states to 657 million, or 28 percent of the underdeveloped world. United States client states (as distinct from actual colonies) then contain 464 million, or 20 percent of the underdeveloped world.

There remain some 873 million people, or 37 percent of the total, in nations usually regarded as relatively independent and politically neutral. The larger nations in this category (those with populations of over 5 million) are Burma, Cambodia, India, Ceylon, Afghanistan, Nepal, Syria, Iraq, Yemen, the United Arab Republic, Algeria, Morocco, Kenya, Tanzania, Sudan, Ethiopia, Uganda, Ghana, and Indonesia. The governments of these nations, whether military, one-party, or multiparty, tend to contain popular nationalist leaders, while those of most of the client states tend either to have been installed by Western powers or to have arisen as a result of military coups that had Western approval. Most of these more independent nations trade with and receive aid from both Western and Communist industrial powers. Most profess to be in some sense socialist. The appeal of their governments is of multiclass, or what Peter Worsley calls a "populist," character.[7] There is a public sector of the economy and an emphasis on national planning, as well as a large private sector dominated by foreign capital.

During the 1950s many liberal social scientists and others hoped that these neutral nations would form a strong Third World that could act independently of the Communist and the Western powers. These hopes have crashed in the past few years, chiefly because of the expansion of American capital and military power, the refusal of European

[7] Peter Worsley, *The Third World* (Chicago: University of Chicago Press, 1965), pp. 118–74.

nations to relinquish their own economic strong-holds, and the neutral nations' failure to raise the standard of living of their burgeoning populations, leading to ever greater dependence on the West.[8] In the past fifteen years, at least 227 million people in sixteen nations have, after a longer or shorter period of relative independence, moved into, or moved back into, a client relationship, usually with the United States. These nations are Guatemala, Honduras, the Dominican Republic, Guyana, Venezuela, Brazil, Argentina, Bolivia, Ecuador, Trinidad and Tobago, South Vietnam, Thailand, Laos, the Congo, Togo, and Gabon. In most of these countries the shift in orientation followed a military coup.

A further 674 million in India, Indonesia, Af-ghanistan, Ceylon, Kenya, and Ghana, which I have classified as "independent," have, more-over, recently moved into much closer depend-ence on the United States, so that their future as independent nations is very uncertain. This is especially the case in Ghana and Indonesia since the recent military coups.

If in fact all these nations are moving into client status, this leaves only 199 million, or 8 percent of the underdeveloped world, in the category of neutral nations, and brings to a total of 1.14 billion, or 48 percent of the underdeveloped world, the people who live in client or near-client states of the United States or in its colonial dependencies. We must also remember that United States capital and military power now exert a strong influence on the colonies and client states of European pow-ers (11 percent of the total), as well as on the re-maining 8 percent of "neutral" states. In these circumstances, United States power can truly be said to be entrenched with more or less firmness throughout the non-Communist underdeveloped world.

Countering this reimposition of Western power, armed revolutionary movements now exist in at least twenty countries with a total population of 266 million. These countries are Guatemala, Peru, Venezuela, Ecuador, Paraguay, Brazil, Honduras, Bolivia, Colombia, Angola, Mozambique, the Congo, Cameroon, Portuguese Guinea, Yemen, Southern Arabia, the Philippines, Thailand, Laos, and South Vietnam. About 501 million people live in seven other countries where unarmed revolution-ary movements or parties have wide support, namely India (especially the states of Bengal and

Kerala), Rhodesia, South-West Africa, South Africa, Nicaragua, the Dominican Republic, and Panama. In more than one third of the underdevel-oped world, therefore, revolution is a considered possibility, while in another third it has already been accomplished. Even in the remaining relative-ly stable colonial, client, or neutral states, a majority of the people are staying poor or growing poorer, while a small minority of rich are growing richer. Populations are increasing, discontent is wide-spread, and revolutionary ferment is probable with-in the next decade or two.[9]

This is the background against which anthro-pologists make their field studies today.

Fundamentally, the contemporary anthropolo-gist's dilemma springs from the fact that much of the non-Western world is in a state of actual or potential revolution against the Western powers and against the kinds of native elites that are sup-ported from the West. The United States govern-ment is the foremost counterrevolutionary force pitted against this revolutionary tide. It is at times aided by European governments, who also have their own counterrevolutionary interests to pro-tect. This means that anthropologists are increas-ingly being caught up in struggles between the powers that fund them and many of the people they are wont to study. This disrupts the whole pattern of relationships that anthropologists have built up over the past eighty years between their own governments and the non-Western objects of their studies. It also faces them with grave kinds of value problems.

Before World War II, anthropologists could console themselves with the thought that neither they nor others could do much to dismantle the existing empires. It therefore behooved the anthro-pologist to analyze the institutions within colonial society as a service to posterity, and to aid reforms

[8] For discussions of U.S. economic and military expansion in the underdeveloped countries, see Robert Wolfe, "American Imperialism and the Peace Movement," *Studies on the Left*, May–June 1966, pp. 28–44; Paul Baran and Paul Sweezy, *Monopoly Capital* (New York: Monthly Review Press, 1966), especially pp. 178–217.

[9] In his study "Hunger" (*Canadian Dimension*, in press), Professor A. G. Frank of Sir George Williams University, Montreal, uses data from the United Nations Food and Agricultural Organization to show that per capita food production has been decreasing in most of the non-Communist, non-Western nations since 1960. His statistics come from the FAO's *The State of Food and Agriculture, 1964* (Rome, 1964). Also on the growing disparity of incomes in non-Communist underdeveloped countries, see Gunnar Myrdal, *An International Economy* (New York: Harper & Row, Publishers, 1956).

where he could. Later, in the 1940s and 1950s, it appeared possible that many colonial societies might gain genuine political *and* economic independence by peaceful means. Today this is no longer the case. Western dominance is continuing under new guises, even expanding and hardening. At the same time, revolutionary movements exist. Events in Vietnam suggest that in at least some areas, non-Western peoples will henceforth be "controllable" from the West only through extermination, if at all. Revolution to overthrow Western dominance in the underdeveloped world increasingly presents *the* alternative to progressive deterioration under Western control.

In these conditions, the practical decisions that anthropologists must make impose value judgments on them as well. For example, in countries where revolutionary movements have arisen or where there is revolutionary ferment among peasants and urban workers, shall the Western anthropologist try to work among these people?[10] Shall he do so even if this involves disobeying or risking offense to his own government? If he is able to gain entry to revolutionary segments of the people, can an anthropologist in fact study them adequately without making political and value commitments, or will his work not then remain wooden and superficial and his problems arid? Shall he remain in the suburbs of the cities among groups who are favorable to the local regime, and at least half favorable to his own government? Shall he, as an applied anthropologist, place himself in the service of his own counterrevolutionary government abroad? Or shall he retire to the remotest hill tribes, if he can still find any, and try to avoid the conflict?

In his home university, shall an anthropologist try to teach about the questions that are shaking world society: the dynamics of latter-day neo-imperialism, for example, or the genesis of guerrilla movements and the conditions for their success? Shall he inquire into the relative efficiency for economic (and spiritual) development of the various communist, "populist," or capitalist models? Or shall he immure himself in the political economies, kinship systems, and religious institutions of preconquest and early colonial societies, or of small local communities in the remaining relatively stable parts of the world? If he sticks to the latter course, by what theoretical criteria is he to justify the limitations of his approach?

To touch on immediate problems, how shall an anthropologist, just back from India or Southeast Asia, counsel the student who comes to him with the confidence that he does not wish to be sent to burn, bomb, or shoot Asian peasants who are fighting for their national independence—or merely hiding in their villages? How for that matter shall he confront the student who, confined from birth in a jingoist and anticommunist frame of thought, is quite ready to do this work? How shall the anthropologist act when he learns that the grades he gives these same students, on the basis of their knowledge of non-Western societies, are to be used by the United States military to determine whether or not they are to be sent to destroy Vietnam?[11]

Unfortunately, many anthropologists seem ill-equipped to respond adequately to these challenges and value problems, being too parochial and specialized and sometimes, indeed, too ignorant of the general state of affairs.

In particular, over the past fifty years, in spite of unquestionably great advances in knowledge of primitive societies, I suggest that anthropology has been weak in two respects.

First, anthropologists have failed to evaluate and analyze, as a world social system and an interconnected political economy, the structure of Western imperialism and the common and variant features of its impact on the non-Western world. In the past few years this defect has been somewhat remedied by a few new studies. The early chapters of Peter Worsley's *The Third World* give an overview of Western colonial expansion, and the later ones an analysis of developments in the new nations of non-Communist Asia and of Africa. Immanuel Wallerstein's *Social Change: The Colonial Situation* ... makes a useful contribution by drawing together relevant extracts and articles by anthropologists, nationalist leaders, and others over

---

[10] For a rare example of such a study, see Donald L. Barnett and Karari Njama, *Mau Mau from Within* (London: MacGibbon & Kee, 1966).

[11] The practice has a special irony for anthropologists. It means that they are now using their students' reception of the knowledge they themselves obtained from non-Western tribal and peasant peoples, in order to select functionaries who will go to exterminate precisely such peoples in Vietnam.

In these circumstances, a few anthropologists have resigned their teaching appointments or have refused to grade their students. Professor Donald L. Barnett of the University of Iowa, for example, an anthropologist and father of four children, has received notice that his pay will be cut off from the day that he fails to hand in his grades. He has refused to submit to this threat, thereby endangering—or more probably, ending—his professional career in America.

the past twenty years. It is remarkable, however, that so few anthropologists have studied modern Western imperialism as a historical epoch and a distinctive social system.

It is true, of course, that anthropologists have made numerous studies of modern social change in preindustrial societies, especially in local communities. They have, however, usually handled them through very general concepts: "culture-contact," "acculturation," "social change," "modernization," "urbanization," "Westernization," or "the folk-urban continuum." Force, suffering, and exploitation tend to disappear in these accounts of structural processes, and the units of study are so small that it is hard to see the forest for the trees. These approaches, in the main, have produced factual accounts and limited hypotheses about the impact of industrial or preindustrial cultures in local communities, but have done little to aid understanding of the world distribution of power under imperialism or of its total system of economic relationships.[12] Until very recently there has also, of course, been a bias in the types of non-Western social units chosen for study, with primitive communities least touched by modern changes being preferred over the mines, cash-crop plantations, white settlements, bureaucracies, urban concentrations, and nationalist movements that have played such prominent roles in colonial societies.[13]

The second weakness I would point to is that in the accumulation of factual detail and of limited hypotheses, we have gradually lost sight of the initial question of the Enlightenment: How can the science of man help men to live more fully and creatively and to expand their dignity, self-direction, and freedom?

Relating this question to the methods and immediate problems of anthropology is of course difficult. Social science is not social philosophy, and tends to become bad social science when it tries to be. Nevertheless, I suggest that social science, like all science, becomes morally and socially either meaningless or harmful unless its skills and knowledge are periodically referred back to the question, "Science for what purpose and for whom?" If we cease to ask this question, we cease to seek wisdom and cease to be intellectuals in any meaningful sense of the word. With the loss of responsibility for our learning, we also cease to be fully social, and therefore human.

Moreover, values do enter anthropological research at many points, whether or not this is recognized. They enter into the selection of problems, the choice of variables, and thus the interpretation of data. I suggest that an anthropologist who is explicit about his own values is likely to frame his problems more sharply and to see more clearly the lines between values and data than one who has not examined his values.

A contrary view of the ethical neutrality of science and of its complete irrelevance to social responsibility is, however, often advanced nowadays in departments of anthropology. In fact, whether consciously or unconsciously, the "ethical neutrality" position seems to be taken up as an excuse for not espousing unpopular viewpoints or getting into controversies. Most anthropologists, for example, make no theoretical objection to applied anthropology. Yet an applied anthropologist both influences policy and also necessarily accepts, at least in part, the broad framework of policy of an administrative body—often, an imperialist government.

In sum, therefore, it must be acknowledged that anthropology has not been and cannot be ethically neutral. Rather, what seems to have happened is that in circumstances of increasing specialization, bureaucratization, and management of research by governments, anthropologists have virtually ceased to ask explicitly what the human goals of their science are. More and more reduced to the status of hired functionaries, they have tended to

---

[12] There is, of course, a large literature on this subject, much of it influenced by Marx. Early studies, besides the classic treatments by J. A. Hobson, Lenin, and Rosa Luxemburg, include Parker T. Moon's *Imperialism and World Politics* (London: Macmillan & Co., Ltd., 1926). More recent works include Paul Baran's *Political Economy of Growth* (New York: Monthly Review Press, 1957); Frantz Fanon's *Studies in a Dying Colonialism* (New York: Monthly Review Press, 1962) and *The Wretched of the Earth* (New York: Grove Press, 1963); and Kwame Nkrumah, *Neo-Colonialism, the Last Stage of Imperialism* (New York: International Publishers, 1966). Such works are not, however, very commonly used in departments of anthropology and seldom appear in standard bibliographies of the social sciences in America.

[13] For this and other criticisms of modern anthropology see *The End of Anthropology?* a paper prepared for the Sociology and Anthropology Working Group of the sixth World Congress of Sociology, by Peter Worsley, Department of Sociology, University of Manchester. Important exceptions to this criticism in the last few years have been A. L. Epstein, *Politics in an Urban African Community* (Manchester: Manchester University Press, 1958); Michael P. Banton, *West African City: A Study of Tribal Life in Freetown* (New York: Oxford University Press, 1957); and Julian H. Steward, *The People of Puerto Rico*. (Urbana: University of Illinois Press, 1956).

make productivity of facts and of mutually un-related hypotheses their goal. The fear of being speculative and "unempirical" (a fear that may bear some relation to the less conscious fear of pro-ducing politically or socially "subversive" theories) has made much current anthropological work frag-mented and dull. In abdicating the search for benef-icent goals for our science, we have ceased to be its masters and have turned into its slaves.

For a speculative and questioning anthropolo-gist in America, the networks of research and teaching within which he must work are increasing-ly repressive. Although part of the responsibility lies with the size, specialization, and complexity of universities, the main sources of constriction stem from the government and the military and indus-trial institutions, which now penetrate education so deeply. This is not surprising. The United States is the world's wealthiest and most powerful nation. It is dedicated to delaying or preventing social change throughout two thirds of the world, and anthro-pologists are either salaried employees of its state governments, or are funded by its federal govern-ment or by private segments of its power elite. While professors need not always actively support current policies, they may be handsomely rewarded if they do so and they are discouraged from effec-tively opposing them. The fact that constraints are usually unofficial and vaguely formulated, and that they operate within a rhetoric of democratic and academic freedoms, only adds to the bafflement and frustration of unconventional scholars.

University teachers seldom publicize painful professional incidents, and rumor is unreliable. To document examples of constraint I must therefore fall back on personal experiences. In October 1962, while employed as assistant professor at a small Eastern university of liberal reputation, I made a speech at a public meeting of students and faculty condemning the American blockade of Cuba. This brought on a furious blast from the university's president in a private interview. It was followed by a false written accusation, lodged with my depart-ment, that I had said I hoped Cuban missiles would destroy American cities. Later came the news, passed to me in private by a group of senior faculty members, that regardless of my colleagues' recom-mendations the university president had decided not to renew my three-year contract in 1964. In 1963, after months of argument and mental turmoil, my husband and I resigned from the university.[14]

Later in 1963 I learned from various parts of the country that the Immigration and Naturalization Service was making private inquiries among my colleagues as to whether they considered me a danger to the security of the United States. (I was at that time a British immigrant of seven years' standing in the United States.) Nothing happened, so my fellow anthropologists must have been con-vinced of my harmlessness. In 1964 I applied for a grant from the National Science Foundation to restudy two South Indian villages after an absence of fifteen years. I wanted in particular to find out why most of the villagers had become Communist supporters. A reply by letter informed me that the Foundation was unable to finance this research. Later, I heard privately that the committee of anthropologists appointed to judge the application had approved it, but that the Department of State had vetoed it on the grounds that federally financed research into the causes of revolutionary move-ments was not thought desirable in India at present.

Nonetheless, in that same year, as later became known, the United States Army allotted four to six million dollars for social science research in thirty-one countries of Asia, Africa, Latin America, North America, and Europe under Project Came-lot, designed to "assess the potential for internal war in national societies,"[15] or in the words of one sociologist, "to learn how to measure revolutionary forces, and to understand the processes by which revolutions are generated."[16] The anomaly sprang, of course, not only from differences of policy be-tween the Department of State and the Army. The researchers under Camelot were intended to dis-cover how to prevent revolutions (a subject known as "insurgency prophylaxis"), while I, with my con-fessed warmth toward Castro's Cuba, might be suspected of sympathy with them. Fortunately, whereas Camelot was canceled in the midst of an international scandal in 1965, I did scrape up the dollars, partly privately and partly from an auxil-iary research award from the Social Science Re-search Council for research of my own choosing, to carry out my work in India. On my return, the State

[14] For further details, see the *Justice* (Brandeis University, Waltham, Mass.), March 26 and April 2, 1963.

[15] I. L. Horowitz, "The Life and Death of Project Camelot," *Trans-Action*, 3, (November–December 1965): 4. [Reprinted earlier in this section.]

[16] William J. Goode, defending the project in the *American Sociol-ogist*, 1 (November 1966): 256.

Department's initial squeamishness did not prevent its research department from immediately writing to request a copy of the first paper I read on the research before a regional conference of anthropologists.

The profession itself, however, seemed less interested. An editor of a firm publishing books in the social sciences told me that American readers "simply would not be interested" in a book dealing with the spread of Communist ideas among Indian villagers. It was not "standard, classical anthropology" and therefore could not command a university market as assigned reading in anthropology and other courses.

These experiences may be atypical. It must be said, however, that American anthropologists in general are now showing deep uneasiness over the temptations and restraints to which their profession is increasingly exposed by the policies of government agencies. In 1965, in the wake of Project Camelot, the American Anthropological Association appointed a Committee on Research Problems and Ethics under the chairmanship of Professor Ralph L. Beals. The committee has since published a report on such matters as "access to foreign areas, governmental clearances, professional ethics, and our responsibilities toward colleagues at home and abroad, the peoples with whom we work and the sponsoring agencies."[17] In a thoughtful and illuminating discussion, the report comments on the damage already done to American anthropology abroad by the Central Intelligence Agency's alleged employment of non-anthropologists in the guise of anthropologists, and by its secret employment of some trained anthropologists who are said to have falsely represented themselves as engaged in anthropological research, in some cases for universities that in fact no longer employed them.

At the same time, genuine anthropological research is now being increasingly curtailed or circumscribed by government restrictions on foreign travel. In August 1965, following the adverse effects of Project Camelot's publicization, President Johnson wrote to the Secretary of State: "I am determined that no Government sponsorship of foreign area research should be undertaken which, in the judgment of the Secretary of State, would adversely affect United States foreign relations." In response to an inquiry from the executive board of the American Anthropological Association, Mr.

Thomas L. Hughes, Director of Intelligence and Research of the State Department, stated in a letter on November 9, 1965: "It does not seem desirable to us to impose on private research projects supported by the National Science Foundation or the National Institutes of Health the review and clearance necessary for foreign affairs research funded by operating agencies [i.e., presumably, by agencies such as the United States Army or the Central Intelligence Agency—K.G.] Neither have we the desire nor the intention of including Fulbright scholarships or National Defense Education Act grants within the scope of our review possibilities."[18]

This information is, however, inconsistent with my own experience with the Department of State and the National Science Foundation in 1964, as recounted above. The report of the Anthropological Association's Committee on Research Problems and Ethics indicates, moreover, that as of January 1967, Department of State clearance *was* required of anyone going abroad under grants or contracts with the Department of Health, Education, and Welfare, or with funds obtained under the terms of the National Defense Education Act, contrary to the information received from Mr. Hughes. Moreover, in "sensitive areas," notably Africa, *every* American scholar is advised to provide an itinerary, list of contacts, and list of methods of pursuing research to the American Embassy in the country and to "comply with Embassy guidance," a set of directives virtually incompatible with normal methods of conducting anthropological research.

It is true that many of the present restrictions apply only to government grants and not to those received from private foundations, and that in the present international climate it is often easier for an anthropologist to carry out his work if he can make it known that he is *not* funded by his government. Nevertheless, it is also true that by far the largest portion of research money comes today from federal agencies, so that an anthropologist who is banned from receiving such funds is severely handicapped. With the addition of these recent restrictions on foreign research to the older ban on research in Communist nations, American anthro-

[17]*Fellow Newsletter* of the American Anthropological Association, 8 (January 1967): 4.
[18]Ibid., p. 5.

pologists have become extremely circumscribed in their possibilities for fieldwork.

Using the report of January 1967 as background, Professor Beals and other members of his committee proposed a "Statement on Problems of Anthropological Research and Ethics" for mail-vote approval by the Anthropological Association's members. In March 1967 the statement received the support of a large majority of the membership. It includes a set of guidelines for sponsoring agencies and for anthropologists. These advocate, among other things, freedom to publish research findings without censorship or interference, refusal by academic institutions to become involved in clandestine activities, readiness of anthropologists to supply information about all aspects of their research to people in their host countries, and the lifting of government restrictions on foreign research that has the approval of the researcher's professional colleagues or academic institution. Anthropologists are also warned of the dangers of receiving funds from the Department of Defense and other "mission-oriented" agencies or from private foundations which do not publish the sources of their funds, and are urged scrupulously to avoid entanglement in clandestine intelligence activities. If such guidelines are in fact respected by anthropologists, the profession will at least save itself from active complicity in police-state methods of foreign penetration and domination, and will reassert its own right of free inquiry—whether or not it proceeds to make use of this right. If the United States government acts on them, it will reverse a twenty-year trend toward restraint of free inquiry in non-Western regions and constriction of anthropology.

The future of anthropology as an independent science is thus very uncertain, especially in America. The recently revealed involvement of a large contingent of anthropologists in the Army's counterinsurgency Project Agile in Thailand gives little reason to hope that the field will soon salvage its autonomy as a humane endeavor.[19] If serious resistance to such corruption of the science is confined to a scattered minority, that minority is likely to be purged one by one and dropped into obscurity. In the universities of the West, the anthropologist's best hope may be his students. These, far outnumbering their elders, are forcing us to reexamine our subject matter, theories, and aims. As they insist on creating a space in which to think freely and to grow in dignity, they will shake the foundations of our academic institutions. With them, we may be able to help in reshaping our own society, and in so doing to find new goals for the science of man.

[19] The *New York Times* reports on the work of 157 anthropologists, engineers, and ordinance specialists at the Thai-American Military Research and Development Center in Bangkok. The *Times* describes Project Agile as "the Pentagon's worldwide counterinsurgency program," concerned with methods of countering guerrilla warfare in Northeast Thailand. "The old formula for successful counterinsurgency used to be ten troops for every guerrilla," one American specialist remarked. "Now the formula is ten anthropologists for each guerrilla." (Peter Braestrup, "Researchers Aid Thai Rebel Fight," *New York Times*, March 20, 1967, City Edition, p. 11.)

Herchelle Sullivan Challenor

No Longer at Ease: Confrontation at the 12th Annual African Studies Association Meeting at Montreal

In 1969, the annual meeting of the African Studies Association literally blew apart. The Association had theretofore been a collection of scholars who shared miscellaneous interests in Africa and who came together annually to deliver learned papers and look over prospective academic employees. At this meeting, a Black Caucus made up of Africans and Americans demanded a major role in the Association in order to end white domination of it and make it more relevant to the concerns, and more responsive to the interests, of Africans. Charges of racism flew from both sides; the whites refused the black demands; and the blacks withdrew. Later, negotiations for a rapprochement were initiated. A range of views was soon expressed in Africa Today, *the journal of the Association. Here we present three—the first from a scholar who is a member of the Black Caucus and espouses its position. The events of that meeting and the positions set forth in our selection by scholars and others are only the tip of an iceberg. The negative response by peoples studied to those who study them in a colonial context is a deep, many-faceted result of a long period of incubation. It is not something that can be talked away. On the willingness and ability to grant its legitimacy and confront its implications forthrightly depends the future of social science in the Third World.*

The Black Caucus disrupted the African Studies Association's 12th Annual Meeting when the organization's Executive Board and voting membership refused to accede to the Caucus' minimal demands regarding the Association's focus and structure. Whereas challenges of this type have become a common phenomenon in universities and at professional meetings, the events at Montreal are singularly significant because of their international implications.

Montreal may go down in history as the harbinger of a new era of pan-Africanism that surpasses in scope and inclusiveness earlier pan-Africanist movements. Unlike the limited scope of the cultural pan-Africanism of the 1900s led by Sylvester Williams and William E. B. DuBois and the geographically restricted post-war political pan-Africanism which galvanized incipient nationalist movements in Africa for the purposes of liberating the continent of colonial rule, the Montreal Black Caucus affirmed the culturo-political interdependence of all African peoples regardless of national origin. We maintained that all peoples of African descent are African peoples; we recognized that despite a difference in form and degree we shared a common historical experience of racial oppression that has substantially distorted our history and culture or even denied its validity; we affirmed that Africa's image and political position in the world affect all of us.

The Caucus' demands were supported not only by a cross section of Afro-American scholars,

students, and professionals working in the field of African affairs, but also by West Indians and resident and nonresident Africans both anglophone and francophone, northern and sub-Saharan.

Paradoxically at the ASA meeting in Montreal, many of those white scholars who have devoted much of their intellectual energy to studying African nationalism failed or refused to recognize the broadly based nature of this bona fide challenge to their legitimacy. Furthermore, they consciously or unconsciously attempted to neutralize what became a ground-swell by using some of the divisive and stalling tactics characteristic of former colonial powers. Ironically, those white "Africanists" who had consistently treated us as black "Africanists" in the past, thereby defining our primary loyalties in their own eyes, suddenly expected us to be "Africanists" who happened to be black and to join them, the "academics," against other blacks.

The Confrontation in Perspective

Whereas we respect the right of the ASA membership to disagree with us, the Black Caucus would prefer that this judgment be based not on assumptions but on a clear understanding of our position. Placed in historical perspective, the events of Montreal were an outgrowth of the ASA Annual Meeting at Los Angeles in 1968. Prior to that time a few black "Africanists" had tried unsuccessfully for several years on an individual basis to persuade the ASA to involve more Blacks in its proceedings. At the Los Angeles meeting, the Black Caucus called upon the ASA to "render itself more relevant and competent to deal with the challenging times and conditions of black people in Africa, the United States and the whole of the black world." Specifically the Caucus asked that steps be taken to increase black participation in all phases of the Association's operations; that the organization's membership be broadened to include more black people particularly those involved in fields closely related to African and Afro-American studies and finally that the ASA "address itself in a meaningful and educational way to changing American public

From "No Longer at Ease: Confrontation at the 12th Annual African Social Studies Association Meeting at Montreal" by Herchelle Sullivan Challenor, from *Africa Today*, Vol. 16, Nos. 5 and 6, 1969. Reprinted by permission.

opinion based on deep racism and ignorance of the black people whom the African Studies Association takes as its subjects." In response to these suggestions the ASA formed an Ad Hoc Committee on Afro-American Issues composed of professors James Gibbs Jr. (Chairman) of Stanford University, Simon Ottenberg of the University of Washington, William Schwab of Temple University, John Henrik Clarke of Hunter College, Adelaide Hill of Boston University, and Dr. Shirley K. Fischer, Staff Associate of the ASA Research Liaison Committee. This Committee, charged with making proposals to implement the Caucus' suggestions, met at least twice during 1968–69 and presented an interim report to the ASA Board meeting in May and a final report to the Board at the Montreal meeting.

In addition to participating in the work of the Ad Hoc Committee on Afro-American Issues, members of the Black Caucus officially established the African Heritage Studies Association at its first annual meeting in June 1969 at Washington, D.C. At that time John Henrik Clarke was elected President of the African Heritage Studies Association. Impressed with the "need for self-help among black scholars" AHSA formulated the following objectives:

1. Reconstruction of African history and cultural studies along Afro-centric lines while effecting an intellectual union among black scholars the world over.
2. Acting as a clearing house of information in the establishment and evaluation of a more realistic African or Black Studies Program.
3. Presenting papers at seminars and symposia where any aspect of the life and culture of African peoples are discussed.
4. Relating, interpreting, and disseminating African materials to elementary and secondary schools, colleges, and universities.

It is within the context of this background colored by the formation of the African Heritage Studies Association and little evidence of the ASA Board's attempts to act on the May interim report of the ASA Ad Hoc Committee on Afro-American Issues that the confrontation at Montreal must be viewed.

The African Studies Association is not just a professional association. Its leaders perform other functions that directly or indirectly affect the lives and livelihood of Africans and Afro-American

scholars and students. Its annual meeting which brings together government officials, journalists, publishers, foundation representatives, businessmen, scholars, students, and members of voluntary associations, serves as a point of contact and a market place where jobs, research funds, ideas, and information are exposed and exchanged. Its members are scholars whose research not only determines or influences at the very least the image of Africa in America but also conditions the kind and scope of much of the written documentation available about the continent. Research completed by its members has provided background material for United States foreign policy decisions in Africa. For these reasons we deemed the ASA annual meeting the proper forum for our demands.

Black Caucus-AHSA Demands at Montreal and Evolution of Events

Essentially the Black Caucus presented the following six demands to the ASA twelve member Executive Board on Thursday morning October 16th.

African peoples attending the ASA Conference have demanded that the study of African life be undertaken from a Pan-Africanist perspective. This perspective defines that all black people are African peoples and negates the tribalization of African peoples by geographical demarcations on the basis of colonialist spheres of influence. . . .

Specifically, in order to reflect this perspective, African peoples demanded that the following changes be made in the ideological and structural bases of the Organization. . . .

1. The ideological framework of the ASA which perpetuates colonialism and neocolonialism through the "educational" institutions and the mass media should be changed immediately.

2. The constitutional procedures, which provide for the election of a predominant white Board of Directors to decide upon the scholarship, study and research of African life should be changed immediately.

3. In accordance with the above the new Board of ASA should be composed of twelve members—six Africans and six Europeans.

4. That the ASA give financial support to the African students of Sir George Williams University in Montreal, Canada who are now political prisoners of a colonialist government, and that the ASA make a strong public statement indicating its abhorrence of the situation.

5. The rules governing the membership of the ASA should be amended so as to allow African scholars total participation in the Association.

6. The criteria for allocation of funds for research and publications on the study of African life should be established by a committee composed of equal numbers of Africans and Europeans.

As negotiations between the Black Caucus delegation and the ASA Board progressed it became clear that the only contentious issue was point three relating to the composition of the Executive Board. After having first maintained that they had no authority to restructure the Board on the basis of equal representation, the ASA Executive Board decided that perhaps they could offer three seats in addition to the two already held by Blacks. One of the black incumbents, Dr. Absolom Vilakasi, a South African professor at American University, and Dr. Elliott P. Skinner, professor at Columbia University and another longstanding member of the ASA openly supported the Caucus' demands during the negotiation sessions. The Board's "token offer of three Africans ... on a twelve member Board of Directors" was considered "irresponsible" and "insulting" by the Black Caucus. As a result the Caucus unanimously agreed to reject the Board's proposal. Our rejection of their offer prompted the Board to convene an assembly of the voting membership of ASA to decide the issue.

It was at this point, as a direct response to the Board of Directors' apparent indifference to the continued participation of the Blacks, that the Caucus voted to unequivocally support the African Heritage Studies Association and to no longer cooperate with the ASA meeting. Black panelists agreed not to present their papers to the body at large but to the Black Caucus. In order to avoid the inconveniences of the unwarranted locking of the room set aside for Caucus meetings, these panels were rescheduled in the hotel suites of black participants. Unfortunately, the pressure of events precluded the ultimate realization of these panel discussions.

Probably the most crucial event in the three day confrontation was the ASA voting membership's rejection of the Black Caucus' demands by a vote of 103 to 97 in its plenary session on Friday afternoon. It is of interest that the ASA, an organization of scholars whose prestige and output depends upon maintaining good relations with Africans both in terms of gaining entry into African countries and obtaining reliable information from them, would have permitted, if for no other than political reasons, their voting membership to go on record as having voted against minimal demands of African peoples. People have argued in defense of the white ASA membership that although a large number of them supported the demands, they were affronted by the tactics of disruption, and therefore could not in good conscience grant the Blacks immediate representation on the Board. If this assessment is true, then it raises a fundamental question of their ability to understand and evaluate societies or events occurring in those societies with which they disagree in principle.

Despite the negative implications of their action, the white ASA membership's rejection of black demands served a positive function. It acted as a catalyst that not only galvanized support of most of those few Blacks who were still wavering in their decision to join the movement but also strengthened the commitment of those already involved.

Let there be no mistake about the broadly based support of the Black Caucus. The leadership of the AHSA that spearheaded the confrontation included resident Africans and Afro-Americans. The Black Caucus-AHSA committee that negotiated with the ASA Board consisted of African, West Indian and Afro-American students and professors, one of whom had been an ASA voting member since its inception. Moreover, the majority of the African visitors invited by the ASA and the Canadian African Studies Committee to attend the Conference supported the substance of the Black Caucus demands. The Caucus' concerns over the white domination of scholarly output on Africa had been expressed by Africans at two earlier International Conferences of Africanists at Dakar. Indication of African support was initially voiced by Gabriel d'Arboussier, a nationalist leader in francophone Africa since the 1940s and currently Senegalese ambassador to Germany. D'Arboussier was slated to deliver the keynote address for the opening session at which time the first statement of black demands was presented. Robert Gardiner, Director of the United Nations Economic Commission for Africa, actively participated in the Caucus' meetings and supported its demands. By Friday noon when the Black Caucus met with the invited African guests to clarify our position in French and in English, they presented a written declaration of support which had been signed by most of the leading African participants. Léon Damas of French Guiana, one of the three original *negritude* poets, along with Aimé Césaire and Léopold Sédar Senghor, read the declaration of solidarity cited below.

We the undersigned participating in a joint annual meeting of the African Studies Association and the Committee on African Studies in Canada, in our capacity as guests of the latter, in face of the incidents which confront the Afro-American participants and the ASA (USA) note that the Africanist Congress held in Dakar in December 1967 strongly criticized the orientation of African studies in two resolutions adopted at the 5th and 6th Committees. We strongly reiterate the view that African studies as conceived within the context of colonialist and imperialist domination of the African continent have served exclusively to reinforce an ideology which serves their domination in the interest of foreign capital used to exploit the African continent. We affirm that the Africanist associations and explicitly the ASA continue to serve the interest of imperialism in the formation and presentation of its policy of exploitation in spite of the aforementioned resolutions. Therefore we strongly support the views and requests voiced by the Afro-American participants regarding the ASA.

The Question of Procedure and Substance

The question of the procedure, tactics, and ultimate objective of the Black Caucus was a pivotal issue. In the eyes of the ASA white membership any challenge to their authority that was not supported by the black ASA voting members had no legitimacy. However, they misinterpreted an expression by some black "Africanists" of nonsupport of tactics to also mean nonsupport of substantive issues. There is an African proverb that says, "When three men are walking down the road the fact that one is walking on the left, one on the right, and one down the center does not mean they are not going in the same direction." The number of black "Africanists" who neither supported the Black Caucus' tactics nor their objectives was negligible.

Our objectives are as follows: (1) to consolidate the African Heritage Studies Association, an organization aimed at the development and exchange of scholarly information about Africa and African peoples. Plans are now under way for our second annual meeting in April 1970; (2) to withhold our participation in ASA until it recognizes our legitimate right to participate in the governance of the organization and the rewards that accrue to its members in terms of research funds, influence, and accessibility to publications; (3) to encourage the United States Government to devise an African policy that is more consistent with the legitimate aspirations of African peoples.

Status of Negotiations

What is the present status of negotiations between the Black Caucus and the African Studies Association? In response to the compromise position proposed by the White Reform Caucus and approved by the ASA membership, the Black Caucus has decided that it will send fifteen delegates who will represent the Caucus and the AHSA on the thirty-man committee provided that six Blacks be appointed as interim members of the ASA Board of Directors. The Reform Caucus' compromise proposal envisions the appointment of an ad hoc committee of thirty comprised of fifteen Whites and fifteen Blacks whose purpose would be to formulate plans for the total restructuring of ASA.

Our conditional acceptance reflects our suspicions about the compromise agreement. These suspicions are based on two factors: (1) the lack of guarantees of the compromise plan and some confusion about the selection of the Blacks who will serve on the Ad Hoc Committee, and (2) the past experiences many of the members of the Caucus have had with negotiations of this type. Let us examine the first point. The compromise agreement proposed an ad hoc committee that will formulate proposals for restructuring the ASA not within a month, but over a period of six months, that is by April 1970. Secondly, these proposals once formulated cannot be operative until they are approved by the ASA voting membership. It is not inconceivable that those same persons who rejected the minimal demands of equal representation on the Board will not be kindly disposed to approve a total restructuring of the organization. Thirdly, there will be no connection between this Ad Hoc Committee and the Executive Board—focus of our original demands—which will carry on business as usual. In addition, there was some uncertainty about who would select the black representatives on the Ad Hoc Committee. Initially we were told that there would be fifteen Whites and fifteen Blacks and that the latter would be selected by the Black Caucus. Then we heard that some Whites deemed it antithetical to their liberal predilections to participate on an all-white delegation representing a white constituency. Therefore, they decided that their delegation of fifteen should include Blacks as well as Whites. By agreeing to this formula, the Whites raised a serious question in our minds about whether the number of Blacks elected to serve with their fifteen would be subtracted from our allotted fifteen, since the original resolution clearly stated that the Ad Hoc Committee would consist of fifteen Whites and fifteen Blacks. The majority group addressed themselves to this issue and agreed that they would accept the Black Caucus' fifteen representatives regardless of the racial composition of their fifteen. Even this solution has negative portents. Are we being set up for a confrontation on the Ad Hoc Committee between our delegation and a group of Blacks legitimized by the white body and therefore representing them?

With respect to the second factor pertaining to past experiences of Black Caucus members, certain facts should be taken into consideration. Our support comes from (1) longstanding members of the ASA who have tried unsuccessfully to persuade the organization's leadership over a period of years to accord more decision making power to Blacks; (2) veterans of the sit-in movement of the early sixties and the leaders of the more recent student demonstrations on university campuses who recall that frequently the opponents' underlying motives for agreeing to negotiations in order to stop demonstrations was to usher in a cooling-off period during which time the opposition would have time to crystallize and the challengers' initial momentum

would be dissipated; and (3) West Indians and Africans who remember the fractionalization of their nationalist movements caused by European supported rival political parties opposed to self determination. The problem is one of perception. Whereas we understand the liberals' view that their compromise proposal is a concession, they must understand that we wonder if it is a trojan horse.

We are no longer at ease. We can no longer accept the continuation of white majority control over those areas which directly affect our lives. Those white conference delegates who spoke of abandoning ASA and trying to create a greater allocation of time for African affairs in other professional associations such as the American Historical Association, the American Political Science Association, and the American Anthropological Association, must realize that we have entered a new era of confrontation politics where there are no sanctuaries. Not only in the United States but also throughout the world majority rule which has been unresponsive to the aspirations of numerical and political minorities is being contested. Just as the Jewish people have joined in support of Zionism, we hereby dedicate ourselves to Black Melanism, a movement which recognizes the interdependence of all peoples of African descent regardless of their nationality and will strive to neutralize any attack on Africa or the culture or person of black peoples anywhere in the world. We consider Africa our homeland but reaffirm our refusal to accept barriers to our opportunities in those countries of which we are citizens.

It is hoped that the Black Caucus and the African Heritage Studies Association position has been clarified. Has it all been a misunderstanding resulting from a lack of communication, or have we understood each other too well?

Pierre L. van den Berghe

The Montreal Affair: Revolution or Racism?

The next selection, from the same issue of Africa Today, *is a letter from a white scholar who deplores the demands of the Black Caucus.*

The 1969 annual meeting of the African Studies Association in Montreal on October 15 to 18 was marked by a successful attempt to disrupt the proceedings of the convention and what seems like an equally successful attempt to change the structure of the organization. Given space limitations, I shall put the stress on interpretation of the events and give only the briefest description of the facts. A "Black Caucus" claiming to speak for the African Heritage Studies Association and locally represented by about forty to fifty people, for the most part Afro-Americans and West Indians in their twenties, interrupted the proceedings of two plenary sessions and several of the panels by getting hold of the microphone and making a series of demands of the African Studies Association. The key structural reform asked for was that the Board of Directors of ASA be expanded from nine to twelve, and that parity of racial representation be established between "Africans" and "Europeans" on the Board. Asked to define these two terms, spokesmen for the group repeatedly stated that "Africans" meant Blacks irrespective of culture or geographical location, while "Europeans" meant Whites whether from America, Europe, Africa, or Australia.

After a lengthy process of negotiation between the Board of Directors of the Association and representatives of the "Black Caucus," the Board acceded to some of the peripheral demands and recommended that the Fellows grant three black seats to the Caucus in an expanded 12-man Board. The Black Caucus rejected this as "insulting" and it was never put to a vote. A straw vote of people present at the Conference agreed by a large majority to accept the principle of racial parity. This meeting was followed by a business meeting of Fellows who rejected that proposal by a narrow margin, but subsequently adopted by a majority of about eight or ten to one a motion to constitute a constitutional review committee consisting of 15 "Africans" and 15 "Europeans" (as racially defined above) with the mandate to recommend a Board of Directors with racial parity. The constitutional amendments to be proposed by that committee are to be voted upon by the entire membership of the Association, and not by the Fellows only. The modalities of electing the 30 members of the committee were later discussed.

In spite of considerable disagreement between members of the Black Caucus, they showed excellent organization and tactical effectiveness in disrupting the convention. I witnessed no physical violence at any stage of the proceedings, but there was a great deal of verbal abuse and racial epithets (such as "honkie") used, and the black group deliberately created an atmosphere of intimidation designed to disorganize resistance, prevent free discussion, and paralyze parliamentary procedure.

So much for a summary of the facts as I saw them. My interpretation of them will necessarily be colored by my ideological position as a socialist and as an antiracist. Basically, I think the "Black Caucus" made three valid points, all of which pointed to the need for the fundamental reform of the Association:

1. The euro-centric and frequently racist character of African scholarship was quite evident until the last few years. Since 1960 or thereabouts, the intellectual climate has changed toward a more afro-centric view of things, but a number of Africanists continue to produce work which might be described as in the "colonial tradition."

2. The almost complete lack of African representation (meaning "citizens of African states") in the Association and its Board of Directors was anomalous, given the concern of its members with the study of Africa.

3. The involvement of many prominent members of the Association with research projects of dubious sponsorship and the misuse of Africanist scholarship to promote the interests of American imperialism were seriously undermining the ostensibly scholarly aims of the Association.

From "The Montreal Affair: Revolution or Racism?" by Pierre L. van den Berghe, from *Africa Today*, Vol. 16, Nos. 5 and 6, 1969. Reprinted by permission.

These three points are entirely nonracial in character, and all three have been made repeatedly and publicly by a number of the Association's members, including myself, quite irrespective of their pigmentation or lack of it. While all these points were made by the Black Caucus, the main thrust of their action was a purely racist one. They successfully implanted into the Association the racist dialectics of American society, making the Association an arena of an essentially American conflict that has only the most tenuous of connections with Africa. While the Black Caucus claimed to speak on behalf of Africa, it was quite clear that most African participants in the conference viewed the Black Caucus as quite irrelevant to Africa, and, indeed, as another neo-colonialist attempt by outsiders to speak on behalf of Africa.

By a clever combination of intimidation and playing on the racial guilt of white American members of the Association, a small totally unrepresentative group of racists succeeded in imposing on the Association a racial definition of the situation, and in stampeding a flock of bewildered self-styled liberals into accepting the principle of apartheid within the Association. In effect, the Association, by voting in favor of the "racial parity" resolution, has constituted itself into a White Caucus.

Pandering to black racism is, of course, the easiest thing for establishment "liberals" to do. It is, in fact, a form of neo-paternalism. I can conceive of no greater abdication of social responsibility both as scholars and as citizens than for American intellectuals to adopt a double standard of judgment depending on whether the racism they face is white or black. Yet, this is precisely what they do all over the country in the hope of working out their guilt and in the fear of being branded racists or reactionaries. The ASA has just given the most glaring display of this sort of irresponsible behavior.

The fundamental need of the ASA was to *Africanize* the Association, not to *racialize* it. It chose the latter course, and by doing so it has become less African and more American than it was before. The ultimate irony of the situation is that the blueprint for an apartheid association which was accepted in Montreal has destroyed whatever shaky legitimacy we had as a group of Africanists.

As I see it, we can follow three courses of action:

1. Disband.
2. Follow the road of apartheid and continue to exist as a group acting out the insane logic of racial conflict.
3. Pull back from the brink, snap out of the state of shock and anomie into which the Montreal meeting threw us, and Africanize our Association along nonracial lines. There, I would suggest that a Board of Directors consisting of six Africans, meaning *citizens of African states*, and six non-Africans would be a step in the right direction.

Obviously, I hope that we shall choose the last course. The first two would mean the end of our Association. I might say in conclusion that I am speaking as an Afro-American with an equal foot on both continents, and as one who hopes that America will indeed become more African by transcending the dialectic of racial conflict as almost every leader of African independence has successfully done in the last decade.

Immanuel Wallerstein
Africa, America, and the Africanists

Last is a letter from a white scholar who recognizes both the legitimacy and the inevitability of the Black Caucus position.

At the Montreal meetings of the African Studies Association (USA) in October, 1969, there was a confrontation between Blacks and Whites. It is difficult to believe that most of the 1000 or so registrants were surprised. But some were unnerved. And many were unhappy.

The initial reactions of the participants to the events were mainly of three kinds: (1) catharsis and satisfaction; (2) bewilderment and anger; (3) anxiety and withdrawal. No doubt it would be happier if I could say these were transitory emotional states, part of a crisis about to be surmounted. I doubt this is so. The crisis of the ASA is of course a pale reflection of a far more fundamental discombobulation of the modern world, and it is likely to become aggravated over the coming years. Rational analysis can illuminate it. Whether or not it will alleviate it remains to be seen.

In the narrow confines of that arena of human action known as the study of Africa, what were the issues of the confrontation? There were three fundamental assertion/demands of the Black Caucus.

One was a demand for a *mea culpa*. In many ways this was the most fundamental. White Africanists were accused of having served the cause of racism in the world; worse yet, of being racists themselves; worse yet, of not being casual racists but deep-rooted racists. And there was scarcely a White at Montreal ready to admit these charges. Most were not even ready to recognize that these charges could have any validity whatsoever.

The second charge, somewhat akin to the first but not identical, was that the work of white scholars has not been relevant to the problems of black men, either in Africa or in the United States, and that it has not been relevant basically because it has not been committed to the cause of black liberation from white domination. Here the black demand met a more mixed response from the Whites. Many reacted to this demand for relevance as they react to all demands for relevance, by argu-

ing one variety or another of the belief in value-free science. But there were many Whites at Montreal who had long since abandoned this concept, and had indeed urged "committed" action upon the ASA in the past: the attempt, which had failed, to get the ASA as a corporate body to condemn *apartheid* in South Africa; the attempt, which was resisted and amended, to get the ASA as a corporate body to condemn links of scholars with the CIA.

The third demand was that Blacks should get a fixed minimum share (in this case 50 percent) of the decision-making posts in ASA. This consumed most of the actual discussion at Montreal. We know the results since they are statistical. A majority of the Fellows present voted for a resolution which established a constitutional reform committee composed on a parity basis, whose work was circumscribed in one way only: that the new Governing Board of ASA must be on a black-white parity basis.

Though the majority of Fellows voted for this resolution, many of them did so feeling they were under duress and others did so only most reluctantly, worried they had violated one of their own most sacred principles, that of the equal rights of all individuals.

I argued at Montreal and will repeat here that a modern democratic society that doesn't find some institutional form to recognize the equal rights of groups along with and in addition to the equal rights of individuals is simply according a constant differential advantage to the dominant group or groups. Put bluntly, quotas of one variety or another may be an essential weapon in restituting other social imbalances so that members of low-ranking groups can in reality get approximately equal treatment with members of high-ranking groups. The African Studies Association has accepted that principle reluctantly. Some day soon, I hope all members will feel that it was a wise and highly meritorious decision, one that met not

From "Africa, America, and the Africanists" by Immanuel Wallerstein, from *Africa Today*, Vol. 16, Nos. 5 and 6, 1969. Reprinted by permission.

only the political needs of the moment but also the moral needs.

There was much muttering in the corridors at Montreal that ASA had just adopted *apartheid*. This is a wrong and pernicious view to take. It comes from a simplistic analysis of superficial similarities. *Apartheid* is a system in which a high-ranking group, the Whites, who are high in income, high in social status, high in education, high in political power, high in control of economic institutions, etc., etc., etc., make sure that there is no accidental breakthrough in this rigid caste system by using the police and judiciary to enforce visible stratified separate treatment. A parity system in ASA for Blacks means that a low-ranking group, the Blacks, who are low in income, low in academic position, low in official status, low in participation on award-granting bodies, etc., etc., etc., get *one* lever to break through a system reputed to be based on individual merit but one in which every Black starts with a negative handicap and in which those Blacks who are exceptional are able to catch up in rewards with those Whites who are mediocre. It is clear that what ASA has just voted for is, in spirit and in fact, the very opposite of *apartheid*.

The demands/assertions are fairly straightforward. Initial reactions have been equally clear. The question most Africanists ask themselves is what is the road ahead? It is clearly rocky.

To begin a confrontation there must be mutual suspicion. To conduct one increases it. To effectuate a compromise does not make it abate; indeed, it could even be said to inflate it still further ("Why were those other guys willing to compromise?"). Furthermore, Africanists do not live in a small closed world resolving their inner disputes. They are part of a larger world, and close to the two most racially explosive segments of it: Africa and America.

Those who are impatient or cannot tolerate anger are devised to grow rhododendrons. They will not survive the turmoil. Those who think they can make it on antacid pills are encouraged to cultivate, for the long-range, a view of optimism, and, for the short-range, low boiling points for all contacts with all friends. A dose of commitment based on faith and at least as much intelligence as a rat in a maze is indispensable.

The African Studies Association, after all, is a minor arena of life. There is the real world beyond it, in which we all live. If ASA had been a haven of peace, to destroy it would have been nefarious. But it was a small building-stone in a larger system that ought to change and is, I am happy to report, changing—if all too slowly. What happened at Montreal was useful for ASA and for all those who were there. I would not exaggerate its import but it was not a negative event. It offered us the possibility of redemption. Since the world has seen a number of previous offers of redemption, we know (empirically) with what lack of enthusiasm such offers are greeted. But it is evidence for a long-range view of optimism that these offers have been made repeatedly. After all, as every believer knows, some men do attain salvation.

Satish Saberwal
The Problem

"Academic colonialism" is a term that has rapidly gained currency in intellectual circles in India. The following article introduced an entire issue of the Indian journal Seminar devoted to a symposium on academic colonialism—Western domination of India's academic and intellectual life—and to the implications of that domination and ways of combating it. This is a clear presentation of the issues as seen by an Indian anthropologist who did his postgraduate work in the United States, taught in Canada, and then returned to India to make his contribution to that hard-pressed country's emergence as a nation of people who are intellectually and emotionally independent as well as politically sovereign.

In a symposium on the Impact of the Cultural Revolution in China, held at the 20th Annual Meeting of the Association for Asian Studies in Philadelphia on March 24, 1968, the first scheduled paper concerned the "Impact on the Party Machine." Its author was Charles Neuhauser of the U.S. Central Intelligence Agency. Other contributors came from the George Washington University, Harvard University, and the University of California, Berkeley. This was an occasion for a dialogue between a CIA man and the academics in the United States. Much commoner is the monologue: the academic speaks, writes, and publishes his books; the CIA man listens, reads, and pursues his agency's goals.

Of academic colonialism, this is one aspect: the academics contribute information—through employment, through contract research, and through sheer publication—used by CIA, Pentagon, and other overt and covert agencies of the United States government to advance its political objective of dominating Afro-Asian countries. The other aspect lies in other forms of dominance—economic, intellectual, and political in different contexts—which North American academics come to exercise over academics and others elsewhere. (I am aware of the many exceptions, and to them I offer my apologies.) Here I examine the sources, the manifestations, and the consequences of this new form of colonialism. The purpose is not to suggest a countervailing policy but rather to provoke a clarification of options and attitudes preliminary to a definition of public policy. The intent is not to be hostile to North American academics but to assess the impact of their research on the integrity and the security of the countries where they do field work.

There are strong reasons to suspect that the covert U.S. agencies use the U.S. social scientists' expertise acquired through field research abroad. This utilization is usually "sanitized" through seemingly respectable organizations; some of the processes became public during the CIA revelations early in 1967. Back in the mid-50s, the Human Relations Area Files, located at Yale University, accepted a contract from the U.S. Army for producing Area Handbooks summarizing information of potential interest to the army. These handbooks were produced under the direction of renowned scholars at a series of distinguished seats of learning in the United States;

apparently no one chose to enquire why *the army* was making huge subsidies for these handbooks on Afro-Asian countries.

Commenting on the matter, a colleague, who observed the activity at close range and who believes this service to the army to have been innocent, says, "I do not think that either the army or the State Department could ever have read the work of the HRAF or they would never have so misunderstood the Southeast Asian situation as to have opposed Ho Chi Minh in the first place." This is credible in view of the evidence concerning the decision-making processes of the U.S. government revealed by James Thomson, Jr., in his paper, "How Could Vietnam Happen? An Autopsy," *The Atlantic Monthly*, April 1968, 47–53. Thomson, who teaches history at Harvard now, gives an inside view. The essential point is that the availability of massive expertise appears to give these decision-makers the feeling of spurious confidence, posing a miscellany of grave threats for people from Guyana to Vietnam.

In the late 50s, a large team of social scientists from the Michigan State University was located in Saigon, doing research intended to aid and strengthen the Diem regime. Financed generously by the U.S. Government, the team provided "cover" for a sizable CIA operatives' contingent. Stories concerning the involvement of academics from the most prestigious campuses in the U.S. in all manner of "counterinsurgency" research, that is, military espionage, are legion; undoubtedly a great many of them are true. The situation worries U.S. social scientists because it threatens their access to future field research.

Free access to data is important for U.S. social scientists who work abroad. A majority of them pursue the data with a detachment that would have done honor to Arjuna, but many recognize the value of their work for manipulating other peoples. Thus, D. S. Greenberg reports: "A study group appointed by the National Academy of Sciences has advised the Department of Defense (DOD) to increase its support and use of research in the social and behavioral sciences."

The study group included social scientists from Harvard, Stanford, Northwestern, and Indiana universities and also a few from such intellectual

'The Problem" by Satish Saberwal from *Seminar* No. 112, (December, 1968). Reprinted by permission of *Seminar*.

brothels as the Rand Corporation; its report says: "To maintain an adequate base for planning and for the conduct of military operations when and where they may occur, the U.S. military establishment must have access to a steady flow of knowledge that originates in social science studies conducted by U.S. and foreign scientists engaged in unclassified research tasks overseas." An elaborate "research strategy for military agencies" is proposed; for example, financial support should be given for:

Social science tasks to be conducted by major U.S. graduate studies centers in foreign areas that utilize U.S. based foreign students in training and research enterprises in the countries of their origin. . . . *These linkages should be sustained over time so that they can serve as channels for* intellectual development with the friendly support of U.S. scholars. [*italics mine*]

Before concluding that this suave prostitution of the social sciences aims only at distant, military contingencies, it is useful to remember the U.S. agents going silently about their business of persuading the politicians, the intellectuals, the soldiers, and anyone else available and raising little problems for governments which fail to submit—when the marines themselves are not helping out—events so routine which now the world has almost ceased to take notice of.

During the past year or so I have engaged in the painful task of confronting a large number of my North American colleagues with the above situation. Many of them suffer and show acute distress. Here are liberal, generous men and women, deeply in sympathy with the Third World, deeply worried over the direction the world is taking and over the U.S. government's part in it. Their situation reminds me of the tragedy and the hopelessness of the white liberal in South Africa, of the humane person in Nazi Germany.

The dilemma hits them in various ways; the case of the Canadian anthropologist who went to Nigeria to study the social organization of the urban unemployed will serve as an example. He undertook this study, he told me, out of a sense of urgency, a missionary feeling: if the African governments fail to understand the implications of growing unemployment, the wrath of the unemployed will overwhelm the governments and produce absolute chaos. In the course of his stay in

Nigeria, the U.S. ambassador there approached him and said, in effect: please continue your fine research; when you have the time, I would appreciate your sending me the names of the leaders of the unemployed. This gentleman was horrified at the request and the contract came to an end. Others comply and keep quiet. Occasionally I encounter the position enunciated by a young anthropologist at the Michigan State University, "Every country looks out for its interests; nothing is wrong with our boys working for the CIA." Got the message?

The past two decades in the United States have seen spectacular increases in the financial support available for the social sciences, especially for research abroad. The individual academic tends to see in this the general North American affluence; that would explain rising salaries but not the explosion in numbers. I have traced above what seem to me to be the imperialist origins of this explosion.

There is, besides, the element of interpersonal dominance—economic, intellectual, and political—involving North American academics. The economic dominance results from their control over large research funds used to employ the "locals." Imtiaz Ahmad offers a Delhiwalla's eye view:

. . . research by some foreign sociologists is developing into a new kind of industry in which the foreign sociologist secures funds for projects in the planning of which his prospective Indian colleagues have no hand; establishes a hierarchy in which he himself assumes the supervisory or editorial role and actual fieldwork is left to raw students who neither have any experience nor any special training for the specific job, and after giving some casual and often only token guidance in the course of the project, collects together the ill-processed data in the form of a hurriedly done report. This naturally results in a three-fold wrong: violence is done to facts in these unbalanced reports, their superficial character affects the understanding of the social reality and it provides a wrong example to Indian research scholars who generally start at the lowest strata of this new hierarchy.

Professor M. N. Srinivas also underlined the gravity of the situation in his Presidential Address to the Conference of Indian Sociologists in October 1967. Economic and intellectual dominance are joined here, and this can have lasting effects. Uncritical internalization of the boss's preferences leads to the colonization of the mind. The point is this: if X assesses Y's ideas and instruments in terms of his own perspective, finds them relevant and adopts them, the situation is free; when X takes Y's ideas without critical appraisal—and therefore without the capacity to grow and to innovate on his own—the relationship is colonial. It is true, of course, that a highly critical attitude smothers ideas and kills the capacity to be creative; thus, a disciplined receptivity which suspends judgment in the initial stages is an important capacity: combined with a subsequent controlled, equally disciplined, capacity for critical assessment, it lays the basis for significant achievement.

The essence lies in the attitude of those who are colonized towards those whom they recognize as their patrons or masters. Most Afro-Asian social scientists' dependence on North American sponsors for research funds is pathetic; its consequences for problem selection, research design, and modes of publication are disastrous. You run around in a vicious circle: you choose a problem to interest the patron abroad; its relevance to your country's needs is minimal; so your country has little incentive to support your enquiry. (Again, my apologies to the many honorable exceptions.) To outgrow the colonization of your mind is painful; but given the will to struggle, the outcome cannot be in doubt.

There is finally the element of political dominance by academicians. It refers to attempts by the "prestigious" foreign academic to use his eminence to influence the political process in the country where he has done research. A spectacular example of this brand of academic colonialism was furnished by Professor Michael Brecher, a political scientist at McGill University, in June 1967. In the wake of the Arab-Israeli conflict, Brecher wrote letters denouncing India's position on this conflict to more than a hundred journals and newspapers all over the world; on a conservative estimate, more than ten million copies of this letter were printed.

In this letter he described himself as one of the "friends of India"; nowhere did he indicate that he was an intensely committed Zionist, with close ties of kinship with Israel, who had recently toured Africa in the company of Premier Levi Eshkol! Not only this. Only a few weeks earlier he had been interviewing M.Ps in New Delhi, doing research on Indian politics. Now he proceeded to write to them individually urging them to reshape India's "sterile policy in West Asia"; again no mention of his Zionist moorings! I cannot doubt that, in choosing the Indian M.Ps to address, Brecher gave careful attention to the factions and cleavages in the Parliament, using information he had so recently secured in a context of academic research, seeking to sharpen the issue in Indian politics to Israel's advantage. All this was done on the stationery of McGill University, but the academics' concept of "academic freedom" seems to extend also to political adventurers in academic masquerades. With two or three honorable exceptions, Brecher's colleagues maintained a judicious silence: India is half-way round the world, Montreal a Zionist strong-hold, and Brecher a powerful campus figure!

The problem, then, is manifold. It requires, first, an explanation from North American social scientists to the constituency of the countries where they do research: in view of the knowledge gained in the past couple of years concerning the operations of the United States government, do they feel they can keep the trust reposed in them when they (and their colleagues) are permitted to do research in an Afro-Asian country? What monitoring procedures do they propose so as to ensure that their colleagues will not carry "academic freedom" into the realm of license, an instrument of colonialist manipulation? What sanctions will they have for this task?

The academics within each Afro-Asian country, in turn, have to confront the question: how does the stimulus of communication with the international intellectual community balance against the hazards resulting from the flow of data concerning our societies into the U.S. war machine? What are our options for improving the balance sheet? How shall we relate our research to the needs of our society, and how shall we communicate its findings to our local constituents, so we may shed our clientship to patrons abroad, a relationship of subservience always and everywhere?

The situation demands sober and balanced assessment, accurate perception and definition of reality, aware that our own judgments are the only ultimate basis for public policy. To the extent that these judgments follow a cold, dispassionate appraisal of all available data, to that extent will our decisions and actions lock with reality.

Gerald D. Berreman
Anthropology and Moral Accountability

As we have seen, anthropologists find themselves unwelcome in many nations of Africa, Asia, and Latin America. They are unwelcome also in many American Indian reservations, in black ghettos, and in Chicano *barrios*. They are unable to do research in many nations and among many peoples. And the situation appears to be fast worsening.

These facts bode ill for anthropology as a discipline and, as surely, they reflect badly upon anthropologists and Americans alike. Yet both characteristically regard themselves as warmhearted, good-natured, well intentioned, egalitarian, easily able to get along with others, and generous. There is a disparity, it seems, between our self-perception and the impressions conveyed to others; between ideals and actions, between intentions and accomplishments. The root of the disparity is the anthropologist's old nemesis, ethnocentrism—the habit of judging others by the standards of one's own group, defining a situation in terms relevant and meaningful to yourself and ignoring factors and interpretations relevant and meaningful to others. When doing anthropological research in another society, this can be disastrous. When I objected to Defense Department funding of the Himalayan Border Countries Project (see the selection "Academic Colonialism: Not So Innocent Abroad"), I was told in a note from an academic administrator of the institute accepting the funds that "the complications you fear because of government funding were actually carefully avoided in our negotiations under ARPA" (ARPA is the Advanced Research Projects Agency of the Department of Defense). He proved to have a sadly clouded crystal ball, for the project was terminated as soon as its funding became known in India. The error lay in assuming that what is believed in the Institute of International Studies in Berkeley will be believed and acted upon by politicians in India. And the political situation in India was such that the source of funds alone foredoomed the project. Research in a politically sensitive problem area, sponsored by the military establishment of a foreign power—the United States—was intolerable. Good intentions, and contractual agreements between the Department of Defense and the researchers which guaranteed academic freedom and nonsecrecy, were simply irrelevant. Project Camelot suffered precisely the same

fate three years earlier. Social scientists have more recently walked into the same quicksand in Southeast Asia, notably Thailand. The lesson seems to be a difficult one to learn, and the reason seems to be that it works against the immediate interests of many social scientists as they define those interests. It curtails their opportunity to do whatever they want to, however they want to, and wherever they want to, in pursuit of science and the rewards which come to its successful practitioners.

Heretofore, American anthropologists have usually made their choices about research and scholarship solely on the basis of their own criteria of scholarship, their own career interests, and the interests of the profession as they define it—and within the context of their own national interests. It is becoming increasingly clear that those days are gone forever. A redefinition of the role of the United States in the world, and hence in the Third World, is emerging, and with it a redefinition of the role of scholars in relationship to governments and the public. Anthropologists are not politicians, but neither are they free of political effect. Their politics remains the politics of truth. But in its pursuit they are now more than ever responsive not only or even primarily to their sources of funds, their government, and their Anglo-American audience, but to the diverse peoples among whom they work. This does not mean that they stretch the truth. It means that they attend to different voices and to additional voices as they seek a broader, more relevant truth. This often entails difficult decisions, agonizing dilemmas, and unpredictable consequences. But they believe that they must move with the times in this direction. If not, the times will move without them and they will find themselves as irrelevant as are many sociologists and historians of race relations in American society, surpassed by the peoples and issues they have studied but have failed to comprehend. To the extent that the anthropologist's comprehension of the human meaning of the experience of the Third World peoples he has studied has been inadequate, the harsh allegations of ethnocentrism, racism, and colonialism carry the sting of truth. To the extent that the anthropologist's comprehension has been or can become genuine, anthropology justifies itself as a scientific and humanistic discipline.

In the context of the Southeast Asian war, and of

exploitation of the Third World and scholarly complicity therein, anthropologists face a crisis of responsibility analagous to that faced by nuclear physicists in the atomic age—smaller, perhaps, but nevertheless analagous—for both have been called upon to put their knowledge in the service of those who do not fully comprehend it or its consequences, yet who may use it for drastic purposes.

In this regard, it may not be overly dramatic nor inappropriate to quote the words attributed to the atomic physicist, Dr. J. Robert Oppenheimer, in a closing statement before his security hearing in 1954, in the play, *In the Matter of J. Robert Oppenheimer:*

I begin to wonder whether we were not perhaps traitors to the spirit of science when we handed over the results of our research to the military, without considering the consequences. Now we find ourselves living in a world in which people regard the discoveries of scientists with dread and horror, and go in mortal fear of new discoveries.

. . . I ask myself whether we, the physicists, have not sometimes given too great, too indiscriminate loyalty to our governments, against our better judgment. . . .

We have been doing the work of the military, and I feel it in my very bones that this was wrong. . . . I will never work on war projects again. We have been doing the work of the Devil, and now we must return to our real tasks.[1]

A good many American social scientists have come to share feelings akin to these, and I believe that more will as time passes.

The ultimate commitment to scholarship in anthropology has as its essential ingredients a deep respect and concern for the people studied, responsiveness to their values, claims, and perspectives, trust in them, and commitment to the truth as it is discovered. It is clear from the material presented in this section that these ingredients are essential if social science research, especially American research, is to continue in the Third World. The moral imperatives now coincide with anthropology's self-interest. Only recognition of this fact can prevent anthropology from becoming a discipline without a subject.

[1] Heinar Kipphardt, *In the Matter of J. Robert Oppenheimer*, trans. Ruth Speirs (New York: Hill and Wang, 1967), pp. 126–127.

4 Race and Racism

Hermann K. Bleibtreu and John Meaney
Race and Racism

James N. Spuhler and Gardner Lindzey
Racial Differences in Behavior

Jean Hiernaux
The Concept of Race and the Taxonomy of Mankind

Benson E. Ginsburg and William S. Laughlin
The Multiple Bases of Human Adaptability and Achievement: A Species Point of View

Jerry Hirsch
Behavior-Genetic Analysis and Its Biosocial Consequences

Benjamin Pasamanick
A Tract for the Times: Some Sociobiological Aspects of Science, Race, and Racism

Hermann K. Bleibtreu and John Meaney
Racial Differences in Behavior: Cultural and Evolutionary Considerations

Races do not exist; classifications of mankind do.   George A. Dorsey

Discussions of the biological origins and characteristics of
subjectively determined races, based exclusively, as they
must be, on evolutionary misconceptions, are useful only
for strengthening culturally determined prejudices against
groups which have reality only in a social, rather than a
biological, sense.   Paul R. Ehrlich and Richard W. Holm

To explore the IQ of dark-skinned children in comparison
with that of light-skinned ones has, it seems to me, as
much scientific significance as exploring the correlation of
any two probably independent characters comparing the IQ
of red-haired children with that of black-haired ones, or of
children with hereditary inclination to obesity with that of
congenitally skinny ones.   Eugene Rabinowitch

Hermann K. Bleibtreu and John Meaney

Race and Racism

Americans can't seem to make up their minds about the importance of racial differences. During the 1950s and '60s the general sentiment seemed to be that everyone was pretty much the same: racial differences were trivial and should be ignored; the guarantee of civil rights and enforced integration would quickly put the "racial issue" in the shade, anyway. The "melting pot," which had apparently solved the Irish, Italian, Jewish (and so forth) "problem" in the past would also solve the Negro and Indian "problem." But quickly, by 1970, it became clear that ethnicization—not integration—was to be the product of a decade of civil rights legislation and aid to the poor (see the section "The Myth of the Melting Pot"). Instead of an end to racism, "racial pride" developed among those so recently designated as the economically, educationally, and socially "disadvantaged." For the first time, the stigma of racial inferiority conferred on others by the middle-class white majority was countered by racial pride. The melting pot idea was totally replaced by vague hopes that a basis for a new coexistence could be worked out. There were those who suggested that the time between slavery and socioeconomic equality with the enslaver has to be a time in which strong group identification takes root, in which feelings of inferiority are supplanted by those of superiority. Thus, ethnicization necessarily precedes integration.

Whether this is simply wishful thinking and rationalization by members of the dominant class who believe that centuries of injustice can be rectified by somewhat

minimizing those injustices remains to be seen. What is certain is that racism blooms afresh in America. While it is considered poor taste, if not un-American, to disparage another for his race, it is quite acceptable to be proud of one's own racial (spelled "ethnic") memberships. "Positive" racism, however, requires that races be represented in various roles and have varying status; "positive" racism requires that we recognize in each other those qualities "known" to be characteristic of our hereditary racial background. But whether "positive" or "negative," racism is a social pathology without scientific meaning.

The Cultural Bias of Racism

Racism is, by definition, a belief that individuals' capacities are predetermined and limited and that their behavior is dictated by their genetic membership in a group identifiable as a race. Moreover, racial characteristics are fixed, and so can only be little or not at all modified by environmental influence such as education, medicine, nutrition, and so forth. A racist sorts individuals into preexisting pigeonholes, ascribing to the individual the characteristics attributed to his race. But there is no reason to label the racist himself with any positive or negative social or moral attributes. It is the nature of his reasoning that makes him a racist, and not the particular likes or dislikes he has for any person or groups of people.

To substantiate the opinion that most Americans

are racists does not require taking a poll of attitudes and prejudices but, rather, determining whether or not most Americans reason like racists. It is the authors' opinion that racist reasoning is the product of typological thinking, which in turn is due to an ignorance of the process of evolution. The need to rationalize injustice and to assure his own superiority gives rise to the attributes with which a racist endows races. Most discussions about race deal with these attributes: is black really beautiful; can Negroes learn as well as whites; are Jews smarter? Such arguments are pointless, since the nineteenth-century reasoning—before we knew anything about populations and genetics—upon which they are based are spurious. Until a knowledge of population genetics becomes part of the public fund, racism will continue to be a part of American culture.

The suggestion that the rather esoteric theoretical findings of one small branch of science—population genetics—can affect a cultural change may appear to be the height of academic conceit. But is it? Western European people used to believe that the sun revolved around the earth, that man was created in 4004 B.C., that species were immutable, and that life was a spiritual and not a physical property. There were important cultural reasons for retaining each of these beliefs, yet all of them have now been replaced by other theories, and their replacement involved a profound change in world view as well as changes in behavior. A replacement of the typological, static concept of race with a populational processual one will also result in a changed point of view and a concomitant change in behavior. To suggest that education affects the way people think and behave only is to say that man's behavior, more than that of any other animal, is the consequence of learning. All the moralizing and humanitarian effort we can muster will not erase racial prejudice. Even substantial findings that refute racial stereotypes will have no real effect on racism, because they will be followed by equally substantial findings in the opposite direction (a back-and-forth practice called "scientific" racism). Until races are recognized as populations in the genetic sense of that term, and until their characteristics are understood in terms of the modern theory of evolution, racism will continue to be a common attribute of Americans.

There are impediments to getting across the necessary scientific ideas that will enable us to come to rational terms with individual and population variation. The problem is not that the ideas themselves are so difficult that they require a specialized education: the ideas can be, and often are, simply and clearly presented in many high-school biology texts. The reason the ideas don't get across and take root is a cultural one. Two major blocks stand in the way: (1) the cultural unacceptability of thinking in terms of distribution and variation instead of absolutes; and (2) the general suspicion of the theory of evolution. They both effectively preclude the acceptance of a modern scientific view of race. Note that neither of these cultural biases can be attributed solely to those who have not been formally educated. They are as entrenched in our higher educational system as in any other part of the culture. In this sense, members of the Academy, nationally recognized educators, and the man in the street are equally children of their culture. Racism, whether it be "scientific"—i.e., presumably free of moral or value judgment—or the "red-neck" variety, is nonetheless racism.

Typological Thinking

In the heads of many Americans resides an image of the type Negro, the type Caucasian, the type American Indian, and so on. These, of course, are stereotypes and do not really exist, but they serve as a model against which one can compare the real thing. Oddly enough, the real person invariably turns out to be less "real" than the model. He's too short, not blond, or does not have blue eyes; the Negro is not dark enough, his hair is too straight. The same kind of stereotyped reasoning also underlies the concept of "pure" race, since every individual who deviates from the Platonic archetype is some sort of a hybrid. These are even less "real" than unmixed variants of the stock or race. All of this is, of course, nonsense. Individuals are members of populations: that is, they originate from a gene pool that has been established by a group which over the generations habitually exchanged mates. Such pools are "leaky" in that people immigrate and emmigrate, yet at any one time an individual consists of a more or less random amalgamation of genes from that pool. Since there are thousands of loci in man and the possibility of multiple alleles at every locus, it is to be expected that, within a population, variation can be great. While the pool can be characterized in terms of gene frequencies and the population members can be described in terms of biological similarities, any one person will only represent a very small amount of the variation which *could* be expressed by the pool.

The human species (i.e., the maximum population), because it is geographically so widespread, is divided up into a number of subpopulations, any two of which might be more or less isolated from one another. Long periods in which there is no exchange of mates between pools which are acted on differentially by forces which change gene frequencies can result in genetically quite distinct populations. This is another way of saying that Homo sapiens is a polytypic species. The difference between even the most remote populations has evidently never resulted in genetic incompatibility, speciation. Gene pools merge, separate, perhaps become isolated for generations, then merge again, and so on. One "frame" in that ongoing film is the race at that moment; a number of generations later, the picture can be very different. As our colleague F. S. Hulse has said, race is simply an episode in the life of a gene pool. That is why a classification of races is such a thankless and biologically meaningless task. Not only are absolute distinctions between geographical races impossible to make—because we are dealing with subpopulations, not species—races themselves may change gradually.

Obviously our culture finds it difficult or mentally uncomfortable to deal with categories that are not clearly distinct from one another and that don't remain stable. The result is that our cultural classifications of race are typological, totally at variance with our scientific concept of population. Any member of the culture is an authority on what a Negro is or what a Caucasian is, but these are cultural categories that may lump individuals from totally different gene pools simply because of some phenotypic similarity. In other words, the cultural category is typological, the scientific category is populational. When that distinction is not kept in mind—and even scientists do not always bother with the distinction—it vitiates valid research on race.

Note how difficult it would be to be a racist and think in populational terms. A typological configuration is doomed when there are no absolute characteristics, only differences in frequencies; no clear-cut boundaries, only gradual shadings of one group into the other; no definite time of origin and no stability, just gradual change.

Anti-Evolutionism

The modern theory of evolution, often labeled the "synthetic theory" because it is a synthesis of theories developed in genetics, taxonomy, and paleontology,

has received little public exposure in America. If taught at all, it is in upper-division college or graduate school. Most high school textbooks avoid the subject altogether, or apply the theory only to plants and animals, leaving it up to the student to conclude that man is a special case. He may not know algebra or physics until he studies it, but the student already has a good deal of "knowledge" to draw on when it comes to evolution. He knows, for example, that evolution is but a "theory" (as opposed to a "fact"), that it is not generally acceptable (even some great scientists don't believe in it), that it is antithetical to Christianity, and that it attempts to prove that man evolved from an ape although the missing link has not been found. On the other hand, there seem to be some acceptable parts of the theory, or at least they agree with common sense: things evolve from simple to complex, from lower to higher in a process that is scientifically identifiable as "progress," with Caucasian man being the most evolved form. Also, that part of the theory about the environment influencing organisms, even man, makes sense. It is obvious that primitive peoples, like aborigines, are in some way a product of the incredibly meager, uncivilized conditions under which they live.

Such nineteenth-century middle-class American views about evolution have now, thanks to our churches and schools, become a part of the public fund of knowledge. They provide the fertile ground upon which racism thrives. Not one of the above statements about evolution is accurate. They all reflect the layman's general awareness of what is considered the evidence for evolution and his almost total ignorance of the theoretical framework in which that data can be interpreted. The accumulation of the "evidence of evolution" provided by fossil men, apes, and human races has proved nothing, in and of itself, yet most texts and popular books on human evolution are loaded with descriptions and pictures of the evidence with hardly any explanation of the evolutionary processes.

The basic tenets of the modern synthetic theory of evolution are quite simple. There is a genetic mechanism which relentlessly pumps out variation. Most variants do not survive or are relatively less successful, reproductively; a few do survive, and reproduce individuals somewhat similar to themselves. He who survives and reproduces the most is obviously best represented, genetically, in future generations. In any given generation, the individuals whose constellation of inherited qualities best suit the existing environment are "selected for"; as environments change, the species is challenged, as it were, to come up with viable new genetic combinations. The exhaustion of a goodly store of genetic variations upon which to draw to meet environmental changes results in extinction. The challenge is for the species to tread a line between overspecialization and overgeneralization: that line is called "adaptation."

The extent to which a population is responding to its environment can often be estimated by measuring the gene changes. Such changes come about by the action of "evolutionary forces": mutation, gene flow, genetic drift, and selection. In many human populations and in experimental animal populations the action of these forces can be measured. This is study of what is called "on-going evolution." It is assumed that these forces acted in the past just as we can prove they are acting today. In other words, differences in human population today (i.e., racial differences) as well as those in the archaeological past must be explained in terms of the action of those four forces.

It is generally agreed that of the four, natural selection has been most responsible for both the racial variation that differentiates subpopulations of the species and the chronological variation that differentiates consecutive populations. We can assume that behavioral differences among human populations are primarily functional; they signify adaptations to different environments, although it is extremely difficult to reconstruct the conditions which were responsible for the measurable variation in either fossil or living populations. There are major problems in the fossil record; for example, it is usually impossible to distinguish racial differences from differences in species. An example of this is the current dispute concerning the number of species of Australopithecines. Do these fossils represent racial variants of one species, or two or more coexisting species? Another example is the problem of whether Homo sapiens evolved out of Homo erectus or whether these are two species that diverged from some common ancestral species.

The analysis of contemporary racial variation is less complex because there is no doubt that we are only dealing with one species. We are therefore able to hypothesize that a variable, such as skin color, is a characteristic of the species which varies in degree of expression across subpopulations and does not signify a basic difference in kind. This is also true of differences in blood groups. These are not absolute differences. The occupying question of modern research into race is a different one: whether selection or chance established these differences. Skin color, for example, may be considered an adaptation if recent findings can be

supported that connect the regulation of vitamin D synthesis with melaninization. It is at least a plausible suggestion. As to most other racial traits—i.e., population characteristics which vary from one population to another—we have so far not been able to suggest testable hypotheses.

Race and Behavior

Differences in the behavior of populations is perhaps the most difficult and undeveloped area of human genetics. We do know that there is less genetic programming for behavior in our species and more dependence on learning than in any other animal. And what is learned—the actual content—differs greatly only among the subpopulations of Homo sapiens. The unique result is that while all men are biologically essentially the same—for example, they are interfertile, they can exchange parts like hearts, they seem to have pretty much the same physiological and nutritional requirements—they may act or behave very differently because they have learned different things. No other animal is faced with this paradox. Cockroaches of the same species, tigers, or wombats have cockroach, tiger, or wombat "world views," because, thanks to their genes, each species "learned" precisely the same things. Individual experience after birth can somewhat modify even the behavior of the lowly roach, but there is simply no comparison to the learning process in man.

The advantage of having your behavior depend on what you have learned is that it allows for great flexibility. Man is geographically the most widespread animal, primarily because of his ability to think up artificial (noninnate) means of compensating for his biological limitations. But this flexibility also has its drawbacks. A dependence on learning, or cultural transmission, is far more risky than dependence on genetic transmission; and even more dangerous is the paradox that members of the same species, simply because they belong to different subpopulations, do not behave in the same way. Their similar biology doesn't automatically signal their brotherhood. They meet and they are strangers.

An ethologist studying the behavior of a certain species of animal may worry that his generalizations too readily gloss over individual variations in that species. The anthropologist, the specialist in the behavior of one species—sapiens—has greater concerns. He cannot make any general statement about the species at all, not so much because of individual differences, but because of the behavioral differences of subspecies, what he calls "cultural differences." It is the culture that provides the individual with his world view through learning, or enculturation, and therefore it is the culture which determines his behavior. Racists tend to miss that point and confuse culture with biology; thus they make the serious taxonomic error of identifying racial differences as differences in species. Because human behavior is mainly dependent on enculturation, behavioral differences among human populations must be only minimally due to genetic differences.

The articles that follow support the position that any argument for racial inferiority or superiority is scientifically untenable. During one period in American history racists sought for support from the churches; today they seek confirmation from science. The extent to which they receive scientific support will depend largely on how well informed our educators and scientists are about population genetics and evolution.

James N. Spuhler and Gardner Lindzey
Racial Differences in Behavior

One of the anthropologist's major tasks has been to explain the meaning of "race." In numerous articles, anthropologists have traced the historical use of the term and attempted to define it. The first two articles in this section reflect contemporary approaches to the concept, delineating some of the differences in the use of the idea of race within the field and reflecting the controversy over whether the concept serves any useful purpose.

Spuhler and Lindzey tell us that, historically, racial classifications have changed from typological to anthropometric, which in turn gave way to the concept of gene frequencies. An interesting distinction is made between the anthropologist's and the geneticist's definition of race, a distinction important to keep in mind when reading any discussions of racial differences in behavior. In many such papers, what groups are really being compared is not always thoroughly discussed; more often than not the races being compared have been grouped on the basis of physical similarity (skin color and some combination of facial features) and no attempt has been made to determine whether or not the groups represent populations.

This chapter begins with a brief discussion of the concept of race, an indication of what we mean by "race," and consideration of how racial differences may be detected. Following this we shall present a general discussion of empirical findings concerning the existence of racial differences in behavior. In conclusion, we shall comment briefly upon the utility of the concept of race for the behavioral scientist.

No reasonable discussion of race differences can commence without at least passing attention to present usage and the rather painful past of the concept of "race." The necessity of such an endeavor is underlined by the sizable number of contemporary scientists who are convinced that the concept of race has no legitimate place in the social or biological sciences. Scholars as diverse professionally as Klineberg, Livingstone, Montagu, and Penrose argue that the concept only misleads and confuses and serves no legitimate scientific purpose. Although representatives of almost every social and biological science at one time or another have decried the use of this concept, it has displayed a tough viability and even now seems on the way to surviving the rash of attacks that followed Hitler's affinity for the term. One may note that the associative link between "race" and "Aryan" is even today strong enough in our society to account

From *Behavior-Genetic Analysis* edited by Jerry Hirsch. Copyright © 1967 by McGraw-Hill, Inc. Reprinted by permission of McGraw-Hill Book Company.

for a good deal of the discomfort that many scientists display in the presence of the term "race."

It was probably inevitable, once mankind had been divided into classes or categories, that some persons would think in terms of an order of quality or merit. It was equally ordained that dictators, demagogues, and elitists would employ such concepts for their own purposes and without regard for their technical meaning. This use of the race concept by "racists" scarcely seems a legitimate argument against the concept if it serves any useful purpose within an empirical discipline, any more than the abuse of genetic concepts in the hands of these same individuals should lead to an abandonment or alteration of these concepts, or the misuse of probability concepts in the hands of an ardent advertising copywriter should influence statistical analysis in the social sciences. In considering the concept of race, we shall limit our attention to its empirical-theoretical significance within behavioral and biological science and largely overlook the social-political impact of the term. In another context the latter issue, of course, could be of primary importance. . . .

The Concept of Race

As a technical term, the concept of "race" has been primarily the property of the anthropologist, although in recent years it has come to play an increasingly influential role in genetics. The original attempt of anthropologists to identify a specified number of races can be viewed as nothing more than an extension of Linnaean, zoological taxonomy. Given the physical diversity of mankind, it seemed only reasonable to subdivide the multitude into classes that were physically more homogeneous than the total population and that shared a common descent. According to this view, the category of human race is the next more specific category beneath the class *Homo sapiens*. Early concern with races was heavily influenced by the conception of "ideal" or "pure" races believed to represent the original ancestors of the many "mixed" classes of individuals which can be observed today. Such a viewpoint is no longer seriously entertained within biological or social science.

It was also logical that these early classificatory attempts should begin with those characteristics that appeared relatively invariant over time in the adult organism and were easy to measure objectively. In view of the link of physical anthropology to archaeology, it was not surprising that the search for a classificatory basis should focus upon attributes that could be measured, even though the subject was no longer living and might not have been living for many centuries. Thus, early efforts at classification emphasized physical measurements, particularly skeletal indices. A typical example is provided by the work by Dixon who used three skeletal indices (cephalic index, length-height index of the skull, nasal index) to classify races. Subsequent investigators were more concerned with "common descent" than Dixon, and many of them employed physical attributes that were not skeletal, such as lip thickness, skin color, eye color, and hair texture. Garn suggests, however, that significant links between the race concept and the theory of evolution have appeared only during the past 10 or 15 years.

The most important development in this area is the recent attempts to link racial classification with physical characteristics that are genetically well understood. The writings of Boyd and Mourant provide the best illustration of this approach, which has leaned heavily upon blood types as its classificatory base. Many arguments have been advanced in support of serological classification, but the decisive factor seems to be the additional power generated by understanding the genetic basis for the attribute. A somewhat enthusiastic statement of the case for a "genetic definition" of race is presented by Boyd:

A classification of men on the basis of gene frequencies has a number of advantages. (1) It is objective. Gene frequencies are determined by straight-forward counting or relatively simple computation from quantitative observations of clear-cut, all-or-none characters. The subjective element which complicates attempts to compare the skin colors of two peoples, for example, does not appear. (2) It is quantitative. The degree of similarity between two populations is not a matter of guess-work, but can be compared by calculating from the frequencies of the genes considered. (3) It makes it possible to predict the composition of a population resulting from mixture in any assigned proportions of two populations of known gene frequencies. (4) It encourages clearer thinking about human taxonomy and human evolution. Emotional bias is less likely to operate than in the case of physical appearances such as stature or skin color. There are no prejudices against genes. It permits a sharp separation of the effects of heredity and environment. In the case of a character like stature, it is difficult to say whether genes or food and climate have contributed more to making two populations alike. In the case of blood groups no such problem arises.[1]

It should be noted that none of the classificatory systems that has any current popularity is strictly actuarial. Although they involve objective indices, these are intended for a trained observer who employs them with a weather eye for geographic location and such. Boyd's classification, for example, does not lean solely upon allelic frequencies but also seems to consider implicitly geographic location, lineage, and past classificatory practice. It appears that modern biometric and psychometric techniques for multivariate classification have not been employed extensively in this area, and the occasional applications have not received wide attention in secondary sources. Nonetheless, beginnings have been made, the most impressive being the recent studies of Cavalli-Sforza, Barrai, and Edwards.

Definitions of race fall into two broad categories, with those advanced by anthropologists usually emphasizing physical similarity and common descent (geographic factors), whereas the definitions proposed by geneticists typically focus upon differences in gene frequencies and breeding isolation. The continuity between the concept of race as applied to man and the concepts of breed or strain as applied to lower animals has often been identified.

An interesting sidelight to problems of definition of race concerns the tendency of many anthropologists of a decade or so ago to assert that the attributes to be used in classifying races must be non-adaptive, that is, make no contribution to the process of natural selection. This emphasis was defended on the grounds that only characters unrelated to natural selection would possess reasonable stability over time. It seems likely that these observers must have been influenced also by an implicit concern lest racial distinction be used as a basis for racial prejudice or racial superiority. The infirmity of their reasoning was pointed out by geneticists, particularly Dobzhansky, and this position has been largely abandoned.

Often the genetic biography of a species is not uniform over its full distribution in space at some particular time. Given the raw materials of inherited variability, the genetic structure of a species depends largely on local selection intensities, on the one hand, and gene flow between different local areas, on the other. If there is much gene flow, local races cannot develop; if there is less, clines may be formed; if still less, local races may differentiate. When the genetic biography is not uniform, it is useful to recognize, and sometimes to name, the races or subspecies within the species.

The biological and anthropological notion of race (= subspecies) which we use is based on stipulative rather than lexical or ostentative definition. In the first instance, "racial differences" are those genetic differences which define "races." It does not follow that the geographic distribution of other genetic traits will be concordant with that of the selected set of traits used to define the racial groupings. It is a separate problem to find out if other genetic differences between populations are "racial." But as Simpson, in commenting on misapprehensions about subspecies, wrote:

. . . subspecies do not express the geographic variation of the characters of a species and are only partially descriptive of that variation. They are formal taxonomic population units, usually arbitrary, and cannot express or fully describe the variation in those populations any more than classification in general can express or fully describe phylogeny. They are not, for all that, any less useful in discussing variation.[2]

Most species of animals with a wide distribution over a variable geographic habitat exhibit more or less distinct geographic races. The existence of such racial differentiation is a token of the biological adaptation of local populations to their local environment. Mayr reports: "Such races are sufficiently distinct in about one-third of the better known species of animals to have been designated as different subspecies. Some widespread species of birds and mammals may have as many as twenty

[1] W. C. Boyd, "The Contributions of Genetics to Anthropology," in *Anthropology Today*, A. Kroeber, ed. (Chicago: University of Chicago Press, 1953), pp. 495–496.
[2] G. G. Simpson, *Principles of Animal Taxonomy* (New York: Columbia University Press, 1961), p. 175.

or thirty or, in exceptional cases, more than fifty rather well-defined races."[3]

The fundamental processes underlying the anthropological concept of race are bisexual reproduction and adaptation through natural selection. A given individual is connected by gametes to representatives of a set of persons which we stipulate as a subspecies, that is, what anthropologists usually call a race. Unlike the individual, this set of individuals (a partially isolated local breeding population or race) is self-perpetuating. This set of persons, largely of common descent, has potentially unlimited longevity; and, unlike the species, this racial population is open to gene flow from the outside.

In the human and other bisexual species, different individuals are heterozygous for different genes even though the gene pool of the breeding population is at equilibrium with the evolutionary forces causing change in gene frequencies. With the trivial exception of monozygous multiple births, all human individuals are unique in genotype. Under random mating with dominance and a few alleles at each locus, much of the variation is hidden in heterozygotes. This large store of hidden variation may be associated with a short-run disadvantage to the local population because of reduced fitness of homozygous deleterious recessives in the prevailing environment while at the same time providing a long-run advantage in the possession of genetic flexibility in meeting environmental change. Since the change in gene frequency over space is gradual, any attempt to separate people sharply into races having exact boundaries and different gene frequencies is arbitrary. The number of races recognized is thus a matter of convenience. It follows that a race does not have an average genotype and therefore it does not have an average phenotype. Thus it is misleading to try to picture a typical or average member of a race. Rather, a race should be defined in terms of the relative frequencies of some of the alleles contained in its gene pool.

Having glanced at the history of the race concept and its typical definition, we now ask: What are the races of man? It is characteristic of questions concerning human taxonomy that they lack clear or definitive answers. Consistently, the human races are sometimes identified as three in number (almost always Negroid, Mongoloid, Caucasoid), sometimes as six (for example, Negroid, Mongoloid,

Caucasoid, Australoid, American Indian, and Polynesian), and in one authoritative volume as thirty. At the present time there is no objective basis for agreeing upon how many racial categories should be employed, although it seems clear that few investigators will wish to be burdened with 30 different classes. Even Garn and Coon in a more recent publication have suggested that contemporary evidence supports a classification involving no more than 10 major races, and still more recently Garn suggested distinguishing between geographic races, local races, and microraces. He has also pointed out that differences in the number of races proposed by investigators are largely to be understood not in terms of disagreement or conflicting claims but rather in terms of different levels or principles of classification that have determined the various systems. His geographic races are nine in number and include Amerindian, Polynesian, Micronesian, Melanesian-Papuan, Australian, Asiatic, Indian, European, and African. Undoubtedly the most interesting classification in the present context is that developed by Boyd on the basis of approximate gene frequencies, primarily for blood types. The distinction he offers is between Early European (Basque), European (Caucasian), African (Negroid), Asiatic (Mongoloid), American, and Australian. In more recent publications Boyd has elaborated this scheme to include 13 races as follows: Early European, Lapp, Northwest European, Eastern and Central European, Mediterranean, African, Asian, Indo-Dravidian, American Indian, Indonesian, Melanesian, Polynesian, and Australian.

It should be noted that the setting apart of the Basques as members of an "Early European" race is of doubtful validity. The Basques who have been blood-typed, being contemporary, are not "earlier" than other living peoples of Europe. They speak a relict language, but the oldest evidence for Iberian language is not as old as that for other languages still spoken in Europe. They have a high frequency of the Rh blood type, but if one uses as many as 12 gene frequencies of the red blood cellular antigens to measure biological affinity, the Basques are not as distinctive from other European populations as are, for example, the Irish and the Sicilians....

[3] E. Mayr, "Races in Animal Evolution," *International Social Science Journal*, 17 (1965): 121–122.

Conclusions

In conclusion, we may say that the concept of race has little importance for the student of human behavior at present. There are areas of human behavior where it is as misleading to refer to "the human being" as it is in comparative animal psychology to refer to "the rat," "the mouse," or "the monkey"; these include the areas of the sensory processes or of the enzyme deficiencies where major genes have high penetrance and nearly constant expression in most environments. In these domains, major genes with clear-cut behavioral consequences may control in most environments a large proportion of the observed variation within and between races. These are the areas in behavioral science where the concept of race—or its biological equivalent—is needed to give a satisfactory account of the observed variation. But the behavioral consequences of such known major genes are not very important for human behavior considered broadly. For the areas of human behavior that are vital in everyday life, for the varieties of behavior that allow individuals to participate satisfactorily in their society, there is no comparable evidence for genetically determined racial differences. Indeed there is at least the possibility that selection acting over the past 2 or more million years has made genes adaptive for symbolic behavior, for behavior associated with language, and consequently has made it very unlikely that such racial differences exist.

The concept of race is likely to remain of small general importance for behavioral science until anthropologists and other students of human biology replace the typological and taxonomic notion of race with a dynamic notion based on the genetic theory of evolution. The possibility of future change in the status of the concept is dependent upon increased activity in an area of research that is procedurally difficult, politically dangerous, and personally repugnant to most psychologists, sociologists, and anthropologists.

Jean Hiernaux

The Concept of Race and the Taxonomy of Mankind

Hiernaux builds his definition of race in a stepwise procedure. He states that if "race" is to be used as a taxonomic term, it must be thought of as a grouping of Mendelian or breeding populations. To Hiernaux, the populations are the units to be classified into races.

Two of the most important features of his article are: (1) the explanation of the differences between typological and what can be termed "populational" concepts of race; and (2) the presentation of racial classifications based on cluster analysis. As we observed earlier, some anthropologists still use a typological approach to race, and it is this very approach which many nonanthropologists utilize whenever race is used as one of the variables being considered.

Hiernaux has been a pioneer in the use of multivariate statistical analyses in anthropology, particularly in the study of interpopulational differences. He feels, on the basis of work with cluster analysis, that the human species cannot really be divided into anything like previous classifications. Perhaps what he returns us to is a definition of "race" as equivalent to "breeding population." This is not, however, the way the term is used by the majority of those who study human variation. Thus we are led to a conclusion like Hiernaux's—racial classifications, even those based on a phylogenetic approach, are arbitrary and really of little use in understanding human variation—and, to a conclusion made by many others, that how a racial classification is made depends upon the classifier's purpose, rather than upon realities.

Introduction

Race has been given numerous definitions. Many of them are similar in meaning, but several modes of thinking about race still persist. Within a single mode, the formulation of the concept may differ, and some vagueness in it is frequent. Moreover, application of the concept of race by an author to a classification of mankind does not always meet the requirements of his own definition.

I do not intend to review the literature on race and human races. Only a few contributions will be cited as examples. I shall attempt, where so many others have failed, to reach the most sensible and useful definition, and this as a development of a previous paper on the subject presented at the sixth International Congress of Anthropological and Ethnological Sciences, Paris, 1960. Once this definition is arrived at, I shall endeavor to apply it to current mankind, in other words to apply the concept of race to a classification of mankind into races.

Toward a Definition of Race

1. *A race is a grouping of persons*. There is common agreement on this point: if every individual belonged to a different race, there would be no need for a concept other than that of the individual. The concept of race is obviously a classificatory one: it tends to reduce the immense number of individuals to a more limited number of classes. As in any classification, a hierarchy of groupings may be conceived, for example, one consisting of three grades called grand race, race, and subrace— or similar terms.

2. *What in Man determines race?* Factors of two orders determine the characters of an individual: heredity and environment. In defining race, do we have to consider the genotype only? Or do we have to consider the phenotype, thus including noninherited characters and the nontransmissible influence of the environment?

All concepts of race are interwoven with that of heredity because all aim to define something that has a tendency, at least, to remain stable from one generation to the next. Suppose two groups of people have identical gene pools, but differ phenotypically because of the imprint of different environments. Would it be useful to call them races A and B, knowing that by reversing the environmental conditions race A would become race B in one generation and vice versa? A negative answer seems evident to me as to many others: in order to be useful, a concept of race must be genetical. When using characters known to be partly sensitive to environmental differences, the concept of race is correctly used only when the genetically induced variability is considered. Coon, Garn, and Birdsell, however, write: "A race is a population which differs phenotypically from all others with which it has been compared."[1] The usefulness of such a concept is much less than that of race as a group of individuals characterized by its gene pool.

3. *How to group individuals?* Two basic answers have been given to this question. One of them is: let us group together all similar individuals, wherever they live or have lived. Analyzing the various views on race, H. V. Vallois shows how widely this way of grouping has been used until recently: "the notion of race . . . may be understood, first of all, as a combination of characters discernible in individuals."[2] For example, G. von Frankenberg writes: "Rasse zweierlei bedeutet 1. Einem komplex erblicher merkmale. . . . 2. Eine gruppe von individuen, die diese merkmale zu besitzen pflegen." ("Race has two meanings. (1) A complex of hereditary characteristics. . . . (2) A group of individuals tending to possess these characteristics.")[3] Though adhered to by a much smaller proportion of anthropologists, this concept of race is still alive today. For example, Wierciński and Czekanowski plead in its favor and recent studies on the Swiss and on the Basques use it. Arguments against the theoretical bases of such a concept of race have been expressed too often to be listed here again; the discussion in *Current Anthropology* of Wierciński's paper sums up most of them. Only one aspect of this concept will be considered here. We know that mankind has evolved and is still physically evolving. The groups of individuals that constitute our taxonomic units must be such as to allow investigation of those evolutionary processes: Those groups must both show a tendency toward secular stability

Reprinted with permission of The Macmillan Company from "The Concept of Race and the Taxonomy of Mankind" by Jean Hiernaux. Copyright © Ashley Montagu, 1968.

[1] *Races* (Springfield, Ill.: Charles C Thomas, Publisher, 1950).
[2] "Race," in *Anthropology Today*, A. Kroeber, ed. (Chicago: University of Chicago Press, 1953), pp. 145–162.
[3] *Menschenrassen und Menschentum* (Berlin: Safari-Verlag, 1956).

and reflect evolutionary change. But a race defined as a group of similar individuals is, by definition, incapable of any change. In each generation it will consist of an artificial grouping of people who happen to share a given constellation of characters.

To me, as to many others, it seems that the only useful way of grouping individuals for anthropological analysis is to group together the people participating within the same circle of matings. Such a group shows a genuine tendency toward stability from generation to generation. If it is closed, sufficiently large, and not submitted to selection, the filial generations will have the same gene pool as the parental ones. In contrast, the offspring of a "racial type" may belong to many other types, each member of it having been conceived by two persons who may largely differ, as a result of Mendelian segregation. Evolutionary forces and events will act against the tendency toward stability of the group just defined, and a quantitative study of this process is possible.

To delimit in an absolute way the circle of matings to which an individual belongs is feasible only in the rare case of a strictly closed panmictic community, that is, in an isolate. In all other cases, the delineation is only relative. If two panmictic groups exchange mates but their members marry within their own group with a higher frequency, the partly permeable barrier to gene flow delineates them—be it of geographical, political, social, religious, or linguistic nature. But if both are surrounded by other groups with which they exchange genes at a lower rate, a barrier of a higher order includes them both. If the frequency of matings between different localities is mainly an inverse function of distance, then the only boundaries that can be traced around each locality are delimited in terms of percentage of intragroup matings and the circles overlap. The only way to group individuals in a biological sense thus often requires a probabilistic criterion for its application.

Let us ignore this difficulty and suppose that we could assign each individual to a demarcated circle of matings, for which the term "population" will be used here. Will we equate the concept of race with that of breeding population as just defined? Our grouping of individuals in one population did not take into consideration their characters in any way, it made no use of any taxonomic procedure, it was offered only in order to constitute a biological unit of study.

If we want to keep the term "race" for taxonomic purposes, it may not be applied to the population. One word is enough for one thing, and a taxonomic class may not be equated with the units to be classified. Race is a much more useful concept if we consider it as a grouping of populations. Numerous authors however equate race and population. For example, S. M. Garn defines a local race as a breeding population and even uses the term "race-population."[4] Dunn and Dobzhansky write: "Races can be defined as populations which differ in the frequencies of some gene or genes."[5] W. Howells finds Dobzhansky's definition: "Races are populations differing in the incidence of certain genes" the most acceptable.[6] These authors also use, explicitly or not, higher taxonomic classes below the human species, for example, Garn uses "geographical race," and at this level they rejoin the concept of race here proposed: a race is a group of populations.

Application of the Concept of Race to a Classification of Mankind

Let us first approach the problem of a taxonomic subdivision of current mankind without any time depth, from a purely classificatory viewpoint. Several objects are put in front of us, and we are asked to reduce their multiplicity into a lesser number of categories. Why are we asked to do so? First because, if successful, it will provide us with an efficient means of a quicker and easier memorization of the attributes of the individual objects. Instead of having to memorize their characteristics object by object, our mind has only to apprehend the general qualities of each class, and within the latter framework the peculiarities of each object. Classification is a natural tendency of the mind, a highly satisfying procedure because it saves much time and pain. Another reason is that it makes generalization possible. If we reduced objects numbered one to 100 into ten classes labelled a to j, themselves grouped in three superclasses A, B, and C, we could speak of superclass B or class d

[4]*Human Races* (Springfield, Ill.: Charles C Thomas, Publisher, 1961).
[5]*Heredity, Race and Society*, rev. ed. (New York: The New American Library, Inc., 1952).
[6]*Mankind in the Making* (Garden City, N.Y.: Doubleday & Company, Inc., 1959).

in terms of what is common to all objects in these groups.

Classification by itself does not produce any new knowledge concerning individual things: it is only a mental operation performed on existing knowledge. If the things are not such as to allow their grouping into classes, the failure to classify them may be felt as frustrating, but it does not imply any loss of knowledge. For some things are not necessarily of a nature to permit classification.

Suppose we consider things by their qualitative aspects alone. For example, they are white or red, square or round, metal or wood. A classification based on the three properties will be useful only if there are several things in at least one of the eight possible classes. If they only differ quantitatively in a continuous scale, the problem is more complex. If we consider just one quantitative property, classification is possible only if the things cluster into several groups located at different heights along the scale. In order to be useful, one more condition must be satisfied: the range occupied by a cluster on the scale may not exceed the length of the empty spaces between it and adjacent clusters. Suppose, for example, we are trying to classify things by their linear size, and that the total range runs from 10 to 70 cm, with an empty space on the scale from 40 to 45 cm. Two clusters appear, but two objects belonging to different clusters (of 39 and 50 cm for example) may be much more alike than they are to many members of their own cluster. If size is considered a criterion of affinity, what is the validity of generalizing about short and long things?

Cluster analysis still applies to the case of more than one quantitative variable under consideration, but the eventual correlations between them have to be taken into account. For two variables, a graphical representation is still possible; a representation in space can be built for three variables; for a higher number of properties we can no more visualize the situation but we can make use, if a number of assumptions are satisfied, of efficient statistics, like the generalized distance (D^2) of Mahalanobis which still permits cluster analysis. Again a classification is serviceable only if clusters do appear, and if intercluster distances are higher than intracluster ones.

Turning now to our problem, human taxonomy, what are the things we wish to classify? Human populations, if we accept the proposed definition of race. They are themselves an assemblage of individuals. For no attribute can they be studied qualitatively: owing to human polymorphism, mankind cannot be subdivided in one group with zero percent and one group with 100 percent frequencies for any one character. The properties used for a classification will therefore be expressed as frequencies or means. Cluster analysis will be the basic taxonomic procedure.

How many characters shall we use for building a classification? If we use very few characters, human variability is such that markedly different classifications may emerge from different sets of characters. A sufficient number of characters must be considered in order to make it improbable that including an additional one would alter the picture; this can be tested with currently known characters and with new ones when discovered.

All characters are not equally efficient for taxonomic purposes. Their efficiency depends in particular on their world range of variation. The wider their interpopulational variability, the lower will be the number required for a consistent classification. As said before, gene pools are what we really want to classify. Gene frequencies are consequently the ideal materials. Characters for which gene frequencies have been computed on a large scale do not unfortunately constitute that array of highly variable features concerning the most variable aspects of man needed for the attempt to achieve a satisfactory classification: Those traits or characters were imposed on us by the accidents of their discovery. Many important aspects of human variation can be studied today only through metric variables that cannot be translated into gene frequencies. Furthermore, the environment intervenes in influencing the expression of most of them, and even if the environmental factor could be removed or controlled, identical effects could result from different gene pools. On the other hand, a set of metric variables can be chosen in order to represent the main variable traits of human morphology (for example from the results of a factor analysis) which are relatively not very sensitive to environment. If the clusters eventually observed from such a set and from a set of currently computable gene frequencies clearly differ, there is a strong suspicion that one or both of them are inadequate for a comprehensive analysis of overall distances.

The ideal technique of the classifier described in this way, the main question may now be asked: Are human populations such that they form clusters within which the distances are less than the inter-cluster distances? Only regional cluster analysis of human populations has been published so far. I am responsible for one of them, made on fifteen populations which fill a circumscribed area in central Africa. Mean interpopulational variability in this area is especially high, a fact that increases the chances of successful classification. In fact, one cluster of two closely related populations (the Tutsi of Rwanda and those of Burundi) is clearly apart, but the remaining thirteen populations allow no further clustering, despite their considerable variability. Represented on a two-dimensional plane, their position would clump without any clear internal cleavage, however great the distance between some of the plotted populations (in terms of classical anthropology, the group includes populations so different as to call the one "Hamiticized Bantu" and the other "Pygmoid"). I am now trying to extend the analysis to all Africa south of the Sahara. Only a crude kind of statistics can be applied owing to the nature of most published data. Only very preliminary statements are permissible at the present stage of development. It can, however, be said that an uncleavable clump, showing jagged edges, is the general picture, with maybe a few isolated clusters (the Bushmen, for example). I doubt that any useful classification will emerge beyond the separation of the eventual few clusters.

Such a situation is surely not peculiar to Africa. The total variability of European populations is less. A superficial examination of published data on Asian anthropology does not give the impression that many isolated clusters would emerge. Clustering would undoubtedly be favored in America by the vastly different origins of its current inhabitants, but the races so defined on a continental basis would lose much of their originality when introduced into the world picture.

Following the above procedure would there emerge something resembling the classical subdivision of mankind into three main groups: Whites, Blacks, and Yellows (or whatever more sophisticated terms are used)? I doubt it. We know of so many populations that do not fit into the picture! Adding more "oids" to this three-fold primary subdivision would not improve it. The subdivision into nine geographic races (i.e. "the taxonomic unit immediately below the species") proposed by Garn is no more satisfactory: it only shifts the problems to a lower level. Just as Indians could not be classed with the Black or White races of the ternary system, numerous populations are unclassifiable in a nine-fold subdivision because they are peripheral to several geographical races. It seems highly probable to me that the more races we create the more unclassifiable populations there would be at fewer and fewer levels of differences, until we should reach a state of subdivision close to an enumeration of all existing populations, i.e., the units to be classified.

Though not based on a systematic testing, my impression is thus that an attempt at a classification of contemporary mankind along the lines here indicated would yield very poor results: an uncleavable mass of populations, however large the constellation they form, and a few isolated clusters, which alone could be called races. This impression was gained from considering monofactorial characters as well as multifactorial ones. Unclassifiability seems to me inherent in the modalities of human variability. What can be built from a detailed knowledge of human variability is a diagnostic key. There are no two identical gene pools nor two phenotypically identical populations. By a system of successive dichotomies any population could be identified, as could also any human being since the probability of finding two identical individuals is exceedingly low (the exception of monozygotic twins is only an apparent one, since genetically they constitute but one individual). But a diagnostic key and an efficient classification are two different devices, though constructed from similar materials.

Many race classifications used today did not result from a cluster analysis, but reflect an attempt to extract from the anthropological data the peculiarities common to most populations of vast geographical areas. This is, for example, the case of the classification into thirteen races falling into seven main groups proposed by Boyd, in which the races are defined by characteristic ranges of gene frequencies. Such a splitting of mankind essentially belongs to a diagnostic key. Its equation to a genuine classification is not clear. The conditions necessary for a valid classification will be examined later.

Probably many will find the requirement of a maximal intracluster distance lower than the minimal intercluster one too exacting. But again what is the usefulness of a classification of races A and B if we know that some populations of race A are nearer to some of race B than to some of their own race?

Though seemingly extreme, the position here expressed concerning the intrinsic resistance of contemporary mankind to any coherent taxonomic subdivision might be partly shared by many who use racial terminology. Th. Dobzhansky, commenting on Livingstone's paper on the nonexistence of human races (in which arguments similar to mine are set forth), agrees that "if races have to be discrete units, then there are no races," but is satisfied by races as a category of biological classification so vague that ". . . how many [races] should be recognized is a matter of convenience and hence of judgement."[7] W. C. Boyd states: "Whatever races we choose to distinguish will be almost entirely arbitrary, and their distribution will depend on the particular characteristic on which we choose to base them."[8] S. L. Washburn expresses the opinion that "since races are open systems which are intergrading, the number of races will depend on the purpose of the classification."[9] Though defining a local race as a breeding population, Garn does not apply this concept when listing local races. For example, he considers the Bantu as a local race, while Bantu breeding populations number more than one hundred. In fact, he applies his former concept of a local race; "our enumeration [of local races] depends on the minimum size of the population units we wish to consider," thus introducing a highly arbitrary element into his system. There seems to be no basic theoretical disagreement between these authors' views and those exposed here. The difference lies in the fact that they consider it useful to separate into discrete units, in a somewhat arbitrary manner, the open intergrading systems that they record (there is no escaping it: if you put a label, be it a name, a letter, or a number, on something, you make it discrete). What I question is this: If any racial classification is arbitrary, for what purpose can it be of any use? Why spend so much time and effort building a classification, knowing that many others, not any worse, could be opposed to it, and that it runs the risk not only of being useless but also harmful by conveying the erroneous impression that it makes generalization possible?

Washburn's answer is: "Race is a useful concept only if one is concerned with the kind of anatomical, genetic, and structural differences which were in time past important in the origin of races. . . . If classification is to have a purpose, we may look backward to the explanation of the differences between people structural, anatomical, physiological differences—and then the concept of race is useful, but it is useful under no other circumstances, as far as I can see." A similar answer is given by M. T. Newman: "If indeed the population is the proper unit for biological study—and we have been told this many times in the past 15 years—much of the older racial work that was not so oriented needs to be rescrutinized, screened, and then appraised against the yardstick of modern populational studies. This is laborious work and would be worth it only for the understanding of phylogeny and race process that come from building a taxonomy from the bottom upward."[10]

Human Taxonomy and Phylogeny

These statements lead us to question the possibility and usefulness of human taxonomy in the light of a criterion not yet referred to here: Racial classification is useful if it reflects phylogeny.

Let us first examine the conditions required for making a phylogenetic classification of populations possible. The basic one is this: Evolution must have taken the form of a growing tree. The current populations represent the terminal twigs; the bough common to several twigs may be called a race, the larger limb common to several boughs corresponds to a higher taxonomic unit, and so on until we reach the trunk which represents the human species. Infraspecific evolution takes this form only when the species splits into several groups which are exposed to different evolutionary forces and events under complete or effective genetic isolation, with eventual further splitting under similar conditions of differentiation in isolation. The process of raciation in this mode of evolution is the same as that of speciation, but represents only its initial stage; speciation is attained when and if the accumulated differences have reached the level at which fertile cross-matings no longer occur even when the subgroups come together again. Under such conditions, if we could follow each population back into the past, it would be possible to build an impregnable phylogenetic classification, which would

[7] "Comment on 'The Nonexistence of Human Races' by F. B. Livingstone," *Current Anthropology*, 3 (1962): 481–494.

[8] "Genetics and the Human Race," *Science*, N 140 (1963): 1057–1064.

[9] "The Study of Race," *American Anthropologist*, 65 (1963): 521–531.

[10] "Geographic and Micrographic Races," *Current Anthropology*, 5 (1963): 189–207.

reflect the dynamics of race formation. Would it be possible to derive a phylogenetic tree from data on contemporary populations? Only if great care is taken in the dynamic explanation of differences. The overall distances used for a horizontal classification may be misleading, especially if few characters are considered: each adaptative feature responds to its own specific environmental stimuli, convergence may occur, and the accident of random drift may, in one generation, strongly differentiate two newly separated populations. The difficulty cannot be bypassed by trying to use non-adaptive characters only: even if they could be identified with certainty, the fact remains that their frequencies are especially sensitive to the long-lasting effects of drift, and we should thus reduce the possibilities of classification, since adaptation is an important process of differentiation. By and large however, if human evolution had been of the type described, a taxonomy built from the current characteristics of human populations would be of great help in the understanding of their phylogeny. Moreover, under such conditions, the chances are large that clear-cut clustering would correspond to characteristic constellations of gene frequencies. The limiting conditions to such a general correspondence between ultimate clusters and characteristic constellations seem to be felt by Boyd who, while defining races by characteristic constellations, writes: "Racial differentiation is the end result of the action of natural selection on the raw material provided by random mutations in a population sufficiently isolated genetically." But the fact is that no nonarbitrary general classification of mankind is available, and what we know of the migratory habits of man, and of the extent to which population mixture took place, altogether explains why no systematic subdivision of races is possible, and eliminates the hope that a general phylogeny-reflecting classification could be constructed. Human evolution did not take the form of a growing tree, at least, not in recent times. The general picture is not one of isolated groups differentiating in circumscribed areas. Mixture occurred many times in many places between the most various populations brought into contact by human mobility. The tendency toward high adaptive specialization was balanced again and again by migration, and by man's power to transform his environment. Even if we could reconstruct the intricate succession of mixtures that contributed to each living population, the final picture would look like a reticulum more than a tree, and a reticulum defies dichotomizing subdivision.

There have always been forces acting toward raciation, but they conduced to genuine races (in the sense of well-individualized clusters of populations) only here and there. I have already cited the Bushmen as a possible race that could emerge from an analysis of African variability; if this is confirmed, it would mean that this group experienced a differentiating evolution combined with a high degree of isolation. The Bushmen are in the long run facing either extinction or disappearance as a race through mixture, while maybe another race is in process of individualization somewhere else in the world. The few genuine races that could emerge from a cluster analysis of living mankind might not be those of tomorrow, nor those of yesterday.

If the preceding views are correct, the recent biological history of mankind can be visualized as an immense irregular reticulum growing upward; here and there at different time levels a stem grows away from the mass but is later embodied by it. Human populations are such that they defy general classification because of their phylogenetic history. To force them to fit into a classificatory scheme by overlooking a large part of the data can only lead to a grossly distorted idea of their phylogeny.

Conclusion

From whatever viewpoint one approaches the question of the applicability of the concept of race to mankind, the modalities of human variability appear so far from those required for a coherent classification that the concept must be considered as of very limited use. In my opinion, to dismember mankind into races as a convenient approximation requires such a distortion of the facts that any usefulness disappears: on the contrary, only the harm done by such practices remains. They tend to force our minds into erroneous channels of thinking, or, if we manage to retain any lucidity, to enter a maze of distinctions and restrictions.

To give up all general racial classifications would mean for anthropology freeing itself from blinkers it has too long worn, and focusing all its energy on its actual goal: the understanding of human variability, as it really is.

Benson E. Ginsburg and William S. Laughlin

The Multiple Bases of Human Adaptability and Achievement: A Species Point of View

At the end of his article, Hiernaux stated that the elimination of attempts at racial classifications would allow us to better understand human variability "as it really is." This implies that a strictly populational approach to the study of human variation gets us closer to reality.

Ginsburg and Laughlin, in the following article, dispense almost completely with race and racial classification, by discussing genetic variability between breeding populations. These authors view races as breeding populations, and so use the term population *instead of* race. *Their article serves as the pivotal point in our set of articles on race, in that it introduces a question considered extensively in the remaining articles—the question of populational, or racial, differences in behavior. Ginsburg and Laughlin make the important point that no sample of individuals can be studied without a knowledge of the population in which they occur—a point that should be borne in mind when considering the kinds of studies criticized in the remaining articles. The question of whether we are dealing with populations seems to be avoided in most discussions of racial differences in behavior.*

Ginsburg and Laughlin are highly critical of two approaches taken when the question of population differences in behavior is raised. The Dichotomy-Dismissal Approach and the Unlike-but-Equal Approach are discussed, and dismissed in favor of a holistic synthesis. What evolves is a rather extensive attempt at a synthetic approach to behavior by a genetically oriented psychologist and a physical anthropologist, an approach which bridges the dichotomy so often thought to exist between culture and biology.

Analyses of Human Diversity

A broad question such as that of man's place in nature cannot be treated at the research level by a single person or a single discipline. Nevertheless, the evidence that is collected by differently trained and oriented workers must be assembled and interpreted. The utilization of a variety of evidence, drawn from different fields, is a generic problem that poses special difficulties when we attempt to examine ourselves. The *zeitgeist* in which we operate is one dominated by a preoccupation with ethical considerations in which one hopes that dispassionate investigation will yield results that are consonant with our moral notions. Where there is an apparent danger of conflict between science and ethic, three modes of operation have been adopted with respect to the areas that interest us here.

The Dichotomy-Dismissal Approach

Here the two major procedures have been:

1. To dismiss the subject of heritable human variability that may extend to behavioral capacities by pointing out that present methodologies and information permit only tentative conclusions to be drawn in this area, and that these are vulnerable to misinterpretation and fraught with political danger.

2. To dichotomize the biobehavioral continuum, dismissing the biological aspects and, assigning to culture the role of determining all that is meaningful in human behavior. Thus, "In general, human variability seems to have had no proven effect on culture."[1]

The practical results, in terms of training students or integrating different kinds of materials, are essentially the same: a serious stultification. For example, Margaret Mead states:

The artificial distinction between culture—as a purely human process—and all forms of learning through experience—in the rest of the biological sector—may have been a necessary device to dispose of theories of racial difference which assumed a racial factor in "Gallic wit" or "Negro musical ability."[2]

"The Multiple Bases of Human Adaptability and Achievement: A Species Point of View" by Benson E. Ginsburg and William S. Laughlin from *Social Biology*, Vol. 13, No. 3, pp. 242–255, 1966. Reprinted by permission of The University of Chicago Press and the authors. © 1966 by The University of Chicago.

[1] J. H. Steward and D. B. Shimkin, "Some Mechanisms of Sociocultural Evolution," in *Evolution and Man's Progress*, H. Hoagland and R. W. Burhoe, eds. (New York: Columbia University Press, 1962), p. 72.

[2] "Cultural Determinants of Behavior," in *Behavior and Evolution*, A. R. Simpson and G. G. Simpson, eds. (New Haven: Yale University Press, 1958), p. 487.

This view had a tremendous influence upon the directions and priorities of anthropological and sociological investigations of the thirties and forties and was given further impetus by the elevation of the pseudoscientific racist writings of Gobineau and Chamberlain to the role of official dogma for the Third Reich. Indeed, the heat generated by the recent suggestion of concerted biological research in the area of human population differences as set forth by Ingle came partly from the crematoria of Auschwitz and Bergen-Belsen and partly from our own segregationist practices in this country. It is as though the recognition of significant biological differences among human population groups necessarily implies immutable distinctions in behavioral capacities that arrange themselves on a superiority–inferiority axis, and that studies of such differences can only lend themselves to racist doctrines. The ethical scientist, afraid of what he might let loose upon the world should he open this Pandora's box, is therefore better advised to turn his attention to other variables and to focus upon the social determinism of important human differences. The latter view has been well epitomized by Paul T. Baker, who states that, "The concept of culture, as defined by some, almost precludes the biology of man from a significant role in his behavior."[3] Biologically speaking, the species Man is the text so far as the identicist is concerned—the genetically partitioned subgroups are merely commentary. Hence, all distinctly human qualities, of whatever degree, become species attributes by definition, and are attainable by any human group under appropriate conditions of the surround.

The Unlike but Equal Approach

Here, the existence of biological differences unequally partitioned among various subpopulations within the human species is taken as a demonstrated fact, but the extension of these differences to include fundamental behavioral capacities is denied or minimized. As T. Dobzhansky points out:

Equality does not mean identity. Equality means equality of opportunity. . . . Race is a category of classification applied to subdivisions of mankind—there are races of man and of animals and plants . . . regardless of whether there is someone who wishes to classify them.[4]

The apposition of competent taxonomy and population genetics to problems of human systematics attempted by many workers has not yet produced a synthesis. Instead, the biology-culture dichotomy is invariably reinstated; and the conclusion, though arrived at on other grounds, is that of the cultural determinist. Human population differences are analyzed in terms of beanbag genetics and referred to as "mere" differences in frequency distributions of genes (although these may include frequencies of 0 or 100 percent as well as very different probabilities for achieving particular combinations, where intermediate values obtain). The implication is that such differences are nonqualitative and that any gene can get to any population, as there are no impenetrable barriers to genetic exchange between any groups within the species. Man's psyche, together with his intellectual capacities are, again, taken to be properties of the entire species, and no significant biological differences in behavioral capacities are therefore reasonable expectations among human subgroups, however classified. Individual differences occur in all populations, but these are, in this view, not selectively arrayed according to geography, pigmentation, or marriage customs. It is as though no genetic changes have occurred in the human species since the dawn of civilization and cultural factors have had no selective influence on the human genotype in almost 200 generations.

This view is, perhaps, most dramatically illustrated in the recent UNESCO report in which 22 scientists representing 17 nations agreed that:

The genetic capacity for intellectual development, like certain major anatomical traits peculiar to the species, is one of the biological traits essential for its survival in any natural or social environment. The peoples of the world today appear to possess equal biological potentialities for attaining any civilization level. Differences in the achievements of different peoples must be attributed solely to their cultural history. [Our italics.][5]

Thus, the matter has been resolved by resolution and the issue of the equality of all peoples made to

[3]"The Application of Ecological Theory to Anthropology," Part 1, *American Anthropologist*, 64 (1962): 15–22.

[4]*Heredity and the Nature of Man* (New York: Harcourt Brace Jovanovich, Inc., 1964).

[5]"Proposals on the Biological Aspects of Race," *UNESCO Courier*, April 1965, pp. 8–11.

rest on the premise of genetic noninvolvement where differences in significant behavioral capacities are concerned. The very description of these differences in the report gives them a hierarchical value and implies that were they to have any genetic basis, some human groups would then be at least statistically inferior to others, a situation that would be philosophically and ethically intolerable to the authors of the report.

The Holistic Synthesis

On this view, "all aspects of any organism may be thought of as 100 percent genetic but not 100 percent determined."[6] The genetic endowment of any organism, which includes its behavioral capacities, represents a potential, the actualization of which involves a series of interactions with environmental factors that restrict the degrees of freedom of this potential. The expressed phenotype at various stages of development, though dependent on what has been encoded in the genome, is not entirely determined by it. To be sure, there are varying degrees of lability between gene and character, but even at the highest level of lability, that of intellectual behavior, limits are set by the genotype. There is no aspect of any organism that is exempted from these biological effects.

Turning from the individual to the group, the human species is seen as a population reticulum in which genetic exchange is much more probably within aggregates united by a common biological and cultural history than between them. Despite the intergradations and diversity that occur in all widely distributed and variable species, there are identifiable phenotypic population clusters resulting from a common breeding history under the influence of selective factors. These coadapted genotypes cannot be thought of as simply the sum of their component parts and are, therefore, not adequately represented by a table listing the frequency of occurrence of each gene. The genomes constituting a population are intradependent environmentally regulated servomechanisms assimilated to an evolved set of phenotypic norms. As such, they are buffered and able to absorb genes from other populations without undergoing a phenotypic change proportional to the amount of genetic infusion. It has, for example, been estimated that American Negroes have an admixture of Caucasian genes that is, minimally, on the order of 30 percent. Although this contributes to the

variability of the population, this infusion is continually being assimilated to the prevailing phenotype, which is not obliterated by it. The corollary to this phenomenon is that a population of sufficient size harbors a great deal more genetic variability than its current phenotypic census would suggest and that, given a selective impetus, such a population can move to other phenotypic norms in a relatively short time using its own genetic resources. These resources are probably most meager with respect to those genes that serve as phenotypic markers, on the basis of which assortative mating occurs, and that are, therefore, under extreme selective pressure for phenotypic constancy. Given a multiplicity of genetic ways of achieving similar phenotypic expression, convergence on the part of genetically diverse partial isolates within a species is to be expected under a common and sustained selection pressure. Man's culture, while an expression of his genetic endowment, also affects it via the assortative mating patterns that result, thus constituting part of a feedback system whose components are continually interacting. To attribute the achievements of peoples solely to their cultural histories, which may be the products of differences as well as similarities in their biological endowments, is, in a dramatic sense, to dispense with the people. The student of culture thereby becomes a paleontologist of behavior, whose fossils are the books, music, technology, and other leavings of human organisms taken as groups—except that most hypotheses regarding the significance of biological factors as contributors to similarities or diversities that might be entertained by the student of fossil behavior of other organisms when he finds consistent differences in the nests built by different species of termites or of birds, for example, are excluded *a priori*.

The Species Reticulum Approach

Biobehavioral Monism

The holistic synthesis that we are attempting here admits of no genetical-cultural dualism, nor does it array biologically based clusters of capacities that may differ statistically among subpopulations in any necessary hierarchical order. Evidence from

[6]B. E. Ginsburg, "Genetics as a Tool in the Study of Behavior," *Perspectives in Biology and Medicine*, 1 (1958): 397–424.

the fields of behavior genetics and ethology provide ample documentation of the biological contributions to behavioral capacities ranging from intelligence to temperament to instinct. Freud faced up to the problem of biological determinism in relation to individual differences, but in practical terms he homogenized these differences and left biology primarily at the instinctual level.

Contemporary comparative psychologists, among them Beach and Lehrman, have gone back to the genome, and have, as D. D. Thiessen has summarized, "... forcefully argued and demonstrated that *behavior is the outcome of genotype developing within a milieu of environmental and social influences*. Instincts, as a result, are translated into species-specific behaviors with unique heritable and experiential components."[7] The mind and the body have thus again become aspects of each other, not only in the sense of traveling in the same conveyance, but also of occupying the same seat.

Wright ... has pointed out that the organization of a species is that of a network, or reticulum, and that the human social organism includes domesticated animals, cultivated plants, and products of technology. In going from gene to society, his successive levels of involvement include the theory of the gene itself; physiological genetics at the cellular level; developmental genetics at the level of the individual; population genetics at the species level; and genetics of behavior at the societal level. At this societal level of organization, cultural anthropology and history deal with human behavior descriptively; while sociology and certain aspects of philosophy deal with it dynamically, and behavior genetics, theoretically. On his analysis, these disciplines are embedded in a matrix whose axes and dimensions are biological, and from which aspects of individual and group behavior are emergent.

Analysis by Comparison

All people belong in museums, Philadelphia lawyers and Eskimo shamans alike, for they are equally exotic to each other. It is a truism derivable both from experience and as a consequence of the practically infinite field for genetic variability attributable to Mendelian recombination under biparental reproduction that no two persons derived from separate ova are genetically alike, nor is it probable that the genetic duplicate of such a person has occurred or will occur throughout the history of

life on earth. Still, Eskimos, as we know them, are not infinitely variable but are distinguishable from other populations. There exists a cluster of traits by which they can be recognized. Those that are not manifest and subject to convergent selection are often used as "tracers." Those that serve as the hallmarks of recognition may be termed "markers" and are of prime importance in assortative mating. As long as these markers remain within normal limits of variability, a great deal of genetic variation for other characters may be carried by the population. In view of the fact that there is a multiplicity of genetic ways of achieving similar phenotypic expression, selective mechanisms can and have acted to buffer or assimilate this variability to the prevailing phenotypic norms. In domestic animals, the practical breeder has taken advantage of this latent variability to create new color varieties, body types, and behavioral constellations through selective inbreeding.

Given the nonpanmictic structure of the human population, in which groups are maintained in partial, and in some cases total, genetic isolation from each other over long periods of time, it is extremely improbable that such subgroups within our species should be genetically alike as populations. Indeed, our evolutionary strength as a species lies precisely in this fact. Such a reticulum of subpopulations within which there is free genetic exchange and between which such genetic exchange is restricted to varying degrees depending upon distance, cultural diffusion barriers, and biological dissimilarities expressed primarily via combinations of marker genes, provides a set of excellent conditions whereby different genetic constellations can be "tried out" in a variety of environmental circumstances and conforms to the conditions that, according to Wright, may be expected to provide the most favorable opportunities for evolutionary advance.

The environments that served as selective agencies by means of which directive effects have been exerted have been consistently dissimilar over considerable periods of time not only with respect to such variables as temperature, altitude, and sunlight, but also with respect to the selective effects of diverse cultures, some of which have placed a premium on attributes having to do with

[7] "Stickleback Zigzags to Monomorphic Marking," *Contemporary Psychology*, 10 (1965): 246–248.

literary, musical, and artistic ability over some 160 or more generations in some genetic stocks, while detecting and selecting for quite different constellations of traits in others. The results of selection experiments with other mammals would suggest, not that populations under such differential pressures would generally develop unique constellations of genotypes (although they might in certain circumstances), but rather that genetic combinations that are adaptive in terms of the demands and opportunities of particular cultures are detected within such cultures and maintained as well as augmented by an assortative mating system that places a premium on these abilities. The frequencies of these genetic combinations are thereby increased.

The differential selective effects of the physicocultural environmental complex are themselves dependent on the biological (i.e., biobehavioral) potential of the population, not only in the ordinary sense of constituting a differential sieve for existing phenotypes, which impose limits upon the selective mechanisms, but also in a very special sense of crossing a biocultural threshold. In order to accomplish the latter, it is necessary for a population to be able to generate enough individuals possessing special and unusual abilities at a particular time and place to make a discovery that has the potential for changing the conditions of life for the group and to translate this potential into actuality. Once such a threshold is crossed, new selective forces are set into motion that extract and fix genetic combinations that would otherwise not be favored, and thereby produce genetic differences that were, in turn, generated by genetic differences that permitted such a threshold to be crossed in the first place.

The detection of such differences, especially when behavioral capacities are involved, can be accomplished only through comparative studies that do not rest on the assumption that the portion of the species reticulum from which the scientists are drawn and with which they are familiar is an adequate sample of the variation existing in the total species reticulum. Otherwise, we are in danger of using the criteria developed in a given culture as measures of abilities for all people in all cultures. Our so-called "intelligence tests" measure attributes that are predictors of success in a certain kind of schoolroom and in other situations requiring verbal and symbolic abilities, relational

manipulations, and various other factors that can be identified and listed. When we make such a test "culture free," we free it (to the extent that we are successful) from dependence on particular kinds of experiences but attempt to specify it to the same ends. If our test may be analogized to a prism, which analyzes light in the visible spectrum, then we can make our prism work for light from various sources and of differing intensities. It does not, however, analyze the nonvisible spectrum. This requires a wholly different instrument in addition to the appreciation that the nonvisible spectrum exists. Comparative studies must attempt to sample the total range of human capacities and should include both similar and dissimilar genotypes in as widely varying environments as possible. Otherwise, we are looking through our instruments at a mirror.

The Meaning of Correlation

Studies of attributes of different peoples provide an important test of the degree to which correlated characteristics are causally related. From the genetic point of view, six major possibilities are apparent:

The first is that where the correlated characteristics are attributable to a common agency. Thus, on the hypothesis put forward by Stockard that the genotype controls the endocrine balance and that this, in turn, is responsible for both body form and behavior, a consistent relationship between somatotype and behavior is to be expected. The second possibility is that the same relationship would hold if the associated effects were determined by the same genes but dependent on different mechanisms. Thirdly, a less invariant relationship would be expected if separate but linked genes were involved, depending upon the degree of linkage. Coadapted mechanisms resting on a more complex genetic base constitute a fourth possibility, as in the case of the AB and Rh blood groups. As a fifth possibility, the pairing of genes through independent selection for their separate effects may also occur; or, as a sixth alternative, such pairing may occur by chance through the vicissitudes of sampling. Data on the invariant occurrence of particular associations of traits in widely different populations as against the possibility of their occurrence in different associations in diverse populations (as well as within a single, variable population) are needed to help eliminate the range over which speculation may occur and also to identify, by means of the differences emerging from such comparative studies, what the traits are that may be considered to be natural units of variation for human beings and how they are distributed in the context of the reticular organization of the human species.

Containers and Contents

The tremendous field for variation afforded by Mendelian recombination in a sexually reproducing species provides an apparatus whereby some aspects of the phenotype may be held relatively constant (as in the case of marker genes on which assortative mating patterns are often based), while others vary widely. Should selection favor a complex of independently heritable characteristics, these may come to be associated in a given population although they have no other dependent connections. In another population some elements of this complex may appear in association with quite different characteristics. As mentioned above, comparisons of populations based on such similarities and differences may be expected to provide clues regarding the natural evolutionary units involved.

Two complications must be considered in relation to the interpretation of such clues: The first is that those morphological, physiological, and behavioral properties that attract our attention constitute only an aspect of the phenotypic expression of the genes on which they depend. To discover the total phenotype resulting from the possession of these genes requires further research. The second is that there is no invariant relationship between genotype and phenotype. Whether one is considering amino acid sequences or behavior, there is more than one genetic route to the same end result. In addition, environmental manipulations may produce similar results (phenocopies) by nongenetic means; and, conversely, genetic deficiencies may be compensated for by environmental intervention (i.e., the administration of insulin to genetic diabetics). The phenotypic topography of a population is, therefore, dynamically complex. Its traits and their associations must be considered from the point of view of a context matrix in which correlations may be due to any of the six relationships to the genetic substratum outlined in the previous section. When one adds the considerations just described to the context matrix (namely, that similar phenotypes may arise convergently from different genetic bases, that any given genotype may be variably expressed depending upon environmental conditions, and that phenocopies can mimic particular genotypes), it is evident that comparative studies must include genealogies, mechanisms, and developmental histories in order to arrive at any sensible interpretation of observed phenomena.

In the genetic sense, both populations and individuals may be considered to be container units with reference to the great variety of genetic materials that can be added or deleted with no perceptible change in the continuity of the population over a span of generations, or, put the other way around, in the external appearances of the range of individual organisms comprising the population. Among the important differences between these kinds of units is the fact that natural selection operates only through populations, not through individuals or types; and populations are what really evolve. Variation for physiological and behavioral characteristics can occur within individuals of a given physical constitution or somatotype, . . . and spurious correlations may be secured by comparing constitution with various physiological and behavioral traits. . . .

Just as traits cannot be adequately treated without a knowledge of the context matrix in which they occur, neither can a sample of individuals be treated without a knowledge of the population context in which they occur. An important part of a population is the matrix of pathways connecting the individuals. Populations consist of related individuals, not separate units such as beans in a bag. The sampling of a population should reflect the nature of this population matrix which may enhance redundancy as a consequence of inbreeding, or of assortative mating, large family size, or the many other conditions that structure the genetic distance between individuals. It is efficient and necessary to define isolates and small populations with reference to the fact that they are intrabreeding communities. Thus, a population is a cluster of genetic pathways whose intersections recombine molecular units of inheritance, some of which develop into living organisms that reproduce. Too much attention has traditionally been given to the end products of the reproductive system of a population, the developed traits of adult males and females most commonly used for morphological, physiological, and serological sampling.

Genetic populations are clusters of individuals who more frequently mate with other individuals within the group than outside. Geographical and cultural boundary-maintaining devices limit the genetic exchange between groups which, if random, would of course dissolve the groups. No two populations are identical, and they may vary in any trait used to characterize the populations. The common definition of a population as an intrabreeding community differing in the frequency of one or more genes from other such communities is uninformative. The stipulation of differing from others is extraneous and raises a multitude of questions such as, in how many genes they should differ and from whom they should differ. The study of migrant and hybrid groups is especially valuable for obtaining information on processes, even though physical differentiation of isolates separated by only one generation is minor compared with groups that have been separated for 8 or 80 generations. There is little point in collecting data on characteristics of people, be they morphological, physiological, serological, or behavioral, unless the genetic relationships between the individuals are known and means for testing hypotheses can be developed. The relationship of sample to population provides an equally valid reason for genealogical study. In small isolates this constitutes no theoretical problem, though it is tedious and time consuming. In metropolitan studies, where assortative mating is a more important factor and various kinds of subgroups are included, theoretical problems require more attention, and various models such as those based upon isolation by distance may be more relevant.

There are many ways of making comparisons between populations, all of which are vitiated if the original population unit is not adequately characterized. The construction of a species standard to which each population can be compared is efficient and objective. The construction of clines or character gradients is still another useful method of comparison, and formal classification involving the estimation of biological distance (numerical taxonomy) between three or more groups is a third major category for describing between-group variation. All of these methods of relational systematics are useful for estimating degrees of similarity and difference, for assessing the distribution of variation, and for testing hypotheses. It should be noted that the explanation of similarity between groups (reflected in comparisons) is not automatically provided by the distributional maps or tables of relative degrees of similarity. The correspondence between similarity and affinity is a problem in relational systematics of populations for which there is a rich body of theory. Confusion between the procedures of defining or delimiting a population, identifying individuals who belong to a population, characterizing a population, and then making comparisons between populations (of which classification is only one method) are common. The enumeration of the number of populations is often more of an inventory than a classification. Classification consists of arranging the populations in a meaningful system. The problem of how many there are to be arranged is a separate and prior problem. All human populations intergrade to some extent, though there are many traits that are confined to a single continent and completely missing in another. Since we are dealing with variation within a single, nonpanmictic species, rather than with different species or with ideal types, intergradation is the rule. The lack of watertight compartments offers no theoretical block to study, though this is sometimes conceived to be so because of the confusion that exists between identifying individuals, on the one hand, and comparing populations, on the other. Paleontologists who work with genera between which there is a decided morphological gap, where identifying individuals and arranging them into series is no problem, have no fewer difficulties in assessing the relational systematics of the taxons with which they work. In the case of human populations, improvement in understanding degrees of relationship between populations is not automatically achieved by the substitution of gene frequency data for morphological data. The classificatory containers can remain the same with change only in the kind of data to be poured into them. Tabulation of gene frequencies is one way of characterizing a limited portion of the variability of a population. The frequency of a gene is not a necessary measure of the significance of that gene in that population. A gene may have the same frequency in two different populations and yet differ in its functional significance in each population because of the frequency of other genes or because of differences in environmental conditions. The trait complex matrix and the population matrix must both be known in order to interpret the significance of the frequency of a gene.

Man: The Self-Domesticating Species

Principles and directions may often reveal themselves clearly in a simplified context where they are difficult to detect in a more complex one. Darwin found it useful to outline the principles of his theory of evolution on the basis of what could be seen and demonstrated with domesticated forms where man himself was the selecting agency. The analogy to domestic animals, and especially to breed formation, is often extended to man but is as often disputed. Dobzhansky, for example, considers the analogy misleading, because selection in dogs, horses, and cattle has included behavioral attributes such as "temperament," "disposition," "intelligence," and "trainability," whereas selection for behavioral attributes in human beings has, on his view, not been parallel. In advancing this point of view, proponents of this concept are assuming the heritability of these aspects of an organism and sufficient genetic variability with respect to these qualities to make them amenable to relatively rapid selection by man but are denying that man, whose behavioral attributes are the most critically adaptive of any mammalian species and form the basis for his ability to live in groups and generate culture, can have developed these behavioral adaptations by similar means.

The position of biobehavioral monism formulated here precludes such a point of view. Most students of evolution would agree with G. G. Simpson that "Behavior is subject to particularly strong selection, and it is probably farthest removed from the genes and also most elaborately polygenic as a rule. Some single-gene determinants of behavior are known, but they are exceptional."[8]

Washburn and Shirek have identified the bridge between behavior and its selection, including man's selection of his own behavior, by pointing out that "There is feedback between behavior and its biological base, so that behavior is both a cause of changing gene frequencies and a consequence of changing biology."[9] Culture, which is a consequence of man's genetic endowment, is also a selective agency. It helps to determine the extent to which assortative mating will occur on the basis of

obvious physical genetic markers. It also detects genetic combinations capable of specialized behavioral performances involved in the evolution of civilization, such as artistic, musical, and mathematical ability, as well as the types of intelligence that are necessary for the production of literature, technology, and art. As these detecting mechanisms improve through the universalization of education, more efficient use can be made of the genetic resources of the population in these regards. By providing attractive niches for the development and execution of these talents, cultures not only detect and develop them, but siphon them off and provide opportunities and impetus for assortative matings, consanguineous and otherwise, based on these criteria, thereby composing and perpetuating useful coadapted gene complexes. The cultures from which ours has evolved have been doing this for upwards of 150 generations—certainly time enough to have exerted selective genetic effects.

These genetic effects have been a source of worry to many students of human population who are concerned that the more intellectually capable segments of a society are outbred by the less capable segments. This is a needless worry on two grounds. The first is minor and is simply that favorable genotypes for the values existing in our culture are constantly being generated from the less advantaged segments of the population. The second is that the numerical proportion of creative minds with specialized capabilities need not be large in order to maintain and advance civilization. They form the keystone of a biobehavioral arch; and as long as there is sufficient sustained assortative mating on the basis of these qualities to keep such a genetic track going, the possibility for shifting its numerical representation as cultural demands change is a potential that the population possesses.

Man as a self-domesticating species may take advantage of a large variety of relatively simple devices in order to exert increasing control over his own genetic potential, on a voluntary basis. These include birth control, abortion, adoption (including prenatal adoption), sperm donor programs

[8]"Organisms and Molecules in Evolution," *Science*, 146 (1964): 1535–1548.

[9]"Human Evolution," in *Behavior-Genetic Analysis*, Jerry Hirsch, ed. (New York: McGraw-Hill Book Company, 1967), pp. 10–21.

(the genetic data from which should be kept on a worldwide basis), and genetic counseling in relation to particular pedigrees, to inbreeding, and to minimizing radiation hazard. These devices can, in turn, provide data on the basis of which more intelligent assessment of alternatives will become increasingly possible and useful, especially as social strictures change. What is important here is that as cultures become more specialized and complex, they provide a multiple-track system demanding different though overlapping biological capacities. While detecting and developing these from an existing genetic base, cultures also encourage assortative matings within these tracks, thereby leading to the formation and retention of particular kinds of genetic combinations on preferential bases. Thus, genetic variability has a demonstrable effect on culture, which, in turn, organizes the genetic pool on the basis of assortative mating systems relevant to the culture.

The Genotypes of Race and Culture

The genetic parsing of experimental animal populations has revealed that they differ markedly with respect to behavioral capacities. Emotionality and aggressiveness in mice, for example, are profoundly affected by infantile manipulation. Both the direction and magnitude of the effects vary according to strain or genotype. Whether there is a critical period for the maximal effectiveness of the applied stimulation and when it occurs, are also strain-specific. A mouse population from which these diverse response patterns to identical stimulation may be extracted is a reticulum whose measures of central tendency have a misleading biological meaning. Selection can quickly extract diverse styles, magnitudes, and directions of responses from such a population, all of which can be assimilated to a variety of physical marker genes. Thus one could, by genetic manipulation, create a population of black mice having a uniform set of responses to the manipulations described, although there is no causal relationship between the coat color and the behavior. One could as easily have associated the color with another behavioral profile. Similarly, the temperament, disposition, and various other behavioral qualities of dogs can be assimilated to one or another physical type. One

of us has been associated with a project that produces dogs to lead the blind, where, possibly because of the image of Rin-Tin-Tin, the demand has been primarily for the German shepherd breed. Many of the foundation animals from which the present stocks on this particular project are derived, although intelligent and highly trainable, were also of a protective and mistrustful disposition and did not transfer easily from one person to another. These qualities, while admirable in a guard dog, are not suitable to one who must be a guide. Neither are they sufficiently reliably modified by conditions of rearing and training. Over approximately 10 generations of selective line-breeding, it has been possible to change the behavioral predisposition within this population while maintaining the characteristic appearance without resorting to cross-breeding, an indication that a good deal of genetic variability had been assimilated to the prevailing phenotype and could be extracted from it to conform to a different set of behavioral norms while retaining the identifying physical marker genes.

Such clusters of buffered genotypes that can assimilate a high degree of potential genetic variability to a prevailing phenotypic profile are typical of natural populations as well, and, as suggested by data on white and Negro populations, between which there is considerable genetic exchange in this country, are also characteristic of man. He is not panmictic either within or between population subgroups variously designated as racial or ethnic. The use of culture as a scanning mechanism that identifies and repackages the bits and pieces of heredity are, in a longer time, analogous to what may be accomplished with mice and dogs in a much shorter time span of more rigorous selection. The recombined genetic constituents are not entirely independent and may be expected to exhibit secondary interaction effects with other factors in the trait context matrix. Thus, the species reticulum, consisting of subpopulations that differ in marker genes and in the probabilities with which particular genetic combinations expressing themselves as identifiable phenotypes are encountered, is partially and flexibly partitioned. No part of it adequately represents the whole, and every substantial part undoubtedly has sufficient genetic resources to move to a new set of phenotypic norms under appropriate selection pressures. These new norms most probably include any phenotype now represented in the species reticulum with the probable exception of those dependent upon marker genes, which may be relatively fixed where the history of selection with respect to the phenotypes they control has narrowed the range of variability.

If one views the entire species reticulum at a given instant in time, it is not to be expected that the nature-nurture or genetic-cultural feedback mechanisms have resulted in convergent clusters of phenotypes at all nodal points. Styles and rates of response to environmental agencies as well as other capacities may differ as well as overlap. Just as the critical period at which early trauma has the greatest effect in a population of mice is genotype-dependent, as are the directions and magnitudes of the effects in question, so the rates, sensitivities, and outcomes of the far more sensitive interactions of human genotypes with respect to emotion, learning, and other behavioral attributes of importance to a social species are probably also biologically variable. Nor must it be taken for granted that the capacities measured by tests extrapolated from the capacities and cultures of one part of the species reticulum are adequate measures for all—either in scaling, or in the definition of what is to be measured. Readiness for assimilating particular kinds of experience may easily vary, as may the capacity for sequential ordering—i.e., objects before symbols, for example. What is an optimal early educational procedure in terms of the prevailing phenotypes of European caucasoids, is not necessarily optimal for Aleuts in order to achieve exactly the same goals. Analogy to animal behavior-genetics would lead us to expect such differences. Parallel hypotheses need to be entertained and investigated in relation to our own species where, precisely because we have confined ourselves to particular measures on particular scales and attempted to homogenize our educational procedures, hierarchical value judgments have been made where none necessarily exist. Instead of investigating a problem in a manner that would best enable us to take advantage of the differences offered by varying portions of our species reticulum, we have, out of misguided condescension involving apology for the fact that some of us measure up better than others in proportion as the scale we use was constructed expressly for us, shut ourselves off from the possibility of both understanding and making better use of the rich and varied resources of our species.

Spade Versus Geotome: Ethical Considerations

The ethical obligations of a research team to the population being studied should be prominently reiterated in the training of personnel as well as in the actual prosecution of studies. These include respect for the dignity and privacy of subjects; compensation for their time and participation; medical, dental, and related services; consultation and exchange of information with learned men; an appreciation of the impact a research team may have on a community; an assessment of the values that remain after the research team departs; and, of course, cooperation with the officials and agencies of the national authority to which the people are responsible. The immediate practical benefits of being studied by teams of dentists, serologists, child-growth specialists, geneticists, nutritionists, anthropologists, et al., is often enhanced by the opportunity to train a member of the community who may continue some data collection and who may use this skill as a source of future compensation or entry to an academic institution. Genetic information as well as general health information is sometimes sought by members of the community as well as local government officials, and the same standards of accuracy and discretion should be applied to all.

A second area in which an ethical obligation is apparent is in the training of the students and other personnel for participation in an international program. Education in human biology of the species, where the genetic unity of the species and understanding of all the variation contained within it is the frame of reference, is an honest and scientifically unqualified undertaking. One of the effective by-products is dissipation of fallacious concepts emerging from the typological models still in use, treatment of human variation in a nonhierarchical reticulum, or the implication that various populations must undergo mixture in order to advance. It is far more effective and much faster to insert scientific and testable ideas into peoples' heads than to delete erroneous ideas already lodged there. The positive facts of evolutionary species biology and the methods for securing and testing them are of value to all members of the species, and they provide the only known basis for intelligently counteracting the arguments of racists and environmentalists.

A third area is that of the reactions to a false dilemma posed by belief in hierarchy and by our egalitarian ethic. The common tendency to read hierarchy into phenomena that are nonhierarchical, and our existing corpus of literature and beliefs in which this "Great Chain of Being" is applied to humans within the species, coupled with the simultaneous espousal of a belief in the worth of all individuals, should not induce us to eschew biobehavioral studies dealing with differences in maturation rates, various kinds of learning, and other special aptitudes. Variation in aptitudes does not indicate position on an ascending scale, any more than underpigmentation indicates position on a hierarchical phylogenetic scale. It does indicate that different populations have emphasized different as well as similar foci in the biobehavioral reticulum as these have been relevant to their adaptive needs and evolutionary history— a reticulum common to the entire species, whose basic elements are found in all groups. An isomorphic analogy is the difference between males and females, ranging from the molecular to the derivative behavioral characteristics. The differences may be considered minor, but there is cause for rejoicing that they exist at all. It would obviously be inapplicable to configure a study of males and females in terms of an ascending scale of nature.

No single scale or frequency is adequate to characterize a population, and tests designed for one population may be inapplicable to all others. All groups need the information resident in other groups, because no single population or national unit contains an adequate sample of the variability of the entire species in forms that we can presently study. The answers to many fundamental biological questions cannot be secured by more intensive study of one or even several populations.

Jerry Hirsch

Behavior-Genetic Analysis and Its Biosocial Consequences

The subject of behavioral differences among races is at present one of the most controversial topics in the study of human variation. The article which follows is the first of two discussions of aspects of such differences. And with this topic considerations of racism develop naturally, for it is behavioral differences with which racists most frequently toy.

An important contribution of the article is the historical review of the old nature-nurture controversy in in terms of what Jerry Hirsch contrasts as extreme views, behaviorism vs. racism. Statements quite similar to those Hirsch quotes and discusses can be heard and read today in the continuing debate over racial differences in IQ. The major part of his paper is devoted to the controversy over the alleged differences in intellectual capacity between blacks and whites in the United States, and particularly to the argument of one instigator of the debate, Jensen.

The major criticism of Jensen's work is his use of the concept of heritability. There are very significant limits to estimates of heritability, and Hirsch states precisely what these limits are. It is important to note that the arguments of Jensen and others stand or fall on these limitations of the concept of heritability. Hirsch concludes that the use of estimates of heritability in the study of human variability is "both deceptive and trivial."

From "Behavior-Genetic Analysis and Its Biosocial Consequences" by Jerry Hirsch from *Intelligence: Genetic and Environmental Influences*, edited by Robert Cancro (1971, pp. 88–104). First published in *Seminars in Psychiatry*, Vol. 2, No. 1 (February 1970). Reprinted by permission of Grune & Stratton, Inc. and the author.

Invited address presented to the XIXth International Congress of Psychology, London, England, July 30, 1969, and dedicated to Prof. Th. Dobzhansky on his 70th birthday.

This work was prepared with the support of Mental Health Training Grant 1 T01 10715–04 BLS for Research Training in the Biological Sciences.

Behaviorism

Over the past two decades the case against behaviorist extremism has been spelled out in incontrovertible detail. The behaviorists committed many sins: they accepted the mind at birth as Locke's *tabula rasa*, they advocated an empty-organism psychology, they asserted the uniformity postulate of no prenatal individual differences; in short they epitomized typological thinking. Many times we have heard quoted the famous boast by the first high priest of behaviorism, John B. Watson:

Give me a dozen healthy infants, well-formed, and my own specified world to bring them up in, and I'll guarantee to take any one at random and train him to become any type of specialist I might select—doctor, lawyer, artist, merchant-chief and yes, even beggar-man and thief, regardless of his talents, penchants, tendencies, abilities, vocations, race of his ancestors.

However, it is only when we read the next sentence, which is rarely, if ever, quoted, that we begin to understand how so many people might have embraced something intellectually so shallow as radical behaviorism. In that all important next sentence Watson explains: "I am going beyond my facts and I admit it, but so have the advocates of the contrary and they have been doing it for many thousands of years."

Racism

Who were the advocates of the contrary and what had they been saying? It is difficult to establish the origins of racist thinking, but certainly one of its most influential advocates was Joseph Arthur de Gobineau, who published a four-volume *Essay on the Inequality of the Human Races* in the mid-1850s. De Gobineau preached the superiority of the white race, and among whites it was the Aryans who carried civilization to its highest point. In fact, they were responsible for civilization wherever it appeared. Unfortunately, de Gobineau's essay proved to be the major seminal work that inspired some of the most perverse developments in the intellectual and political history of our civilization. Later in his life, de Gobineau became an intimate of the celebrated German composer, Richard Wagner. The English-born Houston Stewart Chamberlain, who emigrated to the Continent, became a devoted admirer of both de Gobineau and Wagner. In 1908, after Wagner's death, he married Wagner's daughter, Eva, settled in and supported Germany against England during World War I, becoming a naturalized German citizen in 1916.

In the summer of 1923, an admirer who had read Chamberlain's writings, Adolf Hitler, visited Wahnfried, the Wagner family home in Bayreuth where Chamberlain lived. After their meeting, Chamberlain wrote to Hitler: "My faith in the Germans had never wavered for a moment, but my hope . . . had sunk to a low ebb. At one stroke you have transformed the state of my soul!" We all know the sequel to that unfortunate tale. I find that our modern scientific colleagues, whether they be biological or social scientists, for the most part, do not know the sad parallel that exists for the essentially political tale I have so far recounted. The same theme can be traced down the main stream of biosocial science.

Today not many people know the complete title of Darwin's most famous book: *On the Origin of Species by Means of Natural Selection or the Preservation of Favoured Races in the Struggle for Life.* I find no evidence that Darwin had the attitudes we now call racist. Unfortunately many of his admirers, his contemporaries, and his successors were not as circumspect as he. In Paris in 1838, J. E. D. Esquirol first described a form of mental deficiency later to become well known by two inappropriate names unrelated to his work. Unhappily one of these names, through textbook adoption and clinical jargon, puts into wide circulation a term loaded with race prejudice. Somewhat later (1846 and 1866), E. Seguin described the same condition under the name "furfuraceous cretinism" and his account has only recently been recognized as "the most ingenious description of physical characteristics."

Unhappily that most promising scientific beginning was ignored. Instead the following unfortunate events occurred: In 1866, John Langdon Haydon Down published the paper entitled "Observations on an Ethnic Classification of Idiots."

. . . making a classification of the feeble-minded, by arranging them around various ethnic standards— in other words, framing a natural system to supplement the information to be derived by an inquiry into the history of the case.

I have been able to find among the large number

of idiots and imbeciles which comes under my observation, both at Earlswood and the out-patient department of the Hospital, that a considerable portion can be fairly referred to one of the great divisions of the human family other than the class from which they have sprung. Of course, there are numerous representatives of the great Caucasian family. Several well-marked examples of the Ethiopian variety have come under my notice, presenting the characteristic malar bones, the prominent eyes, the puffy lips, and retreating chin. The woolly hair has also been present, although not always black, nor has the skin acquired pigmentary deposit. They have been specimens of white negroes, although of European descent.

Some arrange themselves around the Malay variety, and present in their soft, black, curly hair, their prominent upper jaws and capacious mouths, types of the family which people the South Sea Islands.

Nor have there been wanting the analogues of the people who with shortened foreheads, prominent cheeks, deep-set eyes, and slightly apish nose, originally inhabited the American Continent.

The great Mongolian family has numerous representatives, and it is to this division, I wish, in this paper, to call special attention. A very large number of congenital idiots are typical Mongols. So marked is this, that when placed side by side, it is difficult to believe that the specimens compared are not children of the same parents. The number of idiots who arrange themselves around the Mongolian type is so great, and they present such a close resemblance to one another in mental power, that I shall describe an idiot member of this racial division, selected from the large number that have fallen under my observation.

The hair is not black, as in the real Mongol, but of a brownish colour, straight and scanty. The face is flat and broad, and destitute of prominence. The cheeks are roundish, and extended laterally. The eyes are obliquely placed, and the internal canthi more than normally distant from one another. The palpebral fissure is very narrow. The forehead is wrinkled transversely from the constant assistance which the levatores palpebrarum derive from the occipito-frontalis muscle in the opening of the eyes. The lips are large and thick with transverse fissures. The tongue is long, thick, and is much roughened. The nose is small. The skin has a slightly dirty yellowish tinge and is deficient in elasticity, giving the appearance of being too large for the body.

The boy's aspect is such that it is difficult to realize that he is the child of Europeans, but so frequently are these characters presented, that there can be no doubt that these ethnic features are the result of degeneration.[1]

And he means degeneration from a higher to a lower race. The foregoing represents a distasteful but excellent example of the racial hierarchy theory and its misleadingly dangerous implications. That was how the widely-used terms Mongolism and Mongolian idiocy entered our "technical" vocabulary. For the next century, this pattern of thought is going to persist and occupy an important place in the minds of many leading scientists.

Alleged Jewish Genetic Inferiority

In 1884, Francis Galton, Darwin's half cousin, founder of the Eugenics movement and respected contributor to many fields of science, wrote to the distinguished Swiss botanist, Alphonse de Candolle: "It strikes me that the Jews are specialized for a parasitical existence upon other nations, and that there is need of evidence that they are capable of fulfilling the varied duties of a civilized nation by themselves." Karl Pearson, Galton's disciple and biographer, echoed this opinion 40 years later during his attempt to prove the undesirability of Jewish immigration into Britain: ". . . for such men as religion, social habits, or language keep as a caste apart, there should be no place. They will not be absorbed by, and at the same time strengthen the existing population; they will develop into a parasitic race."

Beginning in 1908 and continuing at least until 1928, Karl Pearson collected and analyzed data in order to assess "the quality of the racial stock immigrating into Great Britain." He was particularly disturbed by the large numbers of East European Jews, who near the turn of the century began coming from Poland and Russia to escape the pogroms. Pearson's philosophy was quite explicitly spelled out:

Let us admit . . . that the mind of man is for the most part a congenital product, and the factors which determine it are racial and familial; we are not deal-

---

[1] Reprinted in V. A. McKusick, ed., "Medical Genetics," *Journal of Chronic Diseases*, 15 (1962): 432.

ing with a mutable characteristic capable of being moulded by the doctor, the teacher, the parent or the home environment.

The ancestors of the men who pride themselves on being English today were all at one time immigrants; it is not for us to cast the first stone against newcomers, solely because they are newcomers. But the test for immigrants in the old days was a severe one; it was power, physical and mental, to retain their hold on the land they seized. So came Celts, Saxons, Norsemen, Danes and Normans in succession and built up the nation of which we are proud. Nor do we criticize the alien Jewish immigration simply because it is Jewish; we took the alien Jews to study, because they were the chief immigrants of that day and material was readily available.[2]

His observations led him to conclude: "Taken *on the average*, and regarding both sexes, this alien Jewish population is somewhat inferior physically and mentally to the native population." Pearson proclaimed this general Jewish inferiority despite his own failure to find any differences between the Jewish and non-Jewish boys when comparisons (reported in the same article) were made for the sexes separately.

Alleged Black Genetic Inferiority

Quite recently there has appeared a series of papers disputing whether or not black Americans are, in fact, genetically inferior to white Americans in intellectual capacity. The claims and counterclaims have been given enormous publicity in the popular press in America. Some of those papers contain most of the fallacies that can conceivably be associated with this widely misunderstood problem.

The steps toward the intellectual cul-de-sac into which this dispute leads and the fallacious assumptions on which such "progress" is based are the following: (1) A trait called intelligence, or anything else, is defined and a testing instrument for the measurement of trait expression is used; (2) the heritability of that trait is estimated; (3) races (populations) are compared with respect to their performance on the test of trait expression; (4) when the races (populations) differ on the test whose heritability has now been measured, the one with the lower score is genetically inferior, Q.E.D.

The foregoing argument can be applied to any single trait or to as many traits as one might choose to consider. Therefore, analysis of this general problem does *not* depend upon the particular definition and test used for this or that trait. For my analysis I shall pretend that an acceptable test exists for some trait, be it height, weight, intelligence, or anything else. (Without an acceptable test, discussion of the "trait" remains unscientific.)

Even to consider comparisons between races, the following concepts must be recognized: (1) the genome as a mosaic, (2) development as the expression of one out of many alternatives in the genotype's norm of reaction, (3) a population as a gene pool, (4) heritability is not instinct, (5) traits as distributions of scores, and (6) distributions as moments.

Since inheritance is particulate and not integral, the genome, genotype, or hereditary endowment of each individual is a unique mosaic—an assemblage of factors many of which are independent. Because of the lottery-like nature of both gamete formation and fertilization, other than monozygotes no two individuals share the same genotypic mosaic.

Norm of Reaction

The ontogeny of an individual's phenotype (observable outcome of development) has a norm or range of reaction not predictable in advance. In most cases the norm of reaction remains largely unknown; but the concept is nevertheless of fundamental importance, because it saves us from being taken in by glib and misleading textbook clichés such as "heredity sets the limits but environment determines the extent of development within those limits." Even in the most favorable materials only an approximate estimate can be obtained for the norm of reaction, when, as in plants and some animals, an individual genotype can be replicated many times and its development studied over a range of environmental conditions. The more varied the conditions, the more diverse might be the phenotypes developed from any one genotype. Of course, different genotypes should not be expected to have the same norm of reaction; unfortunately

[2] K. Pearson and M. Moul, "The Problem of Alien Immigration into Great Britain, Illustrated by an Examination of Russian and Polish Jewish Children," *Annals of Eugenics*, 1 (1925): 124, 127.

psychology's attention was diverted from appreciating this basic fact of biology by a half century of misguided environmentalism. Just as we see that, except for monozygotes, no two human faces are alike, so we must expect norms of reaction to show genotypic uniqueness. That is one reason why the heroic but ill-fated attempts of experimental learning psychology to write the "laws of environmental influence" were grasping at shadows. Therefore, those limits set by heredity in the textbook cliché can never be specified. They are plastic within each individual but differ between individuals. Extreme environmentalists were wrong to hope that one law or set of laws described universal features of modifiability. Extreme hereditarians were wrong to ignore the norm of reaction.

Individuals occur in populations and then only as temporary attachments, so to speak, each to particular combinations of genes. The population, on the other hand, can endure indefinitely as a pool of genes, maybe forever recombining to generate new individuals.

Instincts, Genes, and Heritability

What is heritability? How is heritability estimated for intelligence or any other trait? Is heritability related to instinct? In 1872, Douglas Spalding demonstrated that the ontogeny of a bird's ability to fly is simply maturation and not the result of practice, imitation, or any demonstrable kind of learning. He confined immature birds and deprived them of the opportunity either to practice flapping their wings or to observe and imitate the flight of older birds; in spite of this, they developed the ability to fly. For some ethologists this deprivation experiment became the paradigm for proving the innateness or instinctive nature of a behavior by demonstrating that it appears despite the absence of any opportunity for it to be learned. Remember two things about this approach: (1) the observation involves experimental manipulation of the conditions of experience during development, and (2) such observation can be made on the development of one individual. For some people the results of a deprivation experiment now constitute the operational demonstration of the existence (or nonexistence) of an instinct (in a particular species).

Are instincts heritable? That is, are they determined by genes? But what is a gene? A gene is an inference from a breeding experiment. It is recog-

nized by the measurement of individual differences—the recognition of the segregation of distinguishable forms of the expression of some trait among the progeny of appropriate matings. For example, when an individual of blood type AA mates with one of type BB, their offspring are uniformly AB. If two of the AB offspring mate, it is found that the A and B gene forms have segregated during reproduction and recombined in their progeny to produce all combinations of A and B: AA, AB, and BB. Note that the only operation involved in such a study is *breeding* of one or more generations and then at an appropriate time of life, observation of the separate individuals born in each generation—controlled breeding with experimental material or pedigree analysis of the appropriate families with human subjects. In principle, only one (usually brief) observation is required. Thus we see that genetics is a science of *differences*, and the breeding experiment is its fundamental operation. The operational definition of the gene, therefore, involves observation in a breeding experiment of the segregation among several individuals of distinguishable differences in the expression of some trait from which the gene can be inferred. Genetics does not work with a single subject, whose development is studied. (The foregoing, the following, and all discussions of genetic analysis presuppose sufficiently adequate control of environmental conditions so that all observed individual differences have developed under the same, homogeneous environmental conditions, conditions never achieved in any human studies.)

How does heritability enter the picture? At the present stage of knowledge, many features (traits) of animals and plants have not yet been related to genes that can be recognized individually. But the role of large numbers of genes, often called polygenes and in most organisms still indistinguishable one from the other, has been demonstrated easily (and often) by selective breeding or by appropriate comparisons between different strains of animals or plants. Selection and strain crossing have provided the basis for many advances in agriculture and among the new generation of research workers are becoming standard tools for the experimental behaviorist. Heritability often summarizes the extent to which a particular population has responded to a regimen of being bred selectively on the basis of the expression of some trait. Heritability values vary between zero and plus one. If the distribution of trait expression among progeny remains the same no matter how their parents might be selected, then heritability has zero value. If parental selection does make a difference, heritability exceeds zero, its exact value reflecting the parent-offspring correlation. Or more generally, as A. R. Jensen says: "The basic data from which . . . heritability coefficients are estimated are correlations among individuals of different degrees of kinship."[3] Though, many of the heritabilities Jensen discusses have been obtained by comparing mono- and di-zygotic twins.

A heritability estimate, however, is a far more limited piece of information than most people realize. As was so well stated by Fuller and Thompson: "heritability is a property of populations and not of traits." In its strictest sense, a heritability measure provides for a given population an estimate of the proportion of the variance it shows in trait (phenotype) expression which is correlated with the segregation of the alleles of independently acting genes. There are other more broadly conceived heritability measures, which estimate this correlation and also include the combined effects of genes that are independent and of those that interact. Therefore, heritability estimates the proportion of the total phenotypic variance (individual differences) shown by a trait that can be attributed to genetic variation (narrowly or broadly interpreted) in some particular population at a single generation under one set of conditions.

The foregoing description contains three fundamentally important limitations which have rarely been accorded sufficient attention: (1) The importance of limiting any heritability statement to a specific population is evident when we realize that a gene, which shows variation in one population because it is represented there by two or more segregating alleles, might show no variation in some other population because it is uniformly represented there by only a single allele. Remember that initially such a gene could never have been detected by genetic methods in the second population. Once it has been detected in some population carrying two or more of its segregating alleles, the information thus obtained might permit us to recognize it in populations carrying only a single allele. Note how this is related to heritability: the trait will show a greater-than-zero heritability in the segregating population but zero heritability in the nonsegregating population. This does *not* mean that the trait is determined genetically in the first population and environmentally in the second!

(2) Next let us consider the ever-present environmental sources of variation. Usually from the Mendelian point of view, except for the genes on the segregating chromosomes, everything inside the cell and outside the organism is lumped together and can be called environmental variation: cytoplasmic constituents, the maternal effects now known to be so important, the early experience effects studied in so many psychological laboratories, and so on. None of these can be considered unimportant or trivial. They are ever present. Let us now perform what physicists call a Gedanken, or thought, experiment. Imagine Aldous Huxley's *Brave New World* or Skinner's *Walden II* organized in such a way that every individual is exposed to precisely the same environmental conditions. In other words, consider the extreme, but *un*realistic, case of complete environmental homogeneity. Under those circumstances the heritability value would approach unity, because only genetic variation would be present. Don't forget that even under the most simplifying assumptions, there are over 70 trillion potential human genotypes—no two of us share the same genotype no matter how many ancestors we happen to have in common. Since mitosis projects our unique genotype into the nucleus, or executive, of every cell in our bodies, the individuality that is so obvious in the human faces we see around us must also characterize the unseen components. Let the same experiment be imagined for any number of environments. In each environment heritability will approximate unity but each genotype *may* develop a different phenotype in every environment and the distribution (hierarchy) of genotypes (in terms of their phenotypes) must not be expected to remain invariant over environments.

(3) The third limitation refers to the fact that because gene frequencies can and do change from one generation to the next, so will heritability values or the magnitude of the genetic variance.

Now let us shift our focus to the entire genotype or at least to those of its components that might co-vary at least partially with the phenotypic expression of a particular trait. Early in this century

---

[3] "How Much Can We Boost IQ and Scholastic Achievement?" *Harvard Educational Review*, 39 (1969): 48.

Woltereck called to our attention the norm-of-reaction concept: the same genotype can give rise to a wide array of phenotypes depending upon the environment in which it develops. This is most conveniently studied in plants where genotypes are easily replicated. Later Goldschmidt was to show in *Drosophila* that, by careful selection of the environmental conditions at critical periods in development, various phenotypes ordinarily associated with specific gene mutations could be produced from genotypes that did not include the mutant form of those genes. Descriptively, Goldschmidt called these events *phenocopies*—environmentally produced imitations of gene mutants or phenotypic expressions only manifested by the "inappropriate" genotype if unusual environmental influences impinge during critical periods in development, but regularly manifested by the "appropriate" genotype under the usual environmental conditions.

In 1946, the brilliant British geneticist J. B. S. Haldane analyzed the interaction concept and gave quantitative meaning to the foregoing. For the simplest case but one, that of two genotypes in three environments or, for its mathematical equivalent, that of three genotypes in two environments, he showed that there are 60 possible kinds of interaction. Ten genotypes in 10 environments generate 10^{144} possible kinds of interaction. In general m genotypes in n environments generate $\frac{(mn)!}{m!n!}$ kinds of interaction. Since the characterization of genotype-environment interaction can only be ad hoc and the number of possible interactions is effectively unlimited, it is no wonder that the long search for general laws has been so unfruitful.

For genetically different lines of rats showing the Tryon-type "bright-dull" difference in performance on a learning task, by so simple a change in environmental conditions as replacing massed-practice trials by distributed-practice trials, McGaugh, Jennings, and Thomson found that the so-called dulls moved right up to the scoring level of the so-called brights. In a recent study of the open-field behavior of mice, Hegmann and DeFries found that heritabilities measured repeatedly in the same individuals were unstable over two successive days. In surveying earlier work they commented: "Heritability estimates for repeated measurements of behavioral characters have been found to increase, decrease, and fluctuate randomly as a function of repeated testing."[4] Therefore, to the limitations on heritability due to population, situation, and breeding generation, we must now add developmental stage, or, many people might say, just plain unreliability! The late and brilliant Sir Ronald Fisher, whose authority Jensen cites, indicated how fully he had appreciated such limitations when he commented: "the so-called coefficient of heritability, which I regard as one of those unfortunate short-cuts which have emerged in biometry for lack of a more thorough analysis of the data."[5] The plain facts are that in the study of man a heritability estimate turns out to be a piece of "knowledge" that is both deceptive and trivial.

The Roots of One Misuse of Statistics

The other two concepts to be taken into account when racial comparisons are considered involve the representation of traits in populations by distributions of scores and the characterization of distributions by moment-derived statistics. Populations should be compared only with respect to one trait at a time and comparisons should be made in terms of the moment statistics of their trait distributions. Therefore, for any two populations, on each trait of interest, a separate comparison should be made for every moment of their score distributions. If we consider only the first four moments, from which are derived the familiar statistics for mean, variance, skewness, and kurtosis, then there are four ways in which populations or races may differ with respect to any single trait. Since we possess 23 independently assorting pairs of chromosomes, certainly there are at least 23 uncorrelated traits with respect to which populations can be compared. Since comparisons will be made in terms of four (usually independent) statistics, there are $4 \times 23 = 92$ ways in which races can differ. Since the integrity of chromosomes is *not* preserved over the generations, because they often break apart at meiosis and exchange constituent genes, there are far more than 23 independent hereditary units. If instead of 23 chromosomes we take the 100,000 genes man is now estimated to possess and we think in terms of their phenotypic trait correlates, then there may be as many as

[4] "Open-field Behavior in Mice: Genetic Analysis of Repeated Measures," *Psychonomic Science,* 13 (1968): 27.

[5] "Limits to Intensive Production in Animals," *British Agriculture Bulletin,* 4 (1951): 217.

400,000 comparisons to be made between any two populations or races.

A priori, at this time we know enough to expect no two populations to be the same with respect to most or all of the constituents of their gene pools. "Mutations and recombinations will occur at different places, at different times, and with differing frequencies. Furthermore, selection pressures will also vary." So the number and kinds of differences between populations now waiting to be revealed in "the more thorough analysis" recommended by Fisher literally staggers the imagination. It does not suggest a linear hierarchy of inferior and superior races.

Why has so much stress been placed on comparing distributions only with respect to their central tendencies by testing the significance of mean differences? There is much evidence that many observations are not normally distributed and that the distributions from many populations do not share homogeneity of variance. The source of our difficulty traces back to the very inception of our statistical tradition.

There is an unbroken line of intellectual influence from Quetelet through Galton and Pearson to modern psychometrics and biometrics. Adolphe Quetelet (1796–1874), the Belgian astronomer-statistician, introduced the concept of "the average man"; he also applied the normal distribution, so widely used in astronomy for error variation, to human data, biological and social. The great Francis Galton followed Quetelet's lead and then Karl Pearson elaborated and perfected their methods. I know of nothing that has contributed more to impose the typological way of thought on, and perpetuates it in, present-day psychology than the feedback from these methods for describing observations in terms of group averages.

There is a technique called composite photography to the perfection of which Sir Francis Galton contributed in an important way. Some of Galton's best work in this field was done by combining—literally averaging—the separate physiognomic features of many different Jewish individuals into his composite photograph of "the Jewish type." Karl Pearson, his disciple and biographer, wrote: "There is little doubt that Galton's Jewish type formed a landmark in composite photography." The part played by typological thinking in the development of modern statistics and the way in which such typological thinking has been

feeding back into our conceptual framework through our continued careless use of these statistics is illuminated by Galton's following remarks: "The word generic presupposes a genus, that is to say, a collection of individuals who have much in common, and among whom medium characteristics are very much more frequent than extreme ones. The same idea is sometimes expressed by the word typical, which was much used by Quetelet, who was the first to give it a rigorous interpretation, and whose idea of a type lies at the basis of his statistical views. No statistician dreams of combining objects into the same generic group that do not cluster towards a common centre, no more can we compose generic portraits out of heterogeneous elements, for if the attempt be made to do so the result is monstrous and meaningless."[6] The basic assumption of a type, or typical individual, is clear and explicit. They used the normal curve and they permitted distributions to be represented by an average because, even though at times they knew better, far too often they tended to think of races as discrete, even homogeneous, groups and individual variation as error.

It is important to realize that these developments began before 1900, when Mendel's work was still unknown. Thus at the inception of biosocial science there was no substantive basis for understanding individual differences. After 1900, when Mendel's work became available, its incorporation into biosocial science was bitterly opposed by the biometricians under Pearson's leadership. Galton had promulgated two "laws": his Law of Ancestral Heredity (1865) and his Law of Regression (1877). When Yule and Castle pointed out how the Law of Ancestral Heredity could be explained in Mendelian terms, Pearson stubbornly denied it. Mendel had chosen for experimental observation seven traits, each of which, in his pea-plant material, turned out to be a phenotypic correlate of a single gene with two segregating alleles. For all seven traits one allele was dominant. Unfortunately Pearson assumed the universality of dominance and based his disdain for Mendelism on this assumption. Yule then showed that without the assumption of dominance, Mendelism becomes perfectly consistent with the kind of quantitative data on the basis of which it was being rejected by

[6] K. Pearson, *The Life, Letters and Labours of Francis Galton*, Vol. II, (Cambridge: Cambridge University Press, 1924), p. 295.

Pearson. It is sad to realize that Pearson never appreciated the generality of Mendelism and seems to have gone on for the next 32 years without doing so.

Two Fallacies

Now we can consider the recent debate about the meaning of comparisons between the "intelligence" of different human races. We are told that intelligence has a high heritability and that one race performs better than another on intelligence tests. In essence we are presented with a racial hierarchy reminiscent of that pernicious "system" which John Haydon Langdon Down used when he misnamed a disease entity "mongolism."

The people who are so committed to answering the nature-nurture pseudo-question (Is heredity or environment more important in determining intelligence?) make two conceptual blunders. (1) Like Spalding's question about the instinctive nature of bird flight, which introduced the ethologist's deprivation experiment, their question about intelligence is, in fact, being asked about the development of a single individual. Unlike Spalding and the ethologists, however, they do not study development in single individuals. Usually they test groups of individuals at a single time of life. The proportions being assigned to heredity and to environment refer to the relative amounts of the variance between individuals comprising a population, not how much of whatever enters into the development of the observed expression of a trait in a particular individual has been contributed by heredity and by environment respectively. They want to know how instinctive is intelligence in the development of a certain individual, but instead they measure differences between large numbers of fully, or partially, developed individuals. If we now take into consideration the norm-of-reaction concept and combine it with the facts of genotypic individuality, then there is no general statement that can be made about the assignment of fixed proportions to the contributions of heredity and environment either to the development of a single individual, because we have not even begun to assess his norm of reaction, or to the differences that might be measured among members of a population, because we have hardly begun to assess the range of environmental conditions under which its constituent members might develop!

(2) Their second mistake, an egregious error, is related to the first one. They assume an inverse relationship between heritability magnitude and improvability by training and teaching. If heritability is high, little room is left for improvement by environmental modification. If heritability is low, much more improvement is possible. Note how this basic fallacy is incorporated directly into the title of Jensen's article "How Much Can We Boost IQ and Scholastic Achievement?" That question received a straightforward, but fallacious, answer on his page 59: "The fact that scholastic achievement is considerably less heritable than intelligence ... means there is potentially much more we can do to improve school performance through environmental means than we can do to change intelligence...." Commenting on the heritability of intelligence and "the old nature-nurture controversy" one of Jensen's respondents makes the same mistake in his rebuttal: "This is an old estimate which many of us have used, but we have used it to determine what could be done with the variance left for the environment." He then goes on "to further emphasize some of the implications of environmental variance for education and child rearing."

High or low heritability tells us absolutely nothing about how a given individual might have developed under conditions different from those in which he actually did develop. Heritability provides no information about norm of reaction. Since the characterization of genotype-environment interaction can only be ad hoc and the number of possible interactions is effectively unlimited, no wonder the search for general laws of behavior has been so unfruitful, and *the* heritability of intelligence or of any other trait must be recognized as still another of those will-o-the-wisp general laws. And no magic words about an interaction component in a linear analysis-of-variance model will make disappear the reality of each genotype's unique norm of reaction. Such claims by Jensen or anyone else are false. Interaction is an abstraction of mathematics. Norm of reaction is a developmental reality of biology in plants, animals and people.

In Israel, the descendants of those Jews Pearson feared would contaminate Britain are manifesting some interesting properties of the norm of reaction. Children of European origin have an average IQ of 105 when they are brought up in individual homes. Those brought up in a Kibbutz on the nursery rearing schedule of 22 hours per day for 4 or more years have an average IQ of 115. In contrast, the mid-Eastern Jewish children brought up in individual homes have an average IQ of only 85, Jensen's danger point. However, when brought up in a Kibbutz, they also have an average IQ of 115. That is, they perform the same as the European children with whom they were matched for education, the occupational level of parents, and the Kibbutz group in which they were raised. There is no basis for expecting different overall results for any population in our species.

Benjamin Pasamanick

A Tract for the Times: Some Sociobiological Aspects of Science, Race, and Racism

In the preceding article, Hirsch discussed the concept of the phenotypic norm of reaction of the genotype. In the article which follows, Pasamanick enumerates many of the environmental factors which must be considered in any discussion of this norm of reaction. In particular, he discusses the development of intellectual capacity in the individual.

The views presented in this paper would be labeled by Ginsburg and Laughlin as the Dichotomy-Dismissal Approach. But despite Pasamanick's environmentalist bias, he makes some interesting points about environmental and cultural influences on behavior. The complexity of the problem is brought forth in reading what Pasamanick has to write about his own research.

Note that the author, like Hirsch, is critical of investigators who call for further research into racial differences in intelligence. He is especially concerned that science continues to involve itself with such issues. Perhaps the most relevant social aspect of the article is Pasamanick's emphasis on the urgency of work on environmental solutions rather than on further research which may or may not have any bearing on the immediate social problems.

As the lukewarm skirmish against poverty gives promise of turning into a hot war of rebellion for justice and equality, the fifth estate—science— rides precipitously into the fray, frequently to add confusion and to protect and give comfort to the establishment.

I would like to take as the thesis for my tract, the 1967 meeting of the National Academy of Sciences, where the smoldering question (implicit or explicit) of Negro inferiority exploded anew. This time the protagonists were Shockley, the Nobel Prize winner for transistor work; Kennedy of Florida State, sponsored by Harlow; and, finally, the Academy itself.

The tired questions at issue again were: Are Negroes genetically inferior? Would an improved environment really improve their social functioning? Are scientists inhibited from investigating these problems? Etc. Etc. What was offered was a new, definitive test, which on further scrutiny turned out to be neither new nor definitive.

Kennedy mentioned very briefly the 75 years of massive studies on Negro intelligence, stating that if there could be individual differences in some characteristics, there could be race differences in intelligence. He pointed to a 20 percent IQ difference between Negroes and whites in the Southeastern states, narrowed to 10 percent by so-called preschool "cultural enrichment" programs. The fact that Negro infants in those states were indistinguishable from white infants for the first two years, he said, "challenges the hypothesis of Pasamanick that one of the major effects of cultural deprivation and its poor prenatal nutritional and medical care is the production of sickly, underweight, and often premature infants who begin life at an inferior level of 'intelligence.'" But he then went on to state that infant tests do not predict school-age test performance anyway.

The test suggested by Kennedy involved placing illegitimately pregnant Negro girls in maternity homes with good prenatal care and diet and then placing their offspring in middle-class Negro homes—using as controls lower-class Negro and white infants left in their biological environment.

But he asked the obvious question himself—Why do such a study "when intelligence tests themselves may not be the most sensitive instrument by which to study the effect of genetics on performance"? Part of his reply was a plea "simply to open the field of inquiry such that honest investigators may make careful study of racial differences in the hope that unique racial factors may be found which might well go undiscovered by default and thus to keep the concept of racial differences in intelligence as an open question." He did stress that as far as he knew "there is no convincing evidence that there are any racial differences in intellectual abilities that are based upon genetic factors."

Some months later a letter commenting on Kennedy's paper appeared in *Science* pointing out that, "Some of the effects of a poor prenatal environment may not show themselves clearly until relatively complex intellectual tasks are presented later in the child's life." The writer pointed to our data indicating "that lower socioeconomic status is associated with dietary deficiencies during pregnancy, lack of adequate medical care during pregnancy and delivery, prematurity, greater maternal and infant mortality" and a higher incidence of maternal complications in nonwhite mothers attributable to their socioeconomic status. Further, that nutrition during pregnancy was associated with intellectual performance in offspring and that the mother's nutritional history and other aspects of her health history even prior to the conception of the child may influence the status of the child. The final point made was that the "attributing to heredity any IQ differences (remaining) on the basis of such studies (as Kennedy's) could hardly be justified, (i) because not all of the known relevant environmental variables would have been controlled, and (ii) because knowledge of the relevant environmental variables cannot be assumed to be complete."

To this Kennedy replied [in the same 1967 issue] "that when ... mothers are given adequate prenatal care, even as late as the second trimester of pregnancy, the findings of Pasamanick do not hold. That is, if the mothers are given a vitamin and dietary supplement and adequate prenatal care, the Negro children, far from being born at a physical disadvantage, are born instead in what appears to be a superior position, as far as the general measures of intellectual and physical health are concerned. Although Pasamanick's study does indeed call attention to the necessity of controlling the prenatal environment, his findings are not consistent with those of almost any well-baby clinic with reports on Negro children born with hospital prenatal care. His findings evidently result from a combination of factors related to extreme poverty in a large city slum with very poor prenatal care."

Kennedy then proposed that "mothers could be eliminated [from his study] if they showed any evidence that massive deprivation had occurred during the first trimester." He did not, however, reply to the issue of preconceptional malnutrition and disease related to socioeconomic variables, which has indeed been heavily implicated in reproductive casualty by Baird in Aberdeen.

Kennedy did acknowledge that "the study might not be definitive, particularly if significant differences between the experimental and control groups were obtained, ... given the use of the null hypothesis."

Before continuing with the next episode in the narrative, I would like to clarify as briefly as possible some of the confused and confusing issues raised in the foregoing and to discuss some biologic factors involved.

Kennedy stated that in the Southeast Negro infants during their first two years progress behaviorally at rates no different from those seen in whites. It is amusing to note that we were the first to demonstrate this more than two decades ago on what was probably a representative, if small, New Haven sample. The New Haven findings were replicated twice on much larger and more obviously representative samples in Baltimore and Columbus.

These are not irrelevant measurements, unpredictive of school-age functioning as Kennedy says.

On the contrary, we and others have demonstrated repeatedly that the prediction of performance on standard intelligence tests given children seven years after testing them as infants is at least as good as the prediction of performance on the same tests given children seven years apart within their school-age period. This is only further proof that the patterns of behavioral development during infancy contain all the precursor ingredients of later behavior, and that any deficiencies in conduction time, perception, central nervous system integration, motor output, etc., can be discovered in infancy. Indeed, we have shown the prediction of such defects to be even better than the prediction of intellectual performance.

It is true that we have found a greater incidence of severe damage in Negro infants related to perinatal events, but this has been insufficient, during infancy, to influence the *mean* quotients of our Negro samples. As a consequence, again contrary to Kennedy, we have never placed any great weight upon prenatal damage as a cause of Negro group intellectual dysfunction during the school years. We had some evidence on the basis of retrospective studies that prenatal damage disorganized all aspects of behavioral functioning, including cognition, but it wasn't until our recent analysis of longitudinal data that we were prepared to elucidate the seemingly paradoxical findings that prenatal damage results in no differences in mean quotients during infancy and yet should be considered as one of the variables involved in school-age differences.

First, I should point out that damaged children were a not inconsiderable fraction of our total. Approximately one eighth of the infants exhibited objective, reliable indices of brain damage. We now know these indices to be valid, for seven years later we found 90 percent of these same children, no matter what their race or economic status, to differentiate clearly on a battery of tests of perceptual, integrational, and motor items. But what we had not fully anticipated was how socioeconomic status, again irrespective of race, would differentially affect these injured children. The group as a whole fell from its early promise of intellectual potential, but it was the children in middle and lower socioeconomic thirds of the group who contributed most to the decline and, as might have been anticipated, largely the children in the lower third who fell most precipitously.

Let us examine a bit more closely the probable course of events leading to this decline and fall. The common explanation offered for the poor showing of lower-class children is lack of stimulation, for which the paradigm is the animal isolation experiments. While this might hold for children in the old orphan asylums, nothing could be less descriptive of the slum child's environment, living as he does in crowded quarters and constantly bombarded by sensory stimuli of all modalities—blaring radios and television sets, extremes of heat and cold, surrounded by active adults and children frequently in disorganized and confusing array—difficult even for the intact child or adult to integrate or inhibit. The injured child with impaired inhibitory, attentional, and integrative capacities responds with aphasias, autism, and extremes of psychomotor excitation, making it difficult, if not impossible, to mature successfully. We have demonstrated, in addition, that he contributes to the further disorganization of his own environment and is subject to repeated illnesses and hospitalizations, so that it is not surprising that we end with a schoolchild with a low IQ, demoralized by constant failure and a distinct handicap to his ghetto schoolmates.

I do not want to overemphasize the contribution brain damage makes to the decline of the group mean IQ but rather to indicate its cost to group functioning and what the needs are for individualized care. But I will return to it after discussing another biologic variable which we can now begin to place in a more precise context.

In our first longitudinal New Haven study we found that a number of commonly implicated social and demographic variables had played no role in influencing infant development. Physical growth was the only variable found to be significantly related to performance. Those infants below the median on height and weight curves, even by 40 weeks of age, were already significantly lower in intellectual potential than those above. Nevertheless, the group *as a whole* had growth curves similar to the best white rates, and at school age had IQs equal to whites. (It is true that those living in segregated areas and attending segregated schools were lower than the others.) We felt justified in assuming the probability of a causal relationship between nutritional intake before and after birth, in turn related to full employment and rationing during the war years, with consequent satisfactory behavioral progress.

Once again, in Baltimore we confirmed precisely the same relationship of physical growth to performance in the Negro group. But two, probably not unrelated, differences from the New Haven findings struck us: first, that the Negro weight curves, even for full-term children, were significantly lower than white curves; second, that by three years of age the Negroes were also falling behind intellectually. A third, most telling finding, was the discovery that the white children did not have this relationship of low physical growth curves to low performance.

We can now, with support from other studies, begin to offer a simple explanation for these seemingly disparate findings. Amongst the whites, at least in Baltimore, physical growth patterns appear to be largely reflections of inherited physique rather than related to nutritional intake; in large measure, and as a group, whites are above that threshold where dietary differences during childhood play a significant role. The Negroes, on the other hand, perched precariously on the low rungs of the economic ladder, are significantly lower than whites in physical growth, and those sufficiently below the threshold exhibit the intellectual consequences of nutritional deprivation, primarily of protein and vitamins. (One can only imagine the devastation occurring in grossly undernourished populations abroad.)

We can also, at this time, begin to outline the probable biochemical and physiologic mechanisms involved. It seems clear that either RNA and/or protein synthesis in the neuron is involved in long-term memory and learning and consequently in behavioral and intellectual functioning. Chronic or intermittent malnutrition could affect this synthesis and thereby have recurrent or permanent effects leading to disorganization or delay in the complex of reciprocal interweaving of developmental patterns which we term intellectual maturation. These effects would be greatest during fetal life, leading to measurable neurologic impairment, with lesser interference during childhood, impairing only intellectual growth in most cases.

We can now begin to fit these two biologic variables of brain damage and malnutrition into the highly interrelated complex of biologic factors (there are other variables such as infection, immunologic responses, toxic substances, etc.) and in turn into the matrix of biopsychosocial factors which cause racial differences in intelligence. And

the biologic variables are probably not the weightiest contributors to malfunction. All we need and can do is list some of the others: the powerlessness, the recurrent blasted hopes, the shame, the fear, the anger, the dirt, the noise, the poor health care, disease, strife, frustration, hunger, idleness, hard work, disorganization, lack of stimulation and dystimulation, and on, and on, and on.

And in how much dysfunction does this seemingly endless spiral result? In Baltimore, where one of the worst ghettos in the country exists, at six years of age the Negro children are only 10 percent behind the whites (and this on a test, the Stanford-Binet, that is strongly biased in its contents against lower-class children). (This is in stark contrast to the 20 percent Kennedy reports in Southeast U.S., indicating that, bad as conditions are in the cities, they are still worse in the South, particularly in the rural areas.) Even further, when the Negroes as a whole are compared to the lower socioeconomic half of the Baltimore whites, they are only 5 percent behind and, were it possible to equate the socioeconomic conditions, there is no doubt there would be no significant differences at all.

In the face of what these children must contend with, day in and day out, and the significant but relatively small differences which become smaller or disappear with even minor improvement in their lot, how can one speak of innate racial inferiority? I can only stand in awe of man's stamina and his resilience in response to the continuous onslaught upon his functioning. I state hesitantly and, probably with some bias, that I believe whites could do as well under the same circumstances.

I would maintain that the successive approximations made to ultimate knowledge of group differences in intellectual functioning make Negro innate inferiority exceedingly implausible and that at this time we know enough of what must be done to erase this infamy. (It is of no little interest that in that long, sad document, the 1968 President's State of the Union message, proposing some crumbs of health care, the heaviest emphasis was on maternal and child health.)

What we can say quite clearly at this time is that, when a sample of Negroes approaches sociocultural comparability to a white sample (and I must add that, because of centuries of discrimination, even under the best of circumstances no precise comparability is currently possible), the Negroes become comparable to the whites in all important aspects—infant and maternal mortality, physical growth, morbidity, and intellectual performance. However, the common reply to this observation is that these samples are biased, containing only individuals at the upper end of the curve of capacity. Such circular polemics lead inevitably to the conclusion that unless and until the Negro achieves full social and economic equality in our society, the definitive test of his capacity is not possible. The challenge to those eager and determined inquirers into scientific truth then becomes one of turning all the strength of their efforts and determination into achieving the type of society in which the definitive test is possible. It is at this point that the crucial decision arises and must be made. Until they accept this challenge we must doubt their intentions and, indeed, their scientific and social integrity.

But I greatly fear that the most common response is that Negroes, because of their capacities, could not reach social and economic equality even if given the opportunity. This is, of course, to prejudge the outcome, and becomes the basis for the self-fulfilling prejudice with which we have been contending. The more ingenious reply is that it would take too long, be too difficult. All the more reason to hasten and devote all our energies to the task, instead of diverting them largely or wholly to trivial investigations of racial differences which lead us back into a meaningless circle of inconclusiveness.

In the light of this analysis, Shockley's call for public debate on Carleton Putnam's racist ideas becomes, indeed, shocking. As for his hoary argument, as old as Galton, that the mean IQ of the population is declining because the genetically inferior families have more children, it can be dismissed along with a whole farrago of nonsense, as it was by the entire genetics department at his university who termed it "pseudoscientific" and falling "between mischief and malice." Studies made in Britain over decades have indicated that, rather than declining, IQs have risen as have physical growth curves. The British, with far less wealth and productive capacity than we, have achieved a lower infant mortality, lower prematurity and complications of pregnancy rates, and a rising intellectual potential merely by a more equitable distribution of their goods and an approach to a better system of social services.

Why do we keep harping on the subject? Why do we respond automatically to every prod into the festering gangrene? Certainly we have little hope of convincing the prejudiced or changing the racist.

Donald Campbell in his essay on stereotype points out that, "In southern legislatures in the last 100 years, the alleged intellectual inferiority of Negroes has played an important role. Removing the belief that Negroes are inferior would not, however, remove the hostility, although it would change the content of the stereotype. Had the World War I test results showing northern Negroes to be more intelligent than southern whites been effectively publicized in the South, opportunistic hostility could certainly have created an image of the northern Negro carpetbagger whose opprobrious traits included shrewdness, trickiness, and egg-headed intellectuality. Remedial education in race relations focused on denying or disproving stereotypes implicitly accepts the prejudiced ingroupers' causal conception rather than the social scientists' and is undermined where actual group differences are found."[1]

I do not wholly agree with this last, but why take the risk? Let me take my cue from the next scene in our tragic comedy.

In November 1967 *Science,* reporting on William Shockley's call for research on the effects of heredity and environment on intelligence, indicated that his call had been uncomfortable for the National Academy of Sciences, adding up "to a loaded question that might be destructively exploited by racists if the Academy even ratified it as the right question." And, in reaction, the Academy's president presented its Council's response in a long statement prepared with the assistance of several eminent geneticists.

The statement began with the nature of certain questions being asked, went on to the difficulties involved in such investigations, and then said on one hand this and on the other hand that. But amongst its conclusions, which were also hedged, it stated:

. . . we question the social urgency *of a greatly enhanced program to measure the heritability of complex intellectual and emotional factors.*

---

[1] "Stereotypes and the Perception of Group Differences," *American Psychologist,* 22 (1967): 817.

Likewise, we question the social urgency of a crash program to measure genetic differences in intellectual and emotional traits between racial groups. In the first place, if the traits are at all complex, the results of such research are almost certain to be inconclusive. In the second place, it is not clear that major social decisions depend on such information.

Wars, past and present, have stimulated research which has proved of benefit to mankind but which cannot, under any circumstances, justify the waging of war. Similarly the centuries-old war against injustice and inequality has taught us much about life processes and human functioning, certainly enough to end most of this strife. The social urgency is to do that which must be done to end the strife, not to ascertain what should be done. And we all know how great is the urgency.

To call, at this time, for more research on racial differences in intelligence is an exercise in futility and callousness. It is analagous to calling in the midst of a slum fire for research on the relationship of racial differences in pigmentation to resistance to burns. We are on the verge of a holocaust and the research has been done.

The concern which drove the National Academy to issue its statement is a very real one. The *Iron Mountain* mentality of brutal repression of demands for a decent life has been endemic in American society since its inception, and is spreading as one of the reactions to our present crisis. We must not ignore it or its concomitant desperate search for scapegoats. The Indian, the Negro, the alien have served in the past, and racism has been its base.

It is sickening to recall that one of the items in the indictment of the Jews drawn up in *Mein Kampf* was that of their defense of racial and ethnic groups and their opposition to the Nazi doctrine of the simian character of the Negro. This doctrine has served its purpose well in justifying slavery and second-class citizenship for the Negro.

Science in its comments upon Shockley hints at another rationalization, "Or will genetic inheritance produce such a low social capacity index that most will perform at frustratingly low social levels?" Mechanization and new methods have made the Negro superfluous in the rural South, condemning him to slow starvation or refugee status in the North. Is there now a suggestion that automation and urban life which require skilled labor and high social capacity indices have made the Negro superfluous in our society, calling for "apartheid" or even "a final solution" of the Negro problem?

Might it be these implications which the Academy Council had in mind, recalling our genocidal efforts upon the American Indian and the more recent cry to bomb a small country "into the Stone Age," when it issued its statement?

We recoil in horror—and in this reaction lies our hope. We are in a crisis—urban, national, global. We, as a society, have striven frantically for control over all animate and inanimate matter in this world, the moon, the planets, and the stars with a system of values based upon self-interest, dead-ending with power as an ultimate good. We have evaded the self-confrontation necessary to reorder our values to achieve a true community and a just society. We can evade it no longer and, uncomfortable as it may be, it is good that it is so.

John Gardner, voicing the concern of all humane people, has said that there are two overriding, immediate items on the agenda of American society—a decent, equal place for the Negro, and peace. The two are, of course, *totally interdependent.* The wherewithal for the jobs, housing, education, health care, and other ingredients of a dignified existence can only come from those tremendous resources now allocated to destruction.

Half of the 160 billions of dollars the world pours into war and preparation for war is expended by our country. This is in violent contrast to the 7 billions from all nations going towards aid to the poverty-ridden countries, for which our contribution continues to fall, now ranking us fifth in proportion to our production. What a world this could be if we reversed these expenditures.

This jeremiad, I know, is only one of many now coming at you from all quarters and indicating the universal shock of recognition of our problem. They are the inevitable first reactions upon which we must build together a reordering or our values and reallocation of our resources. To remain quiet is to lapse into the cynicism or apathy which can follow upon the darkness confronting us. Gunnar Myrdal, who described the American dilemma of inconsistencies within the American dream, returned last year after two decades to offer his final warning against stupid optimism. We must operate from the most realistic view of things as they are and then go forward, because *blind* retreat is no longer possible.

Hermann K. Bleibtreu and John Meaney

Racial Differences in Behavior: Cultural and Evolutionary Considerations

The articles selected for our section on race all emphasize, in different ways, the necessity of understanding racial differences in populational, genetic, and evolutionary terms. Moreover, we have reprinted articles which, in our judgment, best discuss those scientifically difficult topics—intelligence and behavior, and their alleged variability with race.

It has recently been suggested by a number of ranking American scientists that there indeed are racial, genetically based differences in intelligence. This conclusion stems, for the most part, from the correlation between racial phenotypes and IQ, supposedly in the presence of experimentally controlled environmental influence. Although correlational analyses in no way lend themselves to causal interpretation, these scientists have arrived at the conclusion that intelligence varies among human races on the grounds that IQ has a significant degree of heritability. The conclusion has been criticized because environmental influences have not actually been controlled in the intelligence test situation and because the concept of heritability has been misapplied. These criticisms alone, if upheld, devastate the conclusion that races differ in intelligence. But a more profound issue is at stake here than a methodological one: it appears that these scientists are promoting a conclusion which is incompatible with our understanding of raciation or subpopulation formation in man.

In genetic terms, a race is a population. A racial difference is a difference in gene frequency between populations, and gene frequencies are determined solely by the action of selection, sampling error (drift), mutation, and migration. Therefore any statement about a racial difference is an evolutionary statement and requires validation in terms of an evolutionary model. If it is claimed that intelligence is a trait which differs among races, a supporting argument is required, one which explains how, in evolutionary terms, that difference could have come about. If no such scientifically sensible argument can be made, the validity of the initial claim becomes suspect. The scientists who have proposed innate differences in intelligence between American blacks and whites have, perhaps un-

wittingly, made a profound statement about human evolution. Had they been aware of what we already know about racial differences, they would have been more cautious.

It should be noted that anthropologists have never really been involved in cross-cultural intelligence testing. This has been left to psychologists who are not necessarily sensitive to cultural and subcultural differences and whose tests therefore tend to be culture-bound. Thus, the subject with the best understanding of the psychologist's culture is considered the most intelligent. Anthropologists, on the other hand, are particularly impressed by the individual who "knows" a great deal about his own culture. Since no culture is primitive, except in the technological sense, it seems unlikely that enculturation (the process by which the child learns his culture) is mentally less demanding in one culture than another.

Anthropology has gone through three methodological phases in finding traits that vary among the races of man. Before becoming aware of the modern theory of evolution, anthropologists did research into racial characteristics by measuring the kind of traits believed to be little, or not at all, affected by environmental influences. The object was to discover racial markers for taxonomic purposes. Head shape was a great favorite, since it was believed that such a functional trait would be immune to environmental influences and thus represent the pure essence of race. Then, about twenty years ago, influenced by the theory of natural selection, anthropologists reversed themselves completely. The old racial markers were now seen as population variables established by a genetic response to environmental pressures. This launched the "great correlation game." One picked a racial trait (skin color, for example), plotted it on world distribution maps of annual temperature, humidity, sunlight, and so forth, and determined the environmental correlates with the biological variable. Such research contributed little to the understanding and measurement of environmental conditions; for that kind of information, one had to depend on data about weather, some of it of the most general and unsophisticated sort. But huge amounts of data on human variations were accumulated. In particular, information about blood groups was collected, since it was felt that such a genetic trait, of known mode of inheritance, was far more valuable in distinguishing populations than the anthropometric information that had been gathered in equally prolific fashion earlier. But even the use of blood groups did not clarify or simplify the correlation of populational traits with environmental variables.

Finally, less than ten years ago, a third approach to the study of population—"human adaptability studies" —was undertaken. It exactly reverses the correlational methodology, by first identifying an environmental variable—usually a fairly dramatic one like high altitude, desert heat, arctic cold—and then finding the human biological correlate or response. Attempts are then made to determine whether the aborigines living in that extreme environment have special physiological or other characteristics for dealing with the supposed stresses. This kind of research is scientifically superior to the correlational approach because it deals with specific populations living in well-defined environments. Moreover, there is no prior commitment to the idea that environmental variable X produces human physical trait Y. The scope of the research is much wider: it is expected that life under stressful natural conditions, modified by cultural means, depends on a multiplicity of complex yet measurable interactions between the organism and the environment. Some of man's biological responses will be due to adaptations in the genetic sense (i.e., will be products of selection); others will be responses developed during the individual's growth period; others will be even shorter-term accommodations arising from a general biological flexibility. Unlike the proponents of a correlational approach, investigators of human adaptability have been very cautious about suggesting genetic causes for the biological differences they have shown to exist in different populations living in different environmental extremes.

The common goal of all these anthropological approaches—racial marker, correlation, and adaptability—has been to identify the biological differences among human populations living in different geographical areas. And it would appear from the extensive literature on the subject that a tremendous number of differences have now been discovered. Some of these, like the blood groups, are straightforward single gene differences; some, like skin color, eye color, and some morphological features are presumably due to complex genetic differences. Finally, there are all those differences which seem to have a biological component

which in turn may have some sort of genetic basis. In other words, there has been accumulated over the years an extensive inventory of variables which vary among populations—and the search goes on. While this may be thought of as a scientific accomplishment, it is at the same time rather depressing to note that most of the differences discovered so far, and perhaps especially those of a simple genetic nature, evidently are functionally and adaptively trivial. This is not to say that biology does not count nor that selection does not operate in human populations, nor is it to say that the differences that have been found are not scientifically interesting. The point is that most known genetic traits which differentiate the races of man do not seem to influence, positively or negatively, the adaptation of a given population to its environment.

The human being can evidently tolerate great genetic diversity, both within and between populations. We can imagine selection consistently weeding out the extremes but leaving a tremendous amount of expressed diversity which neither hinders nor enhances the survival and procreation of human populations, no matter in what environment it operates. This may mean that selection should be the last, not the first explanation we should reach for in attempting to explain populational differences. Nevertheless, selection provides a clean cause-and-effect kind of explanation that appeals to our Western minds so much more than what appears to be a soft line of reasoning which gives fortuity, or history, and genetic flexibility a role. After all, the startling fact about Homo sapiens is that tens of thousands of years of ever increasing geographical distribution has not resulted in a divergence sufficient to create a new species. Nor are races in any way analogous to breeds—i.e., variants of a species specialized for the performance of certain activities.

The major factor responsible for biological nonspecialization is evidently that mediator with the natural environment that anthropologists call culture. This "artificial" environment, common to all races, may be the major reason why all human gene pools have maintained their similarity even though many have been separated for many thousands of generations. What really differentiates populations is their culture, not their biology. Yet not even the diversity of cultural environments has been great enough to induce genetically specialized populations. This fact has not, however, prevented racists from attempting to raise biological racial differences to the status and magnitude of cultural differences. After all, the modern concept of species is relatively new and the temptation to envision the process of human raciation as a minor form of speciation still exists. This may account for the present emphasis on natural selection as the evolutionary force which explains racial differences—differences suspected of having adaptive significance. But if human raciation is not adaptive, then human races cannot be considered as incipient species.

In anthropology, as well as biology, the word *adaptation* is commonly used but seldom defined.[1] Frequently it is synonymous with "specialization." The organism is said to be "particularly suited" to its environment, a situation which has come about by natural selection. In the genetic sense, "adaptation" can be defined as that state in which the organism, because of its genetic constitution, is responding to the environment in such a way that its chances for reproduction and for living through its reproductive years are maximized. In other words, adaptation makes for maximal fitness, i.e., genetic survival over the generations. By either definition, specialization or genetic survival, adaptation is a concept most difficult to apply to man. What is genetically "good" for a population is not necessarily what is culturally "good." Much cultural practice is obviously inadaptive in the genetic sense. There is no reason why the two should reinforce each other. Whole human populations become extinct for genetically and evolutionarily irrelevant reasons; other populations grow, split, and become dominant for equally fortuitous biological reasons.

Selection itself takes on some peculiar characteristics when applied to human populations. To say that a gene is "selected for" means that one of its alleles is increasing in frequency at the cost of one of its other alleles. Its carriers must have relatively more offspring over the generations. The selective advantage bestowed by a gene provides its host with a more successful way to deal with some environmental obstacle, say, disease, than the individual who does not have the gene and thus dies before or during his reproductive period. But gene frequencies in human populations also increase and decrease because of cultural selection. The chief of the Xavante village leaves a highly disproportionate number of children compared to other village males because he has first sexual access to the village females. Perhaps this is really an example of genetic drift rather than cultural selection, because the genetic effect is a product of a decrease in effective population size. In animal societies the dominant male must also father most of the offspring of the next generation. We assume that his dominant behavior is in itself genetically determined, making this a clear case

of natural selection; in the human case, on the other hand, the characteristics that make one the head man are social rather than biological. The point is that, in human populations, changes in gene frequencies can come about entirely independently of and be irrelevant to any feature of the natural environment. This is another reason why the attempt to find environmental correlates for every human populational difference is misguided.

If populational differences in intelligence really do exist, and if these differences can be shown to have some sort of genetic basis, then what makes intelligence different from any other populational-racial variant? A good deal has been made of the fact that differences in the IQ of black and white populations reach statistical significance. It should be pointed out that this is also true of morphological dimensions, blood group frequencies, physiological performance, and so on. In other words, statistical significance has no bearing on functional or adaptational significance. The statistical significance of racial differences in the length of the ear lobe in no way alters the triviality of either the trait or the finding. Our American culture, of course, overwhelmingly values "intelligence." We attribute many good things to it, especially in academe. In fact, we validate our whole world view by presuming that it is based on our perception of reality and on our rational powers. Therefore no one without our powers—no one not like us, or essentially *not us*—can share our world view, and they cannot do so for genetic reasons. Members of every culture have some claim to absolute exclusiveness, and our idea of intelligence serves this purpose very well. Most Americans would probably agree that the decisive difference between our culture and that of a primitive group is that we are rational in our world view while they are not. Our success and progress is due to our technology, which is the product of our Western brains. We suspect that "backward" societies are in such a state because they lack the mentality to live differently. Selection, whether it was natural or social, must ultimately be a responsible agent in bringing about our truly remarkable superior culture. Everybody knows it takes more intelligence to participate in this culture than in some primitive group's. Moreover, it might be expected that selection is now pretty intensively making for smarter and smarter citizens: the process really got under way long ago with

---

[1]Cultural anthropologists use the term very loosely, to describe everything from barest survival to practices which are lavish embellishments on social and cultural practices dealing with the natural and spiritual environment.

our ancestors, the first civilized people in the world, and it is no wonder that the modern descendants of primitive peoples are a bit behind in the evolution of intelligence.

Now all of this is, of course, nonsense. If there is selection for "brains" it is probably for better functioning of that organ from birth to about the age of nine, when the maturation of the brain appears to be complete. This is probably also about the time that the evolutionary significance of the brain's function is also complete. By that time the child has been through the Herculean task of enculturation. Whatever purpose he uses his brain for after that is—evolutionarily and biologically speaking—fortuitous.

In summary, we can say that at present there is no valid empirical or theoretical basis for the assumption that some races are inferior in general intelligence. Evolution is an enormously slow process, compared to human generations and particularly compared to technological and social change, and it is highly unlikely that middle-class American genes or even "civilization genes" have been established as frequencies in populations. Europeans came out of a primitive forest culture far too recently to attribute the content of the Metropolitan Opera, General Motors, or even Los Angeles to genetic evolution. Whatever genes dwell in the gonads of the leaders of today's "developed" nations, they are genes mainly evolved in the Pleistocene and not after the Industrial Revolution or even after the advent of agriculture.

Thus, if certain genetically based attributes are unequally distributed among the races of man it is doubtful that we can call them responsible for cultural differences found in the world today. There were no doubt times when there was general agreement among the highly technological nations that the quaint island of Japan was yet another example of Oriental inferiority. And there are probably still times now when modern Greeks contemplate the shifts of power to the barbarians of the north who now have the audacity to find their origins in the ancient Greeks.

5 Poverty and Culture

Seymour Parker
Poverty and Culture

Oscar Lewis
The Culture of Poverty

Elliot Liebow
Men and Jobs

Bernard J. James
Social-Psychological Dimensions of Ojibwa Acculturation

Seymour Parker and Robert J. Kleiner
The Culture of Poverty: An Adjustive Dimension

Ulf Hannerz
Another Look at Lower-Class Black Culture

Herbert J. Gans
Culture and Class in the Study of Poverty: An Approach to Anti-Poverty Research

Seymour Parker
Poverty: An Altering View

Since the standards of law—and even of morality—of an affluent society are determined by the affluent members of that society, the poor are, by definition, less law-abiding and less moral, but only because they are less affluent and must therefore adapt to different existential circumstances.   Herbert J. Gans

It is important not to confuse basic life chances and actual behavior with basic cultural values and preferences.   Hylan Lewis

The major reason for the failure of most anti-poverty programs so far is that they require the poor to change their behavior before they have gained the resources that would change their situation.   Lee Rainwater

Seymour Parker

Poverty and Culture

The publication of *The Negro Family* (the Moynihan Report) by the United States Department of Labor has been followed by a storm of controversy. In this and other publications, Patrick J. Moynihan set forth the view that there exists among the American blacks a subculture of poverty that is self-perpetuating. The "disorganization" of the blacks' family life, then, is not only a direct response to discrimination, unemployment, poor housing, and other forms of social deprivation, but is also a way of life—learned early by the black child and reinforced by the social values of his or her immediate group. And so the culture of poverty and the disorganization continue through the generations.

Although similar ideas have been expressed earlier in the literature on the poor, Moynihan's formulation came to the fore at a time of violent social ferment and fierce political controversy. Moreover, although the report deals only with black families, its evidence and arguments are susceptible to extension to all populations living in extreme poverty. It is therefore interesting to examine the type of evidence on which his conclusions are based. There is, of course, ample documentation of the instability of a large segment of black families, but the evidence for the existence of a self-perpetuating subculture of poverty among lower-class blacks rests on a change in one statistical correlation: after 1961, the positive relationship between nonwhite unemployment rates and the incidence of cases of Aid to Families with Dependent Children

(AFDC) decreased. (It should be understood that AFDC is most commonly available to families where one parent—and this is usually the father—is missing.) From this altered statistical relationship, it was inferred that the previous strong relationship between poverty, as measured by unemployment rates, and family disorganization, as measured by AFDC cases, was weakening. In other words, the two phenomena were becoming increasingly independent of each other. Now if this were so, it could mean that while family disorganization in the past may have been predominantly a situational response to extreme poverty, such disorganization might now reflect a self-perpetuating subculture with distinctive norms and values.

However, the inference that the decreased correlation demonstrates the self-perpetuating character of family instability among the poor blacks has been challenged. It has been noted, for example, that although unemployment among nonwhites has indeed declined since 1963, it has remained very high for the young people and may even have risen somewhat. It is precisely among the young that illegitimacy rates (and therefore AFDC) are highest. It has also been pointed out that in 1962 more social casework service to the poor was undertaken by the Social Security Administration; a rise in AFDC cases may have been a consequence of the change in the administrative regulations that made the increased service possible. (It should also be noted that there has been no appreciable change since the end of World War II in the proportion of the national income received by the poorest 40 percent of American families.)

In the heat of the recent controversy over the existence and nature of a subculture of poverty, the position of Moynihan (and Oscar Lewis as well) has been attacked as racist. It is the implication for public policy that has engendered the heat. If the existence of a distinct and self-perpetuating culture of poverty were widely accepted, it is said, public funds might be diverted from programs to create more jobs, more housing, and better schools to more social work and reeducation of a psychiatric nature. Moynihan's interpretation is regarded by many knowledgeable protagonists in the civil-rights battle as a "cop-out" that would jusify a letdown in programs of a bread-and-butter nature that could result in a redistribution of income in this country and lead to significant social change. Moreover, they feel, it serves to sustain the complacency of the more affluent by shifting the onus away from themselves and onto the shoulders of the poor or even their father's fathers.

Still another danger is associated with the theory that there is a culture of poverty, according to its critics. If the poor can be characterized as "disorganized," "deviant," or even "sick," it would then be foolhardy to permit them to share in decisions about the allocation of public funds or to give them any control over their community life, such as in the schools their children attend or the administration of the welfare payments they receive. Such exclusion would blunt the thrust of the civil-rights movement and the more creative poverty programs. This fear is not an idle one: Vice-President Agnew, in a recent speech, observed that control of poverty programs by the poor would be akin to a patient's dictating his medical treatment to the doctor.

Recently there has been a broadening of the attack on sociological analyses of the poor. It has been charged that the assumptions underlying studies of the values, beliefs, and personality characteristics of the poor are biased. The very attempt to make such analyses has been dismissed as irrelevant at best and an attempt to rationalize the status quo at worst. One social scientist recently labelled descriptions of the culture of the poor as "the characteristic way in which those on top describe those on the bottom." Another finds "idiosyncrasies of culture . . . of more interest and use to the tourist than to the advocate of progress and change."

Two interesting alternatives to the concept of the culture of poverty have been suggested by Charles Valentine in *Culture and Poverty*. The first is the idea that there are no significant differences between the cultural norms of the poor and those of the more affluent population; however, the poor are unable to "live up to" their cultural norms because of the severe social disadvantages to which they are exposed:

The distinctive patterns of social life at the lowest income levels are determined by structural conditions of the larger society beyond the control of low income people, not by socialization in primary groups committed to a separate cultural design. Otherwise stated, the design for living received by the poor through socialization is not significantly distinct from that of society as a whole, but that the actual conditions of low income life are importantly inconsistent with actualization of this cultural design.[1]

The second alternative suggested by Valentine is the possibility that the poor may have some "specialized alternative values" that are adopted in response to the necessities of their situation. These are "accepted where contradictions between cultural ideals and situational conditions are sharp."

Other students of the problem raise questions about the function of the "secondary" attitudes often associated with the poor, claiming that resignation, fatalism, small hopes or even hopelessness, and so on, are in fact adaptive responses to an extremely disadvantaged situation. If so, then "secondary" attitudes may be secondary not in the sense that they are weaker or less effective in influencing behavior but rather that they are alternative values in the repertoire of the poor that are activated by the exigencies of specific situations. Whether or not such a configuration of secondary attitudes should be called a "subculture" is a matter of definition.

The importance of research and controversy about the culture of poverty is that it may help us understand the entire range of attitudes and values of the poor and not merely one segment of this range. It is also important to learn about the function of specific values of the poor and in what situations they emerge. Third, we need to know more about how the distinctive attitudes associated with poverty affect the utilization of existing opportunites, if indeed they do affect it. Finally, we need to evaluate the relationship between such distinctive values and public policies and programs.

[1] Charles A. Valentine, *Culture and Poverty* (Chicago: University of Chicago Press, 1968), p. 129.

Although Moynihan himself has borne the brunt of the political implications teased out of his position, he still has raised important questions about the culture of poverty, questions too important to be simply dismissed or discredited as "racist." These questions—and we have introduced some of them here—are of great interest to the social scientist. It should be clear by now, however, that they are not merely academic. The issue of the existence and nature of a culture of poverty is a vital one whose resolution will seriously affect the lives of millions of people. It is one that is being addressed not only in clamorous legislative sessions and street demonstrations but also in scholarly discussion and research. Some of that discussion and research follows.

Oscar Lewis
The Culture of Poverty

It is fitting that the first selection in this series of articles on poverty should be authored by Oscar Lewis, whose writings (The Children of Sanchez *and* La Vida) *first introduced and popularized the concept of a "culture of poverty." Essential to this concept is the idea that poverty is not merely economic deprivation, but also entails cultural and personality traits, some of which are psychologically compensatory and rewarding. Furthermore, like other aspects of culture, such elements are transmitted to the children in the process of socialization, and thus contribute to the perpetuation of poverty itself.*

Lewis is cognizant of the fact that poverty involves severe economic deprivation, much of which stems from the economic organization of the dominant society, and he also makes clear that, despite its compensatory aspects, this subculture involves considerable maladaptive behavior and psychic pain. Lewis does not naively blame the poor for being poor; he notes that the socioeconomic interests and the values of the larger society are causal factors in both the development and perpetuation of poverty. However, his inquiry is directed at an understanding of how these forces influence the lives of those living in poverty and how their adaptations, in turn, influence their receptivity to available opportunities and to change. The questions raised by Lewis set the stage for the controversy and positions that will be explored further in this section.

Although a great deal has been written about poverty and the poor, the concept of a culture of poverty is relatively new. I first suggested it in 1959 in my book *Five Families: Mexican Case Studies in the Culture of Poverty*. The phrase is a catchy one and has become widely used and misused. Michael Harrington used it extensively in his book *The Other America*, which played an important role in sparking the national antipoverty program in the United States. However, he used it in a somewhat broader and less technical sense than I had intended. I shall try to define it more precisely as a conceptual model, with special emphasis upon the distinction between poverty and the culture of poverty. The absence of intensive anthropological studies of poor families from a wide variety of national and cultural contexts, and especially from the socialist countries, is a serious handicap in formulating valid cross-cultural regularities. The model presented here is therefore provisional and subject to modification as new studies become available.

Throughout recorded history, in literature, in proverbs, and in popular sayings, we find two opposite evaluations of the nature of the poor. Some characterize the poor as blessed, virtuous, upright, serene, independent, honest, kind, and happy. Others characterize them as evil, mean, violent, sordid, and criminal. These contradictory and confusing evaluations are also reflected in the in-fighting that is going on in the current war against poverty. Some stress the great potential of the poor for self-help, leadership, and community organization, while others point to the sometimes irreversible, destructive effect of poverty upon individual character, and therefore emphasize the need for guidance and control to remain in the hands of the middle class, which presumably has better mental health.

These opposing views reflect a political power struggle between competing groups. However, some of the confusion results from the failure to distinguish between poverty *per se* and the culture of poverty and the tendency to focus upon the individual personality rather than upon the group—that is, the family and the slum community.

As an anthropologist I have tried to understand poverty and its associated traits as a culture or, more accurately, as a subculture with its own structure and rationale, as a way of life which is passed down from generation to generation along family lines. This view directs attention to the fact that the culture of poverty in modern nations is not only a matter of economic deprivation, of disorganization, or of the absence of something. It is also something positive and provides some rewards without which the poor could hardly carry on.

Elsewhere I have suggested that the culture of poverty transcends regional, rural-urban, and national differences and shows remarkable similarities in family structure, interpersonal relations, time orientation, value systems, and spending patterns. These cross-national similarities are examples of independent invention and convergence. They are common adaptations to common problems.

The culture of poverty can come into being in a variety of historical contexts. However, it tends to grow and flourish in societies with the following set of conditions: (1) a cash economy, wage labor, and production for profit; (2) a persistently high rate of unemployment and underemployment for unskilled labor; (3) low wages; (4) the failure to provide social, political, and economic organization, either on a voluntary basis or by government imposition, for the low-income population; (5) the existence of a bilateral kinship system rather than a unilateral one; and finally, (6) the existence of a set of values in the dominant class which stresses the accumulation of wealth and property, the possibility of upward mobility and thrift, and explains low economic status as the result of personal inadequacy or inferiority.

The way of life which develops among some of the poor under these conditions is the culture of poverty. It can best be studied in urban or rural slums and can be described in terms of some seventy interrelated social, economic, and psychological traits. However, the number of traits and the relationships between them may vary from society to society and from family to family. For example, in a highly literate society, illiteracy may be more diagnostic of the culture of poverty than in a society where illiteracy is widespread and where even the well-to-do may be illiterate, as in some Mexican peasant villages before the revolution.

The culture of poverty is both an adaptation and a reaction of the poor to their marginal position in a class-stratified, highly individuated, capitalistic society. It represents an effort to cope with feelings of hopelessness and despair which develop from the realization of the improbability of achieving success in terms of the values and goals of the larger society. Indeed, many of the traits of the culture of poverty can be viewed as attempts at local solutions for problems not met by existing institutions and agencies because the people are not eligible for them, cannot afford them, or are ignorant or suspicious of them. For example, unable to obtain credit from banks, they are thrown upon their own resources and organize informal credit devices without interest.

The culture of poverty, however, is not only an adaptation to a set of objective conditions of the larger society. Once it comes into existence it tends to perpetuate itself from generation to generation because of its effect on the children. By the time slum children are age six or seven they have usually absorbed the basic values and attitudes of their subculture and are not psychologically geared to take full advantage of changing conditions or increased opportunites which may occur in their lifetime.

Most frequently the culture of poverty develops when a stratified social and economic system is breaking down or is being replaced by another, as in the case of the transition from feudalism to capitalism or during periods of rapid technological change. Often it results from imperial conquest in which the native social and economic structure is smashed and the natives are maintained in a servile colonial status, sometimes for many generations. It can also occur in the process of detribalization, such as that now going on in Africa.

The most likely candidates for the culture of poverty are the people who come from the lower strata of a rapidly changing society and are already partially alienated from it. Thus landless rural workers who migrate to the cities can be expected to develop a culture of poverty much more readily than migrants from stable peasant villages with a well-organized traditional culture. In this connection there is a striking contrast between Latin America, where the rural population long ago made the transition from a tribal to a peasant society, and Africa, which is still close to its tribal heritage. The more corporate nature of many of the African tribal societies, in contrast to Latin American rural communities, and the persistence of village ties tend to inhibit or delay the formation of a full-blown culture of poverty in many of the African towns and cities. The special conditions of apartheid in South Africa, where the migrants are segregated into separate "locations" and do not enjoy freedom of movement, create special problems. Here the institutionalization of repression and discrimination tend to develop a greater sense of identity and group consciousness.

The culture of poverty can be studied from various points of view: the relationship between the subculture and the larger society; the nature of the slum community; the nature of the family; and the attitudes, values and character structure of the individual.

1. The lack of effective participation and integration of the poor in the major institutions of the larger society is one of the crucial characteristics of the culture of poverty. This is a complex matter and results from a variety of factors which may include lack of economic resources, segregation and discrimination, fear, suspicion or apathy, and the development of local solutions for problems. However, "participation" in some of the institutions of the larger society—for example, in the jails, the army, and the public relief system—does not *per se* eliminate the traits of the culture of poverty. In the case of a relief system which barely keeps people alive, both the basic poverty and the sense of hopelessness are perpetuated rather than eliminated.

Low wages, chronic unemployment, and underemployment lead to low income, lack of property ownership, absence of savings, absence of food reserves in the home, and a chronic shortage of cash. These conditions reduce the possibility of effective participation in the larger economic system. And as a response to these conditions we find in the culture of poverty a high incidence of pawning of personal goods, borrowing from local moneylenders at usurious rates of interest, spontaneous informal credit devices organized by neighbors, the use of second-hand clothing and furniture, and the pattern of frequent buying of small quantities of food many times a day as the need arises.

People with a culture of poverty produce very little wealth and receive very little in return. They have a low level of literacy and education, usually do not belong to labor unions, are not members of political parties, generally do not participate in the national welfare agencies, and make very little use of banks, hospitals, department stores, museums, or art galleries. They have a critical attitude toward some of the basic institutions of the dominant classes, hatred of the police, mistrust of government and those in high position, and a cynicism which extends even to the church. This gives the culture of poverty a high potential for protest and for being used in political movements aimed against the existing social order.

People with a culture of poverty are aware of middle-class values, talk about them, and even claim some of them as their own, but on the whole they do not live by them. Thus it is important to distinguish between what they say and what they do. For example, many will tell you that marriage by law, by the church, or by both, is the ideal form of marriage, but few will marry. To men who have no steady jobs or other sources of income, who do not own property and have no wealth to pass on to their children, who are present-time oriented and who want to avoid the expense and legal difficulties involved in formal marriage and divorce, free unions or consensual marriage makes a lot of sense. Women will often turn down offers of marriage because they feel it ties them down to men who are immature, punishing, and generally unreliable. Women feel that consensual union gives them a better break; it gives them some of the freedom and flexibility that men have. By not giving the fathers of their children legal status as husbands, the women have a stronger claim on their children if they decide to leave their men. It also gives women exclusive rights to a house or any other property they may own.

2. When we look at the culture of poverty on the local community level, we find poor housing conditions, crowding, gregariousness, but above all a minimum of organization beyond the level of the nuclear and extended family. Occasionally there are informal, temporary groupings or voluntary associations within slums. The existence of neighborhood gangs which cut across slum settlements represents a considerable advance beyond the zero point of the continuum that I have in mind. Indeed, it is the low level of organization which gives the culture of poverty its marginal and anachronistic quality in our highly complex, specialized, organized society. Most primitive peoples have achieved a higher level of sociocultural organization than our modern urban slum dwellers.

In spite of the generally low level of organization, there may be a sense of community and *esprit de corps* in urban slums and in slum neighborhoods. This can vary within a single city, or from region to region or country to country. The major factors influencing this variation are the size of the slum, its location and physical characteristics, length of residence, incidence of home and land-ownership (versus squatter rights), rentals, ethnicity, kinship ties, and freedom or lack of freedom of movement. When slums are separated from the surrounding area by enclosing walls or other physical barriers, when rents are low and fixed and stability of residence is great (twenty or thirty years), when the population constitutes a distinct ethnic, racial, or language group, is bound by ties of kinship or *compadrazgo*, and when there are some internal voluntary associations, then the sense of local community approaches that of a village community. In many cases this combination of favorable conditions does not exist. However, even where internal organization and *esprit de corps* is at a bare minimum and people move around a great deal, a sense of territoriality develops which sets off the slum neighborhoods from the rest of the city. In Mexico City and San Juan this sense of territoriality results from the unavailability of low-income housing outside the slum areas. In South Africa the sense of territoriality grows out of the segregation enforced by the government, which confines the rural migrants to specific locations.

3. On the family level the major traits of the culture of poverty are the absence of childhood as a specially prolonged and protected stage in the life cycle, early initiation into sex, free unions or consensual marriages, a relatively high incidence of the abandonment of wives and children, a trend toward female- or mother-centered families and consequently a much greater knowledge of maternal relatives, a strong predisposition to authoritarianism, lack of privacy, verbal emphasis upon family solidarity which is only rarely achieved because of sibling rivalry, and competition for limited goods and maternal affection.

4. On the level of the individual the major characteristics are a strong feeling of marginality, of helplessness, of dependence, and of inferiority. I found this to be true of slum dwellers in Mexico City and San Juan among families who do not constitute a distinct ethnic or racial group and who do not suffer from racial discrimination. In the United States, of course, the culture of poverty of the Negroes has the additional disadvantage of racial discrimination, but as I have already suggested, this additional disadvantage contains a great potential for revolutionary protest and organization which seems to be absent in the slums of Mexico City or among the poor whites in the South.

Other traits include a high incidence of maternal deprivation, of orality, of weak ego structure, confusion of sexual identification, a lack of impulse control, a strong present-time orientation with relatively little ability to defer gratification and to plan for the future, a sense of resignation and fatalism, a widespread belief in male superiority, and a high tolerance for psychological pathology of all sorts.

People with a culture of poverty are provincial and locally oriented and have very little sense of history. They know only their own troubles, their own local conditions, their own neighborhood, their own way of life. Usually they do not have the knowledge, the vision, or the ideology to see the similarities between their problems and those of their counterparts elsewhere in the world. They are not class-conscious, although they are very sensitive indeed to status distinctions.

When the poor become class-conscious or active members of trade-union organizations, or when they adopt an internationalist outlook on the world, they are no longer part of the culture of poverty, although they may still be desperately poor. Any movement, be it religious, pacifist, or revolutionary, which organizes and gives.

hope to the poor and effectively promotes solidarity and a sense of identification with larger groups, destroys the psychological and social core of the culture of poverty. In this connection, I suspect that the civil rights movement among the Negroes in the United States has done more to improve their self-image and self-respect than have their economic advances, although, without doubt, the two are mutually reinforcing.

The distinction between poverty and the culture of poverty is basic to the model described here. There are degrees of poverty and many kinds of poor people. The culture of poverty refers to one way of life shared by poor people in given historical and social contexts. The economic traits which I have listed for the culture of poverty are necessary but not sufficient to define the phenomena I have in mind. There are a number of historical examples of very poor segments of the population which do not have a way of life that I would describe as a subculture of poverty. Here I should like to give four examples:

1. Many of the primitive or preliterate peoples studied by anthropologists suffer from dire poverty which is the result of poor technology and/or poor natural resources, or of both, but they do not have the traits of the subculture of poverty. Indeed, they do not constitute a subculture because their societies are not highly stratified. In spite of their poverty they have a relatively integrated, satisfying, and self-sufficient culture. Even the simplest food-gathering and hunting tribes have a considerable amount of organization, bands and band chiefs, tribal councils and local self-government—traits which are not found in the culture of poverty.

2. In India the lower castes (the Chamars, the leather workers, and the Bhangis, the sweepers) may be desperately poor, both in the villages and in the cities, but most of them are integrated into the larger society and have their own *panchayat* organizations (a formal organization designed to provide caste leadership) which cut across village lines and give them a considerable amount of power. (It may be that in the slums of Calcutta and Bombay an incipient culture of poverty is developing. It would be highly desirable to do family studies there as a crucial test of the culture-of-poverty hypothesis.) . . .

3. The Jews of eastern Europe were very poor,

but they did not have many of the traits of the culture of poverty because of their tradition of literacy, the great value placed upon learning, the organization of the community around the rabbi, the proliferation of local voluntary associations, and their religion which taught that they were the chosen people.

4. My fourth example is speculative and relates to socialism. On the basis of my limited experience in one socialist country—Cuba—and on the basis of my reading, I am inclined to believe that the culture of poverty does not exist in the socialist countries. I first went to Cuba in 1947 as a visiting professor for the State Department. At that time I began a study of a sugar plantation in Melena del Sur and of a slum in Havana. After the Castro Revolution I made my second trip to Cuba as a correspondent for a major magazine, and I revisited the same slum and some of the same families. The physical aspect of the slum had changed very little, except for a beautiful new nursery school. It was clear that the people were still desperately poor, but I found much less of the despair, apathy, and hopelessness which are so diagnostic of urban slums in the culture of poverty. They expressed great confidence in their leaders and hope for a better life in the future. The slum itself was now highly organized, with block committees, educational committees, party committees. The people had a new sense of power and importance. They were armed and were given a doctrine which glorified the lower class as the hope of humanity. (I was told by one Cuban official that they had practically eliminated delinquency by giving arms to the delinquents!)

It is my impression that the Castro regime—unlike Marx and Engels—did not write off the so-called lumpen proletariat as an inherently reactionary and antirevolutionary force, but rather saw its revolutionary potential and tried to utilize it. . . .

I have found very little revolutionary spirit or radical ideology among low-income Puerto Ricans. On the contrary, most of the families I studied were quite conservative politically and about half of them were in favor of the Republican Statehood Party. It seems to me that the revolutionary potential of people with a culture of poverty will vary considerably according to the national context and the particular historical circumstances. In a country like Algeria which was fighting for its independence, the lumpen proletariat was drawn into the struggle and became a vital force. However, in countries like Puerto Rico, in which the movement for independence has very little mass support, and in countries like Mexico which achieved their independence a long time ago and are now in their postrevolutionary period, the lumpen proletariat is not a leading source of rebellion or of revolutionary spirit.

In effect, we find that in primitive societies and in caste societies, the culture of poverty does not develop. In socialist, fascist, and in highly developed capitalist societies with a welfare state, the culture of poverty flourishes in, and is generic to, the early free-enterprise stage of capitalism and that it is also endemic in colonialism.

It is important to distinguish between different profiles in the subculture of poverty depending upon the national context in which these subcultures are found. If we think of the culture of poverty primarily in terms of the factor of integration in the larger society and a sense of identification with the great tradition of that society, or with a new emerging revolutionary tradition, then we will not be surprised that some slum dwellers with a lower per capita income may have moved farther away from the core characteristics of the culture of poverty than others with a higher per capita income. For example, Puerto Rico has a much higher per capita income than Mexico, yet Mexicans have a deeper sense of identity.

I have listed fatalism and a low level of aspiration as one of the key traits for the subculture of poverty. Here too, however, the national context makes a big difference. Certainly the level of aspiration of even the poorest sector of the population in a country like the United States with its traditional ideology of upward mobility and democracy is much higher than in more backward countries like Ecuador and Peru, where both the ideology and the actual possibilities of upward mobility are extremely limited and where authoritarian values still persist in both the urban and rural milieus.

Because of the advanced technology, high level of literacy, the development of mass media, and the relatively high aspiration level of all sectors of the population, especially when compared with underdeveloped nations, I believe that although there is still a great deal of poverty in the United States (estimates range from thirty to fifty million people),

there is relatively little of what I would call the culture of poverty. My rough guess would be that only about 20 percent of the population below the poverty line (between six and ten million people) in the United States have characteristics which would justify classifying their way of life as that of a culture of poverty. Probably the largest sector within this group would consist of very low-income Negroes, Mexicans, Puerto Ricans, American Indians, and Southern poor whites. The relatively small number of people in the United States with a culture of poverty is a positive factor because it is much more difficult to eliminate the culture of poverty than to eliminate poverty *per se*.

Middle-class people, and this would certainly include most social scientists, tend to concentrate on the negative aspects of the culture of poverty. They tend to associate negative valences to such traits as present-time orientation and concrete versus abstract orientation. I do not intend to idealize or romanticize the culture of poverty. As someone has said, "It is easier to praise poverty than to live in it"; yet some of the positive aspects which may flow from these traits must not be overlooked. Living in the present may develop a capacity for spontaneity and adventure, for the enjoyment of the sensual, the indulgence of impulse, which is often blunted in the middle-class, future-oriented man. Perhaps it is this reality of the moment which the existentialist writers are so desperately trying to recapture but which the culture of poverty experiences as natural, everyday phenomena. The frequent use of violence certainly provides a ready outlet for hostility so that people in the culture of poverty suffer less from repression than does the middle class.

In the traditional view, anthropologists have said that culture provides human beings with a design for living, with a ready-made set of solutions for human problems so that individuals don't have to begin all over again each generation. That is, the core of culture is its positive adaptive function. I, too, have called attention to some of the adaptive mechanisms in the culture of poverty—for example, the low aspiration level helps to reduce frustration, the legitimization of short-range hedonism makes possible spontaneity and enjoyment. However, on the whole it seems to me that it is a relatively thin culture. There is a great deal of pathos, suffering, and emptiness among those who live in the culture of poverty. It does not provide much support or long-range satisfaction and its encouragement of mistrust tends to magnify helplessness and isolation. Indeed, the poverty of culture is one of the crucial aspects of the culture of poverty.

The concept of the culture of poverty provides a high level of generalization which, hopefully, will unify and explain a number of phenomena viewed as distinctive characteristics of racial, national, or regional groups. For example, matrifocality, a high incidence of consensual unions, and a high percentage of households headed by women, which have been thought to be distinctive of Caribbean family organization or of Negro family life in the U.S.A., turn out to be traits of the culture of poverty and are found among diverse peoples in many parts of the world and among peoples who have had no history of slavery.

The concept of a cross-societal subculture of poverty enables us to see that many of the problems we think of as distinctively our own or distinctively Negro problems (or that of any other special racial or ethnic group) also exist in countries where there are no distinct ethnic minority groups. This suggests that the elimination of physical poverty *per se* may not be enough to eliminate the culture of poverty which is a whole way of life.

What is the future of the culture of poverty? In considering this question, one must distinguish between those countries in which it represents a relatively small segment of the population and those in which it constitutes a very large one. Obviously the solutions will differ in these two situations. In the United States, the major solution proposed by planners and social workers in dealing with multiple-problem families and the so-called hard core of poverty has been to attempt slowly to raise their level of living and to incorporate them into the middle class. Wherever possible, there has been some reliance upon psychiatric treatment.

In the underdeveloped countries, however, where great masses of people live in the culture of poverty, a social-work solution does not seem feasible. Because of the magnitude of the problem, psychiatrists can hardly begin to cope with it. They have all they can do to care for their own growing middle class. In these countries the people with a culture of poverty may seek a more revolutionary solution. By creating basic structural changes in society, by redistributing wealth, by organizing the poor and giving them a sense of belonging, of power, and of leadership, revolutions frequently succeed in abolishing some of the basic characteristics of the culture of poverty even when they do not succeed in abolishing poverty itself.

Elliot Liebow

Men and Jobs

In the previous selection, Oscar Lewis observed that the poor are aware of middle-class values, frequently talk about them, but do not really act on them. This implies that such values are not internalized and that the larger society does not serve as a referent group for purposes of self-evaluation. It assumes a sharp break between the culture of poverty and the larger cultural context. A further implication of Lewis' position is that deviation from the dominant values of society produces few or no feelings of guilt or failure in the poor.

The ethnographic data and conclusions emerging from Tally's Corner *raise serious questions about Lewis' position. Liebow, who spent a few years as a participant-observer on a ghetto streetcorner, draws a poignant picture of the lives of the men there and shows us how their frustrated hopes have contributed to deep feelings of failure. The portrait that emerges indicates that those involved in the culture of poverty do* internalize *many of the dominant society's values. However, in an almost desperate (but largely unsuccessful) attempt to escape the dire psychological con-*

sequences of their failure, they develop alternative ways of behaving. In other words, it appears that middle-class values do influence these streetcorner men, but the serious disabilities and constraints imposed by their socioeconomic situation produce behavior that is far from middle-class. This chapter of Liebow's book also demonstrates the strengths of the participant-observer technique. With it Liebow gained subtle insights into the motivational factors that underlie behavior and into the culture of those he observed.

A pickup truck drives slowly down the street. The truck stops as it comes abreast of a man sitting on a cast-iron porch and the white driver calls out, asking if the man wants a day's work. The man shakes his head and the truck moves on up the block, stopping again whenever idling men come within calling distance of the driver. At the Carry-out corner, five men debate the question briefly and shake their heads no to the truck. The truck turns the corner and repeats the same performance up the next street. In the distance, one can see one man, then another, climb into the back of the truck and sit down. In starts and stops, the truck finally disappears.

What is it we have witnessed here? A labor scavenger rebuffed by his would-be prey? Lazy, irresponsible men turning down an honest day's pay for an honest day's work? Or a more complex phenomenon marking the intersection of economic forces, social values, and individual states of mind and body?

Let us look again at the driver of the truck. He has been able to recruit only two or three men from each twenty or fifty he contacts. To him, it is clear that the others simply do not choose to work. Singly or in groups, belly-empty or belly-full, sullen or gregarious, drunk or sober, they confirm what he has read, heard, and knows from his own experience: these men wouldn't take a job if it were handed to them on a platter.

Quite apart from the question of whether or not this is true of some of the men he sees on the street, it is clearly not true of all of them. If it were, he would not have come here in the first place; or having come, he would have left with an empty truck. It is not even true of most of them, for most of the men he sees on the street this weekday morning do, in fact, have jobs. But since, at the moment, they are neither working nor sleeping, and since they hate the depressing room or apartment they

live in, or because there is nothing to do there, or because they want to get away from their wives or anyone else living there, they are out on the street, indistinguishable from those who do not have jobs or do not want them. Some, like Boley, a member of a trash-collection crew in a suburban housing development, work Saturdays and are off on this weekday. Some, like Sweets, work nights cleaning up middle-class trash, dirt, dishes, and garbage, and mopping the floors of the office buildings, hotels, restaurants, toilets, and other public places dirtied during the day. Some men work for retail businesses such as liquor stores which do not begin the day until ten o'clock. Some laborers, like Tally, have already come back from the job because the ground was too wet for pick and shovel or because the weather was too cold for pouring concrete. Other employed men stayed off the job today for personal reasons: Clarence to go to a funeral at eleven this morning and Sea Cat to answer a subpoena as a witness in a criminal proceeding.

Also on the street, unwitting contributors to the impression taken away by the truck driver, are the halt and the lame. The man on the cast-iron steps strokes one gnarled arthritic hand with the other and says he doesn't know whether or not he'll live long enough to be eligible for Social Security. He pauses, then adds matter-of-factly, "Most times, I don't care whether I do or don't." Stoopy's left leg was polio-withered in childhood. Raymond, who looks as if he could tear out a fire hydrant, coughs up blood if he bends or moves suddenly. The quiet man who hangs out in front of the Saratoga apartments has a steel hook strapped onto his left elbow. And had the man in the truck been able to look into the wine-clouded eyes of the man in the green cap, he would have realized that the man did not even understand he was being offered a day's work.

Others, having had jobs and been laid off, are drawing unemployment compensation (up to $44 per week) and have nothing to gain by accepting work which pays little more than this and frequently less.

Still others, like Bumdoodle the numbers man, are working hard at illegal ways of making money, hustlers who are on the street to turn a dollar any way they can: buying and selling sex, liquor, narcotics, stolen goods, or anything else that turns up. . . .

And finally, there are those like Arthur, able-bodied men who have no visible means of support, legal or illegal, who neither have jobs nor want them. The truck driver, among others, believes the Arthurs to be representative of all the men he sees idling on the street during his own working hours. They are not, but they cannot be dismissed simply because they are a small minority. It is not enough to explain them away as being lazy or irresponsible or both because an able-bodied man with responsibilities who refuses work is, by the truck driver's definition, lazy and irresponsible. Such an answer begs the question. It is descriptive of the facts; it does not explain them. . . .

In summary of objective job considerations, then, the most important fact is that a man who is able and willing to work cannot earn enough money to support himself, his wife, and one or more children. A man's chances for working regularly are good only if he is willing to work for less than he can live on, and sometimes not even then. On some jobs, the wage rate is deceptively higher than on others, but the higher the wage rate, the more difficult it is to get the job, and the less the job security. Higher-paying construction work tends to be seasonal and, during the season, the amount of work available is highly sensitive to business and weather conditions and to the changing requirements of individual projects. Moreover, high-paying construction jobs are frequently beyond the physical capacity of some of the men, and some of the low-paying jobs are scaled down even lower in accordance with the self-fulfilling assumption that the man will steal part of his wages on the job.

Bernard assesses the objective job situation dispassionately over a cup of coffee, sometimes poking at the coffee with his spoon, sometimes staring at it as if, like a crystal ball, it holds tomorrow's secrets. He is twenty-seven years old. He and the woman with whom he lives have a baby son, and she has another child by another man. Bernard does odd jobs—mostly painting—but here it is the end of January, and his last job was with the Post Office during the Christmas mail rush. He would like postal work as a steady job, he says. It pays well (about $2.00 an hour) but he has twice failed the Post Office examination (he graduated from a Washington high school) and has given up the idea

as an impractical one. He is supposed to see a man tonight about a job as a parking attendant for a large apartment house. The man told him to bring his birth certificate and driver's license, but his license was suspended because of a backlog of unpaid traffic fines. A friend promised to lend him some money this evening. If he gets it, he will pay the fines tomorrow morning and have his license reinstated. He hopes the man with the job will wait till tomorrow night.

A "security job" is what he really wants, he said. He would like to save up money for a taxicab. (But having twice failed the postal examination and having a bad driving record as well, it is highly doubtful that he could meet the qualifications or pass the written test.) That would be "a good life." He can always get a job in a restaurant or as a clerk in a drugstore but they don't pay enough, he said. He needs to take home at least $50 to $55 a week. He thinks he can get that much driving a truck somewhere . . . Sometimes he wishes he had stayed in the army . . . A security job, that's what he wants most of all, a real security job . . .

When we look at what the men bring to the job rather than at what the job offers the men, it is essential to keep in mind that we are not looking at men who come to the job fresh, just out of school perhaps, and newly prepared to undertake the task of making a living, or from another job where they earned a living and are prepared to do the same on this job. Each man comes to the job with a long job history characterized by his not being able to support himself and his family. Each man carries this knowledge, born of his experience, with him. He comes to the job flat and stale, wearied by the sameness of it all, convinced of his own incompetence, terrified of responsibility—of being tested still again and found wanting. Possible exceptions are the younger men not yet, or just, married. They suspect all this but have yet to have it confirmed by repeated personal experience over time. But those who are or have been married know it well. It is the experience of the individual and the group; of their fathers and probably their sons. Convinced of their inadequacies, not only do they not seek out those few better-paying jobs which test their resources, but they actively avoid them, gravitating in a mass to the menial, routine jobs which offer no challenge—and therefore pose no threat—to the already diminished images they have of themselves.

Thus Richard does not follow through on the real estate agent's offer. He is afraid to do on his own—minor plastering, replacing broken windows, other minor repairs, and painting—exactly what he had been doing for months on a piece-work basis under someone else (and which provided him with a solid base from which to derive a cost estimate).

Richard once offered an important clue to what may have gone on in his mind when the job offer was made. We were in the Carry-out, at a time when he was looking for work. He was talking about the kind of jobs available to him.

I graduated from high school [Baltimore] but I don't know anything. I'm dumb. Most of the time I don't even say I graduated, 'cause then somebody asks me a question and I can't answer it, and they think I was lying about graduating.... They graduated me but I didn't know anything. I had lousy grades but I guess they wanted to get rid of me.

I was at Margaret's house the other night and her little sister asked me to help her with her homework. She showed me some fractions and I knew right away I couldn't do them. I was ashamed so I told her I had to go to the bathroom....

Thus, the man's low self-esteem generates a fear of being tested and prevents him from accepting a job with responsibilities or, once on a job, from staying with it if responsibilities are thrust on him, even if the wages are commensurately higher....

Lethargy, disinterest, and general apathy on the job, so often reported by employers, has its streetcorner counterpart. The men do not ordinarily talk about their jobs or ask one another about them. Although most of the men know who is or is not working at any given time, they may or may not know what particular job an individual man has. There is no overt interest in job specifics as they relate to this or that person, in large part perhaps because the specifics are not especially relevant. To know that a man is working is to know approximately how much he makes and to know as much as one needs or wants to know about how he makes it. After all, how much difference does it make to know whether a man is pushing a mop and pulling trash in an apartment house, a restaurant, or an office building, or delivering groceries, drugs, or liquor, or, if he's a laborer, whether he's pushing a wheelborrow, mixing mortar, or digging a hole....

A crucial factor in the streetcorner man's lack of job commitment is the overall value he places on the job. *For his part, the streetcorner man puts no lower value on the job than does the larger society around him.* He knows the social value of the job by the amount of money the employer is willing to pay him for doing it. In a real sense, every pay day, he counts in dollars and cents the value placed on the job by society at large. He is no more (and frequently less) ready to quit and look for another job than his employer is ready to fire him and look for another man. Neither the streetcorner man who performs these jobs nor the society which requires him to perform them assesses the job as one "worth doing and worth doing well." Both employee and employer are contemptuous of the job. The employee shows his contempt by his reluctance to accept it or keep it, the employer by paying less than is required to support a family. Nor does the low-wage job offer prestige, respect, interesting work, opportunity for learning or advancement, or any other compensation. With few exceptions, jobs filled by the streetcorner men are at the bottom of the employment ladder in every respect, from wage level to prestige. Typically, they are hard, dirty, uninteresting, and underpaid. The rest of society (whatever its ideal values regarding the dignity of labor) holds the job of the dishwasher or janitor or unskilled laborer in low esteem if not outright contempt. So does the streetcorner man. He cannot do otherwise. He cannot draw from a job those social values which other people do not put into it.

Only occasionally does spontaneous conversation touch on these matters directly. Talk about jobs is usually limited to isolated statements of intention, such as "I think I'll get me another gig [job]," "I'm going to look for a construction job when the weather breaks," or "I'm going to quit. I can't take no more of his shit." Job assessments typically consist of nothing more than a noncommittal shrug and "It's O.K." or "It's a job."

One reason for the relative absence of talk about one's job is, as suggested earlier, that the sameness of job experiences does not bear reiteration. Another and more important reason is the emptiness of the job experience itself. The man sees middle-class occupations as a primary source of prestige, pride, and self-respect; his own job affords him none of these. To think about his job is to see himself as others see him, to remind him of just where he stands in this society. And because society's criteria for placement are generally the same as his own, to talk about his job can trigger a flush of shame and a deep, almost physical ache to change places with someone, almost anyone, else. The desire to be a person in his own right, to be noticed by the world he lives in, is shared by each of the men on the streetcorner. Whether they articulate this desire (as Tally does below) or not, one can see them position themselves to catch the attention of their fellows in much the same way as plants bend or stretch to catch the sunlight.

Tally and I were in the Carry-out. It was summer, Tally's peak earning season as a cement finisher, a semiskilled job a cut or so above that of the unskilled laborer. His take-home pay during these weeks was well over a hundred dollars—"a lot of bread." But for Tally, who no longer had a family to support, bread was not enough.

"You know that boy came in last night? That Black Moozlem? That's what I ought to be doing. I ought to be in his place."

"What do you mean?"

"Dressed nice, going to [night] school, got a good job."

"He's no better off than you, Tally. You make more than he does."

"It's not the money. [Pause] It's position, I guess. He's got position. When he finish school he gonna be a supervisor. People respect him. . . . Thinking about people with position and education gives me a feeling right here [pressing his fingers into the pit of his stomach]." . . .

The streetcorner man wants to be a person in his own right, to be noticed, to be taken account of, but in this respect, as well as in meeting his money needs, his job fails him. The job and the man are even. The job fails the man and the man fails the job.

Furthermore, the man does not have any reasonable expectation that, however bad it is, his job will lead to better things. Menial jobs are not, by and large, the starting point of a track system which leads to even better jobs for those who are able and willing to do them. The busboy or dishwasher in a restaurant is not on a job track which, if negotiated skillfully, leads to chef or manager of the restaurant. The busboy or dishwasher who works hard becomes, simply, a hard-working busboy or dishwasher. Neither hard work nor perseverance can

conceivably carry the janitor to a sit-down job in the office building he cleans up. And it is the apprentice who becomes the journeyman electrician, plumber, steam fitter, or bricklayer, not the common unskilled Negro laborer.

Thus, the job is not a stepping stone to something better. It is a dead end. It promises to deliver no more tomorrow, next month, or next year than it does today.

Delivering little, and promising no more, the job is "no big thing." The man appears to treat the job in a cavalier fashion, working and not working as the spirit moves him, as if all that matters is the immediate satisfaction of his present appetites, the surrender to present moods, and the indulgence of whims with no thought for the cost, the consequences, the future. To the middle-class observer, this behavior reflects a "present-time orientation"—an "inability to defer gratification." It is this "present-time" orientation—as against the "future orientation" of the middle-class person—that "explains" to the outsider why Leroy chooses to spend the day at the Carry-out rather than report to work; why Richard, who was paid Friday, was drunk Saturday and Sunday and penniless Monday; why Sweets quit his job today because the boss looked at him "funny" yesterday.

But from the inside looking out, what appears as a "present-time" orientation to the outside observer is, to the man experiencing it, as much a future orientation as that of his middle-class counterpart. The difference between the two men lies not so much in their different orientations to time as in their different orientations to future time or, more specifically, to their different futures.

The future orientation of the middle-class person presumes, among other things, a surplus of resources to be invested in the future and a belief that the future will be sufficiently stable both to justify his investment (money in a bank, time and effort in a job, investment of himself in marriage and family, etc.) and to permit the consumption of his investment at a time, place, and manner of his own choosing and to his greater satisfaction. But the streetcorner man lives in a sea of want. He does not, as a rule, have a surplus of resources, either economic or psychological. Gratification of hunger and the desire for simple creature comforts cannot be long deferred. Neither can support for one's flagging self-esteem. Living on the edge of both economic and psychological subsistence, the streetcorner man is obliged to expend all his resources on maintaining himself from moment to moment.

As for the future, the young streetcorner man has a fairly good picture of it. In Richard or Sea Cat or Arthur he can see himself in his middle twenties; he can look at Tally to see himself at thirty, at Wee Tom to see himself in his middle thirties, and at Budder and Stanton to see himself in his forties. It is a future in which everything is uncertain except the ultimate destruction of his hopes and the eventual realization of his fears. The most he can reasonably look forward to is that these things do not come too soon. Thus, when Richard squanders a week's pay in two days it is not because, like an animal or a child, he is "present-time oriented," unaware of or unconcerned with his future. He does so precisely because he is aware of the future and the hopelessness of it all.

Sometimes this kind of response appears as a conscious, explicit choice. Richard had had a violent argument with his wife. He said he was going to leave her and the children, that he had had enough of everything and could not take any more, and he chased her out of the house. His chest still heaving, he leaned back against the wall in the hallway of his basement apartment.

"I've been scuffling for five years," he said. "I've been scuffling for five years from morning till night. And my kids still don't have anything, my wife don't have anything, and I don't have anything.

"There," he said, gesturing down the hall to a bed, a sofa, a couple of chairs and a television set, all shabby, some broken. "There's everything I have and I'm having trouble holding onto that."

Leroy came in, presumably to petition Richard on behalf of Richard's wife, who was sitting outside on the steps, afraid to come in. Leroy started to say something but Richard cut him short.

"Look, Leroy, don't give me any of that action. You and me are entirely different people. Maybe I look like a boy and maybe I act like a boy sometimes but I got a man's mind. You and me don't want the same things out of life. Maybe some of the same, but you don't care how long you have to wait for yours and I—want—mine—right—now."

Thus, apparent present-time concerns with consumption and indulgences—material and emotional—reflect a future-time orientation. "I want mine right now" is ultimately a cry of despair, a direct response to the future as he sees it.

Bernard J. James

Social-Psychological Dimensions of Ojibwa Acculturation

The American Indians are one of the most deprived groups in the United States. Their situation is not only one of severe material deprivation; they also suffer what might be called "cultural attenuation."

For a long time, anthropologists and others in contact with the American Indian have argued about the culture of the reservation. Those who believe that the Indian is part of our "cultural pluralism" attempt to understand and explain reservation life and behavior in terms of the perpetuation of aboriginal Indian patterns. One recent government document describes reservations as "a natural way of life, unhurried and undemanding. The competition and bustle of urban society is foreign to tribal customs." Other observers of the same scene hold that Indian culture (as a relatively unique system of functioning social institutions and shared values) can no longer be said to exist. Instead, they see grinding rural poverty with "shades and flavors" of an Indian past. They hold that the romanticizing of reservation life, seeing it as a way of sustaining and even developing Indian culture, merely serves as a rationalization for the continuance of a dehumanizing and dismal poverty.

James, the author of the following article on the

Ojibwa, believes that one cannot understand life on the reservation without an appreciation of "the co-dependent nature of subcultural [Indian] and White institutions." The Indians on the reservation, like the blacks on Tally's Corner, form a negative view of themselves which then provides the social context in which they live and within which they interact with the dominant white society. James views their behavior as an outgrowth of this accommodation to white institutions and attitudes, and not as significantly continuous with an Indian past. In this light, the reservation system is seen to provide white society with a convenient way of dealing with an historically important ethnic minority. But that minority lives in poverty, and in a situation which offers little or no impetus for the development of cultural integrity. In fact, the American Indian's "culture of poverty" is rooted in the reservation system and will last as long as this dependent way of life is perpetuated.

The interpretation of Ojibwa acculturation presented here is an attempt to relate culture to personality through four conceptual levels: institutional patterns that characterize the reservation as a subculture within American culture, role patterns that permit us to identify specific points of conflict between the subculture and its environment, the Indian self-image, and individual response to the contemporary situation in psychological terms. I have attempted to relate factors hitherto more or less ignored in culture-personality studies of the Ojibwa—such as income, public assistance dependency, drinking, and racial prejudice—to the present social-psychological adjustment of the Indian. . . .

A Contemporary Ojibwa Community as a Subculture

The Ojibwa community of Deerpoint is a small village on the Lac Court Oreilles reservation in northern Wisconsin. It has a population registered on tribal rolls as 113 females and 148 males. It is located among numerous lakes which are surrounded by second growth aspen, spruce, pine, and upland hardwood. Fauna include large game such as deer and black bear, though they are kept reduced to scant numbers by over-hunting, and small animals such as fox, rabbit, mink, and game birds. Soils in the area are poor; about 65 percent is

sand or peat unsuitable for ordinary agriculture, the rest is sandy loam.

The village was one of the Ojibwa communities on the reservation that had to be relocated in 1922 with the development of a Chippewa River hydro-electric reservoir. Of 39 dwellings in the village, 10 are log houses, 4 are lapboard and tarpaper structures, and 25 are frame siding buildings in various states of repair. Nine are wired for electric power. Interiors vary; the better frame homes have the usual contemporary furnishings—sofas, upholstered chairs, electric appliances, and such, while the tarpaper and log houses are mostly one- or two-room affairs with rickety furniture, wrought-iron bedsteads, and kerosene-lamp lighting. Heating methods range from automatic gas and oil stoves in a few homes to homemade, oil-drum wood-stoves in others.

Communication between Deerpoint and the outside world is relatively poor. The village has but one telephone, located in the irregularly occupied policeman's house. Only the homes with electricity have dependable radios (television began to reach the village in 1953). Highway traffic flowed through the village in 1951 at about half the rate for the nearest Indian community and a quarter of the rate for the nearest White community. The road through the village was blacktopped in 1953, however, and this has increased traffic since. The community owned ten automobiles, four of which were reliable the year around.

Deerpoint's economy, like that of the reservation generally, is a jerry-built system comprising wage labor, large amounts of public assistance, small amounts of gathering and trapping for commercial purposes, and some business enterprise. Village food supply is supplemented by some hunting, fishing, and gathering, though all three have declined in importance during recent years, and, contrary to what is generally assumed about the Indian "living off of nature," are not of major significance to the life of the village. . . .

Clothing is of the inexpensive type—blue denim, cottons, work-clothes; occasionally more is spent for a quality coat or pair of boots. Clothes are also received through charity or church-sponsored

"Social-Psychological Dimensions of Ojibwa Acculturation" by Bernard J. James. Reproduced by permission of the American Anthropological Association from *American Anthropologist*, Vol. 63, No. 4, (1961).

rummage sales in which, for example, a pair of pants will sell for 50¢.

Several points are clear, I believe, in such data as these. One is that as far as economic criteria are concerned, Deerpoint is a "lower class" community. Another is that most of the earned income of the village comes from work for White employers off the reservation. Such employment is an outreach of White institutions. It is especially important to the social psychology of the community because it continually exposes the Ojibwa to the values and expectations that mediate the relationship of the reservation and its environment.

The latter point is vital and is underscored by data on geographic mobility. There is continuous movement of people leaving and returning to the reservation and there is constant spill-over and assimilation of part of the population into the White culture. Not only are the Ojibwa now living in relatively compact permanent villages, in contrast to aboriginal and contact times, but seasonal movement does not isolate the individual or the family from social contact as it formerly did; it intensifies social relations. . . .

The subcultural status of Deerpoint is reflected in its institutional life. In 1951 and 1952, formal organizational activity in the village was confined entirely to school and mission affairs. The grade school, a new structure with a large gymnasium, enrolled about 60 Indian children in eight elementary grades and employed two White teachers, a White janitor, and an Indian bus driver. The school board was entirely White. . . .

The Catholic Mission's influence in Deerpoint is older and more pervasive than that of the school, but its impact is more economic than religious. Although villagers refer to the community as "all Catholic" (only four adults are reportedly unbaptized), only about 25 village adults, two-thirds women, attend Sunday services regularly. . . .

Two small Indian-owned businesses operated in Deerpoint in 1952. One was a small summer concession that handled ice cream, soft drinks, bread, and some canned goods; the other was a resort establishment that rented six cottages sporadically during the summer and two to teachers during the school year. Compared to more expensive and elaborate resorts in the area, this was a modest operation and had limited economic impact on the village.

The wages paid to village lumberjacks for work in village-owned timber tracts, plus wages drawn for work in tribally-owned reservation cranberry bogs, represent the only remaining Indian business activities that affect the village. . . .

[A]s far as the loss of Ojibwa culture traits is concerned, the village has become deculturated and . . . its minimal appropriation of new culture traits has produced a "poor White" type of subculture in which the conservative-progressive distinction actually operates as a socioeconomic class line. A "poor" family tends to be considered "Indian" in cultural orientation regardless of the loss of Ojibwa cultural habits or techniques.

The point is illustrated by the so-called "Indian custom" marriage. There are sixteen such arrangements in the village. They are casual and permissive, much as was aboriginal "marriage." But it is apparent among young people who know and care little about the old tribal way of life that a liaison may be called "Indian custom" for convenience only, when financial assistance via federal revolving funds are sought, for example. But young people recognize the rationalization involved and also refer to such cohabitation as merely a "shack up."

The subcultural nature of such relations is reiterated when children are born and separation occurs. Such children are not cared for through any indigenous institution comparable to the primitive adoption system. On the contrary, they are supported via Aid to Dependent Children, a form of public assistance to Deerpoint that amounted to slightly more than $7,000 in 1952, nearly half of the public aid received by the village.

The extent to which such ADC abets the frequency of abandonment cannot be easily determined. Public welfare administrators in reservation areas insist that it is a definite contributory factor. In any case, "Indian custom" marriage can no longer be understood merely as a persistent aboriginal trait. Its meaning can only be established by placing it within the modern reservation setting.

Role Conflict in Reservation Subculture

The interaction of the Ojibwa reservation subculture and its environment can be brought into finer focus by examination of several interdependent role patterns in Deerpoint. Each such general role pattern can be conceived, in turn, as a cluster of specific roles.

Economic roles. The necessity of making a living

confronts the adult male in Deerpoint with a variety of role alternatives. If he decides to conform, for whatever reason, to the expectations of local White economic values, he will seek to establish a reputation as a reliable worker, eschewing at the same time the appeal of contradictory native economic pursuits such as "making rice." . . .

Such an individual will avoid job-hopping as much as possible and will prefer steady employment at low wages to itinerant labor or guiding for higher but irregular wages. He will use his income to equip his home with modern appliances, dress his family in conformity to local White standards. Except for his racial identity he may be indistinguishable from local White laborers.

Contrary values define several distinct, but often co-dependent, subcultural economic roles. One is that of the "welfare dependent"; the other is the culturally conservative hunting-gathering role. Typically, the welfare-dependent person does not view public assistance as a temporary form of support but views it as a permanent feature of the reservation situation. He will seek such assistance ("You just go to the [county welfare office] and stand in line.") in the firm conviction that "the government should do something for the Indian." . . .

The hunting-gathering role is similarly tied into attitudes toward the reservation as a refuge, a place where the Indian "at least has his rights." In fact, efforts to play this role in spite of the fact that game and wild foods have been substantially depleted in recent decades indicate very pointedly the force of such beliefs. . . .

Political-legal and civic roles. The political and legal peculiarities of the Ojibwa reservation subculture illustrate the tangle of contradictory expectations that define various civic roles and, in turn, involve various economic and social behavior. . . .

Lac Court Oreilles, originally 69,136 acres, had lost 14,437 acres by 1951 and the reservation was a checkerboard of Indian and White ownership. Deer can be shot out-of-season on White-owned tracts, dragged to a reservation tract to be butchered, then sold illicitly back to Whites. Muskellunge and pike can be speared by the Indians at any time on one end of Lake Chippewa while it is illegal to do so at the other end. Before the repeal of prohibition laws in 1953, White-owned taverns located on alienated tracts sold beer to the Indians in great volume and efforts by reservation authori-

ties to keep the Ojibwa "dry" were comically ineffectual.

The fact that reservation Indians do not pay property taxes adds a further complication to the role of "public spirited citizen." Local Whites complain that they have to "carry" the Indians, pay for their schools, supply large amounts of relief, etc. These attitudes heighten White hostility and prejudice and simultaneously reinforce the Indian's resentment.

Ambiguities and jurisdictional complications of the present legal and administrative status of the reservation frustrate any effort of the Indian to take the role of "equal" or "well informed" citizen. Two individuals in Deerpoint who professed to have made strenuous efforts in the past to "do something for the Indian," one in school district affairs, the other in tribal business committee activity, retreated into cynical indifference as soon as they confronted the myriad complications of their reservation status. ("That Tribal Business Committee is just a rubber stamp.")

Religious role. I have already indicated that native Ojibwa religious beliefs had almost disappeared from Deerpoint by 1951. Six "conservative" households retained remnants of the old interpretation of the supernatural and from them I obtained accounts of the use of "bad medicine" and violated taboos about ten years earlier. And one man in the village occasionally participated in sacred drum ceremonies still held in a small community on the other end of the reservation. But such aboriginal religious elements survived as dislocated bits and pieces of the old way of life and were frequently ridiculed in the village, often within the same family that perpetuated them. In any case, the religious role of "pagan" has disintegrated, except where it has assumed a romantic mutant form under the influence of White commercialism.

The role of Catholic believer, on the other hand, is relatively well-defined in the village and a few individuals meet its expectations rather fully, participating in sacraments weekly, and so on. But the role is beset with disintegrating influences. Parents may, for example, actively encourage their children to become altar boys, to sing in the mission choir, or study for the Holy Orders (three girls from the village have become nuns). But the same parents may plunge weekly into drunken "powwows," during which cursing, violence, vulgarity, and sexual license occur, behavior wholly contradicting that of the "good Catholic" role.

The mission itself is sometimes victim of startling displays of areligiosity. During recent years, for example, a band of carousing villagers broke into the church and its tabernacle in search of wine. The aisles of the building were left littered with beer cans. While such sacrilegious outbursts shock the community, there is no clear evidence that they are triggered by hostile feelings toward the mission. They seem to be the result simply of the lust for drink. The areligious tone of community life is underscored by the complete neglect of the mission cemetery, in contrast to the concern shown for both aboriginal burial sites and local White Catholic cemeteries. Deerpoint's areligiosity is additional evidence of the deculturation that is peculiar to the reservation subculture.

Status and Self-Image

Although values intrude on the reservation ·in a pell-mell and discordant manner, they assume integrated form in several stereotypic images of the Indian. The most obvious of these is a negative stereotype of the Indian as a status inferior, a person who is considered by local Whites to be "dirty," "drunken," "lazy," and "immoral." A counter stereotype of the romantic "Indian" can also be identified. To local Whites he is the "old time," that is, dead Indian who "never lied," "always provided for his family," and so forth; to tourists he is the "Indian" who knows the mysteries of nature, can predict weather months ahead by behavior of birds, has colorful ceremonies, and so on. These stereotypes are crucial to Ojibwa acculturation because they are projected into the vacuum produced by the destruction of aboriginal institutions and they now dominate the reservation's accommodation to its environment.

Unlike the romantic stereotype, the negative stereotype has its roots in the vital empirical referents of existing subcultural conditions. It is the only viable system of values, in fact, mediating the relationship of Indian social life and the dominant culture. As a measure of the status differential that separates the Ojibwa from White culture it is actually an inverted definition of the behavioral change required by assimilation.

The negative stereotype is not simply a product of White imagination or bigotry. It is a White judgment, motivated by White values, concerning White experience with reservation Indians. (For that reason, too, it cannot be exorcized simply by appeals to brotherhood.) The notion that the Indian is "dirty," for example, is based upon White experience with Indian dress, housing, hygiene, disease (especially tuberculosis and venereal infection), and sexual conduct. The relative "inferiority" of the Indian to local Whites can be noted in each instance.

In Deerpoint, for instance, only about six sewing and washing machines operated in 1951; only five of twelve pumps were usable; regular bathing was exceptional. The outdoor privy was the only sanitary facility, and most were filthy and dilapidated. Two-thirds of the village's homes needed repair; all but three frame buildings had lost their paint and were badly weathered. In spite of transportation difficulties, villagers were hospitalized about twice as frequently as Whites. . . . During the '40's, there were reportedly 20 cases of syphillis and 19 of gonorrhea in the community. During 1952, at least 90 percent of the adults had serious dental infections, many with associated rheumatic infections of the joints. During that same period the grade school was closed twice while children infected with lice were treated. . . . From 1931 to 1941, the tuberculosis mortality rate for Wisconsin Indians generally was eight times as high as the total U.S. population's. . . .

The "drunken" element of the stereotype has parallel empirical components. I estimate that the average household monthly expenditure for beer in the village was about $15 and that some families consume half of their cash income for beer and wine. A "powwow" of four or five adults may consume $40 worth of beer in a single week-end. While such rates of alcoholic consumption may not be unusually high in comparison to that of some White homes in the reservation area, it inevitably works a severe hardship on many Indian families, especially when it affects care of children, diet, clothing, and the necessities of life.

As far as the stereotype is concerned, however, it is important to note that Indian drinking is highly visible. Even such humorous features of the stereotype as the claim that "all you need to do to find their towns is to drive onto the reservation and follow the beer cans" has an empirical element. It was possible in 1952 to count from a moving vehicle over three hundred discarded beer cartons per mile (discounting those obscured by grass and undergrowth) on some stretches of reservation road. I observed nothing comparable near local White communities. . . .

Other aspects of the negative stereotype can be examined in parallel fashion. The belief that the Indian is "lazy" relates to White work ethics, to public assistance dependency, to absenteeism and apathy.

The Wisconsin Governor's Commission on Human Rights reports that in 1950 29.5 percent of the Indians of the state required public assistance as compared with 3.9 percent of the Whites. In Sawyer County, Deerpoint's location, the percentage of Indian population receiving public assistance was about twice that of the non-Indian population.

Though absenteeism is frequently cited by Whites as a problem in retaining Indian workmen, it is a factor difficult to study in a controlled fashion outside an industrial situation. My data are anecdotal, such comments as, "You hire them and they do good work. But just when you need them most they don't show up." . . .

The decline of Indian use of reservation agricultural potential also contributes to the belief by Whites that he is "lazy." All but one of the Lac Court Oreilles's approximately 15 small farms that operated during the '20s and '30s have disappeared. Likewise, household gardens, once common, have almost disappeared. . . .

With the decline of gardening, the canning of vegetables also ceased, a valuable support to village diet was lost, and the notion that the Indian refuses to "help himself" reinforced in yet another way.

The Indian is judged "immoral" for reasons that have been discussed above. Sexual conduct is permissive by local White standards (actual White behavior is another matter) and the frequency of illegitimate births (as well as venereal infection) contribute to this component of the stereotype. Aid to Dependent Children accounts for about 40 percent of the public assistance to Deerpoint. To local Whites, such aid connotes both "immorality" and "laziness."

Several principles concerning the development of Indian personality and contemporary behavior can be derived from an examination of the functions of the negative stereotype. It heightens the visibility of status "inferiority," simultaneously generating a desire to escape it. To assimilate, the individual must be "clean," "moderate," "ambitious," and "moral," the converse of the negative stereotype of the Indian. . . .

Movement into White culture is blocked or slowed, however, by powerful forces working against it. Economic and social dependency, real and imaginary "rights," the strong appeal of "land of our own," are several countervailing factors. But racial visibility is perhaps the most significant single barrier to assimilation. The negative connotations that words like "black" and "smokey" have on the reservations, the pecking-order attitude of the Indian toward the Negro, and the manner in which racial concerns boil to the surface during intoxication, all attest to the importance of this dimension of status inferiority. This element of the stereotype is enormously important because it anchors such "inferiority" in the biology of the individual, beyond his control. It thereby blocks adjustment to the very forces that generate the desire to escape subcultural status.

If efforts to assimilate are blocked, either by the rewards for maintaining subcultural affiliation ("rights," public assistance dependency, etc.), or by the punishment of Indian racial visibility, the individual finds himself in an impasse. To the extent that he accepts the values of White culture and defines his goals in terms of them—as inevitably he must to participate successfully in the roles that constitute the subcultural extension of White institutions, he is forced to admit the validity of the stereotype. He is pressed to internalize the negative stereotype as a self-image, to conclude that he is in fact an "inferior" person. . . .

The tortured, devious, and ambivalent responses of the Ojibwa to the subcultural predicament are evidence that the genesis of the modern Indian self lies in the social processes that constitute reservation life, in exactly the sense that George Herbert Mead, in his classic studies, identified the origins of "self." Contemporary personality is an isomorphic psychological version of the contemporary social situation in which it develops.

Contemporary Patterns of Indian Response

Once the outlines of the contemporary reservation situation have been drawn, I believe a good deal of the behavior of the Ojibwa becomes understandable. We can identify contemporary forms of anxiety and its causes. We can indicate . . . the consequences of conflict between culturally induced goals and the means for achieving them. We can also indicate how the Indian seeks to conform to, get around, withdraw from, overwhelm, or escape the predicament he is in.

Anxiety. The anxiety that casts its shadow across the entire gamut of Ojibwa behavior is a product of both the physical deprivations that attend reservation experience ... as well as the conflicts and uncertainties that characterize status inferiority....

In Deerpoint, for example, the ancestral fear of sorcery has been replaced by new, though equally imperious, fears. Threats of an old villager in 1952 to use "bad medicine" on a neighbor were laughed off. But when a village malcontent complained to the government agent about insults of a neighbor, the agent's assurance that he would "keep an eye on the fellow" was quickly dramatized in the community to, "He's being watched. They're watching him."

These anxieties are also involved in the perpetual concern of the Ojibwa about the loss of "Indian hunting and fishing rights," "rights" that are, as I suggested earlier, of less economic than symbolic significance.... But suspicion of "the government" has been generalized and has taken on some of the connotations once reserved for fear of sorcerers. Fear of "papers" and strangers illustrate.

Generalized anxiety is also reflected in the frequency of Indian emotion during drinking, as well as in the indiscriminate nature of drunken hostility. It likewise seems to produce unpredictable little breaches of the status relationship with Whites, a sudden remark by a very deferent guide, for instance, when asked by his White employer to wash out boats: "We shouldn't be your slaves. You should be our slaves!" ...

Assimilation and its barriers. Adult Ojibwa often display clear evidence of their desire to conform to the implied demands of the stereotype....

I had frequent contact in 1951 and 1952 with a dark-skinned, half-breed, middle-aged Ojibwa who lived with an "Indian custom" wife and family and supported his household by odd-jobs, guiding, itinerant labor, logging, and relief. Known as a very "touchy" person he seemed particularly preoccupied with the racial aspects of status inferiority. When "kidded" about his "suntanned neck" by a local White resorter he replied in cold anger, "I may be black on the outside, but I'm White on the inside and that's more than you can say.". . .

Whether or not an individual can conform to White expectations sufficiently to "cross" depends upon his racial visibility, his work habits, and his general cultural affiliation. But under local conditions he must not look "Indian." If he is light-skinned and his dress and mien do not betray him he can assimilate locally. . . .

For most persons, however, such assimilation within the local situation is difficult, if not impossible. For dark-skinned individuals it may be necessary to leave the reservation and attempt to "cross" as a member of an urban minority. Such a course is difficult to follow. Racial visibility may force the individual to identify with minorities as unfavorably placed in the status pecking-order as the Indian. One informant, for example, on one of his few visits to the reservation after having moved to Chicago six years earlier, told me that in the city he was "treated like a nigger" and denied promotions on that account. He attempted, in turn, to avoid telling his son that they were Indian until the boy reached school age and raised questions about his race.

Such thwarted efforts to assimilate increase Indian anxiety toward life away from the reservation and enhance the appeal of the reservation as "land of our own." The consequent increased ambivalence stimulates movement back and forth from city to reservation with further intensification of economic maladjustment....

Drinking. The most frequent cause of loss of emotional control among the Ojibwa is intoxication. During drinking bouts violence may erupt, blunt and bellicose behavior may transform a placid and diffident individual into a crucible of hostility. All the murders that occurred on Lac Court Oreilles during two decades prior to 1952 (reportedly six in number) involved use of alcohol. According to State of Wisconsin Department of Public Welfare data 14 times more Indians than Whites per thousand population come from time to time under jurisdiction of state parole and probation officers, a heavy percentage of such cases involving beatings, disorderly conduct, and threats of bodily harm during drinking.

The violence of the Ojibwa during drinking bouts is by no means a new phenomenon [and has often] precipitated fighting, beatings, and killings. . . . Intoxicated individuals are extremely sensitive and it is a reservation social rule-of-thumb that when a drinking Ojibwa "looks for trouble" he finds it, whether or not he can find someone against whom he carries a grudge. Nevertheless, Ojibwa drinking is almost invariably a social affair. A "powwow" is, in fact, virtually an institutionalized consequence of pay day or "pension day" (when public assistance aid is received). The social function of such drinking is indicated not only by the fact that the obsessional solitary drinker is uncommon but by the fact that volume intoxicants like beer and wine are preferred to concentrated liquors such as whiskey and gin. The social nature of drunkenness on the reservation is also indicated by the actual "content" of the drinking bout. During such affairs, loud talk, shouting, boasting, and vulgar language erupt, a great deal of which concern status "inferiority":

I can get anything I want at that tavern. My name is good anywhere I go!

When (the reservation police man) caught me with that beer, I told him right to his face. "Goddamn you. You got some too, you and that girl of yours." I told him right to his face too....

My data are not sufficiently extensive or precise to prove the point, but the way in which alcohol acts to reduce the sense of isolation and to permit the ventilation of anxieties, would seem to illustrate the connection noted by Horton between excessive drinking and culturally induced anxieties. The striking fact, too, that some Ojibwa seem to get drunk on but a single bottle of beer, when they are neither physically run down nor empty-stomached, suggests that a definite set of expectations is involved in the reservation subculture's definition of a drinking situation. Such pseudo-intoxication helps explain the appearance of truculence and boasting before technical intoxication seems reasonable. It would also explain why many individuals are capable of staying "drunk" for several days on a very limited supply of alcohol. The reinforcement that such pseudo-intoxication provides both for the negative stereotype and the "drunken" element of the "inferior Indian" self-image is further evidence of the interdependence of social and psychological forces on Ojibwa reservations.

The Romantic Response. The Ojibwa's use of a romantic Indian stereotype to counter the negative stereotype of his inferiority is a sufficiently important Indian response to contemporary reservation life to deserve special comment. The romantic counterimage is maintained only because it is shared by both Indians and Whites, because it

functions as a dimension of the status differential between the reservation and its environment. This accounts for much of the appeal of such occupations as guiding, dancing for tourists, and bead work. Thus, a woman that manufactures bead strips for White manufacturers will insist that "Those are Indian designs and we think them up and we ought to get credit for them"—"credit," that is, via White cultural rewards. Authentic Ojibwa bead art has long since been replaced by commercial work whose design is dictated by drugstore canons of taste. The fact [is] that most Wisconsin Ojibwa have no better idea of what native arts constitute than do local Whites....

Broader Implications of the Analysis

Space limitations do not permit me to explore many of the broader theoretical implications of the analysis presented, but I believe the approach outlined points to resolution of several outstanding difficulties. By treating personality as an isomorphic version of social process, after the manner of George Mead, it is possible to describe Ojibwa acculturation through consecutive conceptual levels: self, role, and institution, without positing any disjunction between culture and personality. A reservation acculturation model can thus be defined. Its lineaments would include: (1) the codependent nature of subcultural and White institutions, (2) the relative integration of component role systems in each, (3) the nature of values that operate between the reservations and their environment, and (4) the formation of self as a miniaturized version of the processes that characterize value conflict and accommodation on the reservations....

A cross-reservation application of the analysis suggested has significant implications for such phenomena as "pan-Indianism." Syncretism and survival of various tribal artistic remnants, for example, appears to be the consequence of common subcultural responses to status inferiority rather than the result of any natural affinity of persistent native traits. The Indian appropriates romantic "Indian" roles, in dance, music, or beadwork, because such roles counter stereotypic inferiority, because, that is, they are sustained by romantic values shared by Indians and Whites. The key to pan-Indianism, in other words, appears to lie in social relations between Indians and Whites rather than in relations between tribes.

Policy implications for the conduct of American reservations flow from the interpretation of the Indian subculture I have advanced. I cannot explore these here. But if it is correct to conclude that native cultures have been replaced by reservation subcultures of a "poor-White" type, and an essential functional requirement for their existence, as we know them, is an extreme socioeconomic status differential, prescriptions that attempt to perpetuate this "Indian way of life" may be both unwise and inhumane.

Seymour Parker and Robert J. Kleiner

The Culture of Poverty: An Adjustive Dimension

The "Moynihan controversy" concerning the existence of a subculture of poverty among the poor blacks has been marked by polar positions. There are those who feel that much of the "deviant" behavior of this group is actually "normal" within its context and that it is socially transmitted as a facet of both personality and culture. Others maintain that such behavior is merely an overt behavioral response to extreme poverty and other forms of deprivation. The data in the paper that follows, derived from structured interviews with a large sample of the black population of Philadelphia, indicate that those living in poverty do have some of the attitudes that have been associated with a "subculture of poverty." On the other hand, the data also suggest that such attitudes are but one segment of the group's total range of attitudes and reference values, many of which are shared by the larger society. Further, the evidence indicates that these attitudes may serve to maintain the mental health of a severely disadvantaged people. Thus the findings lend support to an idea found in previous selections on the "culture of poverty," since most of our authors have maintained that the poor have, simultaneously, two sets of values and attitudes: one shared with the larger society, and another set of subcultural "secondary" values which develop in response to the social situation of the poor and help them make the necessary psychological adjustments.

Data are needed before evaluations can be made of potential changes in the poor and strategies for effecting that change. For example, we need to know more about the nature and range of these secondary values, their social and psychological functions, whether or not they are significantly related to the ability of the poor to avail themselves of existing opportunities for betterment, the forces that serve to perpetuate them, and the strength with which they are held. The findings presented here confirm the idea of alternative sets of values among the poor, some of which have important adjustive functions, as we have already said. Nevertheless, they do not constitute a successful buffer against a sense of deprivation and failure. The authors conclude that the subjective values of the subculture will not change significantly until the objective deprivations are removed and a condition of actual equality, and not merely "equal opportunity," is approached.

In the work of social scientists who have used the participant-observer method to study poverty, two conclusions consistently emerge: first that "secondary" values and attitudes of the poor are held concomitantly with (not in lieu of) those shared with the larger society, and secondly that these secondary attitudes are psychologically adjustive.

"The Culture of Poverty" by Seymour Parker and Robert J. Kleiner. Reproduced by permission of the American Anthropological Association from *American Anthropologist*, Vol. 72, No. 3, (1970).

That is, the core of culture is its positive adaptive func-
tion. I, too, have called attention to some of the adap-
tive mechanisms in the culture of poverty—for ex-
ample, the low aspiration level helps to reduce frustra-
tion, the legitimization of short-range hedonism
makes possible spontaneity and enjoyment. . . .

The purpose of this paper is to determine wheth-er values usually associated with the "culture of poverty" are in fact psychologically adjustive and "secondary". . . . This is difficult to demonstrate directly. We will depend on inferences drawn from the data to be presented. Briefly, the research design of this study consists of a comparison be-tween a known mentally ill Negro population and a sample drawn from the Negro community of Phil-adelphia, Pennsylvania. Comparisons will be made of values that have been considered to constitute elements of the "culture of poverty syndrome." The data for both sample populations were an-alyzed according to the income status of the house-hold to which the individual belongs. For heuristic purposes we assumed that attitudes characterizing the "culture of poverty" are adjustive (but not nec-essarily without some psychological costs) for those in the lowest socioeconomic status. It follows that individuals in this stratum who do not have such attitudes will be maladjusted and will ex-perience psychological stress and some degree of psychological impairment. From these assump-tions we derived a number of hypotheses:

(1) Attitudes characterizing the "culture of poverty" are inversely related to income status in a general community population.
(2) Attitudes characterizing the "culture of poverty" are more prevalent in a low-income community population than in a low-income mentally ill group.
(3) A low-income mentally ill group is more similar to a high-income community group than to a low-income community group on attitudes characterizing the "culture of poverty."

We thus hypothesize that attitudes characterizing the "culture of poverty" help people living in poverty (i.e., at the lowest income level) to main-tain their sanity. To some degree, they reflect a "realistic" appraisal of the constraints of their social situation. On the other hand, the lack of realism among the mentally ill and its maladaptive consequences would be demonstrated by an ab-sence of such attitudes and their similarity to a high income community group, which (realistically) has little need for such "adjustive" attitudes.

The second part of our problem is concerned with the "secondary" nature of these distinctive attitudes. If such attitudes are truly secondary and, by implication, not in accord with primary values, then individuals holding them should manifest a type of "painful" compromise. Since a subculture cannot be completely isolated from the prevailing value system, we assumed that the dominant values serve (to *some* degree) as reference points for self-evaluation. It follows that even if the "secondary" values of the Negro poor are adjustive to a con-siderable degree, these individuals will still reflect feelings of failure and self-rejection in some areas of life. Given the logic of this argument, we offer a final hypothesis:

(4) In the community population, there is an inverse relationship between income status and feelings of failure and low self-esteem.

We will try to show that individuals in the lowest income group are *more dissatisfied* with aspects of themselves and their social performance than those in the highest income group. Assuming a well-de-fined and relatively encapsulated *culture* of poverty characterizing the most economically deprived segment of the population would *not* lead to this prediction.

The data reported in this paper are based on re-sponses from a representative sample of Phila-delphia Negroes between twenty and sixty years of age (N = 1489) and a representative group of diag-nosed mentally ill Negroes in the same age range from the same city (N = 1423). The latter consisted of "new cases" admitted to public and private, in-patient and out-patient treatment facilities (in-cluding private psychiatric practice and penal in-stitutions) in the city during a specified time period (i.e., incidence, rather than prevalence figures). The interviews took place during 1960. The opera-tional procedures used in deriving the various mea-sures used in this study will be described below when the relevant data are presented. For purposes of presenting the various tables, groupings will be used based on the yearly income of the head of the household. These consist of three categories: $1,000 or less, $1,001–$2,000, and $3,001 and over.

Table 1. Income Status and Goal-Striving Involvement for Income

Income level	Goal-striving involvement (mean scores)	
	Mentally ill (n)	Community (n)
1	20.72 (278)	8.48 (266)
2	23.74 (620)	15.33 (801)
3	18.20 (261)	24.09 (312)

Chi-square tests of significance: (1) Community (level 1) vs. community (level 3) $t = 3.13$, $P < .005$; (2) Community (level 1) vs. mentally ill (level 1), $t = 2.20$, $P < .02$ (3) Community (level 3) vs. mentally ill (level 1), N.S. (All probability values greater than 0.05 will be considered "not significant.")

All formulations of the "culture of poverty" include the idea that those involved in this situation have low aspirations as a form of realistic adaptation. One measure used to evaluate the first three hypotheses was the respondents' degree of "goal-striving involvement." . . .

This measure incorporates into one formula the discrepancy between level of aspiration and level of achievement, the valence or importance of reaching the particular goal, and the individual's subjective probability of reaching the goal.

As predicted in Hypothesis 1, involvement in goal-striving for income increases directly with income status in the community population (Table 1). As predicted in Hypothesis 2, the mean level of goal-striving involvement is lower in the community sample at the lowest income level than among the mentally ill at this level. Finally, there is no significant difference between the mean level of goal-striving involvement of the mentally ill at income level 1 and the community sample of income level 3, as hypothesized.

The findings reported in Table 1 suggest that having relatively low levels of goal-striving involvement (as an element in the culture of poverty) is adaptive and may serve to minimize the likelihood of mental illness. However, it can be maintained that low levels of goal-striving may not be adaptive if the existing opportunity structure is, in fact, relatively open and provides high potential for upward mobility. Even though there is considerable evidence that for the majority of Negroes at the time of our survey the opportunity structure was *relatively* closed, to gauge the adjustive value of low levels of goal striving one must know how individuals themselves *view* the possibilities for upward mobility. To answer this question, we asked our sample populations to estimate (from precoded responses) the degree to which "being a Negro has been a barrier for you." The responses indirectly indicate the degree to which individuals felt that the opportunity structure was closed to Negroes and also provides a measure of "hopelessness" (as a component of the culture of poverty). We note in Table 2 that in the community population there is a significant inverse relationship between income level and the degree to which the community population feels that "barriers" exist for the Negro. That is, the lower the income level, the higher the tendency to respond that being a Negro constitutes a barrier to getting ahead. Also at income level 1, the mentally ill are significantly more prone than those in the community to report that being a Negro has constituted "no" barrier. Finally, as

Table 2. Being a Negro as a Barrier to Getting Ahead

Perceptions of barrier	Income levels (%)					
	1		2		3	
	III	Community	III	Community	III	Community
Yes, very much or to some degree	21	47	26	35	27	34
Yes, slightly	20	24	15	29	21	26
No, not at all	59	29	59	36	52	40
n	(278)	(266)	(620)	(801)	(261)	(312)

Chi-square tests of significance: (1) By income status in the community $\chi^2 = 11.40$, df = 2, $P < .01$; (2) Community (level 1) vs. mentally ill (level 1), $\chi^2 = 51.60$, df = 1, $P < .001$; (3) Community (level 3) vs. mentally ill (level 1), $\chi^2 = 22.45$, df = 1, $P < .001$.

predicted in Hypothesis 3, the mentally ill at income level 1 differ most from their status peers in the community and resemble most closely the community sample at the highest income status level, although this latter difference is still statistically significant. These findings indicate more directly that those living in poverty are more prone to feel pessimistic about their chances of "making it." However, the mentally ill feel much more optimistic (as do the higher income levels in the community).

We now turn to another measure of the perception of the opportunity structure in the culture of poverty syndrome, the idea that individuals characterized by the "culture of poverty" are less likely to see personal advancement (on the usual social status continua) as a function of personal effort than as a result of "luck" or other related concepts. This attitude undoubtedly implies feelings of powerlessness and a relative inability to control one's fate. Subjects were asked the following: "It has been said that if a man works hard, saves his money, and is ambitious, he will get ahead. How often do you think this really happens?" Table 3 presents the distribution of responses by income level and mental health status.

Viewing these results in terms of the first three hypotheses presented, we note that in the community population, individuals at income level 1 are more likely to be characterized by the attitudes under consideration than those at income level 3. Secondly, at the lowest income status level, individuals in the general community sample are more likely to be characterized by this "culture of poverty" characteristic than the mentally ill. Finally, the mentally ill at the lowest income level

do not differ significantly from those at the highest level in the community. Thus, the first three hypotheses are supported by the data. . . .

Existing characterizations imply that those living in poverty exhibit little interest in maximizing *social status* (in terms of the usual "middle class" status criteria). The measure of this factor was determined by asking subjects to choose between three sets of paired occupations. Each pair consisted of a white-collar job with a relatively low wage attached to it and a blue-collar job with a relatively high wage. It was assumed that a choice of the white-collar job (with the wage penalty attached to it) would indicate a relatively higher need for social status. A choice of the blue-collar position would reflect a "culture of poverty" orientation. Table 4 indicates that for two out of three sets of choices there is a direct relationship in the community population between income status level and tendency to choose the white-collar jobs. All three choices show that those in the community population at the lowest status level are less likely than are the mentally ill to choose the white-collar job. Finally, the mentally ill at the lowest income level do not differ significantly from those in the community at the highest level but resemble most those at income level 2. With respect to the analyses in in Table 4, it can be said that the consistent direction (but not the statistical significance) of the results provides some support for the first three hypotheses.

We now approach the fourth and final hypothesis of this study, which predicts that those living in poverty will show more feelings of failure and negative self-evaluations than those in the higher income groups. As noted previously, this hypo-

Table 3. Perception of the Opportunity Structure

Efficacy of personal effort	Income levels (%)					
	1		2		3	
	III	Community	III	Community	III	Community
Very often	31	17	3	25	33	26
Often or occasionally	60	75	57	69	61	67
Hardly at all	9	9	8	6	7	7
n	(272)	(238)	(678)	(737)	(272)	(369)

Chi-square tests of significance: (1) By income status in the community χ^2 = 7.98, df = 2, P < .02; (2) Community (level 1) vs. mentally ill (level 1), χ^2 = 13.45, df = 1, P < .01; (3) Community (level 3) vs. mentally ill (level 1), N. S.

Table 4. Blue-Collar–White-Collar Occupational Choices

Occupational choices	Income levels (%)					
	1		2		3	
	III	Community	III	Community	III	Community
Choice 1						
Bricklayer (B-C)						
$120 wk.	38	43	31	35	32	33
Teacher (W-C)						
$90 wk.	62	57	69	65	68	67
n	(278)	(267)	(622)	(803)	(260)	(302)
Choice 2						
Machine Operator						
(B-C) $100 wk.	45	50	42	46	43	49
Gov't. Clerk						
(W-C) $80 wk.	55	50	58	54	57	51
n	(278)	(267)	(621)	(802)	(260)	(309)
Choice 3						
Factory Worker						
(B-C) $80 wk.	59	62	62	59	57	58
Sales Clerk (W-C)						
$60 wk.	41	38	38	41	43	42
(Dept. Store)						
n	(278)	(267)	(621)	(789)	(260)	(299)

Chi-square tests of significance: For each choice, three tests of significance were carried out—none was significant.

thesis rests on the assumption that those living in poverty share many of the ("primary") values of the larger society.

In accordance with Hypothesis 4 and logic developed in the previous discussion, we will attempt to determine the respondents' perception of their own positions on a self-anchored striving scale. Each respondent was presented with a diagrammatic representation of a ten-step ladder, the top step being labeled the "best possible way of life" and the bottom step the "worst possible way of life." The individual was asked to specify the components of the "best" and the "worst" ways of life *for him.* Using these two anchor points, instructions were given to select the step that represented his own level of achievement. This hypothesis predicts that a direct relationship exists between income status and perceived position on the striving scale. Table 5 indicates that the results of this analysis are in the predicted direction but that the differences are not statistically significant. However, the difference between status levels 1 and 3, when taken alone, is significant (< 0.05), indicating that those living in the most impoverished group do feel relatively deprived. The fact

that these differences are not as great as one might expect suggests that some accommodation is taking place. . . .

Still another method was used to gauge individuals' perceptions of the extent of their own success or failure. We wished to avoid specifying the criteria of "success" or "failure" because to impose what *we* considered important would have vitiated the intent of the question, i.e., to gauge relative deprivation (in terms of their own "significant" value criteria). Therefore respondents were asked the following question: "On the basis

Table 5. Income Status and Perceived Position on the Self-Anchored Striving Scale

Perceived position striving scale	Income status levels (%)		
	1	2	3
Low (steps 1–3)	7	4	3
Medium (steps 4–6)	36	32	32
High (steps 7–10)	57	64	65
n	(240)	(743)	(375)

$x^2 = 7.55$, $df = 4$, $P < .10$.

of your experiences so far, to what degree would you say you have been 'successful' in life?" Hypothesis 4 predicts a direct relationship between income status level and perception of degree of success. An examination of the data in Table 6 indicates that this prediction is supported and that the differences obtained are statistically significant.

We now turn to self-esteem as determined by perceived discrepancies between one's actual and ideal concepts of self. It is assumed that if those living in poverty do share with the larger society many values related to success and status, they will manifest a relatively devalued self-esteem. If this occurs, it would indicate that the "culture of poverty," despite its adjustive aspects, by no means insulates individuals from an awareness that their position is less than desirable. Put simply, a devalued self-image would imply that the culture of poverty represents a "painful compromise" rather than a "complacent adjustment." In accord with Hypothesis 4, we predict that there is a direct relationship between income status position and self-esteem. In terms of our discrepancy measure, the hypothesis predicts that there is an inverse relationship between income status position and discrepancy between self and ideal-self concepts. For these purposes, seventeen statements pertaining to performance in various social roles (i.e., parental role, spouse role, ethnic-racial role, social-friend role) were presented to all respondents. Preceding all of these statements was the phrase "I am a person who." Precoded response categories were "almost never," "occasionally," "usually," and "almost always." Later in the administration of the questionnaire (in order to "break" a response set), respondents were presented with the same items and the same response categories. However, now these items were preceded by the statement, "I am a person who would like to . . . ." Since a numerical value was attached to the different response categories, we were provided with a quantifiable measure of self-ideal–self-discrepancy. The analyses of the discrepancy scores were grouped and are presented by income status position in Table 7. The data show that although there is a tendency for self-esteem to be directly related to income status position, this tendency is not statistically significant.

Before discussing the implications of these findings for the larger issues posed in the beginning

of this paper, we first summarize the findings as they bear on the hypotheses of this study. The analyses were presented in two parts; the first (related to Hypotheses 1, 2, and 3) dealt with the question of the adjustive nature of attitudes commonly associated with the "culture of poverty." The second part (related to Hypothesis 4) was concerned with the extent to which these adjustive attitudes were "secondary" and insulated individuals from an awareness of failure, low self-esteem, etc. Three of the four measures concerned with the first three hypotheses indicate quite conclusively that in a Negro population attitudes commonly associated with the culture of poverty are inversely related to income status position. These findings, as well as the fact that the mentally ill in the lowest status groups resemble the *highest* income group in the community more than they do the lowest, suggests the adjustive nature of this phenomenon. To quote a popular cliché, it represents a normal reaction to an abnormal situation. It is a way of maintaining sanity—if not middle-class respectability—in "dismal" circumstances.

Table 6. Income Status and Perceived Degree of Success

Degree of success	Income status levels (%)		
	1	2	3
Very or fairly successful	50	54	67
Hardly successful or not successful at all	50	46	33
n	(242)	(743)	(375)

$\chi^2 = 19.23$, $df = 2$, $P < .001$.

Table 7. Income Status and Discrepancy Between Self and Ideal-Self Concepts

Discrepancy between self-concept and ideal-self concept	Income status levels (%)		
	1	2	3
Low (high self-esteem)	33	39	40
Medium	50	46	44
High (low self-esteem)	17	16	16
n	(268)	(706)	(395)

Chi-square: N.S.

In a sense, many mentally ill attempt to maintain "respectability" in a social context that makes it unrealizable.

With respect to Hypothesis 4 (Tables 5 through 7), all analyses are in the predicted direction; two are statistically significant. Although those in the lowest income group showed indications of relatively low self-esteem and feelings of failure, . . . they were not uniformly different from the highest income group. We interpret this as meaning that while the "culture of poverty" is not a self-contained and insulated milieu for its participants, it does serve partially to reduce feelings of failure. The consistent direction of the findings suggests that along with the attitudes considered part of the culture of poverty there also exist simultaneously reference values shared with the larger society that make for feelings of relative failure and militate against a blithe acceptance of low social status and achievement.

It appears that both extreme positions . . . are not supported. Negroes living in poverty *are* characterized by a "subculture of poverty" with its modal (but by no means unique) set of attitudes. The behavior of those living in poverty is associated with underlying value positions and is not merely a series of overt reactions forced on them by the constraints of their social situation. On the other hand, our data also suggest that attitudes characterizing this subculture represent but one segment of the total range of attitudes and reference values, many of which are shared with the larger society. Critics of the traditional culture of poverty descriptions are probably correct in pointing out that middle-class social scientists often focus on this narrow range and ignore the wider attitudinal context. However, they are probably wrong in denying that the behavior of individuals in poverty is related to some internalized values.

The conclusions above should come as no surprise to social scientists who are aware of the research evidence of an interaction between social structure, culture (i.e., values and attitudes), and personality. It seems to us, however, that the demonstration of an adjustive function of the culture of poverty has direct relevance for the policy issue raised previously. Given this adjustive function, a serious attempt to change these "undesirable" values in the direction of middle-class values by psychiatric–social-work–educative methods without prior (or concomitant) efforts to significantly alter social structural realities (i.e., income, employment, housing, cultural patterns that restrict the area of social participation and the exercise of power) is at best doomed. At worst, by encouraging unrealistic goals this approach may increase maladjustment and deviant behavior. It is naive to assume that educative methods by themselves or as preparation for later structural changes would be effective; ultimately such a position represents mere "tokenism." The "culture of poverty" does not arise from ignorance but serves an adjustive function.

The significant question that should have been raised in the Moynihan controversy is *not* whether configurations of attitudes are associated with populations experiencing long-standing poverty and deprivation. Such configurations *do* exist. The significant *academic* issue is only their nature, their boundaries, and their function in the full context of the lives of the individuals involved.

We agree with Rainwater that "sociologists have found it much easier to go to the people of the underclass to find out how they survive than to prove why it is they must survive in those ways."

With regard to the social policy issue, the crucial issue is the most effective method of bringing about desired change. It is here that our findings have most relevance. They support the astute (but unpalatable to many) conclusion that "the central fact about the American underclass—that it is created by, and its existence is maintained by, the operation of what is in other ways the most successful economic system known to man. In any case, one can hope that as a result of the social science efforts to date, 'thinking people' will stop deluding themselves that the underclass is other than a product of an economic system so designed that it generates a destructive amount of income inequality, and face the fact that the only solution of the underclass is to change that economic system accordingly."

Ulf Hannerz

Another Look at Lower-Class Black Culture

Although the following article deals largely with the role of the black lower-class male, it evokes a more general problem. Studies of the culture of poor groups as different as the Puerto Ricans, poor whites, Irish peasants, Mexicans—as well as American blacks—indicate the problematic role of the male as spouse and father. These discussions have centered around the "matrifocal" family and the attendant problems and failures of the males. On the other hand, critics of this position have pointed out that prevailing definitions of the male role often reflect middle-class ideals of family life. Considered within the context of the lives of the poor (in this case, in the black ghetto) should the behavior of the male toward his family be conceptualized as an example of "role failure," as adherence to a different and alternative set of family norms, or as a reaction to a "cultural vacuum" in which middle-class values have been rejected, but not replaced?

Although more data are needed before definitive answers to such questions are available, Hannerz' analysis points to some of the answers. First, the author establishes that the hypothesis of a "culture vacuum" is not tenable. The role of the male in the ghetto family contains an amalgam of both mainstream and ghetto values. Since both sets of values are present in the ghetto, they must conflict with each other at some points. It appears that the performance of the black male cannot be satisfactorily conceptualized either as "role failure" or simply as adherence to an alternative family institution. Once again, as in previous articles in this section, we note that the unique aspects of the culture of poverty cannot be understood apart from the larger social context in which it is imbedded and the reactions of the poor to this context. It is for this reason that the critics of the concept of a culture of poverty point to a need for studies of the value system and exploitive institutions of the larger society.

Ever since the beginnings of the scholarly study of black people in the Americas, there has been an interesting fascination with the differences between the family life of Negroes and that of their white counterparts, the chief difference being seen as the dominant, not to say dominating, role of women in black families.

From E. Franklin Frazier's pioneering 1932 study of *The Negro Family in Chicago* through Melville Herskovits' *The Myth of the Negro Past* in 1941 to the so-called Moynihan Report of 1965, social scientists have been repeatedly rediscovering, analyzing, and worrying over the crucial role of the mother (or grandmother) in the family structure of blacks in the New World. Herskovits saw the centrality of the mother as an African vestige, typical of the polygynous marriage in which every woman, with her offspring, formed a separate unit. Frazier is generally regarded as the first to ascribe to the institution of slavery itself the strongest influence in undermining the stability of marriage, an influence that was later reinforced when blacks encountered what Frazier perceived as the peculiarly urban evils of anonymity, disorganization, and the lack of social support and controls. Moynihan, like Frazier, sees the matriarchal family as being practically without strengths, at least in the context of the larger American society, but his Report emphasizes the ways in which employer discrimination and, more recently, welfare policies have contributed to the breaking up (or foreclosure) of the male-dominated family unit among blacks.

In all of these studies, however, the black *man*—as son, lover, husband, father, grandfather—is a distant and shadowy figure "out there somewhere" ...if only because his major characteristic as far as the household is concerned is his marginality or absence....

This essay is an attempt to outline the social processes within the ghetto communities of the northern United States whereby the identity of streetcorner males is established and maintained. To set the stage and state the issues involved in this essay, I'd like to look at the views of two other observers of the ghetto male. One is Charles Keil, whose *Urban Blues* is a study of the bluesman as a "culture hero." According to Keil, the urban blues singer, with his emphasis on sexuality, "trouble," and

Reprinted from "Roots of Black Manhood" by Ulf Hannerz in *transaction* magazine (now *Society*), October 1969. Adapted from "What Ghetto Males Are Like: Another Look" from *Afro-American Anthropology* edited by Norman E. Whitten, Jr., and John F. Szwed. Copyright © 1970 by The Free Press, A Division of The Macmillan Company. Reprinted by permission.

flashy clothes, manifests a cultural model of maleness that is highly valued by ghetto dwellers and relatively independent of the mainstream cultural tradition. Keil criticizes a number of authors who, without cavilling at this description of the male role, tend to see it as rooted in the individual's anxiety about his masculinity. This, Keil finds, is unacceptably ethnocentric:

Any sound analysis of Negro masculinity should first deal with the statements and responses of Negro women, the conscious motives of the men themselves, and the Negro cultural tradition. Applied in this setting, psychological theory may then be able to provide important new insights in place of basic and unfortunate distortions.

Keil, then, comes out clearly for a cultural interpretation of the male role we are interested in here. But Elliot Liebow in *Tally's Corner*, a study resulting from the author's participation in a research project that definitely considered ghetto life more in terms of social problems than as a culture, reaches conclusions which, in some of their most succinct formulations, quite clearly contradict Keil's:

Similarities between the lower-class Negro father and son ... do not result from "cultural transmission" but from the fact that the son goes out and independently experiences the same failures, in the same areas, and for much the same reasons as his father.

Thus father and son are "independently produced look-alikes." With this goes the view that the emphasis on sexual ability, drinking, and so forth is a set of compensatory self-deceptions which can only unsuccessfully veil the streetcorner male's awareness of his failure.

Keil and Liebow, as reviewed here, may be taken as representatives of two significantly different opinions on why black people in the ghettos, and in particular the males, behave differently than other Americans. One emphasizes a cultural determinism internal to the ghetto, the other an economic determinism in the relationship between the ghetto and the wider society. It is easy to see how the two views relate to one's perspective on the determinants of the domestic structure of ghetto dwellers. And it is also easy to see how these perspectives have considerable bearing on public policy, especially if it is believed that the ghetto family structure somehow prevents full participa-tion by its members in the larger American society and economy. If it is held, for example, that broad social and economic factors, and particularly poverty, make ghetto families the way they are—and this seems to be the majority opinion among social scientists concerned with this area—then public policy should concentrate on mitigating or removing those elements that distort the lives of black people. But if the style of life in the ghetto is culturally determined and more or less independent of other "outside" factors, then public policy will have to take a different course, or drop the problem altogether *qua* problem.

Admittedly, the present opportunity structure places serious obstacles in the way of many ghetto dwellers, making a mainstream life-style difficult to accomplish. And if research is to influence public policy, it is particularly important to point to the wider structural influences that *can* be changed in order to give equal opportunity to ghetto dwellers. Yet some of the studies emphasizing such macrostructural determinants have resulted in somewhat crude conceptualizations that are hardly warranted by the facts and which in the light of anthropological theory appear very over-simplified.

First of all, let us dispose of some of the apparent opposition between the two points of view represented by Keil and Liebow. There is not necessarily any direct conflict between ecological-economic and cultural explanations; the tendency to create such a conflict in much of the current literature on poverty involves a false dichotomy. In anthropology, it is a commonplace that culture is usually both inherited and influenced by the community's relationship to its environment. Economic determination and cultural determinism can go hand in hand in a stable environment. Since the ecological niche of ghetto dwellers has long remained relatively unchanged, there seems to be no reason why their adaptation should not have become in some ways cultural. It is possible, of course, that the first stage in the evolution of the specifically ghetto life-style consisted of a multiplicity of identical but largely independent adaptations from the existing cultural background—mainstream or otherwise—to the given opportunity structure, as Liebow suggests. But the second stage of adaptation—involves a perception of the first-stage adaptation as a normal condition, a state of affairs which from then on can be expected. What was at first independent adaptation becomes transformed into a ghetto heritage of assumptions about the nature of man and society.

Yet Liebow implies that father and son are independently produced as streetcorner men, and that transmission of a ghetto-specific culture has a negligible influence. To those adhering to this belief, strong evidence in its favor is seen in the fact that ghetto dwellers—both men and women—often express conventional sentiments about sex and other matters. Most ghetto dwellers would certainly agree at times at least, that education is a good thing, that gambling and drinking are bad, if not sinful, and that a man and a woman should be true to each other. Finding such opinions, and heeding Keil's admonition to listen to the statements and responses of the black people themselves, one may be led to doubt that there is much of a specific ghetto culture. But then, after having observed behavior among these same people that often and clearly contradicts their stated values, one has to ask two questions: Is there any reason to believe that ghetto-specific behavior is cultural? And, if it *is* cultural, what is the nature of the coexistence of mainstream culture and ghetto-specific culture in the black ghetto?

To answer the first question, one might look at the kinds of communications that are passed around in the ghetto relating to notions of maleness. One set of relationships in which such communications occur frequently is the family; another is the male peer group.

Much has been made of the notion that young boys in the ghetto, growing up in matrifocal households, are somehow deficient in or uncertain about their masculinity, because their fathers are absent or peripheral in household affairs. It is said that they lack the role models necessary for learning male behavior; there is a lack of the kind of information about the nature of masculinity which a father would transmit unintentionally merely by going about his life at home. The boys therefore supposedly experience a great deal of sex-role anxiety as a result of this cultural vacuum. It is possible that such a view contains more than a grain of truth in the case of some quite isolated female-headed households. Generally speaking, however, there may be less to it than meets the eye. First of all, a female-headed household without an adult male in residence but where young children are growing up—and where, therefore, it is likely that the mother is still rather young—is seldom one where adult males are totally absent. More or less steady boyfriends (sometimes including the separated father) go in and out. Even if these men do not assume a central household role, the boys can obviously use them as source material for the identification of male behavior. To be sure, the model is not a conventional middle-class one, but it still shows what males are like.

Furthermore, men are not the only ones who teach boys about masculinity. Although role-modeling is probably essential, other social processes can contribute to identity formation. Mothers, grandmothers, aunts, and sisters who have observed men at close range have formed expectations about the typical behavior of men which they express and which influence the boys in the household. The boys will come to share in the women's imagery of men, and often they will find that men who are not regarded as good household partners (that is, "good" in the conventional sense) are still held to be attractive company. Thus the view is easily imparted that the hard men, good talkers, clothes-horses, and all, are not altogether unsuccessful as men. The women also act more directly toward the boys in these terms—they have expectations of what men will do, and whether they wish the boys to live up (or down) to the expectations, they instruct them in the model. Boys are advised not to "mess with" girls, but at the same time it is emphasized that messing around is the natural thing they will otherwise go out and do—and when the boys start their early adventures with the other sex, the older women may scold them but at the same time point out, not without satisfaction, that "boys will be boys." This kind of maternal (or at least adult female) instruction of young males is obviously a kind of altercasting, or more exactly, socialization to an alter role—that is, women cast boys in the role complementary to their own according to their experience of man-woman relationships. One single mother of three boys and two girls put it this way:

You know, you just got to act a little bit tougher with boys than with girls, 'cause they just ain't the same. Girls do what you tell them to do and don't get into no trouble, but you just can't be sure about the boys. I mean, you think they're OK and next thing you find out they're playing hookey and drinking wine and maybe stealing things from cars and what not. There's

just something bad about boys here, you know. But
what can you say when many of them are just like
their daddies? That's the man in them coming out.
You can't really fight it, you know that's the way it is.
They know, too, but you just got to be tougher.

This is in some ways an antagonistic socialization, but it is built upon an expectation that it would be unnatural for men not to turn out to be in some ways bad—that is fighters, drinkers, lady killers, and so forth. There is one thing worse than a no-good man—the sissy, who is his opposite. A boy who seems weak is often reprimanded and ridiculed not only by his peers but also by adults, including his mother and older sisters. The combination of role-modeling by peripheral fathers or temporary boyfriends with altercasting by adult women certainly provides for a measure of male role socialization within the family.

And yet, when I said that the view of the lack of models in the family was too narrow, I was not referring to the observers' lack of insight into many matrifocal ghetto families as much as I was to the emphasis they placed on the family as *the* information storage unit of a community's culture. I believe it is an ethnocentrism on the part of middle-class commentators to take it for granted that if information about sex roles is not transmitted from father to son within the family, it is not transmitted from generation to generation at all. In American sociology, no less than in the popular mind, there is what Ray Birdwhistell has termed a "sentimental model" of family life, according to which the family is an inward-turning isolated unit, meeting most of the needs of its members, and certainly their needs for sociability and affection. The "sentimental model" is hardly ever realistic even as far as middle-class American families are concerned, and it has even less relevance for black ghetto life. Ghetto children live and learn out on the streets just about as much as within the confines of the home. Even if mothers, aunts, and sisters do not have streetcorner men as partners, there is an ample supply of them on the front stoop or down at the corner. Many of these men have such a regular attendance record as to become quite familiar to children and are frequently very friendly with them. Again, therefore, there is no lack of adult men to show a young boy what men are like. It seems rather unlikely that one can deny all role-modeling effect of these men on their young neigh-

bors. They may be missing in the United States census records, but they are not missing in the ghetto community.

Much of the information gained about sex roles outside the family comes not from adult to child, however, but from persons in the same age-grade or only slightly higher. The idea of culture being stored in lower age-grades must be taken seriously. Many ghetto children start participating in the peer groups of the neighborhood at an early age, often under the watchful eye of an elder brother or sister. In this way they are initiated into the culture of the peer group by interacting with children—predominantly of the same sex—who are only a little older than they are. And in the peer-group culture of the boys, the male sex role is a fairly constant topic of concern. Some observers have felt that this is another consequence of the alleged sex role anxiety of ghetto boys. This may be true, of course, at least in that it may have had an important part in the development of male peer-group life as a dominant element of ghetto social structure. Today, however, such a simple psychosocial explanation will not do. Most ghetto boys can hardly avoid associating with other boys, and once they are in the group, they are efficiently socialized into a high degree of concern with their sex role. Much of the joking, the verbal contests and the more or less obscene songs among small ghetto boys, serve to alienate them from dependence on mother figures and train them to the exploitative, somewhat antagonistic attitude toward women which is typical of streetcorner men. . . .

This sociability among the men seems to be a culture-building process. Shared definitions of reality are created out of the selected experiences of the participants. Women are nagging and hypocritical; you can't expect a union with one of them to last forever. Men are dogs; they have to run after many women. There is something about being a man and drinking liquor; booze makes hair grow on your chest. The regularity with which the same topics appear in conversation indicates that they have been established as the expected and appropriate subjects in this situation, to the exclusion of other topics.

Mack asked me did I screw his daughter, so I asked:
"I don't know, what's her name?" And then when I
heard that gal was his daughter all right, I says,
"Well, Mack, I didn't really have to take it. 'cause

it was given to me." I thought Mack sounded like his daughter was some goddam white gal. But Mack says, "Well, I just wanted to hear it from you." Of course, I didn't know that was Mack's gal, 'cause she was married and had a kid, and so she had a different name. But then you know the day after when I was out there a car drove by, and somebody called my name from it, you know, "hi darling," and that was her right there. So the fellow I was with says, "Watch out, Buddy will shoot your ass off." Buddy, that's her husband. So I says, "Yeah, but he got to find me first!" . . .

Groups of one's friends give some stability and social sanction to the meanings that streetcorner men attach to their experiences—meanings that may themselves have been learned in the same or preceding peer groups. They, probably more than families, are information storage units for the ghetto-specific male role. At the same time, they are self-perpetuating because they provide the most satisfactory contexts for legitimizing the realities involved. In other words, they suggest a program for maleness, but they also offer a haven of understanding for those who follow that program and are criticized for it or feel doubts about it. For of course all streetcorner males are more or less constantly exposed to the definitions and values of the mainstream cultural apparatus, and so some cultural ambivalence can hardly be avoided. Thus, if a man is a dog for running after women—as he is often said to be among ghetto dwellers—he wants to talk about it with other dogs who appreciate that this is a fact of life. If it is natural for men to drink, let it happen among other people who understand the nature of masculinity. In this way the group maintains constructions of reality, and life according to this reality maintains the group.

It is hard to avoid the conclusion, then, that there is a cultural element involved in the sex roles of streetcorner males, because expectations about sex are manifestly shared and transmitted rather than individually evolved. (If the latter had been the case, of course, it would have been less accurate to speak of these as roles, since roles are by definition

cultural.) This takes us to the second question stated above, about the coexistence of conventional and ghetto-specific cultures. Streetcorner men certainly are aware of the male ideal of mainstream America—providing well for one's family, remaining faithful to one's spouse, staying out of trouble, etc.—and now and then everyone of them states it as his own ideal. What we find here, then, may be seen as a bicultural situation. Mainstream culture and ghetto-specific culture provide different models for living, models familiar to everyone in the ghetto. Actual behavior may lean more toward one model or more toward the other, or it may be some kind of mixture, at one point or over time. The ghetto-specific culture, including the streetcorner male role, is adapted to the situation and the experience of the ghetto dweller; it tends to involve relatively little idealization but offers shared expectations concerning self, others, and the environment. The mainstream culture, from the ghetto dweller's point of view, often involves idealization, but there is less real expectation that life will actually follow the paths suggested by those ideals. This is not to say that the ghetto-specific culture offers no values of its own at all, or that nothing of mainstream culture ever appears realistic in the ghetto; but in those areas of life where the two cultures exist side by side as alternative guides to action (for naturally, the ghetto-specific culture, as distinct from mainstream culture, is not a "complete" culture covering all areas of life), the ghetto-specific culture is often taken to forecast what one can actually expect from life, while the mainstream norms are held up as perhaps ultimately more valid but less attainable under the given situational constraints. "Sure it would be good to have a good job and a good home and your kids in college and all that, but you got to be yourself and do what you know." Of course, this often makes the ghetto-specific cultural expectations into self-fulfilling prophecies, as ghetto dwellers try to attain what they believe they can attain; but, to be sure, self-fulfilling prophecies and realistic assessments may well coincide.

On the whole, one may say that both mainstream culture and ghetto-specific culture are transmitted within many ghetto families.

Herbert J. Gans

Culture and Class in the Study of Poverty: An Approach to Anti-Poverty Research

Gans' article illustrates the value of periodically "stepping away from the data" to review and reconsider a body of research. Pursuing some of the points raised in our previous selection, Gans criticizes theories about culture (of poverty or otherwise) that fail to incorporate data about aspirations as well as behavioral adaptations to an "existential situation." Only by understanding the goals people have and how they regard their failure to reach these goals, Gans tell us, can one approach a true assessment of their potential change under specified circumstances.

Liebow and Hannerz both found that among the poor they studied there were considerable discrepancies between their actual situation and their ideals and aspirations, and that feelings of inadequacy stemmed from their failure to bridge the gap. How widespread are these perceptions among the poor? How strongly are they felt? Gans pleads for more research before conclusions are drawn about the potential extent of the resistance of the culture of poverty to situational change. Among his other recommendations for research, three merit special note. First he raises the question of a middle-class bias in those who do research on poverty. He also wonders about the extent to which the cultural differences that do exist between the middle class and the poor might or actually do operate to prevent the poor from taking advantage of even the limited opportunities for improvement available to them. Finally Gans, like others, stresses the importance of studying those conditions in the larger society and those attitudes of its more affluent members that contribute to the perpetuation of both poverty and the culture of poverty.

I. The Moral Assumptions of Poverty Research

Poverty research, like all social research, is suffused with the cultural and political assumptions of the researcher. Consequently, perhaps the most significant fact about poverty research is that it is being carried out entirely by middle-class researchers who differ—in class, culture, and political power—from the people they are studying. . . .

Moreover, poverty researchers, like other affluent Americans, have had to grapple with the question of how to explain the existence of an underclass in their society. In a fascinating paper, Rainwater has recently described five explanatory perspectives that, as he puts it, "neutralize the disinherited" by considering them either immoral, pathological, biologically inferior, culturally different, or heroic. As his terms indicate, these "explanations" are by no means all negative, but they enable the explainers to resolve their anxiety about the poor by viewing them as different or unreal.

Rainwater's list is a sophisticated and updated version of an older, more familiar, explanatory perspective that judges the poor as *deserving* or *undeserving*. This dichotomy still persists today, albeit with different terminologies, for it poses the basic political question of what to do about poverty. If the poor are deserving, they are obviously entitled to admittance into the affluent society as equals with all the economic, social, and political redistribution this entails; if they are undeserving, they need not be admitted, or at least not until they have been made or have made themselves deserving.

The history of American poverty research can be described in terms of this moral dichotomy. Most of the lay researchers of the nineteenth century felt the poor were personally and politically immoral and therefore undeserving. . . .

Social scientists took up the study of poverty in the twentieth century without an explicit political

From Chapter 8, "Culture and Class in the Study of Poverty: An Approach to Anti-Poverty Research" by Herbert J. Gans in *On Understanding Poverty*, edited by Daniel P. Moynihan with the assistance of Corinne Saposs Schelling; © 1968, 1969 by the American Academy of Arts and Sciences; Basic Books, Inc., Publishers, New York. Reprinted by permission of Basic Books, Inc.

agenda and also changed the terminology. They saw the poor as suffering from individual pathology or from social disorganization; they treated them as deficient rather than undeserving, but there was often the implication that the deficiencies had to be corrected before the poor were deserving of help.

This conception of the poor spawned a generation of countervailing research that identified positive elements in their social structure and culture. Although many of the studies were done among the working class populations, the findings suggested or implied that because the poor were not disorganized, socially or individually, they were therefore deserving.

At the present time, the debate over the moral quality of the poor is most intense among the practitioners of public welfare and anti-poverty programs. Today's advocates of undeservingness see the poor as deficient in basic skills and attitudes. Educators who share this view describe them as culturally deprived; social workers and clinical psychologists find them weak in ego strength; and community organizers view them as apathetic. Professionals who believe the poor to be deserving argue that the poor are not deficient but deprived; they need jobs, higher incomes, better schools, and "maximum feasible participation"; "resource strategy equalization" in Lee Rainwater's terms, rather than just services, such as training and counseling in skills and ways of living that lead to cultural change.

Today's social scientists have debated an only slightly different version of the same argument. Some feel that the poor share the values and aspirations of the affluent society, and if they can be provided with decent jobs and other resources, they will cease to suffer from the pathological and related deprivational consequences of poverty. According to Beck's review of the recent poverty literature, however, many more social scientists share the feeling that the poor are deficient. Yet, others, particularly anthropologists, suggest that poverty and the lowly position of the poor have resulted in the creation of a separate lower-class culture or a culture of poverty, which makes it impossible for poor people to develop the behavior patterns and values that would enable them to participate in the affluent society.

Although few social scientists would think of characterizing the poor as deserving or undeserv-ing, at least explicitly, those who argue that the poor share the values of the affluent obviously consider them as ready and able to share in the blessings of the affluent society, whereas those who consider them deficient or culturally different imply that the poor are not able to enter affluent society until they change themselves or are changed. Walter Miller argues that the poor do not even want to enter the affluent society, at least culturally, and his analysis implies that the poor are deserving precisely because they have their own culture. Even so, those who see the poor as deficient or culturally different often favor resource-oriented anti-poverty programs, just as those who feel that the poor share the values of the affluent society recognize the existence of cultural factors that block the escape from poverty. . . .

The Poor: Neither Deserving nor Undeserving

Because of its fundamental political implications and its moral tone, the debate about whether the poor are deserving or undeserving will undoubtedly continue as long as there are poor people in America. Nevertheless, I feel that the debate, however conceptualized, is irrelevant and undesirable. The researcher ought to look at poverty and the poor from a perspective that avoids a moral judgment, for it is ultimately impossible to prove that the poor are more or less deserving than the affluent. Enough is now known about the economic and social determinants of pathology to reject explanations of pathology as a moral lapse. Moreover, since there is some evidence that people's legal or illegal practices are a function of their opportunity to earn a livelihood in legal ways, one cannot know whether the poor are as law-abiding or moral as the middle class until they have achieved the same opportunities—and then, the issue will be irrelevant.

It is also undesirable to view the poor as deserving or undeserving, for any judgment must be based on the judge's definition of deservingness, and who has the ability to formulate a definition that is not class-bound? Such judgments are almost always made by people who are trying to prevent the mobility of a population group that is threatening their own position, so that the aristocracy finds the *nouveau riche* undeserving of being admitted to the upper class; the cultural elite believes the middle classes to be undeserving partakers of "culture"; and many working-class people feel that people who do not labor with their hands do not deserve to be considered workers. Still, almost everyone gangs up on the poor; they are judged as undeserving by all income groups, becoming victims of a no-win moral game in which they are expected to live by moral and legal standards that few middle-class people are capable of upholding. Deservingness is thus not an absolute moral concept but a means of preventing one group's access to the rights and resources of another.

The only proper research perspective, I believe, is to look at the poor as an economically and politically deprived population whose behavior, values—and pathologies—are adaptations to their existential situation, just as the behavior, values, and pathologies of the affluent are adaptations to *their* existential situation. In both instances, adaptation results in a mixture of moral and immoral, legal and illegal practices, but the nature of the mix is a function of the existential situation. Since the standards of law—and even of morality—of an affluent society are determined by the affluent members of that society, the poor are, by definition, less law-abiding and less moral, but only because they are less affluent and must therefore adapt to different existential circumstances.

If the poor are expected to live up to the moral and legal standards of the affluent society, however, the only justifiable anti-poverty strategy is to give them the same access to resources now held by the affluent, and to let them use and spend these resources with the same freedom of choice that is now reserved to the affluent. . . .

II. Poverty and Culture

The argument between those who think that poverty can best be eliminated by providing jobs and other resources and those who feel that cultural obstacles and psychological deficiencies must be overcome as well is ultimately an argument about social change, about the psychological readiness of people to respond to change, and about the role of culture in change. The advocates of resources are not concerned explicitly with culture, but they do make a cultural assumption: Whatever the culture of the poor, it will not interfere in people's ability to take advantage of better opportunities for obtaining economic resources. They take a *situational* view of social change and of personality: that people respond to the situations—and opportunities—available to them and change their behavior accordingly. Those who call attention to cultural (and psychological) obstacles, however, are taking a *cultural* view of social change, which suggests that people react to change in terms of prior values and behavior patterns and adopt only those changes that are congruent with their culture. . . . Clearly, the truth lies somewhere in between, but at present, neither the data nor the conceptual framework to find that truth is as yet available.

The situational view is obviously too simple; people are not automatons who respond either in the same way or with the same speed to a common stimulus. Despite a middle-class inclination on the part of researchers to view the poor as homogeneous, all available studies indicate that there is as much variety among them as among the affluent. Some have been poor for generations, others are poor only periodically; some are downwardly mobile; others are upwardly mobile. Many share middle-class values, others embrace working-class values; some have become so used to the defense mechanisms they have learned for coping with deprivation that they have difficulty in adapting to new opportunities; and some are beset by physical or emotional illness, poverty having created pathologies that now block the ability to adapt to nonpathological situations. Sad to say, there is as yet no research to show, quantitatively, what proportion of poor people fit into each of these categories.

The Shortcoming of the Cultural View of Change

The cultural view of social and personal change is also deficient. First, it uses an overly behavioral definition of culture that ignores the existence of values that conflict with behavior; second, it sees culture as a holistic system whose parts are intricately related, so that any individual element of a culture cannot be changed without system-wide reverberations.

The behavioral definition identifies culture in terms of how people act; it views values as *behavioral norms* that are metaphysical and moral guidelines to behavior, and are deduced from behavior. For example, Walter Miller sees values as "focal concerns" that stem from, express, and ultimately maintain behavior. As he puts it, "the concept 'focal concern' . . . reflects actual behavior, whereas 'value' tends to wash out intracultural differences since it is colored by notions of the 'official' ideal." This definition, useful as it is, pays little or no attention to *aspirations*, values that express the desire for alternative forms of behavior. . . .

But such a definition of culture is not applicable to contemporary western society. Many poor people in our society are also fatalists not because they are unable to conceive of alternative conditions but because they have been frustrated in the realization of alternatives. . . .

At present, there are only enough data to affirm the existence of a divergence between aspirations and behavioral norms and to underline the need for more research, particularly in areas of life other than marriage. In a heterogeneous or pluralistic society, such divergence is almost built in; when a variety of cultures or subcultures coexist, aspirations diffuse freely. Among affluent people, the gap between aspirations and behavioral norms is probably narrower than among poor people; the former can more often achieve what they want. Even if they cannot satisfy occupational aspirations, they are able to satisfy other aspirations, for example, for family life. The poor have fewer options. Lacking the income and the economic security to achieve their aspirations, they must develop diverging behavioral norms in almost all areas of life. Nevertheless, they still retain aspirations, and many are those of the affluent society.

Consequently, research on the culture of the poor must include both behavioral norms and aspirations. The norms must be studied because they indicate how people react to their present existence, but limiting the analysis to them can lead to the assumption that behavior would remain the same under different conditions when there is no reliable evidence, pro or con, to justify such an assumption today. As Hylan Lewis puts it, "It is important not to confuse basic life chances and actual behavior with basic cultural values and preferences." Cultural analysis must also look at aspirations, determining their content, the intensity with which they are held, and above all, whether they would be translated into behavioral norms if economic conditions made it possible.

The second deficiency of the cultural view of change is the conception of culture as holistic and systemic. When a behavior pattern is identified as part of a larger and interrelated cultural system and when the causes of the pattern are ascribed to "the culture," there is a tendency to see the behavior pattern and its supporting norms as resistant to change and as persisting simply because they are cultural, although there is no real evidence that culture is as unchanging as assumed. This conception of culture is also ahistorical, for it ignores the origin of behavior patterns and norms. As a result, too little attention is paid to the conditions that bring a behavior pattern into being—or to the conditions that may alter it. Culture becomes its own cause, and change is possible only if the culture as a whole is somehow changed. . . .

The systemic concept of culture is also inappropriate. Modern societies are pluralist; whether developed or developing, they consist of a diverse set of cultures living side by side, and researchers studying them have had to develop such terms as subculture, class culture, and contra-culture to describe the diversity. Holistic functionalism is irrelevant, too; no culture is sufficiently integrated so that its parts can be described as elements in a system. . . .

An ahistorical conception of culture is equally inapplicable to modern societies. In such societies, some behavior patterns are persistent, but others are not; they change when economic and other conditions change, although we do not yet know which patterns are persistent—and for how long—and which are not. More important, culture is a response to economic and other conditions, it is itself situational in origin and changes as situations change. Behavior patterns, norms, and aspirations develop as responses to situations to which people must adapt, and culture originates out of such responses. Changes in economic and social opportunities give rise to new behavioral solutions, which then become recurring patterns, are later complemented by norms that justify them, and which are eventually overthrown by new existential conditions. Some behavioral norms are more persistent than others, but over the long run, all of the norms and aspirations by which people live are nonpersistent; they rise and fall with changes in situations.

These observations are not intended to question the validity of the concept of culture, for not all behavior is a response to a present situation, and not all—and perhaps not even most—behavior patterns change immediately with a change in a situation. A new situation will initially be met with available norms; only when these norms turn out to be inapplicable or damaging will people change; first, their behavior, and then the norms upholding that behavior. Nevertheless, the lag between a change in existential conditions and the change of norms does not mean that norms are immutable.

An Alternative Conception of Culture

Behavior is thus a mixture of situational responses and cultural patterns, that is, behavioral norms and aspirations. Some situational responses are strictly ad hoc reactions to a current situation; they exist because of that situation and will disappear if it changes or disappears. Other situational responses are internalized and become behavior norms that are an intrinsic part of the person and of the groups in which he moves, and are thus less subject to change with changes in situation. The intensity of internalization varies; at one extreme, there are norms that are not much deeper than lip service; at the other, there are norms that are built into the basic personality structure, and a generation or more of living in a new situation may not dislodge them. They become culture, and people may adhere to them even if they are no longer appropriate, paying all kinds of economic and emotional costs to maintain them. . . .

Not all behavioral norms are necessarily conservative; some may make people especially adaptable to change and may even encourage change. Despite what has been written about the ravages of slavery on the southern Negro, he went to work readily during World War II when jobs were plentiful. Similarly, the southern businessman operates with behavioral norms that make him readier to accept racial change than others; he cannot adhere with intensity to any beliefs that will cut into profit.

To sum up: I have argued that behavior results initially from an adaptation to the existential situation. Much of that behavior is no more than a situational response that exists only because of the situation and changes with a change in situation. Other behavior patterns become behavioral norms that are internalized and are then held with varying degrees of intensity and persistence. If they persist with a change in situation, they may then be considered patterns of *behavioral culture*, and such norms may become causes of behavior. Other norms can encourage change. In addition, adaptation to a situation is affected by aspirations, which

also exist in various degrees of intensity and persistence, and form an *aspirational culture*. Culture, then, is that mix of behavioral norms and aspirations that causes behavior, maintains present behavior, or encourages future behavior, independently of situational incentives and restraints.

Culture and Poverty

This view of culture has important implications for studying the poor. It rejects a concept that emphasizes tradition and obstacles to change and sees norms and aspirations within a milieu of situations against which the norms and aspirations are constantly tested. Moreover, it enables the researcher to analyze, or at least to estimate, what happens to norms under alternative situations and thus to guess at how poor people would adapt to new opportunities.

With such a perspective, one can—and must— ask constantly: To what situation, to what set of opportunities and restraints do the present behavioral norms and aspirations respond, and how intensely are they held; how much are they internalized, if at all, and to what extent would they persist or change if the significant opportunities and restraints underwent change? To put it another way, if culture is learned, one must ask how quickly and easily various behavioral norms could be unlearned once the existential situation from which they sprang had changed?

The prime issue in the area of culture and poverty, then, is to discover how soon poor people will change their behavior, given new opportunities, and what restraints or obstacles, good or bad, come from that reaction to past situations we call culture. To put it another way, the primary problem is to determine what opportunities have to be created to eliminate poverty, how poor people can be encouraged to adapt to those opportunities that conflict with persistent cultural patterns, and how they can retain the persisting patterns that do not conflict with other aspirations.

Because of the considerable divergence between behavioral norms and aspirations, it is clearly impossible to think of a holistic lower-class culture. It is perhaps possible to describe a *behavioral lower-class culture*, consisting of the behavioral norms with which people adapt to being poor and lower class. There is, however, no *aspirational lower-class culture*, for much evidence suggests that poor people's aspirations are similar to those of more affluent Americans. My hypothesis is that many and perhaps most poor people share the aspirations of the working class; others, those of the white-collar lower-middle class; and yet others, those of the professional and managerial upper-middle class, although most poor people probably aspire to the behavioral norms of these groups—to the ways they are living now—rather than to their aspirations.

Under present conditions, the aspirations that poor people hold may not be fulfilled, but this does not invalidate them, for their existence—and the intensity with which they are held—can only be tested when economic and other conditions are favorable to their realization. If and when poor people obtain the resources for which they are clamoring, much of the behavioral lower-class culture will disappear. Only those poor people who cannot accept alternative opportunities because they cannot give up their present behavioral norms can be considered adherents to a lower-class culture. . . .

My definition of culture also suggests a some-what different interpretation of a culture of poverty than Oscar Lewis's concept. If culture is viewed as a causal factor, and particularly as those norms and aspirations that resist change, then a culture of poverty would consist of those specifically cultural or nonsituational factors that help to keep people poor, especially when alternative opportunities beckon.

Lewis's concept of the culture of poverty puts more emphasis on the behavior patterns and feelings that result from lack of opportunity and the inability to achieve aspirations. According to Lewis,

The culture of poverty is both an adaptation and a reaction of the poor to their marginal position in a class-stratified, highly individuated society. It represents an effort to cope with feelings of hopelessness and despair which develop from the realization of the *improbability of achieving success in terms of the values and goals of the larger society. . . .*

Whether or not the families who tell their life histories in Lewis's books adhere to a culture that is a direct or indirect cause of their remaining in poverty is hard to say, for one would have to know how they would react to better economic conditions. Since such data are almost impossible to gather, it is difficult to tell how the Sanchez and Rios families might respond, for example, if Mexico and Puerto Rico offered the men a steady supply of decent and secure jobs. Since almost all the members of the families aspire to something better, my hunch is that their behavioral and aspirational cultures would change under improved circumstances; their culture is probably not a cause of their poverty.

As I use the term culture of poverty, then, it would apply to people who have internalized behavioral norms that cause or perpetuate poverty and who lack aspirations for a better way of life, particularly people whose societies have not let them know change is possible—the peasants and the urbanites who have so far been left out of the revolution of rising expectations. The only virtue of this definition is its emphasis on culture as a causal factor, thus enabling the policy-oriented researcher to separate the situational and cultural processes responsible for poverty.

If the culture of poverty is defined as those cultural patterns that keep people poor, it would be necessary to also include in the term the persisting cultural patterns among the affluent that, deliberately or not, keep their fellow citizens poor. When the concept of a culture of poverty is applied only to the poor, the onus for change falls too much on them, when in reality the prime obstacles to the elimination of poverty lie in an economic, political, and social structure that operates to protect and increase the wealth of the already affluent.

Seymour Parker
Poverty: An Altering View

The history of science is a history of controversy, and the behavioral sciences are no exception. Behavioral scientists have argued causality and the nature of man over and over, in battles involving heredity versus environment, insight versus rote learning, culture versus personality, and so on. Although the accumulation of evidence has proved most such dichotomies to be false, the research sparked by the controversies has resulted in a deeper understanding of people and their problems. I myself suspect that the present controversy, which can be phrased as culture versus situational constraint, is of the very same nature as the earlier issues. Ongoing social behavior results *both* from the individual's cultural adaptations and the constraints of the situation in which he finds himself. The crucial questions have to do with the relative contribution of each to the perpetuation of poverty and the bearing of the answers on public policy.

How can one account for the vehemence of the disagreements that have arisen? There are at least two important factors within the academic world itself: the nature of the academic community and the relationship of academic research to the political process and to public policy. Let us look at both.

In order for the mind of man to comprehend and deal with the complexity of a "booming and buzzing" world, he has had to organize phenomena into a number of separate academic disciplines, each with its own special vocabulary and concepts. Frequently the concepts are abstractions of the same reality that are merely being utilized in different theoretical contexts, but the scholars have been educated to become specialists and are better acquainted with and more comfortable in the context of their own disciplines and their own language. Moreover, their personal as well as professional interests are likely to be bound by their own disciplines. In this atmosphere, concepts are often reified and claims for their exclusive causal role are strongly maintained. Debates become partisan partly because no serious attempt is made to relate the concepts of one discipline to those of another. This problem of academic narrowness is further compounded by the separation of behavioral scientists from the political decision-making arena. Minimally involved in the making of public policy, many scholars are more inclined to investigate problems anchored in their disciplines rather than in the society around them.

Nevertheless, academic problems and research findings of our social scientists often bear importantly on political issues. Research findings are rarely neutral when they enter the arena of politics; and the social scientist, however pure his motivation, eventually finds himself or herself contending the political implications of his or her own research, or of a colleague's. As we saw in the discussion of the Moynihan Report in the introduction to this section, research data and conclusions swiftly become public property, to be used or abused by protagonists in the social arena. When academic findings become enmeshed in the political process, they are often supported or attacked for reasons that have little to do with their validity but, rather, with whether they can be used to bolster or weaken a particular policy.

To understand the storm created around the idea of a culture of poverty more fully, it is also important to have some historical perspective. Many different societies have been aware of poverty. Various are the explanations of poverty that have been offered. In pre-industrial Europe, poverty, though regarded as unfortunate, was considered one of the mysterious workings of God and was, in fact, imbued with an aura of holiness and moral purity. Poverty was considered inevitable, beyond the comprehension of man. The poor were not held to be responsible for their sad state, nor the rich and powerful for theirs. This view permitted the more affluent members of society to express their piety by acts of Christian charity administered through the Catholic Church, and removed from the rich the onus of the poverty of others. Moreover, the giving of charity helped to justify the affluence of the rich and the power of the Church.

With the emergence of the bourgeoisie and the Industrial Revolution, this earlier view was altered. In the conflict that ensued between the rising middle class and the old aristocracy, a new view of man and his situation was required. The newly acquired good fortune of the merchants, traders, and early factory owners was explained on the grounds of personal merit and hard work. The obverse of the coin was that poverty or declining fortune must be due to personal or moral defects. These new views, embodied in Protestantism and in its ethic of personal responsibility, a disciplined exercise of will, and individual effort, effected a radical change in society's attitude toward charity. Since the defects of the poor (with some exceptions, to be sure) were responsible for their unfortunate situation, it was necessary to reeducate them rather than to reward them by charitable contributions of their betters' hard-earned money. This view was incorporated into the English Poor Laws, which were clearly punitive in their intent and which served to insure "labor discipline" in the growing industrial system.

In America, where there was a relatively great need for unskilled labor and unparalleled opportunities for climbing the ladder of success, the Protestant view was especially prevalent. In the land of Horatio Alger, it was particularly easy to conclude that poverty was the result of moral defect. It was only in the latter part of the nineteenth century and particularly during the Great Depression of the 1930s that social critics began to question this view. By then, it had become obvious that business cycles and high levels of unemployment could not be explained away as personal failure.

Now, and since the end of World War II, techno-logical progress has militated even further against the poor. Increasingly, the workers who are needed are skilled, well educated, and highly motivated. There is no social ladder that large portions of the population can climb. The situation has produced a core of poor, locked into poverty, living in what Michael Harrington has aptly termed "The Other America." Urbanization, the decline of the small farm, physical mobility and consequent isolation of immediate families from their other relatives, longevity, all have locked more and more people into poverty-stricken lives. Yet myths die hard, especially when they serve powerful or personal interests, and the view that the poor are inferior and responsible for their own poverty is still widespread. To believe otherwise would shift the burden and the responsibility for the poor onto our social institu-tions and our affluent citizens. In this context, the strong passions and partisan positions that the Moyni-han Report has produced are more understandable.

Aside from academic and historical considerations, there are a number of questions which arise when the concept of a culture of poverty is carefully considered. First, there are problems in defining both "poverty" and "culture." Poverty always involves a pronounced degree of material deprivation, in comparison to the standard of living of the general community. However, there are all kinds of poverty. The poverty of the aged, the migrant worker, the physically handicapped person, the person who lives in a city ghetto, the isolated rural farmer who barely ekes out an existence, and the deserted housewife are all quite different in their etiology and consequences, and they seem to call for different solutions. Poverty has so many facets that it is difficult to talk about "the poor."

Similarly the concept of "culture" is not clearly delin-eated. Herbert Gans, in his chapter reprinted in this section, points out that anthropologists, because their field work has traditionally been with relatively small, isolated, and homogeneous populations, regard "culture" as a cohesive system of interlocking norms and values, a scheme in which all the elements fit with each other and are functionally related. Whatever its virtues in certain situations, this simple formulation does violence to the heterogeneity and conflict within the populations in industrial and urban environments. The "overintegrated" view of culture, as embodied in the work of Oscar Lewis and others who support the idea of a culture of poverty, may have resulted in a somewhat one-sided view of the poor as lacking sensi-tivity to existing dissatisfactions, potential strengths, and aspirations for change. It has led Lewis and others to paint a picture of uniform apathy, low self-esteem, and a lack of ability to visualize, desire, or strive for alternative modes of living. This is illustrated in the statement of a prominent social scientist on the values of the poor:

It is our assumption that an intervening variable medi-ating the relationship between low [status] position and lack of upward mobility is a system of beliefs and attitudes within the lower classes which in turn reduced the very voluntary actions which would ameliorate their low position. To put it simply, the lower class individual doesn't want much success, knows he couldn't get it even if he wanted to, and doesn't want what might help him get success. [1]

Without adopting an idealized and romanticized view of the poor, I think that there is sufficient evidence in some of the readings in this section to seriously ques-tion the position just quoted. While the modern pro-ponents of the concept of a culture of poverty do not place the blame for poverty on the poor, they do focus attention on the characteristics of this population rather than on the institutional arrangements or atti-tudes of the more affluent. From the evidence pre-

[1]H. H. Hyman, "The Value Systems of Different Classes: A Social Psychological Contribution to the Analysis of Stratification," in *Class, Status and Power: A Reader in Social Stratification*, R. Bendix and S. M. Lipset, eds. (New York: The Free Press, 1953), pp. 426–442.

sented in the readings, it appears that the portrayals of the poor presented by Lewis and others with a similar position can be criticized not for being wrong, but for being limited. They virtually ignore the strengths of the poor (e.g., spontaneity, patterns of sharing, the importance of kinship) and their capacity for change. They have little to say about the structural or organizational modifications of society that must occur before the capacity to change can be demonstrated. They show relatively little understanding of the processes and prerequisites of attitudinal change. Social scientists who have become mired in the "changeless" view of the poor usually regard some observed characteristics such as "present-time orientation" and an "inability to delay gratification" as fixed internalized habits that automatically perpetuate themselves.

Herbert Gans also pointed to the failure of many investigators to study what he called "aspirational culture." He notes that it is dangerous to jump to conclusions about values and norms by merely observing overt behavior. Elliot Leibow's *Tally's Corner* provides special evidence of the aspirations of the poor, of their frustration, of their deep dissatisfaction, and of the conditions that make for a high probability of failure when they try to change. His is a poignant documentation of how this frustration leads to what may be called "secondary attitudes," painful adaptations to their seriously disadvantaged situation. Bernard James' description of life on the Indian reservation also amply demonstrates this point. James shows that one cannot understand some of the "undesirable" aspects of Indian behavior as a historical continuity of Indian culture. Values and practices on the reservation are explained mainly as an adaptation to the larger system of economic arrangements and attitudes that surround them. It is misleading to attempt to view either the Indian reservation, the ghetto, or the *barrio* as self-contained social systems or subcultures. They are *subsystems* of the larger society, whose forms will be perpetuated as long as the structure and values of our present society persist. If this view is valid, it would follow that it is futile to contemplate changing the poor without altering the social situation to which they must adjust. To entertain the idea that the poor can change significantly without modifications in the situation in which their behavior is rewarded or punished shows an ignorance of the elementary principles of learning theory.

Another objection that can be leveled against the social scientists who advocate the concept of a culture of poverty is that they may inadvertently be exhibiting a degree of middle-class ethnocentrism. There is little or no evidence that much of the behavior they find distasteful or the attitudes they label "hedonistic" are significantly related to the causes or perpetuation of poverty. They may well be confusing behavior that they find unattractive (because it does not conform to middle-class patterns) with actual impediments to social and economic mobility. Implicit in this ethnocentric view is an idealized image of middle-class people as virtuous, ascetic, hard-working, money-saving, and socially integrated monuments to the Protestant ethic. Little need be said about the anachronistic aspects of this view. It is glib to advocate "changing the poor" without carefully considering the question of what one desires to change them into. Without minimizing the differences between the poor and the affluent, there is considerable evidence that the deviance of a middle-class person, when it occurs, is more apt to be hidden or treated.

We have in this discussion been critical of the concept of a culture of poverty, although there is no doubt that there are considerable differences between the attitudes of the rich and the poor. The concept of a culture of poverty is one-sided insofar as it dwells on negative aspects without concomitant attention to strengths and ability to change. Second, it diverts attention from the societal conditions and population groups that are responsible for much of the behavior of the poor. Third, it implicitly assumes that attitudes represent fixed traits that are self-perpetuating independently of a situation that sustains it. Fourth, it assumes (incorrectly, as we showed in the introduction to this section) that we have empirical evidence linking specific characteristics of the poor with their condition of poverty. Finally, it compares the actual behavior of the poor with that of an idealized middle class.

Whatever merits are associated with the concept of a culture of poverty, we will not be able to truly understand and evaluate the potential behavior of the poor until the social opportunities available to them exist at a much higher level than they do now. Moreover, our understanding of this behavior will remain limited as long as it is viewed in isolation (i.e., as a subcultural entity) without concomitant attention to its position as a subsystem of the larger society. No amount of punishment, moral exhortation, reeducation, or psychotherapy will have an appreciable effect on the tragic and shameful aspect of our affluent society known as poverty. What is required is an enlargement and a shift of focus, from the poor to the larger context which creates their poverty.

6 Schooling: Coping with Education in a Modern Society

John Singleton
Schooling: Coping with Education in a Modern Society

Bud B. Khleif
The School as a Small Society

Jacquetta Hill Burnett
Ceremony, Rites, and Economy in the Student System of an American High School

A. D. Fisher
White Rites versus Indian Rights

Rosalie H. Wax and Murray L. Wax
The Enemies of the People

Stephen S. Baratz and Joan C. Baratz
Early Childhood Intervention: The Social Science Base of Institutional Racism

Carol Talbert
Studying Education in the Ghetto

Manning Nash
The Role of Village Schools in the Process of Cultural and Economic Modernization

Ivan Illich
The Futility of Schooling in Latin America

John Singleton
The Educational Uses of Anthropology

There are several striking differences between our concept of
education today and that of any contemporary primitive
society; but perhaps the most important one is the shift from
the need for an individual to learn something which everyone
agrees he would wish to know, to the will of some individual
to teach something which it is not agreed that anyone has any
desire to know. Such a shift in emphasis could come only
with the breakdown of self-contained and self-respecting
cultural homogeneity.   Margaret Mead

There is too much education altogether, especially in
American schools. The only rational way of educating is to be an
example—of what to avoid, if one can't be the other sort.   Albert Einstein

John Singleton

Schooling: Coping with Education in a Modern Society

Culture has been defined as the shared products of human learning, and so it is natural that cultural anthropologists and ethnographers have become interested in the process by which it is shared and transmitted in modern societies. In their studies of modern education, however, anthropologists have been ambivalent: themselves successful products of a highly developed and formalized system of schooling, anthropologists, though seeming to be studying and questioning that system, have nevertheless often accepted it on faith. They have assumed that the schools fulfill their announced double function, serving as institutions for cultural transmission and as instruments of social change.

Careful ethnographic studies of the schools, recently made, have required that such assumptions be set aside. It is now widely realized that the modern school is no longer, if it ever was, a natural solution to the social problems created by isolation, poverty, and injustice. Indeed, it is now recognized that the schools themselves are a social problem—as students in our own colleges and universities have been telling us for a long time, and as high-school students have been telling us by protesting or dropping out.

But coping with education has never been a simple matter. Each generation of young learners, whether in a primitive or modern society, has had to reconstruct the cultural systems in which it participates. From the learning of language and the accepted rules of social interaction to the mastery of complex technical skills, from the development of a unique relationship with one's parents to the working out of a personal philosophy of the meaning of life, each individual is involved in a creative interaction with the cultural systems that surround him or her. Even acquiring the most basic cultural artifact, language, entails a complex learning process in which the individual develops a personal, as well as cultural, style of expression and communication.

The transmission of the symbols and meanings of human experience—cultural transmission—is a humanizing process. The institutions and customs of formal education, especially in the schools in modern, complex societies, have not, however, been consistently humane or humanizing. Though they are thought to be institutions which educate children to become adults, modern schools often inculcate behaviors more consistent with a student role than an adult role—thus providing for the convenience of the teachers rather than the benefit of the pupils. The schools have, in part, become custodial institutions to keep our children off the streets and out of the job market.

Modern schools have also become sorting devices for social mobility. It is to the extent to which the school labels the individual a "success" that he or she often makes his way in the world. Social status and economic rewards tend to be distributed on the basis of years of schooling, kinds of schooling, degrees received, and all of these tend to depend on the kinds of evaluations given the student by the teacher.

In this role of gatekeepers of social mobility, the schools often reinforce rather than change ascribed social status. This is nowhere more evident than in the experience of certain minority groups within American schools. The social class of one's parents or the identification with recognized minority groups has been consistently associated with academic achievement. Some minority groups have benefited from a particular affiliation with the culture of the schools. Students of Japanese and Jewish ancestry have consistently bested middle-class WASPs (white Anglo-Saxon Protestants) in the classroom. This does not mean that as adults they achieve equal economic or social rewards, but it has been significant in the social opportunities opened to them. Blacks, Chicanos, Puerto Ricans, and Indians, on the other hand, consistently have their lower-class status reinforced as they lose out in the school game.

The differential experience of social and cultural groups with school systems suggests that there is a "culture" of the schools which is, to some extent, isolated from the societies and communities in which they exist. While schools are sometimes described by social scientists as social microcosms of their communities—a system in which the social and cultural structures of the larger society can be studied in manageable context—they must also be understood as a part of an international institutional complex. Modern schools have been distributed around the world, where they remain tributes to Western colonialization.

Many instances of formal schooling in traditional societies, from West African bush schools to the apprenticeship system for transmitting complex navigational skills to Micronesian navigators, have been described in the ethnographic literature. In modern schools there has been a distinct shift of emphasis, from learning to teaching—and a change from a stable pattern of cultural transmission to the teaching of what the parents never knew. Margaret Mead, especially, has pointed out these contrasts between modern and primitive schooling.

Some who have studied the culture of modern schools have naively accepted the modern myth that the school is the most important agency for cultural transmission in the modern world—a highly dubious assumption in view of the current evidence that family, peer group, and neighborhood are far more effective agents for transmitting language, cultural values, attitudes, and customs. The school is, of course, the place where the most formal and explicit attempts to instruct children and adults take place, but it is certainly not the place where one's world view is most definitively shaped.

It is not surprising that those anthropologists who have chosen to study modern schooling in the manner previously reserved for isolated and primitive societies have become disturbed by the gap between ideology and practice in the educational institutions. Education is one of many cultural processes occurring within the school. Political, economic, and social transactions are an integral part of modern schooling; like other social institutions, schools may operate in direct contradiction of their stated goals.

Schooling has thus come to be viewed as a social problem by the anthropologist, in contrast to the popular belief that education is a *solution* to social problems. Jules Henry, in a brilliant anthropological examination of his own society, used data derived from the schools, newspaper advertisements, old people's homes, and elsewhere. He became so disgusted with what he found that he had to call his report "Culture Against Man." It is passionate anthropology and an important radical critique of American society. Ivan Illich, another critic, has suggested that the ultimate obscenity might be "school you!"

Anthropologists have also been drawn into the problems of school management. Some have been willing to prescribe educational reforms for a system in which they have been participants but never participant-observers. Reliable anthropological knowledge, however, is based on extensive and disciplined direct experience with human interactions perceived as data. The prescriptions of anthropologists who have not had this structured experience have been neither good anthropology nor sound advice.

A few anthropologists, whose recommendations are based on systematic studies of schooling, have been helpful when addressing themselves to the problems of coping with education in modern society. The papers in this section are designed to provide a feel for the anthropologist's contributions to our understanding of social problems in schooling—while including admonitions against an easy acceptance of common educational myths.

The specific contributions of anthropology to coping with education that we will emphasize are:

1. That schools are social institutions in our society not unlike other institutions—hospitals, prisons, business concerns, churches, factories, and families. When we view them in this light, we begin to sense

that they have a social existence and reality independent of their avowed function. Schooling may, in this context, be viewed as ritual and ceremony rather than as cultural transmission.

2. That schooling is not the same for students who come from different subcultures of our modern society. This is true of blacks, American Indians, and members of minority groups, who often experience a reinforcement of social discrimination in school rather than an opportunity for liberation. As Illich points out, it is also true in Latin America.

3. That the expansion of schools in the Third World countries that are intent upon economic modernization may not serve the purposes of the people, their governments, or the international agencies that foster educational development.

Our central theme is that education must be studied as a social institution and as a social problem. We have had too many descriptions of students and communities as problems. The culture of poverty has been too easily used as an excuse for the failure of those responsible for the schools. How the *school* fails to meet the expectations of those who support it, rather than how the student fails, must become the focus of ethnographic attention. Our studies must take account of all the functions, implicit and explicit, of the school—baby-sitting and classifying, as well as equalizing, socializing, and educating. We need to determine the ways in which our schools serve or subvert the best goals of our society.

Bud B. Khleif

The School as a Small Society

The challenge to anthropologists who would study schooling in their own society is to break away from "common sense" notions of education, the mythology of education with which they have been surrounded as children, students, and teachers. As "successful" products of the system, they must be especially sensitive about the assumptions which they bring to their study.

In a paper originally written for a symposium on anthropological research methodology in the study of education, Bud Khleif suggests a number of ways in which the school can be viewed as an institution of socialization much like other institutions and organizations in our society which, however, do not publicly proclaim the purpose of education. He offers several models for studying institutionalization of education in schools. We might well begin by applying what Khleif says to the educational institution with which we are most closely connected—the college or university.

This paper is intended as an introduction to the anthropological study of public schools. I explore some variety of approaches which would provide

working hypotheses for the conduct of fieldwork within the schools. I hope that these may be useful in providing new viewpoints for the observation of old institutions, and throughout I focus on potential spots of tension and conflict in the inner workings of public school.

Towards an Ethnography of Public Schools

How are public schools related to the rest of American society? I propose the following:

1. It can be said that whatever is sociologically important happens in the school, that the school is a miniature society. For one thing, the sociology of education is but a study of the issues and achievement of American democracy.

2. Perhaps, the most constant thing about human affairs is change; hence, equilibrium in a social system—regardless of its theoretical boundaries—

Excerpted from Chapter 10, "The School as a Small Society" by Bud B. Khleif in *Anthropological Perspectives on Education* edited by Murray L. Wax, Stanley Diamond and Fred O. Gearing; © 1971 by Basic Books, Inc., Publishers, New York.

is but a case of constant change (homeostasis). In this regard—following Robert E. Park—we can define society as a group of competitive groups that are only in temporary balance. . . . Society in whole and in part continues to be governed by a temporary elite, a minority group which defines other groups and whose self-definition itself is based on ascription of inferiority to other groups. In this sense, we can see that society is but a *negotiated order*—that is, a bargain—and that "status politics"—"the capacity of various groups and occupations to command personal deference"— is an on-going process that permeates society.

3. We can apply the notions of "negotiated order" and "status politics" to the building blocks of social structure, that is, to institutions. An institution may be defined as a processing-plant for people and skills, as a guardian of integrative symbols in society, or—to follow Sumner—as a set of functionaries formally established to deal with the person at various junctures in his life. That is to say that the daily business of institutions is socialization—the family, the school, the church, the factory, and prison. . . . Quite often, educators talk lyrically of small-town America where, in their words, "the home, the church, and the school" were equal in power, complementary to one another, and mere aspects of one another. But you can say that there has been a major shift in the distribution of power among this trinity of institutions, with the school, in many cases, emerging as the most powerful of the three. It can be said that the school has become the major socializing agency in the culture, the chief institution for bringing up a new generation. The school has more children than are found in other institutions and keeps them for a good deal of the day and for a number of years. The school has assumed a multitude of functions; in neighborhoods where the traditional influence of the home and the church is not strong, and in cases of rapid physical or social mobility, the school has become a major stabilizing force in the life of the child. . . .

4. In this new shift in the balance of power between traditional institutions, there has been an interinstitutional acculturation. For example, whereas the church nowadays uses secular methods for staying in business, the school uses sacred terminology in its functions. If you listen to a principal talking in an assembly before the whole school and stressing individualism, democracy, good work-habits, and the like, you would think you were hearing a minister addressing his congregation. The point is that there has been a shift in the sacred-secular dichotomy in society, that society can be viewed as a process, and that the school, although officially a secular institution, does quite often perform a sacred function. In a sense, school teaching can be considered a religious occupation.

5. Now if we take a look at a smaller level of phenomena, we can see that the school system itself can be regarded as a treaty between unequals and that it is permeated with status politics. For one thing, a school system can be viewed as a source of jobs for particular ethnic groups. For example, if you have had any contact with the Boston Irish or were interested in doing field work in the Boston schools, then the school people would smilingly tell you that you ought to meet the "only non-Irish principal in the school system!" In addition, women, as a sociological minority group, are rarely made high school principals and none of them can become superintendents. The same is true of Negroes. . . .

6. (a) The school itself, not only the school system, can also be seen as a treaty between unequals, as a group of competitive groups. There you find the teachers and the taught, administrators and the administered, the rulers and the ruled. Willard Waller has characterized the chief aspect of interaction in the school as being ceremonious fighting between functionaries and clients. Jules Henry, John Holt, Edgar Friedenberg, Murray Wax, Solon Kimball—among others—have described the public school as a rigid bureaucracy run for the convenience of administrators, not students: Peace in the hallways, law and order in the classrooms, written corridor-passes for the student before he can walk down the hall to the library or the toilet, and the label of "cultural deprivation" flung at students by some teachers who can themselves be perhaps more truly described as "culturally deprived." As Goffman says, "What is prison-like about prisons is found in institutions whose members have broken no laws." Patients, prisoners, and students—persons for whom services are organized—have no voice in the operation of hospitals, jails, or schools; if they do, it is only as token participation; their committees and councils are carefully controlled.

(b) In the school, the principal himself may be

regarded as a foreman, mediating between the school system's central office and his school, and between parents, teachers, counselors, and pupils. That seems to be the core of his job. . . . In particular, as every school observer knows, the principal is especially wary of those central-office personnel—often officially designated not as supervisors or inspectors but as subject-matter "consultants" and "coordinators"—who . . . essentially carry news to the central office and engage in informal as well as formal evaluation of principal, teachers, and pupils. School systems—with their scattered units that are administered as if they were citadels or tribal reservations—are run, perhaps more than any other institutions, on the basis of politics and gossip; the principal, for all practical purposes, has to be a master of public relations and an expert on controlling gossip networks.

(c) It can be said that in our society, public-school teaching is a thankless job; the teacher acts not only as an instructor but also as clerk, accountant, cop, recreation leader, embattled soldier, and mother-confessor. She is to be, as her trade-journals enjoin her, omnicompetent and omniscient. Hence, the drop-out problem among teachers is quite high (technically called "teacher turnover"—only kids supposedly drop out; teachers only turn over). In the flight from the classroom up the educational ladder, there are perhaps three avenues: a job as a school administrator, counselor, or research assistant at the school system's research department. . . . As for working in research in the school system, it can be said that this is a very limited possibility. . . .

7. An institution, like a person, has a career. The Dame School of the nineteenth century developed into a Normal School, then into a State Teachers College, then into a State College, then, in some cases, into a State University. . . . Currently, teachers are mostly trained at a state teachers college, . . . at a small private or state college, . . . at a department of education in a small university, . . . or at one of those large warehouses called Colleges of Education. . . . There are still vestiges of the old order, the two-year school. . . . The development of the teacher-training institution and the kind of academic union-cards it offers (M.Ed. or Ed.M., and Ed.D.) may be indicative of who goes into teaching and who stays in it.

As Hofstader has pointed out, education as a discipline was cut off from the intellectual tradition of the university essentially in 1911 when the so-called Committee of Nine—composed mainly of vocational school principals—stressed that the objectives of education were not to be high-brow or intellectual, that is, concerned with the cultivation of the mind in the humanistic tradition, but practical, that is, concerned with vocational training and "citizenship." Later on in 1918, the NEA formally adopted these objectives in a report it issued, called the "Cardinal Principles of Education." Ever since that time, education has been under the thumb of psychology; their alliance has given impetus to the large achievement and IQ testing industry we now have. It is only recently that the isolation of education has been broken; nowadays there is some cooperation between sociologists, anthropologists, and educators.

It should be remembered that at the turn of the century, the country was flooded with poverty-stricken immigrants who came in large groups and necessitated a redefinition of the old settlers as well as raised educational issues. Educators at that time found a new function—civilizing immigrants; hence the emphasis on the practical arts and citizenship. . . . Obviously, the civilizing mission that school teachers are bent on is not ended, for nowadays those to be civilized are *native* strangers: geographically mobile pupils and lower-status Negroes and Whites—dwellers of urban and rural appalachias.

Whereas school teaching used to be an ad hoc occupation for people on their way to becoming lawyers or anthropologists, nowadays entry into it has become more difficult; school teachers tend to be, by and large, career teachers.

Ever since the rise of mass education, the country has needed functionaries who are not as literate as the rest of university graduates and has been willing to meet them half way, that is, grant them a modified form of the B.A., M.A., or the doctorate. James Conant has pointed out the watered-down or dried-up shells of subject-matter called education courses. Everett C. Hughes and David Riesman, among others, have emphasized the dame-school orientation of teachers and the omnicompetence expectations that still prevail in the teacher's work. Whereas some writers have maintained that nationally public-school teachers tend to be drawn from the lower middle-class, others have maintained that now there is an increasing number of bona fide middle-classmen among them, that is, people who have been second-generation American middle-class. School teaching, it can be said, has been a traditional avenue for the social mobility of the peasantry, of both "urban villagers" as Herbert Gans calls them, and of rural ones. This is, of course, not to discount that people of nonrural background or of middle-class origins do go into teaching. The important thing to remember is that a considerable proportion of teachers continue to be converts to the middle-class—Poles, Italians, Irishmen, Negroes, and fifth-to-eighth generation heretofore socially immobile "old stock." Perhaps public school teaching with its multifarious duties and low occupational status can, to a considerable extent, be only performed by converts to the middle-class, as indeed, some schoolmen themselves have asserted. What is sociologically or urban-anthropologically important about this notion is that the instruction of the young, of the new generation, being in part entrusted to converts, ensures, among other things, that competition and achievement continue to be zealously institutionalized in the school and that those who transmit cultural values are themselves paragons of middle-class virtues. That the public school, as a middle-class institution, is partially manned by converts ensures perpetuation of middle-class orthodoxy. No society could ask for better "cultural cops" than converts, and in this lies both the public schools' achievement and limitations!

Metaphors and Phrases

What kind of a place is the school? Educational literature tends to eulogize it as a unique institution, but obviously this is not so. There are similarities between institutions, for example in the way they are governed. In a system of checks and balances, public institutions tend to be governed by laymen and run by professionals. School-board members are not invariably the most "educated" in the community (pity the school superintendent whose board is composed exclusively of ex-teachers!). The same can be said of colleges, hospitals, and prisons, whose boards of trustees are not the most educationally, medically, or criminologically trained. Church trustees are not invariably the most ardently pious or ministerial

either; they represent, like other trustees of public institutions, the more respected and stable elements in the community. This means that educational and other institutions are kept "within the bounds of cost, intensity, and kind that the community . . . can stand and will support," that people who are hired to perform cherished services are kept in check, and that the institution continues to be responsive to the dominant elements in the community. If schools tend to be run by professionally trained middle-classmen, then their boards of trustees tend to be predominantly upper middle-class.

For putting the school within the context of institutional networks in society, a variety of metaphors and descriptive phrases have been employed:

1. As indicated earlier, institutions are processing-plants for people and skills; their chief business is socialization. If socialization is regarded as coterminous with life, then it can be seen that the church, the clinic, the factory, the college, and the prison also engage in socialization, into meeting the person at various contingencies in his life and determining his identity.

2. Institutions, as Malinowski has indicated, have a synthetic rather than a unitary function. What is church-like about the school? What is family-like about it? What is factory-like, hospital-like, and prison-like about it? In some schools—e.g., some slum schools where children are deliberately trained in social amenities as boys lining up outside the classroom to wait for girls to enter, learning to pour tea and serve cookies elegantly—the public school could be regarded as a finishing school or a sort of family. In schools where there is an emphasis on production, the endless test battery-scores and marking business make the school resemble a factory. It is as if teachers were employed on a piece-work basis and—as expected—would resort to rate-busting. On the other hand, some schools do seem like hospitals, with "special adjustment rooms" (as they are called in some places in the Middle West) for emotionally disturbed pupils. Some of these schools, because of recent federal or private grant funds, operate quite often as if they were a Rogerian theological seminary. As for what is prison-like about the school, in some upper middle-class schools, children—because of over-crowded cafeteria facilities—cannot talk while eating their 15-minute

lunch; because of the rule of silence, they develop an elaborate nonverbal system of communication as if they were inmates of a prison or a Tibetan convent. Some slum schools are run as if they were day jails; maximum security is enforced constantly by teachers, principal, and school counselors. In a sense, the school could be studied as a part of the larger socioeconomic system and viewed as a "complicated machine for sorting and ticketing and routing children through life."

3. The school, as Waller maintains, is a "museum of virtue." The dichotomy between the idealized world of the child and the realistic one of the adult is institutionalized in the school. Lower middle-class teachers who, as Riesman maintains, had missed being trained in poise, turn it into a big industry, a zealous quest for the all-rounded and colorless personality. It is as if the mass media never existed or never trained pupils in manners and morals.

4. Schools, as Durkheim points out, are guardians of the national character. Teachers train children in terms of an ideal client, a person suited to what the dominant group in a society likes to see produced.

5. Schools, as Peter L. Berger has said, are churches for drilling children in the religion of democracy. The perceptual sphere of children is narrowed down to focus only on the history—that is, official mythology—of a particular society and a particular social class. In this sense, we can see that stupidity—that is, self-serving ignorance—is, as Jules Henry has shown, institutionalized in the school. That ethnic groups in America, as part of their status politics for social mobility, had to clean up the textbooks and ask to be cut in on a piece of the action in American history is not taught in school, nor in college for that matter.

6. Schools, as Sumner has emphasized, teach the predominant orthodoxy of society, not the full range of beliefs and values in society.

7. The school is not only an academy but a place where the pupil acquires an identity. He is there told what he should do and get, and hence, what he should be. There he learns to make out, to work the system. How a child is turned into a pupil, how a boy is turned into a man under school auspices, and how a girl is turned into a woman would be—as Murray Wax and others have suggested—a worthy object to study in sociology and urban anthropology.

8. Lastly, the schools can be regarded as a political arena for special-interest groups who are bent on social mobility, that is, as job monopolies for occupational as well as ethnic groups. The way schools are run exemplifies the notion that what is true about society at large may also be true about the school as a small society, namely, that it is a group of competitive groups.

Summary and Conclusion

. . . In this paper, no fundamental distinction has been made between sociology and anthropology, especially when it comes to a field-work look at our public schools. In the perspective of the Chicago school of sociology, the sociologist is defined as an anthropologist of his culture. (In this sense, "urban anthropology" is but a delayed form of sociology.) One assumes that to understand what goes on in schools, one has to pull back from the school's culture in order to examine the unobvious things that lie behind the obvious, that is, one has to take the role of the stranger and try to decipher what the natives of the situation take for granted.

Whereas, in general, anthropologists have been fond of gathering detailed accounts of far away places, they have tended to take American society for granted. But perhaps, as Simmel says, the far is near: There is enough of the exotic in American society to make it a worthy concern of anthropology. As Waller has remarked in his study of public schools, "it is not necessary for the students of strange customs to cross the seas to find material." The familiar is but a special case of the unfamiliar.

Jacquetta Hill Burnett

Ceremony, Rites, and Economy in the Student System of an American High School

What happens when an anthropologist decides to study a school in her own society as she might study an isolated tribe in New Guinea? Suspecting that human beings have more similarities than differences, she would look for categories of behavior with which she is familiar. In just this manner, Jacquetta Burnett has written an ethnographic description of a small midwestern American high school. Most interesting to her was the unacknowledged importance of ceremonial and ritual behavior in the activities of the school.

Her paper shows that the study of schooling is not only enlightened by an ethnographic account, but also that a direct contribution to the development of anthropological theory is made when we try to make explicit the evolution of modern society.

Max Gluckman [has] expressed the view that "modern urban life" is correlated with the disappearance of the ritualization of social relations. Gluckman said: "I consider that rituals of the kind investigated by Van Gennep are 'incompatible' with the structure of modern urban life." He goes on to say, with respect to helping people of the secular urbanized world in their transitions from one status to another: ". . . I do not believe that it [i.e., help] can come from the tribal type of *rites de passage* in which social relationships are ritualized to assist persons at what are defined as crises."

On the basis of nearly a year's field work in a small midwestern high school in 1960–61, I wish here not only to present a description of one aspect of the culture of an American secondary school, but also to question on empirical grounds the extinction of ritual as an effective, functional device in urbanized societies. In fact, the empirical extension of the concepts "ceremony" and "ritual" was critical to the analysis of the calendar of events of the high school. . . .

I spent nine months as a participant observer in the school with 110 students, 7 teachers, and a teaching principal. Although I presented myself as a researcher, the students and faculty soon interpreted my activities and assigned me the role of guidance counselor. Throughout the nine-month school term, I observed the students during free periods of the day and during school-sponsored and school-related afternoon and evening activities. I gathered data on the relation between academic work and the student system by observing students in the study halls and in and between classes for several hundred hours.[1]

Ritual and Ceremonial in an American High School

The ceremonies and rites of the American high school which I studied were a regular part of extracurricular or student activities. Beyond the formal organization of work and the ubiquitous informal network of clique relationships, there were associational sets (or student clubs) of three general types that sponsored, planned, and carried out the annual calendar of activities. The most dominant type was formed out of the age-grade statuses in the high school. The second type grew out of the subject matter and work of formal courses in the regular curriculum, though the activities of these associations often seemed far removed from that subject matter. Finally, there was a type formed out of participation in interschool sports competition—a type with only one member, the Varsity Club.

Although teachers participated in these associations and activities as advisors and counselors and stressed their importance in teaching students a "sense of responsibility" (i.e., independence of initiative and decision-making), participation by the teachers was a matter of tradition and expectation, not of contract. The fact that they, as a body, could have withdrawn from participation, emphasized the semiformal character of this extra-

"Ceremony, Rites, and Economy in the Student System of an American High School" by Jacquetta Hill Burnett from *Human Organization* (Vol. 28, No. 1, 1969). Reproduced by permission of the Society for Applied Anthropology and the author.

[1] Van Gennep's schema of separation, transition, and incorporation was analytically helpful when applied to certain parts of the data. See A. Van Gennup, *The Rites of Passage*, trans. M. B. Vizedom and G. L. Caffee (Chicago: University of Chicago Press, 1960).

curricular sector of the institution.

Although the activities and events of the system were patterned into an annual cycle, for each age-grade or year-class status there was a four-year cycle of changing relationships to the annual cycle of student activities. From freshman initiation through sophomore, junior, and senior years, each year-class group experienced increasing opportunities for mobility in the student prestige hierarchy, increasing access as a group to commercial enterprises of the system, increasing financial affluence of the class-group, increasing political power and responsibility for important ceremonial events, and increasing opportunity to engage in student self-regulation of the subsystem. . . .

An Illustration of Student Ritual

Here we will first consider in some detail one of the ceremonies, the pep rally, to illustrate the criteria and data used in analysis of these ceremonial events. The pep rallies involved full assemblage of the high-school body to "work up school spirit," as the explanation usually went, just before an extramural sports event. The pep rally for football season struck me as somewhat more elaborate than the ones preceding basketball. No pep rallies preceded track meets, an incongruity that will be explained later. The rite was a regular, recurrent part of student life and very much a mainstay of the student system.

. . . To understand the systemic significance of ritual, one must take note of who interacts with whom and of the regular habitual order, duration, and temporal distribution of their actions with respect to one another.[2] Human social systems are continuously faced with crisis in their need to change the characteristic modes of interaction to carry out the instrumental requirements of a living system, and to meet shifts in their internal aspects as well as in the external environment. Disturbances, or required changes, in interaction relationships result in crisis and adjustment of the individual or of a group to the new arrangement and frequency of interaction.

Adjustment to change or to crisis may be secured either through associational interaction or through ritual. . . . Crisis is an everyday reality in social systems. . . . Both associational interaction and ritual interaction can be used to restore effective

[2] See E. Chapple and C. S. Coon, *Principles of Anthropology* (New York: Holt, Rinehart and Winston, 1942).

Time Cycles and Phases of Activity

Agricultural Cycle		School Cycle	Athletic Cycle	School Holidays	Rites of Intensification	Rites of Passage*
Summer	August					
	September	First semester				Freshman initiation
		First six weeks	Football		Pep rallies	
Fall	October	Second six weeks	Football		Pep rallies	
					Homecoming	
					Football banquet	
	November	Third six weeks	Basketball	Thanksgiving	Pep rallies	
	December			Christmas	Christmas dance	
	January				New Year's Eve party	
Winter						
		Second semester				
		Fourth six weeks			Pep rallies	
	February		Basketball		Sweetheart dance	
	March	Fifth six weeks	Track	Easter	Athletes' banquet	
Spring	April					
	May	Sixth six weeks	Track		Honors day	Baccalaureate
	June					Graduation
						Alumni banquet
						Senior trip

*The rites of passage are on a four-year rather than an annual cycle.

interactive equilibrium. Rites of passage are used at some points of crisis in the individual life cycle and rites of intensification are used to restore the interactive balance for a group when some change of conditions or disturbance affects all or a part of the members of a system. Through the rituals of the ceremony, rites of passage provide the individual with practice in new orders and distribution of interaction entailed in a change in his status in the system. The ritual in the ceremony of rites of intensification provides group members with a dramatic presentation of habitual relationships associated with the activities of the system. Shifts in required activities bring about crisis through demanding changes in the interaction needed to carry out the activities. A rite of intensification is one functional device for carrying off the shifts in habitual relationships. Pep rallies, then, are ritual means of quickly carrying the students through a transition in interaction from work activity and the everyday relations of daily school life to the characteristically different relationships of extramural athletic events, when students relate to large numbers of members of the community and relate to one another in somewhat different ways.

The course of the events during football season can illustrate the characteristic order and interrelationship of aspects of ceremonial events. Football games were held on Friday evenings around 8:00 P.M. out-of-doors under floodlights. . . . During football season, the order of events of the day ran its familiar course until a special bell rang ten minutes earlier than the usual dismissal bell. At this signal, the entire high-school population, including teachers, assembled in the old gymnasium. When all were assembled, the school principal called the group to order and made a few announcements. Then the cheerleaders, as a group, trotted before the audience, and in well-practiced formation initiated cheers to the students and led them in highly synchronized cheers, first for the team, then for the coaches. They retired and one or two of the varsity players (always either seniors or juniors in class standing) stood before the group and gave a pep talk on the coming game. The talks always ended on a note of determination to strive to win. The player was greeted with a cheer; his talk was sometimes interrupted with cheers and always closed with a cheer from students. Next, the head coach or assistant coach gave a pep talk always concerned with the reputation of this week's oppo-

nent and the good features and improvements in the home team. The coach's talk always closed with a statement of his confidence in the players and their determination to play hard and to play to win. Finally, he usually alluded to the helpfulness toward victory of the spirit and support of the rest of the students. Then, the cheerleaders led the entire student body in more cheers and, as the dismissal bell rang, the students filed out, cheering as they went.

As the girls and boys dispersed to walk home or ride home in bus or car, there was an unusual degree of segregation of boys and girls. The occupants of cars were particularly noticeable for their sexual homogeneity. According to training rules, the players reported to me, the boys on the team were to go straight home to rest and prepare themselves for the game. Those boys were not to engage in interaction with girls from the time they departed from school until after the game. As the boys usually put it, "You aren't supposed to be seen with girls."

The male/female segregation actually began during the pep rally. In the old gymnasium, there were bleachers running the length of the south side of the gym; they were separated into an east and a west side by the entrance and steps leading down into the gymnasium. During pep rallies, the students always sat on the west side of the bleachers; the teachers, except for coaches, always sat on the east side; the coaches sat with their players. The students further segregated themselves: the players sat toward the west end of the west bleachers near the playing floor of the gymnasium; the boys who weren't on the team sat at the back of the west bleachers from the center aisle to the west wall. The girls sat toward the front of the west bleachers nearest the aisle and well separated from the players. The cheerleaders, all girls, sat on the lowest bleachers adjoining the gymnasium floor directly in front of the other girls. The students were further organized spatially through the tendency of students to cluster near one another in clique groups.

During the evening event in the course of the game, the social relations and orders of action that were prominent in the pep rally occurred repeatedly. For example, players were segregated from other students, particularly from girls; cheerleaders initiated and synchronized cheers during the course of the game; and students were not subject to their usual relationship to teachers and other adults. And those who acted as vendors of drink and food, had a different type of relationship with adults.

After home games, a student dance ... was usually held in the gymnasium with music provided on phonograph records. . . .

The mode of activity and interactive relationships characteristic of evening events like this were markedly different from the mode of activity and interaction that characterized the school workday. Clearly, the ritual of the pep rally ceremony could be said to help with the quick transition by organizing, dramatizing, and actively illustrating the change in interaction and relationship.

Other Student Ceremonials

The football banquet marked the end of football season. The banquet—for football players, their coaches, and the school principal and superintendent—was a boisterous, rowdy, stag affair that signaled a change in the characteristic mode of interaction among players. Relationships with other students, among community members, and between players and spectators did not change enough from football to basketball seasons to require ritual dramatization for student body and community. The rite, therefore, involved only the players and the coaches, who were deeply affected by the cessation of certain modes of relationship and interaction.

The Christmas dance and New Year's Eve dance related to the culture-wide temporal event of the Christmas season. They marked the beginning and close, respectively, of a long recess from schoolwork and from regular modes of interaction among students. The Sweetheart Dance anticipated the end of . . . the Friday evening dances that followed home games.

The athletes' banquet, in contrast to the football banquet, was sponsored by parents and attended by parents as well as students and players. It posed an interesting challenge to the view that rites of intensification mark changes in group social relations. One asks why did it occur before, rather than after, track season? The explanation lies in the fact that track meets were held in the afternoon immediately after school rather than later in the evening. Despite several winning track seasons, few students attended, only a handful of adults attended, no money-earning enterprises were operated, and no cheerleaders or other means were used to organize spectator response. Most heads of households drove to nearby cities to their work and, consequently, did not arrive in time for events beginning around half past three in the afternoon. Track meets after school just didn't fit the community time schedule. The significant change in interaction for the community occurred with the cessation of basketball games, which were evening games they could attend. It is this which was marked by a rite of intensification—the community-sponsored athletes' banquet.

Homecoming, which occurred in the fall just a few weeks after the school year began, was an event that brought together students, former students, and the community in general, and that gave expression to every significant relationship in the student subsystem—because successful execution of the ceremony *demanded* the operation of all these relationships. The political dominance of the seniors was reflected in the fact that they were entirely in charge of planning, organizing, and supervising Homecoming. From the building of parade floats, through the ritual beginning of Homecoming with a bonfire and snake dance on Thursday, a parade in town on Friday afternoon, the half-time activities at the football game Friday evening, the decoration of the gymnasium, sponsorship of the Homecoming Dance, to the ritual climax of the Homecoming ceremony with the crowning of the King and Queen of Homecoming, seniors were in charge. But they relied on the cooperation of all the student organizations in the school. By the time the first preparations for Homecoming began in late September, positions in the various associations had been assigned personnel, from presidents to minor standing committees. Homecoming activities were handled within the permanent associations through both special and standing committees. But the structures were not activated and put into motion until Homecoming and its preparation, colored by intensity of feeling, deadline rush, and anxiety for success, touched the whole system with a sense of crisis and the need to mobilize. The organizational system then moved into forward gear as the senior class offered a monetary prize for the best float. The year-class, age-graded associations were the liveliest competitors in that contest. In addition, whether or not they organized to build floats, *all* associations carried out elections to nominate a king and queen candidate—although seniors always won the final crowns. The student council had exercised its function as a control for allocating money-earning enterprises. The community at several points assumed its role of interested, responsive spectator to the knowledge, performances, and products of the high school students.

Details might be added, but it seems clear that Homecoming was a system-wide rite of intensification. The usual role positions of the associations were filled; certain organizations had begun to operate; year-class groups were poised to behave in a new status in relationship to the total system. But without a very dramatic challenge it might have required a long time for the complex interdependencies and synchronization of activity and positional duties to work in smooth, orderly fashion. All these new characteristics of interaction amount to a crisis of the system that is resolved through carrying out a complex event in the form of ritualized, traditional patterns of action and interdependencies. . . . Everyone gets practice in the patterns of action and interaction that will be characteristic of associational work throughout the rest of the year.

Ritual, Ceremony, and the Student Economic System

Turning finally to the manner in which the entire ceremonial system was supported by and related to the student economic system, one must consider a special rite of passage: the senior trip. The senior trip was the main objective in the money-earning activities of each year-class. Every year, after going through several ceremonial events that dramatized the separation of the seniors from the high school system, the senior class departed on a three- or four-day trip. Accompanied only by the class sponsor, bus driver, and their respective spouses, the seniors rode to a resort in the Missouri Ozarks where other senior classes from other high schools also gathered for three or four days of "gay abandon." This was the final event of the school year and the final student activity of the seniors' high school career. . . .

Though the beliefs associated with most of these ceremonial events mentioned above were skimpy to nonexistent, there was a rather more elaborate development of myth in connection with the senior trip. These myths, told more often by boys than girls, centered on tales of curfew violation, smoking, drinking, and sex. Ex-seniors emphatically declared to me that there was much fiction and little fact in these stories. . . .

The senior trip was the keystone of the student economy and the integrating goal of the student system. That this economic goal took priority over all other goals was reflected in the student council's policy of allocating the best and the greatest number of money-making enterprises to the seniors and juniors, in that order. I would not argue that economic motive was the only propelling force of the system. For example, yearning for prestige among their peers and within their immediate social milieu surely impelled students to expend thought, time, and energy in student activities. Yet the economic goal of financing special events of the year welded atomistic desires into group effort. Each student association had a main annual event around which to muster the efforts and economic enterprise of its members. However, the main event around which each year-class association organized its economic activities was the senior trip which was quadrennial rather than annual. By providing motive and direction over a four-year cycle rather than an annual cycle, the senior trip provided the focus for an intergenerational tradition which upperclassmen could transmit to lowerclassmen, thus forming a pattern of enculturation for the student system as a whole.

The most common means of earning money was through selling food, and sometimes services. Except where long tradition had given another association a particularly lucrative resource, class associations, especially seniors, were granted the more profitable enterprises.

The frequent coincidence of entertainment activities and relationships with commercial activities and relationships was a salient characteristic of the system. The most successful entertainment events from the commercial point of view were the athletic events, for the needs of the crowd during the games were fulfilled by the goods sold by student associations. School spirit and school pride notwithstanding, the better the team the bigger the crowd; the bigger the crowd the more popcorn, candy, hot dogs, soda pop, and coffee sold. Thus, a good team, along with star athletes, not only carried responsibility for the reputation of the school *vis-à-vis* other schools; it was an economic asset to the student system.

There were other ways of making money from persons outside the student body than selling refreshments, but most of these required an assemblage of persons from the community. A group could earn money through admissions to dances, but the size of the crowd was critical. The sponsoring group hired an orchestra and a certain minimum attendance was required before the initial investment could be recovered and a profit made. Scheduling the dance after an athletic event was one of the best means of assuring at least this minimum profitable attendance. In light of this relationship it does not seem entirely unwarranted to suggest that between the athletic events and the student systems there was a kind of ecological connection.

Without the participation of adults and community members as spectators, these events would have gradually disappeared from the calendar of events. Through student activities, adults and parents were involved in socialization into that special style we have come to call "independence training." The adult was spectator to the performance, learning, success or failure of the young. Much of this learning was from peers, but it was then tested against the positive or negative response of adults as spectators. The adults in the community, through their interest in local high school athletics and other entertainment events, ultimately influenced and affected the value system of the students in the school—not in a one-to-one, adult-to-young relationship, but through a complex network of influence.

Conclusion

At the empirical level, this study challenges the position that rites and ceremonies of "status change" necessarily disappear with the rise of secular urban institutions. . . .

Some may argue that the rural setting of the high school studied here is a survival from the past and that data from this community are not relevant to the modern urban world. Actually, this type of rural community is a necessary part of the urban scene. The mechanized, market-oriented, commercialized agriculture and the salient presence of commuting by nonfarmers to nearby urban centers for employment declare this community's membership in the broad urban scene and the relevance of this study to urban society. This is the agricultural sector of an urbanized society.

The town and school are admittedly small and highly homogeneous. These facts may limit the extension of any generalization from this setting. We know, however, that elaborate ceremonial cycles characterize secondary schools across the United States, although the interrelationships among ceremonial cycle, the academic work system, clique structure, immediate community, and association structure may vary greatly with the heterogeneity and size of the high school population. But this study does raise the question of what part ritual plays in the multichartered, multigrouped institutions that educate, socialize, and enculturate young people into modern megalopolises.

A. D. Fisher

White Rites versus Indian Rights

American anthropology is historically derived from studies of American Indians. Recent critiques of anthropology have suggested that the implicit acceptance by anthropologists of the colonial relationships of Indians to the surrounding American society has been a severe handicap for those who would see the discipline as a liberating force. It is, therefore, especially

appropriate to point out that recent anthropological studies of Indian education have been exceptional in that they relate to the present social problems of Indians rather than to their past glories.

Going beyond Burnett's analysis of ritual patterns in schools, Fisher shows, through the plight of Canadian Indians, that the modern schooling process itself can be viewed as a ritual of the larger society—functional for only some of its people involved.

Indians have experienced a long period of forced acculturation in the schools of both Canada and the United States. They have rarely had the opportunity or legal right of making schools for their children in the tribal setting. Nor do the schools gain their children entrance into the dominant society. Though Fisher has written little about his own experience, he has been active for the past several years in supporting the attempts of Canadian Indians to gain control of the political and educational institutions to which they have been subjected by the dominant society.

In North America...the belief in increasing educational opportunities as the avenue to social progress has become an article of faith, and "going to school" an assurance of secular salvation akin to "good works" and "saving grace" in other times and other religions....

Yet it is a fact that the propitiation of the gods of learning simply isn't working for vast numbers of Americans and Canadians, especially the poor, the black, and the Indian. Indeed, for those with whom I am most concerned in this essay, the Indian people of Canada, it can be demonstrated that education has been very nearly a total disaster.

Despite a considerable expansion of the number of schools and in the number of years of schooling available to Canadian Indian children, the unemployment rate among them has increased. Between the years 1959–60 and 1962–63, the welfare costs among Alberta's Indian population jumped from $294,625 to $683,080, and a sizeable portion of the latter figure went to unemployed but "educated" Indians. The incidence of unemployment among Indians with education is even more graphically illustrated by comparing the average unemployment of the total Indian population (43 percent) to that of Alberta Indian students who terminated their education in 1964–65 (64 percent).

While these figures clearly indicate that the Canadian Indian fails to use whatever education he receives once his schooling is over, other studies show that he also fails to take advantage of the schooling available to him. For example, in 1965 a study was made of junior high school dropouts at the Blackfoot Indian Reserve, Gleichen-Cluny, Alberta. It was determined that 86 of 168 students, or 51 percent, had dropped out of school in the years since 1961 and of these dropouts, 95 percent left school before they had completed grade nine....

The School as Ritual

...In Euro-Canadian society the school is a "primary institution," in the sense that it is basic and widespread. All Euro-Canadian children are expected to attend school for extensive periods of time and to profit from the experience. It is, in fact and in theory, the major socialization device of the industrialized, urbanized segment of the Canadian population. As such it consumes a tremendous amount of time, substantial amounts of money, and a great deal of energy.

In this paper, then, I define "the school," all formal education from kindergarten to grade twelve or thirteen, as a rite of passage, or rather a series of rites signifying separation from, transition through, and incorporation into culturally recognized statuses and roles. Within the larger chronological rite there are also numerous other rites and ceremonials indicating partial transitions and new role relationships.

This redefinition of the school as a rite of passage is likely to provoke some disagreement. Anthropologists and laymen alike choose to think of ritual and rites of passage as essentially magico-religious activities, and of schools as being only partially or minimally engaged in this type of activity. This is not altogether so. Not all ritual must be magico-religious, nor are schools as institutions, or what goes on in schools, completely free from magico-religious significance. It is quite difficult to categorize ritual activity clearly as to religious content. Further, ritual activity ranges from the purely magical and religious through the pseudorational to rational routine, albeit it is up to the observer to ascertain its rationality. Clearly in any case, there are numerous calendrical and other rites and ceremonies in the public school that signify changes in the student's social life. Thus, the whole educational structure can be envisioned as a long-term ritual marking various changes in the social lives of the individuals. It is difficult for an outside observer to assess their magico-religious or secular content.

Nevertheless, it would be very hard to argue that the majority of Canadian students, parents, and teachers see "education" in a wholly rational light. In a recent study, a noted American educator pointed out that despite scientific knowledge to the contrary the vast majority of public school classrooms in the United States operate on the two-thirds theory (*Trans-action*, 1967): two-thirds of the time someone is talking, two-thirds of the time it is the teacher who is talking, two-thirds of the time the teacher is talking she is lecturing or commenting upon the behavior of children in the classroom. If this is the case in the United States, then Canadian schools, generally, operate on the three-quarters theory, and schools catering to Indians operate on the seven-eighths theory. The involvement of the school in teaching moral-ethical behavior, the continuing belief in "disciplining the mind" through rigid curricula and repetitive testing, the various rites of prayer and of patriotism, indeed, the whole defensive ethos of the school point to the pseudorational nature of the school.

Rites of Passage

More succinctly, one can look at "the school" as a series of "ideological rituals," using "ideological" here in Mannheim's sense, as a means to protect and perfect the existing social system, in contrast to the "utopian" striving for revolutionary change. In this sense the public school in North America is indeed an ideological rite of passage. Educators have long thought [of] the institution of the public school as the common ground that allows immigrant and indigenous groups the wherewithal for intelligent self-government, common mores, and economic perfection and advancement within the ideological system of North American "democratic" society.

There is little doubt that the characteristic form of North American public education is typical of North American society. It exemplifies and reflects the values of that society, and prepares students for urban, industrialized middle-class society. Finally the whole ritual culminates in a pseudo-religious ceremonial known as "Convocation" or "Commencement" in which it tells the ex-student, "Now do it." Those who "can do it" have been certified for that society. From kindergarten or grade one when the child learns who his "helpers" in the school and neighborhood are, to grade

twelve or thirteen when each student is ranked and evaluated on the formalized "external" or Departmental examinations, he passes through a multitude of statuses and plays many roles. The result of the whole process is the development of a particular sort of individual, that is if the process is successful.

But, what would happen if we were to take this ceremonial system out of its context, North American middle-class society, and place it in a wholly or partly alien context such as an Indian reserve? The answer is that unless there were community support for it, it would fail. Let me stress this point. It would be the rite of passage, the rituals recognized and enjoined by middle-class society that would fail; *not the Indian student*.

Since 1944 there has been little doubt among scholars that students of North American Indian ancestry have intelligence adequate for most activities, exclusive of school. Robert Havighurst's well-known 1957 article demonstrates that Indian children perform "about as well" as white children on performance tests of intelligence. More recently, in Charles Ray, Joan Ryan, and Seymour Parker's 1962 study of Alaskan secondary-school dropouts, the authors state: "The conclusion to be derived from the data is that intelligence *per se* cannot be considered a major contributing factor to dropouts and that achievement levels are not markedly different." As this essay is focused primarily on dropouts with Eskimo, Aleut, or Tlingit ethnic backgrounds as contrasted with white children, it appears to indicate that the cause of dropout is elsewhere than intelligence. But where are we to find it?

Thinking in Two Tongues

California Achievement Test scores in Alberta and South Dakota among Plains Cree, Blackfoot, and Sioux Indians indicate that the young Indian starts out *ahead* of his white peers, but then gradually tails off in achievement. Fourth-grade Indians who had averaged 4.3 on achievement tests while their white counterparts scored only 4.1, had by the eighth grade been surpassed by the white students who achieved an 8.1 average while Indian students had one of 7.7. Test scores consistently decline between grades five and seven.... From these patterns of slumping achievement-test scores ... it appears that some sort of difficulty arises in the relationship between "the school" and the pre-pubescent/pubescent Indian. Admittedly, some Indian students drop out later than others but it would appear that in most cases of prolonged schooling it is the enforcement of the School Act that made the difference. The Blackfoot and Blood Indians of southern Alberta, for example, are under considerable compulsion to stay in school. If they do not "fit" the existing academic program, they are enrolled in "pre-employment" courses or in special programs such as "upgrading." It is therefore quite difficult for these students to leave school. The younger student often "solves" this problem by becoming a "trouble-maker" in school (sassing teachers, being truant, refusing to work, etc.) or by becoming "delinquent" outside school (drinking and sexual escapades, fighting and theft). Of these Blackfoot "early dropouts," ages thirteen to sixteen (which is the school-leaving age) 75 percent of the fifteen-year-olds and 70 percent of the sixteen-year-olds were considered "delinquent." Among the older students, ages seventeen, eighteen, and nineteen, the amount of delinquent behavior was radically reduced. Apparently, then, when a Blackfoot student passes the school-leaving age, he can choose to stay or to go, and he generally chooses to go. . . .

Indian expectations of school are conditioned by what the young Indian learns in the environment of his home community. Because what he learns at home often differs widely from what he learns at school, the Indian student is frequently forced to separate the two learning experiences. George Spindler once heard a "successful" Blood Indian say:

I have to think about some things in my own language and some things in English. Well, for instance, if I think about horses, or about the Sun Dance, or about my brother-in-law, I have to think in my own language. If I think about buying a pickup truck or selling some beef or my son's grades in school I have to think in English.

The languages of Blackfoot and English are kept entirely apart; the former is for thinking about basic cultural elements, while the latter is used for school work. The Indian student grows up in a particular society with its own particular role transitions and in the presence of or absence of appropriate ritual recognition of these changes. Since the expectations about ritual and about role

transitions held by any society and recognized as legitimate for that society are peculiar to that society, and to part-societies, at any time the school, as a rite of passage, may become inappropriate to members of a particular society that differs from North American middle-class society. This is what seems to happen to the Indian student.

Identity and Work

Young Blood Indians have certain very specific ideas about what they are and what they are going to be. Among a stratified sample of forty young Bloods the most popular choices of a career or vocation were as follows: ranching, automechanic, carpenter, bronc rider, haying, and farming. All of these occupations can be learned and practiced right on the Blood Reserve. They chose these occupations for two important reasons: knowledge and experience or, in other words, experiential knowledge that they already held. Among the Blackfoot dropouts and "stay-ins" a very similar pattern emerged. They, too, chose occupations that were familiar to them, even if they pertained little to their academic life. And this pattern emerges elsewhere in only slightly different form.

In Harry Wolcott's "Blackfish Village" Kwakiutl study he mentions in passing the response by students to the essay topic, "What I Would Like to Be Doing Ten Years from Now." Almost all the students thought they would be in and around their village. Two of the older girls guessed they would be married and in the village. Farther north, in Alaska, the Ray, Ryan, and Parker study notes that the three primary reasons given for dropping out of secondary school are "needed at home," "marriage," and "wanted to work." Of the secondary reasons, to help at "home," "marriage," and "homesick" were most important. These reasons appear to indicate that the Alaskan dropout was opting out of formal education to return home to what he or she knows. As the authors indicate, "The majority of dropouts saw little relationship between what they were learning in school and jobs that were available to them."

Turning inland from British Columbia and Alaska we note the same phenomenon among the Metis of the Lac La Biche area (Kikino, Owl River, Mission), among the Blackfoot dropouts of Gleichen and Cluny and among the young Blood of southwestern Alberta. In each case the Indian student on the one hand expects to be doing what is now done in the context of his community, and on the other hand sees only a vague, if any, correlation between the demands of formal education in the context of the school and that which he expects to do.

A final point in this regard is made in the Waxes' study of the Pine Ridge Sioux. They state that education and being a good Sioux Indian are two separate processes, if becoming a good Indian is a process at all. They say that the full-bloods think that:

. . . education harms no one, but on the other hand it has almost nothing to do with being a good person. . . . [They] do not seem to be aware that their off-spring are regarded as unsocialized, amoral, or backward by their teachers. That a child could be educated to the point where he would become critical of his kin or attempt to disassociate himself from them is still beyond their comprehension.

In conclusion, these studies show that the expanded educational opportunities for Canadian Indians are not really opportunities at all. For what the school offers is an irrelevant set of values and training. Moreover, the school often comes into direct conflict with certain moral and cultural values of the student. Thus, it is the educational system that fails the student and not the student who fails the system. In trying to be a good and successful Indian, the Indian student must often be a bad and unsuccessful student.

Rosalie H. Wax and Murray L. Wax

The Enemies of the People: Report of an Ethnographer

Like Fisher, the Waxes have been active in working with programs of Indian education. In her paper, Rosalie Wax recounts in detail their interaction with their subjects and their relation to programs designed to change the Indians' situation. The nature of the cultural transactions taking place between Indians and the outside society, represented by the federal government, is quite important. The structure of this article emphasizes the reciprocal and interacting quality of problems between Indians and the outsiders.

There is also an important warning here for those who would go off as reformers and organizers ready to meet the educational problems of another group. Peace Corps volunteers, VISTA volunteers, and even anthropologists recruited to government programs of education and community development have all too often made their own unilateral decisions about the "needs" of the people and the appropriate way to organize to meet these needs. Perhaps we should learn to be equally careful in making prescriptions for our own community schools.[1]

As social scientists and teachers, my husband and I have until very recently believed that the almost impenetrable wall between American Indians and the people and organizations who wish to help them could be crossed or dissolved by proper means of communication. If the Indians who need help could learn how to plug into the right channels, if the White people who man these channels could come to understand Indians, then the stalemate of Indian helplessness, isolation, and bitter poverty might be broken. We realized, of course,

"The Enemies of the People" by Rosalie H. Wax and Murray L. Wax. Reprinted from Howard S. Becker, et al., editors, *Institutions and the Person: Essays Presented to Everett C. Hughes* (Chicago: Aldine Publishing Company, 1968); copyright © Howard S. Becker, et al. Reprinted by permission of the authors and Aldine Atherton, Inc.

[1]As a footnote to this article, we would like to quote from a letter that Murray L. Wax sent to us: "When we sent a copy of the essay to our Oglala Sioux friend, Calvin JumpingBull, he responded 'Lila waste yelo' which in the Lakota language is a salute to an outstanding performance."—Ed.

that, compared to other people in the U.S., the Indians had very little power and, ourselves being professors, we had good reason to appreciate that knowledge is *not* power. Nevertheless, we reasoned, power is hard to acquire without knowledge and knowledge rests on communication.

It was in the spirit of this belief that we participated in many workshops and conferences—both for Indians and for the teachers of Indian children. It was also in the spirit of this belief that we designed and carried out an intensive study of a reservation school situation where academic achievement was notoriously low. There we observed that in some classrooms the children were learning virtually nothing of a scholastic nature. By the fifth or sixth grade they had become adept at disrupting and inhibiting the process of instruction. They feigned stupidity, refused to listen, sharpened pencils loudly when asked to recite, and wrote on the board in letters so small no one could read them. When asked to read aloud they held their books before their faces and mumbled a few incomprehensible words. (The teacher was not aware that other pupils were teasing the reader, by signs and whispers in their native language.)

The efficiency of social organization of these children excited our admiration. Nonetheless, when we talked to their parents we found that most wanted their children to acquire education and, moreover, believed that they were getting it. Investigating further, we found that the parents rarely entered the school and never saw what went on in the classrooms; whereas the teachers, for their part, never visited the parents or attended any of the local Indian social events, such as fairs, dances, give-aways, or bingo parties. Indian elders were not permitted to use the schools for gatherings or entertainments, lest they dirty the floors and destroy government property. Around each consolidated school was a compound in which the teachers lived and kept to themselves.

It seemed to us that if the teachers genuinely wished to educate the Indian children and if the parents genuinely wished their children to be educated, they might do well to break down this elaborate system of *dharma*, get together, and devise means by which the spirited youngsters could be controlled. Among the more radical of our recommendations (though I now consider it the most sensible) was the suggestion that the Indian communities run their own schools with monies

from the federal government. Eccentric and off-beat such schools might be, but they could not teach the children less than now. Among our other or less radical suggestions were that mothers be hired as classroom aides, that parents be invited to social gatherings held at the school, that teachers be given time off to visit parents in their homes, and that Indians sit on the school board.

Having spoken so strongly in favor of involving the Indian parents and communities in the education of their children, we subsequently welcomed the opportunity to observe and report on Head Start Projects among the Indians living in the Dakotas and Minnesota. In these projects, or so it seemed to us, the Office of Economic Opportunity was sponsoring exactly the kind of grass-roots activity that would help to dissolve the wall between the Indian parents and the schools. For example, communities needing aid were to request it. If funds were granted, the projects were to be directed and carried on by the people who had asked for assistance—and not, primarily, by outsiders. Should outside professional assistance be required, the professionals were directed to involve the parents. We were particularly eager to see what was happening in the several Indian communities which, a year before, had been visited by a representative of the Community Action Programs, who had urged the people in the various districts to form committees, make plans for community improvement, and submit them to Washington. We had heard that several communities had prepared such plans and had ourselves seen the one submitted by the Standing Man Community. So far as we know, it is the only poverty program introduced by a poem:

Go in search of the people
Live with the people
Learn from them
Love them
Serve them
Make plans together with the people
Begin with what they know
Build on what they have.

It further explains that:

Many members [of the community] expressed that they had not realized that poverty existed, as so many of them grew up in conditions which are now described as poverty but was not identified as such prior to this time.

and that:

The older people have given their consent to let the young people plan the future of the community. They have said that the younger generation is the one who will have to live with the proposed programs.

The plan included such items as a summer youth program, adult education, and self-help housing. Its budget was extremely modest, and it emphasized that:

the community feels that the programs presented for the Poverty Program Committee can be effective in establishing a foundation for stabilizing the impact of the dominant culture if administered by the people themselves, and thus, maintain the dignity and respect for themselves as Indian people.

It requested, in addition, a professional person

who will help and work with the people in the community [and help] develop able trainees from the local people in the community.

So far as we knew, this program had not yet been funded. On the other hand, we were informed that the OEO expected to establish Head Start projects on this reservation, and, this being so, we were to investigate and report on how this might best be done. Accordingly, on our arrival we began to visit Indian friends and acquaintances in the districts and ask them what they thought about a playschool for 4- and 5-year-olds. Most parents and elders opined that if the hours were not too long and if the teachers were young and happy instead of old and crabby, a school in which the little children could learn and play might be a good thing. Some felt that the children should be taught something about "Indian things," and others, that it would be a good idea if some of the teachers or teachers-helpers spoke the native language. Asking about recent developments, we were told that the newly established program of work for youth (Neighborhood Youth Corps) was a good thing, but that, of course, what the people really needed was work for adult men who had to support families. When we asked about the new and handsome looking Old Peoples Home erected since our last visit, we were told that the old people did not like it and so nobody was living in it now but VISTA workers and some nurses' aides.

After three days, this phase of our investigation was brought to an abrupt close when we dis-

covered, quite by accident, that an elaborate program of Head Start and Child Development Centers was already funded and under way. Curious as to how such a program could exist without any of the people knowing anything about it, we inquired further and were referred to "the VISTA workers." These young people, looking wan and harassed, told us that they had been so busy doing paper work and arranging for the delivery of Head Start supplies, that they had not had the time to leave the Agency Town and get out on the reservation. From them we learned that the existing program had been spearheaded by the (White) Tribal Attorney, with the consent of the Tribal Council. It was now being directed by another White man, who was supervising their work. A highly qualified young White woman with a master's degree in child development had been hired to take charge of instruction. Several of the Head Start schools would be ready to open within a few weeks.

We expressed sincere astonishment at the amount of progress which had been made through the efforts of so few people. Nonetheless, we suggested that the program as it was now being conducted seemed somewhat lacking in community involvement and parental participation. Would it not still be possible to arrange a few meetings at which hours, curriculum, transportation, and other matters might be discussed with the parents? The young people explained that they had suggested this, especially since one of the schools was about to open, and "'the people out there' must be beginning to wonder what it's all about." But the temporary director had vetoed the idea, because, he said, "As soon as 'the people out there' discover that a program has been funded, they will come to my office in droves trying to get jobs for their relatives."

We pointed out that the contract with OEO specifically called for the involvement of parents in the planning of the program and went on to ask to what extent community leaders had been involved. "We haven't been able to find any," said the young folk rather aggrievedly. When, later in the conversation, we named several of the men who had helped to prepare the original "poverty programs," the young peoples' faces hardened with distaste. These men, they confided, were selfish politicians who wanted only to help their family and kin but cared little for the reservation as a whole. "They're not going to get a thing from us." Warming to the subject, the young folk informed us that "we have decided" that the Standing Man Community, which had been making the most fuss of all (apparently, we gathered, by asking what had happened to their poverty program of the year before), was to be taught a lesson. It was to be the last district on the reservation to be granted a Child Development Center.

In subsequent discussions we tried to point out to the young VISTA workers that the grand, overall reservation community with which they were trying to interact did not exist. Instead, the reservation always has been and still is divided into people who call each other Fullbloods and Mixedbloods. Most of the Fullbloods live out on the reservation in small local communities, which they themselves call *tiyospaye* and which were predominantly composed of kin. Each of these small communities maintains an internal organization and economy of extraordinary efficiency. They are extremely poor, but they are also extremely tough and tenacious. On the other side are the Mixedbloods, who, for three generations, have served as mediators between the local bands, or *tiyospaye,* and the larger society. First existing as scouts and traders, they later became entrepreneurs; in recent years, many have become liaison men and federal administrators. Their social organization is much more diffuse than that of the Fullbloods, and, while they are seldom wealthy, they are usually better off than the latter. Since the White and Mixedblood members of the bureaucracy insist (and sometimes believe) that there is only one reservation-wide community, they can and do monopolize all the influential and well-paid jobs. This is not to say that they do not need jobs. But the Fullbloods, who rarely get within reach of a good job, are for the most part, bitterly poor. As in many symbiotic relationships, neither side trusts the other. The Mixedbloods consider the Fullbloods unreliable and backward, because "they are always favoring their relatives." The Fullbloods mistrust the Mixedbloods because they have no (local) community allegiance and so are "not really Indian."

We did not tell the VISTA workers that the Fullbloods do not always regard the members of the Tribal Council as their "representatives" and that, though able and honorable men sometimes sat on the council, it had been created by the Indian Bureau to operate according to the White man's rules. Nor did we tell them that we had small confidence that the Tribal Attorney or the incumbent director of the Community Action Program had any real understanding of the social dynamics of reservation life. The attorney, who is dedicated to helping Indians but has never striven to understand them or to grasp their values, had recently involved the Tribal Council in several elaborate and expensive ventures, like the then uninhabited Old Peoples Home. The director has devoted a lifetime to trying to change the Fullbloods into his conception of good citizens, but he pointedly refrains from attending their social or ceremonial affairs (which would put him on a level of parity with them) and participates instead in the Rotary Club, the Kiwanis, the American Legion, and other organizations whose cultural basis is non-Indian; nor has he learned the native language in which Fullbloods carry on most of their social, economic, and political affairs. We did recommend most strongly to the young people that they get out of the Agency Town and make the acquaintance of the so-called Fullbloods, feeling that if they obtained a more complete picture of the situation, they would be able to make their own judgments. One of the VISTA workers accepted my invitation to accompany me on some home visits. But talking to the Fullblood mothers about their children seemed to make little impression on her. On the ride back to the Agency Town she expressed concern because we had been doing something contrary to the local program, namely, consulting the parents beforehand.

Some five months later, we were again given the opportunity to visit Thrashing Buffalo Reservation and report on the now functioning Head Start Program. By this time the VISTA workers had been replaced by a considerable staff of White people and Mixedbloods. These persons talked about "selling the program to the Indian people" and pointed out that a great deal of work would have to be directed toward the Indian people "in order for them to comply with our attempts and efforts, as workers, to help them." They also stressed the "lack of communication" and complained about the difficulty of making "an effective penetration into the Indian areas." Meanwhile, the Fullbloods were voting with their feet. Some pointed out to us that the Community Action Program directorate in the Agency Town had, as usual, hogged all the funds that might otherwise have flowed directly from the federal government to the people of the *tiyospaye*. When asked what their neighbors thought of the Head Start Programs, they remarked delicately: "Since these programs are not their own programs, they are not too much interested."

At one indoctrination meeting, the few local people who attended were less diffident. They told the CAP representatives that they did not want a nursery school, because 4-year-old children would not grow as they should if taken from their mothers. Besides, without her little children to care for, a mother would feel lost and useless. They regarded with strong disfavor the suggestion that they donate their community building to serve as a Head Start classroom, because (we suspect) they feared that if the school authorities took it over they would never give it back.

A year after its inception, the Thrashing Buffalo Head Start Program was limping along with neither "side" giving an inch. Indeed, the director, an energetic specialist in child development, openly announced that the purpose of the program was to change Indian culture. When members of a *tiyospaye* approached her with the suggestion that some older Indian people be hired to teach some elements of Indian culture, she explained that this is not possible because "nursery age-levels do not permit factual and conceptual learning."

We visited many other Head Start Projects for Indian children, and in most of them we found that the programs had been funded, planned, staffed, and put into operation with virtually no involvement of the children's parents. At several schools the parents had subsequently approached the directors and teachers with complaints and suggestions concerning the operation of the schools. But in every case, the professional staff regarded this parental interest with distress, as if it reflected a failure in either planning or procedure. Parental involvement was defined as the parents' complying with the suggestions of the teachers. Thus, the directors were pleased when the parents made blocks for the children according to the specifications laid down by the teachers, or when the parents, as requested, "volunteered" to accompany the classes on bus trips.

To the directors and teachers we remarked that the complaints and suggestions of the parents could profitably be viewed not as judgments on their professional competence but as opportunities to involve the parents in participation. Meetings might be held in which the various problems and proposals could be discussed and the advice and assistance of the parents might be solicited. If, for example, the parents felt that their children were being "picked on" during free play periods, they might be willing to send more volunteers to watch the children. At this time we did not realize that we were preaching heresy. But two weeks later, when we made the same suggestion at a workshop for teachers of Indian children, we were summarily rebuked by a high school principal, who pointed out that "consulting with parents would detract from the authority of the schools."

Stephen S. Baratz and Joan C. Baratz

Early Childhood Intervention: The Social Science Base of Institutional Racism

Ethnography is not the only anthropological field contributing to the study of schooling. Linguists have recently been developing the implications for education of their findings about language and language learning. Somewhat surprising is the fact that the cultural implications of linguistic analysis, its bearing on the complex relations between minority groups and the dominant society, has been coming in large part from linguists who do not associate themselves with anthropology.

In specific response to the need for finding new and relevant patterns of education for inner-city blacks, there has been some new and intensive work on the structure and patterning of the black dialects of English. Such work has led to new programs for teaching standard English and the language arts in the ghetto, an extension of the linguists' earlier concern with more effective formal teaching of second languages. The linguists have also been active in developing bicultural school programs for American Indians, Spanish Americans, and black Americans.

Linguists have, moreover, been led to identify the cultural biases underlying the new programs of compensatory education, especially those aimed at preschool children. Two of the best spokesmen for this linguistic point of view are the Baratzes. Their article has caused a good deal of controversy in educational circles. It would seem to us that anthropologists have much to learn from it as they relate to their own urban communities.

The editors of the Harvard Educational Review *have written the following about this article:*

Joan and Stephen Baratz examine the underlying assumptions of intervention programs that tacitly label Negro behavior as pathological. They suggest that the failure to recognize and utilize existing cultural forms of the lower-class Negro community to teach new skills not only dooms intervention programs such as Head Start to failure, but also constitutes a form of institutional racism. An illustration of a pathological versus cultural interpretation of Negro behavior is

presented when the Baratzes contrast the interventionists' statements that describe Negro children as verbally destitute and linguistically underdeveloped with current sociolinguistic data that indicate that Negro children speak a highly developed but different variety of English from that of the mainstream standard. The cultural difference model is presented as a viable alternative to the existing genetic inferiority and social pathology models, both of which share the view of the Negro as a "sick white man."

To understand the present political and academic furor over the efficacy—and therefore the future—of such early-intervention programs as Head Start, it is necessary first to examine the basic concepts and assumptions upon which these programs are founded and then to determine whether existing data can support such an approach to the problem of educating children from black ghettoes.

This paper attempts (1) to present an overview of the interventionist literature with particular emphasis on the role of the social pathology model in interpreting the behavior of the ghetto mother, and (2) to illustrate how the predominant ethnocentric view of the Negro community by social science produces a distorted image of the life patterns of that community. The importance of this distortion is that, when converted into the rationale of social action programs, it is a subtle but pernicious example of institutional racism.

This paper is concerned with the goals of intervention programs that deal with altering the child's home environment, with improving his language and cognitive skills, and most particularly with changing the patterns of child-rearing within the Negro home. These goals are, at best, unrealistic in terms of current linguistic and anthropological data and, at worst, ethnocentric and racist. We

"Early Childhood Intervention: The Social Science Base of Institutional Racism" by Stephen S. Baratz and Joan C. Baratz from *Harvard Educational Review*, Vol. 40, No. 1. Reprinted by permission of the authors.

do not question the legitimacy of early childhood programs when they are described solely as nursery school situations and are not based on the need for remediation or intervention; nor do we question such programs when they increase chances for the employment of economically deprived Negroes. Finally, we do not question such programs when they are described as opportunities to screen youngsters for possible physical disorders, even though follow-up treatment of such diagnostic screening is often unavailable.

We wish to examine in more detail, however, the social pathology model of behavior and intelligence in Head Start[1] projects. We shall attempt to demonstrate that the theoretical base of the deficit model employed by Head Start programs denies obvious strengths within the Negro community and may inadvertently advocate the annihilation of a cultural system which is barely considered or understood by most social scientists. Some thirty years ago, Melville Herskovits made the following insightful observation when talking about culturally related behavioral differences:

[We need to recognize the existence of] . . . the historical background of the . . . behavioral differences . . . being studied and those factors which make for . . . their . . . existence, and perpetuation. When, for instance, one sees vast programs of Negro education undertaken without the slightest consideration given even to the possibility of some retention of African habits of thought and speech that might influence the Negroes' reception of the instruction thus offered—one cannot but ask how we hope to reach the desired objectives. When we are confronted with psychological studies of race relations made in utter ignorance of characteristic African patterns of motivation and behavior or with sociological analyses of Negro family life which make not the slightest attempt to take into account even the chance that the phenomenon being studied might in some way have been influenced by the carry-over of certain African traditions, we can but wonder about the value of such work.[2]

It is one of the main contentions of this paper that most, if not all, of the research on the Negro has sorely missed the implications of Herskovits' statement. Rather, research on the Negro has been guided by an ethnocentric liberal ideology which denies cultural differences and thus acts against the best interests of the people it wishes to understand and eventually help.

Socio-political Ideology and Studies of the Negro

Though it has seldom been recognized by investigators, it has been virtually impossible for social science to divorce itself from ideological considerations when discussing contemporary race relations. As Killian has pointed out with reference to the social science role after the 1954 Supreme Court Decision:

Because of their professional judgment that the theories were valid and because of the egalitarian and humanitarian ethos of the social sciences, many sociologists, psychologists, and anthropologists played the dual role of scientist and ideologist with force and conviction. Without gainsaying the validity of the conclusions that segregation is psychologically harmful to its victims, it must be recognized that the typically skeptical, even querulous attitude of scientists toward each other's work was largely suspended in this case.[3]

Social science research with Negro groups has been postulated on an idealized norm of "American behavior" against which all behavior is measured. This norm is defined operationally in terms of the way white middle-class America is supposed to behave. The normative view coincides with current social ideology—the egalitarian principle—which asserts that all people are created equal under the law and must be treated as such from a moral and political point of view. The normative view, however, wrongly equates equality with sameness. The application of this misinterpreted egalitarian principle to social science data has often left the investigator with the unwelcome task of describing Negro behavior not as it is, but rather as it deviates from the normative system defined by the white middle class. The postulation of such a norm in place of legitimate Negro values or life ways has gained ascendance because of the pervasive assumptions (1) that to be different from whites is to

[1]We recognize that no two Head Start projects are exactly alike. Head Start is used here as a generic term for intervention programs designed for under-privileged preschool children.
[2]"The Ancestry of the American Negro," in *The New World Negro* (Bloomington: Indiana University Press, 1966), p. 121.
[3]*The Impossible Revolution?* (New York: Random House, 1968), p. 54.

be inferior and (2) that there is no such thing as Negro culture. Thus we find Glazer and Moynihan stating: "The Negro is only an American and nothing else. He has no values and culture to guard and protect."

Billingsley has taken sharp objection to the Glazer and Moynihan statement, pointing out:

The implications of the Glazer-Moynihan view of the Negro experience is far-reaching. To say that a people have no culture is to say that they have no common history which has shaped and taught them. And to deny the history of a people is to deny their humanity.[4]

However, the total denial of Negro culture is consonant with the melting-pot mythology and it stems from a very narrow conceptualization of culture by non-anthropologists. Social science has refused to look beyond the surface similarities between Negro and white behavior and, therefore, has dismissed the idea of subtle yet enduring differences. In the absence of an ethno-historical perspective, when differences appear in behavior, intelligence, or cognition, they are explained as evidence of genetic defects or as evidence of the negative effects of slavery, poverty, and discrimination. Thus, the social scientist interprets differences in behavior as genetic pathology or as the alleged pathology of the environment; he therefore fails to understand the distortion of the Negro culture that his ethnocentric assumptions and measuring devices have created. The picture that emerges from such an interpretive schema may be seen as culturally biased and as a distortion of the Negro experience.

Liberals have eagerly seized upon the social pathology model as a replacement for the genetic inferiority model. But both the genetic model and the social pathology model postulate that something is wrong with the black American. For the traditional racists, that something is transmitted by the genetic code; for the ethnocentric social pathologists, that something is transmitted by the family. The major difference between the genetic model and the social pathology model lies in the attribution of causality, *not* in the analysis of the behaviors observed as sick, pathological, deviant, or underdeveloped. An example of the marked similarity between the genetic and the social pathology perspectives can be found in the literature concerning language abilities of Negroes.

Language Abilities of Negroes

Language proficiency is considered at length in both the social and the genetic pathology models. This concern is not accidental, but is the result of a basic assumption shared by both the social pathologists and the genetic racists that one's linguistic competence is a measure of one's intellectual capacity.

Thus we find Shaler, who believed in the genetic inferiority of the Negro, writing:

His inherited habits of mind, framed on a very limited language—where the terms were well tied together and where the thought found in the words a bridge of easy passage—gave him much trouble when he came to employ our speech where the words are like widely separated steppingstones which require nimble wits in those who use them.[5]

And later, Gonzales describes the language of the Carolina coastal Negroes called Gullahs in a similar manner:

Slovenly and careless of speech, these Gullahs seized upon peasant English used by some of the early settlers and by the white servants of the wealthier colonists, wrapped their clumsy tongues about it as well as they could, and, enriched with certain expressive African words, it issued through their flat noses and thick lips as so workable a form of speech that it was gradually adopted by other slaves and became in time the accepted Negro speech of the lower districts of South Carolina and Georgia. With characteristic laziness, these Gullah Negroes took short cuts to the ears of their auditors, using as few words as possible, sometimes making one gender serve for three, one tense for several, and totally disregarding singular and plural numbers.[6]

Hunt provides a similar description, but from the social pathology perspective, when he writes of the parents of Negro children:

These parents themselves have often failed to utilize prepositional relationships with precision, and their

[4]*Black Families in White America* (Englewood Cliffs, N.J.: Prentice-Hall, 1968), p. 37.
[5]"The Nature of the Negro," *Arena*, 3 (1890): 23.
[6]*The Black Border* (South Carolina: The State Company, 1922), p. 10.

syntax is confused. Thus, they serve as poor linguistic models for their young children.[7]

And Deutsch, writing on the same subject, states:

In observations of lower-class homes, it appears that speech sequences seem to be temporally very limited and poorly structured syntactically. It is thus not surprising to find that a major focus of deficit in the children's language development is syntactical organization and subject continuity.[8]

Green gives us another example of the deficit orientation of social pathology thinkers:

The very inadequate speech that is used in the home is also used in the neighborhood, in the play group, and in the classroom. Since these poor English patterns are reconstructed constantly by the associations that these young people have, the school has to play a strong role in bringing about a change in order that these young people can communicate more adequately in our society.[9]

Finally, Hurst categorizes the speech of many Negro college freshmen as:

... [involving] such specific oral aberrations as phonemic and sub-phonemic replacements, segmental phonemes, phonetic distortions, defective syntax, misarticulations, mispronunciations, limited or poor vocabulary, and faulty phonology. These variables exist most commonly in unsystematic, multifarious combinations.[10]

Because of their ethnocentric bias, both the social pathologists and the genetic racists have wrongly presumed that linguistic competence is synonymous with the development of standard English and, thus, they incorrectly interpret the different, yet highly abstract and complex, nonstandard vernacular used by Negroes as evidence of linguistic incompetence or underdevelopment. Both share the view that to speak any linguistic system other than standard English is to be deficient and inferior.

Since as early as 1859, when Müller wrote the *History of Ancient Sanskrit Literature*, the racist contention has been that languages (and their cognitive components) could be hierarchically ordered. Müller himself offered German as the "best" language for conceptualization, but it will not surprise anyone to learn that at various times and according to various writers, the "best"

language has been the language of the particular person doing the thinking about the matter. Thus, the ethnocentrism of the social pathology model, which defines a difference as a deficit, forces the misguided egalitarian into testing a racist assumption that some languages are better than others.

The Logic of Intervention

It is important, then, to understand that the entire intervention model of Head Start rests on an assumption of linguistic and cognitive deficits which must be remedied if the child is to succeed in school. The current linguistic data, however, do not support the assumption of a linguistic deficit. The linguistic competence of black children has been well documented in a number of recent investigations.... Many lower-class Negro children speak a well ordered, highly structured, but different, dialect from that of standard English [see table]. These children have developed a language. Thus one of the basic rationales for intervention, that of developing language and cognitive skills in "defective" children, cannot be supported by the current linguistic data.

Nonetheless, the first intervention programs assumed that the causes of a Negro child's failure in school could be counteracted in those months prior to his entrance into school. Data soon became available concerning the effects of Head Start, indicating that three months was not enough time for intervention to be effective.... The social pathologists reasoned that the supposedly progressive deleterious effects of the early environment of the Negro child were so great they could not be overcome in a few months. This argument provided the basis for the extension of Head Start to a full year before school—and by extension into intervention programs which begin earlier and earlier in the child's life and which eventually call for

[7]"Towards the Preservation of Incompetence," in *Research Contributions from Psychology to Community Health*, J. W. Carter, ed. (New York: Behavioral Publications, 1968), p. 31.

[8]"The Disadvantaged Child and the Learning Process," in *Education in Depressed Areas*, H. Passow, ed. (New York: Columbia University Teachers College, 1963), p. 174.

[9]"Dialect Sampling and Language Values," in *Social Dialects and Language Learning*, R. Shuy, ed. (Champaign, Ill.: NCTE, 1964), p. 123.

[10]*Psychological Correlates in Dialectolalia* (Washington, D.C.: Howard University, 1965).

Some Examples of Systematic Variation in Negro Nonstandard English

Variable	Standard English	Negro Nonstandard
Linking verb	He _is_ going.	He___goin'.
Possessive marker	John_'s_ cousin.	John___cousin.
Plural marker	I have five cent_s_.	I got five cent__.
Subject expression	John___lives in New York.	John _he_ live in New York.
Verb form	I _drank_ the milk.	I _drunk_ the milk.
Past marker	Yesterday he walk_ed_ home.	Yesterday he walk___home.
Verb agreement	He run_s_ home.	He run___home.
	She _has_ a bicycle.	She _have_ a bicycle.
Future form	I _will go_ home.	I'm_a go_ home.
"If" construction	I asked him _if he did it._	I ask _did he do it._
Negation	I _don't_ have _any._	I don't got _none._
	He _didn't_ go.	He _ain't_ go.
Indefinite article	I want _an_ apple.	I want _a_ apple.
Pronoun form	_We_ have to do it.	_Us_ got to do it.
	His book.	_He_ book.
Preposition	He is over _at_ his friend's house.	He over _to_ his friend house.
	He teaches _at_ Francis Pool.	He teach___Francis Pool.
Be	Statement: He _is here all the time._	Statement: He _be_ here.
Do	Contradiction: No, he _isn't._	Contradiction: No, he _don't._

From "Teaching Reading in an Urban Negro School System," by Joan C. Baratz, in _Teaching Black Children to Read,_ Joan C. Baratz and R. W. Shuy, eds. (Washington, D.C.: Center for Applied Linguistics, 1969). Reprinted by permission of Joan C. Baratz.

interference with existent family and child-rearing activities.

This expanding web of concern is consistent with the deficit model. Postulation of one deficit which is unsuccessfully dealt with by intervention programs then leads to the discovery of more basic and fundamental deficits. Remediation or enrichment gradually broadens its scope of concern from the fostering of language competence to a broad-based restructuring of the entire cultural system. The end result of this line of argument occurs when investigators such as Deutsch and Deutsch postulate that "some environments are better than others."[11]

With the recognition of failures and limitations within Head Start and like programs with a social pathology base, proponents of intervention call for earlier and earlier interventions in the child's life. This follows from an interlocking set of assumptions which they frequently make:

1. that, upon entering school, the Negro disadvantaged child is unable to learn in the standard educational environment;
2. that this inability to learn is due to inadequate mothering;
3. that the ghetto environment does not provide adequate sensory stimulation for cognitive growth.

The first premise is buttressed by the continued reports of failure of black children in our schools. Indeed, they do not benefit from the standard educational environment. (That does not, however, say anything about whether they are capable of learning generally.) The second premise is an extension of the earlier work on mothering of institutionalized children as reported by Spitz, Goldfarb, Rheingold, and Skeels and Dye. Much of this literature, however, is predicated on the total absence of a mother or mothering agent. Indeed, the Skeels follow-up study indicates that a moronic mother is better than no mother at all. The difficulty in extending this logic to the ghetto child is that _he has a mother,_ and his behavior derives precisely from her presence rather than her absence.

Then too, the sensory stimulation assumption was an over-extension of the earlier work of Kretch et al., where animals were raised in cages with either

[11] C. Deutsch and M. Deutsch, "Theory of Early Childhood Environment Programs," in _Early Education: Current Theory, Research and Action,_ R. Hess and R. Bear, eds. (Chicago: Aldine Publishing Co., 1968).

considerable sensory stimulation or *none* at all. Again, the model was that of absence of stimulation rather than difference in type and presentation of stimulation.

The Inadequate Mother Hypothesis

It is important to understand that the inadequate mother hypothesis rests essentially on the grounds that the mother's behavior produces deficit children. It was created to account for a deficit that in actuality does not exist—that is, that ghetto mothers produce linguistically and cognitively impaired children who cannot learn. Black children are neither linguistically impoverished nor cognitively underdeveloped. Although their language system is different and, therefore, presents a handicap to the child attempting to negotiate with the standard English-speaking mainstream, it is nonetheless a fully developed, highly structured system that is more than adequate for aiding in abstract thinking. French children attempting to speak standard English are at a linguistic disadvantage; they are not linguistically deficient. Speaking standard English is a linguistic disadvantage for the black youth on the streets of Harlem. A disadvantage created by a difference is not the same thing as a deficit!

In addition, before reviewing some of the notions of the inadequate mother hypothesis, it is necessary to stress that the data presented in that literature fail to show anything more than correlations between child-rearing behaviors and school achievement. As has been discussed elsewhere, these correlations cannot be utilized as if they are statements of cause and effect. Although available data do indeed indicate that these culturally different Negro children are not being educated by the public school system, the data fail to show (1) that such children have been unable to learn to think and (2) that, because of specific child-rearing practices and parental attitudes, these children are not able (and, presumably, will never be able) to read, write, and cipher—the prime teaching responsibilities of the public school system.

Nevertheless, the inadequate mother hypothesis has proliferated in the literature of educational psychology. Of chief concern in this literature is the mother-child interaction patterns of lower-class Negroes. Despite the insistence that these patterns are the chief cause of the child's deficits, the supporting data consist almost entirely of either (1) responses to sociological survey-type questionnaires or (2) interaction situations contrived in educational laboratories. There is almost no anthropologically-oriented field work that offers a description of what actually does happen *in the home* wherein the deficit is alleged to arise.

One of the chief complaints leveled against the black mother is that she is not a teacher. Thus one finds programs such as Caldwell's which call for the "professionalization of motherhood," or Gordon's which attempts to teach the mother how to talk to her child and how to teach him to think.

The first assumption of such programs is that the ghetto mother does not provide her child with adequate social and sensory stimulation. However, further research into the ghetto environment has revealed that it is far from a vacuum; in fact, there is so much sensory stimulation (at least in the eyes and ears of the middle-class researcher) that a contrary thesis was necessarily espoused which argues that the ghetto sensory stimulation is excessive and therefore causes the child to inwardly tune it all out, thus creating a vacuum for himself.

More recently, studies of social interaction suggest that the amount of social stimulation may be quantitatively similar for lower-class and middle-class children. Thus, the quantitative deficit explanation now appears, of necessity, to be evolving into a qualitative explanation; that is, the child receives as much or even more stimulation as does the middle-class child, but the researchers feel this stimulation is not as "distinctive" for the lower-class child as it is for the middle-class child. Of course, it is interesting to note here that, except for those environments where social and sensory deprivation are extremely severe or total, a condition which is certainly not characteristic of the ghetto environment, there is not evidence to suggest that the ghetto child is cognitively impaired by his mother's sensory social interactions with him.

It has further been suggested that the ghetto mother manages her home in such a manner that the child has difficulty developing a proper sense of time and space—i.e., the organization of the house is not ordered around regularly occurring mealtimes and is not ruled by the White Anglo-Saxon Protestant maxim "everything in its place, and a place for everything." To the middle-class observer, such a home appears to be disorganized and chaotic, while it is merely organized differently. Thus we have data which tell what the mother does not do, but we are missing the data which describe what she does do and explain how the household manages to stay intact. Again, there is no extant research that indicates that the development of a concept of time is either helped or hindered by a child's growing up in an environment where there are regularly occurring meal and bedtimes. There is, however, a considerable literature concerning cultural differences in the concept of time.

Further, it is continually asserted that the ghetto mother does not talk or read to her child, thus supposedly hindering his intellectual growth and language development. Despite the fact that no study has ever indicated the minimal amount of stimulation necessary for the child to learn language, and despite the fact that *the child has in fact developed language,* the ghetto mother is still accused of causing language retardation in her infant.

The mother's involvement in reading activities is also presumed to be extremely important to the child's development and future school success. The conclusions of many studies of the black ghetto home stress the absence of books and the fact that ghetto mothers rarely read to their children. Although the presence of books in the home may be quite indicative of middle-class life styles, and stories when read may very well give pleasure to all children, there appears to be no evidence which demonstrates that reading to children is essential for their learning to read, or that such reading will enhance their real language development. Although Irwin's landmark study indicates that children who are systematically read to babble more, it does not demonstrate that they are linguistically more proficient than those children who are not read to systematically.

A further factor in the mother's behavior which is continually blamed for deficits in the child is her lack of communication to him of the importance of school achievement. Although the literature presents a great many cases which illustrate that the lower-class mother verbalizes great achievement motivations concerning her children, these verbalizations are largely discredited in the eyes of some psychologists who see little action—for example, helping with homework, joining the PTA—underlying her statement of achievement motivation for her child. (Here, ironically, the supposedly nonverbal mother is now being penalized for her verbal

behavior.) Indeed, her verbalizations tend to exhort the child to behave and achieve in class in relation to some assumed behavioral norm rather than to some educational reward; e.g., learn to read because the teacher says so, not because there are many things that one can learn from books. Nonetheless, there do not appear to be any data which show that preschool children resist learning, avoid schooling, or generally do not wish to achieve in the classroom; nor are there data to suggest that intrinsic motivations (learn for learning's sake) are effective for teaching reading, or that extrinsic ones (do it because I tell you) are not. In fact, the behaviorist literature tends to indicate that different subgroups (i.e., lower-class versus middle-class) respond differently to various reinforcements (for instance, food versus praise).

The recent work of Hess, Shipman, Brophy, and Bear is sure to add considerable fuel to the inadequate mother hypothesis. Hess and his colleagues collected data on 163 black mothers and their four-year-old children. The mothers were divided into four groups: professional, skilled, unskilled-family intact, and unskilled-father absent. Social workers collected data in two extensive home interviews. Later, the mothers and children came to the university where IQ and other formal tests were administered. The mothers were also presented with theoretical situations and asked what they would do or say—e.g., what would you say to your child on his first day of school. In addition, the mothers were asked to teach their children a block-sorting task and to replicate a design on an etch-a-sketch box with their children. The Hess et al. data furnished a good deal of information concerning teaching styles of lower- and middle-class black women. These data, however, were undoubtedly influenced by the fact that the situations in which they were elicited (i.e., interviewing and a laboratory task) are much more typical of middle-class experiences. Nevertheless, many differences in maternal language and teaching styles appeared. It would be a mistake, however, to conclude that these differences in language and teaching style cause the child to be uneducable. What makes him appear "uneducable" is his failure in an educational system that is insensitive to the culturally different linguistic and cognitive styles that he brings to the classroom setting. The school, therefore, fails to use the child's distinct cultural patterns as the vehicle for teaching new skills and additional cultural styles.

One of the major difficulties with the work of Hess et al. lies in their concept of "educability." Superficially this refers to those skills which every child potentially possesses but which presumably are not developed if the mother's behavior is "restricted" and not similar to that of those middle-class mothers who produce children who succeed in school. Those skills which the child potentially possesses, however, are not defined by Hess et al. simply as language development, but rather more subtly as the use of standard English. Concept development is not seen as the development of language for thought (There are, of course, no languages that one cannot think in!) but rather, it is defined in terms of performance on standardized tasks or measures of verbal elaboration. Again, motivation is described not in terms of wanting to read, but rather in terms of books around the house and the use of the public library. "Educability" then, is really defined as specific middle-class mainstream behaviors rather than as the possession of universal processes through which specific behaviors can be channeled. The lower-class mother is *a priori* defined as inadequate because she is not middle-class.

In their discussions of the mothers' language behavior, Hess et al. rely heavily on the concepts of Basil Bernstein, who describes two different communicative styles generally used by lower- and middle-class English children. That the language and teaching behaviors of lower-class Negro mothers are different from those of middle-class mothers is beyond question. That the different behavior leads to cognitive defects has yet to be demonstrated. Carroll has discussed the methodological issue of the relationship of language style to cognition. To say that a particular language has a deleterious effect on cognitive performance, speakers of that language must be tested for cognitive ability on a non-linguistic task—such a task has yet to be developed or tested.

The Hess data, while providing considerable information on maternal behavior differences in lower- and middle-class black women, do not indicate that the children from lower-class homes are any less ready to learn than are the middle-class children, nor do they demonstrate that these children will be less able—especially if they are placed in a school that takes advantage of their experiences, as the present school curriculum does in

certain crucial regards for the middle-class child. The Hess data do show, however, that the behaviors of the middle-class Negro mothers are more typically mainstream and that what these mothers teach their children is more typically within mainstream expectations; therefore, such children tend to perform better in a testing situation— and subsequently in a school situation—which requires mainstream behaviors and heuristic styles than do lower-class children, who have learned something else.

There is much to be learned about maternal teaching styles and how they can be used to help the child function better in interactions with the mainstream culture. Research has indicated how unlike the middle-class mother the lower-class mother is, but there is very little description of who the lower-class mother is and what she does.

The Failure of Intervention

Intervention programs postulated on the inadequacy of the mother or the lack of environmental stimulation fail after an initial spurt in IQ scores. This appears to be an artifact of the methodology, for the first contact with mainstream educational patterns (an agent intervening in the home, a Head Start Program, kindergarten or first grade in the public school) appears automatically to cause an increase in IQ for these children. This artifact is clearly evidenced in the "catch-up" phenomenon where non-Head Start children gain in IQ apparently as a result of exposure to a school environment. The additional observation, that increases in IQ of both Head Start *and* non-Head Start children decrease after second or third grade, is a further indication that early childhood intervention is not where the answer to the failure of children in public school lies.

Interventionists argue that what is needed are school-based programs (Project Follow-Through) which maintain the "gains" of Head Start by changing the nature of the school environment. In effect, this argument is a specious one since it was the intervention program itself which was supposed to insure the child's success in the schools as they are presently constituted. For the early childhood interventionists then to turn around and say that the schools do not do their job in maintaining the increases which the school itself has generated in non-Head Start children (as well as the increases of Head Start children) is indeed to point to the crux of the matter: the failure lies in the schools, not the parents, to educate these children. This clearly indicates that critical intervention must be done, but on the procedures and materials used in the schools rather than on the children those schools service. Intervention which works to eliminate archaic and inappropriate procedures for teaching these children and which substitutes procedures and materials that are culturally relevant is critically needed. It is important to note here that such intervention procedures—e.g., the use of Negro dialect in the teaching of reading—are not ends in themselves. The goal of such procedures is to have the children perform adequately on standardized achievement tests. It is the process, not the goals, of education that must be changed for these children. *The educational problems of lower-class culturally different Negro children, as of other groups of culturally different children, are not so much related to inappropriate educational goals as to inadequate means for meeting these goals.*

It is not, therefore, a particular program for early childhood intervention at a critical period which affects IQ scores. Rather it is the initial contact with mainstream middle-class behaviors that tends to raise temporarily the scores of young children. As the test items, however, begin to rely more and more heavily on the language style and usage of the middle-class, these culturally different dialect-speaking children tend to decrease in test performance. Unlike the behaviors which initially raise IQ scores and which the child learns simply from contact with the middle-class system, fluency in a new language style and usage must be taught formally and systematically for it to be mastered. Indeed, this failure to teach the mainstream language styles and usage by means of the child's already existing system may well explain why the initial test gains of these children are not maintained.

The early childhood programs, as well as public schools, fail in the long run because they define educability in terms of a child's ability to perform within an alien culture; yet they make no attempt to teach him systematically new cultural patterns so that the initial spurt in test scores can be maintained. Educability, for culturally different children, should be defined primarily as the ability to learn new cultural patterns within the experience base and the culture with which the child is already

familiar. The initial test scores of culturally different children must not be misevaluated as evidence of "educability," but rather should be viewed as evidence of the degree to which the child is familiar with the mainstream system upon which the tests are based both in content and presentation.

Because of the misconception of educability and the misevaluation of the test data, interventionists and educators create programs that are designed (1) to destroy an already functionally adequate system of behavior because it is viewed as pathological and (2) to impose a system of behavior without recognizing the existence of a functionally adequate system of behavior already in place. (Thus it is comparable to attempting to pour water into an already wine-filled pitcher.) Education for culturally different children should not attempt to destroy functionally viable processes of the subculture, but rather should use these processes to teach additional cultural forms. The goal of such education should be to produce a bicultural child who is capable of functioning both in his subculture and in the mainstream.

However, since Head Start has disregarded or attempted unknowingly to destroy that which is a viable cultural system, we should not have been surprised by its failure in attempting to "correct" these behaviors. Head Start has failed because its goal is to correct a deficit that simply does not exist. The idea that the Negro child has a defective linguistic and conceptual system has been challenged by the findings of Stewart, Baratz, J., Labov, and by Lesser and his colleagues, who point to the structurally coherent but different linguistic and cognitive systems of these children. Indeed, the deficit model of Head Start forces the interventionist closer and closer to the moment of conception and to the possibility of genetic determination of the behavior now attributed to a negative environment. This position is plaintively described by Caldwell:

Most of us in enrichment . . . efforts—no matter how much lip service we pay to the genetic potential of the child—are passionate believers in the plasticity of the human organism. We need desperately to believe that we are born equalizable. With any failure to demonstrate the effectiveness of compensatory experiences offered to children of any given age, one is entitled to conclude parsimoniously that perhaps the enrichment was not offered at the proper time.[12]

Elsewhere Caldwell refers to what she calls the Inevitable Hypothesis which we interpret as backing up further and further (intervene at four, at three, at one, at three months) until we are face to face with the possibility of genetic differences between Negroes and whites which forever preclude the possibility of remediation or enrichment. We are in Caldwell's debt for such a passionate statement of the real issue at hand. All educators concerned with intervention of any kind and unaware of the culture (and the alternative conceptual framework it offers) respond at a gut level to the implications which the failure of early childhood programs has for the overtly racist genetic model. The frustration due to the failure of intervention programs proposed by the social pathologists could lead to three possible lines of responses from those watching and participating in the unfolding of events. They are:

1. an increased preoccupation with very early intervention, at birth or shortly thereafter, to offset the allegedly "vicious" effects of the inadequate environment of the Negro child;
2. the complete rejection of the possibility of intervention effects unless the child is totally removed from his environment to be cared for and educated by specialists;
3. the total rejection of the environmentalist-egalitarian position in favor of a program of selective eugenics for those who seem to be totally unable to meet the demands of a technological environment—scientific racism.

Suffice it to say that recently we have seen an articulation of all three of these unfeasible positions.

The clearest line of thought currently evident comes from people such as Shaefer, Gordon, and Caldwell, advocating the introduction of specialists into the home who would not only provide the missing stimulation to the child, but also teach the mother how to raise her children properly. Thus, the new input is an intensive attempt to change totally the child's environment and the parent's child-rearing patterns.

But the fear is that even such a massive attempt will still fail to inoculate the child against failure in the schools. Recognizing this, Caldwell pro-

vides the model for intervention programs which take the child completely out of the home for short periods of time for the purpose of providing him with the experiences unavailable to him during his first three years of life. It is only a short distance from this position to Bettelheim's statement advocating total removal of Negro children to kibbutz-like controlled environments in order to overcome the effects of the allegedly negative values and practices of the ghetto—in short, the annihilation of distinctive Afro-American cultural styles.

Finally, the appearance of the scholarly article recently published by Arthur Jensen in the *Harvard Educational Review* represents the attempt of a former social pathologist to deal with the failure of the intervention programs.[13] He may find his position politically distasteful but, for a scientist who lacks a cross-cultural perspective and a historical frame of reference, it is the only way to maintain his scientific integrity. Like most scholars who come to advocate an unpopular thesis, Jensen has done his homework. His familiarity with the data indicates to him the futility of denying (1) that Negro children perform less well on intelligence tests than whites and (2) that Head Start has failed in its intent to produce permanent shifts in IQ which lead to success in the educational system. Since Jensen rejects the social pathology model but retains a concept that describes Negro behavior as defective, it is not at all surprising that he has no alternative other than a model of genetic inferiority.

However, like the social pathologists who had to create an explanation (i.e., inadequate mothering) for a nonexistent deficit, Jensen is also called upon to explain the reasons for a relative theory of genetic inferiority in the American Negro. His argument, similar to those of earlier genetic racists, states that the Negroes who were brought over as slaves "were selected for docility and strength and not mental ability, and that through selective mating the mental qualities present never had a chance to flourish." Interestingly enough, this contention was decimated almost thirty years ago by Melville Herskovits in his book, *The Myth of the*

[12]The Fourth Dimension in Early Childhood Education," in *Early Education*, R. Hess and R. Bear, eds. (Chicago: Aldine Publishing Co., 1968), p. 81.

[13]A. Jensen, "How Much Can We Boost IQ and Scholastic Achievement?" *Harvard Educational Review*, 39 (1969): 187–190.

Negro Past, in which he presents historical and anthropological data to reject the notion of selective enslavement and breeding. It is precisely the absence of a sophisticated knowledge and perspective of cultural continuity and cultural change which has forced both the social pathologists and the genetic pathologists to feel that they have dealt with "culture" if they acknowledge that certain test items are "culture-bound." Such changes represent very surface knowledge of the concept of culture and, in particular, do not deal with subtle yet significant cultural differences. Many social scientists believe that they are dealing with the culture when they describe the physical and social environment of these children. One must not confuse a description of the environment in which a particular culture thrives for the culture itself.

Because historical and political factors have combined to deny the existence of a Negro culture, social scientists have found themselves having to choose between either a genetic deficit model or a deficit model built on an inadequate environment (the "culture" of poverty). However, our view of the current status of research on the Negro in the United States indicates that we are on the brink of a major scientific revolution with respect to American studies of the Negro and the social action programs that derive from them. This revolution began with Herskovits and is being forwarded by the linguistic and anthropological studies of Stewart, Szwed, Abrahams, Hannerz, and others. The basic assumption of this research is that the behavior of Negroes is not pathological, but can be explained within a coherent, structured, distinct, American-Negro culture which represents a synthesis of African culture in contact with American European culture from the time of slavery to the present day.

Since the pathology model of the language and thought of Negroes as it is used in intervention programs has been created by the superimposition of a standard English template on a nonstandard dialect system, producing a view of that nonstandard system as defective and deviant, then the data gathered in support of that pathology view must be totally reevaluated and old conclusions dismissed, not solely because they are nonproductive, but also because they are ethnocentric and distorted and do not recognize the cultural perspective. The great impact of the misuse of the egalitarian model on social science studies of the

Negro must be reexamined.

As long as the social pathology and genetic models of Negro behavior remain the sole alternatives for theory construction and social action, our science and our society are doomed to the kind of cyclical (environment to genes) thinking presently evident in race relations research. Fortunately, at this critical point in our history, we do have a third model available, capable of explaining both the genetic and social pathology views with greater economy and capable of offering viable research and societal alternatives.

The major support for the assertion of a revolution in scientific thinking about the Negro comes from the discovery that the urban Negro has a consistent, though different, linguistic system. This discovery is an anomaly in that it could not have been predicted from the social pathology paradigm. This finding, if we can judge from the incredulity expressed about it by our colleagues, violates many of the perceptions and expectations about Negro behavior which are built into the assumptive base of the social pathology model. This assumptive base, it is argued, has restricted our phenomenological field to deviations from normative behavior rather than to descriptions of different normative configurations. In the present case, it would appear that the defect and difference models of Negro behavior cannot exist side by side without a growing awareness of the need for change and radical reconstruction of our modes of theorizing and conceptualizing about Negro behavior.

However, there may be resistance to adopting the cultural difference model which stems not only from the inherent methodologies of the social pathology theory, but also from the much more vague, and often unexpressed sociopolitical view of the particular investigator seeking to support his view of our current racial situation—views which are unarticulated and therefore unexamined. Thus, the resistance we anticipate may be intensified by the fear that talking about differences in Negro behavior may automatically produce in the social pathologist the postulation of genetic differences. This fear, so often expressed, is related to the real fact that the genetic model itself relied on behavioral differences as the basis for its conclusions about genetic determination. Three points can be made here to deal with this concern: (1) it has not and should not be the role of rational scholarly discourse to dismiss data and knowledge simply because it does not fit a particular ideological position extant at a particular moment in history; (2) differences, which indicate that learning has taken place, are not deficits; and (3) the view of the current social pathology position is in many ways prone to the same criticisms leveled at the genetic pathology model. The current scientific crisis will resolve itself solely on the basis of scholarly research and not ideology or polemic. The basic assumptions of scholarly research must be examined and models tried out that offer more successful and economical explanations.

In summary, the social pathology model has led social science to establish programs to prevent deficits which are simply not there. The failure of intervention reflects the ethnocentrism of methodologies and theories which do not give credence to the cognitive and intellectual skills of the child. A research program on the same scale as that mounted to support the social pathology model must be launched in order to discover the different, but not pathological, forms of Negro behavior. Then and only then can programs be created that utilize the child's differences as a means of furthering his acculturation to the mainstream while maintaining his individual identity and cultural heritage.

Carol Talbert
Studying Education in the Ghetto

One anthropologist, though still a graduate student when this paper was written, has gone deeply into the problem of understanding the interaction between black urban students and their schools. Carol Talbert combined ethnographic and linguistic methodology in her approach to a study of education and in her personal involvement in a project to meet the educational needs of black children. Starting with a research method that made her a sporadic observer in the classroom, she found it necessary to become involved as a teacher, to move into the student's neighborhood, and to develop a new linguistic approach to the teaching of reading and writing.

In her paper, Talbert describes her methodology, criticizing the earlier approach and describing some of the outcomes of her own involvement in teaching. True to her anthropological background, she has become a participant-observer in the home and school community of the children in whom she is interested.

The writer's present attempts to study the learning and language of black children in the inner city are an outgrowth of her own learning experiences in previous studies.

The first of these, a study of schoolchildren outlined and first directed by Jules Henry, was based on "naturalistic observation." Natural observation, as described by Henry in the original outline for the project, is grounded in the traditional anthropological method of studying primitive societies. But there is a difference between natural and naturalistic observation. Natural observation meant living in the native society for an extended period of time, and it involved both observation and participation. Henry himself used this method in studying the Kaingang and the Pilagá in Brazil.

Later in his career, however, Henry turned to the analysis of complex societies, and in the process modified his approach. In his well-known study of the families of autistic children, Henry lived for a week in the children's homes, maintaining an impassive, uninvolved stance. In "Culture Against Man," Henry reported other observations in

"Studying Education in the Ghetto" by Carol Talbert. Unpublished paper prepared for delivery at the 1970 Annual Meeting of the American Educational Research Assn., Minneapolis (March, 1970). Reprinted by permission of the author.

middle-class American schools, homes, and mental hospitals.

It would appear that Henry had decided that prolonged involvement was not necessary to an understanding of people in his own country, the United States. As he has written in defense of naturalistic observations, the unifying theme of investigations in which they are employed is the expression of cultural factors through the lives and personalities of the individuals studied:

The culture of a family is the idiosyncratic expression within a particular family of the values, drives, and attitudes traditional in the culture as a whole. . . . In our culture . . . the values of achievement, competition, money, kindness, solicitude for others, etc., are stressed; they have varying significance in different families.[1]

Now possessing a unicultural view of American families, Henry proposed, in studying the black child and family, to describe the patterns in which lower- and middle-class blacks, like whites, expressed the values and themes of American life. The objective of the study he designed was to relate the teacher's expectations to the pupil's behavior. In four all-black elementary schools and homes in the inner city, as well as in white schools and homes, we began on the first day of kindergarten, recording the interactions between teacher and pupils, paying special attention to the style and content of verbal communication. After three months, each teacher was asked to select four pupils: two who seemed slated for academic success and two who seemed slated for failure. We then visited the homes of these children, observing the spoken communication and the general behavior of the mother toward the child. As a researcher, I visited for short periods (one to two hours a week) in the schools and homes of the selected black children. During this time I engaged the parents and other members of the household, or the teacher, in conversation and informal interviews.

It should be noted that this method was quite successful when the informants were, like the researchers, white and middle-class. Henry's research assistants in middle-class schools quickly became "confidants" and "father confessors." Earlier, when Henry himself had lived with the families of the autistic children, their middle-class parents were receptive to his presence because he had advised them that he was interested in learning more about disturbed children in order to help. Henry felt that there were other reasons, besides the motivation of his informants, to account for his success. Children, being unsophisticated, would not alter their behavior even in the presence of a strange observer; similarly, their parents would also act fairly naturally, thus unconsciously exposing the underlying dynamics of their behavior toward their children.

Nevertheless, in my own work with black children and their teachers and parents, there was no such happy success. The nagging suspicion, which later grew into a conviction, that we were recording and analyzing "paper people," was possibly the most important consequence of the frustrating weekly visits required by the research design. Still, I felt that language was the key to understanding the black child, and I conducted a study of the phonology of first-grade children and their teacher. I then decided to obtain samples of the speech of children who had not yet entered school and, to accomplish this, volunteered my services to a summer Headstart Program as a "speech correctionist." In this capacity, I was a mere citizen without establishment backing—an interesting experience.

The classroom was itself fascinating. The mothers and teachers sat in the front, talking together while the children and the teen-age assistants busied themselves at the tables. It seemed to me that the mothers and teacher were more interested in each other than in the children, a circumstance I was completely unprepared for and of which I was highly critical. The teacher and parents, for their part, were openly suspicious of my understanding of black children. I was reminded that I was using the same old methods and would arrive at the same old evidence of the deficiency of the children. They repeatedly asked, "What are you doing to do to help these children?" There was a great deal of criticism of my permissiveness and open affection for the children, but most of the time I was treated as a nonperson. Since I was not considered a social worker, to be communicated with in some kind of manipulative fashion, I was only a confused person who had to be tolerated.

---

[1] Jules Henry, "Naturalistic Observation of Family Cultures." Unpublished paper presented at the 1958 Symposium on Naturalistic Observation at the meeting of the American Anthropological Association, Washington, D.C., p. 1.

My experience with the children in the Headstart Program was very rewarding. We taped stories and played games the entire morning. Even children who the teacher thought would have trouble speaking and learning to read and write became verbal. Particularly when they spoke about situations and experiences close to home, close to their own lives, the children were highly expressive and spoke as much as any child.

After the summer, I decided to take the advice of the Headstart teacher and drop my role as an impassive researcher. I began to enter new relationships with mothers from the inner city. Though I would be the first to admit that I am still viewed primarily as a resource to be exploited for social and economic advantage because of my ties with the white establishment, I am at least beginning to observe behavior I never encountered in my weekly visits. Much of what I learned is important to a scientific approach to the problems of education and perception of the black child—the relationship between age and status in the black community, for example.

During early childhood, the black child is ubiquitous. Yet the child does not interact with his parents or other adults most of the time; he is nearby, listening to the conversation of the adults, but he is not expected to interrupt or comment. As he or she approaches adolescence and is able to make a substantial contribution to the family (a daughter may mother the younger children or the son may bring money into the home), the young person is accorded adult status and enjoys the freedom of speaking to elders without any risk of ridicule.

The difference in the behavior of youngsters and adolescents sheds light on the Headstart teacher who spent her time talking to parents. It helps to explain the black teachers described in the literature as engaging in minimal conversation with children in the primary grades. On the other hand, in the higher grades, such teachers often chat with the children as if they were equals. This seems to begin at about the time the black child is reaching adult status in his home. We have observed a black male teacher engaging in mild jokes and seductive repartée with one of his thirteen-year-old female students. This same teacher, however, behaved in very different fashion when he felt the situation demanded an authoritative stance. The inherent conflict between his behavior in the two contexts reflects the difference between school's and the black community's definitions of maturity.

The sex of the black child also has social ramifications that are somewhat different in the black community than in the white. Male black children apparently develop fairly cohesive social groups, to the point that they rarely appear anywhere alone, while black girls and women seem to lead a more solitary life. Even when, in kindergarten, girls develop dyadic relationships with each other, they are more interested in gaining the attention and affection of the teacher than they are in each other. The boys, as the school year progresses and they become more and more peripheral to the actual teaching, concentrate more and more on communicating with each other. It should be remembered that the teacher places her pupils in "levels" and then spends most of his or her time with those in the highest level, leaving the rest of the children to while away their time drawing on one sheet of paper or staring into space. The teacher thus makes a contribution to the crystallization of a cultural form having its origins in the community: in the study described earlier, most of those whose failure was predicted by the teacher were boys.

There are other patterns in the black community that bear on the teaching of and research on the black child. The black child is accustomed to the continuous presence of relatives and peers, a finding that bears on the structuring of interviews, therapy sessions, or testing. In the black families that I have observed, the primary communication and learning about the environment goes on between those of similar age and sex. A conversation between a child and an adult has another purpose, either to give the child a task or administer a correction. The child behaves as though he would like to be as unobtrusive as possible and appears to pay close attention to the instructions he is being given, but he often, both at home and in school, prefers a nonverbal response to one that might be incorrect. It would seem that the risk of ridicule is thereby lessened. Small wonder, then, that when confronted by a white adult and asked to perform novel and possibly meaningless tasks, the black child lapses into silence, appears frightened, or becomes sullen. It is tempting to relate this strategy of not responding to a more widespread adaptation having its roots in the historical past. From the days of slavery to the present, black people have coped in a way that appears passive and self-destructive but which in reality serves to protect them from actual destruction by masking their true attitudes and feelings. The change in the black child's behavior when he is in a group became apparent to me when I was tape recording samples of speech. In an effort to reduce the effect of my speech patterns on theirs, I began using "native" interviewers. Almost immediately, the quantity and quality of their speaking soared. I then began to hand the microphone around to different children in turn, allowing them to interview each other. This works even better, except that it is almost impossible to be sure which child's voice one is hearing when the tape is played back because these "nonverbal" children interrupt each other and sometimes all talk at once.

The kind of research I am doing now is a far cry from "naturalistic" observation. Short-term observation is, however, still a widely used technique that is probably most fruitfully applied to the study of functioning and process in bureaucratic institutional structures. Elizabeth Eddy, Louis Smith and W. Geoffrey, and Roger Barker, to name but a few, have observed social processes in school systems, focusing on roles and personal interaction within a particular milieu. Studies such as these describe the confrontation of school and home culture, but their emphasis is on the culture of the school, and no clear distinction between familial patterns and institutional constraints is made. Herbert Kohl and Jonathan Kozol, describing the problems of urban education, also fail to distinguish between black culture and school culture. The middle-class person reading their studies is moved to condemn the harsh black teacher who maintains a quiet classroom, speaking little and to only a few children, bestowing her favors on a few privileged pupils, and in general behaving in an authoritarian manner. I would suggest, on the basis of my own observations, that such descriptions reflect particular aspects of the relationship between the black mother and her child.

Another largely unrecognized source of the frustration and failure of urban education is the lack of congruence between a white middle-class curriculum and the ways in which a black child actually learns. Curriculum guides and teacher-training aids are written with the white middle-class teacher in mind. It is expected that he or she will naturally spend a lot of time explaining and discussing a lesson, for example. It is assumed that the teacher will covertly strive to gain control over her students, that she will "get inside the child's mind." It was evident, from our group's research on white middle-class kindergartens that the teacher's main concern was the fostering of security and group feeling, and the minimization of deviance. To accomplish this without seeming authoritarian, the teacher needs to be continuously and intensely interacting with all the children. Such a view of child training is identical with that held by the white middle-class parent. I need not dwell here upon the often-described insulated, protective, nuclear family; I only wish to remind the reader of its harmony with the instructional patterns of the classroom.

The question that emerges from the present discussion centers around the validity of the hypothesis that cultural norms are shared by all the strata of a complex society. It is my contention that minority groups, rather than sharing all the values of the larger society, may be bringing up their children in ways distinctly different from the majority, ways which become a source of frustration when one pattern conflicts with another, as in education. The tools and techniques of anthropology can make a unique contribution here. An anthropological approach to the social structure of the black community can help us understand black norms, values, and behavior in their own terms. Theories of education which are truly versatile and which could move beyond the class-biased descriptions of "cultural deprivation" could emerge. Were we to view the behavior of different groups of city dwellers as systems of adaptations to environmental and social conditions, we would be enabled to view the families and community organization of the ghetto as ongoing adaptations susceptible to analysis and study rather than to simple description. It might also become possible to ask whether most descriptions of black parents and children are not really descriptions of their adaptation to a white middle-class professional, a condescending interviewer, or an unenlightened do-gooder.

One might ask what, in a black child's past experience with whites, would motivate him to expose and express his inner feelings? Why should a black mother, already experienced with the welfare office and the police department, place any trust in a researcher who visits once or twice a week and promises the alleviation of the child's educational problems? The answer is, of course, that there is little reason for trust or sharing of confidences; moreover, that there is a great likelihood of obtaining information which serves only to support the stereotype of the ghetto family. No one should assume for a moment that black people are naïve about their position in society or about the motivation of most researchers. They are adept at playing games with the researcher and managing to hide their true attitudes.

The most devastating aspect of the educational problem is that the teachers themselves adhere to the stereotype of the "uneducable" and "unmotivated" child. As I observed in a black kindergarten and as others in the research project also noted, the teacher is a most effective agent of society and its stratification, selecting children who are the most middle-class in speech and behavior as the most likely to succeed and investing most time and resources in them. The process of stratifying children begins in kindergarten and usually ends in first grade, when they are sorted into reading "levels."

The white researchers who analyze the education of ghetto children, if they are not to perpetuate the injustices of that education, must rid themselves of their middle-class bias and study the learning and perception of the black child as they would study the patterns of a distinct cultural group. Only then can the patterns of learning of black children be accurately described. Such a stance becomes even more necessary in view of the proximity of black ghettos to middle-class academic institutions. I would suggest that something similar to Piaget's approach to Swedish children be developed for research on ghetto children. I fear that our prejudices, our conscious or unconscious racism, and our faith in traditional tests of intellectual functioning are so entrenched that we must start anew if we are ever to make meaningful inroads and new discoveries.

As anthropologists studying education and culture, we would do well to follow the lead of students of modern linguistics. Certain linguists have taken the position that the English spoken by black Americans is grammatically different from standard American English. There may be deeper differences as well. Analyzing the language of the blacks as a corrupt version of standard English precludes searching for internal rules and new structures; exciting new insights have been gained by rejecting this type of analysis. Anthropologists believe that language and behavior are interrelated and almost inseparable in the development of learning and perception. For this reason, it is imperative that we develop methods which will not intrude our linguistic and behavior systems.

In my own research, in order to obtain more data on the nature of black children's grammar and an understanding of the kinds of textbook content which may be meaningful, I have begun a "Write Your Own Book" program in a housing project in the inner city. Beyond linguistic analysis, it is my long-range hope that experiences such as these will in the near future develop to the point where cognitive and perceptual analyses can be initiated on the black children's own terms and in their own language.

In my "Write Your Own Book" program the children come in voluntarily. They tape stories and jokes, or discuss their views on the tape recorder. Then they write and illustrate stories for us. My two student assistants from the University of Washington and I act as black mothers might. We do not supervise closely; rather, we chat among ourselves and with other adults. We give the older children the tape recorder and allow them to monitor the stories of the younger children. If we do conduct an interview, it is always with a group of children. This setting appears to have a definite effect on the quality of expression found in the recordings. The children are even beginning to lose their fear of recording obscenities or other sensitive statements to which I might react negatively. I am just beginning to introduce a phonetic system of writing to a few of the older children. I do not know at this point whether this will be successful or not, but the difference in written and spoken expression is so great that I feel it necessary to try to tackle this problem.

Though this program has just begun, my experience assures me that no deficit hangs over the inner city in verbal expression, facility, or creativity—when the language used is their own. When they discuss matters and experiences close to their own lives, the interest, motivation, and concentration of the children is extremely high. This "Write Your Own Book" program, incidentally, has had no resources other than those of the inner-city community. We have the support and interest of local community and political organizations and, most importantly, we have the time and energy of those involved.

In summary, I have indicated my own dissatisfaction with attenuated observations based on a unicultural view of American society. I have discussed the differences in behavior in black and white middle-class homes and the educational problems that arise when it is assumed that these differences are inconsequential. I have talked about my own research and what it has taught me. I have pointed out the imperative need to begin to understand black children as they grow and develop in their own families and neighborhoods.

I am urging a return to traditional participant-observation as defined by Charles and Betty Lou Valentine or E. Liebow, for example. The particular political and economic conditions in our urban centers, however, complicate participant-observation. It is necessary, in the context of contemporary social problems, for the researcher to discard the role of uncommitted observer and take something of an activist position if he is to develop the beginnings of an honest reciprocal relationship with the subjects of his study.

Manning Nash
The Role of Village Schools in the Process of Cultural and Economic Modernization

An American educator has suggested that American faith in education has led to a new kind of cultural missionary—the educationary. Around the world, many such American educationaries are actively involved in the development and expansion of both secular and religious school systems. They see the school as an instrument of individual, community, national, and international development. Anthropologists, too, are associated with this movement and have used their ethnographic experience and methodology to study schooling in modernizing societies.

Manning Nash here draws on his experience in Mexico and Guatemala to suggest some of the ways in which village schools have functioned in their communities. It should be obvious that we must know what schools are as local cultural and social institutions before we can suggest ways in which they might be instrumental in achieving particular goals of economic, political, and social development. Work such as this can contribute to more effective technical assistance to education overseas.

When a nation embarks on a deliberate course of modernization there is a clear and broad mandate for the educational system. Education serves as one of the principal means of social transformation. In a newly developing nation education is viewed by the elite and their planning agents as having two chief tasks: (1) to instil the skills required for the movement of the economy from a raw-producing, agricultural-export one toward an industrial, processing, and diversified agricultural economy; and (2) to produce a modern nation of dedicated citizens from a population of peasants who have small experience and understanding of civic, consensual, or mobilization politics. These tasks stem in part from the elite vision of the future and in part from their appraisal of the contemporary social structure.

The universities and secondary schools in nations like Mexico [and] Guatemala . . . are fairly amenable to planning, to elite control, and to government pressure to get on with the tasks of modernization. Of course, I do not mean that

From "The Role of Village Schools in the Process of Cultural and Economic Modernization" by Manning Nash from *Social and Economic Studies* (Vol. 14, 1965). Reprinted by permission of the author and the University of The West Indies Institute of Social and Economic Research.

the government can or does have its way easily with the universities and secondary schools. Indeed, the . . . events in Guatemala during the 1950's, indicate that universities have a built-in dynamic of independence, of resistance, and of political criticism. However, the universities, their faculties, and student bodies are visible, centralized, and, even if opposed to the government or the elite, are at least speaking and acting in the same idiom and in the same universe of expectations as those who seek to find the path and means toward modernity. Universities are, in fact, one of the spearheads of modernity in any developing nation, and however ineffectual they may be at one or another moment, they are ineluctable sources or reservoirs of the culture of modernity and of the skills for economic transformation.

The village schools, on which I concentrate, are in a different relation to the government and the elite, and play a more problematic role in the process of modernization. The village schools are numerous, decentralized, less open for inspection, less amenable to manipulation, and most importantly, they are set into local communities. Higher education, in most cases, forms its own community and relates to the world community of like institutions. But the village school is embedded in an organized local community and it has neither the resources nor the ability to set itself against, or apart, from the social system of which it is but an aspect. Not only is the village school part of a locally organized society, but the community itself is but an aspect of a complex nation, a larger social and cultural system.

In order to assess the possibilities and the probabilities of various local systems of education in the process of social change aimed at speeding modernization, the first tasks are the exploration of the relation of the school to the local community, and the stipulation of the place of the local community in the complex society that is the nation. . . .

In treating Mexico and Guatemala, the data comes from [two communities]. The Guatemalan community is a mixed Indian and Ladino *municipio* in the Western Highlands, and details of its society and culture may be found in *Machine Age Maya.*[1] The Mexican Indian community of Amatenango del Valle is an extreme instance, even for Mexico. These Indian societies are in

a tense bicultural situation and there is much antipathy and hostility. . . .

Amatenango is a municipio with a town center of 1469 persons and a rural periphery of 2529. It is an all-Indian community, and more than 90 percent of its population are born in the municipio and spend their lives there. It is, like other Mayan Indian communities in Meso-America, a distinct local society, united by blood and custom, living on its own territory, and conscious of itself as an ethnic entity. The community makes its living by agriculture on a small plot system combining the subsistence crops of maize, beans, and squash with a cash wheat crop. It also is the pottery producing center for a region between Tuxtla and Comitan. The community has many of the defensive features of the Indian peasantry of Meso-America, but it is none the less tied into the national society in at least three distinct and significant ways. First, the economic ties stemming from its relationship in the regional market economy give rise to the fact of the circulation of Mexican currency, the consumption of items produced in the national economy, the price levels being set by the forces of supply and demand on the larger stage of the region, and tenure of land being defined by the national legal code. Second, like other communities, Amatenango has been the object of special government attention. The *Instituto Nacional Indigenista* (INI) has for more than a decade carried out in this region a program of education, road building, sanitation, medical care, and agricultural and industrial innovation. Amatenango, for example, has a clinic sponsored by INI, a store and credit society, and a piped water system installed by the agency. Thirdly, Amatenango is affected by the politics of Mexico, for the program of "incorporation" of Indians into the national society is implemented or ignored according to shifts in politics at the national level. Also, the *ejido* (government grant of communal land) is in the political arena, and some Amatenangeros have *ejido* land in the hot country about a day's distance from the municipio. And finally, just how the Indian will fare with the police, the courts, and in the myriad legal and contractual relations Indians make with Ladinos is a function of the political climate of the nation as that is

[1] Manning Nash, *Machine Age Maya* (Glencoe, Ill.: The Free Press, 1958).

refracted in the backwoods of Chiapas.

Left on its own,... a community like Amatenango would not have any school at all. For the community itself continuity in culture and development of the skills needed for the maintenance of the society come through the informal means of ordinary socialization and enculturation. What is needed to be an Amatenangero is learned in the local social system, while what is needed to deal with outsiders may be learned in the local school. This puts the school and schooling in perspective: it is an extrinsic agency, part of the larger society, transmitter of a different cultural tradition, and by nature an agent of change and a source of new and wider mental horizons. That the school has not radically transformed the community, or in fact made much of a dent in its illiteracy is a function of two facts: the major concerns of the people of Amatenango, and the character of the incumbent school teacher.

The people of Amatenango are, because of their place in the multiple society and due to the long history of acrimonious ethnic relations in Chiapas, not concerned with becoming Ladinos[2] and the process of acculturation over nearly 400 years has not eroded the ethnic distinctiveness of the society, whatever cultural items and traits they have borrowed and accepted from Ladino society. The Amatenangeros have major interests in making a living, a mundane business of getting along with neighbors, and keeping the proper relations between the society and the supernatural. For these ends, the school counts little. Nothing in the curriculum implements the ends of Amatenango Indians.

The school itself is set in the central square of the town center in an adobe building. The Ladino teacher and his family (his wife and daughters serve as assistant teachers) make their residence in the school compound. About 280 students (130 girls and 150 boys) are usually enrolled in the three grades that the school offers. (There is another school of about 50 students in the rural *barrio* of Madronal.) The major tasks of the school are the teaching of Spanish and the elementary skills of reading and writing. The normal language of the household and the streets of Amatenango is Tzeltal, and if anybody learns Spanish it is as a second language. Men in Amatenango have a much higher fluency in Spanish than do women. By rough percentages, for the town center, better than 85 per-

cent of the men are to some extent bilingual, while just the reverse is true for women.... Among children from six to twelve years of age (in 1959, when all of these data were collected in the field) the percentages of bilinguality of both boys and girls was about 75 percent. What is clear from this figure is that the three or four years of school does instil some basic Spanish language skills in both boys and girls, but that men, because they travel, meet Ladinos, sometimes work for them, and have other contacts with them, while women do not; hence men increase their Spanish over their lifetimes, while the Spanish of the women tends to erode and decay from lack of occasion for use.

The literacy rates, even in the most loosely defined notion of functional literacy, are about 15 percent for the males, and under 5 percent for the females, indicating the difficulty of transfer of the skills from school to everyday life, where they are not called for at all. The only reading matter I ever observed in Amatenango were comic books in simple basic Spanish, an occasional newspaper, and government decrees. Outside of the Indian officials in office, it is safe to estimate that the population of the town center, collectively, spends less than one hour a day in contact with the printed word.

The innovative potential of village education— for the school does follow the national curriculum and does try to instil some history, some geography, some patriotism, and some arithmetic as well as the national language and literature—is thus clearly circumscribed by the total operation of Amatenango as a society with its given value system and its place in a multiple social structure. It is further hampered by the character of the school teacher himself. The teacher and his family are socially isolated from the Indians. At night he locks up his school and his house, and given the numerous guns he has, the place has something of the aspect of a fortress. The analogy is deliberate. The teacher is an alien in the midst of a people he does not understand and does not completely trust. On their side the Amatenangeros neither respect nor trust the school teacher. He leaves on any occasion, his life is tied to the nearby

[2]Persons who speak Spanish as their main language, who dress like members of the national society, and who are culturally identified with it; a cultural and not a biological distinction.—Ed.

city, not the village, and even if he should wish, he could not get into the intimate daily life of the community. He is overbearing, authoritarian, and not particularly gentle in his relations with the Indians. Furthermore he is a state of Chiapas employee, and hence not responsible to the local community, and they in no way influence the conduct or the content of teaching. The school scratches the surface of Amatenango life, because that life is oriented to its own concerns, and because the teacher is a social irritant in an alien community, not the representative, however humble, of a respected *literati*.

What revolutionary or innovative potential schooling may in fact have when it is divorced from the constraints of local society is exemplified by a social experiment carried out in Indian communities about 20 years ago. There was a program of boarding schools (*internados*) instituted by the Mexican government to train some Indians in each community in Spanish speech and literature. Young boys and girls were taken from their families and put into boarding schools and kept from four to six years. Of the ten taken from Amatenango into the program, all are now resident in Amatenango, all of them are still bilingual, and all of them are literate. Furthermore they have worked out to be something of an elite, in the sense that they relate the community to a Ladino world that they understand much better than their fellow villagers, and they have held the top offices in the village civil and religious hierarchy. They have, at least some of the men, moved over to a Ladino style dress, and have a comparatively expanded view of the world. Also some of them have taken on jobs (like store keeper) that no other Indian could handle, and furthermore they are the people who have married outside of the habitual rule of village endogamy. They have married Indian women from other communities who were ladinoized enough to give up traditional Indian costume.

The boarding school experience does indicate that elementary schooling can result in important social change, even for people at the end of multiple society, but that it must be withdrawn from the community constraints, when the community is organized as is Amatenango.

By way of contrast . . . is the Guatemalan Indian community of Cantel. Cantel is a more sophisticated community of Maya Indians in a double sense than is Amatenango. It apparently had a richer Mayan heritage (in the area where Quiché was and is spoken), and it has been in longer, more intimate contact with Guatemalan Ladino society than has Amatenango. If I can hazard a forecast, when the road net around Amatenango now in construction gets to the level that Cantel has enjoyed for 20 years, Amatenango will begin to approximate many of the structural and cultural features of Cantel. The municipio of Cantel is also more populous. Its town center (in 1954, when the field census was taken) had a population of 1,910 and its outlying areas had 6,585 souls. In the town center *(pueblo)*, on which I shall focus, the Indians accounted for 96.2 [percent] of the population, and the remaining 3.8 [percent] were Ladinos. In the pueblo, 17.7 [percent] of the population were engaged in specialist occupations (not all of them full time) and more than a quarter of the work force was in the textile factory just across the river from the town center. In short, the town center was a bustling, cosmopolitan, and specialized place compared to the agricultural village of Amatenango. But still Cantel was a distinct social and cultural entity, both in objective fact and in their self-perception as Cantelenos whose customs were different, not only from Ladinos but, say, from their Zunil, Almolonga, Totonicipan, or Quezaltenango neighbors.

There were in Cantel two schools. One was the national school, the other run by the factory for children of factory workers. The school attendance in Cantel was slightly better than that of Amatenango, . . . but the difficulty of meeting the compulsory attendance of children from age seven to age fourteen was about the same. Where school and work conflict in societies at this level of income, work always wins. Poverty coupled with familial agricultural production has the effect of drawing children out of school as soon as they are useful in the fields. Cantel's schools offered up to sixth grade education. But the enrollment figures are revealing: in the first three grades are 300 pupils; in the fifth and sixth grades combined there are only 20 pupils. Still, the fact that 20 students a year get up to the sixth grade level gives Cantel a greater edge on the modernity and national integration scales than Amatenango.

By the same loose definition of literacy, about 60 percent of the Cantelense are illiterate, and this is about the national average, while Amatenango was above the reported Mexican average. Bilingualism in the town center is much greater for women than it is in Amatenango, and most men can handle elementary Spanish.

The schools are, as they are in Mexico, agencies of the national government, transmitters of the national culture, and divorced from the community in regards of support or of control. The school teacher is a Ladino, somewhat marginal to the community but not so nearly an alien as in Amatenango.

That the schools have not been more of a radical agent of social change than in fact they have been in Cantel is accounted for by two major facts. First, the poverty of the community and the nation keeps many children from more than three years of education, where they barely learn the elementary skills; and secondly the national government is, and has been, hesitant about how to incorporate Indians into the political society of Guatemala. Thus the schools are not seen, nor used as catalysts in social change, but are confined to transmission of elementary skills, some patriotism, and some minor facts about history and geography. But these schools could, if an ideology activated them, if more resources were poured in, if more teachers were assigned, if more books . . . —but why catalogue the needs of any under-developed country?—act more forcefully as agents of change. This requires not only the necessary expenditures, but a clear and definite program among the national segment as to the role of the Indian in Guatemalan society. This program is but vaguely enunciated and defined, and this very hesitancy, plus the lack of scale in investment, keeps the schools in a marginal role in fostering modernity.

One strong index of the impact of both schools and factory on the children of Cantel is found in the occupational aspirations of school children. Interviewing (in 1953–54 when all of the data were collected) 136 boys and girls between the ages of 10 and 15 in both the Pueblo and Pasac schools, for job preferences, revealed the predominance of a preference for artisan or specialist occupations. These occupational aspirations are at variance with the chief uses of manpower in the community and far exceed the foreseeable demand for the kinds of jobs and services selected by school children. What these aspirations seem to indicate is a continuance of the basic community

values of self-employment and economic independence or self-sufficiency. Formerly these values were expressed in terms of land holding, but the pressure of a growing population on a fixed land base has moved the loci of the values to artisan or specialist occupations. This younger generation of school-educated are willing to try occupations which may cut them off from some of the roots of community life and possibly alienate them from the local society. It appears that schooling, even under the restricted conditions of Cantel, does have the potential for social change and mental expansion.

Part of the receptivity to change in the economic sphere among the school-educated of Cantel is intimately linked to the political events of the preceding decade, and points up again the fact that, in multiple societies structured like Guatemala, political events on the national scene are likely to be decisive in social and economic change in local communities. The school can and does act as agency of the national society, and in the interaction between the school and the community lies an important source for receptivity or resistance to change.

In Cantel, the generational differences of the effect of both educational and political change are fairly clearly marked. The older generation lost much influence, power, and respect to the younger more literate and less traditional members of society, and this is echoed even in the consequences of schooling. Of the adults attending a night school for literacy, only one thought of an occupation outside of the traditional roster of Cantel (and, of course, those willing to come to night school on their own for the rewards of literacy represent the most progressive of the older generation). In short, those who are "well built-in" members of the society and of middle age cannot afford the risks of mobility, of loss of social obligation and support, and the adventures of new careers. This generational difference underlines yet another important generalization: in local communities the village school begins to instil different values from those of the local community, but adulthood, the claims of mundane life, the competition of the known with the unknown, and the absence of supporting institutions beyond the schools make these values, in most instances, atrophy and eventually disappear. . . .

Three very general propositions about village

schools in the process of social change may be hazarded on the basis of the foregoing: (1) It is change in the economic, religious, and interpersonal relations on the local and regional levels which are antecedent to change in the educational system. (2) Local schools tend to be conservative agents, transmitting by means that reinforce local tendencies toward stability. (3) Education becomes a force for social change only when the process of social change is well underway.

The practical and procedural consequences of these propositions are fairly self-evident. What is needed is to verify them with a wider sample than that given here. However, it is clear that the diagnostic tools of social science, its abilities to distinguish between types of poverty and types of social system are valuable ingredients in translating any plan into practice, and even in foreseeing, however opaquely, some of the consequences of a given course of action.

Ivan Illich

The Futility of Schooling in Latin America

Having insisted that schooling can be a social problem in modern society, few anthropologists have made this problem explicit. Like most modern men, their faith in education and the cultural institution of the school has been shaken in specific instances more than their faith in education as a general institution of individual development and liberation. A Catholic priest, however, has recently taken the lead in developing concern for the implications of the school as a social institution. Monsignor Illich is specifically occupied with the problems of Latin America and speaks out of the same context as Nash, but with different purposes and conclusions. The questions which he raises and his suggestion of the "futility of schooling" are important to us and should suggest a number of new anthropological approaches in which education would be treated as a social problem.

For the past two decades, demographic considerations have colored all discussion about development in Latin America. In 1950, some 200 million people occupied the area extending from Mexico to Chile. Of these, 120 million lived directly or indirectly on primitive agriculture. Assuming both effective population controls and the most favorable possible results from programs aimed at the increase of agriculture, by 1985 40,000,000 people will produce most of the food for a total population of 360 million. The remaining 320

million will be either marginal to the economy or will have to be incorporated somehow into urban living and agricultural production.

During these same past twenty years, both Latin American governments, and foreign technical assistance agencies have come to rely increasingly on the capacity of grammar, trade, and high schools to lead the nonrural majority out of its marginality in shanty towns and subsistence farms, into the type of factory, market, and public forum which corresponds to modern technology. It was assumed that schooling would eventually produce a broad middle class with values resembling those of highly industrialized nations, despite the economy of continued scarcity.

Accumulating evidence now indicates that schooling does not and cannot produce the expected results. Seven years ago the governments of the Americas joined in an Alliance for Progress, which has, in practice, served mainly the progress of the middle classes in the Latin nations. In most countries, the Alliance has encouraged the replacement of a closed, feudal, hereditary elite by one which is supposedly "meritocratic" and open to the few who manage to finish school. Concomitantly, the urban service proletariat has grown at several times the rate of the traditional landless rural mass and has replaced it in importance. The marginal majority and the schooled minority grow ever further apart. One old feudal society has brought forth two classes, separate and unequal.

This development has led to educational research focused on the improvement of the learning process in schools and on the adaptations of schools themselves to the special circumstances prevailing in underdeveloped societies. But logic would seem to require that we do not stop with an effort to improve schools; rather, that we question the assumption on which the school system itself is based. We must not exclude the possibility that the emerging nations cannot be schooled; that schooling is not a viable answer to their need for universal education. Perhaps this type of insight is needed to clear the way for a futuristic scenario in which schools as we know them today would disappear.

The social distance between the growing urban mass and the new elite is a new phenomenon, unlike the traditional forms of discrimination known in Latin America. This new discrimination is not a transitory thing which can be overcome by schooling. On the contrary: I submit that one of the reasons for the awakening frustration in the majorities is the progressive acceptance of the "liberal myth," the assumption that schooling is an assurance of social integration.

The solidarity of all citizens based on their common graduation from school has been an inalienable part of the modern, Western self-image. Colonization has not succeeded in implanting this myth equally in all countries, but everywhere schooling has become the prerequisite for membership in a managerial middle class. The constitutional history of Latin America since its independence has made the masses of this continent particularly susceptible to the conviction that all citizens have a right to enter—and, therefore, have some possibility of entering—their society through the door of a school.

More than elsewhere, in Latin America the teacher as missionary for the school-gospel has found adherents at the grassroots. Only a few years ago many of us were happy when finally the Latin American school system was singled out as the area of privileged investment for international assistance funds. In fact, during the past years, both national budgets and private investment have been stimulated to increase educational allocations. But a second look reveals that this school system has built a narrow bridge across a widening social gap. As the only legitimate passage to the middle class, the school restricts all unconventional crossings and leaves the underachiever to bear the blame for his marginality.

This statement is difficult for Americans to understand. In the United States, the nineteenth-century persuasion that free schooling insures all citizens equality in the economy and effective participation in the society survive. It is by no means certain that the result of schooling ever measured up to this expectation, but the schools certainly played a more prominent role in this process some hundred years ago.

In the United States of the mid-nineteenth century, six years of schooling frequently made a young man the educational superior of his boss. In a society largely dominated by unschooled achievers, the little red schoolhouse was an effective road to social equality. A few years in school for all brought most extremes together. Those who achieved power and money without schooling had to accept a degree of equality with those who achieved literacy and did not strike it rich. Computers, television, and airplanes have changed this. Today in Latin America, in the midst of modern technology, three times as many years of schooling and twenty times as much money as was then spent on grammar schools will not produce the same social result. The dropout from the sixth grade is unable to find a job even as a punchcard operator or a railroad engineer.

Contemporary Latin America needs school systems no more than it needs railroad tracks. Both—spanning continents—served to speed the now-rich and established nations into the industrial age. Both, if now handled with care, are harmless heirlooms from the Victorian period. But neither is relevant to countries emerging from primitive agriculture directly into the jet age. Latin America cannot afford to maintain outmoded social institutions amid modern technological processes.

By "school," of course, I do not mean all organized formal education. I use the term "school" and "schooling" here to designate a form of child-care and a *rite de passage* which we take for granted. We forget that this institution and the corresponding creed appeared on the scene only with the growth of the industrial state. Comprehensive schooling today involves year-round, obligatory, and universal classroom attendance in small groups for several hours each day. It is imposed on all citizens for a period of ten to eighteen years. School divides life into two segments, which are increasingly of comparable length. As much as anything else, schooling implies custodial care for persons who are declared undesirable elsewhere by the simple fact that a school has been built to serve them. The school is supposed to take the excess population from the street, the family, or the labor force. Teachers are given the power to invent new criteria according to which new segments of the population may be committed to a school. This restraint on healthy, productive, and potentially independent human beings is performed by schools with an economy which only labor camps could rival.

Schooling also involves a process of accepted ritual certification for all members of a "schooled" society. Schools select those who are bound to succeed and send them on their way with a badge marking them fit. Once universal schooling has been accepted as the hallmark for the in-members of a society, fitness is measured by the amount of time and money spent on formal education in youth rather than by ability acquired independently from an "accredited" curriculum.

A first important step toward radical educational reform in Latin America will be taken when the educational system of the United States is accepted for what it is: a recent, imaginative social invention perfected since World War II and historically rooted in the American frontier. The creation of the all-pervasive school establishment, tied into industry, government, and the military, is an invention no less original than the guild-centered apprenticeship of the Middle Ages, or the *doctrina de los indios* and the *Reducción* of Spanish missionaries in Mexico and Paraguay, respectively, or the *lycée* and *les grandes écoles* in France. Each one of these systems was produced by its society to give stability to an achievement; each has been heavily pervaded by ritual to which society bowed; and each has been rationalized into an all-embrac-

Three eras of education: the apprentice, the village school, and the political orator—"Each one of these systems was produced by its society to give stability to an achievement."

ing persuasion, religion, or ideology. The United States is not the first nation which has been willing to pay a high price to have its educational system exported by missionaries to all corners of the world. The colonization of Latin America by the catechism is certainly a noteworthy precedent.

It is difficult now to challenge the school as a system because we are so used to it. Our industrial categories tend to define results as products of specialized institutions and instruments. Armies produce defense for countries. Churches procure salvation in an afterlife. Binet defined intelligence as that which his tests test. Why not, then, conceive of education as the product of schools? Once this tag has been accepted, unschooled education gives the impression of something spurious, illegitimate, and certainly unaccredited.

For some generations, education has been based on massive schooling, just as security was based on massive retaliation and, at least in the United States, transportation on the family car. The United States, because it industrialized earlier, is rich enough to afford schools, the Strategic Air Command, and the car—no matter what the toll. Most nations of the world are not that rich; they behave, however, as if they were. The example of nations which "made it" leads Brazilians to pursue the ideal of the family car—just for a few. It compels Peruvians to squander on Mirage bombers—just for a show. And it drives every government in Latin America to spend up to two-fifths of its total budget on schools, and to do so unchallenged. . . .

Before poor nations could reach [the] point of universal schooling, however, their ability to educate would be exhausted. Even ten or twelve years of schooling are beyond 85 percent of all men of our century if they happen to live outside the tiny islands where capital accumulates. Nowhere in Latin America do 27 percent of any age group get beyond the sixth grade, nor do more than 1 percent graduate from a university. Yet no government spends less than 18 percent of its budget on schools, and many spend more than 30 percent. Universal schooling, as this concept has been defined recently in industrial societies, is obviously beyond their means. The annual cost of schooling a United States citizen between the ages of twelve and twenty-four costs as much as most Latin Americans earn in two to three years.

Schools will stay beyond the means of the developing nations: Neither radical population control nor maximum reallocations of government budgets nor unprecedented foreign aid would end the present unfeasibility of school systems aimed at twelve years of schooling for all. Population control needs time to become effective when the total population is as young as that of tropical America. The percentage of the world's resources invested in schooling cannot be raised beyond certain levels, nor can this budget grow beyond foreseeable maximal rates. Finally, foreign aid would have to increase to 30 percent of the receiving nation's national budget to provide effectively for schooling, a goal not to be anticipated.

Furthermore, the per capita cost of schooling itself is rising everywhere as schools accept those who are difficult to teach, as retention rates rise, and as the quality of schooling itself improves. This rise in cost neutralizes much of the new investments. Schools do not come cheaper by the dozen.

In view of all these factors, increases in school budgets must usually be defended by arguments which imply default. In fact, however, schools are untouchable because they are vital to the status quo. Schools have the effect of tempering the subversive potential of education in an alienated society because, if education is confined to schools, only those who have been schooled into compliance on a lower grade are advanced to its higher reaches. In capital-starved societies not rich enough to purchase unlimited schooling, the majority is schooled not only into compliance but also into subservience.

Since Latin American constitutions were written with an eye on the United States, the ideal of universal schooling was a creative utopia. It was a condition necessary to create the Latin American nineteenth-century bourgeoisie. Without the pretense that every citizen has a right to go to school, the liberal bourgeoisie could never have developed; neither could the middle-class masses of present-day Europe, the United States, and Russia, nor the managerial middle elite of their cultural colonies in South America. But the same school which worked in the last century to overcome feudalism has now become an oppressive idol which protects those who are already schooled. Schools grade and, therefore, they degrade. They make the degraded accept his own submission. Social seniority is bestowed according to the level of schooling achieved. Everywhere in Latin America more money for schools means more privilege for a few at the cost of most, and this patronage of an elite is explained as a political ideal. This ideal is written into laws which state the patently impossible: equal scholastic opportunities for all.

The number of satisfied clients who graduate from schools every year is much smaller than the number of frustrated dropouts who are conveniently graded by their failure for use in a marginal labor pool. The resulting steep educational pyramid defines a rationale for the corresponding levels of social status. Citizens are "schooled" into their places. This results in politically acceptable forms of discrimination which benefit the relatively few achievers.

The move from the farm to the city in Latin America still frequently means a move from a world where status is explained as a result of inheritance into a world where it is explained as a result of schooling. Schools allow a head start to be rationalized as an achievement. They give to privilege not only the appearance of equality but also of generosity: Should somebody who missed out on early schooling be dissatisfied with the status he holds, he can always be referred to a night or trade school. If he does not take advantage of such recognized remedies, his exclusion from privilege can be explained as his own fault. Schools temper the frustrations they provoke.

The school system also inculcates its own universal acceptance. Some schooling is not necessarily more educational than none, especially in a country where every year a few more people can get all the schooling they want while most people never complete the sixth grade. But much less than six years seems to be sufficient to inculcate in the child the acceptance of the ideology which goes with the school grade. The child learns only about the superior status and unquestioned authority of those who have more schooling than he has.

Any discussion of radical alternatives to school-centered formal education upsets our notions of society. No matter how inefficient schools are in educating a majority, no matter how effective schools are in limiting the access to the elite, no matter how liberally schools shower their non-educational benefits on the members of this elite, schools do increase the national income. They qualify their graduates for more economic production. In an economy on the lower rungs of develop-

ment toward United States-type industrialization, a school graduate is enormously more productive than a dropout. Schools are part and parcel of a society in which a minority is on the way to becoming so productive that the majority must be schooled into disciplined consumption. Schooling therefore—under the best of circumstances—helps to divide society into two groups: those so productive that their expectation of annual rise in personal income lies far beyond the national average, and the overwhelming majority, whose income also rises, but at a rate clearly below the former's. These rates, of course, are compounded and lead the two groups further apart.

Radical innovation in formal education presupposes radical political changes, radical changes in the organization of production, and radical changes in man's image of himself as an animal which needs school. This is often forgotten when sweeping reforms of the schools are proposed and fail because of the societal framework we accept. For instance, the trade school is sometimes advocated as a cure-all for mass schooling. Yet it is doubtful that the products of trade schools would find employment in a continuously changing, ever more automated economy. Moreover, the capital and operating costs of trade schools, as we know them today, are several times as high as those for a standard school on the same grade. Also, trade schools usually take in sixth graders, who, as we have seen, are already the exception. They pretend to educate by creating a spurious facsimile of the factory within a school building.

Instead of the trade school, we should think of a subsidized transformation of the industrial plant. It should be possible to make it obligatory for factories to serve as training centers during off hours, for managers to spend part of their time planning and supervising this training, and for the industrial process to be so redesigned that it has educational value. If the expenditures for present schools were partly allocated to sponsor this kind of educational exploitation of existing resources, then the final results—both economic and educational—might be incomparably greater. If, further, such subsidized apprenticeship were offered to all who ask for it, irrespective of age, and not only to those who are destined to be employees in the particular plant, industry would have begun to assume an important role now played by school. We would be on the way to disabuse ourselves of the idea that manpower qualification must precede employment, that schooling must precede productive work. There is no reason for us to continue the medieval tradition in which men are prepared for the "secular world" by incarceration in a sacred precinct, be it monastery, synagogue, or school.

A second, frequently discussed, remedy for the failure of schools is fundamental, or adult, education. It has been proved by Paolo Freire in Brazil that those adults who can be interested in political issues of their community can be made literate within six weeks of evening classes. The program teaching such reading and writing skills, of course, must be built around the emotion-loaded key words of their political vocabulary. Understandably, this fact has gotten his program into trouble. It has been equally suggested that the dollar-cost of ten separate months of adult education is equal to one year of early schooling, and can be incomparably more effective than schooling at its best.

Unfortunately, "adult education" now is conceived principally as a device to give the "underprivileged" a palliative for the schooling he lacks. The situation would have to be reversed if we wanted to conceive of all education as an exercise in adulthood. We should consider a radical reduction of the length of the formal, obligatory school sessions to only two months each year—but spread this type of formal schooling over the first twenty or thirty years of a man's life.

While various forms of in-service apprenticeship in factories and programed math and language teaching could assume a large proportion of what we have previously called "instruction," two months a year of formal schooling should be considered ample time for what the Greeks meant by "schole"—leisure for the pursuit of insight. No wonder we find it nearly impossible to conceive of comprehensive social changes in which the educational functions of schools would be thus redistributed in new patterns among institutions we do not now envisage. We find it equally difficult to indicate concrete ways in which the noneducational functions of a vanishing school system would be redistributed. We do not know what to do with those whom we now label "children" or "students" and commit to school.

It is difficult to foresee the political conse-

quences of changes as fundamental as those proposed, not to mention the international consequences. How should a school-reared society coexist with one which has gone "off the school standard," and whose industry, commerce, advertising, and participation in politics is different as a matter of principle? Areas which develop outside the universal school standard would lack the common language and criteria for respectful coexistence with the schooled. Two such worlds, such as China and the United States, might almost have to seal themselves off from each other.

Rashly, the school-bred mind abhors the educational devices available to these worlds. It is difficult mentally to "accredit" Mao's party as an educational institution which might prove more effective than the schools are at their best—at least when it comes to inculcating citizenship. Guerrilla warfare in Latin America is another educational device much more frequently misused or misunderstood than applied. Che Guevara, for instance, clearly saw it as a last educational resort to teach a people about the illegitimacy of their political system. Especially in unschooled countries, where the transistor radio has come to every village, we must never underrate the educational functions of great charismatic dissidents like Dom Helder Camara in Brazil or Camilo Torres in Colombia. Castro described his early charismatic harangues as teaching sessions.

The schooled mind perceives these processes exclusively as political indoctrination, and their educational purpose eludes its grasp. The legitimation of education by schools tends to render all nonschool education an accident, if not an outright misdemeanor. And yet, it is surprising with what difficulty the school-bred mind perceives the rigor with which schools inculcate their own presumed necessity, and with it the supposed inevitability of the system they sponsor. Schools indoctrinate the child into the acceptance of the political system his teachers represent, despite the claim that teaching is nonpolitical.

Ultimately, the cult of schooling will lead to violence. The establishment of any religion has led to it. To permit the gospel of universal schooling to spread, the military's ability to repress insurgency in Latin America must grow. Only force will ultimately control the insurgency inspired by the frustrated expectations which the propagation of the school-myth enkindles. The maintenance of the present school system may turn out to be an important step on the way to Latin American fascism. Only fanaticism inspired by idolatry of a system can ultimately rationalize the massive discrimination which will result from another twenty years of grading a capital-starved society with school marks.

The time has come to recognize the real burden of the schools in the emerging nations, so that we may become free to envisage change in the social structure which now make schools a necessity. I do not advocate a sweeping utopia like the Chinese commune for Latin America. But I do suggest that we plunge our imagination into the construction of scenarios which would allow a bold reallocation of educational functions among industry, politics, short scholastic retreats, and intensive preparation of parents for early childhood education. The cost of schools must be measured not only in economic, social, and educational terms, but in political terms as well. Schools, in an economy of scarcity invaded by automation, accentuate and rationalize the coexistence of two societies, one a colony of the other.

Once it is understood that the cost of schooling is not inferior to the cost of chaos, we might be on the brink of courageously costly compromise. Today it is as dangerous in Latin America to question the myth of social salvation through schooling as it was dangerous 300 years ago to question the divine rights of the Catholic kings.

John Singleton

The Educational Uses of Anthropology

Anthropologists and those with whom they associate have begun to declare the relevance of their work to the problems of coping with education in a modern or modernizing society—and it should be obvious that there is still a large field of research and action left for anthropologists and anthropologically oriented participants. Those associated with schooling—especially the teachers and students—will *not*, however, benefit from a new form of imperialism. Most insidious, especially when the intentions are honorable, is the disciplinary imperialism of the anthropological tribe. Anthropologists must subdue the messianic spirit with which they proclaim the newest answer, i.e., anthropology, to one of the world's oldest professions, teaching. We must carefully assess the source of our expertise and avoid giving misleading academic labels to personal feelings and to what seems like common sense in the light of our own cultural surroundings. There are many ways in which our discipline and our disciplined knowledge and approach in anthropology can be of use.

First, a large number of undergraduate anthropology majors become public-school teachers. At the same time, future teachers are being directed to college courses in anthropology. We should ask what difference the study of anthropology will make to them in their future school roles. Has anthropology been taught as we would want them to teach?

As Postman and Weingartner have suggested in their provocatively titled critique of contemporary education, *Teaching as a Subversive Activity*, there is a need for "a new education that would set out to cultivate . . . experts at 'crap detecting.' . . . We are talking about the schools' cultivating in the young that most 'subversive' intellectual instrument—the anthropological perspective. This perspective allows one to be part of his own culture and, at the same time, to be out of it. One views the activities of his own group as would an anthropologist, observing its tribal rituals, its fears, its conceits, its ethnocentrism. In this way, one is able to recognize when reality begins to drift too far away from the grasp of the tribe."[1]

[1]Neil Postman and Charles Weingartner, *Teaching as a Subversive Activity* (New York: The Delacorte Press, 1969), pp. 3–4.

There is a message here for all teachers—especially those who teach teachers. It is that anthropology, which is relevant to the social problems of our time and place, can contribute a perspective to education which is more important than specific content.

The favorite and traditional subjects of anthropology—the evolution of man and culture, the structure of language and communication, the appreciation and study of cultural difference, the reconstruction of our past through archaeology, the biological nature of our being, and the basic patterns of human society—are now being taught in our elementary and secondary schools. Anthropologists have begun to produce text materials and to train teachers for transmitting what we know about these topics. But how can a teacher teach anthropology without an anthropological perspective? One of the basic ways is to help the teachers view their own social tribe and institution, the school, in cultural perspective. Teachers can only convey that subversive perspective if they have examined their own tribal institutions in the same way that they expect students to examine theirs.

A second way in which the anthropologist can be important to education is to shift his focus, in interpreting the interplay between the administrators and the administered, from the colonial setting to the school. The anthropological viewpoint is especially valuable in settings where multicultural and cross-cultural interactions of teachers, students, and curriculum—the hallmark of modern education—take place.

George Spindler has discussed "cultural therapy" for classroom teachers who convey discriminatory cultural messages to their students. Theodore Brameld goes further with an "anthropotherapy" which will provide for "the theory and practice of descriptive and prescriptive human roles." It is unrealistic, however, to expect that new anthropological cadres will be produced in sufficient numbers to meet the need. Thus, ways must be found of transmitting the anthropological message in new and wider channels. The recent workshop of the American Anthropological Association, suggested by students and directed to the process of getting more relevant anthropological knowledge into the mass media, is most appropriate.

The third relationship of anthropology to education is both the most traditional and the most radical—the anthropological study of education. Research is the traditional core activity of the academic "tribes" called disciplines, but anthropological research into education and schooling in modern society is a new

research preserve. It has been considered somewhat demeaning in the academic world to be associated with the professional study of education, and it is indicative of the conservatism of anthropology that the other social sciences have staked out the educational preserve earlier and in richer detail—sociology, economics, and political science, not to mention psychology, which early captured a formal affiliation with the field by gaining representation in schools of education and teachers' colleges.

It is important, therefore, that anthropologists and educationists are now coming together to serve their common needs. No longer is there a one-way street of charitable contributions from anthropology to education; the self-interest of anthropology itself is now at stake as education and schooling are revealed as productive sites for anthropological research. The formation of the Council on Anthropology and Education within the American Anthropological Association in 1968 was a formal recognition of this joint effort, and the Council's *Newsletter* is a source of information on activities in this field.

Anthropologists who are turning to the study of education as a social institution and as a social problem are finding several analytical frameworks that are appropriate for their purpose. The papers in this section illustrate several attacks. The approach used by Khlief and by Burnett should be useful in any educational setting; Willard Waller's *The Sociology of Teaching*, a classic outline of schools as social institutions in Pennsylvania during the early 1930s, is in the same vein. Those who wish to examine the function of schooling in the context of the larger society can find in the papers by Fisher, Nash, and Illich suggestions that could well be elaborated. One hopes, indeed, that a number of anthropologists will pick up Illich's suggestion that there is a "cult of schooling" and begin to examine specific varieties of schooling in the same way that anthropologists have studied religious traditions. Unlike Illich, they need not fear the "cult of schooling" as the devil incarnate—it is only necessary that they accord this cult the same objective study previously reserved for more explicitly acknowledged religious phenomena.

Educational change, like other varieties of social change, also deserves attention. The Waxes and the Baratzes have suggested some important models for the critical understanding of innovations in schooling. The anthropologist as educational innovator is a new role. If there is a sound foundation of anthropological knowledge, such as Talbert brought to the early teaching of reading and writing, there is ground for further encouragement.

Perhaps the most important problem of American education today is the need to find ways to make public schooling a truly multicultural enterprise. To accomplish this end, we need more concrete information about the educational experiences of the minority groups in our society. Specific conceptual frames for anthropological research in this area would include:

1. *Education as an instrument of socialization.* An emphasis on the processes of socialization as they are experienced by children in both the school setting and outside it suggests that we can differentiate roughly between: (a) primary socialization—the intimate socialization of children to family, sex, and community roles that occurs in familial and primary group contexts; (b) secondary socialization—the development of attitudes and behavior transmitted by schools, peer groups, religious organizations, and other social institutions in which school-age children participate and in which they learn to be members of the community; and (c) tertiary socialization—into adult vocational, religious, and social roles.

Careful studies of secondary and tertiary socialization in schools attended by minority children would have to include the ways in which such children are confronted in the school with their minority-group identity and the conflicts with the majority society that are transmitted directly or indirectly by the school's educational program, learning materials, teachers, and fellow students. Spindler, in *Education and Culture*, has described, for example, the subtle way in which a school counselor communicated their minority-group status to Mexican-American students who were selecting their high-school courses.

The concepts of secondary and tertiary socialization will allow us to avoid the assumption that schooling is just an institutionalized form of socialization to adult roles. They should make us sensitive to the ways in which schools educate children to their roles as pupils. This typology will also help us make sense of such statements as Fisher's that the school is "the major socialization device of the industrialized urbanized segment of the Canadian population." It means that the school is the major instrument of generally accepted *secondary* socialization and implies that the processes of *tertiary* socialization are also significantly present. As he points out, this is not true for the Canadian-Indian population; the secondary socialization of the school is not accepted by the Indian community in Alberta in the same way it is accepted in the mainstream communities of Canada.

Studies of secondary and tertiary socialization might well be as highly organized as previous cross-cultural studies of primary socialization, but they would have to include comparisons of minority and mainstream cultural patterns.

2. *Language, conceptual style, and learning.* The Baratzes and Talbert have emphasized the importance of language in educational programs. Rosalie Cohen has described the systematic and patterned ways in which the schools actively discriminate against large groups of children on the basis of the underlying conceptual style with which they relate to their environment. Two contrasting cognitive styles—analytic and relational—seem to be associated with linguistic and cultural difference.

So discrepant are the analytic and relational frames of reference that a pupil whose preferred mode of cognitive organization is emphatically relational is unlikely to be rewarded in the school setting either socially or by grades regardless of his native abilities and even if his information repertoire and background of experience are adequate.[2]

She goes on to point out that the relational conceptual style not only hampers the child in the school setting, but that the experience of school disables the child in his home and community. This fact seems especially poignant if we realize that the relational conceptual style discouraged by the school is closely related to creative ability. It is important, thus, to determine the differences between the two cognitive styles, the differential patterns of participation and success in school that might be attributable to such differences, and the ways in which schools can change to develop rather than discourage such skills.

The systematic study of minority-group language patterns is, of course, a major approach to the study of cognitive or conceptual style. As Charles Valentine writes: "In view of all the academic and popular interest in the supposed verbal disabilities of the poor, and the many policy implications, particularly with respect to education, this could be a most important contribution of ethnography among the poor."[3]

---

[2] "Conceptual Styles, Culture Conflict, and Nonverbal Tests of Intelligence," *American Anthropologist* (October 1969): 830.

[3] *Culture and Poverty* (Chicago: University of Chicago Press, 1968), p. 185.

Differences of conceptual style imply different patterns of learning. Rosalie Cohen suggests that schools must abandon the assumption that there is a single method for knowing and go on to devise multiple-method learning environments. Cultural patterns of learning deserve intensive exploration.

3. *Adolescent initiation, identity, and education.* The important contrasts between pre- and postpubertal educational patterns in some primitive societies has been suggested by C. W. M. Hart. There, the degree of difference in regulation, personnel, atmosphere, and curriculum underscores the fact that adolescent children were typically taught in initiation schools "the whole value system of the culture, its myths, its religion, its philosophy, its justification of its own entity as a culture."[4] Citizenship, rather than technology, was the prime subject matter, and training involved a restructuring of the participant's identity from child to adult. Some primitive societies, like our modern educational systems, stretch out the period of training for initiation over many years; our difference is in considering such training to be vocational rather than cultural induction.

When the postpubertal schooling of minority-group youth in modern societies is studied, we ought to consider the variety and intensity of identity conflicts produced. Such children are confronted with conflicting patterns of cultural identity, and the ways they resolve this conflict, if they do, are worthy of central concern. The discontinuities in educational experiences and expectations that are associated with social definitions of maturation and those that are associated with minority-group status intersect in patterns which must be especially difficult for the adolescent.

4. *Differential patterns of participation.* We know that some minority groups, like blacks in the United States and the *burakumin* (outcastes) in Japan, are systematically underrepresented in the higher, noncompulsory levels of schooling. We should suspect, however, that even where compulsory schooling brings everybody into the school, minority-group children will interact with the school in systematically different ways. An ethnography of minority-group education should seek to describe these patterns, their effect on the life of the student, and their implications for socially defined standards of success in both the smaller community and the larger mainstream society.

In this context it is also important to delineate differential participation by minority-group teachers in the educational system, differential relations of minority-group parents with the school, and the effect of minority-group school administrators. Even studies of undisadvantaged ethnically distinguished groups in the system will be important. It is obvious, for instance, that the interaction of Jewish teachers with black and Puerto Rican children in Harlem classrooms involves the cultural patterns of at least three American minority groups compounded in interaction with the school roles of the participants and a mainstream cultural ideology represented by the school. As we dig into these complex settings, we can only untangle the patterns by using all the ethnographic tools we can bring to bear.

5. *Out-of-school schooling.* In studying modern education, it is important that we not limit ourselves to accredited schools. There are many kinds of schooling, or organized programs of teaching and learning. In the United States, antipoverty programs have often been based on schooling for new jobs. Black nationalists have organized programs for teaching a new black identity to children. Churches, YMCAs and YWCAs, Boy and Girl Scouts, and others are typical organizations of the mainstream society. Formal and informal schooling for vocational induction, as conducted by labor unions, employers, employment agencies, or professional associations, must be studied from the inside. Since some minority groups are disadvantaged by their systematic exclusion from such programs, entrance restrictions as well as the experiences of those accepted should be studied.

The range and variety of schooling open to minority-group youth should be an important part of every community-centered educational ethnography.

6. *Management of diversity.* Social diversity, rather than uniformity, characterizes modern society. The social management of diversity then becomes a relevant question in considering integration and separation.

Patterns of schooling are instrumental in managing diversity just as they are instrumental in transmitting some of the symbols of cultural unity. In studying minority-group education, we might well accept the diversity-management model of schools and systematically describe the ways in which choices and requirements for diversity are transmitted to children. Counseling, discipline, and the separation of curricula into vocational and academic curricula are traditional methods of managing diversity. Bilingual and

---

[4] In *Education and Culture*, George Spindler, ed. (New York: Holt, Rinehart & Winston, Inc., 1963), p. 419.

bicultural models of schooling are newer experiments. Community-centered ethnographic studies of innovative school models are badly needed, if we are to gain a better understanding of their relation to stability and change in the community; but although anthropologists have applauded the models, I know of no systematic ethnography in such a context.

Americans are noted for their faith in education (meaning public schooling) as the instrument for solving otherwise unsolvable social problems in their own and other societies. We all need to know the social limitations of the school. Anthropologists are well used to the study of ritual and myth, though slow to approach educational institutions on these terms. It is time they did. Comparative studies of education, discrimination, and poverty in a crosscultural context will help us understand the social nature of poverty and the complex processes of cultural transmission, continuity, and change. Applying our research to the problems posed by educational policy makers should lead to: (1) a better understanding of the social advantages of cultural differences; (2) a greater ability to make common schooling a multicultural enterprise for all participants, not just for minority-group members; (3) a more realistic view of what the school can accomplish as an instrument of social policy; and (4) an unromantic analysis of educational innovations to see if they are meeting the goals they proclaim.

7 Violence

Bernard J. Siegel
Violence

Robert A. LeVine
Gusii Sex Offenses: A Study in Social Control

June Nash
Death as a Way of Life: The Increasing Resort to Homicide in a Maya Indian Community

Alan R. Beals
Cleavage and Internal Conflict: An Example from India

Arthur E. Hippler
The Game of Black and White at Hunters Point

Asen Balikci
Conflict and Society

Bernard J. Siegel
Violence and Social Change

Granted that we know . . . how to redistribute land in units which can support the use of modern agricultural machinery; how to locate industrial plants in relation to population and resources; how to utilize the local food supplies to provide a nutritional diet; how to reorganize town planning and water use so as to avoid the principal epidemic and endemic diseases in the world. Granted that we know all this, what will be the cost in terms of the human spirit? How much destruction of old values, disintegration of personality, alienation of parents from children, of husbands from wives, of students from teachers, or neighbour from neighbour, of the spirit of man from the faith and style of his traditional culture must there be? Margaret Mead

Bernard J. Siegel
Violence

The history of civilization is among other things a history of violence. The founders of Sumeria are thought to have come as conquerors from the East. The history of ancient Greece is a history of war, not only between the Greeks and the rest of the civilized world but among the various political subdivisions of the Greeks themselves. Rome's history is one of conquest, enslavement, and the bloody putting down of revolts. The history of the Catholic and Muslim Churches is the history of persecutions suffered and inflicted. The period of Great Explorations that began in Europe at the end of the fifteenth century touched off progressively frequent confrontations between peoples of diverse interests, knowledge, beliefs, values, and social organization. There is seemingly no end of examples of hostilities between groups—colonial wars of conquest, revolutionary social movements—and seemingly no geographic boundary. The Zulu have warred with their neighbors in South Africa, and peasants have rebelled and been put down in medieval Europe and Japan, in Latin America, and in Southeast Asia. The infrequency with which citizens of primitive societies communicate with the world outside has, as its concomitant, great anxiety in encounters with strangers. Such individuals usually lack a common knowledge of rules for peaceful interaction and are therefore likely to think of aliens as nonhuman and potentially dangerous to their very existence. Avoid them if you can; kill them if you must.

Despite the little we know of the histories of most of these societies, it is occasionally possible to trace the forces that have led to the emergence of patterned hostilities among them. The Fore, one of many horticultural peoples who live in the highlands of New Guinea, are a case in point. Prior to their recent contact with Australians they lived in once isolated settlements that progressively cleared the forests of unregenerating trees, until they began to compete with similar groups for the once abundant land. First sporadic, then more regular, fighting broke out. Many factors operated in a linked fashion to lead almost inexorably to this outcome. Among them we can cite the following: the compact soils that rendered very difficult the reworking of plots cleared of virgin forest by slash-and-burn with stone adzes, the substitution of fast-growing taro for slow-growing yams, the increase of population, and the type of native forest cover. Here we see an intimate relation among food, tools, geography, ecological processes, and, ultimately, endemic warfare. The case is instructive.

Violence is also frequently reported *within* stable peasant societies. The recent histories of Sicily and Sardinia are studded with cases of assault and murder. A study of the settlements that developed around commercial agriculture in nineteenth-century Brazil has revealed many cases of violence, apparently stemming from endemic tensions or strains within groups with relatively integrated cultures. In these settlements, amicable relations among people who shared the same rules and values were frequently terminated by stabbings and killings. Violence occurred between neighbors as they argued about land and resources for its cultivation, between economically interdependent groups, among in-laws with conflicting economic interests, and in still other contexts.

Anthropologists, moreover, have amply documented the fact that disputes, including acts of violence, occur with sufficient regularity—even in very isolated, small, and little differentiated societies—to require deterrent and regulatory measures. The forms such measures take vary with the society. Where clans and lineages have an important economic and protective function, each guarding its own interests, they may retaliate for any injury, however accidental, inflicted upon their members. The support that kinsmen give to an offending relative, on the other hand, is tempered by the cost of feuds to the society as a whole. Kinsmen may kill a constant offender rather than suffer continuing diminution.

Perhaps even more disturbing than war or feuding, certainly far less well understood, are the high or increasing rates of violence within groups—rape, assault and battery, murder, suicide, and the like. These acts are commonly attributed to social disorganization, a proliferation of unweighted alternatives, weakened moral purpose, ambiguous social goals, conflicting values, and anomie—a state in which the norms and values of the group exert little force upon the individual or, conversely, exert certain pressures toward deviant behavior upon a number of individuals. They are all evidence of disaffection, disillusion, and social disorder in the face of varying degrees and kinds of stress and challenge.

Any of these conditions and the social processes that generate them may lead to innovation and peaceful change. They may also result in rebellion, in efforts to transform society by violent means, in nonviolent pursuit of values alternative to those of a dominant group, or simply in indecision and an incapacity to act in constructive ways.

People confronted with many new alternatives, of which none is clearly to be valued over the others, frequently make no consistent social commitment. When they continue to reside in settlements with a traditional culture they tend to behave in unconventional and destructive ways. Picuris, a Pueblo Indian settlement in northeastern New Mexico, appears to be a case in point. This once was a relatively large community of its kind—Coronado attributed to it a population of about three thousand in the sixteenth century. Encroachments and interference, first by Spanish and then by Anglos, then led to a drastic reduction in numbers, and today the population, now stable, is about one hundred. The satisfactions that citizens once achieved from a way of life that demanded much communal responsibility have been considerably diminished, however, by the existence of alternative occupations. Each generation of adults has found it increasingly difficult to weigh the advantages of traditional versus alien life styles, even though their early training makes the wish to leave the pueblo an anxiety-ridden one.

Indecision, heavy drinking coupled with frequent physical assault, and irresponsibility in local affairs are endemic. The experience of Picurenses, by no means unique, may yield insights into one mode of response to stress and disaffection in the larger society. A sudden increase of permissiveness, the making possible of all things, may preclude *any* consistently satisfying choice.

The selections from the anthropological literature that follow are intended to illustrate several types of violent within-group responses to environmental pressures and challenges. They stress the social and personal factors that enter into such behavior. We are further restricting our purview here to the comparative evidence of physical aggression which is more pervasive than periodic, which is characteristic of groups and varies historically in incidence, and which can be viewed largely in terms of the cultural and material forces that act upon the individual's social behavior. Not included are examples of the search for the genetic roots of aggression that might help account for man's readiness for combative and violent behavior. Whether or not the search proves to be successful, the social and cultural context of human actions will account for the rates, kinds, and redirecting of violence in society. No amount of inherited aggressive impulses can explain, for example, historical fluctuations in the frequency of conflict and violence in the same population. For several centuries before 1825, England was said to have had the bloodiest record of murder, rape, and criminal attack in all of Europe. Compare that record with its present image as one of the most orderly Western nations.

Moreover, violence within groups is not a single class of things. Civil or internecine warfare, successful bloody revolutions (a rare phenomenon), factional disputes and fighting, attacks upon person including the self, and apparently senseless, sudden, and unprovoked brutality stemming from psychological disorder are different kinds of things, and cannot be explained in terms of one theory.

Conflict and violence are not the only solution to social strains, to technological and external changes. Other outcomes in this ongoing adaptive process, also well documented in the anthropological literature, are disorganization, social movements (often peaceful), rapid change with minimal conflict, the development of more or less well-regulated schisms, and efforts to create more satisfactory social identities. The reader is instructed to look for a common set of interrelated factors that inform all of these processes. Violence, in short, must be viewed in relation to nonviolence, as change must be viewed in relation to continuity.

Robert A. LeVine

Gusii Sex Offenses: A Study in Social Control

While the specific data for this paper relate to the colonial period in Africa, in what is now Kenya, the factors involved in the definition of rape as a social issue are of general relevance under any circumstances. Here LeVine describes the sadistic impulses of males in relation to females—as symbolized in sex relations— who come from segments of society hostile to those of the male. Under traditional circumstances, the expression of aggression between members of hostile social categories is effectively controlled, but with the greater opportunity for physical contact between boys and girls, there is also a greater frequency of coercive sexual intercourse without diminution of hostility. LeVine's discussion provides insight into the occurrence of rape in our own society and elsewhere.

Among the Gusii of southwestern Kenya, the high frequency of rape is a major social problem and has been a source of concern to British administrators and Gusii chiefs for over twenty years. In this paper I shall inquire into the causes of that situation and attempt to formulate some general hypotheses concerning the control of sexual behavior in human societies. . . .

Evidence for the high frequency of rape among the Gusii is not entirely impressionistic. An extremely conservative estimate of the annual rate of rape (including indecent assault) indictments based on court records for 1955 and 1956 yields the figure of 47.2 per 100,000 population. During the same period the annual rate in urban areas of the United States was 13.85 per 100,000 (rural areas, 13.1). On the basis of the relatively few serious rape and defilement indictments entered at the Resident Magistrate's Court, it is possible to make a limited comparison of the Gusii with the major adjacent tribal groups, the South Nyanza Luo and the Kipsigis. During 1955–56 the Gusii (1948 population: 237,542) accounted for thirteen such indictments, the South Nyanza Luo (1948 population: 270,379) for six, and the Kipsigis (1948 population: 152,391) for four. Though the figures are small, they clearly indicate the Gusii lead over the other two groups in number of rape indictments relative to population size. Thus on a comparative basis it is possible to state that the contemporary rate of reported rape among the Gusii is extraordinarily high. It should be noted that the years chosen for comparison, 1955 and 1956, were locally recognized as being high years but by no means the worst on record. In 1937 a mass outbreak of rape created a law enforcement emergency and induced the District Commissioner to threaten a punitive expedition. In 1950 the number of rapists convicted was so great that the district prison facilities were not adequate to hold them. The great amount of rape, then, is a problem of unusual persistence in Gusiiland. . . .

Sex Antagonism in Gusii Society

The Gusii are a Bantu-speaking people practicing agriculture and animal husbandry in the Kenya highlands just east of Lake Victoria. They are strongly patrilineal and have a segmentary lineage system with a high degree of congruence between lineages and territorial groups. Before the onset of British administration in 1907, clans were the most significant political units and carried on blood feuds. Each of the seven Gusii tribes consisted of one or more large, dominant clans and a number of smaller clans and clan fragments. Clans of the same tribe united for war efforts against other tribes, but feuded among themselves at other times.

Each clan, although an independent military and territorial unit, was exogamous and patrilocal, so that wives had to be imported from clans against which feuds had been conducted. The Gusii recognize this in their proverb, "Those whom we marry are those whom we fight." Marriages did not mitigate the hostilities between clans on a permanent basis; in fact, women were used by their husbands' clans to aid in military operations against their natal clans. . . .

The clearest expression of the interclan hostility involved in marriage can be found in the *enyangi* ceremonial. Enyangi is the final ceremony in a Gusii marriage and can be performed either shortly after the start of cohabitation or any number of years later, even after the children have grown up. During the ceremony, iron rings (*ebitinge*) are attached to the wife's ankles and are never removed until the death of her husband or her wilful desertion of him. The practice of enyangi is rapidly disappearing in many areas of Gusiiland, partly because of its expense and partly because many girls become nominal Christians to escape the indignities described below. However, the attitudes and emotions expressed in the traditional rite persist in the contemporary situation. Mayer, who witnessed the ceremony on several occasions, has described its setting as follows:

Enyangi *opens with formal contests between the two groups of affines—a wrestling match for the men and a dancing competition for the women. Afterwards, a strictly obligatory seating arrangement separates bride's from groom's people, who must face each other across the space occupied by the sacred beer pots—the groom's party under the surveillance of the "watcher" whose special task is to avert quarrels.*[1]

On the following day the groom in his finery returns to the bride's family where he is stopped by a crowd of women who deprecate his physical appearance. Once he is in the house of the bride's mother and a sacrifice has been performed by the marriage priest, the women begin again, accusing the groom of impotence on the wedding night and claiming that his penis is too small to be effective. He attempts to refute their insults. The next day bride and groom go to the latter's home. The groom enters the door of his mother's house but when the bride attempts to follow she is met by a bellicose crowd of women who keep her at the door for a long time. They scream insults at her, mock her, pinch her, sometimes even smear dung on her lips. Throughout it all she must remain silent. Some brides have been kept at the door for so many hours that they have given up and returned home. Usually, however, the bride is allowed in and treated with kindness thereafter. . . .

The enyangi ceremony allows the expression of hostility which in-laws must never give vent to under ordinary circumstances and is indicative of the interclan tensions which are involved in every Gusii marriage. Inevitably, it is the bride who experiences this tension in its most acute form. She must move from her childhood home into the enemy camp; she must sever allegiance to her native group and develop loyalty to an opposing group. It is not surprising, then, that girls are ambivalent toward marriage. On the one hand, they yearn for it because women can only achieve security and prestige in Gusii society through legitimate motherhood and especially through bearing numerous sons. On the other hand, they have heard the folk tale in which the innocent bride discovers her parents-in-law to be cannibalistic ogres, and other similar tales; they all know of girls who have returned to their parents claiming that their in-laws were witches who tried to lure them into witchcraft. They are thus as frightened by the prospect of marriage as they are attracted to it.

The fears of the bride are institutionalized in her traditional resistance to being taken to the home of the groom. Among the adjacent Luo and other East African tribes, it is customary for kinsmen of the bride to fight with kinsmen of the groom and at-

"Gusii Sex Offenses: A Study in Social Control" by Robert A. LeVine. Reproduced by permission of the American Anthropological Association from *American Anthropologist* Vol. 61, No. 6 (1959).
[1] Philip Mayer, "Privileged Obstruction of Marriage Rites Among the Gusii," *Africa*, 20: 123.

tempt to prevent her departure. With the Gusii, however, it is the bride herself who resists, or who hides herself in a nearby house, and her father, having received the bridewealth cattle by this time, may even help persuade her to go if her reluctance appears to be sincere. Five young clansmen of the groom come to take the bride; two immediately find the girl and post themselves at her side to prevent her escape, while the others receive the final permission of her parents. When it has been granted, the bride holds onto the house posts and must be dragged outside. Finally she goes, crying and with her hands on her head. Her resistance is token and not really intended to break off the marriage, but it expresses the real fears of every Gusii bride.

When the reluctant bride arrives at the groom's house, the matter of first importance is the wedding night sexual performance. This is a trial for both parties, in that the impotence of the groom may cause the bride to break off the marriage, and the discovery of scars or deformities on the bride's body (including vaginal obstruction) may induce the groom to send her home and request a return of the bridewealth. The bride is determined to put her new husband's sexual competence to the most severe test possible. She may take magical measures which are believed to result in his failure in intercourse. These include chewing a piece of charcoal or a phallic pod commonly found in pastures, putting either of these or a knotted piece of grass under the marriage bed, and twisting the phallic flower of the banana tree. The groom is determined to be successful in the face of her expected resistance; he fortifies himself by being well fed, which is believed to favor potency, by eating bitter herbs, and nowadays by eating large quantities of coffee beans, valued as an aphrodisiac. His brothers and paternal male cousins give him encouragement and take a great interest in his prospects for success. Numerous young clansmen of the groom gather at the homestead in a festive mood; chickens are killed for them to eat and they entertain themselves by singing and dancing while waiting for the major events of the wedding night.

The bride usually refuses to get onto the bed: if she did not resist the groom's advances she would be thought sexually promiscuous. At this point some of the young men may forcibly disrobe her and put her on the bed. The groom examines the bride's mouth for pods or other magical devices designed to render him impotent. As he proceeds toward sexual intercourse she continues to resist and he must force her into position. Ordinarily she performs the practice known as *ogotega*, allowing him between her thighs but keeping the vaginal muscles so tense that penetration is impossible. If the groom is young (by traditional standards, under 25), the young men intervene, reprimand the bride, and hold her in position so that penetration can be achieved on the first night. An older groom, however, is considered strong enough to take care of himself, and the young men wait outside the door of the house, looking in occasionally to check on his progress. It is said that in such cases a "fierce" girl in the old days could prevent the groom from achieving full penetration as long as a week. Brides are said to take pride in the length of time they can hold off their mates. In 1957, a girl succeeded in resisting the initial attempts of her bridegroom. His brothers threatened and manhandled her until she confessed to having knotted her pubic hair across the vaginal orifice. They cut the knot with a razor blade and stayed to watch the first performance of marital coitus by the light of a kerosene pressure lamp.

Once penetration has been achieved, the young men sing in jubilation and retire from the house to allow the groom to complete the nuptial sexual relations. They are keenly interested in how many times he will be able to perform coitus on the first night, as this is a matter of prestige and invidious comparison. He will be asked about it by all male relatives of his generation, and the bride will also be questioned on this score when she returns to visit her own family. It is said that the groom's clansmen also question the bride, in order to check on the groom's account of his attainment. Six is considered a minimally respectable number of times and twelve is the maximum of which informants had heard. They claimed that it was traditional to achieve orgasm twelve times but that performances were lower in recent years.

The explicit object of such prodigious feats is to hurt the bride. When a bride is unable to walk on the day following the wedding night, the young men consider the groom "a real man" and he is able to boast of his exploits, particularly the fact that he made her cry. One informant quoted some relevant conversation from the *enyangi* ceremony which is performed at a later time. At the bride's home the insulting women say to the groom:

You are not strong, you can't do anything to our daughter. When you slept with her you didn't do it like a man. You have a small penis which can do nothing. You should grab our daughter and she should be hurt and scream—then you're a man.

He answers boastfully:

I am a man! If you were to see my penis you would run away. When I grabbed her she screamed. I am not a man to be joked with. Didn't she tell you? She cried—ask her!

The conception of coitus as an act in which a man overcomes the resistance of a woman and causes her pain is not limited to the wedding night; it continues to be important in marital relations. Wives in monogamous homesteads never initiate sexual intercourse with their husbands, and they customarily make a token objection before yielding to the husbands' advances. . . .

There is good reason to believe that the reluctant sexual pose of Gusii wives is not feigned in all cases. Young husbands claim to desire coitus at least twice a night, once early and once toward dawn. In a number of monogamous marriages, however, this rate is not achieved, primarily due to the stubborn resistance of wives. Every community contains some married women with reputations for refusing to have intercourse with their husbands for up to a week at a time. Such husbands are eventually moved to beat their wives and even send them back to their parents. I knew of one case of this kind in which the wife's distaste for coitus was the only major source of conflict between husband and wife. Among monogamous wives who do not have anti-sexual reputations, refusal to have intercourse with their husbands usually occurs when they have quarrelled over something else. Since family modesty prescribes the performance of intercourse in the dark after the children have fallen asleep, wives enforce their refusal by pinching a child awake if the husband is insistent. Such evidence suggests that for some Gusii wives the resistant and pained behavior in marital intercourse does not represent a conventional pose or an attempt to arouse their husbands but a sincere desire to avoid coitus.

On the basis of the Gusii case alone, it is difficult to arrive at a satisfactory solution to the problem of whether the sadomasochistic aspect of the Gusii nuptial and marital sexuality is inexorably con-nected with, and a reflection of, the antagonism of intermarrying clans. Many of the above facts point to such a connection, but it is noteworthy that there is at least one culturally patterned form of express-ing heterosexual antagonism within the clan. This is the practice of "arousing desire" (*ogosonia*) which Mayer has described in some detail. When Gusii boys undergoing initiation are recuperating from their circumcision operation, adolescent girls of the same clan come to the seclusion huts, dis-robe, dance around the novices in provocative attitudes, challenge them to have intercourse, and make disparaging remarks about the genitals of the boys. The latter are of course incapable of coitus, and the girls are well aware of this. According to Mayer, "Most Gusii think that the purpose of *ogosonia* is to cause pain. The girls have their triumph if a resulting erection causes the partly-healed wound to burst open, with acute pain to the novice." Here, then, is the use of sexuality to inflict pain occurring between girls and boys of the same exogamous clan. It could be argued that the adoles-cent girls have already developed the attitudes appropriate to the wedding night and apply them to the nearest males whom they know to be in a uniquely vulnerable sexual condition. In any event, the practice of ogosonia indicates that the antagonism of Gusii females toward male sexuality and their view of sexual intercourse in aggressive terms are components of a general pattern of be-havior not limited to the marital relationship.

Regardless of what other conclusions can be drawn from the foregoing descriptions of institu-tionalized forms of sex antagonism, one major point has been established: Legitimate hetero-sexual encounters among the Gusii are aggressive contests, involving force and pain-inflicting be-havior which under circumstances that are not legitimate could be termed "rape." In the following sections I shall discuss the conditions which lead to the performance of such behavior under illegiti-mate circumstances.

Sex Restrictions Within the Clan

. . . Before proceeding to premarital sexuality of an interclan nature, we must consider three other outlets for males possible within the local group, i.e., masturbation, homosexuality, and bestiality. Masturbation is punished by parents and, accord-ing to all reports, never practiced by Gusii boys except the ones in boarding schools who have learned it from members of other cultural groups. Gusii men consider homosexuality almost inconceivable and could not recall cases of it. If the practice occurs at all, it is extremely rare and certainly not socially condoned. Bestiality, on the other hand, is familiar to Gusii men. It is impossible to estimate its incidence, but everyone interviewed could recall cases of it from different localities, and one case of it appears in the records of the Resident Magistrate's Court. When a boy of early adolescence, up to sixteen, is discovered having intercourse with a goat or a cow, punishment is light, as it is assumed that the youth is attempting to find out if he is potent in a rather harmless way. The animal is considered defiled and is either killed or traded to an alien cultural group, the Luo or Kipsigis. If the animal belonged to someone other than the boy's father, it must be replaced. The son is warned against such activity by his father and sometimes by other elders as well. Nevertheless, it is probably performed clandestinely by many boys who are never caught at it. When a boy older than about sixteen is found having intercourse with an animal it is taken more seriously and treated in the same manner as incest within the nuclear family, or as mental disorder. The assumption in such cases is that the ancestor spirits forced the individual to commit the act by way of retaliation for some ritual misdeed such as omitting a funeral sacrifice. He is taken to a diviner (*omoragori*) who usually prescribes a sacrifice. Despite the formal assumption of supernatural responsibility, if the individual has had any history of sexual misconduct he will become the subject of hostile gossip. Furthermore, the necessity of replacing the defiled cow adds to the punishment, for cows are valuable and expensive. Thus a youth whose bestiality has been revealed on one occasion is unlikely to repeat it unless he has developed a strong preference for animals as sexual objects.

The evidence presented in this section points to the conclusion that the sexual activity of the Gusii youth within his own community and even in other communities of the same clan is drastically limited. Married women are barred to him by the rules of marital fidelity and the sanctions supporting them; unmarried girls are available when he is unsure of his virility, but as he grows older he turns from them in fear of the consequences of incest. Animals are also available to him in his earlier years but are pro-

hibited as continual sexual objects. All of these restrictions within the clan are enforced by the moral sanctions and legal penalties which the clan as an extended kin unit, and its component communities as groups of closely related kin, can use to effect conformity to group norms.

Changing Patterns of Premarital Sexual Behavior

. . . Nowadays most Gusii young people of both sexes have sexual intercourse before marriage. They may meet under a variety of circumstances, some of which have already been mentioned. When a girl visits her father's sister, it is expected that a half-brother or paternal cousin of her father's sister's son will attempt to seduce her. She may refuse, and in any case the act must be kept secret from members of the parental generation, but apparently such liaisons do occur. At marriage dances, too, youths establish contacts with girls whom they try to seduce. Both situations are only occasional, however; the boy must go to the marketplace for the more frequent social mixing which leads to sexual adventures.

Each marketplace has its day of the week when activity is greatest and trading goes on; this is when girls dress up and go in groups to sell some family produce and be seen by boys. The boys and young men also attend, singly and in groups, looking for attractive girls. In the 1930s the young people used to perform traditional dances in the marketplace on market days but this was banned after the 1937 outbreak of mass rape and has never been resumed. Youths approach strange girls, often through girls they already know or through male friends who know them. There is an initial period of small talk in which the girl may immediately reject the boy by claiming that she is married or by assuming a cold and aloof attitude. If she is friendly and laughs, however, the boy is encouraged and may begin some sexual joking. If the girl is favorably inclined to him she will respond in kind, usually using terms of obscene abuse. The boy may grab her arm and attempt to pull her away from the group but she will refuse, at least until he buys her a present in one of the market shops or treats her to some food. Even then he may not succeed in detaching her from the other girls, and he will let her go after arranging a rendezvous and possibly promising a phonograph party. She may agree to the assignation but not show up, in which case the youth will try to woo her later with more gifts and provocative exhortations. Eventually she meets him at a small party in his house or in a secluded part of the bush or forest. . . .

It is assumed that the girl will resist and have to be forced even if she desires intercourse. The Gusii girl avoids looking into the eyes of her seducer during coitus, and some go so far as to cover their faces with their dresses. Some Gusii girls cry out of shame and revulsion after intercourse and, unlike Moraa of the fantasy, may refuse to repeat the act on the same occasion. They often become panicky about discovery of the illicit act and the possibility of a premarital pregnancy.

With respect to a premarital sexual activity, three types of Gusii girls may be distinguished. The first type is stigmatized as a "slut" because she has achieved a reputation for promiscuity. This type of girl engages in intercourse with men and boys she knows very slightly, and after relatively little persuasion. With her, resistance in coitus is probably conscious role-playing designed to please her lover. Some girls of this type occasionally take on a number of young men in succession. Although she is in demand as a sexual partner, a girl with this sort of reputation is considered highly undesirable as a wife and is ordinarily not married with bridewealth unless her marriage takes place at an early age before her reputation has spread. She is likely to elope from the home of her father or legitimate husband and live as the concubine of one man after another.

The second, and probably modal, type is that of the girl with real ambivalence about engaging in premarital intercourse. She desires it but is careful not to be taken advantage of. Thus she will not meet privately with a boy until after he has bestowed numerous gifts upon her from the market; these may be head scarves, bananas, and candy. She rejects the advances of some boys whom she finds unattractive. Her accessibility for sexual liaisons also depends on her moods and the skill of her would-be seducer. Sometimes she is unapproachable; on other occasions, such as a marriage dance, her resistance may be easily broken down, especially by a dashing young man who serenades her on the guitar. She engages in provocative be-

havior, mostly of a hostile sort such as sexual joking, but is determined not to be publicly compromised and not to give away her sexual favors until she has received tangible rewards and flattering attention from her prospective lover. With her, resistance in coitus is partly conscious role-playing and partly an expression of real fears and hostility. This type of girl, if her sexual activity is not discovered and does not result in premarital pregnancy, is considered desirable as a wife, for the marriage intermediary (*esigani*) will have no scandal to report to the groom. The prospective husband and his family do not want the intermediary to pry so deeply into the girl's affairs that he reports her casual liaisons; if she has been discreet enough not to acquire a reputation as a "slut," then he ordinarily informs them that she is chaste. There is no inspection of the hymen, for the husband does not desire knowledge of his wife's premarital experience so long as she is considered a proper girl.

The third type of Gusii girl is the one in whom sex anxiety and hostility toward men outweigh heterosexual desires. Such a girl may acquire a reputation for rejecting sexual advances and eventually be avoided by boys in the marketplace, though her desirability as a wife is in no way diminished. Ordinarily, a girl of this type continues going to the market with the other girls and meets numerous boys who know neither her nor her reputation. Despite her fear of sexuality she enjoys the gifts, the flattery, the attention from the boys, and thus tends to exploit her suitors without giving them the sexual satisfaction they desire in exchange. Though she may even refuse sexual overtures at wedding dances and scold the young men who make them, it appears that most girls of this type do occasionally have intercourse before marriage. When they do, their resistance and crying is probably commensurate with their real feelings, and they are more likely to cover their faces during coitus and be overcome with remorse afterwards. It seems likely, though I have no definite evidence on this point, that such girls become the difficult wives who restrict marital sexual activity and who quarrel over it with their husbands.

Although Gusii girls vary in their reactions to the premarital situation, there are common features which characterize a majority of them. They enjoy the initial phase of the relationship with a young man in which they are given gifts and fervently wooed, and many of them attempt to prolong this phase in order to obtain more goods and attention, regardless of whether or not they intend to comply with the wishes of the would-be seducer. Many of the girls seem to enjoy inflicting frustration on a male or at least putting him in a position of subordination, and this is also indicated by their provocative and hostile sexual abuse of the young men they meet in the marketplace. Premarital sexual affairs are extremely brittle, being terminated after a boy and girl have had intercourse once or twice, so the girls have opportunities to go through the early stages of seduction over and over again. Another behavior pattern common to all young Gusii females, except the most extreme girls of type one, is sexual inhibition and some degree of distaste for the act of coitus. While this is variable from one individual to another, Gusii girls as a group exhibit a greater degree of inhibition and anxiety about sexual intercourse than do girls of surrounding tribes. . . .

To recapitulate: the spatial and military barriers to interclan premarital sexual activity in Gusiiland have disappeared as the result of British pacification of the area and rapid population growth. The barriers that now exist reside not so much in the structure of the situation as in the behavior of Gusii females, whose sexual inhibitions and antagonism to males (learned in childhood and enforced in adolescence) present young men with a different set of obstacles to premarital sexual outlet. It is possible to seduce girls, but seduction requires social and musical skills as well as money. Even the most adept seducers are rarely able to obtain sexual partners more than twice during a week, and youths who are less attractive, skillful, and wealthy may go for several weeks at a time without heterosexual intercourse. When premarital intercourse occurs, it has many behavioral similarities to rape, but so long as the eventual acquiescence of the female is won, the act will not be considered rape by Gusii cultural standards. In the following section the several conditions are described which can result in the female refusing to acquiesce.

Types of Sex Offenses

The typical Gusii rape, so far as I can determine from anecdotal evidence (court records being deficient in this respect), is committed by an unmarried young man on an unmarried female of a different clan. There are some cases in which married men and married women are involved in rape, and also those in which both rapist and victim have the same clan affiliation, but these appear to be relatively infrequent. Futhermore, rapes of married women or of girls in the same clan as the rapist are more likely to be settled locally without resort to the courts, so that they probably form a very small proportion of the high rate of rape indictments which is in question here. Thus I shall concentrate on explaining interclan rape involving unmarried persons. On the basis of the conscious intent of the rapist, three types of Gusii rape may be distinguished: rape resulting from seduction, premeditated sexual assault, and abduction.

1. *Rape resulting from seduction.* Since the typical Gusii seduction bears a strong behavioral similarity to rape, it is only necessary to understand the conditions under which Gusii females who are being seduced decide to bring the act to the attention of the public and eventually to the authorities. First of all, the standard reluctant pose of the Gusii girl provides many opportunities for a young man to misunderstand her motives. Although she may sincerely want to reject his advances because she finds him unattractive or because of her own current fears, the young man may confidently assume she is pretending and proceed to use physical force to achieve his aim. If her revulsion or fear is great enough she may cry for help and initiate a rape case. Such misunderstandings can be due to the eagerness of the youth and his consequent inability to perceive her subtle cues of genuine rejection, or to the girl's failure to make the signs of refusal in unequivocal fashion.

Second, fear of discovery is ubiquitous in Gusii seduction. Opportunities for privacy exist, but a couple may be seen going off together. If they are engaging in intercourse out of doors, someone may pass nearby and either actually observe them or arouse their fears of being seen. When this happens, a girl who was originally willing may decide to save her reputation by crying out (or reporting it later), pretending that she was being raped. Although this may be considered pseudo-rape, such cases appear to be common in societies in which rape is considered a crime and probably inflate the rates of rape indictments in all of them. . . .

Finally, as mentioned above, Gusii girls who

have no desire for sexual relations deliberately encourage young men in the preliminaries of courtship because they enjoy the gifts and attention they receive. Some of them act provocative, thinking they will be able to obtain desired articles and then escape the sexual advances of the young man. Having lavished expense and effort on the seduction of an apparently friendly girl, the youth is not willing to withdraw from the relationship without attempting to obtain sexual favors. If the girl is of the third type described above, rape may easily result. . . .

Thus, the similarity of Gusii seduction to rape, the communication difficulties arising out of this similarity, the girls' anxiety about their reputations and consequent fear of discovery, and the provocative behavior by girls whose motivations are not primarily sexual—all of these contribute to turning the would-be seducer into a rapist.

2. *Premeditated sexual assault.* In some cases Gusii youths decide to obtain sexual gratification from girls by force with no semblance of a friendly approach. One or more boys may be involved in an attack on a single girl. Usually the object is to frighten her first so that she will not cry or resist; for this reason young (11 to 13 years old) and easily frightened girls are more likely to be chosen as victims. The boys disguise themselves by draping cloaks or skins over their heads, hide at a place out of hearing distance of the nearest homesteads, and dart out from behind bushes when the girl comes walking by collecting firewood or carrying a pot of water. Sometimes they beat her badly and tear her clothing. Girls are brought into court with lacerations and bites inflicted by sexual attackers. They may drag her off to the hut of one of them, and there force her into coitus. They intend to let her go eventually, but they may hold her for a couple of days. By this time her father has gone to the chief for the services of Tribal Policemen in finding the attackers. If the policemen track them down in time, the case is more likely to be brought to the Resident Magistrate's Court, since rupture of the hymen and other signs of attack are common in this type of rape.

3. *Abduction.* When a Gusii man lacks the economic means for a legitimate bridewealth marriage and does not have the personal attractiveness or seductive skill needed to persuade a girl to elope with him, he may resort to desperate measures. Determined to obtain a mate, he enlists the aid of some clansmen in an attempt to abduct a girl from a different clan. Sometimes the girl is one he knows fairly well but who has refused to live in concubinage with him. The young men act for him as they would in a legitimate marriage, accosting the girl and taking her away by force. Under these conditions, however, they take pains not to be seen by the girl's parents or anyone else of her community. Another difference is that the girl's resistance is sincere, since she desires a legitimate marriage or concubinage with a man she finds unusually attractive. The young men frequently are rough on her, beating her and tearing her clothes. When she arrives at the home of her would-be lover, he exhorts her in peaceful terms to remain with him until bridewealth can be raised to legitimize their union. Her refusal is ignored in the hope that she will eventually acquiesce, and the wedding night sexual contest is performed, with the clansmen helping overcome her resistance. If she does not escape and report the offense to her father, the latter will eventually come with Tribal Policemen and arrest the abductor.

The type of abduction described is not to be confused with elopement in which the girl is willing to go despite her father's ire at being deprived of bridewealth. Such cases are entered in the Tribunal Courts under a customary law offense, "Removing a girl without the consent of her parents." In the abductive rape which is of interest here, the girl is not a willing accomplice and must be forced into sexual relations not only on the first night but subsequently as well. This type of case results in an indecent assault indictment.

Of the three types of rape described above, two are unlawful versions of patterns which are normally law-abiding and socially acceptable by Gusii standards. The first type develops out of seduction, which has gained acceptance as a culture pattern when kept within the bounds of discretion; the third type is an imitation of traditional wedding procedures, but lacking the legitimizing bridewealth and the consent of the bride and her parents. In both cases there is a close parallel between the criminal act and the law-abiding culture pattern to which it is related. The question arises, why does an individual commit the criminal version of the act rather than its law-abiding counterpart? I have attempted to show how various limitations on the premarital sexual behavior of Gusii males tend to make them sexually frustrated and hence inclined to a less discriminate use of the aggressive aspects of accepted sexual patterns. The occurrence of the abductive type of rape, however, poses an important question: if difficulty of premarital access to females is what frustrates Gusii males, what prevents them from marrying at an earlier age and thus solving their problem in a law-abiding way? . . .

The Bridewealth Factor in Sex Offenses

A legitimate Gusii marriage requires the transfer of cattle (and goats) from the father of the groom to the father of the bride. The number of animals transferred is a matter of individual agreement between the fathers but it is influenced by the prevailing bridewealth rate in Gusiiland. The rate has fluctuated throughout the years from as many as twenty cows to as little as one cow. Reduction in the rate resulted from a severe cattle epidemic, in one case, and from actions taken by traditional and British authorities, in other cases. Despite attempts by authorities to control it, the Gusii bridewealth rate has a tendency to rise which can only be understood in terms of the uses to which bridewealth is put.

The father of the bride receives in one lot most of the bridewealth animals before he allows his daughter to live with her prospective mate; installment payments are not ordinarily permitted. Bridewealth given in marriage for a girl is most often used to procure a wife for her uterine brother (or in some instances for her half-brother or father), and her father is concerned lest the number of animals he accepts for her marriage will prove insufficient to obtain a wife for her brother at a later time. Fearing that the bridewealth rate will rise between the two marriages, the father of the bride demands more cattle than the current rate and thereby helps to bring about a rise. The resulting inflationary spiral has continued in the face of temporarily effective decreases brought about by authoritative action in 1903, 1920, 1937, and 1948, and despite an apparent decrease in the total number of cattle available for marriage payments. Since the British administration prohibited inter-tribal cattle raiding in the first decade of the century, the Gusii have been deprived of one traditional source of livestock for use in bridewealth. In recent years, overcrowding of the land and un-availability of pasturage have tended to effect a reduction in Gusii herds. Yet fathers tenaciously insist on cattle (rather than cash or other currently valued commodities) for their daughters in bridewealth, and in fact demand larger numbers of them now than fathers did 40 years ago.

One consequence of the inflation in bridewealth rates and the reduced availability of cattle is that young men who come from cattle-poor families and who do not have uterine sisters old enough to be married, must postpone their own marriages. They can wait until their sisters grow up (if they have sisters), secure a loan from close patrilineal kinsmen, or attempt to raise money to buy cattle through wage labor. (The minimal bridewealth rate in 1957 was equivalent to the total wages a Gusii plantation worker would receive in 40 months.) Meanwhile, fathers attempt to marry off their daughters as secondary wives to wealthy old men. Among the poorer young men, the enforced postponement of marriage creates a group who reach their late twenties or early thirties before they can afford marriage. A majority of Gusii males marry between 18 and 25, but there are numerous men who are unmarried at later ages and even some who never have legitimate wives. Some of these unfortunates persuade girls to elope without the payment of bridewealth, and such concubinage has been increasing despite efforts by girls' fathers and the courts. Inevitably, however, there are men who lack the economic means for a legitimate marriage as well as the attractiveness and seductive arts needed to convince a girl to elope. In desperation a man of this type may resort to abductive rape as described in the preceding section.

The relationship between excessive bridewealth demands and rape is not a conjectural one. In 1936–37, the bridewealth rates were up to 8 to 12 head of cattle, 1 to 3 bulls, and 8 to 12 goats. This was the highest they had been since before the great cattle plague of the 1890s. Many young men could find no legitimate way of getting married, and they resorted to cattle theft and all types of rape. On one market day in Kisii township, a large group of young men gathered and decided to procure mates for themselves by abduction. They grabbed girls in the marketplace and carried them off. Many of the girls returned home after being raped. The incident precipitated action by the administration. . . .

Under the orders of the District Commissioner, the Gusii elders present at the meeting swore an oath to reduce the amount of bridewealth demanded to 6 cows, 1 bull, and 10 goats. The reduction was effective until 1942, when the rate resumed its upward trend. By 1950 high bridewealth rates resulted in a serious outbreak of rape again, though without the dramatic or organized qualities of the earlier one. Further efforts at control of bridewealth have been made by the African District Council, but with ephemeral success. In 1956, one of the years covered in the figures on rate of rape indictments presented earlier, bridewealth rates averaged 10 head of cattle in the area studied, but wealthy, older men were giving considerably more. All in all, it is likely that the high rate of rape indictments in Gusiiland is in part a function of the economic barrier to the marriage of young men created by excessive bridewealth demands.

Discussion

The foregoing analysis of the etiology of rape in Gusiiland may be summarized as follows: Normal forms of sexual intercourse among the Gusii involve male force and female resistance with an emphasis on the pain inflicted by the male on the female. This general heterosexual aggression appears to be related to the hostility of exogamous clans, since marriage is the prototype of a heterosexual relationship in Gusii culture. Regardless of its origin, the aggressive pattern of sexuality is not entirely pretense but shows clear signs of involving sadistic and masochistic impulses on the part of some Gusii individuals. Rape committed by Gusii men can be seen as an extension of this legitimate pattern to illegitimate contexts under the pressure of sexual frustration. The sexual frustration of Gusii young men is due to effectively enforced restrictions on intraclan sexual activity,

the sexual inhibitions and provocative behavior of Gusii girls, and high bridewealth rates which force postponement of marriage. Prior to British administration of Gusiiland, rape was not such a problem because interclan controls were as effective as intraclan controls. Pacification of the district, however, has eliminated the threat of force and the spatial distances between clan settlements, increasing opportunities for interclan heterosexual contact in the face of greatly diminished penalties for interclan rape. Had Gusii girls proved uninhibited, promiscuity rather than rape would have been the consequence of pacification. However, Gusii values favor restriction of premarital sexuality and the burden of enforcing this restriction now falls upon the girls themselves rather than upon their clansmen. Thus the contemporary system of sanctions operating in Gusii society is not adequate to control the effects of the factors motivating men to commit rape.

If the above analysis is valid, there are four factors in the Gusii situation which should be found in any society with a high frequency of rape: (1) severe formal restrictions on the nonmarital sexual relations of females; (2) moderately strong sexual inhibitions on the part of females; (3) economic or other barriers to marriage which prolong the bachelorhood of some males into their late twenties; (4) the absence of physical segregation of the sexes. This last condition distinguishes high rape societies from societies in which women are secluded and guarded, where rape is not feasible and homosexuality may be practiced instead. These four factors should be regarded as necessary but not sufficient conditions for a high frequency of rape, as they may also be found in societies having prostitution or other functional alternatives.

June Nash

Death as a Way of Life: The Increasing Resort to Homicide in a Maya Indian Community

Here, June Nash provides evidence of the relationship between a dramatic increase in violence (in this case, homicide) and the weakening or elimination of the values that underlie the effective operation of "law and order" in an Indian peasant community of Mexico. She suggests that when we discuss an increase in the incidence of violence we must also ask who kills whom and why. In this society we see some causal relations between economic competitiveness, reactions to new administrative machinery, the erosion of the social controls that have in the past reduced open conflict, and an increase in homicide.

The social impact of homicide has caused some analysts to treat it and its supposed inverted complement, suicide, as one kind of behavior with a single meaning, ignoring Durkheim's caveat that behavioral rubrics categorize diverse phenomena. Here I shall analyze the variety of strategies involved in killing in a Mexican community, which I shall call Teklum (the Tzeltal term for village), and endeavor to show how rules of behavior are expressed in killing and in attempts to avoid being killed. Further, I shall endeavor to point out what these indicate about structural and organizational changes both within the community and in its relations with the wider society. Since suicide is absent, except for a single case of a madman, I have restricted my enquiry to homicide.

Teklum is a predominantly Indian township of Mexico. The population of the town center—about 1,900—includes only one Ladino, or non-Indian, family, that of the school-teacher. The sense of community is limited to people living in the center and in the four nearby hamlets (*barrios*).

The town center is divided physically and socially into two endogamous sections, called "upper" and "lower." The outlying hamlets are linked to the nearest section by social and economic ties. The civil and religious posts of the town are, in local theory, apportioned evenly between the sections.

This was in fact true until the 1950s; for each of the ranked posts had a paired complement, so that both sides of the dual division were represented, and the single posts of president and *síndico* (the president's administrative assistant) were alternated for each three-year term between the upper and lower sections.

But with the recent increase in dealings between the national and regional administrative centers and the local communities, recruitment into office as president and síndico has come to depend upon the candidates' possessing a knowledge of Spanish, literacy, and familiarity with the ways of Ladino society. Because of the relative scarcity of such skills, selection of these two officials has tended to ignore the former residence requirements relating to the dual division. Along with this change in the criteria for selecting these officials has come a decrease in the power and the authority exercised by the *principales*—elders from each side of the dual division who rose to their position by passing through all of the lower offices in the hierarchy—and a corresponding increase in the importance of the presidency.

This dual division also affected the structure of the curing profession. The curers are men who can overcome sickness caused by witchcraft because of their possession of an animal spirit (*swayohel*) and their knowledge of ritual. In each of the two sections of the town was a leading curer (*statal ʔuʔul*) who, by virtue of his age, experience, and recognized authority, was able to control entry into the profession. Their function was to prevent as well as cure, for the leading curers were also charged with guarding their section against the entry of witchcraft. In the last two decades, leadership by recognized elder curers from each side of the dual

"Death as a Way of Life: The Increasing Resort to Homicide in a Maya Indian Community" by June Nash. Reproduced by permission of the American Anthropological Association from *American Anthropologist*, Vol. 69, No. 5 (1967).

division has been lost, and along with it control over limiting the practicing of curing.

It is in the context of these structural divisions that social change and its behavioral indices must be analyzed.

Homicide—an act viewed as a delict in national Mexican law—has in the past two decades become an accepted strategy in social interaction. It is part of the expectations of the society upon which members predicate their own code of behavior and in terms of which they react to others. Gossip not only fails to suppress homicide, but serves to create a consensual base for condoning it. The corpse is referred to as "the one who had the guilt," ?a stukel smul, and even when knowledge of the particular act is lacking, certain assumptions are made: the killer was someone in the community; the victim provoked the killer. In listing crimes, informants sometimes failed to mention killing, or they included it after witchcraft, theft, or adultery. Homicide is considered a *reaction* to crime, not a crime in itself.

The rate is phenomenally high—up to 251.2 per 100,000. . . .

Figures prior to 1950 are not apt to be accurate, for only since that time have there been adequate reporting and checking of township records. In the following tabulation, the marked increase in the annual number of homicides since 1960 represents a real increase.

1950	1	1958	1
1951	0	1959	1
1952	1	1960	4
1953	1	1961	7
1954	1	1962	6
1955	0	1963	7
1956	1	1964	4
1957	4	1965	9

In order to assess the meaning of its remarkable increase during the 1960s, I have proceeded along two lines of enquiry. First, I have analyzed the circumstances surrounding the deaths in as many cases as my informants could remember. Variations in the components of homicidal acts— the setting, agents, purpose, and outcome—suggested the different assumptions underlying each case. Secondly, I have correlated the different kinds of homicide with structural and organizational changes in the community. The analysis of cases in Section I summarizes the patterned components of behavior. The social environment providing the cues to the actors is explored in Section II.

I. The Patterned Components of 37 Homicide Cases

. . . One-half the total number of killings occurred to those between the ages of 34 to 50. However, as the six victims aged 60 and over indicate, survival to a late age does not ensure that one will die a nonviolent death. The age of the victim may be correlated with motive, insofar as some events leading to conflict occur only at certain times in the life cycle. Thus, betrothal conflicts involved only young men, while victims accused of witchcraft were older: 27 was the age of the youngest, and 16 out of the 18 men killed as witches were over 34. Cattle theft, on the other hand, occurred thoughout the age range.

Eight of the victims—more than one-fifth of them—were curers, a much higher proportion than their share in the total population, for there are only about a dozen now living in the town center of 1,900.

There is a personality type recognized by the community as distinctive of those who "get themselves killed." When they see a man who is abusive while drunk, who brags of his power and of that of his animal spirit, they will remark: "That man is going to wake up dead." When such a man is killed, no one complains, even among his immediate relatives. . . . When I asked why women do not get killed, the response was, "They don't look for trouble."

Where the killing takes place and its timing in the diurnal cycle are directly linked. All of the homicides in the streets of the town were committed at night, while those in the roads out of town near the milpa occurred in the late afternoon or evening. In providing privacy and security from discovery, the darkness of night is functionally equivalent to distance from the town center during the daytime. When I suggested that the killings might be reduced if the town would connect the lights that had been installed in the streets, the response was that when they had been in use, killings had increased. The lights helped the killer find his victim, perhaps lying out in the road after a drinking session. He would shoot out the light and then kill his victim.

The only killings in which considerations of space or time were ignored were those in the cantina during a drunken brawl, for in contrast to the usual killing their onset was unpremeditated.

The timing of homicide is related also to the annual cycle: 14 homicides occurred during the fiestas in the town or in a neighboring town. The drunkenness of the fiestas provides an appropriate occasion for killing an enemy, although a drunken brawl is in itself rarely a sufficient motive (two cases). Other opportune times are after a curing ceremony (six cases) and after the gathering of cures during an epidemic (two cases), when people have drunk a great deal and their motive is fresh in their mind.

The settings in which homicides occur indicate that a killer is expressing not his own bravery but rather his fears. Wounds are frequently inflicted from the rear, and often the victim is outnumbered and set upon by a group. The victim is sometimes invited to drink with his killer(s), and in this session he is disarmed psychologically and physically. Alcohol reduces the chance of his effective reaction, and this is important when a knife or machete is used. Shotgun killings are done at a distance and do not require this tactic, although it may still be employed. For drinking serves to reduce the killer's own fears. Drink "heats the blood" and makes unusual behavior possible. One killer, in recounting his act, was not trying to prove bravery, but rather his own good judgment and cool-headedness. The killer fired at the victim while he was sleeping, his back turned to the door, and killed him. The shot also entered the arm of the sleeping man's wife. She saw the killer as he left the scene, but testified in court that she had seen no one. She was, in effect, accepting his verdict that her husband was a witch. This homicide was not regarded by the killer or by anyone else as a heroic act, nor was the killer in recounting it attempting to emphasize anything other than the necessity of the act.

Instrumentality: Weapons and Wounds

gun	14
machete	6
gun and machete	4
knife	3
knife and gun	1
knife and machete	1
knife and stone	1
hatchet	1
nail	1
sandals	1
??	4

The variety of weapons reduces the question of any technological determinism to a minimum. The actual weapon used seems to be a matter of convenience. When more than one is used, it is usually evidence that the assailant had helpers. The nail is unusual. It was hammered into the jaws of a man who had entered the curing profession at an age considered too young. The attack on the jaws of the victim seems related to the power of speech and to the location of the soul in the tongue, wherein lies the particular power of the curer. This possibily suggested the mode of attack.

The instruments used to kill are carried by the farmers of this area most of the time. The men go to their milpa with a machete strapped to their side, a shotgun slung over their shoulder, and sometimes even a knife stuck in their waistband. They frequently interrupt work to hunt birds, rabbits, and deer. The shotgun does not excite suspicion or comment when it is seen. The men of Teklum are technologically prepared to kill in the course of an ordinary day's work.

The number of wounds and the thoroughness with which the job is done suggest not so much the fury of the assailants as the fear motivating their act. In a witch-killing, it appears to be thought necessary to hack up the victim completely so that his power is effectively ended: one witch was cut into 32 pieces; another had 166 wounds.

The death acts drawn up in the local courthouse have been increasingly specific in their statements as to the wounds inflicted ever since the government's intervention in the case of an accidental death in 1950. The local authorities were threatened with a fine of 600 pesos if the details were not properly recorded. The careful measurement of the body in relation to the road and to neighboring milpas and the measurement of the size and depth of the wounds provide the screen of complicity that wards off further investigation by federal authorities and preserves local independence. There is never any questioning of suspects or attempt to solve the crime by officials....

Who Kills and Why

The only universal factor among the killers is sex— only men kill. Women do not kill nor are they killed in Teklum. This does not mean that they are not subject to as many tensions or abuses as men, or that these have no channels for expression. Women work through men by agitating them to homicide. Sometimes revenge is delayed, for the agents chosen by women may be children who must reach maturity before accomplishing the deed. . . .

Neighbors are a significant group in witchcraft killing. . . . They are the informal judges of suspected witches, and it is frequently they who kill a man considered to be a witch. When the curers accuse a man of causing epidemics, his neighbors are usually the executors. For this reason, most people try to neutralize the hostility of their neighbors by establishing *compadrazgo*, or godparental, relations with them.

Ten of the 37 homicides here reported were committed by immediate consanguineal or affinal relatives of the victim. The high frequency of killings involving brothers or brothers-in-law (8 cases) suggests a locus of high tension in these relationships. Male siblings comprise the closest cooperating group. Cooperation between brothers is obligatory when wheat is to be threshed, a house built, or a roof rethatched. If a brother or brother-in-law is unavoidably absent, he must pay a substitute. Brothers, or sons and fathers, are the only relationship pairs who work the milpa in common and share the harvest. Bilateral inheritance, with equal division of land and house to both male and female offspring, means that brothers-in-law are potentially equivalent in the competition for goods as well as in their obligation to cooperate. A man kills his sister's husband if the husband is abusive to the woman or to members of the family (two cases). The brother figures not only as a lethal opponent, but also as the man who avenges one's own death. . . . When someone has been killed for witchcraft, his brothers are expected to accept the verdict or to avenge the killing. . . .

Motivations include both the instrumental reason and the rationalization for the act. The complexity of motivation is correlated with the multiplicity of social ties existing between any two people. For example, when a man shoots his father for failure to provide him with his bride price, but feels justified and expects social approval because his mother on her deathbed accused the father of having provoked her illness by witchcraft, . . . it is impossible to assign a single primary cause. . . .

In one-half of all the cases reported, the motive attributed for homicide is suspicion of witchcraft. . . . Almost all sickness in the community is believed to be caused by witchcraft (the term for witch and witchcraft, *ʔak'čamel*, means "giver of sickness"). The family of a sick person consults the local curers, who pulse the patient. The witch "has left his signature in the blood" of the patient, and by pulsing him the curer can "hear and feel" who the witch is. His procedure is to ask the patient to tell what troubles he has had with his neighbors and relatives, and as the patient recites the names of the people with whom he has had conflict, the pulse jumps. As in the use of the lie detector, this indicates where there is high affect; in Teklum it is interpreted as positive indicator of the guilty person, the witch. If the curer gets drunk enough, he may reveal the name of the witch, but he usually prefers not to—I know of at least three cases, one of which is reported here, in which the man who announced the name of the witch was killed by the person he accused. The family may then check the consultation with curers in neighboring towns or even in the departmental capital. Since these distant curers are not inhibited by fear of the witch, they name the guilty one. The family, or the patient, may broadcast their suspicions, even announcing the consultation over the loudspeakers in the local liquor shops. If the patient dies, a member of the family may act on these suspicions and kill the witch. If he should kill the witch while the patient is still alive, it is believed that the patient will die.

Killing men for cattle theft (six cases) is a relatively recent occurrence. It has put homicide on the market: the associations of cattle-owners have hired killers in three of the six cases. In addition to the killer's fee, they pay the fine to release him from prison. Fines for homicide have increased in the past five years—from 1,000 to 3,000 pesos—but not sufficiently to price the murder of cattle thieves out of the market. A good bull is worth 1,500 pesos, and the threat of further loss by theft seems to justify the expenditure of fees and fines. When the cattle-owners lose some of their herd, they go to spiritualists or to San Miguel, the talking saint of Ixtapa, to find out who did the stealing. Since such evidence does not hold up in court, legal settlement is not attempted. Legal action, moreover, would create an enemy who might seek revenge. A Ladino secretary of the town center who had lost a bull accused a man of stealing his cattle and demanded 500 pesos in compensation. By receiving the money he jeopardized his safety, and eventually he had to leave town.

The Resolution of the Case

It is nearly impossible to find witnesses to homicide. Of these 37 cases, 28 resulted in no action being taken by the authorities, and in five cases where the killers went to jail, they were released with the payment of minimal fines. In the calculations of the townspeople, it is hardly worth risking one's neck to get such a minimal revenge.

However, this does not mean that homicide goes unnoticed in the community. After a killing the widow sings of the life of the dead man. If she is in agreement with the verdict arrived at by the killer and others, she will deny knowledge of what he has done, or even suggest that she too was aware of what harm he has caused (one widow implied that her husband, killed as a witch, was responsible for the death of four of her six children). If she objects to the verdict, she sings of what a good man he was and how blameless. She will then air her own suspicions in the following weeks as to who killed her husband.

Following the funeral, when the women have left the cemetery, the men sit at the grave. As they measure out a liter of liquor and pass it around, they advance hypotheses as to who did it. The consultations with curers prior to the death of the supposed victims of a witch will be introduced as evidence. (Some degree of consensus may have been built up beforehand, in witch-killings, by the public broadcast of accusations noted above.) The focus of the discussion is not so much on who killed the dead man, but whether he was indeed a witch. This kind of mock trial occurs after every funeral, since it must be decided who caused the sickness. Emotions run very high as the liquor is passed around, and accusations are made, sometimes against those present. It was after a funeral that one man killed his son for accusing him of having caused the death of the son's child, who was being buried.

In the weeks following a homicide, it is discussed at all the drinking sessions in the homes or in the town hall. Eventually an authoritative version begins to emerge. Those who have defended the victim then keep silent, and the affair "rests in peace." Avenging the death of a man judged to have been a witch, so far as I know, has never been done. . . .

Rules for Surviving

The patterning of the selection of victims and the circumstances of homicide provide the basis for formulating a set of rules that can ensure survival. The long-range rules of survival, in the words of an elder at the occasion of the death of his godchild, are:

lekon kak'o ta kwenta me?tat
I pay respect to my elders.

hun ku kihtz'in kalničan
I greet my younger brothers and my children (classificatory extension of kinship terms).

spisil kak' ta kwenta
To all I give respect.

ha? hič lekotik. Ma taltik milel ma taltik čamel
Thus I fare well. I have not been killed, nor have I been sick.

A good man is of one heart, and he shows it by his humility or "very soft heart." He can drink with friends on either side of the dual division of the town, and he is called upon in many household fiestas to greet the guests of the house-owner.

But the man who is "very strong of heart," who "fails to take people into account," who "abuses people," has means of survival despite the many threats to his life. He surrounds himself with a circle of *compadres*, or godparents; he especially picks out curers, both to mitigate the use of their power against him, and for them to serve as intermediaries if he should have enemies with animal spirits. When a threat becomes imminent, he may stay within his house or limit his range of activities to a very circumscribed area, always taking a weapon when he does go out. He will usually try to limit his drinking, or give it up entirely. These short-range rules of avoidance are clearly indicated by the circumstances in which killings occur: in the hills or at night, when the victim is under the influence of liquor.

These 37 cases of homicide reveal a regularity in the kinds of people and situations involved. The victims are most often men who assert power, principally curers, or men who violate standards of behavior by abusiveness or theft. Their killers are often linked to them by kinship or neighborhood, the bonds in which tensions are greatest. The regularity of time and place of homicide suggests the precautions that can be taken to avoid being killed if one has an enemy. The general failure of the community social-control agents to bring negative sanctions against a killer indicates that homicide is an accepted solution for interpersonal conflict. The structural setting that validates this behavior is discussed below.

II. Structural Change and Social Control

Case analysis, useful for discerning certain patterns, is inadequate for understanding the interrelationships among a variety of social changes in the community. An increasing rate of homicide of this magnitude indicates fundamental changes in the social matrix in which individual decisions are made: it suggests not only a rise in the tensions that provoke conflict, but an undermining of the social-control mechanisms for channeling them. The perception of these changes by the members of the society makes for shifts in the individual calculi, grossly measured in changes in the rate of behavior. In order to understand the interrelated problems of the sources of increasing tensions and the reasons homicide is chosen as a means of resolving them, I have reconstructed the course of social change in the period from 1935 to 1965.

Increasing Social Tensions

New economic enterprises have increased wealtl differences in the community. The best measure ol this is the increase in cattle-holding, which is a socially approved way of spending money. Twenty-five years ago, there were only a half-dozen men with cattle, and they had only one or two head each. Today, one of the herders in the community has 200 head of cattle, and 75 percent of the households have one or more each.

Cattle-herding is a "new" industry in the sense that instead of just having a team of oxen to help with agricultural labor, men are breeding cattle for profit. Because the cattle roam freely, there is much loss, and this leads to accusations of theft. I have never heard such accusations directed against anyone outside the community; crime as well as positive moral relationships is confined within the boundaries of this corporate community. Suspected cattle thieves are killed by the cattle-owner or by a killer hired by the cooperative of cattle-owners. Such killings account for six of the 37 cases analyzed above.

The illicit distilling of liquor has also added to the town's prosperity. The liquor industry was introduced about 15 years ago, but the number of distillers has increased from 5 to 40 in the last five years. From an enterprise formerly meeting only local market needs, contraband liquor is now sold as far away as the coastal area and across the border in Guatemala. A cooperative of distillers has reduced the frictions that immediately followed the introduction of liquor-distilling. The cooperative pays the fines of any member caught distilling, and in addition threatens to use group action against informers, who were formerly tempted to earn the 200 pesos offered by federal agents. But the envy aroused by the sight of those who profit from this enterprise, as with the cattle industry, is a covert cause for personal attacks on other grounds.

A third enterprise, trucking, has caused a realignment of political interests in factions associated with two truck-owning cooperatives. Membership in one of the cooperatives, or patronage of one of the two trucks, arouses the enmity of members of the other cooperative. Several threats have been made on the lives of the owners and the operators, but the only damage done has been to tires.

The tensions resulting from the introduction of these new enterprises cannot be fully measured by the deaths attributed to direct economic conflict. Wealth differences resulting from the new enterprises excite envy, and with it come accusations of witchcraft. In this community, witchcraft killing does not perform the normative function of reducing wealth differentiation that Kluckhohn saw operating among the Navaho, since it is the poor man who is killed as a witch, not the rich man. The slaying of the envious witch exacerbates the economic differentiation that provides the seedbed for conflict.

Another new source of tension is found in the growing demand for political leadership or even independence from the township by the *ejido* colonies formed since land reform went into effect in 1937. The inept maneuvers of two founders of the ejido colonies in hot country resulted in two homicides.... The increasing strength of these hamlets will mean that more attempts will be made in the future to gain political equality and/or independence. Whether this will result in increasing homicides will depend on social-control agencies external to the Indian communities.

Homicide occurring as a direct result of economic and political competition represents a new strategy in the community. The decision to kill rather than to use other negative sanctions is related to the social-control mechanisms discussed below.

Changing Mechanisms of Social Control

A system of social control rests not only on the exercise of negative sanctions, but on the sense of personal security derived from confidence in the institutions of control. In Teklum, the maintenance of control was formerly centered in the guardianship against malevolent spirits held by the ancestor spirits and the curers. The "police force," made up of ten Indians of the town who served without pay for a year, acted as errand boys more than as guardians of public safety. The townspeople conformed to the cultural code of behavior because of a sense that their welfare was being cared for.

More recently, the breakdown of certain structural features and competition between new and old leaders have undermined nonviolent methods for the maintenance of social control. These changes will be discussed in terms of (1) the organization of the curing profession, (2) conflict between the curers and the civil authority, and (3) how both the curing profession and the civil authority are affected by the breakdown of the old dual division of the town.

(1) *Organization of the curing profession.* Perception of structural changes in the curing profession and their effect on attitudes are indicated in the following statement by an informant.

Formerly there were not many curers. Only two— one in the low side and the other in the high side. They alone spoke together. They walked every night, looking and watching over the pueblo to see that no illness was brought in, checking to see who was bringing it and to see if there was any illness of God [reference to contagious diseases]. They saw which of the children had a soul [reference to the third soul, the swayohel or animal spirit, which gives the power to cure and to do evil].

If anyone wanted to be cured, they bathed them, cured them, and in a little while people got better because there was good illness only. If later on it turned into a disease of the devil, with their animal spirit they seized the force of the illness.

When there was a contagious disease, and a witch "brought heat," and the children began to die, the two curers alone consulted and waited to see who had brought the evil and where they lived. One of them
went to the town hall and gave an account of the fact that they had taken care of the evil and gotten rid of it. It was not necessary to gather together the pueblo —only the two knew what was the matter and how to care for it.

The [two] leader curers of each section alone ordered other curers. No one else could enter curing until permitted by the leaders. They continued in power until they died, and then one of the younger curers took over.

Beginning in 1940, more curers started to enter on their own accord. The elder curer had died, and his successor was not recognized. People saw that someone could pulse, and so they would ask him to cure.

Now when there is an epidemic, the president orders the curers to gather together. The curers look for the man who has "brought the heat." And then they kill him. Formerly it was not so.

The statement points to two interacting features of change within the curing profession: (1) the loss of leadership and of control over entry into the profession and (2) the loss of faith in the guardianship function of the curers. The effect of these changes has been to reduce security and the maintenance of social control.

Formerly the recognized leader of the curers in each section of the dual division legitimized entry of new curers and expelled those who abused their power. When these curers died, there was no one of sufficient power to replace them. In listing curers who are active today, there is no agreement as to who the leading curers are or even as to whether there are leaders.

Loss of leadership in the curing profession has led to competiton among the curers. . . .

The present competition among the curers to assert their power by telling such stories or by displaying fearlessness in the bullfights held in community fiestas is symptomatic of the disruption caused by the breakdown in the hierarchy of the profession. When curing was a controlled profession, abusive conduct by the curers was minimized, but the new curers are reputed to use their power for their own gain. The following story is typical:

J, born in Tetikil, went to live in hot country. A friend invited him to drink. J, who was reputed to be a curer, said to his friend when they were half drunk, "Do you want to 'take out' a girl?" His friend said, "No, how can you?" "Pendejo!" J replied, "I can because I have an animal [swayohel]." "What one?"

asked his friend. "You won't be afraid?" asked J. And then he put his shirt and hat on the floor, spoke three words (my friend didn't say what), and raised his hat and shirt, and a horse appeared. He did this again and a bull appeared. He was a great ʔak'čamel [witch]. He stole a great deal. He was killed by five bullets.

Such stories of curers "who walk on both sides" are favorites in the drinking sessions of Teklum. The power of curers inspires fear, so much so that some of the town presidents have been afraid of putting them in prison.

The open competition between curers serves to undermine the faith of the people in their guardianship function. This function was believed to have been acquired by the leaders from the ancestors, who were said to live in a cave in a hill near the town, from which came the progenitors of the present townspeople. To carry out this guardianship function, the animal spirits of the two leading curers roamed the streets at night, when the evil spirits were out, each one remaining within the limits of his own side of the dual division. In this role, the two major curers were called the *meʔilta-tiletik*, a term derived from the one referring to the ancestors.

The loss of faith in the guardianship function of the curers was coincident with the loss of belief in the presence of the meʔtiktatik. Some deny that the meʔtiktatik live in the cave anymore, and others say they just appear on the day of their fiesta, the Day of the Cross in the Catholic calendar. This fiesta formerly was an important event in establishing the guardian power of the leader curers, since they were the only ones who dared enter the cave and talk to the ancestors. But this fear and this belief have gone. In 1960 one young man of the pueblo entered the cave on the day of the fiesta, when the curers were "deceiving the people" in claiming that they were talking to the ancestors; the fact that he dared enter the cave indicates an ambient distrust (in part resulting from verbal attacks by the priest, who at that time was gaining more power in the town). By now, on the Day of the Cross the church and civil officials, the women prayermakers, and an assistant of the priest, the *fiscal,* go to the cave, but the curers are no longer present, even as bystanders. The curers have tried to buttress belief in the guardianship of the ancestors by claiming that a nephew of the ancestors

is now in residence in the cave and that they are in communication with him. But these claims are met with expressions of disbelief by the people. Almost everyone is convinced not only that the curers do not now talk with the ancestors, but that the ancestors no longer look over them from the watchout hill outside their cave.

The loss of control by the curers is dramatized in the long passage quoted above contrasting the past and present treatment of epidemics. Formerly the two leaders of the curers consulted together and announced to the president that they had rid the town of evil. Now the curers as a group are ordered to come before the civil authority. There, in a long examination called *ʔič yoʔtan*—"taking the heart"—in which 18 liters of liquor are consumed, the assembled curers and civil authorities decide who among them is responsible for bringing in the witchcraft that is causing the epidemic. Later in the evening, one of the curers is usually killed.

(2) *Conflict between the curers and the civil authority.* The competition between the curers and the civil authority can be traced in a series of incidents beginning in the '30s and culminating in an open confrontation in the spring of 1966.

The first incident occurred in 1932, when the town was still part of the neighboring Ladino township:

F went and asked permission of the authorities to kill his enemy, a curer, who he thought was bewitching his brother-in-law. The president went to the house of the suspected witch with the order to imprison him. He said they were going to take him to the neighboring township center to put him in jail. The group of authorities set off with the suspected witch. On the way, another group met them and asked them where they were going. The president replied, "To H." The group that had encountered them asked if they would like a drink to heat their body. They gave one cup, and then another. Then they cut up the suspected witch with a machete and put his body in the cave of the ancestors. When the widow enquired the next day where her husband was, the president said that the man must have gone to the finca.

The ambush by the killers was prearranged in the town court, and the president covered their deed when questions were asked.

In 1940, the leading curer of the lower section was president. When he killed a man who accused him of being a witch, he was put in the local jail by the judge and then removed to the departmental capital. During his term of imprisonment an epidemic broke out in the town; it was attributed to witchcraft supposedly practiced by him and by two other curers who remained in town. These two were then imprisoned. After they were set free, all three men were killed in different episodes involving accusations of witchcraft. Permission to act as executioners was granted by the civil authority.

In the past, the public review of a case before a killing probably served to minimize homicide, since permission was not always granted. Since 1953, when a large highway first linked the town to the departmental capital and communication between this center of justice and the local township increased, the civil authority has not given permission, and prior review of witchcraft cases occurs only with epidemics.

The final incident in which the civil authority confronted the curers occurred in the spring of 1966. The president accused one of the curers of cutting short his life by lighting candles in the mountains. The curers were called together to hear the threat and to go to the hill to look at the evidence. The accused curer remained at home pleading that he was sick. He was warned not to pursue his witchcraft, and as yet there has been no use of violence on either side. This open confrontation without the use of violence may indicate a change in the strategy of conflict with the growing power of the president.

(3) *Breakdown of the dual division.* The loss of internal controls in the curing profession and the conflict for power and control by the civil officials and the curers are related to a more fundamental change in the social structure of the community. Formerly the division of the town into two sections provided a channel for opposition as well as cooperation. Recruitment into leadership positions in both the civil hierarchy and the curing hierarchy was based upon residence. The system provided checks and balances in the exercise of power, for the two principales—one from each section of the dual division—were supposed to act as watchdogs over the curers. The shift in the locus of social control from the principales to the president has been marked by the open confrontation with the curers.

The authority of the president, however, depends on the use of legal sanctions of prison sentences and fines imposed by extracommunity enforcement agencies in the departmental capital. The weakness of these sanctions—the fine for homicide is 1,000 to 3,000 pesos or three to five years' imprisonment—means that these threats do not have a controlling effect on people's decisions to act. Homicide, carried out by individuals who feel themselves to be threatened, is a supplementary mechanism for social control. Cast in the idiom of witch-killing, homicide is the quasi-official execution of a community threat.

The breakdown in the former structural controls has not been compensated for by the intervention of extracommunity institutions. Attempts to circumvent killing are made by the priest, who counsels against it, warning that the killer will acquire the sins of the man he kills, and by the talking saint of Ixtapa, whom the Indians consult when they are pressed and who advises them to wait—their enemy will be killed for them. This advice is not sufficient to forestall all killings. Motivated by fear, some men still seek to eliminate the object of their fear. The sense of the guardianship of the ancestors and their intermediaries, the curers, is lost along with the intervention of the civil authorities. The individual reacts, using his own means and trying to get sufficient consensus to avoid reprisal.

Alan R. Beals

Cleavage and Internal Conflict: An Example from India

Beals discusses the symbolic expression of strain, or potential cleavage, aggression, and conflict in the social relations within villages in India. He asserts, in effect, that cultural solutions of social problems are never perfect, and that they are most likely to involve conflict when conflict is seen as more worthwhile than submitting to strainful cooperation or conventional subordination. His article suggests the circumstances in which party conflict can be regulated short of radical change.

Within each human group there is a set of commonly understood symbols attached to every generally experienced form of behavior which places it somewhere along a continuum between aggression and assistance and which has no necessary connection with the actual nature of the behavior. A man with a sharp instrument may represent a doctor, a fellow play actor, or an enemy. When a segment of a group reacts to the behavior of another segment, it chooses a behavior symbolizing, among other things, some degree of aggression or some degree of assistance. That one segment takes the trouble to respond to another segment is a sufficient indication that the responding segment hopes to achieve some particular value or set of values through its response. Hence, if an aggressive response is made to an aggressive behavior, thus initiating conflict, it can be assumed that calculation or experience has indicated that the communication of aggressive intent is most likely to lead to value realization.

Because the behavior of any two segments of a group must be in sufficient conformity to reality to permit the survival of both, it can be assumed that the choice of conflict as a mode of interaction is ordinarily rational. In any group which survives over a period of time, it can be expected that interaction between individuals and subgroups within it will be patterned in such a way that conflict occurs only under specified conditions and within definite limits. Built into the cultural tradition must be rules of the game which maintain a balance of power and insure that the degree of conflict which develops does not interfere significantly with the realization of values.

That conflict within established groups has been brought into harmony with the value system and with survival needs permits such conflict to be described as functional in the sense that it becomes a cultural pattern which mutually reinforces other cultural patterns. This should not be taken to mean that conflict is the most adaptive response possible, for it always involves the direction of energy toward the control of group members and away from the solution of survival problems. In the same way, incompatibilities between the milieu within which the group carries out its operations and the cultural tradition which directs and interprets the group's operations lessen the efficiency of the group. This, essentially, is the difference between what is happening and what people in the group think is happening or hope will happen. In similar fashion efficiency is reduced when the belief, value, and behavioral systems which comprise the cultural tradition are not self-consistent or when they are mutually inconsistent. Such conflicts, incompatibilities, and inconsistencies have been defined elsewhere as strains.

Use of the term "strain" is based upon the belief that strains represent the imprint upon the cultural tradition of stresses which have arisen in the relationship of the cultural tradition to its milieu and have not been solved or wiped out. In realistic terms, when a stress develops, the group has the choice of either altering the cultural tradition in order to bring it into conformity with the new reality or altering the milieu in order to bring it into conformity with the cultural tradition. When the milieu cannot be altered and when altering the cultural tradition means the abandonment of a cherished value, the common tendency is to make the change in fictional or symbolic terms. This can

"Cleavage and Internal Conflict: An Example from India" by Alan R. Beals from *Journal of Conflict Resolution,* Vol. 5, No. 1 (1961). Reprinted by permission of *The Journal of Conflict Resolution* and the author.

be done by denying the existence of the stress, leaving the cultural tradition intact but incompatible with the environment, or by accepting the stress and amending the cultural tradition so that it becomes inconsistent.

When a mother says to her child, "Don't touch that, it's hot," she is conveying to him a fragment of the cultural tradition involving belief, value, and behavior. If the statement is compatible with reality, the child will be burned when he touches the object. In this case, the cultural tradition is reinforced by the environment and the mother's statement symbolizing assistance is likely to be accepted as such by the child. If the object is not hot, the mother has two choices of action. She can accept the inconsistency and direct aggression against the child saying, "I don't care whether it's hot or not, you do as I tell you." This creates an inconsistency within the cultural tradition and opens up possibilities for counteraggression and resulting conflict. The mother's other choice is to convince the child that the object actually is hot in some extraordinary manner. This creates an incompatibility between the cultural tradition and the milieu but eliminates the possibility of conflict because the mother's actions cannot be interpreted as aggressive.

The choice between the development of inconsistencies and the development of incompatibilities suggests that a distinction can be made between cultural traditions. One type of cultural tradition offers a Barmecide feast of symbols and values which have relatively little connection with reality; the other type offers values and symbols which are compatible with reality but not consistent among themselves. The first type of tradition gives rise to a tightly organized group within which primary value stress is placed upon conservation of the group and of the cultural tradition. The second type, loosely organized, gives rise to a loosely organized group within which primary value stress is placed upon the achievement of realistic values even at the expense of the group and the cultural tradition. Although many cultural traditions and groups fall between these two types, the distinction offers a means of predicting which societies will tend to develop internal conflict in response to new situations, and which societies, exposed to the same kind of new situation, will postpone the development of conflict by denying the new reality.

In general, proneness to conflict can be thought of as a function of the degree to which strain is present within a particular cultural tradition and of the particular varieties of strain which happen to be present. But before conflict, or an extension of existing conflict, can occur, stress must be applied. Assuming that a stress has developed of an order sufficient to create conflict within a particular group, but not sufficient to determine where that conflict will occur within the structure of the group, it appears likely that the locus of the resulting conflict will be greatly influenced by the distribution of strains within the group. Ordinarily conflict will tend to occur in those relationships between individuals or subgroups which carry the greatest degree of strain. The extent to which conflict will take on an organized character, permitting it to be described in terms of parties or schisms, is dependent upon whether or not the existing pattern of strains involves individual or subgroup relationships. For example, strain in the relationships between husband and wife and parent and child is present in most societies, but the contributors to such relationships rarely form separate subgroups. Conflict within such relationships is unlikely to lead to the formation of separate parties representing male against female or parent against child unless there are separate male and female organizations or a well-developed system of age-grade societies. On this basis, two patterns of strain can be postulated: *atomistic* where conflict tends to occur in the relationships between individuals and *schismatic* where conflict tends to break out in the relationships between subgroups.

That strain produces relationships which are unsatisfying or which fall short of expectations is not, by itself, sufficient to produce conflict. The initiator of conflict must have some grounds for believing that the resulting conflict will be more fruitful than the relationship of cooperation or subordination which the conflict relationship replaces. Because conflict represents a desire to change a traditionally established relationship, it is not likely to have a successful outcome unless it leads to the formation of two opposed parties within the group. If such a cleavage cannot be developed and a large part of the group remains neutral, the neutral group is likely to reinforce traditional values and require a return to the pre-existing relationship. A cleavage, then, is a pattern of strain, expressed in the alignment of subgroups, which encourages the development of conflict by holding out the possibility of a dichotomization of the group. Presumably the likelihood of conflict between two subgroups is greatest when it cannot be arbitrated or controlled by any third subgroup or influenced by the overlapping or shifting of membership. There must also be a relationship of interdependence between the subgroups so that control of the members of one subgroup is essential to value realization on the part of the other.

Some of these hypotheses concerning the patterning of subgroup interrelationships and the development of cleavages can be applied to an explanation of conflict relationships within villages in India. Typically, Indian villages contain a relatively small number of kinds of subgroups. These are castes, lineages, neighborhoods, households, informal clique groups, recreational groups, work groups, and social classes. Ordinarily, the basis of social class is a division between landlords, small farmers and tenants, and landless laborers. Very often the number of subgroups in a particular village is reduced by the fact that the membership of the different kinds of subgroups coincides. A caste may occupy a particular neighborhood or it may be composed of a single lineage or it may represent most of the membership in a particular social class. In the same way, work groups may be formed by members of a single lineage, of a single caste, or of a number of castes. Conflict between the different types of subgroups appears to be of rare occurrence and is probably ruled out by the fact that any individual belongs to all or nearly all of the types. Usually conflict in India is described as taking place between lineages within a caste, between castes, or between classes.

The villages to be considered belong to a group of thirty villages located in Gulbarga District in Southern India. These thirty villages are closely linked through kin relationships, economic interdependencies, and a shared governmental structure. Within the common tradition established by these and other similar limitations upon the development of differences between villages, villages differ in size, in the distribution of castes within each village, and in the amount and kind of cooperation and conflict which occur. As these are neighboring villages, it can be assumed that they share a single cultural tradition which is substantially replicated in each of the villages. For the most part, the same techniques for handling conflict and the same basic strains can be expected to be present in all thirty villages.

Replication of the same cultural tradition over a wide area carries with it the implication that unique environmental and historical factors will be encountered which place some villages under a greater degree of stress than others. In particular, the arrangement of subgroups in the different villages is determined by historical factors which have influenced the extent to which particular castes are represented in each. Economic factors have influenced size and created differences in social class composition. Because the area farmed effectively by each village is limited by the fact that fertilizer must be carried from village to field in a two-wheeled cart, population size is greatly influenced by the per-acre productivity of the soil within a four- or five-mile radius of the village. Although the size and distribution of castes and social classes in each village are largely beyond the control of its residents, the problems posed by variations in caste and class must be handled within the confines of the regional culture using commonly accepted techniques.

Conflict ordinarily develops initially between two individuals one of whom is robbed, beaten, murdered, or arrested. If a village has a united and decisive leadership, conflict stops there. If such leadership is not present, the two enemies gather allies and extend the field of their conflict until most of the population of the village is involved. At this point the village acquires the reputation of having "parties." Relationships between parties take the form of stealing each other's grain, injuring each other's cattle, cuckolding each other, beating each other with cudgels, and, ultimately, in riot and murder. Individuals who attempt to maintain neutrality are frequently robbed or beaten.

Violent as party conflict often is, it rarely has the effect of creating a cessation of cooperative effort within the village. The parties remain, there are periodic outbreaks, but on many occasions opponents work together or play together. When cooperation does occur between opponents, it usually has little reference to problems of survival. The essential informal cooperation involved in guarding one another's fields, protecting one another's cattle, or aiding persons in difficulty is largely absent where there are parties. Emphasis is laid instead upon community endeavors requiring public, organized cooperation.

One of these forms of public cooperation is the performance of a *jatra* or interlocal festival to which other villages are invited in the role of guest. Organization of a *jatra* involves an immense expenditure of cooperative effort in accumulating funds and preparing entertainments and rituals. Another form of cooperation involves the development of a stereotyped hostility relationship to an "enemy" village. This hostility is expressed through competitive intervillage wrestling and weightlifting at times when both villages are guests at the same *jatra*. These wrestling matches often culminate in rioting and loss of life. Public cooperation also takes place in the organization of song groups and drama companies. Finally, cooperation is expressed through the organization of village-wide religious ceremonies and the construction of schools, roads, wells, reservoirs, or temples.

Inasmuch as such cooperative projects cannot be undertaken unless conflict is, at least temporarily, brought to a halt, the projects can be said to represent devices available within the regional culture for the control and suppression of conflict. To be sure, such devices are not always effective. Village ceremonies sometimes become riots and those who practice dramas in the evening often practice theft before dawn. The completion of temples, schools, and wells is often rendered impossible by conflict.

The development of conflict is also influenced by landlords and government officials. The landlord is important because he lends money and seed to others and can compel his followers to follow his lead in the initiation or cessation of conflict. He also has influence over police constables and government officials and can use them to force compliance to his wishes. The government officials within the village are a headman and an accountant. If these two men operate jointly to control conflict, parties are unlikely to develop. If these two men are in opposition, parties are almost certain to develop. If a village is small, it is unlikely to possess a powerful landlord or to be capable of providing appropriate conveniences to visiting government officials. It is thrown largely upon its own resources for the handling of conflict. Conflict in larger villages receives much closer government control and supervision, but where there are a number of competing, politically powerful, landlords, the police authority of the government cannot be used effectively.

The thirty villages discussed here fall into four size categories: seven villages have between 92 and 137 households; nine have between 168 and 307 households; and eight have between 379 and 512 households. These four categories will be referred to as hamlets and as small, medium, and large villages. Population data indicate that there are normally about five persons per household.

Among the seven hamlets, none report any significant incidence of conflict. Three hamlets have "a few quarrels" one has "quarrels and thefts." Hamlets are rarely visited by government officials and the police have made arrests in none of them during the last five years. There is no indication that conflict between parties or any other kind of violent conflict has occurred in any of them. None of the three smallest hamlets has engaged in any of the forms of public cooperation. Among the four larger hamlets, one has repaired a reservoir, three have drama companies, two have song groups, and one, the largest, has a *jatra*. There appears to be a fairly direct relationship between size and the relative involvement in conflict and public cooperation. Although the hamlets can be divided into subgroups on the basis of caste and to some extent on the basis of social class, it appears likely that these subgroups are too small to function effectively as social units. The homogeneity and interdependence generated by the small size of the hamlets are evidently effective in ruling out internal conflict.

In marked contrast to the hamlets, the six small villages display great activity, with one exception. In the exceptional case, over half of the population consists of recent converts to Christianity from a low ranking caste. The absence of both conflict and cooperation in this village may be traceable to an abandonment of shared village and traditional values—essentially a division into two hamlets.

The remaining five small villages are all divided by party conflict. Three report the frequent occurrence of fights; four report many thefts; four report frequent quarrels; and in four, police arrests have been made within the last five years. All five villages report many forms of cooperative activity: three have *jatras*; three have "enemy" villages with whom they have engaged in bloody riots; three have recently rebuilt temples; one has a volleyball team; one has built a public well; one has built a school; two have singing groups; and one has a drama company.

It appears probable that these villages are too large to control conflict through the use of informal mechanisms and too small and powerless to control conflict through appeals to higher authority. In all five cases, conflict originated within a single dominant caste having between forty-seven and sixty-seven percent of the population and spread to include the entire village. The conflict is generally the result of a quarrel between intermarrying lineages having to do with the payment of wedding expenses or ill-treatment of a spouse, or it is the result of a quarrel between members of the same lineage over the inheritance of property. In either case, the conflict is between kinsmen who are supported by other kinsmen and by friends and neighbors from other castes. It is to be noted that the only way of dividing these small villages into two more or less equal halves is by dividing the dominant caste. Conflict between the dominant caste and all others is ruled out by the heterogeneous nature of the other castes.

Among the medium-sized villages, only five have public conflict—four have parties and one has had three arrests for murder in a five-year period. The almost total absence of conflict in five of the villages is attributed to the presence of strong landlords or headmen who have persons who disobey them arrested or beaten. None of the four villages which have parties has dominant castes. In every case, the reported conflict is between members of different castes. In two cases, conflict is between castes of approximately equal rank and size. In another case, there are two castes of equal size but of greatly different rank. Here, conflict broke out initially within the high ranking caste and then shifted to conflict between the high ranking and low ranking castes. The presence of a large high ranking caste and of a large low ranking caste evidently creates lines of horizontal and of vertical cleavage with a resulting tendency toward an alternation of the locus of conflict. In the fourth case, there are no clear-cut lines of cleavage. The village is composed almost entirely of small farmers belonging to a number of different castes which are approximately the same size. Possibly the groups in conflict are neighborhoods.

Two of the ten villages have sizable populations of landless laborers which would permit their dichotomization along class lines. One of the villages is the one that had three murders; the other reports little internal conflict but has participated in a riot in which eight people were killed. It is suspected that the relative absence of modern influences upon the region and the almost absolute power of the landlord group has a tendency to suppress conflict along lines of horizontal cleavage.

Among the ten medium villages there is some relationship between the degree to which conflict is present and the degree to which the villages are engaged in public cooperation. Four villages which report quarreling as the only type of conflict present are engaged in a total of seven cooperative enterprises. The four villages which report the presence of parties are engaged in a total of eighteen cooperative ventures. Though eight of these ventures were reported by a single village, the difference remains intriguing even when that village is removed from consideration.

Four of the ten medium villages report quarreling as their only form of conflict. No information is available for one of these villages. The remaining three do not have cleavage along caste lines. All three are dominated numerically by between four and six castes of intermediate rank and of about equal size. A fifth village, which reported the presence of thefts and quarrels, has a numerically dominant caste. The failure of conflict to develop within the dominant caste is attributed by people in the village to the presence of determined village officials. Another important factor may be the presence of a mining operation within the village lands. Employment in the mine may have weakened those economic interdependencies which make it possible for members of opposing parties to recruit participants from other castes or economic levels.

Parties are reported to exist in six of the seven large villages. The smallest reports that party conflict ceased when an elected village council was formed. All seven of the villages possess numerous representatives of the landlord class and it is likely that the conflict stems largely from the economic and political competition of these men. In four of the six cases, party conflict follows well-marked lines of cleavage. In two of these cases, the cleavage is between castes of approximately equal rank and strength. In the third case, it is within a single dominant caste comprising seventy-five percent of the population. In the fourth case, nearly three-fifths of the population is landless, and the conflict follows economic lines.

In the two cases where lines of cleavage are not strongly developed, one village has no party conflict and the other village has conflict mainly within the landlord group. This last village has a basically triangular social organization with a sizable number of wealthy landlords, a large number of prosperous small farmers, and a large number of landless laborers. It is suspected that the prosperity of the small farmer group makes it possible for a considerable proportion of them to ignore the political conflict of the large landlords.

All seven large villages have active forms of public cooperation, but the pattern has changed from one of general contribution by members of every household to one of individual contribution by landlords or government organized councils or cooperative societies.

In giving consideration to the nature of conflict among the thirty villages described above, it must be noted that, despite its sometimes violent character, the conflict tends to be patterned and regulated through forms of public cooperation and through the intervention of police and landlords. It is also regulated by patterns of intermarriage between villages which make every village jealous of its reputation as a good place to give one's daughter in marriage. The importance of the factor of intermarriage cannot be overstated. It is this that leads people in a particular village to do everything in their power to suppress any conflicts which develop within the village. Whenever there is a third party to a developing situation of conflict, it is always in the best interests of the third party to bring the conflict to an end. This would not be the case if the conflict were dysfunctional or if it were the means of effecting a radical change in the social organization of the group. Cultural stability could not be maintained if party conflict were to lead to lasting victory for either side.

Among the thirty villages, party conflict seems to have developed almost entirely in cases where strain had been produced by variations in size and where it was possible to form alignments and coalitions which divided the village into two nearly equal parts. This is most clearly demonstrated by the fact that villages with dominant castes have conflict within the dominant caste and villages which lack dominant castes have conflict between castes. It is suggested that there is a level of strain characteristic of all thirty villages which leads to a propensity for conflict. Where regulatory devices are effective, as in the hamlets and medium villages, or where there are no lines of cleavage, conflict cannot become permanently established.

It is also noteworthy that conflict centers about permanent kin and caste relationships which have a permanent unchanging membership rather than around relatively fluid neighborhood or clique groups. This, again, excludes the possibility of any action which might change the membership of the parties and thereby upset the balance of power.

In this discussion, an attempt has been made to suggest a means of defining and identifying strain. In particular, an attempt has been made to indicate how patterns of strain, expressed as cleavages within groups, influence the development of conflict. Within a single subregion of India, it has been indicated that particular geographical and historical conditions affecting population size and the distribution of castes have placed certain villages under stress. In this case, hamlets and medium-sized villages have relatively little conflict, small and large villages have a great deal. Where villages do have conflict, it appears to follow well-marked lines of cleavage. Although the conflict within the thirty villages is contained and regulated, there is an implication that under changing circumstances, the development of fresh conflict and the intensification of existing conflict would tend to follow existing lines of cleavage. Finally, the purpose of this paper has been to present a preliminary analysis of a particular body of data and to indicate some of the possibilities inherent in a particular line of thought.

Arthur E. Hippler

The Game of Black and White at Hunters Point

*Like many suburbs, Hunters Point is a bedroom com-
munity. There the comparison ends. The ghetto dwellers who live there are not there by design but because
they feel they can afford to live nowhere else. They
share a minimal sense of community, since the institutions which might serve them—whether educational, recreational, or service-centered—are poor or
nonexistent; further, they lack the political means by
which to strive to meet common needs and wants. The
enforced idleness of many and the cumulative frustrations that find few constructive outlets lead to much
aimless behavior. Conflicts that inevitably occur are
difficult to control, among other reasons because of
the lack of local leadership. Occasionally, as we see
in Hippler's article, a conflict may be intensified to the
proportions of a riot; when that happens, no one
within the territory has the power to regulate or resolve
it. Blacks who have succeeded in other urban regions
are culturally and socially very distinct from the ghetto
dwellers; despite their prestige, they have no moral
authority. Intervention by officials of the larger community is largely unsuccessful because of the restricted
communication between the blacks and whites in
Hunters Point, their distorted understanding of each
other, and their fears of each other's violence. Every
aggression by black or white reinforces these views,
in a process that sociologist Robert Merton has termed
the "self-fulfilling prophecy." When outbreaks occur,
they must subside almost of their own weight.*

*The experience of Hunters Point underscores
the problems imposed by lack of organization (the
residents are largely an aggregate, shoved into a given
space), frustration, and a lack of commitment to the
peaceful regulation of conflict. Hunters Point is what
it is because of its relation to the larger community.*

Hunters Point is a depressed and isolated district
in the southeastern section of San Francisco. It
is adjacent to the Hunters Point naval shipyard
where some of the residents work. Generally,
though, unemployment is widespread. There are
still people living in shanty dwellings erected as
"temporary" housing during World War II. Housing in general is inadequate or substandard, and the
whole district is defined by the City Housing
Authority as an official low-income area. Many,
if not most, of the residents draw some form of
public assistance. Nearly all of them are black.
Less notorious than Oakland, on the other side of
the Bay, the district is usually ignored until some
act of violence or a crusading newspaperman
brings it to public attention. Casual violence is
certainly prevalent; so are prostitution and nar-
cotics-dealing. It is a true ghetto, despised and
neglected as far as possible by the rest of the city.
Its votes have been taken for granted by the Demo-
crats, ignored by the Republicans. It is poorly
serviced: garbage collection is irregular; public
transport is inadequate. Hunters Pointers are
clearly an outcast community in San Francisco.

In September 1966 rioting broke out there after
a black teen-ager named Matthew Johnson had
been shot dead by a white policeman while running
away from a car that he and two friends had abandoned. The policeman (also named Johnson) suspected the car to be stolen and had failed to get the
boy to stop. The disturbance which followed lasted
for five days. I was doing participant field work in
the area both before and after these events;
Hunters Point is, I think, one of the few communities involved in the series of urban disturbances of the sixties to have engaged the attentions
of such a researcher at such a time. While I cannot
propose solutions, I hope I can help to clarify the
complex interaction out of which such disturbances grow, and particularly to show some of the
ways in which urban blacks and whites perceive
themselves and each other and how these perceptions determine relations between them.

Social scientists have described at length the
personal and social disorders among black Americans and have attributed them to centuries of
subjugation by whites. Demands made of them
both before and since the abolition of slavery have

created, through the enforced absence of the male, a matrifocal family structure. Because of this, it is held, black males have strong but unconscious feelings of ineffectuality and castration, while women have to cope with fears of desertion by their men. These fears are realistic enough in Hunters Point, where 50 to 80 percent of families have no resident male. The women protect themselves by showing aggressive independence, and the men, attacked as potential nonproviders and deserters, often defend themselves—and open the way to welfare grants for their children—by actually abandoning their families. Moreover, these insecurities are intensified by internalized self-contempt. Blacks despise themselves because for years they have been despised by whites. The black American situation is a vicious cycle. Bad education is caused both by a realistic indifference to scholarly achievement and by expectations that blacks will fail—expectations built into the school system and the minds of its personnel, many of whom are poor teachers and nearly all of whom are white. Bad education (and lack of motivation) itself contributes to a low income level. Since white domination has forced acceptance of the consumer ethic on blacks, they are further frustrated by not having access to the material goods which validate that ethic.

Individuals growing up against such a background face continual evidence of their infantile status in white eyes but have no certain status of their own to grasp as an alternative. Many therefore take an image of themselves which derives in part from their own defensive psychological needs and in part from the fantasies of whites: the image of the hypersexual, hyperaggressive "Bad Nigger." In this way they can support themselves against recognizing how passive they are—"I'm a *bad* motherfucker." Alternatively, they may repress emotion—"Man, I don't feel nothing"—or show covert and overt concerns about sexual potency. These stances all help to buttress their precarious image of themselves. The blacks of Hunters Point have menial jobs in a white world. They see the police, the guardians of that world, as "enemies." Such internal organization that exists is dominated by middle-aged matriarchs. The young can be expected to respond to all this in several ways. Passivity, bravado, and explosive reaction are three stages of response, but elements of all three can be seen in any one. Passivity can be a revolt, bravado gives only the form of manliness, and explosive violence is rarely organized. In the case of Hunters Point, the violence included the first two elements as well.

Social Control and the Police

The Hunters Point resident police are Housing Authority police. They do not belong to the San Francisco Police Department, and being essentially private police, they are theoretically limited in what laws they may enforce and where. They have the same right of arrest as any private citizen. Though their captain is a municipal police force inspector assigned to the Potrero Hill Station, San Francisco police rarely entered Hunters Point before the riot.

The Housing Authority police actually seem to function as a buffer between Hunters Point residents and adequate police protection. Indeed, the residents complain bitterly, not of the brutality of the racially integrated Housing Authority police, but of their refusal to give meaningful police protection. The tenants point out that the main job of the police seems to be to let people into their houses (after they have inadvertently locked themselves out) for a five dollar fee.

Them kids come into the halls shootin' them craps and turnin' over the fire extinguishers, and you call the cops and they tell you, "Don't worry they's just kids." I used to walk from the bus stop in 1946, and up to 1950, but I haven't for a long time now; sometimes they come and grab your purse and they insult you and throw things. The cops, they never come when you call.

I called them when these boys throwed rocks through my window. That policeman, he say, "What do you expect me to do about it?"

They don't care, you know they don't, long as no one gets killed, they don't even interfere in fights. They just drives by like they don't see nothin'.

Moreover, these police have a "bad attitude" toward the tenants. In the tenants' terms, this means "looking down on" them, verbally abusing them, and in general making their distaste for the tenants obvious. This "bad attitude," the tenants feel, merely reflects the attitude of the city and the Housing Authority.

The inspector in charge of the Hunters Point

police, the liaison to the Potrero Hill Station, admits that the Housing Authority police rarely request help from the Potrero Hill Station except in cases of extreme emergencies such as murder (which he claims is no more frequent here than in the rest of the city, although there is a real reluctance on the part of the Housing Authority police to discuss crime rates in Hunters Point). The inspector says it is a quiet place with nice folks and "just like any other middle-class area of the city."

After delivering himself of these opinions he went on to reminisce about the good old days when there was a lot more fighting in the city.

Everybody used to fight a lot then; there was a lot of fight clubs. Everybody knew how to box and you could have some real good fights on Saturday night. We didn't care as much about fighting then as we do now, people I guess just get more nervous about simple little fights than we used to. It used to be lots of fun. People shouldn't get so upset by a little fighting nowadays, but I guess things have changed a lot. It's the same with all this talk about Bay pollution. Heck, we used to swim right near the sewer outlets; if you'd see a big one coming [a piece of human excrement] you'd just yell and duck.

The inspector was, of course, suggesting that although the general opinion of Hunters Point is that it's a dangerous place with a great deal of fighting, it is no different from the fighting he remembers as a boy in the Irish Mission district. More importantly, his suggestion that there was no particular problem of any type in Hunters Point showed that he wanted to relieve the Hunters Point police, as well as the city police, of their responsibilities, but apparently also to reduce racist attitudes which he obviously felt originated in white beliefs about those "dangerous Negroes."

The patrolmen themselves have a somewhat different attitude.

I been here 12 years and I could tell you some hair-raising stories about these people. Some of 'em—not all mind you 'cause there's some good ones—but some of 'em are no better'n animals. Yeah, you could find a lot of trouble if you go looking for it, but I don't. No, sir, I don't go looking for trouble—let 'em knock their own heads together.

But both positions have the same result: a tendency to lessen police activity within Hunters Point.

Crime and Underpolicing

What constitutes a crime in Hunters Point? The police do not regard the kind of boisterous behavior frequently complained about by tenants (noisy parties, gambling in halls and stairways, and the like) as a police matter. They feel that "this is not an upper-class neighborhood," a judgment based on the common sense observation that behavior is different in this neighborhood than it is in some others, and that it would only harass the population unnecessarily (and make police work harder) to police it strictly. Sophisticated as this view may be, it implies to many residents a paternalistic and racist attitude. Some tenants are infuriated that more or less illegal disturbances are thought to be tolerable since the people in Hunters Point "don't know no better." Yet at the same time, many of the same people are just as infuriated by attempts to enforce middle-class morality because they are aware of the racial and cultural prejudices that underlie such attempts.

Another reason why police are less active in Hunters Point than in other areas is that they cannot apply the common "on the beat" technique of harassing "suspicious-looking" people and people who are known to have criminal records or to associate with criminals. Clothing and appearance indicate only too well the "suspiciousness" of most of the young people in Hunters Point, while the criterion of prior criminality is meaningless since a large percentage of them have some record and many others do not only because of police leniency or luck. Verbal aggression and insulting gestures are so common that there is no official response to these either, though naturally they intensify hostility between police and tenants. In other parts of town automatic suspicion falls on young, male, and poor blacks who seem sullen and aggressive. In Hunters Point so many fit this description that no one stands out.

This leaves the police with only their spies, or their own memories, to determine who should be watched. But in a neighborhood where police spies are despised even more than in most, and where black solidarity is gradually growing, few reliable informants exist. The Housing Authority police are often also frustrated in their attempts to solve the crimes that do occur. The most common complaints that can be acted on are of thefts and personal assaults, with thefts being far more common. But since theft is so common, disposal apparently so easy, and the culprits so unlikely to be caught, the police characteristically do not try; in many cases (according to the residents) they do not even respond to reports. Moreover, most police, whether Housing Authority or city, correctly perceive the police-tenant relationship as a racial one and dread a massive incident that might arise as a result of some chance encounter, which is exactly what occurred. To avoid such encounters they involve themselves in the community as police only when no other alternative seems possible.

All these factors have resulted in observable underpolicing in Hunters Point. But as a result of this very inactivity, police behavior may on occasion swing to the other extreme. Frustration and recognition of their own reduced importance may lead to periodic outbursts of excessive police brutality. Only so often can police fail to catch teen-age thieves who escape them on foot before they lose control.

But the Hunters Point residents' response to underpolicing is still a key factor in the climate that preceded the riot. They assume, often correctly, that police think of them merely as "animals" and don't care what they do to each other so long as they stay "on the Hill." They also feel that police do not become involved because they are afraid of the power and manliness of Hunters Point males. This is an attractive view because it corresponds with the "superspade" image, and it is partly correct in that many policemen do have such a fear. Indeed, in Hunters Point both groups are partly accurate in interpreting the attitudes of each other. This leads not to greater tolerance but to more and more unbearable tensions, which seem to need periodic release in outbursts of aggression on both sides.

The infamous Watts riots came before the Hunters Point riot, and Hunters Point residents commented at length on the Los Angeles situation. It was seen as a powerful expression of Negro strength, though in fact nearly all the victims of the riot were Negro. "We really showed them gray bastards" seems incongruous in the face of the fact that very little violence was directed against "grays" (Caucasians), with the exception of absent shop-owners. Negro rioters in Watts did not leave Watts to attack whites. They simply did what Negroes have traditionally done and turned the violence as much on themselves as on others.

This is an even clearer pattern in San Francisco.

The police, however, aware of the hostility towards them, are concerned about symbolic as well as real aggression. If it is true that frustration and prejudice combine to create explosive acts by police, they are able to do so even more among Negro males, and not all such aggressiveness is symbolic. While "being a man" is extremely important to the young Negro male, and his friends confirm him continuously as a "man," the police have a tendency not to treat him at all like a man. He is called "punk," "nigger bastard," and a variety of other obscene and degrading expressions. These threats hit too close to home for many teen-age Negro males. Many arrests and charges of "resisting arrest" or "assaulting an officer" originate from unbearable tongue-lashings by police which humiliate and emasculate young Negro males.

Police-resident relationships, then, are predictably unpredictable and unsatisfactory. The residents see police action as racially oppressive and police inaction as stemming from indifference or fear. These views are correct enough to receive support from each new confrontation. In this situation the police cannot be expected to enforce general social sanctions so that the community accepts them.

Community Control

Public opinion as an alternative form of social control in Hunters Point is as ineffectual as the police. It mainly affects those younger than teenage and over 50. Teen-agers, older teen-agers, and people in their twenties—that is, those most likely to be involved in gambling, heavy drinking, fighting, and theft—are least likely to be affected. This is true for several reasons. First, Hunters Point is not truly a community in the sense that its residents consciously try to identify with their neighbors. It is merely a place to live—or more accurately to sleep. Especially for young men and women, since they spend little time there, it does not represent "home" in any secure sense. Young men and women spend as much time as possible on Third Street at the foot of the Hill in the record shops, hamburger stands, bars, and other amusement places that fill the street. Many try to spend most of their time in the Fillmore (another predominantly

Negro district in San Francisco) or downtown. In Hunters Point itself there is nothing to do. Outside of playgrounds for children there are no organized amusement centers on the Hill.

Young males especially can afford to ignore the complaints of middle-aged women, since it is one of the few ways in which they can exhibit independence and superiority over females. Older blacks in general rightly see in the behavior of the young a reversal of the American Protestant tradition to which they themselves belong. While there was by the summer of 1967 little of the distinctive visual characteristics of black self-awareness, such as the "natural" hair style, the new standards were those of cool detachment, involving occasional drug use on the one hand, and rowdy male exhibitionism on the other.

The final major sanctioning agency in Hunters Point is the Housing Authority, but its main power, that of simply removing tenants (sometimes arbitrarily), is rapidly being reduced. In the absence of any other effective form of social control, then, what sanctions exist have come to correspond to the standards of the young, who are increasingly aware of the conflict between black and white, and are the more inclined to believe that what hurts a white man is justifiable on that account alone.

The Riot: 128 Hours

The police report of the incident is in the form of a very well organized pamphlet entitled *128 Hours,* the total length of the disturbance. This pamphlet details from the official police point of view the chronology of events during the disturbance. The report implies that the situation was handled by the San Francisco police in an orderly and dignified fashion and that at no time was the situation inadequately understood by the police, who exhibited a general aura of competence. This report is at variance with some of the descriptions by individual police officers (none of whom can be named at this time for fear of prejudicing their positions) and is also at variance with the implications of the public press and the reportage of individuals who were present and/or arrested. Clearly these were not necessarily objective. Yet the police have an obvious vested interest as well. It is certain, however, that the police action

did *not* result in any deaths after that of Matthew Johnson.

Johnson was shot on Tuesday, 27 September, in a lot off Navy Road, which runs through Hunters Point. A large crowd of people immediately gathered there. This crowd broke up in about two hours (4:00 P.M.). But, fearing Watts-style violence, the police tried to use so-called community leaders (black members of the city's Human Rights Commission) and confronted them with 70 or so black youths at a meeting in the Economic Opportunity Center on Third Street, just outside the Hunters Point housing site itself. Predictably, the Negro middle-class "community leaders" had absolutely no impact on the local young men except to incense them further. The latter cared only that Officer Johnson be punished for "murder." This was understandable, but apparently not to the police.

The young men, consciously aware of their own economic deprivation, unconsciously responding to their precarious self-image, and emboldened by the action of Negroes in Watts, were making every attempt to assert themselves in the face of this traditionally feared element of the white community (the police). They had also learned to despise successful middle-class Negroes as "Uncle Toms." Success in the white world is de facto evidence of "Tomming" to these young men.

The police now turned to the head of Youth for Service, supposedly an organization of ex-gang youths who operated as a liaison between the police and the fighting gangs. This too, of course, was doomed to failure as the police had been misled by their belief that the Youth for Service leader controlled anything at all; gangs no longer existed in Hunters Point as a focus of any fighting activity or organizational strength.

A third tactical error was made in bringing Major John Shelley of San Francisco to address the crowd at Third Street near the Bayview Community Center. He indicated that Officer Johnson had been suspended pending an investigation of the incident. But the individuals who by this time were thinking in terms of "making their own little Watts" cared very little for the appearance of the mayor, who showed that he felt this one incident was central to the riot and that he was incapable of understanding the basic roots of discontent and its meaning in Hunters Point. Additionally, Mayor Shelley and other civic leaders, standing on the dignity of their offices, could not understand that their refusal to be "moved by violence" was interpreted as indifference and hate by the residents. As one of the rioters said some days later: "Shit man, that the first time the white motherfucker ever come down here to Hunters Point. Fuck man, we should riot every week, that get something out of that motherfucker." In fact, the desire to move "the man" by violence, which would also negate personal feelings of inadequacy, was a core element of the situation.

Even more tragically, the Negro middle-class leadership failed to see that their presence could do no good and that they were not leaders of Hunters Point at all. They did not understand what the dispute was about, and they had no power to change the social situation. They expressed the view: "If they only realized what is being done for them and what we're all trying to do, they wouldn't riot." It was apparent that these "leaders" did not see that the "what was being done for them" was itself part of the package of frustrations leading to the disturbance.

The most eminent "Negro political leader" in the city, and the only one on the Board of Supervisors of the city, a man with a past record of leadership in the NAACP and as a defense lawyer in civil rights cases in the city, went with the mayor to Hunters Point to address the rioters and to try to calm them. If anything, he was greeted with greater antagonism than the mayor.

Rocks were thrown at the entourage, some of them narrowly missing both the mayor and the Negro supervisor, and the latter was completely unable to make himself heard. As one Hunters Pointer later put it,

That cocksucker forget he's black, but when we put them fuckers on the run, they sure let him know at City Hall right away. Sheeit, man, who the fuck he think he's foolin?

The Hunters Pointers felt that they saw the situation more realistically than the supervisor who was "fooling" himself into believing that he was actually accepted as an equal.

After a night of sporadic rioting, the "community leaders" (self-selected as well as those selected by the police and mayor) were unable to handle the situation. The police gave them a time limit on Wednesday afternoon. If at the end of an hour and a half they were still unable to control the situation, there would be police action in force to do so. These community leaders, many of whom were part of the matriarchal structure, as well as ministerial and poverty workers who were not part of it, were completely unable to control the situation. *There was nothing that they were empowered to offer the rioters in return for their stopping the riot which was even half as great as the reward for rioting itself.* Vague promises could not compensate for abandoning the sense of power which the riot gave its participants.

The police now called on the National Guard and other units of the Highway Patrol. At about 5:44 P.M. there was an incident which insured that the riot would not be brought under control quickly. Interestingly, the police report notes this incident in passing in the narrative section, and in the official police log of activities it is not noted at all, although it is the one incident all police officers involved in the riot and all Hunters Point residents recall. Police, in response, as they alleged, to gunfire being directed toward them from the Bayview Community Center, began to open fire on it. After riddling this frame building with every caliber of gun available, the police entered only to find several cowed and huddled children of pre-teen age and no evidence of any shooting or weapons in the building. The police did not kill any of the rioters, but the community now felt they wanted to and that they could expect no mercy. In fact, as well as overtly expressed antiblack attitudes, the police did engage in at least some willful property damage. Numerous bullet holes on a building 100 feet away from the community center indicate that it was gratuitously used as a target by police marksmen. Officers' reports confirm that some of their colleagues competed to see who could hit the gutter spout on top of the building. According to the reports, "Have you got your nigger today?" was a typical question, even though there seems to have been rather little shooting at people per se.

But not only was there some intentional shooting at unnecessary objects because of sport, some shooting occurred as a result of panic which struck the police officers (according to reports from individual police officers themselves). Just prior to the shooting, an officer was hit by a rock on his forehead. A small cut was opened, and the rumor was quickly passed, "They got one of our guys," and an unnamed sergeant gave the order to fire at the Bayview Community Center. Many officers did so in panic.

This panic shows the extent to which white people in San Francisco have stereotyped notions of a Negro threat that far exceeds the evidence. These notions, which result in part from the projection of hatred onto Negroes and guilt over mistreatment of Negroes, has continued in full force even among police, who should actually be the more aware of the fact that Negro aggressiveness is almost always directed against other Negroes.

But by now the police were in no position to make discriminations between "good" Negroes and "bad" Negroes. Some Negro police officers, especially those in plain clothes, even after being identified, were mistreated and manhandled as well as attacked with derogatory racial epithets, as were (from their own reports) any number of otherwise inoffensive Negro middle-class types whose sin lay in the fact that they were the wrong color at the wrong time (one Negro informant was arrested and subsequently dismissed from his job although he was never convicted).

The Police Community Relations Unit, the very arm of the police force which was supposed to deal with minority groups, and whose head (since resigned) has an excellent reputation even among some of the most incorrigible criminals in the Hunters Point area, was not called into the area. Apart from the officer permanently attached to the area from the Community Relations Unit, no officer from this unit was assigned, according to members of the unit. Some officers on the force, both in and out of the unit, believe that this is because of racism in the department, or more mildly, a distrust of "soft tactics" when dealing with rioters.

However, the police undoubtedly considered the residents as riotous and dangerous long before they had become so, and this perception determined the actions of the police and finally the actions of the rioters. The police tend unconsciously to reinforce a Negro's fantasy image of himself as aggressive or dangerous in everyday encounters. In a riot, this will happen faster and more intensely. Moreover, in a riot there are no easy techniques of identification of friend or foe for the police to use except skin color, which becomes the sole criterion. Black skin equals rioter, white skin equals friend, so that there is even less chance to form a more sophisticated perception.

The next four days saw the riot continue with a decreasing incidence of violence and then finally peter out. A few fires were set, some windows broken; there was some looting along Third Street, but primarily the riot consisted of large numbers of "uncontrolled" Negroes moving along the streets. The damage, compared with riots in comparably sized cities, was minimal (several hundred thousand dollars), as were the casualties (ten civilians reported as victims of gunshot wounds with no serious casualties for the police or other antiriot personnel).

Perhaps the best indication of how passive the Negro response was in Hunters Point and how unreasonable the massive fears of whites is that there were less than half a dozen assaults recorded by Negroes against whites in the course of five days of rioting. Far more violent acts than throwing bricks from a distance at police officers, breaking store windows, and sporadic looting are possible in a large metropolitan area with a significant Negro population. There must have been some restraining factor other than the police at work. We suggest it was the internalized fear of whites, so difficult to break down, coupled with a "holiday mood." The riots were as much attempts to strengthen self-image as direct expressions of hatred and dissatisfaction with whites.

The police's reaction is an interesting one. Until the beginning of the sixties, the police had dealt with Negro youths from Hunters Point by isolating them in Hunters Point. As one officer described his customary way of dealing with Negroes out of bounds, "Get back up on the Hill where you belong nigger. If I see your black ass down here again, I'll shoot it off." At the outbreak of the riots, though they were more or less city-wide, the same tactic was used. Negroes, no matter who they were or why they were in the Third Street area, were either arrested or pushed physically back up the Hill.

Even "moderate responsible" Negro adults feared that Negroes were being herded into Hunters Point so that they could be bombarded by naval vessels in the Bay. The fear was increased when an aircraft carrier in the Bay was seen passing Hunters Point. Panic, fear, and a sense of total isolation from the United States as a social system typified the feelings of many residents.

When I was a boy in the army, I mean, man they was bringing in 90 millimeter recoilless rifles against us. I was scared. Man, that was what we was trained to use against the enemy. And that's what I was now—the enemy. I was just waiting for that carrier to send over planes and bomb us like they do in Vietnam.

However, there was some positive response as well. By Thursday the police report notes that youth peace patrols had been formed by some of the young men in Hunters Point, among them the few truly effective community leaders, who were aided as best they could be by the severely hampered Police Community Relations Unit supposedly attached to the Hunters Point area.

In spite of official approval for this group, many police officers saw those of their colleagues who supported it as "coddlers" who were trying to legitimize illegitimate Negro youth organizations (lumping together in their minds the nonexistent "bopping gangs," the poverty workers, and other political activists). If blacks were automatically enemies, then to allow groups of them to do what the police could not do was bound to antagonize the more prejudiced members of the force.

Immediately after the riot, many residents of Hunters Point clearly hoped that the incidents of that fall would lead to greater solidarity among the different community groups and that many of the young men who had distinguished themselves in peace-making activities would gain prestige and power in the community.

The Aftermath

Not only did this not happen, the opposite occurred. Even greater community disintegration resulted. The general belief that "nobody cares" and "it's too late to do anything" became widespread. Because they used military weapons and troops, the authorities were perceived by the residents as making full-scale war. Even "Uncle Toms," notorious for their pro-white attitude, have openly begun to state that they see whites as racists. Some residents have consequently formulated grandiose plans of "war" against white society or purchased small arms "to take some of them with us." Others who see these plans as deluded have simply given up hope and withdrawn.

The blatant and exclusive use by the police of the color criterion to decide whether or not to "rough you up" makes it very difficult for Negroes to continue communicating with whites in Hunters Point. Very few community organizations are still func-

tioning. Even the long-existing Bayview Community Center now counts many pessimistic and cynical "time-servers" among its staff, and there is general feeling that it will soon close.

Very few people in Hunters Point now discuss the riots. Teen-agers and young adult males now believe more strongly that they are seen as truly dangerous. This desperately-wanted recognition has failed to remedy the causes of the feelings of inadequacy for which it compensates.

The white community has a fiction of its own for coping with this problem. Immediately after the riots, a consortium of local business leaders offered 2,000 jobs for Hunters Point youths, to try to alleviate the severe unemployment problem. The jobs were to be channeled through the Youth Opportunity Center. These promises of steady full-time or part-time work were made in October of 1966. By June 1967, 19 of these jobs had actually materialized.

As one of the staff at the Youth Opportunity Center indicated,

It is no longer possible to get the kids here to be enthusiastic about going for jobs—or waiting for all those jobs to come through. They just don't believe it will happen. They are right! After the first big rush of kids coming here for jobs after the riots, when no jobs happened, they just stopped coming. It's just as well; we don't have anything for them.

Probably the clearest aspect of the riot is that both black and white were and still are unable to see how deep are the disorders underlying this almost impotent attempt at self-assertion. Seriously in doubt of their own worth, and anyway denied the means of expressing it, young Negro men (and some women) in Hunters Point, without plan or forethought, drifted into an inept and inadequate revolt. At the same time, frightened beyond reason, perhaps through guilt, and certainly through their own paranoid projections and inadequate understanding of Hunters Point residents, the whites (police) underreacted, reacted wrongly, and finally overreacted to this confrontation.

Yet, there is something about the Hunters Point riots and white reaction to them that suggests that the United States had already institutionalized some method of handling these perceptions and misperceptions in symbolic form. Whites, on the whole, feel city-burnings to be too expensive to tolerate; Negroes generally seem to feel the danger of police reaction to be too dangerous to tolerate. Thus, both groups have compromised upon the "black militant aggressor" scenario as a substitute. In this scenario, young powerless Negroes are permitted the secondary rewards that riots give them. Permitted and indeed encouraged by whites to mouth revolutionary shibboleths, they are also allowed the *form* but not the *substance* of real manhood, independent thought, and revolutionary political action. Meanwhile, more quiescent Negroes are given the opportunity of either decrying this "violence" and supporting their own passive role or of saying "I told you so" and thus at a distance identifying with the militants and safely, though vicariously, "bugging whites."

Sympathetic whites are permitted the luxury of indulging bravado militants while avoiding any dramatic structural changes that would give substance to the form of black power. Unsympathetic whites are permitted anger, fear, and their own traditional paranoid concerns over "dangerous Negroes" and can view with alarm this formal rather than substantive militance.

Thus, the American game of black and white is played out. The perceptions and misperceptions of both races tend to stabilize race separation. Leakage out of this system is available only to a few "white" Negroes. Whites will fully integrate only nondangerous non-Negro Negroes.

A clear illustration of this is the increasingly prevalent belief among both black and white leaders that "separation" must precede "real integration." Black power separatism in this context is a "good thing," since only in "separation" can the black self-image improve. In fact, of course, Negroes and whites have *always* been separated in the United States. This "new" notion is surely no more than an attempt to formalize in the North what has always been true in the South. Until large numbers of Negroes began to live in the North, northerners could avoid dealing with their own racist feelings. Now, rather than face this racism openly and attempt to understand the cultural differences and psychological attitudes upon which this racism is based, whites are retreating from the problem by fostering separatism.

This, of course, fits the unconscious needs of some Negroes. Unable to "get into the game," except as white Negroes, many have taken on an outspoken "dangerous Negro" image. This helps overcome those feelings of inadequacy we have discussed. In this way, in an era of what appears to be very dynamic change in race relations in the United States, the status quo is actually maintained.

Hunters Point was early in the series of summer riots in the United States. The ones which followed became fiercer, partly because black youths felt that they had to do something "real bad to whitey" in order to feel more powerful, and partly because the white response came increasingly to be based on the "law and order" myth. If this chain reaction were to continue, then social catastrophe would certainly result. It would become plausible to predict full race war and concentration camps. But at any rate, the expected explosion in the cities in the summer of 1969 did not occur; and while militant blacks will no doubt develop more sophisticated techniques of action, it is likely that in the foreseeable future such action will remain symbolic. But if whites sustain their misperceptions and react without being aware of *what* black actions symbolize, then Americans can expect the worst.

Asen Balikci
Conflict and Society

Although most knowledgeable observers of the Eskimo people characterize them as generous, friendly, and generally optimistic in outlook, violence is by no means absent from their societies. The Netsilik, a Polar Eskimo people who live in one of the world's most inhospitable environments, today reveal one of the highest incidences of homicide (excluding infanticide) and suicide of any Eskimo society from Alaska to Greenland.

It is difficult to trace the causes of Netsilik violence and to determine what impact external influences have had upon their lives. However, the Netsilik case reveals the difficulty a people have in coping with environmental threat when they have only a simple social structure, a weak, almost anarchic, political organization, and no formal leadership roles. In other words, their situation approximates that of groups, such as the Gusii and the Teklum Maya described earlier in this section, whose capability of exercising control over conflict and disapproved aggressive behavior has been seriously weakened by external pressures.

Practically any minor or trivial event could produce a quarrel and lead to overtly aggressive behavior, the more so if personality factors provided a suitable setting for it. Though in this regard the Netsilik were no different from any other people, on some occasions they responded rather quickly to aggression, as the following cases illustrate.

Innakatar was an elderly woman with a little adopted girl and a grown-up son who was living as a second husband with a younger woman named Itiptaq in an adjoining igloo. One day Innakatar's little daughter pissed on Itaptaq's bed, wetting the sleeping skins. Itiptaq scolded the girl, who started crying. Her mother didn't like this and started a quarrel with the younger woman. Itiptaq lost her temper and Innakatar answered: "Don't scold my little girl, just come and fight with me." They started hitting each other on the face, just like men. Soon cuts and blood covered their faces as they fought noiselessly on. After a while Itiptaq said: "You are getting in a bad shape, bleeding a lot, I don't want to hit you any more" (meaning that Itiptaq was getting scared and in pain and wanted to find a way to give up the fight). Innakatar, feeling

strong, answered: "If I feel anything I will give up, just hit me a few more times." Innakatar was the obvious winner, though both of them were badly cut up around the face.

In another case, Itimangnerk and Utuytoq were joking partners and good friends. One day they were fishing salmon trout at Nuvuteroq on King William Island. They were using the special spring fishing technique which consisted of cutting two parallel rows of holes through the fjord ice and, with leisters in hand, running from one row to the other as a school of fish passed under. Utuytoq asked Itimangnerk to cut him a fresh fish to eat while he was running between the fishing holes. Itimangnerk, who was also hungry, cut up two fishes, one from his own and one from Utuytoq's. The latter thought that both fishes were from his own catch, and got angry for this very trivial reason. Itimangnerk thought that Utuytoq was only joking and laughed. Utuytoq took the argument seriously and hit Itimangnerk on the chest. A real fight followed, until they were separated by Mangalukut, who was fishing nearby.

Obviously quarrels of this sort could and did arise among the Netsilik at any time and apparently for most insignificant reasons. Though in many cases such quick explosions were probably the expression of already existing tensions, in other situations the reaction seems quite spontaneous. Almost always after the exchange of blows, however, peace was re-established and the enemies of a minute before parted good friends.

Mockery or derision was one behavioral trait among the Netsilik that frequently provoked resentment and hostilities. But derision was special because, while it caused resentment and anger, at the same time the threat of derision caused a fear of being laughed at and so it acted as a kind of control, keeping deviant behavior in check. The consequences of incessant mockery could lead to violent reactions, as ... in the case of Iksivalitak.... He killed Amarualik because the latter was constantly making fun of him. This was an unusually extreme reaction, however, and usually mockery provoked only a derisive answer from the other party; and any real enmity established most often found expression in fist fights or formal song duels. Excessive boasting was another form of indirect aggressive behavior. It was not really aimed at anyone in particular, but it diminished the social and manly importance of the others by enhancing one's own prestige.

Impinging upon sexual privileges, failure to give a girl promised for marriage, wife stealing, jealousies implicit in wife exchanging, ambiguities in polyandrous alignments—in sum, competition for sexual access to women in all its multiple forms—constituted another important factor leading to conflict. It is clear that the settings in which these jealousies and competitions arose depended on the highly variable total social situations. Other jealousies led also to strife. The more successful hunters were often surrounded by feelings of jealousy which were skillfully concealed and found expression in secretly performed sorcery. Fast kayakers were especially likely to be envied, and slower hunters used to throw evil spells on their kayaks. Many cases from the Netsilik area have been recorded illustrating these feelings of envy. The following was observed by Rasmussen:

An elderly man, Itqilik, discovered quite by chance that an old woman at the village had for a long time been stealing salmon from his son's catch and hiding the fish in a grave. She was jealous that his son was a better and luckier fisherman than her own, and so she was trying to kill him by magic; for it is believed that a man will quickly die if any of his hunting spoils come in contact with the dead or dead men's possessions. Yet all the time the old woman was plotting against the life of the young man, her relations with both him and his father were of the most cordial kind.[1]

According to recent observations it was during midwinter, when the people were most weary of the long nights and intense cold, that malicious backbiting was most frequent. One often heard then that such-and-such a neighbor always had more food, had caught more foxes, more bears, etc. Certain persons, particularly women, were naturally of a more jealous nature than others. They would keep quiet for long periods and then all of a sudden one night they would give free expression to their envy in front of some trusted person.

There is a general rule among the Netsilik and, as a matter of fact, among most Eskimo groups, that no undue appropriation of important natural resources should take place by individuals or families. People have the right to hunt wherever they wish and nobody is entitled to exclude others from a hunting area that he himself is using. Any infringement upon this basic rule is bound to provoke strong resentment and sometimes leads to strong reaction. The following case, which is probably legendary and impossible to date, illustrates this point.

An elderly man, N., used to camp alone with his wife and three grown-up sons at Oadliq, a crossing point for caribou west of Pelly Bay and an excellent hunting area. One day when N. was alone in his tent three hunters arrived there with their kayaks to catch caribou. They were coldly received by N., who told them: "Nobody should come here unless they want to look at the sky" ("looking at the sky," meaning to lie dead on the ground with the face turned up to the sky). The people said nothing, but went down to the lake shore where they waited until N.'s sons returned and then killed them. N. went insane with anger and ran about screaming, until the three hunters killed him also. After these murders the lake was open for hunting to everybody.

There is another general rule among the Netsilik according to which all able-bodied men should contribute to hunting, and the returns of the hunt should be shared according to established custom. Any activity in exception to this rule was bound to provoke criticism, various forms of conflict, and frequently social ostracism. Such an exception was the lazy hunter, whom the Netsilik called *nuniurut*. They were not usually less skillful than the others— on the contrary, some *nuniurut*, when necessity demanded, were very good in the chase—but they were incurably lazy. While the temporarily disabled hunter was generally helped with gifts of food, nobody liked sharing with the *nuniurut*.

Innaksak had a grown-up son by the name of Tutyaq who was married to the daughter of Kablalik. They all lived together with Tutyaq's grand-

---

[1] Knud Rasmussen, *The Netsilik Eskimos: Reports of the Fifth Thule Expedition.* Vol. VIII (Copenhagen, 1931), p. 200.

mother, an assertive woman well in control of food distribution in the large family. Kablalik was a stranger to the area, having come to live with the group when his daughter married Tutyaq. He was a lazy man, generally disliked and despised. His situation was aggravated by the fact that, being a stranger, he was ignorant of the local hunting grounds and had to depend closely on the others for whatever hunting he did do. Having established camp on the sea ice one evening, the women of the group separated from the men for the evening meal as custom demanded. Tutyaq invited Kablalik, who didn't have any food, to join Innaksak's igloo for a meal. Then Tutyaq went to visit his grandmother, who was with all the other women. The grandmother was furious when she learned that Tutyaq had invited Kablalik to eat, and in her rage she hit Tutyaq with her snow beater. She then went immediately to Innaksak's igloo and started quarreling with Kablalik. Innaksak remained passive until Tutyaq arrived on the scene, when his father started scolding him very sharply. Tutyaq attempted to answer but another older man stopped him and the quarrel finally died out.

It is evident from this case that lazy hunters were barely tolerated by the community. They were the objects of back biting and ostracism for a long time until the opportunity came for an open quarrel. Stingy men who shared in a niggardly manner were treated similarly. Sometimes the social position of a lazy hunter could save him from overt community hostility. Such was the case of Higak, a thief, incurably lazy, and a bad hunter besides because of his poor vision. He was avaricious and almost everybody hated him; but since he was a shaman, people feared his protective spirits and avoided hurting him, although nobody gave him any food. Higak eventually established a strange partnership with Krasovik, an excellent and highly successful hunter, in which Higak sent his protective spirits to help Krasovik hunt, in exchange for which Krasovik shared his catch with the shaman.

These were the most usual causes of conflict—mockery, jealousy, laziness, and minor misunderstandings. Once a conflict situation had been created and left unresolved, secondary causes for quarrels often arose. The social atmosphere of fear and suspicion previously described constituted an excellent ground for the seeds of hostility and persecution to grow in. This process was considerably aided by the Netsilik ability to conceal malicious intentions and hostile feelings in order to prevent possible reprisals by magic and sorcery. On the surface camp life proceeded smoothly, but hidden tensions were such that the slightest incident could set off aggression at any time. A traveler among the Arviligjuarmiut described the following situation to Steenhoven:

I. traveled on Kellett River together with A., S., and some others, who on their sleds had been visiting their caches. The weather was beautiful and we walked to and from each other's sleds, while the sleds were moving all the time. A. was seated on the back of S.'s sled and the latter sat in front of him. A. was eating a fish. I was driving my sled behind his. One moment when S. was turning towards his dogs or so, I saw A. suddenly make a lightning stab with his knife at S.'s back—a would-be stab, to be sure. Then he immediately looked around himself. But I looked already in another direction. S. is the son of I. and it was known that A. and I. did not get along well. It was my impression that this stab had been prompted by an altogether subconscious impulse and that A. only became aware of it after he had done it. I believe he could just as well have really stabbed S. out of these subconscious feelings of resentment.[2]

Theft, although cheerfully practiced in relation to strangers, practically never occurred among camp fellows. Household objects were few anyhow and their owners well known, which made theft in the camp virtually impossible to conceal. There are cases, however, of property destruction, obvious expressions of hatred. Two recent cases involving the destruction of another's cache were recorded by Steenhoven. The first case took place at Thom Bay, where two unrelated children had demolished the household cache of an absent family. Apparently this had been done because the owner of the cache had once refused food to the children's families when they were hungry. In the second case two related children totally destroyed the household cache of an elderly man during his absence from camp. The motive here seems to have been related to the jealousy the children's fathers were known to feel for the privileged position occupied by the victim in the community. In both cases

[2] Geert van den Steenhoven, *Legal Concepts Among the Netsilik Eskimos of Pelly Bay, N.W.T.* (Ottawa: Northern Co-ordinator and Research Centre, Department of Northern Affairs and National Resources, NCRC–59–3, 1959), p. 73.

children acted as their fathers' emissaries, allowing the adults to later disclaim any responsibility for the act.

Murder was the most extreme form of aggression among the Netsilik. It was committed in two ways: physically, by knife or gun, or supernaturally. Killing with magic was by no means the prerogative of shamans only. The Netsilik knew of a whole arsenal of aggressive magical techniques available to practically anybody. Many deaths were therefore attributed to revenge by evil spirits. Here we shall analyze only physical murder, as described by Steenhoven. The desire to steal a certain woman was the most frequent cause for attempted or successful murder. Ambivalences inherent in some polyandrous arrangements leading to murder would be included in this general category. Motives related to an individual's prestige in the community reflected by excessive mockery, bullying, or resentment constitute another category of causes for murder.

Among the seven relatively recent murder cases recorded by Steenhoven five contain information on the killing technique employed. Two men were shot from behind, apparently unaware of any plans afoot to kill them; one was shot while asleep; another was stabbed in the back with a knife while driving on a sledge; still another victim knew his murderer's intent yet did nothing to forestall it. It is remarkable indeed that all the men but one were killed from behind and by surprise. Murderers were evidently careful to avoid a struggle. Further, with one exception, all the murderers were men, although some might have been influenced by women. As for the exception, it was the woman Merkreaut, who shot her sleeping husband, apparently because she did not want to live with him any more.

With the probable exception of the murderess Merkreaut, all other six cases indicate that the decision to kill was slow and deliberate. The potential murderers waited for the appropriate moment to come, then killed with determination. The following case further illustrates the premeditated nature of most murders.

Ikpagittoq was married to Oksoangutaq's sister. They were Netsilik and in the spring they lived on the west coast of Pelly Bay, where they hunted seals. Not far from their camp lived Saojori, a particularly strong man from the Aivilik country, with his two wives. Saojori, although a stranger in this area, frequently boasted that he feared nobody and that no man would dare attack him. Ikpagittoq encouraged Oksoangutaq, who was single, to kill Saojori and take his wives. So one morning the two brothers-in-law walked to Saojori's tent and were told by his wives that Saojori was hunting seals. The two men went out and found Saojori on the ice at the very moment when he was about to catch a seal. Saojori guessed the evil intentions of his visitors, and so he held the seal with one hand and kept the other free to grab his knife if he needed to defend himself. The visitors apparently were very friendly and helped to drag the seal to the shore, where Saojori extracted the liver for a quick meal. Then he went down to the beach to wash his hands, still holding his knife between his teeth, ready for defense. As he knelt down at the water, Ikpagittoq attacked him from behind, trying to throw him to the ground. A struggle developed, while Oksoangutaq stood by watching until the embattled Ikpagittoq shouted at him, "You said you wanted to kill this man, what are you waiting for?" Oksoangutaq stepped up and pushed his knife into Saojori's neck, killing him on the spot. After the murder the two men went inland to hunt caribou; on returning home, they sent Oksoangutaq's sister to Saojori's tent to inform his two wives about the murder. One of the wives was very frightened and ran away with her child. Oksoangutaq had no trouble catching her, and made her his wife. This woman, being an Aivilik, some time later expressed a desire to return to her country and visit her parents. Oksoangutaq agreed. When they reached her father's igloo, she invited her new husband to come in. After some hesitation he walked in, holding his knife in hand. Apparently two Aivilik men had planned to kill him, but they didn't succeed; and Oksoangutaq returned safely to Pelly Bay.

Oksoangutaq's decision to kill was taken calmly, motivated by self-interest and executed at the appropriate moment. Strangely enough, in all the historical cases recorded not a single instance of successful physical revenge occurs, although intentions for revenge are clearly expressed by close relatives of the victim even years after the murder has taken place. There are, however, numerous cases of revenge by supernatural means, though the evil spell may take a long time, sometimes years, before reaching the culprit and accomplishing the original intention of revenge. No specification is made as to the nature of the murderer's death. He may drown, starve to death, or die from sickness; invariably his death is attributed to the spirits charged with the mission of bringing revenge.

The community, in reaction to an accomplished murder, appears on the surface to be remarkably calm and somewhat indifferent. Witness the affable reception of the murderer Oksoangutaq in Aivilik. It is, however, likely that this apparent indifference hides deeper feelings. Clearly the idea of revenge existed, not as an absolute obligation, but definitely as a possibility and a right, albeit a vague one. As an informant put it recently: "It takes away even one's sleep—this fear and tension because of possible revenge." And there was a special camp area, Fort Ross, extremely isolated in the northern part of Boothia Peninsula, where murderers fearing revenge often went to stay for a few years after the homicidal act, waiting for passions to calm down. Now, the community could not passively watch a murder followed by a revenge which in turn could provoke a third homicide and lead to a chain reaction. Every murder signified the loss of a highly needed seal hunter. The community had to intervene and did so. . . .

A stranger in the camp, particularly if he was traveling with his wife, could become easy prey to the local people. He might be killed by any camp fellow in need of a woman. In ancient times such assassinations led to the formation of revenge parties consisting of the relatives of the victim, resembling war expeditions. The following story was told recently by Irkrowaktoq, a middle-aged man from Pelly Bay; he affirmed that the case took place before the arrival of Sir John Ross's ship in the area.

Ugak was an elderly Netsilik who had land around Boothia Isthmus. He had three sons: Kujaqsaq, Anarvik, and Neruqalik. Around Pelly Bay there lived a group of Arvilik whose headman was Kukigak. His son was Anganuak. The feud seems to have started with the murder of old Ugak by Kukigak's people. The Netsilik were outraged, and they formed a revenge party which set off for Pelly Bay. They were known as excellent archers and practiced their marksmanship all the way along the road. As the Netsilik party approached Kukigak's hunting grounds, they saw his son Anganuak at a distance watching a breathing hole. They decided not to kill Anganuak, who then ran ahead to warn his camp. Kukigak immediately sent his two sons away in the opposite direction, toward the Aivilik country (presumably to escape death). When Kujaqsag reached Kukigak's camp he sent his mother ahead to tell the Arvilik people that his party had come to fight. The old woman did so and Kukigak answered: "They will not fight." The woman pointed out: "They have their weapons ready." Kukigak answered: "They will not use them." In spite of which both groups started preparing for the fight. Kukigak didn't have special weapons for fighting, so he got his caribou-hunting gear together. A young man originally from the Netsilik country had been living with the Aivilik, and Kukigak invited him to fight with them, but he refused to fight his relatives. The two groups lined up to face each other, and the first to fall was a sick Arvilik man who had a large opening on his clothing right in the middle of the chest. An arrow hit him there and he died immediately. Then Kujaqsaq saw his father-in-law in the Arvilik group. The old man cried: "I don't want to kill my son-in-law!" Kujaqsaq answered, "If you don't want me to kill you, then get out of the way." And the old man left the battleground. A massacre followed, many Arvilik men died, and Kukigak was mortally wounded. Dying, he said, "When we kill one man we don't kill any more, you people don't want to listen to us." Kujaqsaq answered: "I remember when you were ten men to kill my father, so don't say anything like that." Kukigak was then brought to his igloo, where Kujaqsaq's mother visited him, commenting: "What is wrong with the people, when they meet, they always fight." Kukigak asked one of his two wives to give the old woman a bag full of precious iron objects, possibly as a request for mercy. Kukigak's last wish was to be buried at Kangerk, in a big stone grave, and for all his people to play around it (meaning to camp in this same area, which would indicate that he had had an honorable death).

We have fragmentary information on smaller revenge parties that were formed in the general Netsilik area against the Aivilik and the Garry Lake people living inland. The degree of detail in some of this case material may reasonably be considered as historical truth. As Rasmussen remarked, the Eskimos pride themselves on good memories and are particularly trustworthy in storytelling. Consequently we can safely draw a certain number of conclusions. Physical revenge in traditional times did exist following the murder of defenseless strangers. The feuding groups were usually distantly located. The revenge party was organized by a headman (generally a close relative of the victim) and consisted of his kindred, organized as an action group. There was a formalized pattern for intergroup fighting, involving a messenger, preparations, distribution of the people in two rows facing each other, the choice of valuable opponents, preference given to bows and barbed arrows, etc. The objective of the revenge party was not just to kill the original murderer but members of his kindred as well. In a sense the members of the kindred shared responsibility for the murder.

Why then the absence of physical revenge in the recent historical cases described by Steenhoven? First, it seems that most of these murders involved camp fellows. In this instance, a community could not allow internal feuding, which could result in the loss of vitally needed seal hunters, leading to hardship for everyone in the group. Second, with the introduction of firearms, individual families could get by much more easily, and so the murderer could flee to Fort Ross and remain there for a prolonged period, thus escaping revenge. Third, by the early 1920s, the Royal Canadian Mounted Police had made their presence felt. The police discouraged feuding, and pursued the murderers themselves, often satisfying the desire for revenge in this way.

The Netsilik used various strategies to control or resolve conflict. These were either ambivalent and temporary or decisive and permanent. Gossip falls into the first group. My recent field observations indicate that every Netsilik individual was surrounded by a circle of gossipers who watched his behavior and were ready to comment on it. This undoubtedly helped to check deviancy. Yet it sometimes happened that a man was so provoked by malicious backbiting that he reacted aggressively, answering gossip with gossip or engaging in evil magic. In this case, the means that were supposed to check misbehavior just generated more trouble. Mockery and derision worked the same way. Fear of derision might have stopped an individual engaged in aggressive action, but if he was pushed too far, there was always the chance that he would retaliate and initiate a derisive action of his own, with dangerous consequences. This could also hold true for the fear of magic. Two men who were quarreling might stop short, each afraid that the other might become so angered he would

perform some secret act of aggressive sorcery. This same fear, however, might lead either party to assume that the other already had resorted to a magical attack of some sort, leading him to go ahead with magical activity of his own in retaliation. Thus fear of sorcery, instead of resolving the conflict, simply makes it covert.

The Netsilik knew of a number of rather formalized techniques for peacemaking that were positive in the sense that usually they brought conflict into the open and resolved it in a definitive manner. These techniques were fist fights, drum duels, and approved execution.

Any man could challenge another to a fist fight for any reason. Usually they stripped to the waist and the challenger received the first blow. Only one blow was given at a time, directed against temple or shoulder. Opponents stood without guard and took turns, the contest continuing until one of the fighters had had enough and gave up. This seemed to settle the quarrel, for, as one informant put it: "After the fight, it is all over; it was as if they had never fought before."

As well as its use in the wife-exchange practice, the song duel was a ritualized means of resolving any grudge two men might hold against each other. The songs were composed secretly and learned by the wives of the opponents. When ready, the whole group assembled in the ceremonial igloo, with a messenger finally inviting the duelists. As was the case with all drum dancing, each wife sang her husband's song in turn, while the latter danced and beat the drum in the middle of the floor, watched by the community. The audience took great interest in the performance, heartily joking and laughing at the drummers' efforts to crush each other by various accusations of incest, bestiality, murder, avarice, adultery, failure at hunting, being henpecked, lack of manly strength, etc. The opponents used all their wits and talent to win the approval of the assembly. Here is an example of a derisive song collected by Rasmussen:

A certain Ilukitsoq Arnarituat from Itivnarssuk (Back's River region) had in a song accused Nakasuk of being a poor hunter. Nakasuk, who is the leading man, whom everybody at the villages at Iluileq relies on, hits back by first ironically painting himself as a bad hunter, that his wife has to beg for food and clothing from her neighbours. Then he chastises and mocks his opponent for sexual excesses and impotence, and

concludes with a description of how he once, quite
alone and sitting on the ice, had held a bearded seal
on his harpoon line and killed it.

I will now put together
What is to be my song which nobody wants to sing
Thus—they were only pitiable
The women—these
Who on the neighbours had to run
Like women whom a provider were forced to lack.
This is what I would like to recall:
He it was—my big song-fellow
Because he tried to get at me.
He—my big song-fellow (Ilukitsoq)
Properly forestalling me—prating about everything
* he could think of*
Pattered out words—sang a song of derision
At the festival house here—by the side of it;
His eyes were not boldly raised—how was it he
* behaved?*
When I happened to hear about him—I almost
* made you better than you are*
For the sake of your helpfulness—once
I, who am not accustomed to help
Men—in the right way.
And so I think I now can answer
In the festival house's room
When I sing mockingly—when I doughtily begin to
* patter out the words*
I can usually answer—for I am one about whom
* nothing is heard*
As I am one devoid of anything untrustworthy.
What was it? On the sea's ice
For your daughter-in-law Teriarnaq—yonder
You conceived immoral desires
And yearned for her.
You are one with brief thoughts—and your
* thoughts never go to*
Your wife, poor Akta;
(Your penis) That, to be taken with the hand, that,
* fondly desired*
When it really felt a yearning it needed no help
And certainly, it could at that time—
But towards your wife—the desired one
You had to have help from Savinajuk—there,
Your great helping spirit there
He had to help you, when you were really going to;
When I heard this of you—I did not think of you as
* one*
I need fear!
But what was that? At Itivnarssuk over there on the
* land*

People say that your sister Inugpanguaq
On your way at night
Was felt by you, indeed, was squeezed by you!
When I heard that of you, I did not feel much
* inclined to remember you*
In that way—I used to look out for
Arnarituat from Winerfik's summit
I used to look out for him
And wished he would appear at last—through
Aimarqutaq bay there
On his way to our land—and not simply rest
* content with sending songs of derision*
To Imeriaq's bay—I tried to cross his path.
But I suppose you had no one to go with you—of
* kinsmen*
Or women who are pretty.
At Putuggut and Nuvavssuit islands
At Arfangnak islands and Umanaq's sound
A big bearded seal through its breathing hole I got
* hold of*
No hunting companion (was there) down there
It was Arnarituat's vainly tried for, that there
Which I got hold of there
Quite alone, sitting—out there![3]

Contests involving derisive songs constituted remarkable efforts to resolve conflict in several ways. First, this was a formalized procedure involving preparation and a controlled succession of actions. Apparently free rein was given to the expression of aggressive feelings, yet they have to be molded in verse form. Second, conflict is brought out into the open, with society present to act as arbiter. But society did not act as a judge, separating right from wrong or condemning culprits or absolving innocent individuals. Most of the derisive songs recorded by Rasmussen contained no reference to private grudges. It was rather the whole personalities of the opponents that were evaluated through their performances. The more biting and witty the song, the better was the reaction of the audience. Society stimulated the free expression of aggressive feelings. Song duels thus undoubtedly had a cathartic value for the individual opponents, and in this particular sense conflicts became "resolved." Sometimes one or both of the opponents at the end of a song duel continued to feel enmity. When this was the case, they often decided

[3] Rasmussen, pp. 342–345.

to resume fighting, this time with their fists. This definitely settled the matter.

Execution or approved homicide was another important technique used to control socially undesirable aggression. From time to time there was trouble with insanity, an individual starting to behave in an increasingly strange and dangerous manner, physically menacing and hitting other people. Or sometimes dangerous sorcerers became old and bitter, and took to performing malevolent magic against even their close relatives. These people seemed to hate everybody and to have no mercy even for children. Obviously they constituted a serious threat to the peace of the camp, and a stop had to be put to their vicious activities. Often shamans used their supernatural helpers to neutralize an evil sorcerer. There are two historic cases of approved physical execution. The first was recorded by both Rasmussen and Steenhoven. The latter version is more detailed and is reproduced below. The informant is Kringorn, born in 1905 and living at Pelly Bay:

Around 1922—I was about sixteen years of age—we were living in a large winter house near Lake Willerstedt. I recall the following camp members: my grandparents Aolajut and Kukiaut; their younger son Krimitsiark, who always accompanied his parents; their oldest son Kokonwatsiark; their younger sons Abloserdjuark and Arnaktark; Igjukrak, who was Aolajut's cousin and married to the latter's sister Nujakrit; Igjukrak's two sons-in-law Nerlongajok and Magnerk. All were accompanied by their wives and children. There were also non-relatives in the same camp, but I was early adopted by my grandparents. My father Kokonwatsiark (alias Ubloriaksugssuk) was the "oldest" of the camp. I was early adopted by my grandparents and I lived therefore under the supervision of my uncle Krimitsiark. It was around the darkest time of the year and the camp was preparing to move from the lake, where they had been fishing, on to the sea to hunt seal. The women were busy sewing clothing and thawing meat to be consumed during the journey.

Krimitsiark and Magnerk had already helped Arnaktark to pack forward some six miles, and Magnerk stayed with him there, so as to keep an eye on him; for Arnaktark had suffered the last months from psychic disturbances for the first time in his life. But after two days, Arnaktark disappeared and Magnerk set out to find him. But he failed to locate him and returned to the main camp to inform the family, upon which Kokonwatsiark and Abloserdjuark started searching, also without success. Shortly after, Arnaktark must have returned to his igloo and that same night he stabbed his wife Kakortingnerk in her stomach. She fled on foot with her child on her shoulders, and after arriving at the main camp she told what had happened.

They started to fear that he might stab again at someone they loved, and they discussed what should be done. The discussion was held among family, and it was felt that Arnaktark, because he had become a danger to them, should be killed. Kokonwatsiark said that he would carry out the verdict himself and the others agreed. Old father Aolajut was not supposed to do it, because Arnaktark was his own son; but if Kokonwatsiark for some reason would not have done it, the next oldest, Abloserdjuark, would have offered himself to do it. After the decision was taken, Kokonwatsiark notified the non-relatives, because they also were afraid. All agreed that there was no alternative.

Then the entire camp broke up: Aolajut, Kokonwatsiark, Abloserdjuark, Nerlongajok and Igjukrak traveled to Arnaktark's igloo, and Krimitsiark led the others and the women and children along another route to the new camp at the coast. Upon arrival at Arnaktark's place, the latter was standing outside, and Kokonwatsiark said to him: "Because you do not know very well any more (have lost control of your mind), I am going to 'have' you." Then he aimed at his heart and shot him through the chest. Then they moved on to join the others at the coast. His grave is yonder, towards the end of Willerstedt Lake.[4]

The second case was recorded both by Steenhoven and myself, though from different informants. My version is presented below. A few preliminary details had been already gathered by Rasmussen, who noticed that the old woman Krittark was heartlessly treated by her son-in-law Mikaluk (Arverk). She was poorly clad and often dragged behind when the sleds moved ahead. Apparently Mikaluk could not do better, since he had barely enough clothing skins for his wife and children.

According to my informant, Nakasuk was Krittark's daughter. Nakasuk had two co-husbands,

---

[4] Steenhoven, pp. 53–54.

the young Mikaluk and Tingerjak, who was older and had decided to leave the household to marry another woman. Krittark also had a son. Krittark literally hated everybody; she made trouble all the time, using her powers as a sorceress. She stabbed her own son with a knife through the wrist. She used to remove the amulets from the children's clothes for no apparent reason. Repeatedly she cut small pieces of fur from people's clothing and hid these in graves, trying to cripple them. Her daughter finally became frightened when she thought that her mother might bewitch her husband Mikaluk, and so she decided that Mikaluk should kill Krittark. It happened in winter during a migration. Krittark lagged a short distance behind, then sat down to rest, her back turned to the sled. At that very moment Nakasuk asked Mikaluk to kill the old woman, which he did, shooting her through the head. Krittark's spirit later became an evil ghost and tried repeatedly to take revenge and kill Nakasuk. Several years later Nakasuk saw a fish with a big head in a lake. She thought this was her mother's spirit bringing death to her, and she died a year later.

Both cases indicate that gratuitous aggressiveness and insanity could not be tolerated indefinitely. There came a point when drastic measures had to be taken, even if it meant execution. The fatal decision was taken informally within the circle of relatives present in the camp. It seems that non-relatives abstained from getting involved, and if the situation became too dangerous, they preferred to move away. The execution was always carried out by a close relative. This was considered a duty and had the advantage of avoiding any possibility of revenge. There were thus extreme instances when, in the absence of established courts and rigid judicial procedures, the kindred could act in an informal manner to judge and impose the death sentence when necessary. It should be emphasized, however, that the kindred's capacity to act as arbiter was applicable only to the most critical situations when camp peace could not be maintained by any other means.

There was one other very important strategy for conflict resolution or, better, for conflict avoidance. This strategy consisted simply of withdrawal. Whenever a situation came up in which an individual disliked somebody or a group of people in the band, he often pitched his tent or built his igloo at the opposite extremity of the camp or moved to another settlement altogether. This is common practice even today. A reading of the topographical distribution of the dwellings in a large camp reveals not only the alignments of kinsmen living close by, but also the affinities and hostilities of the camp fellows. People who like each other stay together, those who do not live apart. An additional detail is significant in this respect. If for any reason two families who are not on friendly terms have to camp close by, the openings of their dwellings will face in opposite directions, indicating that there is no intercourse between the two families. The opposite is true if the families like each other. Dwelling distribution therefore becomes a very good guide to the social preferences of a Netsilik community. As old quarrels are mended and new hostilities arise, fresh alignments emerge. It is by no means an uncommon sign to see a family pack its belongings and move from one part of the camp to another to adjust to its friendship alignments.

In dealing with aggression in the Netsilik community, the whole field of social control was characterized by flexibility. Highly variable personality and situational factors make it impossible to establish any arbitrary connections between wrongdoing and sanction. But this does not mean, as Steenhoven supposed, that "formal anarchy" prevailed. Netsilik society did have behavioral norms, mostly concerned with the broad interests of the community as a whole. There were definite obligations with regard to food procurement and food sharing. Freedom of access to important natural resources was also essential. When camp stability was endangered by individuals who disregarded these community interests, or upset the social balance by disruptive aggressive activity or by evil sorcery or insanity, the community did take action—even to the extreme of execution, if it was needed.

Bernard J. Siegel
Violence and Social Change

Not all civil violence is a product of social upheaval or change in the physical and social circumstances to which people had made more or less workable cultural adaptations. At what we may call the tribal level of organization, for example, agricultural and pastoral methods of producing food often brought into conflict groups competing for scarce resources. Hostilities and warfare therefore were not uncommon, although they were mitigated by the custom of marrying outside of one's closer kin and descent groups. Political allegiances among constituent tribal local groups were in any case weak, and security was gained primarily through one's kin. Because so many spouses came from groups that were potential enemies, one of the major concerns of the tribesmen was repairing the peace. In such situations, tensions between spouses are likely to be endemic. The Gusii of Kenya are a good example.

The Gusii case has implications of a more general theoretical nature. LeVine points out two sets of conditions—one spatial, the other relating to training and socialization—which regulate sexual intercourse. For the special cultural factors that govern relations among the Gusii clans we can substitute any other social, economic, and political processes that impede or facilitate interaction between the sexes at different ages. Similarly, we can observe the beliefs and practices involved in bringing up the young elsewhere, hypothesize the outcomes, and then test them in terms of their correlations with the varying factors.

LeVine also describes the importance of change in the environmental context (sometimes referred to as "the external system") of personal behavior, in this case the imposition of the Pax Britannica during colonial times in Kenya. What ensued was a removal of the barriers to contact between young unmarried males and females of different clans, coupled with residual feelings of anxiety and antagonism between the sexes. The result was a significant increase in rape. One might consider, in this light, the changing definitions of rape in our own society in the wake of much greater opportunities for premarital relations and of changing attitudes toward sexual expression among adolescents. Statutory rape laws (intercourse with a girl under the age of eighteen with or without consent) have become almost meaningless unless the act is initiated by a strange male.

Indeed, all the studies in this report on violence reveal that there is an increase in overt conflict and violence as a direct response to new environmental stresses which, by exacerbating the prevailing strains, tensions, and inconsistencies within a society, cause the means of regulating disputes to lose their effectiveness. Beal's data from India suggest that the forces which might generate open conflict by overriding the cooperative enterprises that suppress divisiveness arise in relation to the size of the population and the presence or absence of new external factors such as governmental officials or the opening of a mine. In a Maya Indian community of southern Mexico, June Nash informs us, competition for new forms of wealth and between traditional and new sources of power have eroded the people's confidence in nonviolent ways of controlling a conflict of interests. As a result, homicide has become a common way of handling disputes, "a way of life," and people are encouraged, for their own security, to stay at home at night, much as New Yorkers find that discretion is the better part of valor and do not walk the streets after dark. And the Maya Indians stay home for much the same reason— a loss of a faith in the institutions that control behavior that endangers others.

These and numerous other cases disclose one other important fact, namely, that while things may seem to fall apart, in the sense that life becomes increasingly unpredictable and dangerous, such a period appears to be a phase, a point in a trajectory of events over time. Those who live through this period experience great dissatisfaction with the state of their culture. At the same time one can take hope from the varied efforts that are being made—social movements, attempts to redefine or create a vigorous social identity, and so forth—to create a more satisfying society. Meanwhile the transition may involve many painful episodes.

The vast preponderance of change—technological innovation, for example—has occurred by other than violent means. However dramatic and pervasive revolutions are, violent transformations of a social order are rare. On the other hand, changes in the physical circumstances of group life commonly generate conflict or disorganization. We are especially aware of the dynamic role that warfare plays in industrialized states, not only as it stimulates technological innovation but also as it fosters the growth and specialization of bureaucracies, the destruction, consumption, and development of resources, the challenging of once cherished values, the forced migration, and so forth. Nevertheless, to concentrate on warfare as a prime mover or prime consequence of change, even in the modern world, would be to obscure the processes that operate more generally in this respect.

In what follows I want to attend briefly to a few, probably universal, conditions infusing the human condition that, in conjunction with each other, help explain a wide range of "troublesome" outcomes in the process of change. If we accept one of the most readily demonstrable axioms about culture, namely that the solution of social problems inevitably creates other problems—as our opening quotation from Margaret Mead implies—we shall be better able to seek and cope with the probable consequences of our actions and to pursue our long-range goals more successfully. We may also learn to think of all systems of belief and forms of society as simply points in time, of lesser or greater duration, in transition to something else. Neither do afflictions of the moment spell doom for all time, nor does a more equitable distribution of benefits create permanent utopias.

Strains Within Groups

Conventional solutions to the problems engendered by social life are never perfect. No matter how imperative that there be some regularity in human relations and in the commitment to the values that support them, they are never equally satisfying to all members of the group. The exercise of authority in all manner of situations, from the family to government, creates strains whatever form it takes. Even the egalitarian character of primitive bands involves conventions of sharing and subordination of individual to group welfare that is coercive for citizens in good standing. Some of the major strains among the Teklum Maya are reflected in the relations between victims and their murderers. In villages in India and at Hunters Point they lie elsewhere.

In all groups we may expect cleavages to occur at these points of strain. Destructive attacks against the person (including oneself—suicide) are a response to the feeling that external controls are useless or ineffectual in promoting one's own welfare. Riots are escalations of aggressive behavior that symbolize a general malaise at a given moment, and which occur when authoritative controls governing open conflict are disavowed or lacking. Under these circumstances, organizational forces cease to operate until the collective energy of the participants has been dissipated or controls have been reinstituted. Another response to the feeling that society is an ineffective or even helpful influence on one's life is to voluntarily remove oneself from one's own group and create a new lifestyle. Emigration, the hippie syndrome, and the youth culture are cases in point. Increases in destructive behavior—heavy drinking, murder, rape, arson, suicide—also bear witness to the increase in depth and breadth of these feelings. And such feelings themselves reflect the intensification of strains in conventional relationships and between conflicting beliefs and values.

A society and its culture cannot be understood simply as an inventory of its customs and members. Beliefs bear some relation to one another; groups and individuals act in terms of reciprocity and accommodation. Indeed, even technology does not consist simply of a set of tools and techniques but, more importantly, of the manner in which they mutually affect one another—who makes them, who has access to their use, how they affect the organization of activities. In this sense, all societies and cultures are integrated in one degree or another. Each custom serves to limit the forms that other customs may take. Each activity similarly limits the forms of an individual's participation in other activities.

But integration, like problem solving, is never perfect. It may include, or come to include, many inconsistencies and dissatisfactions. There are times when certain values or ideologies can provide a degree of balance, and the gains of abiding by them may make it possible to endure inherently tension-producing situations. Beals has described this situation in India. As circumstances change—as the size of the village and the number of competing landlords increases, for example—the balance is disturbed, and cleavages manifest themselves in frequent party conflicts. But despite the inherent inequalities of class and caste differences, of landlords, tenants, and farmers, most violent forms of conflict will soon be brought under control because people have agreed that is more satisfactory than undergoing continual attack and counterattack in the interim until a new state of affairs prevails.

External Change

Beginning with the cultivation of food products, human populations have so extensively altered the environments they exploited that the alterations themselves have profoundly affected subsequent adaptations. In time, the exploitation of resources led to efforts to control an ever greater number of differing environments, so that once rather self-sufficient societies became involved in complex interactions with others. Consider how, in varying ways, Indian villages depend upon other villagers and regional governments for their welfare. (As a more homely example, imagine the complex network of interdependent relations an American family requires to get food and set a meal on the table.)

Outside groups—other villagers, tribesmen, ethnic groups, nations—are the most important external stimulus for change. They suggest new alternatives and thus bring to the fore the strains within the group. Regularly recurring or established contacts require patterned accommodations for the use of resources. This has been accomplished in varied ways: trade, marriage exchanges, the enlargement of kin and political units, moving to other territories, emulating others, adopting more efficient techniques and struggling against attempted domination, and by yet other means.

Predatory expansion and conquest have led to complex political and social systems, especially under colonialism. The peace established by force, often for long periods of time, usually required the curtailment of customary activities. The results have been far-reaching; the Gusii of Kenya are only one example. The head tax imposed by the British in parts of colonial Africa, to give another example, impelled many able-bodied men to move considerable distances for varying periods of time in order to seek wage work. Although for some this was a welcome alternative to traditional occupations and responsibilities, the removal of a large segment of the vigorous population disrupted the agricultural production that depended upon their labor. Many young men who would have expected, as part of the bride-price, to labor for several years in the fields of their wives' parents were absent. Depleted of its most competent work force, village agriculture often languished. Conflicts over respective rights and duties erupted, and their resolution created extensive changes in local villages.

Economic factors that encourage the migration of young married couples can have the same effect as political factors. A comparison of contemporary marriage and family relations in central-north Italy and America reveals profound contrasts in such matters as the length of engagements, the exercise of parental authority, and the care of the aged. In all these respects the strain between the generations and among kinfolk are far less pronounced in Italy, where occupational opportunities tend to keep the majority of young adults near their parents and close relatives.

The termination of imperial controls in various parts of the world and the subsequent creation of new nations has imposed yet other demands for accommodation among native ethnic groups whose mutual antagonism had been suppressed. The civil war in Nigeria in 1970 was only one of several bloody conflicts that have erupted between ethnic groups that have struggled with each other for power. But such hostilities are not inevitable, nor are intertribal relations the only problems encountered in the Third World. The rapid growth of old and new cities has challenged immigrants from the villages. Social reorientation is demanded of them. They are required to learn values associated with new occupations (scheduling of time, for example); they have new needs; their political consciousness is awakened. An assortment of voluntary associations for meeting their needs has evolved, frequently in peaceful ways. These same associations, however, align individuals in conflicting camps and complicate the problems of peaceful governance. There is conflict, also, over duties felt toward or reaffirmed by village kinsmen.

Interaction of Internal and External Forces

The seeds of change and violence lie within and among the broad domains discussed above. No culture is static, although a small scale, relative isolation, and a simple technology impart to some societies a high degree of stability and equilibrium with nature. In the absence of knowledge about alternative ways of doing and thinking about things, individuals are most often persuaded to behave as they are expected to. The rearing they receive further disposes them to respond emotionally according to these expectations. The more limited their knowledge, the more their security hinges upon conventional responses which control conflict.

Nevertheless, internal tensions and external stresses inhere in group life. Certain members of any community, under a given set of conditions, will feel mounting dissatisfaction with the status quo. Natural increase of the population may produce this result; so may improved transportation and communication. More than one observer has commented that new roads have constituted a major catalyst for social change by bringing new alternatives to people's attention. Marked increases in personal violence form part of this process. Indeed, physical violence is a significant indicator of transition states. If we examine at a deeper level the events that led to the riot at Hunters Point, for example, we learn that what seems to be one among many urban regions in San Francisco is, in effect, an unorganized aggregate of people seeking more effective organized means for meeting their needs. Among the Netsilik Eskimo, Gusii, and Teklum Maya, a rather sudden rise in the incidence of violence reflects, on the other hand, the disorganization of groups that once expressed a relatively strong sense of community. In certain contexts, groups of citizens may employ violence as a deliberate instrument of social policy. In other contexts these same kinds of groups will assert a strong positive sense of identity around emotionally charged symbols (religious, ethnic, or racial, for example) in an essentially defensive and nonviolent manner. In the United States, the Black Muslims, certain American Indian tribes, and the Mennonites are cases in point. All of these modes of adaptation to changing external conditions are responses to the need for greater social organization when that organization is threatened, weakened, or ineffective in enabling citizens to achieve what they consider to be a satisfactory way of life.

Since culture depends upon communication, perhaps the single most important product of the technological revolution of our time is the tremendous increase in the frequency of communication of the diverse peoples of the world. Everywhere individuals must respond to a fantastic volume of unceasing messages—messages which have sometimes aroused people to new possibilities but which have more often brought to the surface potential cleavages within and between groups. For some time, then, until parties to conflict accept common agents of control, dispute will be unusually frequent and poorly regulated. Some groups, weak in relation to the dominant social forces, can still muster sufficient leadership to close ranks. They reduce conflict by controlling the messages available to members, thus isolating themselves despite the breakdown of environmental barriers to communication. The result is not so much the development of a world community and a world culture as it is a forceful pride in difference. The challenge of our own time thus lies in the mutual accommodation of differences within a framework of striving for ever more satisfying modes of cultural adaptation.

The studies reported in this section have depicted commonly recurring periods in the life of diverse societies, when conflicts about ends and means override consensus and render the regulation of dispute temporarily ineffectual. The general conditions that lead to a resort to violence as a solution of conflict cut across cultural boundaries. The experiences of others, therefore, should help us better understand our own in this respect. They should, in the final analysis, invoke an optimistic view, not because life is without struggle, but precisely because many forms of physical violence are indicators of efforts to achieve more satisfactory forms of cultural adaptation.

8 Our Troubled Environment

Michael H. Crawford
Our Troubled Environment

Isaac Asimov
The End

Estie Stoll
Crowding

Stanley Milgram
The Experience of Living in Cities

Barry Commoner, Michael Corr, and Paul J. Stamler
The Causes of Pollution

James V. Neel
Lessons from a "Primitive" People

Carl Jay Bajema
The Genetic Implications of Population Control

Michael H. Crawford
Some Environmental Problems for Physical Anthropologists

The great question of the '70s is: Shall we surrender to our surroundings or shall we make peace with nature and begin to make reparations for the damage we have done to our air, to our land, and to our water?   Richard M. Nixon

If nothing is done and present trends continue, there is serious danger that famine, which has already taken hold in India in 1966, will spread over most of the Third World. After India, the most vulnerable areas are East Pakistan, Java, Egypt (where there is starvation already), the Maghreb (the North African countries), the Middle East, the Sahel of the Western Sahara (where harvests are scanty), and the Andes from Chile to Mexico; and after that the Caribbean, the Sertao (Northeast) of Brazil, and perhaps even Anatolia in Turkey.   René Dumont and Bernard Rosier

Are we selecting for genetic types only those who can satisfy their aesthetic needs in congested cities? Are the Davy Crocketts and Kit Carsons who are born today being destined for asylums, jails, or suicide?   La Monte Cole

Michael H. Crawford

Our Troubled Environment

Virtually no one living in industrial societies today has escaped the discomforts associated with overcrowding and pollution—the favorite beach which is condemned as unsafe, the strong chlorine taste of tap water, the seeming omnipresence of crowds of strangers and strange noises, the foul-smelling air which has become a permanent condition. It is not necessary to read the newspapers to be convinced of our environmental crisis. Unless it is resolved there is a strong likelihood of the extinction of the human species.

The topic is so vast that it is not possible to cover it exhaustively within this section, or indeed in a single volume, and we have therefore selected six articles on critical ecological problems which face us today. Out of the welter of issues which urgently besiege us, we have chosen three broad areas: overpopulation, pollution, and aggression.

Overpopulation

What was once mentioned by Malthus and discussed by a few intellectuals has become a crusade. One reason for the slowness with which overpopulation has emerged as one of man's greatest problems is that, until the beginning of the industrial revolution, the world population was increasing slightly because of the high rate of mortality. Then, with medical and sanitary progress and the eradication of many infectious diseases, there was a reduction in mortality,

resulting in a very rapid increase in the world population to the present level of approximately 3.5 billion. At current rates of increase, the figure is expected to double by the year 2000. According to Paul Ehrlich, even the present world population is five times too large, so that the environment is "over-stretched," and a future increase to seven billion persons may result in mass starvation, epidemics, and war.

"Notice that people don't smile at us the way they used to?"

David Harbaugh

Pollution

While some people blame pollution almost entirely upon overpopulation, others suggest that technological developments are equally to blame. They argue that even with the arrest of population increase and with stable consumption, environmental degradation will persist.

Technological developments are exploited by Madison Avenue advertisers, who mold public attitudes through saturation advertising and who have been accused, by Philip Abelson among others, of sabotaging environmental reform efforts. In a recent press release, Stewart Udall and Jeff Stansbury concluded that "our cities, rivers, and air have gone sour on us partly because we sat ga-ga before our TV sets and soaked up the huckster's pitch that happiness is a non-return six pack."

The dangers of environmental pollution first became obvious to many in the 1940s and 1950s, when increases in radioactivity were detected after nuclear testing. The movement to ban nuclear testing was given further impetus when measurable increases in the level of strontium-90—a radioactive element, chemically similar to calcium, which is concentrated in bone and is thought to lead to the development of leukemia—were detected in the milk consumed by American children. Recently, Ernst Sternglass has proposed that fallout from atmospheric tests of nuclear explosives is responsible for an appreciable fraction of the fetal and infant mortality in this country, basing his statement on an analysis of patterns in infant and fetal mortality across the United States which correlated with levels of fallout. The extent of the mortality has been questioned, but it indeed appears that increases in radiation do result in elevations of infant and fetal mortality. The primary hazard, however, is that the incidence of chromosomal breakages and mutations is also associated with increases in the dosage of radiation. Since mutations provide the raw material for the action of natural selection, increases in mutation rates are of the utmost significance.

Air pollution knows no boundaries, but is most dangerous and distasteful in cities, where human populations and industry converge. In addition to the discomfort it creates, air pollution has been shown by the World Health Organization to be harmful to health. Automobile exhaust emissions are particularly harmful to persons with upper respiratory sensitivities and diseases, such as asthma, bronchitis, and emphysema. Several hydrocarbons which are present in the atmosphere are known to be carcinogenic, although the concentrations necessary to produce cancer of the lungs are unknown.

Another probable effect of continual and massive utilization of fossil fuels for energy is the liberation of large quantities of carbon dioxide into the atmosphere, thus raising the earth's surface temperature. Also contributing to the buildup of carbon dioxide levels and of cloud cover are the emissions of jet planes, which release more than a ton of water when burning one ton of jet fuel.

In the last few years, the discovery that mercury pollutants have entered the food chain of man has caused much concern. Mercury pollution has reached dangerous levels in certain regions of the United States. Among the many warnings that have been issued, for example, is one from public health officials to pregnant women not to eat fish caught in the San Francisco Bay Delta. Methyl mercury is bound to protein, forming a stable molecule which remains in fish for several years. Mercury concentrations in fish are approximately 5000 times the concentrations found in surrounding water. When contaminated fish have been eaten in large amounts, mercury is absorbed into the intestine and transported throughout the human body. It tends to concentrate in the cerebellum, the calcarine fissure of the visual cortex; lesser amounts may diffuse into the frontal lobe. Methyl mercury interferes with cellular division and is believed to cause chromosomal abnormalities, but the chief danger is that high concentrations in the brain may result in disorders of vision, balance, and personality—as they did in the hat-making centers of America, where the workers absorbed some of the mercury they used in making the hats. Now, a half century after the discovery that madness was an occupational disease among Danbury's hatters, it has been estimated that American industry is losing as much as fifty pounds of mercury a day.

At one time, many of the pollutants that we now damn served useful functions. DDT, which helped eliminate malaria through programs of spraying, has only recently been found to be toxic to man—causing cirrhosis of the liver and brain damage at high concentrations. And the buildup of toxic pesticides disrupts the ecological balance of other species because the reduction of one species of pest may be accompanied by damage to a predator population which in turn permits the proliferation of new pests. The dilemma of this ecological relationship between species and the environment has been summarized by Barry Commoner: "There is no such thing as a free lunch; everything is connected with everything else; everything goes somewhere."

Besides the chemical pollution of the environment, people are faced with a barrage of extraneous sensory stimuli which might be called "sensory pollution." The city dweller, in particular, experiences a wide range of such stimuli, from the blaring of automobile horns to the multi-colored, flashing neon lights, to the pungent odor of barbecued chicken emanating from a little restaurant down the block. The distinctiveness of urban life is not the presence of any one of these pollutants, but the simultaneous assault of all of them on the senses and, ultimately, the brain.

Aggression

There are two schools of thought about the biological and evolutionary origins of aggression. The first, based on the writings of Konrad Lorenz and popularized by Robert Ardrey, contends that man is inherently an aggressive animal and that aggression was transmitted to him by his hominoid ancestors. Ardrey, in particular, presents early man as a fearless hunter-killer, with a propensity for aggression.

According to the second school of thought, aggression is not considered to be innate or under genetic control but, instead, a response to a particular stress. In discussing the possible connections between stress and violence, W. M. S. and C. Russell have said:

Every [technological] advance, changing the relationship between human societies and their natural surroundings and resources, has made possible an increase in population. As a result man has been under virtually continuous social inequality, tension, and violence. Hence some people have supposed that these evils are the normal, inherent lot or nature of man.[1]

[1] *New York Times*, August 16, 1970, p. 53.

"The air I breathe is filthy, my food is poisoned, my automobile is a gas-guzzling behemoth, my school taxes have doubled, the Internal Revenue Service plans to take the fillings out of my teeth, my wife is fifty-three and pregnant, my dog bit a lawyer's kid, my son steals, my mother-in-law is a Communist, my daughter ran off with a fink, and now you tell me that if I don't back up and let you have the right-of-way I'll be in trouble."

Drawing by Booth; © 1972 The New Yorker Magazine, Inc.

The Russells have termed this condition the "Sardine Syndrome," and they point out that, historically, whenever technologically advanced populations have become short of natural resources they have entered a population crisis, resulting in violence and stress. Now, Paul Ehrlich, in an interview in *Playboy*, has said that the world's oil reserves are nearing deple-tion and will be consumed within a hundred years. Natural sources of minerals such as lead, tin, zinc, copper, and nickel are expected to disappear within the next two hundred years. In the light of such predictions, the Russells' analysis portends large-scale warfare and, possibly, a nuclear holocaust.

Isaac Asimov
The End

There are two views on the gravity of our ecological crisis. Some scientists, such as René Dubos, are optimistic and believe that nature will spring back from our abuses. Others take a more pessimistic view and argue that it is too late to reverse the damage to our ecology and that mankind is doomed to extinction. Asimov can be placed with the latter group. Asimov refutes the arguments of the optimists who contend that modern science and technology will continue to increase food production and find new food sources to accommodate a population of several times the present rate, documenting with horrifying clarity the imminent doom. Unfortunately, his view may be the one closer to reality.

Among other things, I am a prophet by profession. That is, I predict the future and get paid for doing so. There is a catch, of course: I don't cheat, so there is a sharp limit to my usefulness. Since I make no passes over a crystal ball, lack the services of a henchman in the spirit world, have no talent for receiving revelation, and am utterly free of mystic intuition, I can't tell anyone which horse will win the Derby, or whether his wife is cheating on him, or how long he will live.

All I can do is look at the world as steadily as possible (a difficult enough task these days), try to estimate what is happening, and then make the basic assumption that whatever is happening will continue to happen. Once that is done, I can make very limited predictions. I can tell you, for instance, about when the Derby will no longer be run at all, about when it will cease to matter whether any-one's wife is cheating on him, and, most of all, how long all of us (with perhaps inconsiderable exceptions) are going to live.

For instance, I look at the world today and I see people, lots of them. Concerning these people, there are two things to say: (1) there are more people now than have ever before existed at any one time, and (2) these people are increasing in numbers at a faster rate now than ever before in history.

Just as an example, in the time of Julius Caesar the total number of people on earth was probably something like 150,000,000 and the world population was increasing at the rate of perhaps 0.07 percent per year (100,000 per year). Latest estimates put the population at 3,650,000,000, or 24 times what it was in Caesar's time, and it is increasing at a rate of nearly 2 percent per year, 30 times the ancient rate. The earth is now gaining people at a rate of 70,000,000 a year so that *it takes us only two years to add to the population a number equal to all those who lived on the planet in the palmy days of Rome.*

The question is: What does this mean for the future?

The doom-cryers, of whom I am one, cry "Doom!" The optimists, on the other hand, talk about modern science and the utilization of hybrid grain and fertilizers. They talk of distilling the ocean for fresh water, of fusion energy, and of the colonization of other planets. Well, why not? Let's grant everything the optimists want and take a look at some figures.

If we accept 3,650,000,000 as the population of the earth today and allow an average of 100 pounds per person (some are small, some are children) then the total mass of human flesh and blood is equal, at present, to about 180,000,000 tons. It is also estimated that the number of people on earth (and therefore the mass of human flesh and blood) is increasing at a rate that will cause it to double in 35 years. Let me then introduce a mathematical equation—not because any of you absolutely need it but because, without it, I will be accused of pulling figures out of a hat. The equation is:

$$(180,000,000)\ 2^{x/35} = y\ (\textit{Equation 1})$$

This equation will tell us the number of years, x, it will take to reach a mass of human flesh and blood equal to y, if we start with earth's present population and double it every 35 years. To make the equation easier to handle we can solve for x and we get:

$$x = 115\ (\log y - 8.25)\ (\textit{Equation 2})$$

Using this second equation, we can ask ourselves the following question: How many years will it take to increase our numbers to the point where the total mass of humanity equals the total mass of the Universe?

I introduce this question because I assume that no optimist will ever dream of arguing that man can possibly reach this point, so that it will represent an ultimate limit beyond cavil. It may be, of course, that the time it will take to achieve this fantastic end is so long (trillions of years, do you suppose?) that there is no point in discussing it. Well, let's see . . .

The universe consists (as a rough estimate) of 100 billion galaxies, each one containing 100 billion stars about the size of our own sun, on average. The mass of the sun is about 2.2 billion billion tons, so the mass of the known universe in tons (throwing in some extra mass to allow for

"The End" by Isaac Asimov from *Penthouse* (January, 1971). Reprinted by permission of the author.

planets, interstellar dust, and so on) is perhaps the figure 3 followed by 50 zeroes (or 3×10^{50} in mathematical lingo). If we set this equal to y in equation 2, then log y is equal to 50.48. Subtract 8.25 from this and multiply the difference by 115 and we find x is equal to 4.856.

So, at the present rate of increase in human population, the mass of humanity will equal the mass of the known universe in 4,856 years. By 6826 A.D. we shall reach absolute dead end.

A period of 4,856 years is long, certainly, in comparison to an individual life, but if it takes only that much time to run out of universe (rather than the trillions of years that might have been suspected) then there has to be the queasy feeling that the actual limit will come sooner. After all, even the most starry-eyed idealist wouldn't think we could colonize all the planets of all the stars of all the galaxies . . . let alone convert the stars themselves into food—all in the next few thousand years.

Actually, during that period, we are almost certain to be confined to the planet earth. Even if we colonize the rest of the solar system, it is beyond hope that we can transfer sizable portions of the human population to such forbidding worlds as the Moon and Mars. So suppose we ask ourselves how long will it take (at the present rate of human increase) for mankind to attain a mass equal to no more than that of our own planet. The earth's mass is 6,600 billion billion tons, and if that is taken as y, then log y is 21.82. Throwing that into the equation, we find that x equals 1,560.

In 1,560 years, at the present rate of increase—that is, by 3530 A.D.—the mass of humanity will be equal to the mass of the earth. Will any optimist in the audience raise his hand if he thinks that mankind can possibly achieve this in any circumstances?

Let's search for a more realistic limit, then. The total mass of living tissue on earth today is estimated to be something like 20 million million tons, and this cannot really increase as long as the basic energy source for life is sunlight. Only so much sunlight reaches earth; only so much sunlight can be used in photosynthesis; and therefore only so much living plant tissue can be built up each year. The amount built up is balanced by the amount destroyed each year, either through spontaneous death or through consumption by animal life.

Animal life may be roughly estimated as one-tenth the mass of plant life or about two million

tons the world over. This cannot increase either, for if, for any reason, the total mass of animal life were to increase significantly, the mass of plants would be consumed faster than it could be replaced, as long as sunlight is only what it is. The food supply would decrease drastically and animals would die of starvation in sufficient numbers to reduce them to their proper level.

To be sure, the total mass of *human* life has been increasing throughout history, but only at the expense of other forms of animal life. Every additional ton of humanity has meant, as a matter of absolute necessity, one less ton of nonhuman animal life.

Not only that, but the greater the number of human beings, the greater the mass of plants that must be grown for human consumption as food (either directly, or indirectly by feeding animals destined for the butcher) or for other reasons. The greater the mass of grains, fruits, vegetables, and fibers grown, the smaller the mass of other plants on the face of the earth.

Suppose we ask, then, how many years it will take for mankind to increase in numbers to the point where the mass of humanity is equal to the present mass of all animal life? Remember that when that happens there will be no other animals left—no elephants or lions, no cattle or horses, no cats or dogs, no rats or mice, no trout or crabs, no flies or fleas.

Furthermore to feed that mass of humanity, all the present mass of plant life must be in a form edible to man; which means no shade trees, no grass, no roses. We couldn't afford fruits or nuts because the rest of the tree would be inedible. Even grain would be uneconomic, for what would we do with the stalks? We would most likely be forced to feed on the only plants that are totally nutritious and require only sunlight and inorganic matter for rapid growth—the one-celled plants called algae.

Well, then, if the total mass of animal life is two million million tons, log y equals 12.30 and x works out to 466. This means that by 2436 A.D. the last animal (other than man) will have died, and the last plant (other than algae) will also have died.

By 2436 A.D. the number of human beings on earth will be 40 trillion or over 8,000 times the present number. The total surface of the earth is equal to about 200,000,000 square miles, which means that by 2436 A.D. the average density of the human population will be 200,000 per square mile.

Compare this with the present density of Manhattan at noon—which is 100,000 per square mile. By 2436 A.D. even if mankind is spread out evenly over every part of the earth—Greenland, the Himalayas, the Sahara, the Antarctic—the density of population will be twice as high *everywhere* as it is in Manhattan now.

Imagine a huge world-girdling complex of high-rise apartments (over both land *and* sea) for housing, for offices, for industry. The roof of this complex would be given over entirely to algae tanks containing an ocean of water, literally, and 20 million million tons of algae. At periodic intervals there would be conduits down which water and algae would pour to be separated; with the algae dried, treated, and prepared for food, the water would be returned to the tanks above. Other conduits, leading upward, would bring up the raw minerals needed for algae growth, consisting of (what else?) human wastes and finely chopped up human corpses.

Even this limit, quite modest compared to the earlier suggestions of allowing the human race to multiply till its mass equalled that of the universe or merely that of the earth, is quite unbearable. Where would we find any optimist so dead to reality as to believe that in a space of four and a half centuries, we can build a planetary city twice as densely populated as Manhattan?

To be sure, all this is based on the assumption that the increase in human population will continue at its present rate indefinitely. Clearly, it won't. Something will happen to slow that growth, bring it to an utter halt, even reverse it and allow the human race to decrease in numbers once more. The only question is what that something will be.

To any person surely the safest way of bringing this about would seem to be a worldwide program for voluntary limitation of births; with the enthusiastic participation of humanity as a whole. Failing this, the same result will inevitably be brought about by an increase in the death rate—through famine, for instance. The question is: How much time do we have to persuade the people of earth to limit their births?

Anyone can see that global birth control will not be achieved easily. There are stumbling blocks. There are important religious bodies who object strongly to the utilization of sex for pleasure rather than for progeny. There are long-standing socio-logical traditions that equate many children with strong national defense, with help around the farm and home, with security in parental old age. There are long-standing psychological factors which equate many children with a demonstration of masculine virility and wifely duty. There are new nationalist factors which cause minority groups to view birth control as a device to limit *their* numbers in particular, and to view unlimited births as a method for outbreeding the establishment and "taking over."

So how much time do we have to counter all this?

If it were a matter of population alone, we might argue that even if things went on exactly as they are science would keep us going for 466 years anyway, till man was the only form of animal life left on earth. Unfortunately, it isn't a matter of population alone. Take energy, for instance. Mankind has been using energy at a greater and greater rate throughout his existence. Partly this reflects the steady increase in his numbers; but partly this also reflects the advance in the level of human technology. The discovery of fire, the development of metallurgy, the invention of the steam engine, of the internal combustion engine, the electric generator, all meant sharp increases in the rate of energy utilization beyond what could be accounted for by the increase in man's numbers alone. At present, the total rate of energy utilization by mankind is doubling every 15 years, and we might reasonably ask how long that can continue.

Mankind is currently using energy, it is estimated, at the rate of 20,000,000,000,000,000,000,000 (twenty billion billion) calories per year. To avoid dealing with too many zeroes, we can define this quantity as one "annual energy unit" and abbreviate that as AEU. In other words, we will say that mankind is using energy now at the rate of 1 AEU a year. Allowing a doubling every 15 years and using an equation similar to that of Equation 2 (which I will not plague you with, for by now you have the idea) you can calculate the rate of energy utilization in any given year and the total utilization up to that year.

Right now, the major portion of our energy comes from the burning of fossil fuels (coal, oil, and gas) which have been gradually formed over hundreds of millions of years. There is a fixed quantity of these and they cannot be re-formed in any reasonable time. The total quantity of fossil fuels thought to be stored in the earth's crust will liberate about 7500 AEU when burned. Not all that quantity of fuel can be dug out of the earth. Some of it is so deep or so widely dispersed that more energy must be expended to get it than would be obtained from it. We might estimate the energy of the recoverable fossil fuels to be about 1000 AEU.

If that 1000 AEU of fossil is all we will have as an energy source, then, at the present increase of energy utilization, we will have used it up completely in 135 years; that is, by 2105 A.D. If we suppose that those reserves of fossil fuel which seem unrecoverable now will become recoverable in the next century or so then that will give us about 45 years more at the ever increasing rate and we will have till 2150 A.D.

Of course, it is not fossil fuels only that we can work with. There is energy to be derived from nuclear fission of uranium and thorium. The total energy from recoverable fission fuel is uncertain but it may be 100 times as great as that from fossil fuels, and that will give us 135 years more and carry us to 2285 A.D.

In other words, in 315 years, or a century and a half *before* we have reached the ridiculous population limit of having mankind the only form of animal life, we will have utterly run out of the major energy sources we use today—assuming things continue as they are going.

Are there other sources? There is sunlight which brings earth 60,000 AEU per year, but we'll need that for the algae tanks. There is fusion power, the energy derived from the conversion of the heavy hydrogen atoms (deuterium) of the oceans to helium. If all the deuterium of the ocean were fused, the energy released would be equal to 500,000,000,000 AEU, enough to keep us going comfortably, even at an endlessly accelerating rate, to a time well past the population limit of the planetary double-Manhattan. (It will bring about a problem as to what to do with all the heat that will be developed—thermal pollution—but there are earlier worries.)

Energy will not be the real limit of mankind, *if* we can harness controlled fusion in massive quantities. We haven't done it yet, but we're on the trail and presumably will do it eventually. The question now is: How much time do we have to make fusion possible, practical, and massive?

We ought to do it before our supply of fossil and fission fuels gives out, obviously, and that means we will have 315 years at most (unless we manage to limit population and energy utilization before then).

That sounds like time enough, but wait. The utilization of energy is inevitably accompanied by pollution, and the deterioration of the environment through a rate of pollution that will double every 15 years may bring a limit much sooner than that imposed by the disappearance of energy sources.

But we want to deal only with the inevitable. Suppose we bring pollution under control. Suppose we block the effluent of chemical industries, control smoke, eliminate the sulphur in smoke and the lead in gasoline, make use of degradable plastics, convert garbage into fertilizer, and mine for raw materials. What then? Is there any pollution that cannot possibly be controlled?

Well, as long as we burn fossil fuels (and only so can we get energy out of them) we must produce carbon dioxide. At the moment, we are adding about 8 billion tons of carbon dioxide to the atmosphere each year by burning fossil fuels. This doesn't seem like much when you consider that the total amount of carbon dioxide in the atmosphere is about 2,280 billion tons or nearly 300 times the quantity we are adding per year.

However, by the time all our fossil fuel is gone, in 2150 A.D., we will have added a total of 60,000 billion tons of carbon dioxide to the atmosphere, or better than 25 times the total quantity now present in the air. A little of this added supply might be dissolved in the oceans, absorbed by chemicals in the soil, taken up by a faster-growing plant life. Most, however, would remain in the atmosphere.

By 2150 A.D., then, the percentage of carbon dioxide in the air would rise from the present 0.04 percent to somewhere in the neighborhood of 1 percent. (The oxygen content, 500 times the carbon dioxide, would be scarcely affected by this change alone.)

This higher percentage of carbon dioxide would not be enough to asphyxiate us, but it wouldn't have to. Carbon dioxide is responsible for what is called the "greenhouse effect." It is transparent to the short waves of sunlight, but relatively opaque to the longer waves of infrared. Sunlight passes through the atmosphere, reaches the surface of the earth and heats it. At night, the earth reradiates heat as infrared and this has trouble getting past the carbon dioxide. The earth therefore remains warmer than it would be if there were no carbon dioxide at all in the atmosphere.

If the present carbon dioxide content of the atmosphere were merely to double, the average temperature of the earth would increase by 3.6°C. We might be able to stand the warmer summers and the milder winters but what of the ice-caps on Greenland and Antarctica? At the higher temperatures, the ice-caps would lose more ice in the summer than they would regain in the winter. They would begin to melt year by year at an accelerating pace and the sea-level would inexorably rise. By the time all the ice-caps were melted, the sea-level would be at least 200 feet higher than it is and the ocean, at low tide, would lap about the 20th floor of the Empire State Building. All the lowlands of Earth, containing its most desirable farmland and its densest load of population would be covered by the rolling waters.

At the rate at which fossil fuels are being increasingly used now, the ice-caps will be melting rapidly about a century from now. To prevent this, we might make every effort to switch from fossil fuel to fission fuel, but in doing that, we would be producing radioactive ash in enormous quantities and that would present an even greater and more dangerous problem than carbon dioxide would.

The outside limit of safety, thanks to pollution, no matter *what* we do (short of limiting population and energy consumption) is only 100 years from now. Unless we develop massive fusion power by 2070, the face of the earth will be irremediably changed, with enormous damage to mankind.

But do we even have that century in which to maneuver if we don't limit population? It is not just that population is increasing, but that it is growing even more unbalanced. It is the cities, the metropolitan agglomerates, that are increasing their loads of humanity, while the rural areas are, if anything, actually decreasing in population. This is most marked in the industrialized and "advanced" areas of the world, but it is making itself felt everywhere, with increasing force, as the decades slip by.

It is estimated that the urban population of the earth is doubling not every 35 years, but every *eleven* years. By 2005 A.D. when the earth's total population will have doubled, the metropolitan population will have increased over ninefold.

This is serious. We are already witnessing a breakdown in the social structure; a breakdown that is concentrated most strongly in just those advanced nations where urbanization is most apparent. Within those nations, it is concentrated most in the cities, and, in particular, in the most crowded portions of those cities.

There is no question but that when living beings are crowded beyond a certain point, many forms of pathological behavior become manifest. This has been found to be true in laboratory experiments on rats, and the newspaper and our own experience should convince us that this is true for human beings also.

Population has been increasing as long as the human race has existed, but never at the present rate, and never under conditions of such fullness-of-earth. In past generations, when a man could not stand the crowds, he could run away to sea, emigrate to America or Australia, move toward the frontier. But now the earth is filled up and one can only remain festering in the crowds, which grow ever worse.

And does social disintegration increase merely as the population increases, or as the level of urbanization increases? Will its level double only every 35 years or even only every 11 years? Somehow, I think not. I suspect that what counts in creating the kind of troubles we see about us— the hostilities, angers, rebellions, withdrawals—is not just the number of people swarming about each individual, but the number of interactions possible between an individual and the people swarming about him.

For instance, if A and B are in close proximity, they may possibly quarrel: but an A–B quarrel is all that is possible. If A, B, and C, are all in close proximity, then A may quarrel with B or with C; or B may quarrel with C. Where two individuals may have only one two-way quarrel, three individuals may have three different quarrels of this sort, and four individuals six different quarrels. In short, the number of possible interactions increases much more rapidly than the mere number of people crowded together does. If the metropolitan areas increase ninefold in population by the year 2000 then I suspect that the level of social disorder and disintegration will increase (at a guess) fiftyfold, and I feel pretty sure that society will not be able to bear the load.

I conclude, then, that we have only the space of

the next generation to stop the population increase and reorganize our cities to prevent the pathological crowding that now occurs. We have 30 years—till 2000 A.D.—to do it in and that estimate is rather on the optimistic side, if anything. Unfortunately, I don't think that mankind can fundamentally alter its ways of thinking and acting within 30 years even in the most favorable conditions; and the conditions are far from favorable. As it happens, those who dominate human society are, generally, old men in comfortable circumstances, who are frozen in the thought-patterns of a past generation, and who cling suicidally to the way of life to which they are accustomed.

It seems to me, then, that by 2000 A.D. or possibly earlier, man's social structure will have utterly collapsed, and that in the chaos that will result as many as three billion people will die.

Nor is there likely to be a chance of recovery thereafter, for in the chaos the nuclear buttons are only too apt to be pushed, and those who survive will then face an earth which will probably be poisoned by radiation for an indefinite period into the future.

And as far as human civilization is concerned, that will be

THE END

Estie Stoll
Crowding

Although the effects of crowding on various mammalian species has been demonstrated, little is known about the social and physiological effects of crowding on man. Psychologists and physiologists uncritically extend findings from studies of mice and rats to man, despite investigations which suggest qualitative and quantitative differences in the response of Homo sapiens to overcrowding. Most notable of these differences is the increase in fertility associated with overcrowding in man, in contrast to a decrease in natality found in animal populations. As A. H. Esser warns, population density is not necessarily the same as crowding in human populations. For example, population density in Hong Kong is extremely high, but the "pathological behavior" associated with crowding occurs at low frequencies.[1]

Thus, researchers must exercise caution when applying animal studies to the understanding of crowded man. Species-specific responses must be taken into account when attempting to deduce the mechanisms causing pathological behavior under crowded conditions, as must the social context, which may ameliorate or aggravate the intensity of the crowding response.

In the following article, Estie Stoll briefly reviews some of the recent studies of crowding in man and in several other species and relates the findings to contemporary social problems in the United States.

Medieval theologians were obsessed with the number of angels able to dance on the head of a pin, but modern scholars are much more preoccupied with *human* spatial requirements in urban society. Overcrowding is often blamed for the higher rates of crime, suicide, infant mortality, and other physical, mental, and social disorders in urban areas compared to rural areas. But because crowded cities often contain the poorest and most depressed populations, "it is important that the effects of crowding, not crowding in conjunction with poverty, malnutrition, noise, and filth be clearly understood," write Drs. Paul Ehrlich, Stan-

"Crowding" by Estie Stoll from *The Sciences,* Vol. 11, No. 6, (October 1971). © 1971 by The New York Academy of Sciences. Reprinted by permission.
[1] A. H. Esser, "Toward Definition of Crowding," *The Sciences,* 11 (1971): 4.

ford biologist, and psychologist Jonathan Freedman, of Columbia University (*New Scientist and Science Journal*, April 1, 1971). Although crowding may have specific negative effects on animals, extrapolating human response from animal studies is risky, they warn.

Crowded Out of Adult Roles

For the past 38 months, Dr. John B. Calhoun of the National Institute of Mental Health has studied the relationship between population dynamics and social death in an inbred strain of house mice. Mice were placed in five universes of increasing size, each universe containing one, two, four, eight, or sixteen cells. Each cell provided an optimum spatial environment for only nine adult mice, but enough food and water for up to 225. Initially, population expanded rapidly and normal social groups were formed, but as crowding intensified, behavioral pathology developed. When population density reached 18 times the optimum—160 mice per cell—all reproduction ceased.

The sequence of events was the same in each universe. Population grew so rapidly that adults couldn't incorporate the maturing young into the social system. In each cell, there were rarely more than three dominant males; stressed by too many competing males, the behavior patterns of the dominant animals dissolved and they were unable to protect lactating females and their young. Forced to protect themselves, these females became "masculinely aggressive"—both toward males and their own offspring—and lost their capacity to build proper nests or protect their infants. Deprived of proper mothering, the new generation of mice never developed the capacity for social participation.

Some of the young, nonterritorial males began to congregate in exposed public living spaces; sedate and withdrawn, they moved only to eat or drink and were highly aggressive if disturbed. Other infantilized males returned to nesting boxes and associated only with females or similarly emasculated males. Dr. Calhoun calls these mice the Beautiful Ones because they were unscarred by the wounds of normal male aggressive behavior. By the time population density reached its maximum, all the older, active males had died and all recently-born males were Beautiful Ones.

Density and Species Death

Both males and females "fail to mature socially. Behaviorally, they continue into adult life as juveniles without the capacity for either mating or aggression; their normal adult roles never emerge," Dr. Calhoun writes in "Environment and Society in Transition" (*Annals of the New York Academy of Sciences*, June 1971). "Where there is no physical escape from a closed environment and where no capacity for elaboration of roles prevails, social death may mark up to 95 percent ... of the population."

"The result of major importance is not that stress builds up as crowding increases, but that the terminal animals become *unstressed*," Dr. Calhoun told *The Sciences*. "Even at peak density, most animals are unstressed, because they are solely involved in autistic-like behavior and aren't cognizant of or participators in the social scene. There is a total breakdown in the community's capacity to conduct the social relations necessary for the perpetuation of the species."

Can the behavior of overcrowded house mice yield predictions about the human crowding response? Dr. Calhoun suggests that it may, if we do not seek exact parallels. Under stress, he points out, each species tends to lose its most complex behavior first. Mice stopped reproducing; men and women would probably lose the capacity to acquire, create, and assimilate complex ideas. "The system of human relationships would collapse because our system requires utilization of complex ideas to survive," he warns. To alleviate human crowding pressures, he urges the proliferation of well-coordinated social roles and contacts—i.e., the creation of simulated "conceptual space" as a partial substitute for our shrinking physical territory. "The planet Earth is becoming progressively a closed system within which there is no physical escape. If adequate measures are not taken to provide habitable conceptual space, the prevalence of social death and morbidity will increase . . ." (*Annals*, NYAS).

Crowding and Adrenal Stress

Negative responses to crowding are not limited to mice. When Philadelphia's Zoological Gardens began breeding stocks in 1950, health and behavior patterns of several species were adversely altered.

Within two years, a thriving colony of nutria (*Myocaster coypu*) began to decline. The rodents became dwarfed and infertile and 75 percent of the males were fatally injured by aggressive cagemates. Within seven years, the colony was extinct. Autopsies revealed hugely hypertrophied adrenal cortexes, suggesting that crowding stress had triggered overproduction of adrenal hormones, indirectly causing group death.

Survival by Reduction

A confined colony of white-tail deer (*Odocoileus virginanus*) at the Zoo recovered its viability only after reproduction had ceased entirely and crowding was relieved by the death of half its members. Again, autopsies revealed enlarged adrenals. In nature, white-tail deer associate in small groups only for breeding or temporary protection. "These associations do not continue, however, a fact which aids in understanding the responses of these animals to having been maintained as a group of increasing size," Dr. Herbert L. Ratcliffe, Director of the Penrose Research Laboratory at the Zoological Society of Philadelphia observed (*Proceedings of the American Philosophical Society*, Aug. 1968). He found the crowding responses in these animals particularly striking because of the "similarity between living conditions for the Zoo species, and the social landscape of densely populated urban areas."

Crowding in Nature

Among wild rabbits in confined areas of their natural habitat, crowding adversely affected liver, spleen, kidneys, and endocrine glands; aggression and sexual activity increased, but reproductive capacity declined, according to Dr. Kenneth Myers of the Commonwealth Scientific and Industrial Research Organization, Division of Wildlife, Canberra City, Australia. Young rabbits were stunted, and adults born into high-density environments the year before also had impaired health. "The 'density syndrome' in mammals is a reality," probably influenced by genetic inheritance and social experience, Dr. Myers told the 135th AAAS meeting in 1968.

Ducks, Density, Disease

In white Pekin ducks, crowding has been related to the development of amyloidosis by Dr. Daniel Cowan and Mr. William C. Johnson, pathologists at Michigan State University. Amyloidosis affects species ranging from mice to human beings; it appears as an accumulation of waxy-protein in vital organs, and kills one duck in ten on breeding farms. It may also adversely affect survival in crowded wildlife preserves. The MSU study examined 72 healthy Pekin ducks randomly separated into nine density groups; 24 single ducks, 12 duck-pairs, and three flocks of eight ducks each, with cage-space allotments of 1.25 square feet, 2.50 square feet, or 3.75 square feet per bird. Within eight months, 44 percent of the ducks had amyloidosis, ranging from 21 percent of isolated birds to 71 percent of flocked animals. The severest cases were twice as common among flock members, but animals died only when crowding was most intense—in flocks with 1.25 square feet of space per bird. "Space allotment is of far less importance than the number of birds in a cage of any given size," the Michigan team reports (*Laboratory Investigation*, Vol. 23, No. 5, 1970). Thus, a single duck in the smallest cage, though more cramped, was less disease-prone than flock members penned in an area eight times larger; in confinement, the latter had no way of escaping the aggressive physical contacts used to establish group hierarchy. Probably, "adaptation is a highly unstable situation and ... considerable neural and endocrine activity is necessary to maintain any sort of physiologic equilibrium. This activity may be responsible in some way for the deposition of amyloid," the investigators suggest. Paradoxically, in each flock, one duck did not develop amyloidosis; they postulate that he may have been dominant and less subject to social stress.

"Crowding appears to cause amyloidosis in ducks much as crowding and frustration appear to cause ulcers in people," says Dr. Cowan. Crowded ducks also became fearful, did a lot of squawking, and displayed stereotyped, repetitive movements, he told *The Sciences*. "Ducks, like people, need space to withdraw and be by themselves occasionally. If ducks are not allowed to do this, their behavior deteriorates and physical symptoms appear."

Dominance may provide relief from crowding

stress in human as well as animal society. There are "spatial correlates of status levels, and, conversely, social correlates of spatial position," Dr. Robert Sommer, University of California psychologist told the AAAS in 1968. "In the barnyard the top chickens have the greatest freedom of space and can walk anywhere, while lower birds are restricted to small areas and can be pecked by other birds wherever they go. In human society, the social elite possess more space in the form of larger home sites, more rooms per house, and vacation homes. In addition, they have greater spatial mobility and more opportunities to escape when they become tense, uncomfortable, or bored."

Variations in the Human Species

Although responses to crowding may reveal basic territorial needs that man shares with other species, cultural values, social status, ethnic ties, and individual factors alter human territorial requirements. Schizophrenics are apparently more sensitive to physical closeness than are healthy people, displaying a measurably larger "body-buffer zone," the "area surrounding each individual which represents the boundaries to what is felt as 'inner' versus what is felt as 'outer'," says psychiatrist Mardi J. Horowitz of the University of California (*Archives of General Psychiatry*, Vol. 11, 1964).

Clinicians at the U.S. Medical Center for Federal Prisoners have also observed that "physical proximity to another inmate was at least as powerful a trigger of violence as were threats, thefts or other more overt provocations," Dr. Augustus F. Kinzel told the American Psychiatric Association in 1969. An Attending Psychiatrist at the New York State Psychiatric Institute, Dr. Kinzel conducted a very limited study of six nonviolent and eight violent prisoners; the latter had significantly larger body-buffer zones. "Many repeatedly violent individuals have a permanent abnormality of body image. They behave as if their bodies are extended farther into the space around them. Thus to intrude on their personal space is to intrude on their bodies. It is unclear whether this is due to a breakdown in their perception of their skin barrier, such that the sense of 'inner' and 'outer' is poorly delineated, or whether they erect a kind of body shell around themselves as a primitive defense against touching." His findings were

reinforced by a study of 36 randomly selected Maryland prisoners whose past histories of aggression corresponded with the size of their body-buffer zones. The study suggests that "There is every indication that in man as well as in animals physical closeness is intimately related to intraspecies aggression" (*American Journal of Psychiatry*, June 1971).

Outside the institutions that deliberately herd men together, human responses to crowding vary enormously; one culture may value close auditory links between members, others require social insulation and design their dwellings accordingly. Displacement from a familiar territory adds still another variable to the human response. "Poor, uneducated people have a much lower tolerance for being displaced than people of the middle class. Even a move across the street can be traumatic because it alters the pattern of social relationships," writes Dr. Edward T. Hall, Professor of Anthropology at Northwestern University (*Ekistics*, March 1969). Thus, city design and urban renewal must contend with a complexity of spatial needs and responses.

Crowding Stress in the Ghetto

Human crowding may have been a crucial factor in the black ghetto riots of the 1960s, suggests geographer John Adams, after analyzing the riot patterns of seven midwestern cities in a study sponsored by Pennsylvania State University. From the downtown business district to the suburban edge, most large metropolitan areas are marked by concentric zones of progressively improved housing. Migrants, the very poor, and the aged are clustered near the core, where housing is old, crowded, and cheap. Traditionally, upwardly mobile families move to newer, more spacious, and more expensive quarters in the outer zones, relieving inner-city crowding by vacating apartments for the poor who remain behind. But this "invasion-succession" process failed during the sixties, says Dr. Adams, currently Associate Professor of Geography at the University of Minnesota. During that decade, government-insured mortgage interest rates rose from about five to ten percent, to counteract the inflation partly due to the expanded Indo-Chinese war, and suburban home construction declined. In 1963, 1.6 million new private houses were started; only 1.2 and 1.5 million were begun in 1966 and 1968, respectively. Normal outward migration declined, fewer apartments were vacated to accommodate growing ghetto populations, and inner city crowding intensified (*Economic Geography*, in press).

Destruction by Urban Renewal

Pressures were compounded by unregulated urban renewal programs and highway construction during the 1950s and early 1960s, Dr. Adams says. Deteriorated black ghettos, strategically located between the business district and affluent suburban consumers, were prime targets for road construction and housing demolition. Their inhabitants were also politically powerless to avert projects beneficial to outsiders but detrimental to themselves. "There was no agency to coordinate population movements and housing in metropolitan areas. Housing was torn down in the core, forcing residents to move outward before they could afford more expensive housing and faster than residents of the middle circles were moving outward. The result was a squeeze in the middle," where violence ultimately broke out. At the riot hearings conducted by Senator John McClellan, Governor Romney of Michigan attributed Detroit's civil disorders in part to highway construction, which had removed large housing tracts and put a strain on adjacent communities (*Riots, Civil and Criminal Disorders Hearings,* U.S. Govt. Printing Office, 1967–69).

Reversing the rising vacancy trend of the previous decade, annual average vacancy rates for the U.S. fell precipitously during the 1960s. The shoe pinched most for families with teen-agers, who need more space than younger children and who also are more militant in their demands, says Dr. Adams. In the crowded middle urban areas where riots flared, limited suburban migration had resulted in a particularly high concentration of 10-to-20-year-old males; the McClellan commission found that half of the arrested rioters were teen-agers.

Density, Frustration, Aggression

Paradoxically, violence did *not* erupt in the poorest ghetto cores, but in lower-class and lower middle-class black neighborhoods lying between severely depressed areas and affluent suburbs. In these middle zones, crowding and high expectations—fed by the optimistic rhetoric of the New Frontier and the Great Society—increased simultaneously. Though the median income of nonwhites rose and the percentage of nonwhite incomes below the poverty line fell during the 1960s, racial discrimination prevented prosperity from measuring up to expectations. "A sense of betrayal of expectations brought grievances into focus"; crowding merely crystallized and exacerbated frustration. In Cleveland, Cincinnati, Detroit, Kansas City, and Milwaukee, population had increased at a faster rate than available housing, and violence erupted in the middle zones. There, ambitious blue-collar blacks were unable to attain the middle-class prosperity flaunted by the mass media.

In Detroit, for example, there were riots in only two black neighborhoods, Kercheval and 12th Street; in the latter, housing starts remained static or decreased but population rose from 22,000 to 38,000. In St. Louis and Minneapolis, civil disorders may have been averted, according to Dr. Adams, because population did not outstrip the available housing (*Research in the College of Earth and Mineral Sciences,* The Pennsylvania State University, 1970). Since the mid-sixties' riots in the U.S., "there has been public reaction to leaving people homeless. Laws have now changed to ensure that displaced people have suitable places to live before their old homes are torn down. And where necessary, these people are given moving expenses," Dr. Adams notes. Although in most cities low-cost housing is still scarce and dislocation remains a problem, such laws as the Federal Housing Act of 1964 are of some help. The Act authorizes family relocation allowances of up to $500, and moving or property-loss reimbursement of up to $200, sums that are more significant in the Midwest than in the East, Dr. Adams told *The Sciences.* To prevent future unrest, he urges building new housing at the suburban edges, as well as in downtown ghetto cores, to permit adequate outward migration and a steady transfer of vacated apartments to the inner-city poor. "We see the ghetto as a small expanding world located within the metropolis—itself a larger and expanding spatial unit. As these spatial changes occur, either society must regulate them or the society will be regulated by their consequences."

The Root of All Evils?

Although high population density has been linked to war and to crime, these complex events probably demand more complex explanations. The Organization of American States attributed the war between El Salvador and Honduras in 1969 to the former's need for spatial expansion; El Salvador had a population of 782 people per square mile of arable land compared to Honduras' 155. Drs. Ehrlich and Freedman disagree with the OAS interpretation, contending that the need for jobs and natural resources far outweighed the need for space.

Superficially, there is an apparent relationship between crowding and crime; in cities with more than 250,000 population, the overall crime rate is five times greater, and the violent crime rate 11 times greater than in rural areas. But New York has a lower incidence of violent crimes than Los Angeles, which is only a fifth as densely populated. Studies of *comparable* metropolitan areas with varying densities indicate that urban crime does not depend on high density alone (*New Scientist and Science Journal*, Apr. 1, 1971).

In the Laboratory

To isolate the effect of crowding on human performance and behavior, Drs. Ehrlich and Freedman began a series of controlled density experiments in 1968. They found that groups of subjects placed in cramped or spacious quarters were equally capable of performing "tasks ranging from tediously simple and routine to rather interesting and complex, from totally nonintellectual to highly creative," Dr. Freedman told the American Psychological Association in September. But when social interaction rather than individual performance was tested, crowding had a pronounced, sex-related effect. One Ehrlich-Freedman experiment grouped men and women of various ages, ethnic backgrounds, incomes, and educational levels in small or large rooms for four-hour periods. After a brief acquaintance, they served as mock juries for taped courtroom cases, then completed a questionnaire evaluating their companions and the experience as a whole. All-female juries judged the experience more favorably and were more lenient jurors in a small room; all-male juries reacted more positively in larger spaces. But in mixed male-female groups, the degree of crowding had no apparent effect on men, women, or the group as a whole. Drs. Ehrlich and Freedman conclude that "all-male juries or cabinets or international conferences should probably be avoided, or at least be given spacious quarters. Better still, women should be included, not only to give them equal representation, but because apparently any negative effects of crowding disappear when the sexes are mixed." They suggest that "there is little evidence that population density per se produces dramatic effects (negative or positive) among human beings," but depend "on the particular situations and the types of behavior involved."

Stanley Milgram

The Experience of Living in Cities

Milgram's article offers a coherent explanation for the existence of certain behavior characteristic of the city dweller. He borrows a concept from systems analysis— overload—which he defines in terms of a system's inability to cope with all inputs simultaneously, thus requiring a set of priorities and decisions about processing them. People in analogous situations, he argues, permit the passage of only certain stimuli to the brain and selectively block the passage of others. The use of unlisted telephone numbers by city people, or the existence of welfare departments, are thus adaptations—mechanisms designed to protect the individual from extraneous sensory inputs and so to prevent overload and stress.

When I first came to New York it seemed like a nightmare. As soon as I got off the train at Grand Central I was caught up in pushing, shoving crowds on 42nd Street. Sometimes people bumped into me without apology; what really frightened me was to see two people literally engaged in combat for possession of a cab. Why were they so rushed? Even drunks on the street were bypassed without a glance. People didn't seem to care about each other at all.

This statement represents a common reaction to a great city, but it does not tell the whole story. Obviously cities have great appeal because of their variety, eventfulness, possibility of choice, and the stimulation of an intense atmosphere that many individuals find a desirable background to their lives. Where face-to-face contacts are important, the city offers unparalleled possibilities. It has been calculated by the Regional Plan Association that in Nassau County, a suburb of New York City, an individual can meet 11,000 others within a 10-minute radius of his office by foot or car. In Newark, a moderate-sized city, he can meet more than 20,000 persons within this radius. But in midtown Manhattan he can meet fully 220,000. So there is an order-of-magnitude increment in the communication possibilities offered by a great city. That is one of the bases of its appeal and, indeed, of its functional necessity. The city provides options that no other social arrangement permits. But there is a negative side also, as we shall see.

Granted that cities are indispensable in complex society, we may still ask what contribution psychology can make to understanding the experience of living in them. What theories are relevant? How can we extend our knowledge of the psychological aspects of life in cities through empirical inquiry? If empirical inquiry is possible, along what lines should it proceed? In short, where do we start in constructing urban theory and in laying out lines of research?

Observation is the indispensable starting point. Any observer in the streets of midtown Manhattan will see (i) large numbers of people, (ii) a high population density, and (iii) heterogeneity of population. These three factors need to be at the root of any sociopsychological theory of city life, for they condition all aspects of our experience in the metropolis. Louis Wirth, if not the first to point to these factors, is nonetheless the sociologist who relied most heavily on them in his analysis of the city. Yet, for a psychologist, there is something unsatisfactory about Wirth's theoretical variables. Numbers, density, and heterogeneity are demographic facts but they are not yet psychological facts. They are external to the individual. Psychology needs an idea that links the individual's experience to the demographic circumstances of urban life.

One link is provided by the concept of overload. This term, drawn from systems analysis, refers to a system's inability to process inputs from the environment because there are too many inputs for the system to cope with, or because successive inputs come so fast that input A cannot be processed when input B is presented. When overload is present, adaptations occur. The system must set priorities and make choices. A may be processed first while B is kept in abeyance, or one input may be sacrificed altogether. City life, as we experience it, constitutes a continuous set of encounters with overload, and of resultant adaptations. Overload characteristically deforms daily life on several levels, impinging on role performance, the evolution of social norms, cognitive functioning, and the use of facilities.

The concept has been implicit in several theories of urban experience. In 1903 George Simmel pointed out that, since urban dwellers come into contact with vast numbers of people each day, they conserve psychic energy by becoming acquainted with a far smaller proportion of people than their rural counterparts do, and by maintaining more superficial relationships even with these aquaintances. Wirth points specifically to "the superficiality, the anonymity, and the transitory character of urban social relations."

One adaptive response to overload, therefore, is the allocation of less time to each input. A second adaptive mechanism is disregard of low-priority inputs. Principles of selectivity are formulated such that investment of time and energy are reserved for carefully defined inputs (the urbanite disregards the drunk sick on the street as he purposefully navigates through the crowd). Third, boundaries are redrawn in certain social transactions so that the overloaded system can shift the burden to the other party in the exchange; thus,

"The Experience of Living in Cities" by Stanley Milgram from *Science,* Vol. 167, pp. 1461–1468 (March 13, 1970). Copyright © 1970 by the American Association for the Advancement of Science. Reprinted by permission.

harried New York bus drivers once made change for customers, but now this responsibility has been shifted to the client, who must have the exact fare ready. Fourth, reception is blocked off prior to entrance into a system; city dwellers increasingly use unlisted telephone numbers to prevent individuals from calling them, and a small but growing number resort to keeping the telephone off the hook to prevent incoming calls. More subtly, a city dweller blocks inputs by assuming an unfriendly countenance, which discourages others from initiating contact. Additionally, social screening devices are interposed between the individual and environmental inputs (in a town of 5000 anyone can drop in to chat with the mayor, but in the metropolis organizational screening devices deflect inputs to other destinations). Fifth, intensity of inputs is diminished by filtering devices, so that only weak and relatively superficial forms of involvement with others are allowed. Sixth, specialized institutions are created to absorb inputs that would otherwise swamp the individual (welfare departments handle the financial needs of a million individuals in New York City, who would otherwise create an army of mendicants continuously importuning the pedestrian). The interposition of institutions between the individual and the social world, a characteristic of all modern society, and most notably of the large metropolis, has its negative side. It deprives the individual of a sense of direct contact and spontaneous integration in the life around him. It simultaneously protects and estranges the individual from his social environment.

Many of these adaptive mechanisms apply not only to individuals but to institutional systems as well, as Meier has so brilliantly shown in connection with the library and the stock exchange.

In sum, the observed behavior of the urbanite in a wide range of situations appears to be determined largely by a variety of adaptations to overload. I now deal with several specific consequences of responses to overload, which make for differences in the tone of city and town.

Social Responsibility

The principal point of interest for a social psychology of the city is that moral and social involvement with individuals is necessarily restricted. This is a direct and necessary function of excess of input over capacity to process. Such restriction of involvement runs a broad spectrum from refusal to become involved in the needs of another person, even when the person desperately needs assistance, through refusal to do favors, to the simple withdrawal of courtesies (such as offering a lady a seat, or saying "sorry" when a pedestrian collision occurs). In any transaction more and more details need to be dropped as the total number of units to be processed increases and assaults an instrument of limited processing capacity.

The ultimate adaptation to an overloaded social environment is to totally disregard the needs, interests, and demands of those whom one does not define as relevant to the satisfaction of personal needs, and to develop highly efficient perceptual means of determining whether an individual falls into the category of friend or stranger. The disparity in the treatment of friends and strangers ought to be greater in cities than in towns; the time allotment and willingness to become involved with those who have no personal claim on one's time is likely to be less in cities than in towns.

Bystander Intervention in Crises

The most striking deficiencies in social responsibility in cities occur in crisis situations, such as the Genovese murder in Queens. In 1964, Catherine Genovese, coming home from a night job in the early hours of an April morning, was stabbed repeatedly, over an extended period of time. Thirty-eight residents of a respectable New York City neighborhood admit to having witnessed at least a part of the attack, but none went to her aid or called the police until after she was dead. Milgram and Hollander, writing in *The Nation*, analyzed the event in these terms:

Urban friendships and associations are not primarily formed on the basis of physical proximity. A person with numerous close friends in different parts of the city may not know the occupant of an adjacent apartment. This does not mean that a city dweller has fewer friends than does a villager, or knows fewer persons who will come to his aid; however, it does mean that his allies are not constantly at hand. Miss Genovese required immediate aid from those physically present. There is no evidence that the city had deprived Miss Genovese of human associations, but the friends who might have rushed to her side were miles from the scene of her tragedy.

Further, it is known that her cries for help were not directed to a specific person; they were general. But only individuals can act, and as the cries were not specifically directed, no particular person felt a special responsibility. The crime and the failure of community response seem absurd to us. At the time, it may well have seemed equally absurd to the Kew Gardens residents that not one of the neighbors would have called the police. A collective paralysis may have developed from the belief of each of the witnesses that someone else must surely have taken that obvious step.[1]

Latané and Darley have reported laboratory approaches to the study of bystander intervention and have established experimentally the following principle: the larger the number of bystanders, the less the likelihood that any one of them will intervene in an emergency. Gaertner and Bickman of The City University of New York have extended the bystander studies to an examination of help across ethnic lines. Blacks and whites, with clearly identifiable accents, called strangers (through what the caller represented as an error in telephone dialing), gave them a plausible story of being stranded on an outlying highway without more dimes, and asked the stranger to call a garage. The experimenters found that the white callers had a significantly better chance of obtaining assistance than the black callers. This suggests that ethnic allegiance may well be another means of coping with overload: the city dweller can reduce excessive demands and screen out urban heterogeneity by responding along ethnic lines; overload is made more manageable by limiting the "span of sympathy."

In any quantitative characterization of the social texture of city life, a necessary first step is the application of such experimental methods as these to field situations in large cities and small towns. Theorists argue that the indifference shown in the Genovese case would not be found in a small town, but in the absence of solid experimental evidence the question remains an open one.

More than just callousness prevents bystanders from participating in altercations between people. A rule of urban life is respect for other people's emotional and social privacy, perhaps because physical privacy is so hard to achieve. And in situations for which the standards are heterogeneous, it is much harder to know whether taking an active role is unwarranted meddling or an appropriate response to a critical situation. If a husband and wife are quarreling in public, at what point should a bystander step in? On the one hand, the heterogeneity of the city produces substantially greater tolerance about behavior, dress, and codes of ethics than is generally found in the small town, but this diversity also encourages people to withhold aid for fear of antagonizing the participants or crossing an inappropriate and difficult-to-define line.

Moreover, the frequency of demands present in the city gives rise to norms of noninvolvement. There are practical limitations to the Samaritan impulse in a major city. If a citizen attended to every needy person, if he were sensitive to and acted on every altruistic impulse that was evoked in the city, he could scarcely keep his own affairs in order.

Willingness to Trust and Assist Strangers

We now move away from crisis situations to less urgent examples of social responsibility. For it is not only in situations of dramatic need but in the ordinary, everyday willingness to lend a hand that the city dweller is said to be deficient relative to his small-town cousin. The comparative method must be used in any empirical examination of this question. A commonplace social situation is staged in an urban setting and in a small town—a situation to which a subject can respond by either extending help or withholding it. The responses in town and city are compared.

One factor in the purported unwillingness of urbanites to be helpful to strangers may well be their heightened sense of physical (and emotional) vulnerability—a feeling that is supported by urban crime statistics. A key test for distinguishing between city and town behavior, therefore, is determining how city dwellers compare with town dwellers in offering aid that increases their personal vulnerability and requires some trust of strangers. Altman, Levine, Nadien, and Villena of The City University of New York devised a study to compare the behaviors of city and town dwellers in this respect. The criterion used in this study was the

---

[1] S. Milgram and P. Hollander, "Murder They Heard," *Nation,* 198 (June 15, 1964): 602.

willingness of householders to allow strangers to enter their home to use the telephone. The student investigators individually rang doorbells, explained that they had misplaced the address of a friend nearby, and asked to use the phone. The investigators (two males and two females) made 100 requests for entry into homes in the city and 60 requests in the small towns. The results for middle-income housing developments in Manhattan were compared with data for several small towns (Stony Point, Spring Valley, Ramapo, Nyack, New City, and West Clarkstown) in Rockland County, outside of New York City. . . . In all cases there was a sharp increase in the proportion of entries achieved by an experimenter when he moved from the city to a small town. In the most extreme case the experimenter was five times as likely to gain admission to homes in a small town as to homes in Manhattan. Although the female experimenters had notably greater success both in cities and in towns than the male experimenters had, each of the four students did at least twice as well in towns as in cities. This suggests that the city-town distinction overrides even the predictably greater fear of male strangers than of female ones.

The lower level of helpfulness by city dwellers seems due in part to recognition of the dangers of living in Manhattan, rather than to mere indifference or coldness. It is significant that 75 percent of all the city respondents received and answered messages by shouting through closed doors and by peering out through peepholes; in the towns, by contrast, about 75 percent of the respondents opened the door.

Supporting the experimenters' quantitative results was their general observation that the town dwellers were noticeably more friendly and less suspicious than the city dwellers. In seeking to explain the reasons for the greater sense of psychological vulnerability city dwellers feel, above and beyond the differences in crime statistics, Villena points out that, if a crime is committed in a village, a resident of a neighboring village may not perceive the crime as personally relevant, though the geographic distance may be small, whereas a criminal act committed anywhere in the city, though miles from the city-dweller's home is still verbally located within the city; thus, Villena says, "the inhabitant of the city possesses a larger vulnerable space."

Civilities

Even at the most superficial level of involvement—the exercise of everyday civilities—urbanities are reputedly deficient. People bump into each other and often do not apologize. They knock over another person's packages and, as often as not, proceed on their way with a grumpy exclamation instead of an offer of assistance. Such behavior, which many visitors to great cities find distasteful, is less common, we are told, in smaller communities, where traditional courtesies are more likely to be observed.

In some instances it is not simply that, in the city, traditional courtesies are violated; rather, the cities develop new norms of noninvolvement. These are so well defined and so deeply a part of city life that *they* constitute the norms people are reluctant to violate. Men are actually embarrassed to give up a seat on the subway to an old woman; they mumble "I was getting off anyway," instead of making the gesture in a straightforward and gracious way. These norms develop because everyone realizes that, in situations of high population density, people cannot implicate themselves in each others' affairs, for to do so would create conditions of continual distraction which would frustrate purposeful action.

In discussing the effects of overload I do not imply that at every instant the city dweller is bombarded with an unmanageable number of inputs, and that his responses are determined by the excess of input at any given instant. Rather, adaptation occurs in the form of gradual evolution of norms of behavior. Norms are evolved in response to frequent discrete experiences of overload; they persist and become generalized modes of responding.

Overload on Cognitive Capacities: Anonymity

That we respond differently toward those whom we know and those who are strangers to us is a truism. An eager patron aggressively cuts in front of someone in a long movie line to save time only to confront a friend; he then behaves sheepishly. A man is involved in an automobile accident caused by another driver, emerges from his car shouting in rage, then moderates his behavior on discovering a friend driving the other car. The city dweller, when walking through the midtown streets, is in a state of continual anonymity vis-à-vis the other pedestrians.

Anonymity is part of a continuous spectrum ranging from total anonymity to full acquaintance, and it may well be that measurement of the precise degrees of anonymity in cities and towns would help to explain important distinctions between the quality of life in each. Conditions of full acquaintance, for example, offer security and familiarity, but they may also be stifling, because the individual is caught in a web of established relationships. Conditions of complete anonymity, by contrast, provide freedom from routinized social ties, but they may also create feelings of alienation and detachment.

Empirically one could investigate the proportion of activities in which the city dweller or the town dweller is known by others at given times in his daily life, and the proportion of activities in the course of which he interacts with individuals who know him. At his job, for instance, the city dweller may be known to as many people as his rural counterpart. However, when he is not fulfilling his occupational role—say, when merely traveling about the city—the urbanite is doubtless more anonymous than his rural counterpart.

Limited empirical work on anonymity has begun. Zimbardo has tested whether the social anonymity and impersonality of the big city encourage greater vandalism than do small towns. Zimbardo arranged for one automobile to be left for 64 hours near the Bronx campus of New York University and for a counterpart to be left for the same number of hours near Stanford University in Palo Alto. The license plates on the two cars were removed and the hoods were opened, to provide "releaser cues" for potential vandals. The New York car was stripped of all movable parts within the first 24 hours, and by the end of 3 days was only a hunk of metal rubble. Unexpectedly, however, most of the destruction occurred during daylight hours, usually under the scrutiny of observers, and the leaders in the vandalism were well-dressed, white adults. The Palo Alto car was left untouched.

Zimbardo attributes the difference in the treatment accorded the two cars to the "acquired feelings of social anonymity provided by life in a city like New York," and he supports his conclusions with several other anecdotes illustrating casual, wanton vandalism in the city. In any comparative study of the effects of anonymity in city and town,

however, there must be satisfactory control for other confounding factors: the large number of drug addicts in a city like New York; the higher proportion of slum-dwellers in the city; and so on.

Another direction for empirical study is investigation of the beneficial effects of anonymity. The impersonality of city life breeds its own tolerance for the private lives of the inhabitants. Individuality and even eccentricity, we may assume, can flourish more readily in the metropolis than in the small town. Stigmatized persons may find it easier to lead comfortable lives in the city, free of the constant scrutiny of neighbors. To what degree can this assumed difference between city and town be shown empirically? Judith Waters, at The City University of New York, hypothesized that avowed homosexuals would be more likely to be accepted as tenants in a large city than in small towns, and she dispatched letters from homosexuals and from normal individuals to real estate agents in cities and towns across the country. The results of her study were inconclusive. But the general idea of examining the protective benefits of city life to the stigmatized ought to be pursued.

Role Behavior in Cities and Towns

Another product of urban overload is the adjustment in roles made by urbanites in daily interactions. As Wirth has said: "Urbanites meet one another in highly segmental roles.... They are less dependent upon particular persons, and their dependence upon others is confined to a highly fractionalized aspect of the other's round of activity."[2] This tendency is particularly noticeable in transactions between customers and individuals offering professional or sales services. The owner of a country store has time to become well acquainted with his dozen-or-so daily customers, but the girl at the checkout counter of a busy A & P, serving hundreds of customers a day, barely has time to toss the green stamps into one customer's shopping bag before the next customer confronts her with his pile of groceries.

Meier, in his stimulating analysis of the city, discusses several adaptations a system may make when confronted by inputs that exceed its capacity to process them. Meier argues that, according to the principle of competition for scarce resources, the scope and time of the transaction shrink as

[2]L. Wirth, "Urbanism as a Way of Life," *American Journal of Sociology*, 44 (1938): 1.

customer volume and daily turnover rise. This, in fact, is what is meant by the "brusque" quality of city life. New standards have developed in cities concerning what levels of services are appropriate in business transactions.

McKenna and Morgenthau, in a seminar at The City University of New York, devised a study (i) to compare the willingness of city dwellers and small-town dwellers to do favors for strangers that entailed expenditure of a small amount of time and slight inconvenience but no personal vulnerability, and (ii) to determine whether the more compartmentalized, transitory relationships of the city would make urban salesgirls less likely than small-town salesgirls to carry out, for strangers, tasks not related to their customary roles.

To test for differences between city dwellers and small-town dwellers, a simple experiment was devised in which persons from both settings were asked (by telephone) to perform increasingly onerous favors for anonymous strangers.

Within the cities (Chicago, New York, and Philadelphia), half the calls were to housewives and the other half to salesgirls in women's apparel shops; the division was the same for the 37 small towns of the study, which were in the same states as the cities. Each experimenter represented herself as a long-distance caller who had, through error, been connected with the respondent by the operator. The experimenter began by asking for simple information about the weather for purposes of travel. Next the experimenter excused herself on some pretext (asking the respondent to "please hold on"), put the phone down for almost a full minute, and then picked it up again and asked the respondent to provide the phone number of a hotel or motel in her vicinity at which the experimenter might stay during a forthcoming visit. Scores were assigned the subjects on the basis of how helpful they had been. McKenna summarizes her results in this manner:

People in the city, whether they are engaged in a specific job or not, are less helpful and informative than people in small towns; ... People at home, regardless of where they live, are less helpful and informative than people working in shops.[3]

However, the absolute level of cooperativeness for urban subjects was found to be quite high, and does not accord with the stereotype of the urbanite as aloof, self-centered, and unwilling to help strangers. The quantitative differences obtained by McKenna and Morgenthau are less great than one might have expected. This again points up the need for extensive empirical research in rural-urban differences, research that goes far beyond that provided in the few illustrative pilot studies presented here. At this point we have very limited objective evidence on differences in the quality of social encounters in city and small town.

But the research needs to be guided by unifying theoretical concepts. As I have tried to demonstrate, the concept of overload helps to explain a wide variety of contrasts between city behavior and town behavior: (i) the differences in role enactment (the tendency of urban dwellers to deal with one another in highly segmented, functional terms, and of urban sales personnel to devote limited time and attention to their customers); (ii) the evolution of urban norms quite different from traditional town values (such as the acceptance of noninvolvement, impersonality, and aloofness in urban life); (iii) the adaptation of the urban dweller's cognitive processes (his inability to identify most of the people he sees daily, his screening of sensory stimuli, his development of blasé attitudes toward deviant or bizarre behavior, and his selectivity in responding to human demands); and (iv) the competition for scarce facilities in the city (the subway rush; the fight for taxis; traffic jams; standing in line to await services). I suggest that contrasts between city and rural behavior probably reflect the responses of similar people to very different situations, rather than intrinsic differences in the personalities of rural and city dwellers. The city is a situation to which individuals respond adaptively....

Conclusion

I have tried to indicate some organizing theory that starts with the basic facts of city life: large numbers, density, and heterogeneity. These are external to the individual. He experiences these factors as overloads at the level of roles, norms, cognitive functions, and facilities. These overloads lead to adaptive mechanisms which create the distinctive tone and behaviors of city life. These notions, of course, need to be examined by objective comparative studies of cities and towns.

[3] W. McKenna and S. Morgenthau, unpublished research prepared at Graduate Center, The City University of New York.

Barry Commoner, Michael Corr, and Paul J. Stamler

The Causes of Pollution

Several factors are contributing to the degradation of the environment: increasing population, increasing consumption, and technology. In the article that follows, the relative importance of these three factors is examined, and the conclusion is that pollution depends upon technology more than the other two factors. Some of the sources of mercury pollution, among other kinds, are discussed in the article.

If the authors are right, control of population growth would provide only minor relief, and is therefore a necessary but not sufficient condition for reversing present ecological trends.

Until now most of us in the environmental movement have been chiefly concerned with providing the public with information that shows that there *is* an environmental crisis. In the last year or so, as the existence of the environmental crisis has become more widely recognized, it has become increasingly important to ask: How can we best solve the environmental crisis? To answer this question it is no longer sufficient to recognize only that the crisis exists; it becomes necessary, as well, to consider its causes, so that rational cures can be designed.

Although environmental deterioration involves changes in natural, rather than man-made, realms —the air, water, and soil—it is clear that these changes are due to human action rather than to some natural cataclysm. The search for causes becomes focused, then, on the question: What actions of human society have given rise to environmental deterioration?

Like every living thing on the earth, human beings are part of an ecosystem—a series of interwoven, cyclical events, in which the life of any single organism becomes linked to the life processes of many others. One well-known property of such cyclical systems is that they readily break down if too heavily stressed. Such a stress may result if, for some reason, the population of any one living organism in the cycle becomes too great to be borne by the system as a whole. For example, suppose that in a wooded region the natural predators which attack deer are killed off. The deer population may then become so large that the animals strip the land of most of the available vegetation, reducing its subsequent growth to the point where it can no longer support the deer population; many deer die. Thus, in such a strictly biological situation, overpopulation is self-defeating. Or, looked at another way, the population is self-controlled, since its excessive growth automatically reduces the ability of the ecosystem to support it. In effect, environmental deterioration brought about by an excess in a population which the environment supports is the means of regulating the size of that population.

However, in the case of human beings, matters are very different; such automatic control is undesirable, and, in any case, usually impossible. Clearly, *if* reduced environmental quality were due to excess population, it might be advantageous to take steps to reduce the population size humanely rather than to expose human society to grave dangers, such as epidemics, that would surely accompany any "natural" reduction in population brought about by the environmental decline. Thus, if environmental deterioration were in fact the ecosystem's expected response to human overpopulation, then in order to cure the environmental crisis it would be necessary to relieve the causative stress—that is, to *reduce* actively the population from its present level.

On these grounds it might be argued as well that the stress of a rising human population on the environment is especially intense in a country, such as the United States, which has an advanced technology. For it is modern technology which extends man's effects on the environment far beyond his biological requirements for air, food, and water. It is technology which produces smog and smoke; synthetic pesticides, herbicides, detergents, and plastics; rising environmental concentrations of metals such as mercury and lead; radiation; heat; accumulating rubbish and junk. It can be argued that insofar as such technologies are intended to meet human needs—for food, clothing, shelter, transportation, and the amenities of life—the more people there are, and the more active they are, the more pollution.

Against this background it is easy to see why some observers have blamed the environmental crisis on overpopulation....

Some observers, for example M. P. Miller, chief of census population studies at the U.S. Bureau of the Census, believe that in the U.S. environmental deterioration is only partly due to increasing population, and blame most of the effect on "affluence."

Finally, some of us place the strongest emphasis on the effects of the modern technology that so often violates the basic principles of ecology and generates intense stresses on the environment....

To begin with, it is necessary to define the scope of the problem, both in space and time. As to space, we shall restrict the discussion solely to the United States. This decision is based on several factors: (a) The necessary data are available—at least to us—only for the United States. (b) The pollution problem is most intense in a highly developed country such as the United States. (c) In any study involving the comparison of statistical quantities, the more homogeneous the situation, the less likely we are to be misled by averages that combine vastly different situations. In this sense, it might be better to work with a smaller sample of the pollution problem—such as an urban region. Unfortunately, the necessary production statistics are not readily available except on a national scale.

As to time, we have chosen the period 1946–68. There are several reasons for this choice. First, many current environmental problems began with the end of World War II: photochemical smog, radiation from nuclear wastes, pollution from detergents and synthetic pesticides. Another reason for choosing the post-war period is that many changes in production techniques were introduced during this period. The upper limit of the period is a matter of convenience only; statistical data for the two most recent years are often difficult to obtain.

We shall thus be seeking an answer to the following question for the period 1946–68 in the United States: What changes in the levels of specific pollutants, in population size, in environmental impact per unit of production, and in the amounts of goods produced per capita have occurred?

Changes in Pollution and Population Levels
Curiously, the first of these questions is the most difficult to answer. Probably the best available data

relate to water pollution.... For the United States as a whole, in the period of 1946–68 the total nitrogen and phosphate discharged into surface waters by municipal sewage increased by 260 percent and 500 percent respectively.

Here are some additional data which, although sparse, are suggestive of the sizes of recent changes in pollution levels. As indicated by glacial deposits, airborne lead has increased by about 400 percent since 1946. Daily nitrogen oxide emissions in Los Angeles County have increased about 530 percent. The average algal population in Lake Erie—one response to, and indicator of, pollution due to nutrients such as nitrate and phosphate—increased about 220 percent. The bacterial count in different sectors of New York harbor increased as much as 890 percent. Such data correspond with general experience. For example, the extent of photochemical smog in the U.S. has surely increased at least ten-fold in the 1946–68 period, for in 1946 it was known only in Los Angeles; it has now been reported in every major city in the country, as well as in smaller areas such as Phoenix, Arizona, and Las Vegas, Nevada.

Rough as it is, we can take as an estimate of the change in pollution levels in the United States during 1946–68 increases that range from two- to ten-fold or so, or from 200 to 1,000 percent.

The increase in U.S. population for the period 1946–68 amounts to about 43 percent. It would appear, then, that the rise in overall U.S. population is insufficient by itself to explain the large increases in overall pollution levels since 1946....

Combined Factors of Population and Production

...A rough measure of overall U.S. production is the Gross National Product (GNP).... GNP has increased about 126 percent in that time and GNP per capita has increased about 59 percent. As a first approximation, then, it would appear that the overall increase in total production, as measured by GNP, is also insufficient to account for the considerably larger increases in pollution levels. However, since the GNP is, of course, an average composed of the many separate activities in the total production economy (including not only agricultural and industrial production and transportation, but also various services), a true picture of the relationship between production and environmental pollution requires a breakdown of the GNP into, at the least, some of its main components.

Under the auspices of the Committee on Environmental Alterations, of the American Association for the Advancement of Science (AAAS), we have begun to collect some of the relevant data for a joint AAAS–Scientists' Institute for Public Information study of the environmental effects of power production. . . .

Several interesting relationships emerge from Table 1. One is that in many cases, the growth in utilization of a particular product is counterbalanced by the reduction in the use of a similar one, the total use of that class of material remaining constant. An example is fiber (or textile) consumption. Total per capita use of fibers of all types increased very slightly (6 percent). However, the major sources of fiber, cotton and wool, declined in per capita consumption by 33 percent and 61 percent respectively. The difference was made up by a very large increase—1,792 percent—in wholly syn-

thetic (noncellulosic) fibers. Thus, we can find in Table 1 a series of pairs in which one item has substituted for another: nonreturnable beer bottles for returnable bottles; plastics for lumber; detergents for soap; truck and air freight for railroad freight; motor vehicles for work animals. Moreover, certain of the other indicated increases in per capita utilization are a result of such substitutions. Thus, mercury use increased partly because chlorine production increased; chlorine production has increased largely because it is heavily used to produce synthetic organic chemicals, which are in turn needed to produce plastics and synthetic fibers. Similarly, one reason for the increase in cement production is the substitution of truck traffic for rail traffic, which necessitates large-scale construction of highways. In the same way, one reason for increased electric power production is the increased production of chemicals, aluminum, and cement, all of which have high demands for power. As we shall see below, most of these changes turn out to be, in environmental terms, unfortunate.

Table 1. Changes in Production or Consumption Per Capita

Item	Period	% Increase	Item	Period	% Increase
Nonreturnable beer bottles	1946–69	3,778	Newsprint (consumption)	1950–68	19
Mercury for chlorine and sodium hydroxide products	1946–68	2,150	Meat (consumption)	1946–68	19
			New copper	1946–68	15
Noncellulosic synthetic fiber (consumption)	1950–68	1,792	Newspaper news (space)	1950–68	10
			All fibers (consumption)	1950–68	6
Plastics	1946–68	1,024	Beer (consumption)	1950–68	4
Air freight—ton-miles	1950–68	593	Fish (consumption)	1946–68	0
Nitrogen fertilizer	1946–68	534	Hosiery	1946–68	−1
Synthetic organic chemicals	1946–68	495	Returnable pop bottles	1946–69	−4
Chlorine gas	1946–68	410	Calorie (consumption)	1946–68	−4
Aluminum	1946–68	317	Protein (consumption)	1946–68	−5
Detergents	1952–68	300	Cellulosic synthetic fiber (consumption)	1950–68	−5
Electric power	1946–68	276			
Pesticides	1950–68	217	Railroad freight—ton-miles	1950–68	−7
Total horsepower	1950–68	178	Shoes	1946–68	−15
Wood pulp	1946–68	152	Egg (consumption)	1946–68	−15
Motor vehicle registration	1946–68	110	Grain (consumption)	1946–68	−22
Motor fuel (consumption)	1946–68	100	Lumber	1946–68	−23
Cement	1946–68	74	Cotton fiber (consumption)	1950–68	−33
Truck freight—ton-miles	1950–68	74	Milk and cream (consumption)	1946–68	−34
Total mercury (consumption)	1946–68	70	Butter (consumption)	1946–68	−47
Cheese (consumption)	1946–68	58	Railroad horsepower	1950–68	−60
Poultry (consumption)	1946–68	49	Wool fiber (consumption)	1950–68	−61
Steel	1946–68	39	Returnable beer bottles	1946–69	−64
Total freight—ton-miles	1950–68	28	Saponifiable fat (for soap products)	1944–64	−71
Total fuel energy (consumption)	1946–68	25	Work animal horsepower	1950–68	−84
Newspaper advertisements (space)	1950–68	22			

Certain large and basic categories, the necessities of life—food, clothing, and shelter—merit special attention. . . .

Surprisingly, for the period 1910 to 1968, there were very few overall changes in per capita consumption of food materials, especially in the period of interest to us. In 1946–68, total calories consumed dropped from about 3,390 per person per day to about 3,250 per person per day, while protein consumption declined slightly from 104 grams per person per day to about 99 grams per person per day.

It should be remembered that these are *consumption* data, whereas the data of interest in connection with environmental stress are those for *total production* (the difference being represented by storage of farm products and the balance of exports and imports). The difference represents, for instance for the year 1968, no more than about 3 percent of the total value of farm production; the consumption data consequently present a fairly accurate picture of farm production.

The total production figures do in fact reflect the trends evident in per capita consumption. Thus, total grain production, including grain used for meat production, decreased 6 percent in the 1946–68 period. The figures on declining protein intake tell us that increased meat consumption is more than balanced by declines in other types of protein intake, for instance of eggs, milk, and dry beans. Of course, the increased use of beef and other meat (about 19 percent per capita) does represent some increase in affluence. On the other hand, there has been a corresponding decline in another indicator of affluence, the use of fruit. Taking these various changes into account, then, there is no evidence of any significant change in the overall affluence of the average American with respect to food. And, in general, food production in the U.S. has just about kept up with the 43 percent increase in population in that time.

A similar situation exists with respect to another life necessity—clothing. The following items show either no significant change in per capita production, or a slight decline: shoes, hosiery, shirts, total fibers (i.e., natural plus synthetic), and total fabric production. . . . So that population increase by itself is not sufficient to explain the large increases in environmental pollution due to production of these items.

In the area of shelter, we find that housing units occupied in 1946 were 0.27 per capita, and in 1968, 0.30 per capita, an increase of 11 percent, although there was some improvement in the quality of units. Again, this change, even with the concurrent 43 percent increase in population, is simply not enough to match the large increases in pollution levels.

Another set of statistics also allows us to arrive at an estimate of the "affluence" factor. These relate to average personal expenditures for food, clothing, and housing (including purchased food and meals, alcoholic beverages, tobacco, rents and mortgage payments, house repairs, wearing apparel, but excluding furniture, household utilities, and domestic service). Such expenditures, adjusted for inflation, increased, per capita, about 27 percent between 1950 and 1968. Again, this increase when multiplied by the concurrent increase in population is insufficient to produce the large increases in pollution levels. It is important to note that these expenditures comprise a sector which represents about one-third of the total United States economy. . . .

Environmental Impact

. . . The activities which have sharply increased in per capita production in the period 1946–68 . . . fall into the following general classes of production: synthetic organic chemicals and the products made from them, such as detergents, plastics, synthetic fibers, rubber, pesticides and herbicides; wood pulp and paper products; total production of energy, especially electric power; total horsepower of prime movers, especially petroleum-driven vehicles; cement; aluminum; mercury used for chlorine production; petroleum and petroleum products.

Several remarks about this group of activities are relevant to our problem. First is the fact that the increase in per capita production (and also in total production) in this group of activities is rather high—of the order of 100 to 1,000 percent. This fact, together with the data already presented, is a reminder that the changes in the U.S. production system during the period 1946–68 do not represent an across-the-board increase in affluence or prosperity. That is, the 59 percent increase in per capita GNP in that period obscures the fact that in certain important sectors—for example, those related to basic life necessities—there has been rather little change in production per capita, while in certain other areas of production the increases have been very much larger. The second relevant observation about this group of activities is that their magnitude of increased production per capita begins to approach that of the estimates of concurrent changes in pollution level.

These considerations suggest, as a first approximation, that this particular group of production activities may well be responsible for the observed major changes in pollution levels. This identification is, of course, only suggested by the above considerations as an hypothesis, and is by no means proven by them. However, the isolation of this group provides a valuable starting point for a more detailed examination of the nature of the production activities that comprise it, and of their *specific* relationship to environmental degradation. As we shall see in what follows, this more detailed investigation does, in fact, quite strongly support the hypothesis suggested by the more superficial examination.

Nearly all of the production activities that fall into the class exhibiting striking changes in per capita production turn out to be important causes of pollution. Thus wood pulp production and related paper-making activities are responsible for a very considerable part of the pollution of surface waters with organic wastes, sulphite, and, until several years ago, mercury. Vehicles driven by the internal combustion engine are responsible for a major part of total air pollution, especially in urban areas, and are almost solely responsible for photochemical smog. Much of the remaining air pollution is due to electric power generation, another member of this group. Cement production is a notorious producer of dust pollution and a high consumer of electrical energy. The hazardous effects of mercury released into the environment are just now, belatedly, being recognized.

The new technological changes in agriculture, while yielding no major increase in overall per capita food production, have in fact worsened environmental conditions. Food production in the United States in 1968 caused much more environmental pollution than it did in 1947. Consider, for example, the increased use of nitrogen fertilizer, which rose 534 percent per capita between 1946 and 1968. This striking increase in fertilizer use did not increase total food production, but improved the crop yield per acre (while acreage was reduced) and made up for the loss of nitrogen to the soil due to the increasing use of feedlots to raise animals (with resultant loss of manure to the soil). For reasons which have been described elsewhere, this intensive use of nitrogen fertilizer on limited acreage drives nitrogen out of the soil and into surface waters, where it causes serious pollution problems. Thus, while Americans, on the average, eat about as much food per capita as they used to, it is now grown in ways that cause increased pollution. The new technologies, such as feedlots and fertilizer, have a much more serious effect on pollution than either increases in population or in affluence.

One segment of the group of increasing industrial activities in the period 1946–68, that comprising synthetic organic chemicals and their products, raises environmental problems of a particularly subtle, but nevertheless important, kind. In the first place, most of them find a place in the economy as substitutes for—some might say, improvements over—older products of a natural, biological origin. Thus synthetic detergents replace soap, which is made from fat—a natural product of animals and plants. Synthetic fibers replace cotton, wool, silk, flax, hemp—all, again, natural products of animals and plants. Synthetic rubber replaces natural rubber. Plastics replace wood and paper products in packaging. In many but not all uses, plastics replace natural products such as wood and paper. Synthetic pesticides and herbicides replace the natural ecological processes which control pests and unwanted weeds. Both the natural products and their modern replacements are organic substances. In effect, we can regard the products of modern synthetic organic chemistry as manmade variations on a basic scheme of molecular structure which in nature is the exclusive province of living things.

Because they are not *identical* with the natural products which they resemble, these synthetic substances do not fit very well into the chemical schemes which comprise natural ecosystems. Some of the new substances, such as plastics, do not fit into natural biochemical systems at all. Thus, while "nature's plastic," cellulose, is readily degraded by soil microorganisms and thus becomes a source of nutrition for soil organisms, synthetic plastics are not degradable, and therefore accumulate as waste. Automatically they become environmental pollutants. Because there is no natural way to convert them into usable materials, they either accumulate as junk or are disposed of by burning—which, of course, pollutes the air. Nondegradable synthetic detergents, with a branched molecular structure that is incompatible with the requirements of microorganisms which break down natural organic materials, remain in the water and become pollutants. Even degradable synthetic detergents, when broken down, may pollute water with phenol, and add another important water pollutant—phosphate—as well. Thus, these synthetic substitutes for natural products are, inevitably, pollutants.

Because of the considerable similarity of the basic biochemical systems in all living things, an active, but synthetic, organic substance such as a pesticide or herbicide is bound to influence not only the insect or weed which it is supposed to control, but also, to some extent—and often in unanticipated ways—a wide range of other organisms that make up the ecosphere. Such substances are, in effect, drugs. When they are introduced in massive amounts into the environment they become a kind of ecological drug which may affect fish, birds, and man, in unwanted, and often harmful, ways.

The point to be emphasized here is that the modern replacements for natural products have become the basis for the new, expansive production activities derived from synthetic organic chemicals, and are, by their very nature, destined to become serious environmental pollutants if they are broadcast into the environment—as, of course, they are.

There is, however, another way in which synthetic organic materials are particularly important as sources of environmental pollution. This relates not to their use but to their production. Let us compare, for example, the implication for environmental pollution of the *production* of, say, a pound of cotton and a pound of a synthetic fiber such as nylon. Both of these materials consist of long molecular chains, or polymers, made by linking together a succession of small units, or monomers. The formation of a polymer from monomers requires energy, part of which is required to form the bond that links the successive monomers. This energy has to be, so to speak, built into the monomer molecules, so that it is available when the inter-monomer link is formed. Energy is required to collect together, through cracking and distil-

lation, an assemblage of the particular monomer required for the synthetic process from a mixture such as petroleum. (That is, the process of obtaining a pure collection of the required monomer demands energy.) And it must be remembered that the energy requirement of a production process leads to important environmental consequences, for the combustion required to release energy from a fuel is always a considerable source of pollution.

If we examine cotton production according to these criteria, we find that it comes off with high marks, for relatively little energy capable of environmental pollution is involved. In the first place the energy required to link up the glucose monomers which make up the cotton polymer (cellulose) is built into these molecules from energy provided free in the form of the sunlight absorbed photosynthetically by the cotton plant. Energy derived from sunlight is transformed, by photosynthesis, into a biochemical form, which is then incorporated into glucose molecules in such a way as to provide the energy needed to link them together. At the same time photosynthetic energy synthesizes glucose from carbon dioxide and water. Moreover, glucose so heavily predominates as a major product of photosynthesis that the energy required to "collect" it in pure form is minimal—and of course is also obtained free, from sunlight. And in all these cases the energy is transferred at low temperatures (the cotton plant, after all, does not burn) so that extraneous chemical reactions such as those which occur in high temperature combustion—and which are the source of air pollutants such as nitrogen oxides and sulfur dioxide—do not occur. In fact, the overall photosynthetic process takes carbon dioxide—an animal waste product, and a product of all combustion—out of the air.

Now compare this with the method for producing a synthetic fiber. The raw material for such production is usually petroleum or natural gas. Both of these represent stored forms of photosynthetic energy, just as does cellulose. However, unlike cellulose, these are nonrenewable resources in that they were produced during the early history of the earth in a never-to-be repeated period of very heavy plant growth. Moreover, in order to obtain the desired monomers from the mixture present in petroleum a series of high-temperature, energy-requiring processes, such as distillation and evaporation, must be used. All this means that the production of synthetic fiber consumes more nonrenewable energy than the production of a natural fiber such as cotton or wool. It also means that the energy-requiring processes involved in synthetic fiber production take place at high temperatures, which inevitably result in air pollution.

Similar considerations hold for all of the synthetic materials which have replaced natural ones. Thus, the production of synthetic detergents, plastics, and artificial rubber inevitably involves, weight for weight, more environmental pollution than the production of soap, wood, or natural rubber. Of course, the balance sheet is not totally one-sided. For example, at least under present conditions, the production of cotton involves the use of pesticides and herbicides—environmental pollutants that are not needed to produce synthetic fibers. However, we know that the use of pesticides can be considerably reduced in growing a crop such as cotton—and, indeed, must be reduced if the insecticide is not to become useless through the development of insect resistance to the chemicals—by employing modern techniques of biological control. In the same way, it can be argued that wool production involves environmental hazards because sheep can overgraze a pasture and set off erosion. Again, this hazard is not an inevitable accompaniment of sheep-raising, but only evidence of poor ecological management. Similarly, pollution due to combustion could be curtailed and thus reduce the environmental impact of synthetics.

Obviously, much more detailed evaluations of this problem are needed. However, on the basis of these initial considerations it seems evident that the substitution of synthetic organic products for natural ones through the efforts of the modern chemical industry has, until now, considerably intensified environmental pollution.

Two other members of the group of production activities which have shown considerable growth per capita during the period 1946–68, like synthetic organic chemical products, add to pollution problems through their very production. One of these is aluminum, a metal which has increasingly replaced steel (in cans, for example). Aluminum is refined by passing an electric current through the molten ore, and it is therefore no surprise that the total energy required to produce a pound of aluminum (29,860 British thermal units, or BTUs) is about 6.5 times that required to produce a pound

of steel (4,615 BTUs). Taking into account that the weight of an aluminum can is less than that of a steel can of equal size, the power requirements are still in the ratio of more than 2 to 1. Of course, a total evaluation of the "pollution price tag" attached to each of these cans requires a full evaluation of the pollutants emitted by steel mills and aluminum refining plants. Nevertheless, with respect to one important part of the environmental cost—air pollution due to power production and fossil fuel consumption, the new product, aluminum, is a far greater environmental polluter than the old one, steel.

This brings us to a distinctive and especially important aspect of the environmentally related changes in production which have taken place in the 1946–68 period—electric power production. Electric power production has been noteworthy for its rapid and accelerating rate of growth. Total power production has increased by 662 percent in the period 1946–68; per capita power production has increased by 436 percent. Electric power production from fossil fuels is a major cause of urban air pollution; produced by nuclear reactors it is a source of radioactive pollution. Regardless of the fuel employed, power production introduces heat into the environment, some of it in the form of waste heat released at the power plant into either cooling waters or the air. Ultimately all electric power, when used, is converted to heat, causing increasingly serious heat pollution problems in cities in the summer. One of the striking features of the present U.S. production system is its accelerating demand for more and more power—with the resultant exacerbation of pollution problems.

Affluence and Increased Production

What is striking in the data discussed above is that so many of the new and expanding production activities are highly power-consumptive and have replaced less power-consumptive activities. This is true of the synthetic chemical industry, of cement, and of the introduction of domestic electrical appliances.

It is useful to return at this point to the question of affluence. To what extent do these increased uses of electric power, which surely contribute greatly to environmental deterioration, arise from the increased affluence, or well-being, of the American public? Certainly the introduction of an appliance such as a washing machine is, indeed, a valuable contribution to a family's well-being; a family with a washing machine is without question more affluent than a family without one. And, equally clear, this increased affluence adds to the total consumption of electric power and thereby adds to the burden of environmental pollutants. Such new uses of electricity therefore do support the view that affluence leads to pollution.

On the other hand, what is the contribution to public affluence of substituting a power-consumptive aluminum beer can for a less power-demanding steel can? After all, what contributes to human welfare is not the can, but the beer (it is interesting to note in passing that beer consumption per capita has remained essentially unchanged in the 1946–68 period). In this instance the extra power consumption due to the increased use of aluminum cans—and the resulting environmental pollution—cannot be charged to improved affluence. The same is true of the increased use of the nonreturnable bottle, which pollutes the environment during the production process (glass products require considerable fuel combustion) and pollutes it further when it is discarded after use. The extra power involved in producing aluminum beer cans, the extra power and other production costs involved in using nonreturnable bottles instead of reusable ones, contribute both to environmental pollution and the GNP. But they add nothing to the affluence or well-being of the people who use these products.

Thus, in evaluating the meaning of increased productive activity as it relates to the matters at issue here, a sharp distinction needs to be made between those activities which actually contribute to improved well-being and those which do not, or do so minimally (as does the self-opening aluminum beer can). Power production is an important area in which this distinction needs to be made. Thus, the chemical industry and the production of cement and aluminum, taken together, account for 18 percent of the present consumption of power in the United States. For reasons already given, some significant fraction of the power used for these purposes involves the production of a product which replaces a less power-consumptive one. Hence this category of power consumption—and its attendant environmental pollution—ought not to be charged to increased affluence. It seems likely to us that when all the appropriate calculations have been made, a very considerable part of the recent increases in demand for electric power will turn out to involve just such changes in which well-being, or affluence, is not improved, but the environment and the people who live in it suffer.

Transportation is another uniquely interesting area for such considerations. At first glance changes in the transportation scene in the United States in 1950–68 do seem to bear out the notion that pollution is due to increased affluence. In that period of time the total horsepower of automotive vehicles increased by 260 percent, the number of car registrations per capita by 110 percent, the vehicle miles traveled per capita by 100 percent, the motor fuel used per capita for transportation by 90 percent. All this gives the appearance of increased affluence —at the expense of worsened pollution.

However, looked at a little more closely the picture becomes quite different. It turns out that while the use of individual vehicles has increased sharply, the use of railroads has declined—thus replacing a less polluting means of transportation with a more polluting one. One can argue, of course, that it is more affluent to drive one's own car than to ride in a railroad car along with a number of strangers. Accepting the validity of that argument, it is still relevant to point out that it does *not* hold for comparison between freight hauled in a truck or in a railroad train. The fuel expenditure for hauling a ton of freight one mile by truck is 5.6 times as great as for a ton mile hauled by rail. In addition, the energy outlay for cement and steel for a four-lane expressway suitable for carrying heavy truck traffic is 3.5 times as much as that required for a single track line designed to carry express trains. Rights-of-way account for a considerable proportion of the environmental impact of transportation systems. In unobstructed country requiring no cuts or fills, a 400-foot right-of-way is desirable for an expressway, while a 100-foot right-of-way is desirable for an express rail line (in both cases, allowing for future expansion to more lanes or two rail lines respectively). Then, too, motor-vehicle-related accidents might be included in environmental considerations; in 1968 there were 55,000 deaths and 4.4 million injuries due to motor vehicle accidents, while there were only about 1,000 railway deaths, almost none of them passenger deaths. Aside from the loss of life and health, motor vehicle accidents are responsible for the expenditure of $12 billion a year on automobile insurance, which is equivalent to 16 percent of total personal consumption expenditures for transportation. In the case of urban travel it is very clear that efficient mass transit would be not only a more desirable means of travel than private cars, but also far less polluting. The lack of mass transit systems in American cities, and the resulting use of an increasing number of private cars is, again, a cause of increased pollution that does not stem from increased affluence.

It seems to us that the foregoing data provide significant evidence that the rapid intensification of pollution in the United States in the period 1946–68 cannot be accounted for solely by concurrent increases either in population or in affluence. What seems to be far more important than these factors in generating intense pollution is the *nature* of the *production* process; that is, its impact on the environment. The new technologies introduced following World War II have by and large provided Americans with about the same degree of affluence with respect to basic life necessities (food, clothing, and shelter); with certain increased amenities, such as private automobiles, and with certain real improvements such as household appliances. Most of these changes have involved a much greater stress on the environment than the activities which they have replaced. Thus, the most powerful cause of environmental pollution in the United States appears to be the introduction of such changes in technology, without due regard to their untoward effects on the environment.

Of course, the more people that are supported by *ecologically faulty technologies*—whether old ones, such as coal-burning power plants, or new ones, such as those which have replaced natural products with synthetic ones—the more pollution will be produced. But if the new, ecologically faulty technologies had *not* been introduced, the increase in U.S. population in the last 25 years would have had a much smaller effect on the environment. And, on the other hand, had the production system of the U.S. been based *wholly* on sound ecological practice (for example, sewage disposal systems which return organic matter to the soil; vehicle engines which operate at low pressure and temperature and therefore do not produce smog-triggering nitrogen oxides; reliance on natural products rather than energy-consumptive synthetic substitutes; closed production systems that prevent environmental release of toxic substances)

pollution levels would not have risen as much as they have, despite the rise in population size and in certain kinds of affluence.

The Case of Mercury

All of the foregoing discussion is based on overall statistical data rather than on the specific analysis of any particular source of pollution. While such an approach is useful, it is also important to develop data of a more specific kind. This is, of course, a huge task. It calls for a detailed study of the nature of present production technologies and the specific ways in which they affect ecologically important processes. Such studies have hardly been begun; nevertheless it is useful to discuss, at least in a tentative way, a specific example as a means of testing the conclusions derived from the more general statistical evidence.

The use of mercury in the chemical process industries is an informative example. Here its use reflects the increasing value of electrochemical processes, in which electricity is employed to effect chemical reactions, for mercury is unique in combining certain valuable chemical properties (for example, that it forms an amalgam with metals, such as sodium) with a capacity to conduct electricity. This led, for example, to the introduction in the United States about twenty years ago of a much improved process for producing caustic soda and chlorine. Since both of these substances are very widely used in the manufacture of the numerous synthetic chemical compounds that have been massively produced in the last 30 years, the rapid increase in the use of mercury in an application which permits losses to the environment is one consequence of the increased production of synthetic substances since World War II. Moreover, several major plastics are produced by processes catalyzed by mercury. Plastics production increased about 200 percent in 1958–67; during that time the use of mercury as an industrial catalyst also increased about 200 percent. In that same period the mercury used in chlorine production increased about 210 percent. These recent changes reflect the trend, beginning with the close of World War II, toward massive technical innovation and intensification of production in the chemical industry (which was discussed in more general terms above). The magnitude of this effect is sharply reflected in the data for the consumption of mercury for electrochemical production of chlorine: an increase of 2,150 percent in the period 1946–68.

These considerations provide an opportunity to test the degree to which population and affluence participate in the generation of environmental pollution by mercury. As already indicated, for the period 1946–68, the U.S. population increased about 43 percent; in the period 1958–68 it increased about 15 percent. In these periods total U.S. consumption of mercury increased 130 percent and 43 percent respectively. A good deal of mercury consumption involves uses in which the mercury is more or less permanently contained (for example, incorporation of mercury into electrical instruments—although here, too, it becomes important to ask where broken thermometers and burned-out fluorescent and other mercury-containing lamps are disposed of; if they are burned on a dump or in an incinerator, mercury vapor will pollute the air). However, it is perhaps more important to examine uses in those industries, such as chemical processing, which do result in environmental release of mercury. In this connection the following figures are relevant: In 1946–66, use of mercury in the chemical process industries increased about 224 percent; between 1958 and 1968 it increased about 250 percent. These data are sufficient to indicate that the increased industrial activities which are involved in mercury pollution cannot be accounted for by concurrent changes in the U.S. population. Nor can they be accounted for by the contribution of mercury consumption to increased affluence. As indicated earlier, per capita GNP increased about 51 percent in 1946–66. At the same time, the per capita use of mercury in chemical processing increased 250 percent for all chemical processing and 2,100 percent for chlorine production alone. In effect, goods now produced in the United States which are derived from chemical process industries involve a considerably greater use of mercury than previously. Thus the increased use—and release to the environment—of mercury reflects changes in industrial chemical technology rather than increased population or affluence.

The Primary Cause

These considerations and the ones discussed earlier in connection with agriculture, synthetics, power, and transportation, allow us, we believe, to draw the conclusion that the predominant factor in our industrial society's increased environmental degradation is neither population nor affluence, but the increasing environmental impact per unit of production due to technological changes.

Thus, in seeking public policies to alleviate environmental degradation it must be recognized that a stable population with stable consumption patterns would still face increasing environmental problems if the environmental impact of production continues to increase. The environmental impact per unit of production is increasing now, partially due to a process of displacement in which new, high-impact technologies are becoming predominant. Hence, social choices with regard to productive technology are inescapable in resolving the environmental crisis.

James V. Neel
Lessons from a "Primitive" People

In this article, James Neel describes in general terms some of the results of intensive investigations by a University of Michigan research team of three "primitive" South American populations—the Xavante, the Yanomama, and the Makiritare. Neel demonstrates the efficacy of such studies to the problems faced by modern society.

Biomedical studies of so-called primitive groups offer unique opportunities to study the genetic structure and population dynamics of populations ancestral to modern man. However, these populations have been exposed to European trade items; therefore they are not pristine nor completely isolated from the viruses and bacteria prevalent in urban populations. Hence, the "lesson" to be learned is by analogy only. The hunting and gathering populations ancestral to man are extinct; nevertheless we can study the mechanisms of evolution in such societies.

The field of population genetics is in a state of exciting intellectual turmoil and flux. The biochemical techniques that are now so freely available have revealed a profusion of previously hidden genetic variability. The way in which this variability arose and is maintained in populations—to what extent by selection, past and present, and to what extent by simple mutation pressure—is currently a topic of intensive discussion and debate, and there is little agreement among investigators as to which are the most promising approaches to the questions. At the same time, it is becoming increasingly clear that the breeding structure of real populations—especially those that approximate the conditions under which man evolved—departs so very far from the structure subsumed by the classical formulations of population genetics that new formulations may be necessary before the significance of this variation can be appraised by mathemathical means.

Some 8 years ago, as the new population genetics began to emerge, my co-workers and I began the formulation of a multidisciplinary study of some of the most primitive Indians of South America among whom it is possible to work. Scientists in the program ranged from the cultural anthropologist to the mathematical geneticist. The general thesis behind the program was that, on the assumption that these people represented the best approximation available to the conditions under which human variability arose, a systems type of analysis oriented toward a number of specific questions might provide valuable insights into problems of human evolution and variability. We recognize, of course, that the groups under study depart in many ways from the strict hunter-gatherer way of life that obtained during much of human evolution. Unfortunately, the remaining true hunter-gatherers are either all greatly disturbed or are so reduced in numbers and withdrawn to such inaccessible areas that it appears to be impossible to obtain the sample size necessary for tests of

hypothesis. We assume that the groups under study are certainly much closer in their breeding structure to hunter-gatherers than to modern man; thus they permit cautious inferences about human breeding structure prior to large-scale and complex agriculture. . . .

Within the context of his culture and resources, primitive man was characterized by a genetic structure incorporating somewhat more wisdom and prudence than our own. How he arrived at this structure—to what extent by conscious thought, to what extent through lack of technology and in unconscious response to instinct and environmental pressures—is outside the purview of this presentation.

The studies to be described have primarily been directed toward three tribes: the Xavante of the Brazilian Mato Grosso, the Makiritare of southern Venezuela, and the Yanomama of southern Venezuela and northern Brazil. At the time of our studies, these were among the least acculturated tribes of the requisite size (> 1000) in South America.

The four salient points about the Indian populations that we studied to be emphasized in this presentation are (i) microdifferentiation and the strategy of evolution, (ii) population control and population size, (iii) polygyny and the genetic significance of differential fertility, and (iv) the balance with disease.

Microdifferentiation and the Strategy of Evolution

The term "tribe" conjures to most an image of a more or less homogeneous population as the biological unit of primitive human organization. We have now typed blood specimens from some 37 Yanomama, 7 Makiritare, and 3 Xavante villages with respect to 27 different genetic systems for which serum proteins and erythrocytes can be classified. A remarkable degree of intratribal genetic differentiation between Indian villages emerges from these typings. . . . To some extent—an extent whose precise specification presents some difficult statistical problems—

these [differences] result from stochastic events such as the founder effect of E. Mayr, sampling error, and genetic drift. But we have also begun to recognize structured factors in the origin of these differences. One is the "fission-fusion" pattern of village propagation, in consequence of which new villages are often formed by cleavages of established villages along lineal lines (fission), and migrants to established villages often consist of groups of related individuals (fusion). A second such factor is a markedly nonisotropic (that is, a nonrandom and "unbalanced") pattern of inter-village migration. A third factor will be discussed below (see "Polygyny and genetic significance of differential fertility"). . . .

Population Control and Population Size

The total human population apparently increased very slowly up to 10,000 years ago. If we may extrapolate from our Indian experience, the slowness of this increase was probably not primarily due to high infant and childhood mortality rates from infectious and parasitic diseases (see "The balance with disease"). We find that relatively uncontacted primitive man under conditions of low population density enjoys "intermediate" infant mortality and relatively good health, although not the equal of ours today. However, most primitive populations practiced spacing of children. Our data on how this spacing was accomplished are best for the Yanomama, where intercourse taboos, prolonged lactation, abortion, and infanticide reduce the average *effective* live birth rate to approximately one child every 4 to 5 years during the childbearing period. The infanticide is directed primarily at infants whose older sibling is not thought ready for weaning, which usually occurs at about 3 years of age. Deformed infants and those thought to result from extramarital relationships are also especially liable to infanticide. Female infants are killed more often than male infants, which results in a sex ratio of 128 during the age interval 0 to 14 years. An accurate estimate of the frequency of infanticide still eludes us, but, from the sex-ratio imbalance plus other fragmentary information, we calculate that it involves perhaps 15 to 20 percent of all live births.

There have been numerous attempts to define the development in human evolution that clearly separated man from the prehominids. The phenomena of speech and of toolmaking have had strong proponents, whose advocacy has faltered in the face of growing evidence of the complexity of signaling and the ingenuity in utilizing materials that are manifested by higher primates. Population control may be such a key development. . . . I conclude, as has been suggested elsewhere, that perhaps the most significant of the many milestones in the transition from higher primate to man—on a par with speech and toolmaking—occurred when human social organization and parental care permitted the survival of a higher proportion of infants than the culture and economy could absorb in each generation and when population control, including abortion and infanticide, was therefore adopted as the only practical recourse available.

The deliberate killing of a grossly defective child (who cannot hope for a full participation in the society he has just entered) or of the child who follows too soon the birth of an older sibling (and thereby endangers the latter's nutritional status) is morally repugnant to us. I am clearly not obliquely endorsing a return to this or a comparable practice. However, I am suggesting that we see ourselves in proper perspective. The relationship between rapid reproduction and high infant mortality has been apparent for centuries. During this time we have condoned in ourselves a reproductive pattern which (through weaning diarrhea and malnutrition) has contributed, for large numbers of children, to a much more agonizing "natural" demise than that resulting from infanticide. Moreover, this reproductive pattern has condemned many of the surviving children to a marginal diet inconsistent with full physical and mental development.

We obviously cannot countenance infanticide. However, accepting the general harshness of the milieu in which primitive man functioned, I find it increasingly difficult to see in the recent reproductive history of the civilized world a greater respect for the quality of human existence than was manifested by our remote "primitive" ancestors. . . .

Polygyny and Genetic Significance of Differential Fertility

The three Indian tribes among whom we have worked are polygynous, the reward in these non-material cultures for male achievement (however judged) and longevity being additional wives. This pattern is found in many primitive cultures. As brought out in the preceding section, women seem to be committed to a pattern of child spacing, which in the Yanomama results, for women living to the age of 40 years, in a lower variance in number of reported live births than in the contemporary United States. By contrast with our culture, then, the mores of these primitive societies tend to minimize the variance of number of live births per female but maximize the variance of number of children per male.

One of our objectives is to understand the genetic consequences of polygyny. The translation of generalizations such as the above into the kind of hard data that can be employed in either deterministic formulations or stochastic procedures based on population simulation designed to explore the genetic consequences of polygyny has proved quite difficult. . . .

The *possible* genetic implications of polygyny are clear, but some of the facts necessary to a meaningful treatment are still lacking. Thus, one of our projected future investigations is an attempt to contrast certain mental attributes of polygynous with nonpolygynous males. In many respects, Indian culture is much more egalitarian than our own. The children of a village have the same diet and, by our standards, a remarkably similar environment. There are minimal occupational differences, and we do not find the differentiation into fishing villages, mining villages, or farming communities encountered in many cultures. Even with allowance for the happy accident of a large sibship, the open competition for leadership in an Indian community probably results in leadership being based far less on accidents of birth and far more on innate characteristics than in our culture. Our field impression is that the polygynous Indians, especially the headmen, tend to be more intelligent than the nonpolygynous. They also tend to have more surviving offspring. Polygyny in these tribes thus appears to provide an effective device for certain types of natural selection. Would that we had quantitative results to support that statement!

The Balance with Disease

Inasmuch as viral, bacterial, and parasitic diseases are commonly regarded as among the important agents of natural selection, a particular effort has been directed toward assaying the health of primitive man and the characteristics of his interaction with these disease agents. We have reported that the Xavante are, in general, in excellent physical condition, and we have similar unpublished data on the Yanomama and Makiritare. In terms of morbidity, perhaps the most important disease is falciparum malaria, which is probably a post-Columbian introduction. Fortunately for our view of the health of the pre-Columbian American Indian, we can find villages in which malaria does not seem to be a problem. . . . Although infant and childhood mortality rates are high by the standards of a civilized country such as present-day Japan, they are low in comparison with India at the turn of the century, especially since there was probably gross underreporting in the data from India. . . . One way to view the differences between these three [cultures] is that the advent of civilization dealt a blow to man's health from which he is only now recovering. . . .

The pattern of acquisition of immunity to endemic diseases in the Indian and possibly other primitives can already be seen to differ in a number of respects from the pattern in most civilized communities. Among the Xavante and Yanomama, for example, we find gamma globulin levels approximately two times those in civilized areas. Newborn infants presumably possess a high measure of maternal antibody acquired transplacentally. From the first, these infants are in an intimate contact with their environment that would horrify a modern mother—or physician. They nurse at sticky breasts, at which the young mammalian pets of the village have also suckled, and soon are crawling on the feces-contaminated soil and chewing on an unbelievable variety of objects. Our thesis is that the high level of maternally derived antibody, early exposure to pathogens, the prolonged period of lactation, and the generally excellent nutritional status of the child make it possible for him to achieve a *relatively* smooth transition from passive to active immunity to many of the agents of disease to which he is exposed. The situation is well illustrated by the manner in which concomitantly administered gamma globulin reduces the impact of a rubeola vaccination while still permitting the development of effective immunity. To be sure, civilized tropical populations also have relatively high globulin levels, so that there should be high placental transfer of passive immunity; however, because of the higher effective birth rate, the child of the civilizado is seldom nursed as long as the Indian child and thus falls prey to weanling diarrhea and malnutrition.

By his vaccination programs, then, modern man is developing a relatively painless immunity to diseases, similar in some ways to the manner in which the Indian seems to have developed immunity to some of his diseases. A danger for both groups is the sudden appearance of a "new" disease. Burnet has described some of the possible consequences for civilized societies in the appearance in the laboratory of strains of pathogens with new combinations of antigenic and virulence properties, and Lederberg has labeled this threat as one of the hidden dangers in experiments related to biological warfare. At the other extreme, we have recently witnessed at first hand the consequences of a measles epidemic among the Yanomama, known from antibody studies to be a "virgin-soil" population with respect to this virus. Although the symptomatic response of the Indian to the disease may be somewhat (but not markedly) greater than our own, much of the well-recognized enhanced morbidity and mortality in such epidemics is due to the secondary features of the epidemic—the collapse of village life when almost everyone is highly febrile, when mothers cannot nurse their infants, and when there is no one to provide for the needs of the community. After witnessing this spectacle, I find it unpleasant to contemplate its possible modern counterpart—when, in some densely populated area, a new pathogen, or an old one such as smallpox or malaria, appears and escapes control, and a serious breakdown of local services follows.

This relative balance with his endemic diseases is only one aspect of the generally harmonious relationship with his ecosystem that characterizes primitive man. . . .

A Program

. . . In the light of our recent experiences among the Indian tribes, I shall now briefly consider some possible emphases in human genetics in the immediate future. . . . My suggestions are rather conservative; they are designed to preserve what we have rather than to promote unreal hopes of spectacular advances. They constitute in many respects an attempt to recreate, within limits, certain conditions that we have observed. These suggestions do not stem from any romanticism concerning the noble savage: Indian life is harsh and cruel, and it countenances an overt aggressiveness that is unthinkable today. Obviously the world should not return to a state of subdivision into demes of 50 to 200 persons constantly involved in a pattern of shifting loyalties and brutal conflict vis-à-vis neighboring demes. Nor are we likely to return to polygyny, with number of wives in part a function of one's "fierceness"—demonstrated by a series of duels with clubs or stylized bouts of chest poundings. Clearly we do not wish to abandon modern medical care to permit natural selection to have a better opportunity to work. But there are other, less disruptive aspects of primitive society for which there is a modern counterpart. These are enumerated below as a series of principles.

Stabilization of the Gene Pool

First principle: Stabilize the gene pool numerically. Throughout the world, primitive man seems to have curbed his intrinsic fertility to a greater extent than has the civilized world in recent centuries. Exactly how those curbs were relaxed with the advent of civilization is unclear, but the agricultural revolution undoubtedly played a part. Although it is currently fashionable to indict the great religions, on the basis of the Old Testament injunction to "be fruitful and multiply," their precise role (until recent times) is in my opinion unclear. The remaining pockets of dissent with the principle of population limitation are rapidly disappearing; the next 5 years will convince even the most reluctant. But by what precise formula should population limitation be accomplished? I have previously urged a simple quota system, set at three living children per couple on the thesis that failure to marry, infertility, and voluntary limitation to less than three would result in a realized average of approximately two children who reach the age of reproduction. I now wonder whether failure of contraception will not result in so many well-intentioned persons exceeding their quota that these guidelines are not sufficiently stringent; I would therefore amend the earlier suggestion to include provision for voluntary sterilization after the third child. You will recognize that this proposal implies relative stabilization of the present gene pool, a move that will tend to conserve all our present bewildering diversity but hinder evolution. It makes no value judgments about any specific group. There would be less opportunity for changes in gene frequency than with present patterns of differential fertility.

Such a policy cannot succeed if some religions and governments simply continue their present half-hearted admonitions and leave the rest to science, while other religions and governments actually oppose effective population control. What has been signally lacking thus far is a clear statement at every possible level of responsibility of the implications of continuing the present rate of population increase. Also lacking has been an administrative framework within which all peoples move toward population control simultaneously, thus dispelling deep-rooted fears that some sectors are being subjected to a subtle form of genocide. Bills now pending in the U.S. Congress— S. 2108, S. 2701, S. 3219, S. 3502, H.R. 11550, H.R. 15165—carry the hope that the United States will shortly be facing these questions much more forthrightly than in the past.

Protection of the Gene Pool

Second principle: Protect the gene against damage. If, as we have implied, polygyny among the Indian has eugenic overtones, there is no acceptable modern counterpart in view. However, we can at least protect the gene pool from obvious damage. The world of primitive man is remarkably uncontaminated. This fact, plus his lower mean age at reproduction, probably results in lower mutation rates than our own, but we have no direct evidence.

Until recently, the principal concomitant of civilization that appeared capable of damaging the gene pool was an increasing exposure to radiation. Now concern is shifting to the many potentially mutagenic chemicals being introduced into the environment as pesticides, industrial by-products, air contaminants, and so forth. The magnitude of this problem is currently undefined. About 6 percent of all newborn infants have been found to have defects partially or wholly of genetic origin. Let us assume that half of these defects (3 percent) result from recurrent mutation. Doubling the mutation rate would *eventually* double that 3 percent.

For all the work that has been done on the genetic effects of radiation, involving both man and experimental organisms, there still remain large areas of ambiguity, especially as regards the effects of low-level, intermittent, or chronic-type doses, such as characterize most human exposures. . . .

The technical advances of the past 20 years now render it possible and feasible to screen a representative 20 proteins in newborn infants for evidence of mutational damage; hence we need no longer rely, as in the studies at Hiroshima and Nagasaki, on the potential genetic effects of the atomic bombs, on such imprecise indicators of genetic damage as congenital malformations, survival rates, and sex ratio. A society that can afford to send man to the moon surely has the resources and the intelligence to monitor itself properly for increased mutation rates. If a significant increase is detected, however, the task of identifying the responsible agent or agents will, because of the many possibilities, be extremely difficult, and that agent, when identified, may be so relevant to the welfare of society that, as with radiation, the goal will be to minimize rather than to eliminate exposures. Despite these difficulties in detection and control, immediate steps to determine the facts are needed.

Genetic Counseling and Prenatal Diagnosis

Third principle: Improve the quality of life through parental choice based on genetic counseling and prenatal diagnosis. Both the pressures on the social system and its services and the increasing demands of society on the individual render it imperative that full advantage be taken of all morally acceptable developments that promise to minimize the number of unfortunate individuals incapable of full participation in this complex society. We will not return to infanticide, but there are ethical alternatives. Genetic counseling, which defines the high-risk family, represents one such development. In the past, once the identification had been made, the individuals who wished to limit the entry of defective children into the population had only two alternatives: to practice birth control or to apply for voluntary sterilization. Recently the possibilities inherent in prenatal diagnosis based on fetal cells obtained through amniocentesis during the first trimester of pregnancy have been receiving active attention. Where accurate diagnosis is possible and the presence of a defective fetus is established, the parents can be offered an abortion, usually with reasonable prospects of a normal child in the next pregnancy. Thus far the conditions that can be accurately diagnosed in the very early stages of pregnancy and the numerical impact of these entities are relatively small.

The moral issues that are involved cannot be evaded, and it is better in this time of reappraisal for society to face them forthrightly. At what point is the artificial termination of a pregnancy no longer ethical, even when the fetus concerned is incapable of marginal participation in society? Just what defects are of such gravity as to justify intervention? To what extent should persuasion be employed in implementing these new possibilities? In my opinion, once the principle of parental choice of a normal child is established, it seems probable that in large measure the parental desire for normal children can be relied on to result in the purely voluntary elimination of affected fetuses.

Realizing the Genetic Potential of the Individual

Fourth principle: Improve the phenotypic expression of the individual genotype. It is a sobering thought that the relatively egalitarian structure of most primitive societies, plus the absence of large individual differences in material wealth, seems to ensure that, within the culturally imposed boundaries, each individual in primitive society leads a life (and enjoys reproductive success) more in accord with his innate capabilities than in our present democracy. In the difficult times ahead, society clearly needs the fullest possible participation of all its members. In the past, a very major effort has gone into the provision of special services for the physically and mentally handicapped. A retreat from such compassion is unthinkable, but it is apparent that a similar effort directed toward realizing the genetic potential of the underprivileged or the gifted would have far more impact on the solution of our problems.

Much of the thrust of the geneticist and those with allied interests has been directed toward the treatment of specific genetic diseases. Obviously these efforts need not only to be continued but to be greatly expanded. And equally obviously, the Indian contributes no insight into a program in this field of endeavor. Others are

speaking eloquently to the needs and potentialities of this type of investigation.

But an even greater effort should be directed toward what I have elsewhere termed "culture engineering," which merges at one extreme with the euphenics of Lederberg. There is presumably an environment (or group of environments) in which the still poorly understood potentialities of the human animal find the fullest and most harmonious expression. Although our present environment-culture reduces the impact of a number of previously important causes of mortality and morbidity, it creates a host of other "casualties of our times." The challenge to culture engineering is, of course, greatest in the realm of the mind. It is not enough to think in terms of better schools and more attractive housing; the subtle and lasting influence of prenatal and early postnatal influences is becoming increasingly apparent. Experimental mammalian models are yielding fascinating evidence on the complexity of these interactions. It is doubtful whether our precipitous and helter-skelter attacks on our present world will yield an optimum environment. We cannot escape the consequences of the peculiar position in which we have placed ourselves; we must now cautiously and reverently accept the full responsibility for shaping our own world.

Summing Up

The foregoing principles constitute an extremely conservative program in human genetics, which advocates for the present a return to as many of the features of the population structure under which we evolved as is consistent with our present culture. The urgent need to understand the biomedical and social significance of human genetic variability as a basis for an eventual, more definitive program should be clear, and yet we seem to be retreating from support of the necessary research while we are squandering billions in pursuit of dubious military goals.

There has been no mention in this presentation of that brand of genetic engineering concerned with controlled changes in transmissible genetic material. This omission is not due to oversight or limitations of time. My thesis is clearly a plea for a profound respect for ourselves and the system in which we function. It would be inconsistent with that thesis to suggest that, with our present limited knowledge of the human genome, we should in the near future think of intervening to alter it in ways we cannot completely understand. Research along these lines with experimental organisms is inevitable and desirable—but I question the wisdom of attempting, in the foreseeable future, to apply the results of that research to man.

The past decade has witnessed spectacular triumphs in the "inner space" of the cell and the "outer space" of the cosmos. Perhaps this decade will in retrospect be seen as the first of many decades of spectacular advances in our understanding of "*intermediate* space"—the biosphere—the space defined as that narrow life-supporting zone wherein occur the interactions between intact humans and other organisms and their environment which by definition are an ecosystem. As we realize the full complexity of intermediate space, it seems very probable that the scientific challenge to produce new knowledge will be equaled by the challenge of integrating the applications of that new knowledge smoothly into the ecosystem. In the most sophisticated way we can summon, we must return to the awe, and even fear, in which primitive man held the mysterious world about him, and like him we must strive to live in harmony with the only biosphere that we can be certain will be occupied by our descendants.

Carl Jay Bajema

The Genetic Implications of Population Control

Many methods for population control have been proposed, and each one could have different genetic and evolutionary consequences. Here, Carl Bajema contrasts the genetic and evolutionary implications of voluntary population control with a program initiated through legislation. The author discusses the possibility that, on a short-term basis, a voluntary program motivated by propaganda or some reward system may accomplish population control with minimal genetic consequences.

Introduction

Each generation of mankind is faced with the awesome responsibility of having to make decisions concerning the quantity and quality (both genetic and cultural) of future generations. Because of its concern for its increasing population in relation to natural resources and quality of life, America appears to be on the verge of discarding its policy favoring continued population growth and adopting a policy aimed at achieving a zero rate of population growth by voluntary means. The policy that a society adopts with respect to population size will have genetic as well as environmental consequences.

Human populations adapt to their environments genetically as well as culturally. These environments have been and are changing very rapidly, with most of the changes being brought about by man himself. Mankind has, by creating a highly technological society, produced a society in which a significant proportion of its citizens cannot contribute to its growth or maintenance because of the limitations (both genetic and environmental) of their intellect. The modern technological societies of democratic nations offer their citizens a wide variety of opportunities for self-fulfillment but find

From "The Genetic Implications of Population Control" by Carl Jay Bajema from *Bioscience*, Vol. 21, No. 2 (January 15, 1971). Reprinted by permission of the author.

that many of their citizens are incapable of taking advantage of the opportunities open to them.

American society, if it takes its responsibility to future generations seriously, will have to do more than control the size of its population in relation to the environment. American society will have to take steps to insure that individuals yet unborn will have the best genetic and environmental heritage possible to enable them to meet the challenges of the environment and to be able to take advantage of the opportunities for self-fulfillment made available by society.

The question of genetic quality cannot be ignored for very long by American society because it, like all other human societies, has to cope with two perpetual problems as it attempts to adapt to its environment. First, American society has to cope with a continual input of harmful genes into its population via mutation (it has been estimated that approximately one out of every five newly fertilized human eggs is carrying a newly mutated gene that was not present in either of the two parents). The genetic status quo can be maintained in a human population only if the number of new mutant genes added to the population is counterbalanced by an equal number of the mutant genes not being passed on due to the nonreproduction or decreased reproduction of individuals carrying these mutant genes. Otherwise, the proportion of harmful genes in the population will increase. Second, American society has to adapt to a rapidly changing environment. For instance, the technologically based, sociocultural, computer age environment being created by American society has placed a premium on the possession of high intelligence and creativity. Our society requires individuals with high intelligence and creativity to help it make the appropriate social and technological adjustments in order to culturally adapt to its rapidly changing environment. On the other hand, individuals require high intelligence and creativity in order that they, as individuals, can cope with the challenges of the environment and take advantage of the opportunities for self-fulfillment present in our society.

The proportion of the American population that already is genetically handicapped—that suffers a restriction of liberty or competence because of the genes they are carrying—is not small. Therefore the genetic component of the human population-environment equation must be taken into account as we attempt to establish an environment that has a high degree of ecological stability and that maximizes the number of opportunities for self-fulfillment available to each individual human being.

Genetic Consequences of American Life Styles in Sex and Reproduction

American life styles with respect to sex and reproduction are currently in a tremendous state of flux and are changing rapidly. This makes it very difficult to accurately predict the genetic consequences of these life styles. Yet, because these life styles determine the genetic make-up of future generations of Americans, it is necessary that we evaluate the genetic consequences of past and present trends and speculate concerning the probable genetic consequences of projecting these trends into the future. Only then will we be able to determine the severity of the problem and to determine what steps, if any, need to be taken to maintain and improve the genetic heritage of future generations.

American society has developed modern medical techniques which enable many individuals with severe genetic defects to survive to adulthood. Many of these individuals can and do reproduce, thereby passing their harmful genes on to the next generation and increasing the frequency of these genes in the population. At present, there is no indication that heredity counseling decreases the probability that these individuals will have children. The life styles of these individuals with respect to reproduction is creating a larger genetic burden for future generations of Americans to bear.

The effect of American life styles in sex and reproduction on such behavioral patterns as intelligence and personality is much less clear. For instance, during most of man's evolution natural selection has favored the genes for intelligence. The genes for higher mental ability conferred an advantage to their carriers in the competition for survival and reproduction both within and between populations. Thus the more intelligent members of the human species passed more genes on to the next generation than did the less intelligent members, with the result that the genes for higher intelligence increased in frequency. As Western societies shifted from high birth and death rates toward low birth and death rates, however, a breakdown in the relation of natural selection to achievement or "success" took place.

The practice of family planning spread more rapidly among the better educated strata of society resulting in negative fertility differentials. At the period of extreme differences, which in the United States came during the great depression, the couples who were poorly educated were having about twice as many children as the more educated couples. The continued observation of a negative relationship between fertility and such characteristics as education, occupation, and income during the first part of this century led many scientists to believe that this pattern of births was a concomitant of the industrial welfare state society and must make for the genetic deterioration of the human race. This situation was, in part, temporary. The fertility differentials have declined dramatically since World War II so that by the 1960s some women college graduates were having 90 percent as many children as the U.S. average. A number of recent studies of American life styles in reproduction, when taken collectively, seem to indicate that, as the proportion of the urban population raised in a farm environment decreases, as the educational attainment of the population increases, and as women gain complete control over childbearing (via contraception and induced abortion), the relationship between fertility and such characteristics as income, occupation, and educational attainment will become less negative and may even become positive.

The only two American studies which have related the intellectual ability (as measured by IQ) of an individual to his subsequent completed fertility have found the relationship to be essentially zero or slightly positive. Further analyses of the data of these two studies indicate that it is difficult to infer the relationship between intelligence (as measured by IQ) and fertility from group differences in fertility with respect to income, occupation, and educational attainment because there is so much variation within these groups with respect to intelligence.

The overall net effect of current American life styles in reproduction appears to be slightly dysgenic—to be favoring an increase in harmful genes which will genetically handicap a larger proportion of the next generation of Americans. American life styles in reproduction are, in part,

a function of the population policy of the United States. What will be the long-range genetic implications of controlling or not controlling population size in an industrialized welfare state democracy such as America?

Genetic Implications of Policies Favoring Continued Population Growth

Most contemporary human societies are organized in such a way that they encourage population growth. How is the genetic make-up of future generations affected by the size of the population? What will be the ultimate genetic consequences given a society that is growing in numbers in relation to its environment? One possible consequence is military aggression coupled with genocide to attain additional living space. This would result in genetic change insofar as the population eradicated or displaced differs genetically from the population that is aggressively expanding the size of its environment. The displacement of the American Indians by West Europeans is an example of this approach to the problem of population size in relation to the environment. Throughout man's evolution such competition between different populations of human beings has led to an increase in the cultural and genetic supports for aggressive behavior in the human species. Violence as a form of aggressive behavior to solve disagreements among populations appears to have become maladaptive in the nuclear age. It will probably take a nuclear war to prove this contention.

If one assumes that military aggression plus genocide to attain additional living space is not an option open to a society with a population policy encouraging growth in numbers then a different type of genetic change will probably take place. Most scientists who have attempted to ascertain the probable effect that overcrowding in a welfare state will have on man's genetic make-up have concluded that natural selection would favor those behavior patterns that most people consider least desirable. For instance, René Dubos, in discussing the effect of man's future environment on the direction and intensity of natural selection in relation to human personality patterns, states that:

Most disturbing perhaps are the behavioral consequences likely to ensue from overpopulation. The ever-increasing complexity of the social structure will make some form of regimentation unavoidable; freedom and privacy may come to constitute antisocial luxuries and their attainment to involve real hardships. In consequence, there may emerge by selection a stock of human beings suited to accept as a matter of course a regimented and sheltered way of life in a teeming and polluted world, from which all wilderness and fantasy of nature will have disappeared. The domesticated farm animal and the laboratory rodent in a controlled environment will then become true models for the study of man.[1]

The genetic and cultural undesirability of either of these two alternative outcomes for mankind makes it imperative that societies move quickly to adopt policies aimed at achieving and maintaining an optimum population size that maximizes the dignity and individual worth of a human being rather than maximizing the number of human beings in relation to the environment.

Genetic Implications of Policies Favoring Control of Population Size by Voluntary Means

There is strong evidence that contemporary societies can achieve control of their population size by voluntary means, at least in the short run.

What will be the distribution of births in societies that have achieved a zero population growth rate? In a society where population size is constant—where each generation produces only enough offspring to replace itself—there will still be variation among couples with respect to the number of children they will have. Some individuals will be childless or have only one child for a variety of reasons—biological (genetically or environmentally caused sterility), psychological (inability to attract a mate, desire to remain childless), etc. Some individuals will have to have at least three children to compensate for those individuals who have less than two children. The resulting differential fertility—variation in the number of children couples have—provides an opportunity for natural selection to operate and would bring about genetic change if the differences in fertility among individuals are correlated with differences (physical, physiological, or behavioral) among individuals.

The United States is developing into a social

welfare state democracy. This should result in an environment that will evoke the optimal response from the variety of genotypes (specific combinations of genes that individuals carry) present in the population. It is questionable, however, as to whether a social welfare state democracy creates the type of environment that will automatically bring about a eugenic distribution of births resulting in the maintenance or enhancement of man's genetic heritage. It is also questionable as to whether a social welfare state democracy (or any society for that matter) will be able to achieve and maintain a zero population growth rate—a constant population size—by voluntary means.

Both Charles Darwin and Garrett Hardin have argued that universal compulsion will be necessary to achieve and maintain zero population growth. They argue that appeals to individual conscience as the means by which couples are to restrain themselves from having more than two children will not work because those individuals or groups who refused to restrain themselves would increase their numbers in relation to the rest, with the result that these individuals or groups with their cultural and/or biological supports for high fertility would constitute a larger and larger proportion of the population of future generations and *Homo contracipiens* would be replaced by *Homo progenetivis*.

Hardin raises this problem in his classic paper, "The Tragedy of the Commons," when he states:

If each human family were dependent only on its own resources; if the children of improvident parents starved to death; if, thus, overbreeding brought its own "punishment" to the germ line—then there would be no public interest in controlling the breeding of families. But our society is deeply committed to the welfare state, and hence confronted with another aspect of the tragedy of the commons.

In a welfare state, how shall we deal with the family, the religion, the race, or the class (or indeed any distinguishable and cohesive group) that adopts overbreeding as a policy to secure its own aggrandizement? To couple the concept of freedom to breed with the belief that everyone born has an equal right to the commons is to lock the world into a tragic course of action.[2]

[1] René Dubos, *Man Adapting* (New Haven, Conn.: Yale University Press, 1965).
[2] Garrett Hardin, "The Tragedy of the Commons," *Science*, 162 (1968): 1243–1248.

The only way out of this dilemma according to Hardin is for society to create reproductive responsibility via social arrangements that produce coercion of some sort. The kind of coercion Hardin talks about is mutual coercion, mutually agreed upon by the majority of the people affected. Compulsory taxes are an example of mutual coercion. Democratic societies frequently have to resort to mutual coercion to escape destruction of the society by the irresponsible. Mutual coercion appears to be the only solution to the problem of pollution. If Hardin is right, it may also be the only solution for any society that is attempting to control the size and/or the genetic make-up of its population.

Hardin's thesis has been questioned on the basis that children are no longer the economic assets they once were in agrarian societies. Rufous Miles has argued that, given today's postindustrial economy, children are expensive pleasures; they are economic liabilities rather than assets. Miles points out that:

There is no conflict, therefore, between the economic self-interest of married couples to have small families and the collective need of society to preserve "the commons." It is in both their interests to limit procreation to not more than a replacement level. Unfortunately, couples do not seek their self-interest in economic terms alone, but in terms of total satisfactions. They are "buying" children and paying dearly for them. The problem, therefore, is compounded of how to persuade couples to act more in their own economic self-interest and that of their children; how to assist them in obtaining more psychological satisfactions from sources other than large families; and how to replace the outworn and now inimical tradition of the large family with a new "instant tradition" of smaller families.[3]

As pointed out earlier in this paper, there is some evidence to support the contention that as American society becomes more urbanized, achieves higher levels of educational attainment, and allows its citizens to exercise complete control over their fertility, reproductive patterns will develop which will lead to a zero or negative population growth rate and a eugenic distribution of births. If this prediction is correct, then there will be no need for the adoption of mutual coercion—compulsory methods of population control—by American society in order to control the size and/or genetic

quality of its population. If, on the other hand, these reproductive patterns do not develop or are transitory, it may very well be that reproduction will have to become a privilege rather than a right in social welfare state democracies in order to insure that these societies and their citizens do not have to suffer the environmental and genetic consequences of irresponsible reproduction.

What might the genetic consequences be if a society had to resort to mutual coercion—had to employ compulsory methods of population control—to control its numbers?

Genetic Implications of Compulsory Population Control

There are a number of methods by which compulsory population control can be achieved. Mutual coercion could be institutionalized by a democratic society to ensure that couples who would otherwise be reproductively irresponsible are restricted to having only two children. Compulsory abortion and/or sterilization could be employed to guarantee that no woman bears more children than she has a right to under the rules set up by society.

A democratic society forced to employ mutual coercion to achieve zero population growth will probably assign everyone the right to have exactly two children. Because of the fact that some individuals will have only one child or will not reproduce at all, it will be necessary to assign these births needed to achieve replacement level to other individuals in that population. The assignment of these births could be made at random via a national lottery system. The result would probably be genetic deterioration. While those individuals who have less than two children would constitute a sample of the population with above average frequencies of various genetic defects, the selective removal of their genes would probably not be sufficient to counterbalance the continual input of mutations. Thus the result would probably be genetic deterioration even if the environment remained constant. If the environment were changing (this is about the one thing we can always count on—a constantly changing environment), the population would become even more geneti-

[3] Rufous Miles, "Whose Baby Is the Population Problem?" *Population Bulletin*, 16 (1970): 3–36.

cally ill-adapted because those individuals in the society that are best adapted to changing environments and to the new environments would not be passing more genes on to the next generation on a per person basis than those individuals less well adapted.

What kinds of eugenics programs could be designed for a democratic society where mutual coercion is institutionalized to ensure that couples who would otherwise be irresponsible are restricted to having two children?

One compulsory population control program designed to operate in a democratic society that has eugenic implications is the granting of marketable licenses to have children to women in whatever number necessary to ensure replacement of the population (say 2.2 children per couple). The unit certificate might be the deci-child or 1/10 a child and the accumulation of ten of these units, by purchase or inheritance or gift, would permit a woman in maturity to have one child. If equality of opportunity were the norm in such a society, those individuals with genetic make-ups that enable them to succeed (high intelligence, personality, etc.) would be successful in reaching the upper echelons of society and would be in the position of being able to purchase certificates from the individuals who were less successful because of their genetic limitations. The marketable baby license approach to compulsory population control, first discussed by Kenneth Boulding in his book *The Meaning of the Twentieth Century*, relies on the environment, especially the sociocultural environment, to do the selecting automatically, based on economics. The marketable baby license approach would probably bring about a better genetic adaptation between a population and its environment. Remember, the direction and rate of genetic change is, to a great extent, a function of the social structure of the human population. The marketable baby license approach ensures that those people selected in society are those who are most successful economically. To ensure genetic improvement society would have to make sure that achievement and financial reward are much more highly correlated than they are at the present.

Another compulsory population program that a democracy might adopt would be to grant each individual the right to have two children and to assign the child-bearing rights of those individuals unable or unwilling to have two children to other individuals based on their performance in one or more contests (competition involving mental ability, personality, sports, music, arts, literature, business, etc.). The number of births assigned to the winners of various contests would be equal to the deficit of births created by individuals having less than two children. Society would then determine to a great extent the direction of its future genetic (and cultural) evolution by determining the types of contests that would be employed and what proportion of the winners (the top 1 percent or 5 percent) would be rewarded with the right to have an additional child above the two children granted to all members of society.

A society might even go further and employ a simple eugenic test—the examination of the first two children in order to assure that neither one was physically or mentally below [the] average which a couple must pass before being eligible to have additional children. The assignment of additional births to those individuls who passed the eugenic tests then could be on the basis of a lottery, marketable baby licenses, or contests, with the number of licenses equaling the deficit of births created by individuals who, at the end of their reproductive years (or at time of death if they died before reaching the end of their reproductive years), did not have any children or who only had one child.

The programs designed to bring about a eugenic distribution of births that have been discussed so far may prove to be incapable of doing much more than counteracting the input of harmful mutations. In order to significantly reduce the proportion of the human population that is genetically handicapped, a society may have to require that each couple pass certain eugenic tests before being allowed to become the genetic parents of *any* children. If one or both of the prospective genetic parents fail the eugenic tests, the couple could still be allowed to have children via artificial insemination and/or artificial inovulation, utilizing human sperm and eggs selected on the basis of genetic quality. Such an approach would enable society to maintain the right of couples to have at least two children while improving the genetic birthright of future generations at the same time.

Successful control of the size and/or genetic quality of human populations by society may require restrictions on the right of individual human beings to reproduce. The right of individuals to have as many children as they desire must be considered in relation to the right of individuals yet unborn to be free from genetic handicaps and to be able to live in a high quality environment. The short-term gain in individual freedom attained in a society that grants everyone the right to reproduce and to have as many children as they want can be more than offset by the long-term loss in individual freedom by individuals yet unborn who, as a consequence, are genetically handicapped and/or are forced to live in an environment that has deteriorated due to the pressure of human numbers.

Conclusion

Each generation of mankind faces anew the awesome responsibility of making decisions which will affect the quantity and genetic quality of the next generation. A society, if it takes its responsibility to future generations seriously, will take steps to ensure that individuals yet unborn will have the best genetic and cultural heritage possible to enable them to meet the challenges of the environment and to take advantage of the opportunities for self-fulfillment present in that society.

The way in which a society is organized will determine, to a great extent, the direction and intensity of natural selection especially with respect to behavioral patterns. The genetic make-up of future generations is also a function of the size of the population and how population size is regulated by society. The genetic implications of the following three basic types of population policies were explored in this paper: (1) policies favoring continued population growth; (2) policies aimed at achieving zero population growth by voluntary means; and (3) policies aimed at achieving zero population growth by compulsory measures (mutual coercion mutually agreed upon in a democratic society). If societies adopt compulsory population control measures, it will be for the control of population size and not for the control of the genetic make-up of the population. However, it is but a short step to compulsory control of genetic quality once compulsory programs aimed at controlling population size have been adopted. The author personally hopes that mankind will be able to solve both the quantitative and qualitative problems of population by voluntary means. Yet one must be realistic and consider the alternatives. This is what the author has attempted to do in this paper by reviewing the genetic implications of various population control programs.

Michael H. Crawford

Some Environmental Problems for Physical Anthropologists

Population

The most important challenge presently facing mankind, it would appear, is to arrest the growth of population. Failure could mean war, social disintegration, starvation, epidemics, and a general deterioration in the quality of life. We have seen from Bajema's and Asimov's reviews of the possible genetic consequences of failure to control our population increase, that when countries attempt to solve the problem of overpopulation by genocide or warfare, the defeated nation is either totally annihilated or assimilated by the victorious group. Genetically this implies either a loss of material, or possibly miscegenation on a large scale. Genocide and the subsequent loss of genetic information from the world gene pool is deleterious because of the reduction of genetic variability, which is advantageous in an ever changing environment. Miscegenation, however, results in the maintenance of the greatest amount of variability while lowering the probability of the segregation of rare, recessive alleles into homozygous genotypes.[1]

Although the most logical method of arresting the growth of population is through some method of

[1] For more information on population genetics, see the section "Race and Racism."

voluntary contraception which would limit family size to two offspring, Paul Ehrlich, when recently asked whether family planning could cut the birth rate and reduce population to the optimum level, responded that the problem around the world is not the unwanted babies—but the wanted ones. This is, in part, the difficulty of instituting a successful family program and the reason that some form of legislation may be required to contain the population explosion. The success of a voluntary program of birth control depends upon its efficacy in altering the attitudes and values in the society by means of a carefully organized propaganda campaign, including appeals to patriotism and advice on the economic advantage of having fewer children to care for. Small families might become the happy, healthy, admired families, and large ones the result of social irresponsibility.

G. Hardin has remarked that if the choice of restraining from having more than two children is left to couples, those who refuse to limit their numbers would constitute a larger proportion of the gene pool of the future, while the socially conscious individuals would not be numerically as well represented. There is no evidence, however, to suppose that this would lead to any deterioration of the gene pool, and no need for governmental attempts at so-called genetic quality control. Limitations in population size are desirable but we do not know all of the possible repercussions and by-products of selective breeding. And few of us would be willing to actively promote or encourage the development of the negative utopias envisioned by Aldous Huxley in *Brave New World* and George Orwell in *1984*. Since we cannot be certain what kinds of people would be best suited to tomorrow's world the safest course is to promote the maintenance of the greatest possible amount of variability—racial, ethnic, and individual.

Aggression

In the opening essay of this section, the author compared the conflicting theories of Lorenz and the Russells about the biological or evolutionary origin of aggression. Although their hypotheses appear to be contradictory, they are equally valid approaches. Lorenz and Ardrey are correct in stating that man has the genetic capacity for violence and aggression. This capacity is probably not limited to man but is found in most animal species. The Russells are also correct in their view that aggression and violence occur under stressful conditions such as overpopulation or food

shortage (see the section on "Violence"). Aggression, like any complex behavior, is the sum total of the interaction between environmental stimuli and the biological structures of the organism polygenically controlled. Undoubtedly there are differences among individuals, populations, and species—differences in the degree and form that aggression takes—determined by morphological and endocrinological variation. The Russells stress the environmental conditions which cause aggressive acts, while Lorenz and Ardrey explain the universality of aggression on the basis of genetics and morphology. The apparent contradiction is purely a matter of emphasis.

Pollution

Sources of pollution of the environment can be summarized as follows:

I. Air pollution
   A. Automobile emissions
   B. Industrial
   C. Nuclear explosions
   D. Airplane exhausts

II. Water pollution
   A. Industry—mercury, detergents, production by-products
   B. Insecticide spraying—DDT
   C. Oil leakage
   D. Eutrophication due to soil fertilization and detergents
   E. Private homes
   F. Nondegradable consumer goods

III. Organismic pollution
   A. Food preservatives
   B. Drugs and medicines
   C. Polluted water

IV. Sensory pollution
   A. Auditory
   B. Visual
   C. Olfactory

The key to successful pollution control is strict legislation prohibiting industrial emission of particulate pollutants and permitting only low levels of gaseous emissions. Many American cities have good antipollution laws and fail to enforce them. Industries have blackmailed communities by threatening to leave and move their payrolls elsewhere if the laws are stringently enforced. But if pollution laws and their enforcement were uniform throughout the country, there would be no advantage in moving to another region.

Automobiles must be required by law to be equipped

with antipollution devices, and leaded gasoline should be removed from the market. Public transportation must be improved in order to eliminate the necessity for driving to the already dangerously congested and polluted urban areas. All of these suggestions are merely delaying tactics, buying us more time until non-combustion engines can be developed. Instead of spending millions of dollars developing SSTs or ABM systems which become obsolete upon completion, the government could subsidize the research and development of nonpolluting engines. Just how they should be developed is controversial. Some critics of the electric motor claim that the pollution caused by generating the electricity for recharging the batteries would be greater than that caused by present automobile exhausts. This may be accurate when the generators operate on the principles of combustion, but other sources of energy could be tapped for this purpose—either solar radiation or the heat from the core of the earth, which could be reached by drilling. Additional research is needed before such methods can be used.

Similar legislation and enforcement is necessary to control the pollution liberated by supersonic jets and tankers which spill oil into our seas. If the polluters were forced to pay the costs of remedying their transgressions, there would be no industrial polluters!

Government has actually made some progress in controlling a number of pollutants which were shown to cause adverse effects in man. These include atmospheric nuclear tests, indiscriminant spraying of DDT, and the sale of drugs such as thalidomide, which has been shown to cause congenital abnormalities. But more stringent regulations are needed against noise pollution, visual pollution, and eutrophication. Communities should forbid the erection of unsightly, neon light advertisements. Billboards must go. Some attempts must be made to muffle sound, through research into the acoustic properties of objects, like garbage cans, which are ritually "clanked," dropped, and reverberated while the city dweller tries to sleep.

Research

The articles in this section were written by psychologists, geneticists, science popularizers, plant physiologists, and ecologists; not by anthropologists. Although there is a paucity of anthropological literature in this area, there are several lines of relevant research open to anthropologists, especially those with a biological orientation.

The primary contribution of biological anthropology to the population problem is in the understanding of the effects of overcrowding. Although a great deal of information is available on overcrowding among infrahuman animals, little is known about this phenomenon in man. Calhoun's classical studies on crowded rats in "behavioral sinks" have revealed great behavioral alterations and pathologies. Similar results have been observed after the experimental or natural crowding of various other mammalian species.

In humans, however, culture plays an important role in the interpretation of the response to overcrowding as well as in its magnitude. The personal space required by a person may be dictated both by learning and by a physiological reaction to bodily heat emission. People may have inherited from their hominoid ancestors some of the regulatory mechanisms which govern their need for personal space. Nonhuman primates might be experimentally tested as to the size of their personal space and the strength of their response to violations of it. Research into the underlying mechanism governing personal space in man appears to be highly promising.

Many questions about the biological effect of pollution cannot be answered at present. We do not know the concentrations of the various chemical pollutants necessary to cause either physiological disturbances in the organism or mutagenesis or carcinogenesis. We do not know whether all chemical pollutants are additive in their action, like radiation, or whether they detoxify in the body without serious aftereffects. We do not know the long-term results of the continual sensory bombardment of the city dweller. Biological anthropologists, in collaboration with other specialists, may be able to make valuable contributions in several of these areas.

Some anthropologists have taken a phylogenetic approach to the question of human aggression, while others have attempted to draw analogies from observations of the behavior of infrahuman animals or from selected aberrant human groups. Of these three approaches the phylogenetic is probably the least satisfactory, for it is based on fragmentary evidence and phylogenetic interpretations are therefore highly questionable. Assertions by paleontologists, such as L. S. B. Leakey, that aggression in early man must have begun only with the appearance of tools are speculation.

Studies of aggression in animals are more fruitful, although their applicability to man is only by analogy. Field studies yield comparative information about the variability of aggressive behavior within and between populations, suggesting the degree of interaction between environment and the genetic components of the trait. Experimental work with animals has located the brain areas controlling different aspects of aggression, but the study of aggression in animals is still a frontier, and many questions are still unanswered.

Man, by his nature, is not a good experimental subject, particularly in the study of aggression. Learning and experience color the manifestation of aggressive behavior and so complicate any analysis of possible biological determinants. Aside from intensive studies of brain pathology due to accidents, warfare, and surgery, there has been little opportunity to explore the biological basis of aggressive behavior in man. With the exception of the XYY prisoners, the study of aggression in individuals with chromosomal abnormalities has not, to my knowledge, been investigated. To date, even such fundamental steps as the definition of aggression and the reduction of aggressive behavior to some kind of quantifiable unit have not been accomplished. There are many possibilities for future anthropological research in this area.

Finally, there is the question of the resilience of the environment: How massive does ecological disruption have to be before the biosphere fails to return to its original condition? How much environmental insult can the earth tolerate before the damage is irreparable? The pessimists and prophets of doom claim that the earth has already reached a point of no return and that it is only a question of whether the world ends with a bang or expires with a cough. At a congress of World Federalists, U Thant, the former Secretary-General of the United Nations, warned: "The degradation of our environment is now so serious that unless immediate measures are taken, the very capacity of the planet itself to sustain life will be in doubt."

An optimist, René Dubos, is convinced that all is not lost and that the ecological damage to the earth is reversible. He cites, as an example, the metamorphosis that the environment of London has undergone during the last twenty years. For two hundred years London was the most polluted city in the world, famous for its pea-soup fogs, a melange of moisture and pollutants. This fog tripled the normal death rate for four consecutive days in 1952; shortly thereafter, strict antipollution laws were passed. Slowly the air and water cleared and the birds and wild life returned to the parks of London. The city has not experienced the pea-soup fog for a number of years, and in 1970 had 50 percent more sunshine than ten years before. The ecological rejuvenation of London has prompted René Dubos to remark: "Nature is immensely resilient . … and bounces back from our abuses."

9 Intervention: Changing the System

Art Gallaher, Jr.
Intervention: Changing the System

Fred Gearing
The Strategy of the Fox Project

William F. Whyte and Allan R. Holmberg
Human Problems of U.S. Enterprise in Latin America

Garth N. Jones
Strategies and Tactics of Planned Organizational Change: Case Examples on the Modernization Process of Traditional Societies

Lauriston Sharp
Steel Axes for Stone-Age Australians

Allan R. Holmberg
The Research and Development Approach to the Study of Change

Anthony F. C. Wallace
Revitalization Processes

Art Gallaher, Jr.
On Changing the System

In an important sense this world of ours is a new world, in which the unity of knowledge, the nature of human communities, the order of society, the order of ideas, the very notions of society and culture have changed and will not return to what they have been in the past. What is new is new not because it has never been there before, but because it has changed in quality. One thing that is new is the prevalence of newness, the changing scale and scope of change itself, so that the world alters as we walk in it, so that the years of man's life measure not some small growth or rearrangement or moderation of what he learned in childhood, but a great upheaval.   Robert Oppenheimer

Art Gallaher, Jr.

Intervention: Changing the System

The contemporary rhetoric of the young continually reaffirms Oppenheimer's notion that "the world alters as we walk in it." In this regard there is continuity between the young of this and previous generations in our society. However, the concerns expressed by the young today differ markedly from those expressed by the young or old of other generations.

No longer, for example, do we hear debate about planning versus laissez-faire nonintervention, or about whether change ought or ought not to occur. Both planning and change are normative conditions in the greater society. The new concerns are about the directions taken by our society, and the pace of change—so fast that it seems to catch people up in currents swift enough to be disorienting.

The signs are explicit. Today's youth demand involvement—*human intervention designed to make a difference in the human condition*. And the evidence for this demand abounds. To mention only a few activities commonplace in the student culture these days: "free university," confrontation politics, student demand for greater involvement by the university in the "real" problems of society, "Nader's Raiders," and the "radical caucuses" which challenge the self-serving premises of professional scientific societies.

These developments follow naturally from the events of recent years. Such domestic problems as economic, racial, ethnic, class, and political conflicts have created unprecedented strains within all our institutions. At the same time, external events—such as Korea, Vietnam especially, and our burgeoning political commitments abroad—have added to domestic strains in ways that cause many to doubt our ability to set priorities. Attempts over the years to manage these strains have led to profound transformations in our society and to many innovations in our international spheres of influence. Change is everywhere apparent. It has had to be that way because the accommodative needs of the society have made it so; it will continue that way because the current generation, born in conflict and having known nothing other in its society's internal and external relations, will continue to press for modification. Moreover, people of all ages and levels increasingly express a personal, vested interest in decisions that bear ultimately on their chances in life.

There is, then, no doubt among the young nor the old regarding the wisdom of planning, but there is doubt about the wisdom of those who are doing the planning. Change is ubiquitous in American society, but those who are to inherit the social system are bent on not taking that system for granted.

It is not surprising, therefore, that today there is no shortage of people and organizations ready and willing to intervene to modify the life style of others. The desire to help, to become involved, to convince others of what is wrong with them and best for them, is a modern social movement of considerable force. The interventionists who would make all the necessary corrections in the social order present themselves in a cacophony of claims and counterclaims. It is, in fact, hard to know the players without a scorecard! They try to convince that their legitimacy derives from *their* auspices—they are the public sector, or the private sector, they represent the marketplace, or science, or religion; that their acceptance should rest in *their* motives, such as peace or conflict, the reduction or substitution of power, or philanthropy; that their success inheres in *their* tactics and strategies, such as altruism, induction, deduction, seduction, or armed force. These elements are all there, in the arguments of interventionists, and they converge especially in a bewildering crescendo on those who are most often the targets for assistance, who are the most vulnerable—the poor, the powerless, the dissident, the disaffected, and the rejected of society. It is, in fact, the style of the day to intervene in the lives of the dispossessed. It is precisely because the practice is so widespread that issues concerning intervention are being raised in all quarters (see, for example, the section "Anthropology and the Third World"). The desire to correct social ills and the unbounded enthusiasm which is brought to the task are not, after all, unquestionable credentials nor necessarily an adequate reason for intervention.

There are, then, special concerns which, when translated into responsibilities, are not to be taken lightly by those who intervene to give direction to the lives of others. And the biggest responsibility of all is to *know*. "Knowing," in this context, means understanding one's own motives as intervener, including those of interested second parties if they are present, and understanding the desires of those who will experience modification in their life styles. One cannot assume that one's unique experience, presumed superior knowledge, divine inspiration, or other claims to omnipotence are adequate to the task. One of the lessons of history, not to be forgotten in the current rush toward greater involvement, is that those who advocate and intervene are often less concerned with solving the problems of a target population than they are with finding solutions to their own. This is no less true of nation-states than individuals, no less true of missionaries than revolutionaries. Those presumptuous enough to intervene should pause long enough to discover whether their intentions correspond to the needs of those whom they presume to help. If not, the verdict of time comes down heavily upon them.

If we reduce what we have just said to the most appropriate summative principles, we are talking, of course, of the need for adequate communications. In the end, it is by this route that the kind of knowing that we have been discussing, cultural knowledge, comes. And communication, it must be recognized, is not one person's shouting loudly, nor even speaking softly, *at* another; it is in turn listening to what that person has to say. Only then are his desires, attitudes, sentiments, and his conceptions of his own problems revealed. This kind of intimate and private sharing, in which one also gives of oneself in kind, is to know the other in a very special sense. Even this, however, is not enough. For as Robert Redfield reminded us several years ago, real communication depends also on one's developing a unique kind of hearing aid—to hear the sound of one's own voice, not as it falls upon one's own ears, but as it falls upon the ears of the listener. To achieve this is not only to know the listener but, perhaps more importantly, to know oneself as well.

The kind of knowing suggested above reduces the compulsion of people to help their friends without first listening to their problems. It is indeed frustrating to be presented with solutions to problems of which one is not aware; more so to be presented with answers to questions that are not yet asked. Both are mistakes common to interventionists; in either case, the likelihood of confused and misinterpreted motives, and hence conflict, is great. It follows that those who intervene to reduce tensions should be especially careful that by their actions they do not add to waters already troubled.

Human social life consists of elements which are related, and to change even one is to modify some others. To "know" the other as we have suggested enables the intervener to comprehend and foresee some of the consequences of the changes that he hopes to achieve.

In the articles that follow, we turn our attention to some of the problems posed by intervention. Our ground is the understanding of culture change that has been gained by anthropologists, especially of directed or planned change; our figures against that ground are those who would intervene actively and purposefully in the lives of others. Our concern is not to provide a formula for success; no such formulas are known. But we can gain, from anthropological insight, some understanding which should enable us to make more enlightened judgments about intervention designed to change the system. The ethics of intervention, beyond the responsibility to "know" are not discussed here; for these important considerations the reader is referred to "The Social Responsibility of the Anthropologist."

Our articles are drawn from the anthropological literature on the nature of short-term cultural change. They are arranged to provide some understanding of (1) the conditions conducive to direct intervention, (2) models of intervention in the social system, and (3) the consequences of intervention in a system already undergoing change.

Fred Gearing
The Strategy of the Fox Project

In 1948, six students from the University of Chicago, doing research among the Fox Indians in central Iowa, decided to try to help the Indians solve their problems. Fred Gearing, an anthropologist who was at that time one of the students, tells us how they set about it. The strategies employed, which subtly emphasized confrontation tactics and teasing an awareness of needs and goals out of the target population, is now considered an action anthropology model of social intervention.

We will be acting in the Fox community and in surrounding white Iowa communities in the coming years. Our plan of action derives from a hypothesis about the nature of the Fox problem. We see that problem as residing in the relations between the Fox and their neighbors. We think the Fox and nearby whites have slipped into a vicious circle.

The total activities of the Fox project in the coming three or four years will be a refinement and test of that hypothesis.

I will first characterize that vicious circle. Then I will outline the strategy in our coming attempts to break into that circle and change its nature.

You will find to the right a schematic diagram of the vicious circle. It will probably help if you follow that diagram.

I enter the vicious circle, in this description, from the left. You see a circle reading: Fox self-organization and a square reading: Whites believe Fox are lazy. Items in circles refer to behavioral phenomena (or inferences from them); items in squares refer to more purely mental or verbal phenomena—ideas and attitudes. Where the two overlap as in this instance, the meaning is that the idea springs, in important degree, from the behavior. So, I begin with a behavioral item, the Fox self-organization, and a belief item, Whites believe Fox are lazy.

Deep-seated psychological differences between Indians and non-Indian Americans have been suggested by scores of students. Most often the difference has been characterized by the terms shame and guilt. Our strong impression is to accept the contrast. We descriptively characterize it in terms of self-organization. In terms of self-organi-

zation, Anglo-Americans seem to adopt as they mature a personal, ideal self. That self is a more or less consistent collection of virtues. The life careers of white men are, ideally, a ceaseless effort to make the real self coincide with that ideal self. Restated in terms of ethos, a—perhaps the—primary ethical principle of Anglo-American society is virtue. In spite of individual and class variation, and in spite of the doubtlessly true reports of decreasing inner-directedness, and in spite, even, of variation within the Fox community, contrast with the Fox is striking. The Fox individual does not seem to create such an ideal self; he does not see himself as *becoming* at all; he is. Restated in terms of ethos, the primary ethical principle of the Fox is harmony.

The effects of that contrast are great. White individuals, if psychologically healthy and not self-consciously marginal, can engage in a sustained effort in a single direction over a long period of time, and—here is the crux—they can do so more or less independent of their group. In contrast, a Fox is guided almost exclusively by his moment-to-moment relations with others; he bridles under

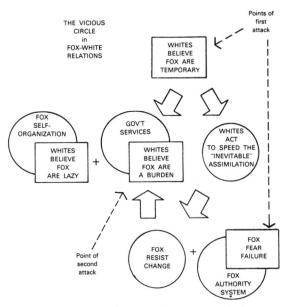

"The Strategy of the Fox Project" from *Documentary History of the Fox Project* by Fred Gearing. Reprinted by permission of University of Chicago Press and the author.

long-term, rigid work schedules; he becomes listless in situations requiring isolated self-direction.

Whites who know Fox Indians almost invariably interpret the contrasting work patterns as laziness, and unreliability. And, omitting perhaps the value judgment bound up in that English word, it *is* laziness. (But conversely, of course, the Fox look at white men and say they are aggressive and selfish.)

When white men make the judgment that the Fox are lazy, that is devastating enough to the relations between the groups. (In white society it seems to be far worse to be lazy than stupid, for instance.) But the effects of that judgment are compounded by the added fact that—moving now to the right on the diagram—the Fox are seen as a burden on honest, hard working taxpayers. The federal government does finance two services in the Fox community—education and, minimally, health. Most whites exaggerate the facts considerably and see the Fox as living off some sort of dole. The idea of lazy people living off of taxpayers' money is something less than tolerable to Iowa farmers when they think of it, which is fairly often.

Because the situation is intolerable, there is a strong disposition to see it [as] temporary. America has had the experience of the melting pot. (You will see that I am now arguing the connection to the second element of the vicious circle on your diagrams.) But America also has a tradition of cultural pluralism. There is a very wealthy colony of German pietists less than 100 miles from the Fox— the Amanas, who made freezers until they sold the name for a fabulous sum. Iowans do not feel that that German colony is temporary, or that it should be. But an Iowan simply does not entertain the idea that the Fox are here for more than, as they put it, another generation.

Once the idea is intrenched, that the Fox are temporary, important actions follow (the third element in the circle). If there is an inevitable process of assimilation under way, then, if one is to do anything, he will attempt to speed the process. Whenever debates arise as to what to do, [the] argument is over whether to spend money in order to create opportunities for the Fox to move upward, or whether to quit spending anything at all and thereby force them to move upward. And, of course, Fox individuals are evaluated according to how far along that imagined line of progress they seem to have individually traveled.

The Fox live in very close contact with the neighboring whites and they are in intimate contact with the government. So the effects of that continual pressure from whites are great. The effects are a marked degree of resistance to change. (I have now moved to the lower right-hand corner of the diagram.)

On one level, that Fox resistance to change reflects a positive evaluation of a life. But it is much more. It reflects a sense of threat. The Fox value their school and wish not to lose it and wish not to have it merged with schools in nearby towns. They want their lands to remain in protected status. They are instantly opposed to any suggested changes—in their school system, in their trust status, in the jurisdiction of their law and order. They oppose the idea of change, irrespective of the substantive details which never really get discussed. They do this because they fear failure—generically.

They fear failure because they have often failed. They have often failed because white society demands, in effect, that the Fox do things the white way. And there are basic structural reasons why the Fox simply cannot. The Fox *can* undertake the tasks—they run a pow wow each year which clears several thousand dollars and involves the coordinated efforts of at least 200 persons. But they must do it their own way.

Those basic structural reasons are the Fox authority system. In Fox social organization, authority roles are all but nonexistent. As Miss Furey has said, the Fox cannot effectively choose a course of action except in the absence of all overt opposition.

Fox tribal government under the Indian Reorganization Act is based on majority rule. Majority rule means that majorities exercise authority over minorities. It doesn't work. White men have gotten the Fox started on cooperative handicraft production and sale, based on majority rule. That didn't work. The pow wow organization has, on paper, a host of grand-sounding, authoritative positions such as president, treasurer, etc. But the organization actually functions the Fox way—by leisurely discussion until overt opposition disappears. That works.

On the whole, white-initiated activities have been organized in a hierarchical arrangement of authority and the Fox have failed. Failing repeatedly and having mixed feelings about what the white man calls progress in the first place, the Fox have settled down to a grand strategy of holding the line. Having set on that course, they tend, through time, to become more of a financial burden. So the beginning of the vicious circle is rejoined.

Turn now to what we plan to do about it. The word attack connotes much more aggressiveness than we are likely to exhibit. But in the upper right-hand corner on your diagrams you read: points of first attack. We have the hope that something can be done by simple verbal communication—education. Education is the first attack.

One prong on the diagram points to the white belief that the Fox are temporary. This historical record makes a pretty good case, we think, that one cannot assume the Fox, or any Indian group, is *inevitably* temporary. We hope that, if we say that often enough and to enough of the right people, it will have detectable effect. Further, some of those people can be affected by pointing out the undesirable results on the Fox when white men act *as if* the Fox are temporary.

But, according to the vicious circle, white men believe the Fox are temporary because, in part, they believe the Fox are lazy and are a burden. I will return to the Fox burden later. What to do about the belief in Fox laziness? We intend to do nothing directly. Rather, by talking about certain other facets of Fox life, we hope to reduce white man's preoccupation with that laziness. We imagine that it would be futile to tell almost any white man that laziness is only culture. After all, we white men hold that work is a virtue; and faith in that is extremely basic in the operations of white society. But there are other areas of Fox life which are now understood and positively valued by the neighbors of the Fox. And there are still other facets of Fox life which, though now misunderstood by whites, could come to be understood and positively valued with relative ease, we think. Iowans say, for example, that the Fox are poor farmers. We think Iowans could be interested in learning that the Fox aren't farmers at all.

In short, we have our focus on the white belief that the Fox are temporary and want to correct that. In order to do so, we will try to draw the attention of whites away from the highly resistant belief that the Fox are lazy and toward more easily valued aspects of Fox life.

Now, turning to the second prong of this first attack, we will attempt, again by verbal communication, to reduce the Fox fear of failure. Some success has already been recorded when we have experimentally talked to Fox individuals about so-called failures in terms of their authority system. Almost invariably the failures occurred because some Fox wasn't authoritarian; he wasn't authoritarian because it would have been indecent to be. The Fox value those patterns of authority highly; they usually combine them with other things under the term, freedom. In one recorded instance, we had written something about the authority patterns, and a Fox had read the article and he came to us quite excited about it. It was apparent that the Fox individual had made the logical connection between that valued freedom and past failures he had experienced. This, no doubt, for the first time; and quite obviously, to his great relief.

To the degree that such understanding becomes general and internalized, the Fox should be better off. That understanding will help relieve their anxieties about past failure and help them to better select future undertakings. It should *help* restore their self-confidence.

The Fox will best come to understand their own social structure through contrasting it with that of white society. We plan such activities as an informal adult education program as alluded to by Mr. Marlin. This would be in the Fox community and would cover the history of their relations with the federal government. The subject is of intense interest to them. In examining with them such things as particular treaties, there will be ample opportunity to attempt to explain Fox and white behavior in terms of culture and social organization. This may be the first time an adult education course on civics has been attempted in an Indian community.

In these first, verbal, attempts to break into the vicious circle, we expect uneven results. The Fox will probably learn more about whites (and about themselves) than whites will learn about the Fox. Fox interest is more pressing. However, the very failure of whites to understand should present further opportunities to demonstrate to the Fox the nature of white society.

One footnote before turning to the second point of attack. I should not leave the impression that all the learning is going from us to them. We expect to learn much more than we now know about both societies by the very act of discussing the contrasts between them.

The second point of attack will begin soon after the first and continue concurrently with it as shown on the diagram; the main focus here is on the fact and fiction of the Fox burden. We intend in this second approach to restructure certain situations so as to create learning experiences. In some instances, the new situations will be designed to demonstrate facts about Fox or white behavior. In others, situations which are threatening will be altered if possible so as to create a better atmosphere for learning.

As an example of creative situations which demonstrate facts, we tried, with some success, a small experiment in cooperative farming. The experiment demonstrated to the participants (including us) some facts about cooperative endeavor under the Fox authority system. I spent many hard hours in a hot Iowa corn field and I cannot discover any subconscious sabotage on my part. But I would mislead if I did not admit to some secret pleasure in the low level of economic success of the project. The lack of economic success confirmed an important hypothesis—and confirmed it as much for the participating Fox as for us. In the future, in regard to such situations which demonstrate facts, we plan to encourage undertakings which seem workable ones, and assist in the implementations when asked. So much for situations which will demonstrate facts.

The threatening situations have more pervasive effects. And more hinges on our hopes to alter them. The matter of government health and education services are especially damaging as they stand today. It is unlikely that the Fox will have sufficient tribal income in the foreseeable future to pay for those services. The federal government's withdrawal policy has created great anxiety among both the Fox and nearby Iowans. The Fox fear they will lose the services. The Iowans fear the costs will be shifted to them. Furthermore, you will recall the important effects, in the vicious circle, of the white man's picture of the Fox as a burden. We think that the fact of government subsidy could be altered in a way which would remove those bad effects. The threat of withdrawal to both Fox and Iowans, and the picture of the Fox as a burden could be greatly altered by establishing a permanent tribal fund large enough to pay the costs of those services from

income from the fund. We are willing, if and when the Fox are ready, to undertake political action with them to the end of getting such a fund appropriated by Congress. The odds are clearly not great. We do not rule out the possibility of Fox self-sufficiency without such a fund but the prospects are very remote.

In summary, we have hopes of breaking into the vicious circle and, through trying, of reaching a more adequate and precise analysis of the relations between the Fox and their neighbors. We will undertake two sets of actions in the attempt. Through education, we will try to alter certain ideas; our focus is primarily on the white belief that the Fox are temporary and the Fox fear of failure. Through changing situations, we will attempt to assist the learning processes; our focus here is primarily on Fox financial dependence.

You perhaps have noticed that throughout we have left the resistant white beliefs, such as the idea that the Fox are lazy, alone. We do not intend to come directly to grips with them. It is felt that one or both of two things will happen to them, assuming a degree of success in our other efforts: Some will become less important and some less true. As for the ideas about Fox laziness, we count more on the first. The idea will be less important because it will be no longer joined with the idea of the Fox being a burden.

A key index of success will turn on how much we are able to increase Fox self-confidence. That self-confidence and its most basic element—the greater Fox understanding of Fox and white behavior—should make it possible for the Fox to adjust their own behavior sufficiently to cope with the white world, especially in the economic sphere. By adjusting we mean self-conscious actions—acting—doing things deliberately for desired ends. It is clear that this sort of change differs radically from the basic change that would be required of whites—to recognize that work is not an absolute virtue. It is clear, too, that the changes we expect of the Fox are not the sort of basic changes that are generally thought of when one speaks of acculturation.

William F. Whyte and Allan R. Holmberg

Human Problems of U.S. Enterprise in Latin America

Intervention is often the attempt of members of one group to direct change in another. Since all culture is learned and therefore varies to some extent in different groups, the possibility that such intervention will produce problems is great. Part of the difficulty is that not all of his culture patterns are explicitly recognized by an individual. There are some he is not aware of, called "implicit" by the anthropologist, which influence him. He "naturally" bases his judgment largely on what is familiar. Such tendencies toward ethnocentrism are to be discouraged in favor of the premise that to help another one should first understand the other. Whyte and Holmberg make this point by contrasting Latin American and North American patterns of culture, both explicit and implicit, and establish the related premise that to adequately know the other requires first to know oneself.

The Contrast of Cultures

To be effective in Latin America, the North American must understand the culture within which he lives and works. But that is not all. He must also understand the culture of his native land. "Know thyself!" is the first injunction philosophers give to those who seek to understand other people. For the North American away from home, this means not only a knowledge of his individual personality but also of the culture in which it was formed. . . .

Cultures are best described in terms of comparison and contrast, and that will be our approach in this chapter. . . .

Class Structures

Human relations in any society, of course, are patterned by its social structure. Here in the United States one of the principles upon which our social system rests is the belief (even though it may be a fiction) that "all men are created equal." Consequently we live in a fairly open and socially mobile society, one in which it is relatively easy for an individual of energy, ability, and character, although of humble economic and social backgrounds, to rise high in the prestige and respect system. This does

not hold true to the same degree for most Latin-American cultures. These were originally founded on an assumption that society consists of a natural hierarchical order in which a few are born to rule and many are born to serve. As a result of this, social relationships in Latin America are more rigidly structured than they are in the United States, and are patterned along the lines of dependence and submission rather than independence and freedom. . . .

The gap between the elite and the masses, for example, has not been bridged, as it has in the United States, by a large and dominant middle class whose values are fundamentally democratic. Rather in much of South America the aristocratic tradition still holds sway and a well-defined middle class has yet to emerge. . . . People who today fall between the high and the low status groups have not yet crystallized into a group we may properly term a middle class. . . . Since it is relatively new, this [middle] group is heterogeneous in composition. It may include everything from a rural storekeeper or teacher to a cabinet minister or scholar. It also lacks an ideology of its own. In values it identifies with both the upper and the lower classes. While it is true that a middle class with a fairly uniform value system is almost certain to emerge in Latin America, the final product is not likely to be a duplicate of the middle class in the United States because of other fundamental differences between the cultures of Latin America and those of the United States. . . .

Types of Individualism

A second point of difference between Latin America and the United States has to do with the relationship between the individual and society and the concept of the individual himself. Almost everyone who has written about the cultures of Latin America has called attention to the phenomenon called personalism, a characteristic, which, like

"Human Problems of U.S. Enterprise in Latin America" by William F. Whyte and Allan R. Holmberg from *Human Organization* (Vol. 15, No. 3, 1956). Reproduced by the permission of the Society for Applied Anthropology and the authors.

the outlook on the structure of society, was inherited from the mother country of Spain. In a sense, personalism may be regarded as a variety of individualism, but it is not the same kind of individualism that is either practiced or preached here in the United States. In Latin America it is more than the doctrine that the individual, and not society, is of paramount importance in human life. Personalism goes even deeper than this. Not man in the abstract, but man in the concrete, becomes the center of the universe. And the concrete man in the center of the universe is the person himself.

Manifestations of this phenomenon of personalism are found on every hand. Much of the economic life in the rural areas is based on the personal relation between *patrón* and *peón*. There is almost everywhere a distrust in the large and impersonal corporation because such an organization is regarded as being over and above the individuals who are members and employees of it. One cannot talk to, argue with, or deal personally with banks, governments, or insurance companies. They themselves have no life, no vitality, no souls. Only people are possessed of such characteristics, and these are the things in life that count. Even in matters of social organization it is the personal relationship between members of class or caste groups that is important. The same is true in political life; almost everywhere in Latin America politics is shot through with the exaltation of, and identification with, the leader—the *caudillo*—at the expense of principles or party platforms.

In the realm of ideology and religion we see manifestations of the same phenomenon. For most Latin Americans, particularly the folk peoples of rural areas who constitute the most numerous group in the total population, God is a kind of vague entity like a corporation. He is a hazy and inaccessible power with whom it is impossible to deal directly. Consequently, He gets little direct attention in religious life. The same is not true of the saints, however. They act as intermediaries between God and man and are viewed as real people with whom it is possible to personalize relations. That is why they play such a significant role in religious life all over Latin America. Not only individuals but whole villages and nations have patron saints, and the relationship between devotees and saints is always a highly personalized one. In most areas of Latin America saints are treated as highly respected human beings, and in religious life one frequently identifies his fortunes in life with a particular saint, just as in politics one may do so with a particular political leader.

The tendency and desire to personalize relations in Latin America extends even to the relationship between people and inanimate objects. This is particularly noticeable today in those areas undergoing rapid modernization. Anyone who has recently travelled in a country like Mexico or Peru, for example, cannot help but note that such pieces of modern equipment as trucks are given personal names by their owners, and that these, like people, are sometimes baptized. The importance of personal relations in Latin America would thus seem to suggest that whenever it is planned to introduce modern changes, of whatever kind, the more one can take advantage of the value of personalism the more successful the proposed change is likely to be.

The differential emphasis and value placed on the personalized relation in Latin America as compared with the United States can hardly be overemphasized. Here we tend to assign high value to the status and role which an individual occupies; we tend to respect an office which he holds or a position which he fills, such as the presidency of the country, or the head of a large corporation. This, however, does not seem to be so much the case in most of Latin America, where prime emphasis is placed on the person who occupies the office, on the individual who holds the position. It is more the particular human being, the unique personality, that becomes the focus of attention and respect and not so much the status and role which he occupies. To a large extent, of course, this difference in emphasis is a reflection of a difference in the concept of the individual himself. Here an individual, despite his personality, is deserving of respect because of his position; there an individual, despite his position, is deserving of respect because of his personality. This is borne out by the emotional reactions that accompany a breach of these norms. In the United States a violation of the dignity of an office is considered a serious offense; in Latin America an insult to the personal dignity of an individual constitutes the supreme affront....

In many cases, the North American will be annoyed by . . . a statement [directed against him] but will not see any necessity for counteraction. His point of view is reflected in the children's saying: "Sticks and stones will break my bones, but names can never hurt me." In Latin America, names do hurt. An unanswered attack is thought to leave a grievous injury to the personal dignity of the individual. So the private citizen may counterattack with a suit for defamation of character. The public official may use his control to suppress the free speech of his critic.

The U.S. conception of individualism does not emphasize the personal dignity of the individual in this same way. To us, individualism means a collection of rights of men: the right of the individual to express himself, to get ahead in the world, to do what he wants to do, and so on. It means also the belief that the individual, by his own efforts, can achieve "success"—and therefore should be respected for what he has achieved.

With us, individualism means competition for position in an organization, but it does not mean distrust of the organization itself. More so than earlier generations, North Americans now accept organizations (small and especially large) as inevitable parts of life. . . .

Family Organization

Another point of prime significance for an understanding of human relations problems in Latin America is the high value placed on the family as an institution and on kinship relations in general. While the family, of course, is a fundamental institution in all societies, in Latin America kinship and family play a more significant role in the patterning of human relations than they do in the United States. Descent and family name are highly significant distinguishing marks of an individual in Latin America, particularly in those countries where the aristocratic tradition still prevails.

The significance of kinship in Latin America is well exemplified in a type of family organization which still persists there. In addition to the nuclear family, relatives are frequently organized on an extended family basis. The patrilineal type of extended family was introduced from Spain during the Colonial period and it still remains a major type of family organization, particularly in rural areas where it is not uncommon to find a large number of relatives sharing a single household. In general, because of the restricted nature of social (and until recently geographical) mobility, it has been possible in most of Latin America to maintain intimate kinship relations outside of the immediate family. Even in urban and industrial areas the extended family system has not completely broken down, as it pretty largely has in the United States, although this type of family organization is not particularly well-adapted to the confines of city life.

The recognition of a blood tie involves serious commitments and obligations, for it is through the family and the bonds of kinship that one makes his way in the world. It is no secret that in Latin America businesses are run by families, that nepotism is practiced in government, and that wealthy and aristocratic families are highly inbred. The family is the one institution to which loyalty is almost always expressed. This does not mean that relationships within the family are all harmonious, for the opposite is often true, but pride in family name is so great that to the outside world, at least, the family presents a united front of friendly cooperation. Indeed, in fighting his battle against the world, the Latin American can always turn for aid to the family, the one institution on which he can depend. . . .

In the United States, the family plays a much smaller role in the organization of society. In the first place, family to us generally means the nuclear family of man and wife and their children. To be sure, we recognize aunts and uncles, cousins, and nieces and nephews, but we feel no strong obligations to them. In many cases, we may not see these relatives for months or even years. The extraordinary geographical mobility of our people has made it impossible to maintain anything approximating an extended family system. Even the grandparents are generally expected to live apart from their children and grandchildren. . . .

We expect the family to provide the child with the equipment necessary to make a promising start on a career. Beyond this point, we do not assume that the family has any obligation. It is up to the individual.

We recognize that people in the United States often get ahead because of the personal "pull" of family or friends. While this is a fact of life, it is also a condition of which we generally disapprove. We all know men who have had the opportunity to reach a high position in industry through friendship or family connections and yet have struck out to make careers in other organizations where they would not have the personal advantages. Such men feel that they cannot call themselves successful unless they can say that they have gained their success by their own efforts. As family businesses have given way to corporations in the United States, the importance of family connections has actually declined. Thus the evolution of our institutions has supported our beliefs in free competition and success through individual effort. . . .

Man and Woman

In connection with the family, some mention should be made of the relationship between the sexes. On the whole, Latin America has been and still is a male-dominated society. This does not mean that men are necessarily regarded as superior to women in all departments of life, but the notion of the equality of the sexes, like the equality of people, is certainly not a part of the cultural heritage. On the contrary, there has always been a fairly sharp separation, recognized by both sexes, between the roles of women and those of men in Latin-American society. Consequently, double standards, one for the male and another for the female, are almost everywhere applied—in work, in play, and in sex. Moreover, in recent times there has been considerably less tendency by one sex to encroach on the spheres of influence of the other in Latin America than there has been in the United States, although this pattern appears to be changing rapidly.

By and large, Latin America is still a man's world. Everywhere manliness is a virtue. To be a *macho*, a whole man, full of physical energy, sexual prowess, honor, and pride is still the dominant ideal, not only for the men themselves, but for the women as well when seeking a mate or training a child. The *conquistador*—free, romantic, fearless, and strong—remains the model to which most young men aspire.

By contrast, women live in a much more restricted world. "Woman" in the abstract was a sacred word to the Spaniards and Portuguese who conquered the southern Americas. And so it is to most Latin Americans today. Values of the age of chivalry still persist. It is perhaps for this reason that an outsider often gains the impression that the relations between the sexes in Latin America are surrounded by a kind of perpetual aura of mystery, romance, and charm. Just how far this is true, however, is quite another matter. . . .

Attitudes of sacredness towards women . . . do not apply to all relationships outside of the family and especially to women of lower social status.

Women outside of the family or immediate social group were created to be enjoyed and are fair game for every man. Thus men often seek sexual satisfaction outside of the confines of the family. A wife exists primarily for the purpose of raising a family; a mistress, for the purpose of diversion and pleasure. Thus a double standard of sex morality and behavior exists between husband and wife. This is formalized in a system of concubinage that is recognized among almost all strata of Latin-American society with the exception perhaps of some Indian groups. While its practice is limited by the economic resources of the husband—it is thus probably more prevalent among the upper-class groups—it is certainly acknowledged as an institution by both husband and wife. . . .

Another institution in Latin America which affects the relations between men and women, and which is quite widespread among the middle and lower social groups, is the consensual union. In spite of the deep influence of the Catholic church, it has made little impression in some areas as far as the sacrament of marriage is concerned. Nor has the law. In some rural villages that have been studied, largely of *mestizo* or mixed-blood population, as many as 60 percent of the men and women living together as husband and wife are not married either by church or state. While there is little evidence to indicate that this type of marriage is less stable than the religious or legal type, it does represent a departure from the norm in the United States.

Actually, the institution of the consensual union is apparently sometimes preferred by women to a legal or religious marriage. It offers them more freedom than they are allowed under the marriage laws of church or state. This is nicely demonstrated by the case of a servant girl in the Andes who gave birth to a child without benefit of marriage. When asked by her mistress why she did not marry the father of the child, she replied, "No, I do not want to do this; it would give him the legal right to beat me and take my salary as well."

The institutions of concubinage and the consensual union in Latin America, as indeed everywhere, create serious human relations problems, to say nothing of kinship complications. Offspring of such unions, of course, are illegitimate. Neither they nor their mothers receive legal protection, as do legitimate children and lawfully wedded wives, unless the father eventually takes steps to recognize them legally. Moreover, even though little social stigma attaches to illegitimacy in Latin America (particularly if the status of one's father is high), nevertheless, the social and psychological problems arising from this state are often tragic, as they are to be sure almost everywhere. Among the poorer classes one frequently encounters a lone woman who has several children, each of whom has been sired by a different man. Having been abandoned and having no other means of support, such a woman must try to form another liaison if she can. But often she is unable to do so and is left alone with her children in poverty and despair. Her plight is sometimes eased as some of the children reach working age and pitch in to help her. Under these conditions her children grow up without even knowledge of who their fathers are. In Latin-American society, which fervently espouses the sacredness of family life, this situation causes severe conflicts in the growing child and he often matures with an abnormal love attachment to his mother and a deeply hostile attitude towards his father. Even in a normal family situation these attitudes sometimes arise because of the strong authoritarian role that it is possible for the father to play with respect to both wife and children.

In the United States, males do not hold the dominant position characteristic of Latin America. Within the household, woman is coming more and more to play the dominant role. This involves not only the major share in disciplining the children but also a sharing with the husband of many household tasks. The husband who helps with the dishes and other chores is looked upon with wonder and condescending amusement by Latin-American men. (Latin-American women, however, may find these traits more to be valued than to be laughed about.)

U.S. women also have achieved something close to equality in standards of sex behavior. The old double standard seems to be losing its force. To be sure, the woman who has sex relations outside of marriage is more subject to social disapproval than the man. But this seems to be more a difference in degree than in kind. Furthermore, at least in the middle class, it is expected that the husband will remain sexually faithful to his wife. The expectation is often violated, to be sure, but the violation generally takes the form of sporadic affairs. Concubinage or a long-term relationship with a mistress is a rare phenomenon in our country. Furthermore, the woman feels free to divorce her husband if she sufficiently resents his sexual—or other—behavior. The Catholic prohibition on divorce applies here as well as elsewhere, but U.S. Catholics are more likely to violate it than are people in predominantly Catholic countries.

Man is still dominant in most fields of business and the professions, but here woman has attained a closer approach to equality than perhaps anywhere in the western world. The same can be said for political life.

Authority and the Common Man

In the United States we grow up with strong egalitarian beliefs. We glorify the common man, "the regular guy" who doesn't "put on airs." We hold to the strong belief that we should take people on their own individual merit and should not recognize inequalities in status. Inevitably we do react in terms of status differences, but nevertheless, our strong egalitarian beliefs do affect our behavior in at least two important ways.

These beliefs give dignity to the "common man," and they make it easier for us to establish reasonably comfortable informal relations among individuals who differ markedly in social status. For example, the worker who is president of his local union does not expect to associate with the plant manager at the country club, but, in their contacts inside the plant, the two men may be on an informal basis in which they talk and joke about a number of things beyond the immediate business at hand.

In Latin America, there has been frequent contact among people of different status levels, and yet, in the past, such contacts have tended to follow a standard, formalized pattern such as we find in the relationship between master and servant. As new situations arise where the master-servant relationship is clearly not appropriate, we can expect Latin Americans to have more difficulty in establishing a comfortable informal relationship across class lines than is the case in the United States. The process of moving up in society always involves some dropping of earlier social ties. In Latin America, with a more stratified society, the break is sharper than it generally is in the United States. We often find that an individual is promoted primarily because of the degree of trust he has built up from his immediate associates. When he then strives to cut himself off from them, he loses the main asset for which he was recognized. . . .

Our beliefs . . . involve a suspicion of authority. We do not assume that, because Jones holds a position of authority, Jones is therefore probably correct in the actions he takes. We are more likely to take the opposite assumption and require that Jones prove his right to hold that position by the quality of his actions. Furthermore, we feel that it is the manly thing to stand up to authority—that you ought to speak right up and tell the boss when you think he has been wrong. Of course, we do not always do this, but the strong belief that it should be done can be illustrated often in our literature.

This attitude toward authority also affects the man in authority. We often find U.S. executives behaving as if they felt somewhat guilty about being in authority and being greatly concerned about winning the support of their subordinates.

In Latin America, we can assume, in general, a greater tendency to accept the authority of the boss. This does not necessarily mean that Latin-American workers will be content with actions of the boss which would be offensive to North American workers. They may be just as resentful, but they are less likely to challenge authority directly, in a face-to-face situation. At the same time, the Latin-American boss—at least if he comes from a social status higher than his subordinates—is less likely than the North American to have self-doubts regarding the justification of his own authority. On the other hand, the Latin American who rises from humble origins to a supervisory position may have even greater anxieties over his authority than does his North American counterpart. Such a Latin-American supervisor may hesitate to wield his authority at all, or he may go to the other extreme and become highly autocratic.

Local Action Versus Centralization

Latin America differs from the United States in the degree of centralization which prevails and is accepted as a natural part of life. This is found not only in government but is also reflected in the pattern people develop to solve their problems. We place a high value on face-to-face, local problem solving. We believe that problems should be solved, as far as possible, by people actually facing those problems. This belief can be traced back to the earliest years of our country. The original

Plymouth colony was a voluntary association. . . .

The North American feels that this approach applies equally well to problems beyond the sphere of government. For community problems, for the regulation of a profession, and for all sorts of activities, the North American calls together a voluntary association of the people concerned. Furthermore, we have the optimistic belief that every problem must have a solution and that the people facing it can solve it if they just talk it out.

Much more than the Latin Americans, we try to avoid referring our local problems to some remote and higher authority. The pattern of thinking we use in problem solving conforms to the organizational level at which we feel problems should be solved. We like to try to solve problems in terms of the practical details rather than in terms of some general, abstract principle.

We also rely upon face-to-face problem solving in the relations among people at different levels of the industrial hierarchy. This means that we expect the subordinate to discuss his problems directly with his superior. To put it in a more technical way, the North American has a greater tendency to initiate action up the line of the organization than do people who grow up in a more rigidly stratified society. . . .

Forms of Expression

The North American feels that a directness in his language should go along with the direct face-to-face relationship. We value frankness as a virtue and diplomacy as having a questionable moral standing. To be sure, people recognize that diplomatic and tactful behavior may be necessary to achieve our goals, yet, at the same time, we are inclined to feel that human nature is really not as it should be on this point. We think you really ought to be able to tell a man frankly face-to-face what you think of him.

We also value simplicity and brevity of expression. We say, "Get to the point. Don't beat around the bush."

The Latin American differs with us in these respects. He does not look upon frankness as a virtue. He places a much higher value on courtesy. He tends to express himself in such a way that personal relations will remain harmonious—at least on the surface. Our simplicity and brevity may seem abrupt to him. He tends to couch his statements in a much more elaborate framework. . . .

The Kidding Pattern

We must give special attention to one characteristic U.S. form of expression—the kidding pattern —for it is the sort of thing that may get us in trouble in Latin America.

If you have the kind of society in which people are encouraged to be frank and come right out with what they feel, you need some sort of safety valve to protect personal feelings. To us, kidding is a very important safety valve. It enables us to say things to other people that we may really mean but in a manner that does not hurt them—*providing they are familiar with our kidding customs.* . . .

In kidding, we are saying to the other fellow, in effect, "You're not really as good as you think you are." This is said in a joking way, but it has a tendency to bring people down a peg. This may be a pitfall in Latin America. The North American manager is in a superior position in his dealings with most Latin Americans. In an effort to establish an informal relationship, he may not recognize that his kidding has a depreciating effect. What we take in a joking way may perhaps be reacted to by a Latin American as an effort of a North American to subordinate him.

Does this mean we must abandon kidding altogether? It means that we must at least be aware of the danger of giving the impression of subordinating the other individual to us.

Work and the Values of Life

Almost everyone who has written about the cultures of Latin America has pointed out that one of their most outstanding characteristics is a deep and central focus on a way of life which we may perhaps best characterize by the Spanish terms *fiesta* and *siesta*. In fact, so much attention has been directed to these values in Latin-American culture—often to the exclusion of others—that in the popular literature, at least, we are led to believe that the average Latin American lives a life of almost nothing else but *fiesta* and *siesta*.

In most of Latin America work is necessary for some people at least, but it is not a particularly esteemed or dignified activity. It is nothing in itself to be rewarded for. It is rather a necessary burden that must be borne by some people as part of the pattern of living. Particularly unfortunate are those who must perform the undignified hard labor of everyday life, but that is the way of the world. It is the nature of things that some are born to leisure and others are born to work, even though the latter may not be particularly happy with their lot nor value the work activities they perform. Thus on the part of socially mobile people, who were not fortunate enough to be born to the leisure class, there is almost everywhere in Latin America a tendency to avoid the stigma of manual labor, for it identifies one with the lower class. A true gentleman, if he works at all, works only with his mind. He regards it as undignified to dirty his hands on anything that is identified with physical labor.

The reason for such attitudes toward work, of course, is simply that higher value is assigned to other activities. There is much more to life than work, than the humdrum activities of everyday life. These are a necessary part of living, to be sure, but they are not the things in life that count. There is something more dramatic, more poetic in the universe than can be captured through the routine activities of life. It is rather through deep emotional feeling and expressive behavior that one experiences the greatest rewards in life.

Among the large mass of people in Latin America it is through the institution of the *fiesta*, particularly the religious *fiesta*, that these values are perhaps best expressed. Enormous amounts of time, energy, and money go into the celebration of particular festive events. In some rural villages, as much as a third of one's time, apart from Sundays, may be spent in *fiesta* activity. And much of the rest of one's time may well be spent in working for the next *fiesta*.

Part of the reason for this is that one not only gains emotional and spiritual satisfaction from participation in festive activity but social status and prestige as well. In fact, in many areas of Latin America the *fiesta* is the central institution around which the rest of the culture revolves. And the *fiesta* is primarily a consumption institution. In other words, its adherents produce primarily to consume and not to save for a rainy day. In many areas people actually undergo a great deal of economic stress in order to fulfill *fiesta* obligations. To economists and businessmen especially, this may seem like irrational behavior. It certainly does not fit the classic model of economic man. Understanding it lies in appreciating the fact that the Latin American places higher esteem on emotional gratification and spiritual values than on the pursuit of wealth for wealth's sake.

What has just been said is not only true of the mass of people in Latin America but is characteristic of the élite as well. Almost everywhere poets, philosophers, musicians, artists, and novelists abound; by contrast there are relatively few natural and technical scientists. This reflects a strong bias for the humanities as a field of interest and study. There is everywhere a preference for ideas rather than things, for abstract theory rather than empirical research; for armchair speculation rather than precise experiment; for deductive reasoning rather than inductive thought. This is further reflected in the contributions made to world culture by the Spaniards and Latin Americans, which include some notable examples of literature and art but relatively little of great distinction in the field of science.

Our country was settled predominantly by Protestants who brought with them the Puritan view of work as a means of salvation. Men are judged according to how hard they work. The wealthy man does not have to work in order to support his family, but his need to work is just as great as it would be if it involved bread and butter. He needs to keep busy in order to act out his role as a responsible citizen in our society.

We tend to divide life into two parts: work and play. We accept play as a necessary part of life but attach no moral value to it. We expect the individual to work first and play when the work is done. Furthermore, we justify play in terms of work, saying that a man should get some regular play so that he will be in shape to do a better job. . . .

We can say that North Americans do display, on the average, a stronger interest in money rewards and profits than do their Latin-American counterparts. However, the contrast is not so extreme as it is often represented to be.

North Americans also tend to set a higher value on the material comforts of life such as automobiles, modern indoor plumbing, household appliances, and so on. This emphasis exposes us to two possible dangers in Latin America. In the first place, we may find ourselves judging other peoples largely in terms of the presence or absence of these material comforts in their communities—a standard which they will find highly insulting. In the second place, we may limit our social orbit to the best hotels in the leading cities, where these material comforts are amply provided—and where foreigners chiefly congregate. There is no surer way to gain the dislike of another (especially a poorer) people than to insist ostentatiously and inconveniently on the expensive foreign luxuries of one's own way of life.

When it comes to the possession and distribution of money, the contrast runs in the opposite direction. We do *not* assume that a man has a right to make or inherit a fortune and to use the money exclusively for the pleasure of himself and his family. So powerful are our egalitarian ideals that most wealthy men begin to feel guilty unless they are using some of their money to promote the general welfare of their country—or of the world. The great American philanthropic foundations grew out of this feeling of obligation to make wealth serve the common interest.

Where a hierarchical social order is an accepted part of life, as in some parts of Latin America, it is natural that the wealthy individual does not feel the same obligation to share with his people as does the North American. This does not mean that the wealthy Latin American is less generous than the North American. He may spend and give his money away freely, but he tends to do it on a more personal basis, helping family, friends and, those who are—and may become—dependent upon him. Thus, one of the effects of distributing his wealth is the extension of his personal influence. On the other hand, the North American, feeling the general social obligation that goes with egalitarian beliefs, tends to dispense his money through impersonal organizations so that he himself is cut off from personal contact with the recipients of his generosity.

Probably this contrast could be seen more sharply a few years ago. Today there is growing evidence of wealthy Latin Americans contributing to broad social purposes, well beyond the reaches of their personal influence.

Fatalism Versus Optimism

A final point, deserving of special emphasis, is the general outlook on life characteristic of the large mass of people in Latin America. This can hardly be described in terms other than fatalistic or pessimistic. Unlike the United States, which was founded on a philosophy of work and constant progress, Latin America was founded on a religious philosophy in which such notions played little part. The prevalent view held in Spain and introduced into Latin America was that, for the large mass of people at least, this was a naturally ordained world of inequality, oppression, and suffering which if endured according to holy scripture, however, would produce its reward in the end—eternal bliss in heaven. There was little that one could do to change this static state of affairs. Thus one had to resign himself to his fate and his destiny; one had to put himself in the hands of higher powers and hope for the best through religious activity.

Such views as these strongly took root in Latin America and still dominate much of the scene today. Most Latin Americans take a dim view of the world. This is particularly true of peasant populations. The world is a harsh place to live in, full of frustration and pain. One is constantly castigated in his struggle for life. This is nicely illustrated by the remark made by an Andean peasant who was surveying a wheat field that had just been completely destroyed by a hail storm. "God castigated us like never before," said he, implying that one was always castigated in life but that this had been a particularly severe instance of it.

Other types of behavior bear witness to the same point of view. In some parts of rural Latin America, for instance, children's funerals are frequently accompanied by music, drinking, and dancing—elements of the *fiesta*. While there is always sorrow on the death of a child, it is accompanied by mixed feelings of joy, for the child goes directly to heaven where he will have to bear no more sufferings of this world. The general preoccupation with tragedy in Latin America is a manifestation of the same phenomenon. Indeed, suffering has become noble and death itself an honor.

It is perhaps in part due to such attitudes as these that Latin Americans sometimes seem unwilling to assume personal responsibility, especially in cases of failure. One is constantly at the mercy of forces beyond his control so that if something goes wrong the responsibility lies there, not with oneself. If someone misses an appointment some force beyond his control prevented him from making it on time; if someone misses a train or a plane, it is they that are at fault, not he.

Garth N. Jones

Strategies and Tactics of Planned Organizational Change: Case Examples on the Modernization Process of Traditional Societies

Approximately two thirds of the world's people share social systems that are defined as "peasant" or "traditional." They comprise a large part of the Third World alluded to in an earlier section. Because they lag behind the industrial age, and because the level of production of food and other goods is usually static, such societies have been and are the target of many development schemes. In the article that follows, Garth Jones reviews the strategies and tactics for planned change in Third World societies. His findings are no less applicable to many situations involving ethnic minorities in the United States.

Strategy of Pressure

This involves the use or show of some kind of force to fulfill predetermined objective(s). Those who are influenced accept displacement of their own judgment and act upon that provided by a superior.

Two case examples will now be discussed to illustrate the use of this type of strategy.

In northern Nigeria, the home of the Hausa tribe, sleeping sickness reached endemic conditions. Field surveys showed that in some areas up to 40 percent of the inhabitants had the disease. Tests revealed that the disease could be controlled by cutting the brush along the streams in which the tsetse fly, the carrier of the disease, bred. The Hausa people disbelieved that sleeping sickness was carried by the fly. Moreover, they regarded certain patches of brush along the streams as sacred and inhabited by spirits who would be angry if their abodes were disturbed. The clearing of the brush was successfully carried out only when pressure was applied by the British colonial officials through the traditional framework of native authority.

While the disease was virtually eliminated, the Hausa people never associated this fact with the cutting of the brush. This was a measure imposed upon them by force from higher authority. Inasmuch as this practice was not incorporated into their cultural system, there were strong indications that this activity would discontinue after the withdrawal of British rule. In sum, the germ theory of disease was beyond their comprehension or willingness to understand. British officials, therefore, felt the strategy of pressure was the only alternative to eradicate the disease.

The Hausa case, although successful as far as short-run goal achievement is concerned, left the administration in a perplexing position in reference to the long-run situation. Another case using the strategy of pressure may be noted where the long-run goal was not left in such a precarious position.

The Gadsden Purchase territory is the home of the Papago Indians, a primitive Indian desert tribe. The severe problem of existence for the Papagos was the dearth of drinking water, and the whole pattern of their lives was built around a simple technology to satisfy this need. Their primary sources of water were from natural ponds in the Arroyos (stream channels without streams until a hard rain) fed by the summer rains. The water was muddy, and the source highly unreliable. In 1915, the United States Indian Bureau started to drill wells in the reservation, but this activity was hampered by a lack of funds. When the Civilian Conservation Corp burgeoned in the 1930's it was possible to drill a large number of wells in areas not yet penetrated by the Indian Bureau.

A spokesman of a village found in one of the driest regions of the reservation was opposed to the sinking of a well within the village area. The village council backed him up. Relations between the Anglo authorities and the Indians were good. The Anglo administrators were caught in a choice of actions. They could respect the local leadership and not drill the well, or they could drill the well and in so doing destroy the existing local leadership. The administrators chose the latter action. They felt that the value of a permanent source of good sanitary water outweighed the value of an individual leader or at the best a few leaders.

In a peculiar quirk of events the anti-forces were caught at night using the well water, and thus discredited in their own community. Since then there has been no opposition to the use of the well.

In summary, it may be useful to compare both cases. The central problem in these cases was to institute technological change in an administered group belonging to a culture other than agent of change (administrators) against the opposition of the administered group's leadership. This is a typical situation of colonial government or societies which have strong minorities. In both cases, the objectives to some degree were achieved: (1) the breeding places of the tsetse fly were destroyed and thereby the incident of the disease of sleeping sickness reduced, and (2) the well was drilled and equipped and the local inhabitants used the water.

At this point, the two cases depart in their common features. Change was completely incorporated into the particular Papago village (i.e., the use of well water); whereas it was doubtful that the Hausa people would continue the practice of cutting the brush along the streams when British Colonial authorities withdrew. However, in both cases the strategy of pressure was successfully used to achieve goals. The only question is the length of time that the goals will be maintained.

Strategy of Stress Induction

This strategy includes any effort (strain or distortion) directed toward disturbing the equilibrium of an organizational system in order to prepare that

"Strategies and Tactics of Planned Organizational Change: Case Examples in the Modernization Process of Traditional Societies" by Garth N. Jones from *Human Organization* (Vol. 24, No. 3, 1965). Reproduced by the permission of the Society for Applied Anthropology and the author.

system for change. The consequence may be a modified system or a complete breakdown in the system that, in turn, develops into a new system.

Traditional societies are particularly susceptible to stress induction in the change process. The case example used here to illustrate this point does not measure up to all of the dimensions of a case on planned organizational change. In spite of its weaknesses, for our purposes, it does make an excellent portrayal of the use of the strategy of stress induction.[1]

The goal for a certain element of an Indian community in Guatemala was to achieve revitalization of its cultural system. The community, Santa Cruz Chinautla, consisted of a total population of 1,672, of which 92.8 percent were classified as Indians of the Pokoman-speaking dialect and the remainder were *Ladinos*, i.e., those with Spanish-Guatemalan orientation. Each of these groups constituted strong cultural systems with the *Ladinos* for many years prior to the revolution of 1944 in the dominant political position. This had led to considerable cultural degeneration of the Indian culture. Central to the Indian culture was a well-established community organization called the *Cofradia* system, the "law of the saints." This organization appeared to be a fusion of Mayan and Catholic traditions, and was deeply ingrained into the Indian power structure and community affairs.

The newly established constitutional democratic practices of the revolution provided the vehicle by which the Indian cultural group gained complete control of the community government in the second municipal election in 1947.

The rise of the Indians to power brought new and unsuspected crises within the Indian community. The leaders in the *Cofradia* system saw in this political setting a favorable climate by which to regain their power in and reestablish their old ways of life. However, the Indian Community was not as fully integrated as formerly and out of this grew two Indian groups: (1) the conservative or supporters of the *Cofradia* system, and (2) the radical or the members of the liberal Catholic and the Protestant elements not strongly committed to the *Cofradia* system.

The period from 1944 to 1955 was one full of a series of stress situations for the three principal groups found in Santa Cruz Chinautla: the *Ladinos*, the conservative Indians, and the radical Indians. With each major stress situation, most of them in-

curred by political forces, there occurred for each individual group a period of reorganization. For the radical Indians and the *Ladinos* the reorganization was of a short duration. For the conservative Indians, however, the stress continued a sequence of reactions analogous to the after effects of a physical disaster. The group, elated by national conditions favorable again for Indian self-government and patterns of life, revitalized its traditional social system. Whether or not this was desirable for the demands of the larger community and the nation constitutes another matter. Significant is that the outcome appears typical for folk, peasant, or underdeveloped communities. The agent of change and the client system will have to wrestle with the question as to whether or not within the revitalized system there is also found a cultural residue in favor of change. In this particular case, the author felt that he saw such a residue.

Normative Strategies

This category of strategies places emphasis upon normative power as a major source of control. Compliance rests primarily upon the internationalization of directions accepted as proper and legitimate. The techniques of control are usually the manipulation of symbolic rewards, employment of leaders, manipulation of symbols, and administration of rituals.

In this group two types of strategies have been selected for illustration purposes: the strategy of participation and the strategy of education/training.

The preliminary studies of Jones and Niaz revealed that normative strategies were widely employed in all types of organizations. Two case examples will be used to illustrate the use of these strategies.

Strategy of Participation

This strategy is no more than involving the individuals concerned into the decision-making process before the actual change is introduced. On the surface this may appear to be a type of strategy not generally suitable for traditional societies. In

---

[1] A more typical case on the use of this strategy within the dimensions of this article is later described under the strategy of education/training, the Vicos case.

other words, because of strong cultural commitment to traditional values, other types of strategies appear, off-hand, to be more effective to induce change. The case discussed here conveys the opposite lesson. The endeavor failed because the agents of change did not early involve the client system in the change process.

This case takes place in the same setting and time as a previous one discussed under the strategy of pressure, i.e., the drilling of a well in the reservation of the Papago Indian reservation in the Gadsden Purchase Territory.

The goal was to introduce a new agricultural practice into the social system of the Papago Indians. The Indian Bureau learned of the practice in Sonoran Mexico of utilizing flood waters from a single storm in such a manner as to raise one crop a year on a commercial basis.

This was called the *bolsa* system. The Spanish word *bolsa* means pocket. The water was literally run into a pocket and left there to soak into the ground, after which the land was plowed and harrowed and well-pulverized, and the seed planted.

The Papago Indian extension division saw possibilities for this system, and with the assistance of the Civilian Conservation Corp constructed, with a sizable investment of energy and capital, a *bolsa*. After several years of frustrations, the project completely failed for technical reasons. Subsequent investigation revealed, among other things, that the *bolsa* was poorly engineered and constructed, climatic conditions in the reservation were not suitable for such an agricultural practice, and an inadequate source of water existed for the acreage prepared for cultivation.

Early, the Indians realized these weaknesses, and, although receptive to Anglo innovations, reverted to their old agricultural practices. In this case they understood better than the Anglo technicians what were the best agricultural practices.

In summary, "the attempt failed because the administrators did not master the technique they borrowed before introducing it." Furthermore, they "did not bring the people into the planning . . . with the result that further technical difficulties developed which could have been avoided." These miscalculations were further compounded because the agents of change were outside of the client system's culture, and unexpected and uncontrollable conditions emerged that they could not cope with in an adequate manner.[2]

Strategy of Education/Training[3]

Great hopes have been placed upon this strategy as a primary means for planned organizational change. However, education and training are fraught with many problems. They are frequently slow and expensive means, and much time is usually consumed before any effectiveness can be determined. Furthermore, these approaches are often employed without any previous sound conceptualization of the needs of the social system. The development and the effective application of human skill and knowledge constitute a persistent problem in organizational settings. This is particularly a difficult matter in traditional societies. An extensive chain of events is usually necessary before anything of significance results.

First, people must be taught basic skills. This is usually a simple matter; but more in the total educational/training process is involved. The first cannot succeed (this is the second process) unless certain habits, attitudes, and ways of thought and behavior have been created. People must learn to be scientific and progressive in outlook instead of living by ancestral laws and long-tried rules of thumb. Thirdly, the education/training must be grafted upon the old; old values, for example, cannot be discarded overnight.

One of the outstanding success stories of planned organizational change, in which education/training played a crucial role, is the transformation of a semi-feudal Indian hacienda in Peru into a progressive democratic community within a five-year period. This experience was the result of an unusual arrangement between the Peruvian government and Cornell University. The endeavor (Peru-Cornell project) operated as a joint enterprise of the Department of Sociology and Anthropology of Cornell University and the Indigenous Institute of Peru. Its primary aims were scientific: the study of the processes and consequences of com-

[2] Henry F. Dobyns, "Blunders with Bolsas," *Human Organization*, 10 (Fall 1951): 25–32.

[3] In technical terms there is a difference between education and training. However, for this article the two words are used together to relate to the institutional processes (school, family, religious organizations, management training programs, etc.) whereby the accumulated ideas, standards, knowledge, technology, and techniques of society are transferred from one person to another. Involved is not only the overall development of the individual for the "good life," but also preparing the individual to meet better certain job requirements of an organization.

munity development. The project proposed to build into the experiment a more productive and effective social system, and to contribute to the development of a more capable and confident people. All of this was to be accomplished within a short period of time, say five years!

The state of affairs of the *hacienda*, Vicos by name, was not a happy one. The hacienda was over 30,000 acres, in the highlands of Northwestern Peru, and inhabited by some 2,000 Quechua-speaking Indians who had a minimum of contact with modern civilization.

Power was so concentrated in the hands of a single person, the patron, that the villagers' fate depended almost entirely upon him. Villagers had almost no say in governmental affairs.

The standard of living was a bare minimum; health and nutritional levels were extremely low; educational facilities (and consequently skills) were almost completely lacking; resistances to the outside world were high, and attitudes toward life were static and pessimistic.

The approach employed was an integrated one. Although a number of strategies were used, two played predominate roles: (1) stress induction and (2) education/training. In fact, it is difficult to separate these two strategies.

The results accomplished by the agents of change within a five year period were astounding. Let us use the words of the authors to sum up the case:

The Vicosinos, after 400 years of peonage, are about to gain control of their own destiny. . . . In October, 1956, democratically, by direct vote of all of its citizens, and for the first time in its history, the people of Vicos elected their own delegates to assume the direction and management of community affairs. At the same time, the Peruvian Government is making it possible for the Vicosinos to purchase the lands on which they have lived as serfs since the Spanish Conquest.[4]

They go on to say that all of this was accomplished with very little expenditure of outside funds, and note four reasons why this situation occurred:

1. The administration took steps to relieve some of the most severe stresses felt by the people. . . . This made it possible for the people to have faith in the administration.

2. The administration developed a program of con-

sultation and delegation of responsibility so as to stimulate the development of Indian leadership.

3. The administration and Indian leaders developed a program of education and training, so that the people could gain the knowledge they needed to build a better community.

4. Steps 2 and 3 made it possible for the people themselves to have faith in themselves. There resulted a self-propelling social system, in which the benefits people achieved through their own efforts released new hopes and energies, and those hopes and energies in turn produced further rewards.[5]

In final summary, in five years an apathetic and disorganized people were transformed into a dynamic and progressive community. The agents of change had successfully compressed time in a constructive fashion.

Utilitarian Strategies

These strategies are characterized by control over material resources and rewards through the allocation of increased contributions, benefits, and services. These are available to the client system when it performs in a manner prescribed by the agent of change. Two types of such strategies have been selected for discussion: strategy of placement and strategy of empiricism.

The joint research of Niaz and Jones has not been very fruitful in finding cases using these types of strategies in traditional or transitional societies. On the other hand, a survey of anthropological and related literature indicates that such strategies have frequently been employed to facilitate and bring about change. It appears that scholars and practitioners alike involved with traditional societies have not taken the time to write up case experiences employing these types of strategies. To illustrate the use of these strategies, it will be necessary to include case examples which took place in industrial type societies.

Strategy of Placement

This strategy could involve two sets of circumstances. One is to assure affected members of a

[4] William F. Whyte and Allan R. Holmberg, "Human Problems of U.S. Enterprise in Latin America," *Human Organization*, 15 (Fall 1956): 18.
[5] Ibid.

group that they will be taken care of in case of any social changes such as the reduction of employees because of a technological innovation. The other is the placing of the right person(s) in strategic positions when change is desired.

An excellent case example of the former situation occurred in the California State Department of Employment when this agency converted from conventional punch card and electronic accounting machine processing to the newly developed electronic data processing machines. Before this change occurred all permanent employees were assured that none of them would be laid off. Such employees would be transferred to positions elsewhere in the state government or the reduction in force would result as a result of normal personnel turnover. Because of this assurance, the new operation was smoothly installed without incurring any resistance by employees.

During Henry Ford's last years, the Ford Motor Company was near collapse. Henry Ford had a strange relationship with Harry Bennett, a gun-toting character who was all-powerful in the organization. When Henry Ford's grandson, Henry Ford II, became President of the Ford Motor Company he placed able and trustworthy persons in important positions formerly occupied by Harry Bennett and his gang of toughs. The result saved the company, and brought it back to such a position that it became a strong competitor.

Strategy of Empiricism

New practices can frequently be incorporated into a social system on the basis of objective and empirical proof of their value to the system. A good case example of acceptance and rejection of new agricultural practices took place in a small, relatively isolated Costa Rican village, San Juan Norte. In this village attempts were made to introduce three new agricultural practices: the use of chlordane, the cultivation of home vegetable gardens, and the cultivation of POJ sugar cane (*Proefstation Oost Java*, a variety of sugar cane).

In 1951, extension students introduced chlordane, an insecticide, into the village to combat pests. This practice was accepted by the villagers when it was demonstrated to them that it was an effective means to combat insects, particularly ants.

Whereas the introduction of chlordane into the agricultural practices was a success, the same was not the case for the cultivation of home vegetable gardens. This venture failed largely for the reasons that the chlordane endeavor succeeded. No objective proof was furnished as to the feasibility of planting gardens. The agent of change, a school teacher, attempted to cultivate a garden. He made an intensive campaign among villagers and managed to enlist the help of part of them. All attempts failed for a variety of reasons, and therefore provided no empirical evidence as to the feasibility of this agricultural practice.

The POJ sugar represents a good example of spontaneous change. Fifteen years after the Costa Rican Ministry of Agriculture took steps to disseminate throughout the country the POJ variety of sugar cane, this variety appeared in San Juan Norte. However, its direct introduction was not undertaken by any agent of change, but spontaneously by a villager. Its acceptance was largely conditioned by objective proof of the efficiency of the new variety.

This case concluded that three basic conditions should exist to insure acceptance of an item by a social group: (1) "A need for the item must be felt by the members," (2) the item "must be compatible with their culture," and (3) "the people must have proof of its workability or effectiveness."[6]

Other Change Techniques

In a narrower sense, agents of change employ what is termed here as tactics to facilitate change. This is the maneuvering of forces of various types into positions of advantage. Frequently, this is accomplished in connection with a strategy. In other cases, tactics are used by themselves and may be regarded as strategies.

In this article three types of tactics are noted: (1) action research, (2) technical modification, and (3) marginality. Representative case examples will now be discussed.

Tactic of Action Research

In recent years there has occurred a growing number of accounts where research personnel have become directly involved as manipulator in the

[6] M. Alers-Montalvo, "Cultural Change in a Costa Rican Village," *Human Organization*, 16 (Winter 1957): 2–7.

change process. This type of action research was used in the previously discussed Vicos case. The researchers in this change situation laid out approximately "130 specific lines of research and development, each matched to a specific developmental goal such as the diversification of agriculture, the development of community leadership, etc."[7]

Another interesting case of this nature occurred in Guatemala. Research on nutrition required that school children in several villages receive a different combination of nutrients and submit periodically to examinations to determine their nutritional status. This experiment was threatened by noncooperation on the part of key persons in several of the villages. An anthropologist was brought into the case to determine the cause of the trouble and to overcome the resistance. Anthropological research disclosed that the growing resistance to the experiment could be attributed to the projects' close identification with one of the two opposing factions in the villages. Effective means were subsequently devised, based upon research, to overcome this resistance.

Tactic of Technical Modification

Cases may be noted where changes in the traditional structure of organizational systems have resulted in an overall increase in performance. An illustration of this type of technical modification occurred in the traditional organizational structure of the Kagor tribe in Northern Nigeria. This tribe today may well be the most heavily literate tribal unit in the northern part of Nigeria. The secret of the Kagor's successful development was the planned redefinition of chieftainship carried out under the competent leadership of a village chief (in power at the time the case was written) through councils modeled around traditional tribal institutions and behaviors.

The institution of chieftainship was introduced by the British Colonial authorities, and was initially incompatible with the Kagor's traditional social structure. It was responsible for considerable social dysfunctionalism, and the admission of undesirable elements. Under the leadership of the chief of the Kagor tribe, the incompatible features were identified and removed and other elements introduced to foster integration and development of the social structure.

Tactic of Marginality

Anthropological literature is full of examples where acculturated bilinguals have served a very useful function in the change process because they share the value systems of their own society and that of the innovating society. Such persons have been skillfully employed in the medical program among the Navaho Indians.

In 1956 the Cornell University Medical College established a project of training a small group of Navaho health aides in the middle of the Navaho reservation. The primary purpose was to enable anthropologists to observe the development of the roles of bilinguals in each society in the performance of their work as health aides.

These persons proved to be a positive asset, and provided the vehicle for which significant changes were made and goals accomplished.

This tactic functioned in practice within a broader framework of reference which is conceptualized in this article under two strategies: communication and empiricism.

The acculturated bilinguals were able to bridge effectively the gap of communication, and the transmissions of new technology in the medical field into the social organization of the Navaho. This task was made easier by the highly practical value system of the Navaho. To him "knowledge is power," and, if it can be demonstrated to him that the health aid could facilitate the relief of pain and illness he willingly accepts medical treatment.

General Conclusions

The frame of reference of this article rests upon empirical analysis, i.e., through the research technique of content analysis strategies and tactics of planned organizational change are isolated and defined and some evaluation is made of their roles in the processes of change in traditional societies.

Only an exploratory view of this approach, largely for two reasons, could be taken in this article. First, this research methodology employed is new in this area. Secondly, there is only a limited

[7]Besides the previous references, see Allan R. Holmberg, "The Research and Development Approach to the Study of Change," *Human Organization*, 17 (Spring 1958): 12–16 and "Reaching the Heart of South America," *Saturday Review*, 45 (November 3, 1962): 55–62.

number of suitable cases on the subject of planned organizational change.

Nevertheless, evidence to date certainly indicates that pragmatic strategies and tactics are available to facilitate organizational change in traditional societies. In other words, by skillfully employing such strategies and tactics it is possible, in a constructive fashion, to telescope and compress the processes of change and development of traditional communities to meet better the needs of modern world society.

The common technique to accelerate change for traditional societies has been through the programs of community development. These programs have been designed to reach village people and to make more effective the use of local initiative and energy for increased production and better living standards. In all of these programs there is a need to adapt improved knowledge and technology to the behavioral patterns of village people, or vice versa. This connotes organizational change, in most cases, of far-reaching consequence.

In final note, it is firmly believed that modern man, equipped with the knowledge of behavioral science, can to a considerable extent control and direct organizational changes rationally, intelligently, and effectively for the goal of a better life. It is hoped that this brief sketch of one possible "bag of tools" may be useful particularly in the hands of community development practitioners toward this end.

Lauriston Sharp
Steel Axes for Stone-Age Australians

Those who have the temerity to give direction to the lives of others have much to learn from Lauriston Sharp's article. Here is a classic example of a well-intended, seemingly minor intervention which produced shock waves so intense that an entire social system verged on disintegration. The society described is a tightly integrated one—that is, one in which the institutions have a high degree of "fit." The account supports our point that intervention imposes the obligation to anticipate the consequences of one's actions.

Like other Australian aboriginals, the Yir Yoront group which lives at the mouth of the Coleman River on the west coast of Cape York Peninsula originally had no knowledge of metals. Technologically their culture was of the old stone age or paleolithic type. They supported themselves by hunting and fishing, and obtained vegetables and other materials from the bush by simple gathering techniques. Their only domesticated animal was the dog; they had no cultivated plants of any kind. Unlike some other aboriginal groups, however, the Yir Yoront did have polished stone axes hafted in short handles which were most important in their economy.

Towards the end of the 19th century metal tools and other European artifacts began to filter into the Yir Yoront territory. The flow increased with the gradual expansion of the white frontier outward from southern and eastern Queensland. Of all the items of western technology thus made available, the hatchet, or short handled steel axe, was the most acceptable to and the most highly valued by all aboriginals.

In the mid 1930s an American anthropologist lived alone in the bush among the Yir Yoront for 13 months without seeing another white man. The Yir Yoront were thus still relatively isolated and continued to live an essentially independent economic existence, supporting themselves entirely by means of their old stone age techniques. Yet their polished stone axes were disappearing fast and being replaced by steel axes which came to them in considerable numbers, directly or indirectly, from various European sources to the south.

What changes in the life of the Yir Yoront still

"Steel Axes for Stone-Age Australians" by Lauriston Sharp from *Human Organization* (Vol. 11, No. 2, 1952). Reproduced by the permission of the Society for Applied Anthropology and the author.

living under aboriginal conditions in the Australian bush could be expected as a result of their increasing possession and use of the steel axe? . . .

Relevant Factors

If we concentrate our attention on Yir Yoront behavior centering about the original stone axe (rather than on the axe—the object—itself) as a cultural trait or item of cultural equipment, we should get some conception of the role this implement played in aboriginal culture. This, in turn, should enable us to foresee with considerable accuracy some of the results stemming from the displacement of the stone axe by the steel axe.

The production of a stone axe required a number of simple technological skills. With the various details of the axe well in mind, adult men could set about producing it (a task not considered appropriate for women or children). First of all a man had to know the location and properties of several natural resources found in his immediate environment: pliable wood for a handle, which could be doubled or bent over the axe head and bound tightly; bark, which could be rolled into cord for the binding; and gum, to fix the stone head in the haft. These materials had to be correctly gathered, stored, prepared, cut to size, and applied or manipulated. They were in plentiful supply, and could be taken from anyone's property without special permission. Postponing consideration of the stone head, the axe could be made by any normal man who had a simple knowledge of nature and of the technological skills involved, together with fire (for heating the gum), and a few simple cutting tools—perhaps the sharp shells of plentiful bivalves.

The use of the stone axe as a piece of capital equipment used in producing other goods indicates its very great importance to the subsistence economy of the aboriginal. Anyone—man, woman, or child—could use the axe; indeed, it was used primarily by women, for theirs was the task of obtaining sufficient wood to keep the family campfire burning all day, for cooking or other purposes, and all night against mosquitoes and cold (for in July, winter temperature might drop below 40 degrees). In a normal lifetime a woman would use the axe to cut or knock down literally tons of firewood. The axe was also used to make other tools or weapons, and a variety of material equipment required by the aboriginal in his daily life. The stone axe was essential in the construction of the wet season domed huts which keep out some rain and some insects; of platforms which provide dry storage; of shelters which give shade in the dry summer when days are bright and hot. In hunting and fishing and in gathering vegetable or animal food the axe was also a necessary tool, and in this tropical culture, where preservatives or other means of storage are lacking, the natives spend more time obtaining food than in any other occupation—except sleeping. In only two instances was the use of the stone axe strictly limited to adult men: for gathering wild honey, the most prized food known to the Yir Yoront; and for making the secret paraphernalia for ceremonies. From this brief listing of some of the activities involving the use of the axe, it is easy to understand why there was at least one stone axe in every camp, in every hunting or fighting party, and in every group out on a "walk-about" in the bush.

The stone axe was also prominent in interpersonal relations. Yir Yoront men were dependent upon interpersonal relations for their stone axe heads, since the flat, geologically-recent, alluvial country over which they range provides no suitable stone for this purpose. The stone they used came from quarries 400 miles to the south, reaching the Yir Yoront through long lines of male trading partners. Some of these chains terminated with the Yir Yoront men, others extended on farther north to other groups, using Yir Yoront men as links. Almost every older adult man had one or more regular trading partners, some to the north and some to the south. He provided his partner or partners in the south with surplus spears, particularly fighting spears tipped with the barbed spines of sting ray which snap into vicious fragments when they penetrate human flesh. For a dozen such spears, some of which he may have obtained from a partner to the north, he would receive one stone axe head. Studies have shown that the sting ray barb spears increased in value as they move south and farther from the sea. One hundred and fifty miles south of Yir Yoront one such spear may be exchanged for one stone axe head. Although actual investigations could not be made, it was presumed that farther south, nearer the quarries, one sting ray barb spear would bring several stone axe heads. Apparently people who acted as links in the middle of the chain and who made neither spears nor axe heads would receive a certain number of each as a middleman's profit.

Thus trading relations, which may extend the individual's personal relationships beyond that of his own group, were associated with spears and axes, two of the most important items in a man's equipment. Finally, most of the exchanges took place during the dry season, at the time of the great aboriginal celebrations centering about initiation rites or other totemic ceremonials which attracted hundreds and were the occasion for much exciting activity in addition to trading.

Returning to the Yir Yoront, we find that adult men kept their axes in camp with their other equipment, or carried them when travelling. Thus a woman or child who wanted to use an axe—as might frequently happen during the day—had to get one from a man, use it promptly, and return it in good condition. While a man might speak of "my axe," a woman or child could not.

This necessary and constant borrowing of axes from older men by women and children was in accordance with regular patterns of kinship behavior. A woman would expect to use her husband's axe unless he himself was using it; if unmarried, or if her husband was absent, a woman would go first to her older brother or to her father. Only in extraordinary circumstances would she seek a stone axe from other male kin. A girl, a boy, or a young man would look to a father or an older brother to provide an axe for their use. Older men, too, would follow similar rules if they had to borrow an axe.

It will be noted that all of these social relationships in which the stone axe had a place are pair relationships and that the use of the axe helped to define and maintain their character and the roles of the two individual participants. Every active relationship among the Yir Yoront involved a definite and accepted status of superordination or subordination. A person could have no dealings with another on exactly equal terms. The nearest approach to equality was between brothers, although the older was always superordinate to the younger. Since the exchange of goods in a trading relationship involved a mutual reciprocity, trading partners usually stood in a brotherly type of relationship, although one was always classified as older than the other and would have some advantage in case of dispute. It can be seen that repeated and widespread conduct centering around the use of the axe helped to generalize and standardize these sex, age, and kinship roles both in their normal benevolent and exceptional malevolent aspects.

The status of any individual Yir Yoront was determined not only by sex, age, and extended kin relationships, but also by membership in one of two dozen patrilineal totemic clans into which the entire community was divided. Each clan had literally hundreds of totems, from one or two of which the clan derived its name, and the clan members their personal names. These totems included natural species or phenomena such as the sun, stars, and daybreak, as well as cultural "species": imagined ghosts, rainbow serpents, heroic ancestors; such eternal cultural verities as fires, spears, huts; and such human activities, conditions, or attributes as eating, vomiting, swimming, fighting, babies and corpses, milk and blood, lips and loins. While individual members of such totemic classes or species might disappear or be destroyed, the class itself was obviously everpresent and indestructible. The totems, therefore, lent permanence and stability to the clans, to the groupings of human individuals who generation after generation were each associated with a set of totems which distinguished one clan from another.

The stone axe was one of the most important of the many totems of the Sunlit Cloud Iguana clan. The names of many members of this clan referred to the axe itself, to activities in which the axe played a vital part, or to the clan's mythical ancestors with whom the axe was prominently associated. When it was necessary to represent the stone axe in totemic ceremonies, only men of this clan exhibited it or pantomimed its use. In secular life, the axe could be made by any man and used by all; but in the sacred realm of the totems it belonged exclusively to the Sunlit Cloud Iguana people.

Supporting those aspects of cultural behavior which we have called technology and conduct is a third area of culture which includes ideas, sentiments, and values. These are most difficult to deal with, for they are latent and covert, and even unconscious, and must be deduced from overt actions and language or other communicating behavior. In this aspect of the culture lies the significance of the stone axe to the Yir Yoront and to their cultural way of life.

The stone axe was an important symbol of

masculinity among the Yir Yoront (just as pants or pipes are to us). By a complicated set of ideas the axe was defined as "belonging" to males, and everyone in the society (except untrained infants) accepted these ideas. Similarly spears, spear throwers, and fire-making sticks were owned only by men and were also symbols of masculinity. But the masculine values represented by the stone axe were constantly being impressed on all members of society by the fact that females borrowed axes but not other masculine artifacts. Thus the axe stood for an important theme of Yir Yoront culture: the superiority and rightful dominance of the male, and the greater value of his concerns and of all things associated with him. As the axe also had to be borrowed by the younger people it represented the prestige of age, another important theme running through Yir Yoront behavior.

To understand the Yir Yoront culture it is necessary to be aware of a system of ideas which may be called their totemic ideology. A fundamental belief of the aboriginal divided time into two great epochs: (1) a distant and sacred period at the beginning of the world when the earth was peopled by mildly marvelous ancestral beings or culture heroes who are in a special sense the forebears of the clans; and (2) a period when the old was succeeded by a new order which includes the present. Originally there was no anticipation of another era supplanting the present. The future would simply be an eternal continuation and reproduction of the present which itself had remained unchanged since the epochal revolution of ancestral times.

The important thing to note is that the aboriginal believed that the present world, as a natural and cultural environment, was and should be simply a detailed reproduction of the world of the ancestors. He believed that the entire universe "is now as it was in the beginning" when it was established and left by the ancestors. The ordinary cultural life of the ancestors became the daily life of the Yir Yoront camps, and the extraordinary life of the ancestors remained extant in the recurring symbolic pantomimes and paraphernalia found only in the most sacred atmosphere of the totemic rites.

Such beliefs, accordingly, open the way for ideas of what *should be* (because it supposedly *was*) to influence or help determine what actually *is*. A man called Dog-chases-iguana-up-a-tree-and-barks-at-him-all-night had that and other names because he believed his ancestral alter ego had also had them; he was a member of the Sunlit Cloud Iguana clan because his ancestor was; he was associated with particular countries and totems of this same ancestor; during an initiation he played the role of a dog and symbolically attacked and killed certain members of other clans because his ancestor (conveniently either anthropomorphic or kynomorphic) really did the same to the ancestral alter egos of these men; and he would avoid his mother-in-law, joke with a mother's distant brother, and make spears in a certain way because his and other people's ancestors did these things. His behavior in these specific ways was outlined, and to that extent determined for him, by a set of ideas concerning the past and the relation of the present to the past.

But when we are informed that Dog-chases-etc. had two wives from the Spear Black Duck clan and one from the Native Companion clan, one of them being blind, that he had four children with such and such names, that he had a broken wrist and was left handed, all because his ancestor had exactly these same attributes, then we know (though he apparently didn't) that the present has influenced the past, that the mythical world has been somewhat adjusted to meet the exigencies and accidents of the inescapably real present.

There was thus in Yir Yoront ideology a nice balance in which the mythical was adjusted in part to the real world, the real world in part to the ideal preexisting mythical world, the adjustments occurring to maintain a fundamental tenet of native faith that the present must be a mirror of the past. Thus the stone axe in all its aspects, uses, and associations was integrated into the context of Yir Yoront technology and conduct because a myth, a set of ideas, had put it there.

The Outcome

The introduction of the steel axe indiscriminately and in large numbers into the Yir Yoront technology occurred simultaneously with many other changes. It is therefore impossible to separate all the results of this single innovation. Nevertheless, a number of specific effects of the change from stone to steel axes may be noted, and the steel axe may be used as an epitome of the increasing quantity of European goods and implements received by the aboriginals and of their general influence on the native culture. The use of the steel axe to illustrate such influences would seem to be justified. It was one of the first European artifacts to be adopted for regular use by the Yir Yoront, and whether made of stone or steel, the axe was clearly one of the most important items of cultural equipment they possessed.

The shift from stone to steel axes provided no major technological difficulties. While the aboriginals themselves could not manufacture steel axe heads, a steady supply from outside continued; broken wooden handles could easily be replaced from bush timbers with aboriginal tools. Among the Yir Yoront the new axe was never used to the extent it was on mission or cattle stations (for carpentry work, pounding tent pegs, as a hammer, and so on); indeed, it had so few more uses than the stone axe that its practical effect on the native standard of living was negligible. It did some jobs better, and could be used longer without breakage. These factors were sufficient to make it of value to the native. The white man believed that a shift from steel to stone axe on his part would be a definite regression. He was convinced that his axe was much more efficient, that its use would save time, and that it therefore represented technical "progress" towards goals which he had set up for the native. But this assumption was hardly born out in aboriginal practice. Any leisure time the Yir Yoront might gain by using steel axes or other western tools was not invested in "improving the conditions of life," nor, certainly, in developing aesthetic activities, but in sleep—an art they had mastered thoroughly.

Previously, a man in need of an axe would acquire a stone axe head through regular trading partners from whom he knew what to expect, and was then dependent solely upon a known and adequate natural environment, and his own skills or easily acquired techniques. A man wanting a steel axe, however, was in no such self-reliant position. If he attended a mission festival when steel axes were handed out as gifts, he might receive one either by chance or by happening to impress upon the mission staff that he was one of the "better" bush aboriginals (the missionaries definition of "better" being quite different from that of his bush fellows). Or, again almost by pure chance, he might get some brief job in connection with the mission which would enable him to earn

a steel axe. In either case, for older men a preference for the steel axe helped change the situation from one of self-reliance to one of dependence, and a shift in behavior from well-structured or defined situations in technology or conduct to ill-defined situations in conduct alone. Among the men, the older ones whose earlier experience or knowledge of the white man's harshness made them suspicious were particularly careful to avoid having relations with the mission, and thus excluded themselves from acquiring steel axes from that source.

In other aspects of conduct or social relations, the steel axe was even more significantly at the root of psychological stress among the Yir Yoront. This was the result of new factors which the missionary considered beneficial: the simple numerical increase in axes per capita as a result of mission distribution, and distribution directly to younger men, women, and even children. By winning the favor of the mission staff, a woman might be given a steel axe which was clearly intended to be hers, thus creating a situation quite different from the previous custom which necessitated her borrowing an axe from a male relative. As a result a woman would refer to the axe as "mine," a possessive form she was never able to use of the stone axe. In the same fashion, young men or even boys also obtained steel axes directly from the mission, with the result that older men no longer had a complete monopoly of all the axes in the bush community. All this led to a revolutionary confusion of sex, age, and kinship roles, with a major gain in independence and loss of subordination on the part of those who now owned steel axes when they had previously been unable to possess stone axes.

The trading partner relationship was also affected by the new situation. A Yir Yoront might have a trading partner in a tribe to the south whom he defined as a younger brother and over whom he would therefore have some authority. But if the partner were in contact with the mission or had other access to steel axes, his subordination obviously decreased. Among other things, this took some of the excitement away from the dry season fiesta-like tribal gatherings centering around initiations. These had traditionally been the climactic annual occasions for exchanges between trading partners, when a man might seek to acquire a whole year's supply of stone axe heads. Now he might find himself prostituting his wife to almost total strangers in return for steel axes or other white man's goods. With trading partnerships weakened, there was less reason to attend the ceremonies, and less fun for those who did.

Not only did an increase in steel axes and their distribution to women change the character of the relations between individuals (the paired relationships that have been noted), but a previously rare type of relationship was created in the Yir Yoront's conduct towards whites. In the aboriginal society there were few occasions outside of the immediate family when an individual would initiate action to several other people at once. In any average group, in accordance with the kinship system, while a person might be superordinate to several people to whom he could suggest or command action, he was also subordinate to several others with whom such behavior would be tabu. There was thus no overall chieftainship or authoritarian leadership of any kind. Such complicated operations as grass-burning animal drives or totemic ceremonies could be carried out smoothly because each person was aware of his role.

On both mission and cattle stations, however, the whites imposed their conception of leadership roles upon the aboriginals, consisting of one person in a controlling relationship with a subordinate group. Aboriginals called together to receive gifts, including axes, at a mission Christmas party found themselves facing one or two whites who sought to control their behavior for the occasion, who disregarded the age, sex, and kinship variables of which the aboriginals were so conscious, and who considered them all at one subordinate level. The white also sought to impose similar patterns on work parties. (However, if he placed an aboriginal in charge of a mixed group of post-hole diggers, for example, half of the group, those subordinate to the "boss," would work while the other half, who were superordinate to him, would sleep.) For the aboriginal, the steel axe and other European goods came to symbolize this new and uncomfortable form of social organization, the leader-group relationship.

The most disturbing effects of the steel axe, operating in conjunction with other elements also being introduced from the white man's several subcultures, developed in the realm of traditional ideas, sentiments, and values. These were undermined at a rapidly mounting rate, with no new conceptions being defined to replace them. The result was the erection of a mental and moral void which foreshadowed the collapse and destruction of all Yir Yoront culture, if not, indeed, the extinction of the biological group itself.

From what has been said it should be clear how changes in overt behavior, in technology and conduct, weakened the values inherent in a reliance on nature, in the prestige of masculinity and of age, and in the various kinship relations. A scene was set in which a wife, or a young son whose initiation may not yet have been completed, need no longer defer to the husband or father who, in turn, became confused and insecure as he was forced to borrow a steel axe from them. For the woman and boy the steel axe helped establish a new degree of freedom which they accepted readily as an escape from the unconscious stress of the old patterns—but they, too, were left confused and insecure. Ownership became less well defined with the result that stealing and trespassing were introduced into technology and conduct. Some of the excitement surrounding the great ceremonies evaporated and they lost their previous gaiety and interest. Indeed, life itself became less interesting, although this did not lead the Yir Yoront to discover suicide, a concept foreign to them.

The whole process may be most specifically illustrated in terms of totemic system, which also illustrates the significant role played by a system of ideas, in this case a totemic ideology, in the breakdown of a culture.

In the first place, under pre-European aboriginal conditions where the native culture has become adjusted to a relatively stable environment, few, if any, unheard of or catastrophic crises can occur. It is clear, therefore, that the totemic system serves very effectively in inhibiting radical cultural changes. The closed system of totemic ideas, explaining and categorizing a well-known universe as it was fixed at the beginning of time, presents a considerable obstacle to the adoption of new or the dropping of old culture traits. The obstacle is not insurmountable and the system allows for the minor variations which occur in the norms of daily life. But the inception of major changes cannot easily take place.

Among the bush Yir Yoront the only means of water transport is a light wood log to which they cling in their constant swimming of rivers, salt creeks, and tidal inlets. These natives know that tribes 45 miles further north have a bark canoe. They know these northern tribes can thus fish from midstream or out at sea, instead of clinging to the river banks and beaches, that they can cross coastal waters infested with crocodiles, sharks, sting rays, and Portuguese men-of-war without danger. They know the materials of which the canoe is made exist in their own environment. But they also know, as they say, that they do not have canoes because their own mythical ancestors did not have them. They assume that the canoe was part of the ancestral universe of the northern tribes. For them, then, the adoption of the canoe would not be simply a matter of learning a number of new behavioral skills for its manufacture and use. The adoption would require a much more difficult procedure; the acceptance by the entire society of a myth, either locally developed or borrowed, to explain the presence of the canoe, to associate it with some one or more of the several hundred mythical ancestors (and how decide which?), and thus establish it as an accepted totem of one of the clans ready to be used by the whole community. The Yir Yoront have not made this adjustment, and in this case we can only say that for the time being at least, ideas have won out over very real pressures for technological change. In the elaborateness and explicitness of the totemic ideologies we seem to have one explanation for the notorious stability of Australian cultures under aboriginal conditions, an explanation which gives due weight to the importance of ideas in determining human behavior.

At a later stage of the contact situation, as has been indicated, phenomena unaccounted for by the totemic ideological system begin to appear with regularity and frequency and remain within the range of native experience. Accordingly, they cannot be ignored (as the "Battle of the Mitchell" was apparently ignored), and there is an attempt to assimilate them and account for them along the lines of principles inherent in the ideology. The bush Yir Yoront of the mid-thirties represent this stage of the acculturation process. Still trying to maintain their aboriginal definition of the situation they accept European artifacts and behavior patterns, but fit them into their totemic system, assigning them to various clans on a par with original totems. There is an attempt to have the myth-making process keep up with these cultural changes so that the idea system can continue to

support the rest of the culture. But analysis of overt behavior, of dreams, and of some of the new myths indicates that this arrangement is not entirely satisfactory, that the native clings to his totemic system with intellectual loyalty (lacking any substitute ideology), but that associated sentiments and values are weakened. His attitudes towards his own and towards European culture are found to be highly ambivalent.

All ghosts are totems of the Head-to-the-East Corpse clan, are thought of as white, and are of course closely associated with death. The white man, too, is closely associated with death, and he and all things pertaining to him are naturally assigned to the Corpse clan as totems. The steel axe, as a totem, was thus associated with the Corpse clan. But as an "axe," clearly linked with the stone axe, it is a totem of the Sunlit Cloud Iguana clan. Moreover, the steel axe, like most European goods, has no distinctive origin myth, nor are mythical ancestors associated with it. Can anyone, sitting in the shade of a *ti* tree one afternoon, create a myth to resolve this confusion? No one has, and the horrid suspicion arises as to the authenticity of the origin myths, which failed to take into account this vast new universe of the white man. The steel axe, shifting hopelessly between one clan and the other, is not only replacing the stone axe physically, but is hacking at the supports of the entire culture system.

The aboriginals to the south of the Yir Yoront have clearly passed beyond this stage. They are engulfed by European culture, either by the mission or cattle station subcultures or, for some natives, by a baffling, paradoxical combination of both incongruent varieties. The totemic ideology can no longer support the inrushing mass of foreign culture traits, and the myth-making process in its native form breaks down completely. Both intellectually and emotionally a saturation point is reached so that the myriad new traits which can neither be ignored nor any longer assimilated simply force the aboriginal to abandon his totemic system. With the collapse of this system of ideas, which is so closely related to so many other aspects of the native culture, there follows an appallingly sudden and complete cultural disintegration, and a demoralization of the individual such as has seldom been recorded elsewhere. Without the support of a system of ideas well devised to provide cultural stability in a stable environment, but admittedly too rigid for the new realities pressing in from outside, native behavior and native sentiments and values are simply dead. Apathy reigns. The aboriginal has passed beyond the realm of any outsider who might wish to do him well or ill.

Returning from the broken natives huddled on cattle stations or on the fringes of frontier towns to the ambivalent but still lively aboriginals settled on the Mitchell River mission, we note one further devious result of the introduction of European artifacts. During a wet season stay at the mission, the anthropologist discovered that his supply of tooth paste was being depleted at an alarming rate. Investigation showed that it was being taken by old men for use in a new tooth paste cult. Old materials of magic having failed, new materials were being tried out in a malevolent magic directed towards the mission staff and some of the younger aboriginal men. Old males, largely ignored by the missionaries, were seeking to regain some of their lost power and prestige. This mild aggression proved hardly effective, but perhaps only because confidence in any kind of magic on the mission was by this time at a low ebb.

For the Yir Yoront still in the bush, a time could be predicted when personal deprivation and frustration in a confused culture would produce an overload of anxiety. The mythical past of the totemic ancestors would disappear as a guarantee of a present of which the future was supposed to be a stable continuation. Without the past, the present could be meaningless and the future unstructured and uncertain. Insecurities would be inevitable. Reaction to this stress might be some form of symbolic aggression, or withdrawal and apathy, or some more realistic approach. In such a situation the missionary with understanding of the processes going on about him would find his opportunity to introduce his forms of religion and to help create a new cultural universe.

Allan R. Holmberg

The Research and Development Approach to the Study of Change

In the selection that follows, Holmberg describes an intervention more extreme than that just presented, a model embodying the maximum use of authority and control—indeed, in retrospect, an experiment in producing revolutionary change in microcosm. In this unusual case we share the very warm and human experience of an anthropologist who became the patrón *on a Peruvian hacienda called Vicos, assuming virtual authority over the two thousand peasants who lived there, as well as responsibility for their welfare. (For a similar experience, see "A Case for Intervention in the Field," by Bernard Gallin, in the first section of this book.) The experience proved that this model of intervention can produce impressive change, and quickly; it also showed that such success can be threatening to vested interests. We are, in the end, left with a nagging doubt about the efficacy of a model of limited revolution.*

I

What I have to say on the question of values in action stems largely from a rather deep and personal involvement with this question for the past five years. In 1952, quite by design, although unexpectedly and suddenly, I found myself in the delicate position of having assumed the role of *patrón* (in the name of Cornell University) of a Peruvian *hacienda*, called Vicos, for a period of five years, for the purpose of conducting a research and development program on the modernization process.

"The Research and Development Approach to the Study of Change" by Allan Holmberg. Reproduced by the permission of the Society for Applied Anthropology and Laura H. Holmberg, executrix for the Estate of Allan R. Holmberg from Vol. 17, No. 1 1958 *Human Organization*.

As you can readily imagine, such action on my part clearly shook (or perhaps I should say shocked) the Board of Trustees—to say nothing of the some 2,000 residents of the *hacienda* and no few of my anthropological colleagues—to the extent, I might add, that had events subsequently taken other turns than they eventually did, I would probably not be writing this and would be much more in disgrace as an anthropologist and human being than I presently am. Moreover, had I known then what I now know, I am not so sure that I would be willing to repeat the experience, even though it has been one of the most rewarding ones of my whole professional career. My doubts lie not so much with the fruitfulness or legitimacy of the research and development, as contrasted with the strictly research, approach to the study of the social process but more with the wear and tear that it might cause to the inadequately financed or inadequately staffed anthropologist or other behavioral scientist who is brash enough to attempt to apply it, especially in a foreign area. On this point I shall have more to say later. For the moment, suffice it to say that having recently retired—again quite by design—from playing the dual role of God and anthropologist (the status of Vicos has recently changed from a dependent to an independent community) and having again assumed the role of a plain anthropologist, I find the change in status a highly comforting one. Nevertheless, on the basis of the past five years of experience at Vicos, I remain convinced that the interventionist or action approach to the dynamics of culture, applied with proper restraint, may in the long run provide considerable payoff in terms both of more rational policy and better science. My concern here, therefore, will be with some of the reasons why I believe this to be the case. What, then, are some of the implications—the advantages and disadvantages, the gains and losses—of the application of the research *and* development approach to the study of change, both from a value and scientific point of view?

II

On the question of values—in the ethical sense—I really have little to say, more than to state my stand. No one—professional or layman—can scientifically justify intervention into the lives of other people, whether they be of his own kind or of a different breed. However, by its very nature, the social process is an influencing process among individuals and social groups, one upon which the very existence of society depends. It is no less a necessary condition for the study of social life. Even the most "pure" anthropologist imaginable, conducting his research with "complete" detachment and objectivity, cannot avoid influencing his subjects of study or in turn of being influenced by them. In some instances, I believe, this has led to very salutory effects, both on anthropologists and their informants. Certainly the science of anthropology has been greatly enriched by those informants who were influenced by anthropologists to become anthropologists, even though it may be more questionable, perhaps, that native cultures have been correspondingly enriched by those anthropologists who were influenced by their informants to go native. While this may seem beside the point, I simply want to emphasize the fact that influence and consequently the values which motivate that influence are always part of the process of human interaction and while they can be studied by science, their validation must rest on other grounds.

This does not mean that any anthropologist—pure or applied—can manipulate his subjects without restraint. Some code of ethics must govern his behavior, as the Society for Applied Anthropology long ago recognized. In the case of Vicos, however, where power was held by us, this became an especially delicate issue because having assumed the role of *patrones* we expected and were expected to intervene in the lives of the people. It was at this point that the question of values entered and it was at this point that it was very necessary to take a value stand. What then was this stand?

I long ago made the decision for myself, which is shared by a great many people and communities of the world, that the best kind of a community in which to live is one that is, to quote Aldous Huxley, "just, peaceable, morally and intellectually progressive" and made up of "responsible men and women." To my way of thinking, and I am by no means unique in this view, the best way of approaching this Utopian state of affairs is to pursue as a goal the realization of basic human dignity to which every individual is entitled. And by basic human dignity I mean a very simple thing: a wide rather than a narrow sharing of what I regard as positive human values, some expression of which, as Professor Harold Lasswell has so clearly shown, is found in every society and towards a wider sharing of which, if I interpret Professor Robert Redfield correctly, the broader course of civilization itself has been moving for a considerable period of time.

For lack of better terms of my own to express the meaning I wish to convey, let me again refer to Lasswell who speaks of the following categories of value: power, wealth, enlightenment, respect, well being, skill, affection, and rectitude. The wide sharing of such values among members of the Vicos community was essentially the overall basic value position and policy goal to which we subscribed. In other words, everyone, if he so desired, should at least have the right and the opportunity, if not the responsibility, to participate in the decision-making process in the community, to enjoy a fair share of its wealth, to pursue a desire for knowledge, to be esteemed by his fellowmen, to develop talents to the best of his ability, to be relatively free from physical and mental disease, to enjoy the affection of others, and to command respect for his private life. While no such value stand, of course, can ever be validated by science we and a surprising number of Vicosinos, as I have said elsewhere, and, as revealed by a baseline study, believed them "to be good and desirable ends."

Movement towards such goals, of course, rests on a couple of fundamental assumptions (or better, expectations) in which I happen to have a very strong faith: (1) that human traits are such that progress can be made towards the realization of human dignity, and (2) that the natural order (physical nature) is such that with greater knowledge and skill, human beings can turn it progressively to the service of social goals.

In stating this overall value position, I have not meant to suggest that movement towards these goals can occur only through a single set of institutional practices. Like most anthropologists I subscribe to the doctrine of the relativity of culture and I firmly believe that people have the right of self-determination, as long as they respect that right in others. From the very beginning at Vicos we recognized this principle. In short, we used our power to share power to a point where we no longer hold power, which is just as matters should be.

Before leaving these value and policy matters let me simply cite a few of the developmental changes that have come about as a result of the application of the research *and* development approach to change at Vicos:

1. *Organization.*
1952. Vicos had an *hacienda*-type organization. Outside renters not only had free use of *hacienda peones* for labor and personal services, but also of their animals and tools. Power was concentrated in the hands of *patrón*.
1957. *Hacienda* system and free services have been abolished; new system of community organization now in march is based on shared interests and local control.

2. *Land Ownership.*
1952. No title to land, although Vicosinos had tried on numerous occasions to purchase the land on which they had been living as *peones* for 400 years.
1957. Based on reports of development by the Cornell-Peru Project, the Institute of Indigenous Affairs asked the Peruvian Government to expropriate Vicos in favor of its indigenous population. This expropriation has now taken place.

3. *Local Authority.*
1952. Under the *hacienda*-type organization there were no responsible secular authorities within the community.
1957. The Vicosinos have organized a board of their own delegates elected from each of 6 zones of the *hacienda*. They have the legal responsibility for the direction of community affairs.

4. *Income.*
1952. The indigenous community of Vicos had no source of income of its own.
1957. Former *hacienda* lands are now farmed for the public good, providing a steady income for the payment of lands and the development of public service.

5. *Education.*
1952. In the aspect of education Vicos had a very small school, with one teacher, 10–15 students.
1957. Vicos now possesses the most modern school in the whole region, recently made a *nucleo escolar*, with a capacity of 400 students. There are now 9 teachers and about 200 students, many of whom have had five years of continuity in school.

6. *Production.*
1952. Low economic production—each *hectare* of potato land produced a value of only $100.

1957. Each *hectare* of potato land is now producing a value of $400–$600.

7. *Health Facilities.*

1952. There were no modern health facilities.

1957. A modern health center has been built by the Vicosinos and a neighboring community; a clinic is held twice a week and a public health program is underway.

Most of the cost of these developments have been borne by members of the community themselves.

As a final development outcome I should perhaps mention that the Cornell-Peru Project has had considerable impact outside of the area of Vicos. When originally undertaken there was not a single project of its kind in Peru. At the present time, the Institute of Indigenous Affairs is directing five programs of a similar nature in other areas of the country. And attached to all are Peruvian anthropologists, many of them trained in part at Vicos.

But more important have been the effects on the outside produced by the Vicosinos themselves. Word of their freedom has got around. Let me cite but one example. Recently an *hacienda* community, in conditions similar to those obtaining at Vicos in 1952, sent a commission to Vicos for advice. Their *hacienda*, a public one as Vicos has been, was about to be rented at public auction for a period of ten years and they were desirous of freeing themselves from service to a *patrón*. One of the ways in which this can be done is for the residents of an *hacienda* to rent it directly from the government themselves. But in the case of this community sufficient funds were not immediately available.

The Vicosinos sent a return commission to *Huascarán*, a fictitious name for the community under discussion. On the recommendation of this commission the community of Vicos, which had funds in the bank, lent the community of Huascarán sufficient money to rent their *hacienda* directly from the government, thus freeing them from service to a *patrón*. More than that when the commission from Vicos first went to Huascarán they noticed that the Huascarinos planted their fields by somewhat antiquated methods and suggested more modern methods of agriculture which were originally introduced into Vicos by the Cornell-Peru Project. These are the kind of developmental effects that give the applied anthropologist an occasion for joy.

III

Now what of the scientific implications of the research and development approach to the study of change?[1] Here again I take a positive view, particularly in a situation like Vicos, where it was possible to work in a complete cultural context, where it was possible to specify social goals for almost all aspects of culture, and where it was possible for the anthropologist to maintain some control over the interventions and variables involved. In such an environment, hypotheses can be tested by comparing actual goal achievement with predicted goal achievement.

Actually in the natural sciences, research and development are inseparable. It is even common to join them in one formal project as is the case in many technologically advanced industries, in government, and in private institutions. But whether formally joined or not, scientific discovery is sooner or later inevitably put to the test of success or failure through the application of research results in engineering and technology. In other words, a great strength of, if not a necessary condition for, natural science is feedback through development.

Anthropology, like other behavioral sciences, profits little from such corrective feedback. In part this is because it is not systematically employed in social decision-making, as let us say, physics is employed in missile or building construction. But even if it is employed the results are either not fed back to the anthropologist or they are fed back too slowly to facilitate rapid scientific advance. Moreover, research and development work in behavioral science are seldom joined, even though they were to some extent in Vicos, for the systematic exploitation of their reciprocal benefits, as they are in the research and development laboratories of the natural sciences. To get the feedback necessary for rapid advance in a behavioral science like anthropology, policy is needed, even if policy does not need science.

The connection between research and development in anthropology and other behavioral sciences is probably even closer than it is in the natural

---

[1] Much of the material here has been revised from an unpublished document prepared by Harold Lasswell, Charles Lindblom, John Kennedy, and myself, entitled "Experimental Research in the Behavioral Sciences and Regional Development." In a sense they should be regarded as joint authors of this section.

sciences. In science, as everyone knows, every generalization is both an insight and a prediction, even though its explicit statement is usually cast in one form or another. Now when a generalization on behavior is communicated to people who are also its subjects, it may alter the knowledge and preferences of these people and also their behavior. Thus a scientific generalization on behavior, by altering behavior, appears to falsify or obsolesce itself. This is called "pliancy factor" by my philosophical colleague at Cornell, Max Black.

In general this complication has been viewed as a cross that the behavioral scientist must bear. Actually, a generalization about behavior is not falsified when predictions based upon it are made obsolete when the subject to whom it is made known prefers to modify himself rather than to conform to an earlier prediction. It is simply that the possibility of modification of behavior must be taken into account and turned to scientific advantage. In the continuous interplay between scientific generalization and goal-seeking behavior, the insight-feedback of a scientific generalization can be employed both for goal revision and as empirical data for research. This is one of the great advantages of the research and development approach. Perhaps an example will illustrate what I mean.

One of the developmental goals of the Vicos program was to bring decision-making bodies of the community up to a level of competence at which we, the *patrones,* could be dispensed with but without the community's falling victim to its most predatory members as has sometimes been the case. Thus, arrangements had to be made for group survival and stability and, through controlling the complexity of the problems dealt with and by other devices, the groups gradually brought to their highest level of competence. This required that hypotheses be formulated and acted upon— hypotheses concerning the requirements of viability and competence of groups. Once acted upon the hypotheses were tested by their results. Hence each successive developmental step was a step in the isolation of another variable for research.

Concretely, both development and research interests merge in following the consequences of such successive steps as the following, at least some of which were taken for one group of potential decision-makers at Vicos: (1) the group was asked for advice in the settlement of land disputes; (2) it was invested with prestige by calling public atten-

tion to its role; (3) the group was given the opportunity to settle land disputes; (4) the group was provided, through skilled observers, the feedback of an understandable analysis of its performance; (5) the *patrón* was withdrawn from the group meeting, reserving only the right to veto under certain conditions; (6) the jurisdiction of the group was enlarged with gradually decreasing veto.

While this detail is much abbreviated, it suggests how research on the developmental steps provides an opportunity for the dogged pursuit of whatever variables one wishes to isolate. Every insight into the variables can be put to a test; and, where predictions are disappointed, a reformulation of the hypothesis can be followed by a further test until predictions are no longer disappointed. By no means will all the unknowns of human behavior become unveiled, but development requires correct insights, hypotheses, and analytic models. It compels their never-ending revision until they pass the test of application.

The essence of the connection between research and development in this illustration is that each developmental intervention—say, introducing legal principles by which land disputes might be resolved—is both a necessary step towards reaching community goals and in the research sense a method of varying the group situation to isolate another variable in group dynamics—in this instance isolating the effect of introducing formal principles against which individual cases are to be judged. It is precisely because of feedback to the researcher from the development application that research needs development just as much as development needs research.

Whatever the particular example, the story is much the same. The researcher is compelled to follow through, to keep on trying for the refinement of an hypothesis or model that will stand the test of application. If, for example, he wants to know what is necessary to break down prejudice between Indians and Mestizos, his research is not terminated when he has tested one popular hypothesis and found it invalid, because his developmental objectives require that he try a whole series of interventions until prejudice begins to decline.

In the case of Vicos, attempts were made in collaboration with several colleagues[2] to lay out about 130 specific possible lines of research and

[2]See footnote 1.

development, each matched to a specific developmental goal such as the diversification of agriculture, the development of community leadership, the reduction of social distance between Indians and Mestizos, the increase of educational opportunities for both children and adults, etc. Wherever possible an attempt was made to make fairly precise statements about the goals in question. To lay out the various possibilities in order subsequently to develop a strategy of research and development, each line of possible intervention was represented in a semi-diagrammatic way by a column on a very large bulletin or map board taking up the walls of a room. The diagram below represents how 3″ × 5″ cards were used to lay out visually the research and development sequences, subject to constant revision as research and development continues:

An ideological goal or end point

A corresponding institutional goal or end point

Program plans for probes, pretests, interventions, and appraisals

Present ideological situation with respect to above goals summarized

Present institutional situation with respect to above goals summarized

Record of past interventions

Base line ideological situation

Base line institutional situation

At the top of the column is posted for some end-point date the particular goal in question to be reached. At the bottom of the column are posted the counterpart institutional and ideological situations found at the base line period before interventions. Above them are summarized any interventions so far made, and above them the present institutional and ideological situation with respect to this one line of development. The remainder of the column is given over to a proposed schedule of probes, pretests, interventions, and appraisals.

By utilizing such a method, interventions are not likely to be hit or miss and their developmental and research gains can be fully appreciated. Scheduling them requires the careful appraisal of the facts describing the existing situation and trends, probes of readiness of the community to take the proposed step, pretests of interventions on a small scale, then the intervention itself and subsequent appraisal, which in turn becomes the first step in a still further intervention. Hence in diagrammatic terms, the upper part of the column, including the goals themselves, is constantly undergoing revision on the basis of the growing lower part of the column representing past experience.

To illustrate the distinctiveness of research, where the whole life of the community is available for study, as it was to a considerable extent in Vicos, it may be helpful to visualize a great many columns such as have just been described, set side by side. The interrelationships among these columns can hardly go unnoticed, and it becomes both possible and necessary to consider these interrelationships in devising a research and development strategy.

One more thing should be said about this contextual mapping in a research and development approach to change. It makes possible, for *development,* an economy of intervention. For example, one way in which to reduce social inequality between Mestizos and Indians is to schedule public functions in Vicos attractive enough to draw neighboring Mestizos in and then conduct these functions in such a way as to break down the traditional acceptance of segregation. One can conceive of an experiment along this line that might test the hypothesis that prejudice between Indians and Mestizos will be reduced by contact under conditions of social equality.

Now with reference to quite a different goal of reducing communal binges, movies are an effective competitor with alcohol because the Vicosinos prefer to be sober when watching a movie. Movies are also an obvious method for adult education, including literacy. Finally, the importation and showing of films may become the nucleus of a small-scale experiment in Indian entrepreneurship. Hence a variety of lines of desirable research and development converge on a movie program for Vicos. Actually such an experiment is now underway at Vicos and a skillful plan for introducing movies into the community may turn out to be a strategically sound intervention because many birds may be killed with one small stone.

I have now said enough to indicate what I believe some of the value and scientific implications of the research and development approach to the study of change to be. Most of what I have said is positive and I have not suggested that this approach be applied to the exclusion of others. My greatest doubts about it, on the basis of my experience at Vicos, stem from the unlikelihood of mobilizing sufficient funds and personnel to do a research and development job well. It is a man's job that a boy cannot be sent to do. I hope that the powers supporting research will soon take cognizance of this fact.

Anthony F. C. Wallace
Revitalization Processes

Anthropologists view short-term cultural change (two or three generations), as basically a sociopsychological process. In the selection that follows, Wallace uses personalistic constructs to depict the response of the members of a group when they perceive severe disorganization in their culture. Recovery is perceived as the rapid acceptance of innovation; the process is deliberate, organized by members of the group. The crisis situation described here, more common than first appears, is one that demands rapid intervention.

. . . Even during periods of stable moving equilibrium, the sociocultural system is subject to mild but measurable oscillations in degree of organization. From time to time, however, most societies undergo more violent fluctuations in this regard. Such fluctuation is of peculiar importance in culture change because it often culminates in relatively sudden change in cultural *Gestalt*. We refer, here, to revitalization movements, which we define as deliberate, organized attempts by some members of a society to construct a more satisfying culture by rapid acceptance of a pattern of multiple innovations.

The severe disorganization of a sociocultural system may be caused by the impact of any one or combination of a variety of forces that push the system beyond the limits of equilibrium. Some of these forces are: climatic or faunal changes, which destroy the economic basis of its existence; epidemic disease, which grossly alters the population structure; wars, which exhaust the society's resources of manpower or result in defeat or invasion; internal conflict among interest groups, which results in extreme disadvantage for at least one group; and, very commonly, a position of perceived subordination and inferiority with respect to an adjacent society. The latter, by the use of more or less coercion (or even no coercion at all, as in situations where the mere example set by the dominant society raises too-high levels of aspiration), brings about uncoordinated cultural changes. Under conditions of disorganization, the system, from the standpoint of at least some of its members, is unable to make possible the reliable satisfaction of certain values that are held to be essential to continued well-being and self-respect. The mazeway of a culturally disillusioned person, accordingly, is an image of a world that is unpredictable, or barren in its simplicity, or both, and is apt to contain severe identity conflicts. His mood (depending on the precise nature of the disorganization) will be one of panic-stricken anxiety, shame, guilt, depression, or apathy.

An example of the kind of disorganization to which we refer is given by the two thousand or so Seneca Indians of New York at the close of the eighteenth century. Among these people, a supreme value attached to the conception of the absolutely free and autonomous individual, unconstrained by and indifferent to his own and alien others' pain and hardship. This individual was capable of free indulgence of emotional impulses but, in crisis, freely subordinated his own wishes to the needs of his community. Among the men, especially, this ego-ideal was central in personality organization. Men defined the roles of hunting, of warfare, and of statesmanship as the conditions of achievement of this value; thus the stereotypes of "the good hunter," "the brave warrior," and "the forest statesman" were the images of masculine success. But the forty-three years from 1754, when the French and Indian War began, to 1797, when the Seneca sold their last hunting grounds and became largely confined to tiny, isolated reservations, brought with them changes in their situation that made achievement of these ideals virtually impossible. The good hunter could no longer hunt: the game was scarce, and it was almost suicidally dangerous to stray far from the reservation among the numerous hostile white men. The brave warrior could no longer fight, being undersupplied, abandoned by his allies, and his women and children threatened by growing military might of the United States. The forest statesman was an object of contempt, and this disillusionment was perhaps more shattering than the rest. The Iroquois chiefs, for nearly a century, had been able to play off British and French, then Americans and British, against one another, extorting supplies and guarantees of territorial immunity from both sides. They had maintained an extensive system of alliances and hegemonies among surrounding tribal groups. Suddenly they were shorn of their power. White men no longer spoke of the League of the Iroquois with respect; their western Indian dependents and allies regarded them as cowards for having made peace with the Americans.

The initial Seneca response to the progress of sociocultural disorganization was quasi-pathological: many became drunkards; the fear of witches increased; squabbling factions were unable to achieve a common policy. But a revitalization movement developed in 1799, based on the religious revelations reported by one of the disillusioned forest statesmen, one Handsome Lake, who preached a code of patterned religious and cultural reform. The drinking of whiskey was proscribed; witchcraft was to be stamped out; various outmoded rituals and prevalent sins were to be abandoned. In addition, various syncretic cultural reforms, amounting to a reorientation of the socioeconomic system, were to be undertaken, including the adoption of agriculture (hitherto a feminine calling) by the men, and the focusing of kinship responsibilities within the nuclear family (rather than in the clan and lineage). The general acceptance of Handsome Lake's Code, within a few years, wrought seemingly miraculous changes. A group of sober, devout, partly literate, and technologically up-to-date farming communities suddenly replaced the demoralized slums in the wilderness.

Such dramatic transformations are, as a matter of historical fact, very common in human history, and probably have been the medium of as much culture change as the slower equilibrium processes. Furthermore, because they compress into such a short space of time such extensive changes in pattern, they are somewhat easier to record than the quiet serial changes during periods of equilibrium. In general, revitalization processes share a common process structure that can be conceptualized as a pattern of temporally overlapping, but functionally distinct, stages:

I. *Steady State.* This is a period of moving equilibrium of the kind discussed in the preceding section. Culture change occurs during the steady state, but is of the relatively slow and chainlike kind. Stress levels vary among interest groups, and there is some oscillation in organization level, but disorganization and stress remain within limits tolerable to most individuals. Occasional incidents of intolerable stress may stimulate a limited "correction" of the system, but some incidence of individual ill-health and criminality are accepted as a price society must pay.

II. *The Period of Increased Individual Stress.* The sociocultural system is being "pushed" progressively out of equilibrium by the forces described earlier: climatic and biotic change, epidemic disease, war and conquest, social subordination, acculturation, internally generated decay, and so forth. Increasingly large numbers of individuals are placed under what is to them intolerable stress by the failure of the system to accommodate the satisfaction of their needs. Anomie and disillusionment become widespread, as the culture is perceived to be disorganized and inadequate; crime and illness increase sharply in frequency as individualistic asocial responses. But the situation is still generally defined as one of fluctuation within the steady state.

III. *The Period of Cultural Distortion.* Some members of the society attempt, piecemeal and ineffectively, to restore personal equilibrium by adopting socially disfunctional expedients. Alcoholism, venality in public officials, the "black market," breaches of sexual and kinship mores, hoarding, gambling for gain, "scapegoating," and similar behaviors that, in the preceding period, were still defined as individual deviancies, in effect become institutionalized efforts to circumvent the evil effects of "the system." Interest groups, losing confidence in the advantages of maintaining mutually acceptable interrelationships, may resort to violence in order to coerce others into unilaterally advantageous behavior. Because of the malcoordination of cultural changes during this period, they are rarely able to reduce the impact of the forces that have pushed the society out of equilibrium, and in fact lead to a continuous decline in organization.

IV. *The Period of Revitalization.* Once severe cultural distortion has occurred, the society can with difficulty return to steady state without the institution of a revitalization process. Without revitalization, indeed, the society is apt to disintegrate as a system: the population will either die off, splinter into autonomous groups, or be absorbed into another, more stable, society. Revitalization depends on the successful completion of the following functions:

1. Formulation of a code. An individual, or a group of individuals, constructs a new, utopian image of sociocultural organization. This model is a blueprint of an ideal society or "goal culture." Contrasted with the goal culture is the existing culture, which is presented as inadequate or evil in certain respects. Connecting the existing culture

and the goal culture is a transfer culture: a system of operations that, if faithfully carried out, will transform the existing culture into the goal culture. Failure to institute the transfer operations will, according to the code, result in either the perpetuation of the existing misery or the ultimate destruction of the society (if not of the whole world). Not infrequently in primitive societies the code, or the core of it, is formulated by one individual in the course of a hallucinatory revelation; such prophetic experiences are apt to launch religiously oriented movements, since the source of the revelation is apt to be regarded as a supernatural being. Nonhallucinatory formulations usually are found in politically oriented movements. In either case, the formulation of the code constitutes a reformulation of the author's own mazeway and often brings to him a renewed confidence in the future and a remission of the complaints he experienced before. It may be suggested that such mazeway resynthesis processes are merely extreme forms of the reorganizing dream processes that seem to be associated with REM (rapid-eye-movement) sleep, which are necessary to normal health.

2. Communication. The formulators of the code preach the code to other people in an evangelistic spirit. The aim of the communication is to make converts. The code is offered as the means of spiritual salvation for the individual and of cultural salvation for the society. Promises of benefit to the target population need not be immediate or materialistic, for the basis of the code's appeal is the attractiveness of identification with a more highly organized system, with all that this implies in the way of self-respect. Indeed, in view of the extensiveness of the changes in values often implicit in such codes, appeal to currently held values would often be pointless. Religious codes offer spiritual salvation, identification with God, elect status; political codes offer honor, fame, the respect of society for sacrifices made in its interest. But refusal to accept the code is usually defined as placing the listener in immediate spiritual, as well as material, peril with respect to his existing values. In small societies, the target population may be the entire community; but in more complex societies, the message may be aimed only at certain groups deemed eligible for participation in the transfer and goal cultures.

3. Organization. The code attracts converts. The motivations that are satisfied by conversion, and

the psychodynamics of the conversion experience itself, are likely to be highly diverse, ranging from the mazeway resynthesis characteristic of the prophet, and the hysterical conviction of the "true believer," to the calculating expediency of the opportunist. As the group of converts expands, it differentiates into two parts: a set of disciples and a set of mass followers. The disciples increasingly become the executive organization, responsible for administering the evangelistic program, protecting the formulator, combatting heresy, and so on. In this role, the disciples increasingly become full-time specialists in the work of the movement. The tri-cornered relationship between the fomulators, the disciples, and the mass followers is given an authoritarian structure, even without the formalities of older organizations, by the charismatic quality of the formulator's image. The formulator is regarded as a man to whom, from a supernatural being or from some other source of wisdom unavailable to the mass, a superior knowledge and authority has been vouchsafed that justifies his claim to unquestioned belief and obedience from his followers.

In the modern world, with the advantages of rapid transportation and ready communication, the simple charismatic model of cult organization is not always adequate to describe many social and religious movements. In such programs as Pentecostalism, Black Power, and the New Left, there is typically a considerable number of local or special issue groups loosely joined in what Luther Gerlach has called an "acephalous, segmentary, reticulate organization." Each segment may be, in effect, a separate revitalization organization of the simple kind described above; the individual groups differ in details of code, in emotional style, in appeal to different social classes; and, since the movement as a whole has no single leader, it is relatively immune to repression, the collapse of one or several segments in no way invalidating the whole. This type of movement organization is singularly well adapted to predatory expansion; but it may eventually fall under the domination of one cult or party (as was the case, for instance, in Germany when the SS took over the fragmented Nazi party, which in turn was heir to a large number of nationalist groups, and as is the case when a Communist party apparatus assumes control of a revolutionary popular front).

4. Adaptation. Because the movement is a revolutionary organization (however benevolent and humane the ultimate values to which it subscribes), it threatens the interests of any group that obtains advantage, or believes it obtains advantage, from maintaining or only moderately reforming the status quo. Furthermore, the code is never complete; new inadequacies are constantly being found in the existing culture, and new inconsistencies, predicative failures, and ambiguities discovered in the code itself (some of the latter being pointed out by the opposition). The response of the code formulators and disciples is to rework the code, and, if necessary, to defend the movement by political and diplomatic maneuver, and, ultimately, by force. The general tendency is for codes to harden gradually, and for the tone of the movement to become increasingly nativistic and hostile both toward nonparticipating fellow members of society, who will ultimately be defined as "traitors," and toward "national enemies."

True revolutions, as distinguished from mere coups d'état, which change personnel without changing the structure, require that the revitalization movement of which they are the instrument add to its code a morality sanctioning subversion or even violence. The leadership must also be sophisticated in its knowledge of how to mobilize an increasingly large part of the population to their side, and of how to interfere with the mobilization of the population by the establishment. The student of such processes can do no better than to turn to the works of contemporary practitioners such as Che Guevara and Mao Tse Tung for authoritative explications and examples of the revolutionary aspect of revitalization.

5. Cultural transformation. If the movement is able to capture both the adherence of a substantial proportion of a local population and, in complex societies, of the functionally crucial apparatus (such as power and communications networks, water supply, transport systems, and military establishment), the transfer culture and, in some cases, the goal culture itself, can be put into operation. The revitalization, if successful, will be attended by the drastic decline of the quasi-pathological individual symptoms of anomie and by the disappearance of the cultural distortions. For such a revitalization to be accomplished, however, the movement must be able to maintain its boundaries from outside invasion, must be able to obtain internal social conformity without destructive

coercion, and must have a successful economic system.

6. Routinization. If the preceding functions are satisfactorily completed, the functional reasons for the movement's existence as an innovative force disappear. The transfer culture, if not the goal culture, is operating of necessity with the participation of a large proportion of the community. Although the movement's leaders may resist the realization of the fact, the movement's function shifts from the role of innovation to the role of maintenance. If the movement was heavily religious in orientation, its legacy is a cult or church that preserves and reworks the code, and maintains, through ritual and myth, the public awareness of the history and values that brought forth the new culture. If the movement was primarily political, its organization is routinized into various stable decision-making, and morale-and-order-maintaining functions (such as administrative offices, police, and military bodies). Charisma can, to a degree, be routinized, but its intensity diminishes as its functional necessity becomes, with increasing obviousness, outmoded.

V. *The New Steady State*. With the routinization of the movement, a new steady state may be said to exist. Steady-state processes of culture change continue; many of them are in areas where the movement has made further change likely. In particular, changes in the value structure of the culture may lay the basis for long-continuing changes (such as the train of economic and technological consequences of the dissemination of the Protestant ethic after the Protestant Reformation). Thus in addition to the changes that the movement accomplishes during its active phase, it may control the direction of the subsequent equilibrium processes by shifting the values that define the cultural focus. The record of the movement itself, over time, gradually is subject to distortion, and eventually is enshrined in myths and rituals which elevate the events that occurred, and persons who acted, into quasi- or literally divine status.

Two psychological mechanisms seem to be of peculiar importance in the revitalization process: mazeway resynthesis and hysterical conversion. The resynthesis is most dramatically exemplified in the career of the prophet who formulates a new religious code during a hallucinatory trance. Typically, such persons, after suffering increasing depreciation of self-esteem as the result of their inadequacy to achieve the culturally ideal standards, reach a point of either physical or drug-induced exhaustion, during which a resynthesis of values and beliefs occurs. The resynthesis is, like other innovations, a recombination of pre-existing configurations; the uniqueness of this particular process is the suddenness of conviction, the trancelike state of the subject, and the emotionally central nature of the subject matter. There is some reason to suspect that such dramatic resyntheses depend on a special biochemical milieu, accompanying the "stage of exhaustion" of the stress (in Selye's sense) syndrome, or on a similar milieu induced by drugs. But comparable resyntheses are, of course, sometimes accomplished more slowly, without the catalytic aid of extreme stress or drugs. This kind of resynthesis produces, apparently, a permanent alteration of mazeway: the new stable cognitive configuration, is, as it were, constructed out of the materials of earlier configurations, which, once rearranged, cannot readily reassemble into the older forms.

The hysterical conversion is more typical of the mass follower who is repeatedly subjected to suggestion by a charismatic leader and an excited crowd. The convert of this type may, during conversion display various dissociative behaviors (rage, speaking in tongues, rolling on the ground, weeping, and so on). After conversion, his overt behavior may be in complete conformity with the code to which he has been exposed. But his behavior has changed not because of a radical resynthesis, but because of the adoption under suggestion of an additional social personality which temporarily replaces, but does not destroy, the earlier. He remains, in a sense, a case of multiple personality and is liable, if removed from reinforcing symbols, to lapse into an earlier social personality. The participant in the lynch mob or in the camp meeting revival is a familiar example of this type of convert. But persons can be maintained in this state of hysterical conversion for months or years, if the "trance" is continuously maintained by the symbolic environment (flags, statues, portraits, songs, and so on) and continuous suggestions (speeches, rallies, and so on). The most familiar contemporary example is the German under Hitler who participated in the Nazi genocide program, but reverted to *Gemütlichkeit* when the war ended. The difference between the resynthesized person and the converted one does not lie in the nature of the codes to which they subscribe (they may be the same), but in the blandness and readiness of the hysterical convert to revert, as compared to the almost paranoid intensity and stability of the resynthesized prophet. A successful movement, by virtue of its ability to maintain suggestion continuously for years, is able to hold the hysterical convert indefinitely, or even to work a real resynthesis by repeatedly forcing him, after hysterical conversion, to reexamine his older values and beliefs and to work through to a valid resynthesis, sometimes under considerable stress. The Chinese Communists, for instance, apparently have become disillusioned by hysterical conversions and have used various techniques, some coercive and some not, but all commonly lumped together as "brain-washing" in Western literature, to induce valid resynthesis. The aim of these communist techniques, like those of the established religions, is, literally, to produce a "new man."

It is impossible to exaggerate the importance of these two psychological processes for culture change, for they make possible the rapid substitution of a new cultural *Gestalt* for an old, and thus the rapid cultural transformation of whole populations. Without this mechanism, the cultural transformation of the 600,000,000 people of China by the Communists could not have occurred; nor the Communist-led revitalization and expansion of the USSR; nor the American Revolution; nor the Protestant Reformation; nor the rise and spread of Christianity, Mohammedanism, and Buddhism. In the written historical record, revitalization movements begin with Ikhnaton's ultimately disastrous attempt to establish a new, monotheistic religion in Egypt; they are found, continent by continent, in the history of all human societies, occurring with frequency proportional to the pressures to which the society is subjected. For small tribal societies, in chronically extreme situations, movements may develop every ten or fifteen years; in stable complex cultures, the rate of a society-wide movement may be one every two or three hundred years.

In view of the frequency and geographical diversity of revitalization movements, it can be expected that their content will be extremely varied, corresponding to the diversity of situational contexts and cultural backgrounds in which they develop. Major culture areas are, over extended periods of time, associated with particular types: New Guinea and Melanesia, during the latter part of the nineteenth and the twentieth centuries, have been the home of the well-known "cargo cults." The most prominent feature of these cults is the expectation that the ancestors soon will arrive in a steamship, bearing a cargo of the white man's goods, and will lead a nativistic revolution culminating in the ejection of European masters. The Indians of the eastern half of South America for centuries after the conquest set off on migrations for the *terre sans mal* where a utopian way of life, free of Spaniards and Portuguese, would be found; North American Indians of the eighteenth and nineteenth centuries were prone to revivalistic movements such as the Ghost Dance, whose adherents believed that appropriate ritual and the abandonment of the sins of the white man would bring a return of the golden age before contact; South Africa has been the home of the hundreds of small, enthusiastic, separatist churches that have broken free of the missionary organizations. As might be expected, a congruence evidently exists between the cultural *Anlage* and the content of movement, which, together with processes of direct and stimulus diffusion, accounts for the tendency for movements to fall into areal types.

Art Gallaher, Jr.
On Changing the System

In the introduction to this section, we made the point that interventionists must know themselves, those they represent, and those who are the target of contemplated changes—and that communication between the parties involved is the element critical to knowing. The selections that followed described the conditions for intervention, important models of intervention, and the ultimate consequences of intervention. We move now to an elaboration of what has gone before, to see what can be learned from it.

It is reassuring, to those of us who are concerned with American society, to remember that change is not new to us. From the beginning we have been under the influence of Western ideas of progress. Building upon these, we have altered our values and even oriented many of them toward the future. Moreover, we have a rich cultural base and an achievement-oriented society. All these factors form a background for further change. In the foreground is our concern about the social issues explored in this volume. The result has been a sharp acceleration in our rate of cultural change, especially since the end of World War II. Americans today, but especially youth, face a literally mind-boggling choice of alternative experiences. It is even thought that the very plentitude of choices is a cause of the alienation felt by so many.

As we observed earlier, much of our present concern with cultural change arises from our attempts to cope with critical incidents, both domestic and international, in our society. The nature of such incidents during the past two decades (from the Korean War on) has been such that more people than ever before could respond personally. To put it another way, both international and domestic issues have been, and continue to be, visceral. They involve the frustration of wars not popular and not won. They include conflicts rooted in race, ethnicity, class, age, and hunger, which are all threatening to oneself, no matter what one's level in the social system.

The main concomitant of this visceral response is a greater sensitivity to needs, personal and collective, on the part of greater numbers of people. This volume is, in fact, dedicated to the delineation of such needs and their translation into social issues. The issues are many, and awareness of them is high; precisely the kind of environment that is most conducive to intervention. *Intervention, directed change,* and *planned change* are all synonyms for that situation in which someone, or some group, interferes actively and purposefully in the social behavior of others. The "others" may be part of the social system of those who are intervening, or they may live in a different society. In either case, the concerns are the same: those who intervene consciously select elements in the social life of others and, by stimulating the acceptance of innovations, inhibiting the practice of prior patterns of behavior—or, as is frequently the case, doing both

simultaneously—manage the direction of change.

It does not matter what the basis for intervention; in the end it has political consequences. This is a fact of life not to be ignored by interventionists, even those suffused with altruism. Because there are political consequences, the problem of "knowing" referred to earlier assumes additional importance. All of us who intervene, whether as anthropologists doing research or as those who are interested in directly changing the system, must keep in mind that our actions are potentially a part of the political arena.[1] Attempting to make some assessment of how our actions will fare in the political arena is increasingly being viewed as a must. It is at this point—when the activist employs theory developed by the anthropologist as a basis for the formulation of social policies—that the activist and the anthropologist may be most closely aligned; in the opinion of some, should be as one. This point is brought out clearly in the section of this volume on "Poverty and Culture," where the concept of a "culture of poverty" is examined against its implications for social planning.

One final point on the politics of intervention: probably more intervention occurs in our lives through the aegis of government than from all other sources combined. Government may either serve as the initiator of interventionist activity or provide the means whereby others can do so. In a rural community that I studied some years ago, and which I call Plainville, the central authority of government was found to be the main innovative force working among the people. Although this is not what the community had desired in the beginning, most of its members realized long ago that the problems were too complex to be resolved by the customary internal adjustments. Since many of the problems of this community were generic rather than unique, government at all levels developed innovative apparatus; because many problems were generic, government bodies initiated direct intervention on their own and rationalized it as in the public interest. This is not to imply that the community was a helpless and passive recipient of whatever came its way. It was not, and on occasion it flexed its own political muscle to oppose or modify; in the end its greatest strength was displayed by its refashioning of many of the innovations to make them fit local norms. In still other cases, where opposition was great but not as strong as the sanctions available to the interventionist, the

[1] For an example of the political aspects of intervention, see "The Life and Death of Project Camelot," by Irving Louis Horowitz, and "The Established Order: Do Not Fold, Spindle, or Mutilate," by Marshall Sahlins, in the section "Anthropology and the Third World."

community accommodated itself to the situation by accepting the innovations only until the stimulus or sanction was withdrawn. I suggest that this kind of change is spurious, as opposed to genuine change, i.e., the kind that modifies values. The kind of accommodative change which I am labeling "spurious" is not an uncommon response in target populations that feel themselves vulnerable; it is also not uncommon in situations where the reward accompanying an innovation provides some immediate gratification or has more value than the innovation itself.

Our comments on the politics of intervention suggest that interventionists sometimes control sanctions to insure compliance with their wishes. This brings us to the matter of intervention tactics and strategies, variables crucial to the final acceptance or rejection of innovations. Since the selection of strategies and tactics is more often determined by ideology than it is by situation, our concern is with ideologies.

The ideological issue ultimately resolves itself into the argument about means versus ends and which is more important. We can refer to one end of this continuum, that is to one type of intervention, as the *pragmatic* strategy.[2] This strategy is concerned mainly with creating a climate conducive to gaining the acceptance of an innovation. Tactics flowing from this approach are based on a large body of literature in anthropology supporting the notion that people more readily accept changes that: (1) they can understand and perceive as relevant; and (2) they have had a hand in planning. This is a clinical model, one of the clearest examples of which is the so-called *action anthropology*. The pragmatic interventionist is one whose tactics and strategies are geared mainly to means rather than ends. Following the model, the interventionist takes his definition of the problem from those who seek assistance, and works from there.

We can refer to the other type of intervention strategy as *utopic*. In this case the interventionist's role is mainly one of manipulation to gain the acceptance of a change. His basic premise is that results are best achieved by doing things to, or planning for, people— rather than with them. Tactics designed to gain acceptance of the innovation involve the use of positive and negative sanctions to insure compliance. As we indicated earlier, this strategy is apt to be invoked when the target is in a subordinate position or the intervener presumes that his expertise is not to be questioned. The utopic interventionist is one whose tactics and strategies are geared mainly to ends, rather than means. The major advantage of the model is that

change can be effected quickly, whereas the pragmatic interventionist's strategy requires more time.

Although there are points to be made for and against each of these models of intervention, the data incline more toward the pragmatic model as insuring the greater opportunity for genuine cultural change. On the other hand, the conservation of time, energy, money, or other resources may dictate at least an initial strategy more akin to the utopic. Again, this is particularly true where the target population has a well-developed dependence upon either internal or external authority. Indications are, however, that contemporary planners are pitching their strategies and tactics somewhere between these two ideological postures.

Tied closely to strategies and tactics is the need to understand the consequences of intervention in the social system undergoing change. There are consequences that derive mainly from the actions of the intervener; secondly, there are consequences that inhere in the nature of the innovation accepted into the social system.

The role of interventionist conveys an image to the target population: it is upon his authority that one should depend to achieve the right result. The bases for an attitude of dependence toward the interventionist are, of course, situational; they reside in the expertise represented by the intervener's credentials, in the power represented by his sanctions, or in his connections with other sources of assistance. The results he achieves may have the effect of continuing the attitude of dependency, with the ultimate possibility that it becomes a norm in the social system. Now, if the intent was to provide an immediate gain for the target population, then disengagement becomes a problem, perhaps not possible without crippling the social system, even leaving it in a worse state than it was. On the other hand, if the intent was to structure the role of the interventionist into the target social system, the problem is to live up to the authority upon which people have been asked to depend.

This brings us to a related matter, that the interventionist conveys to the target population an expectation of change. This is, of course, what intervention is customarily all about. However, if the interventionists —perhaps only to convince the population of their efficacy—pushed their claims for success too enthu-

---

[2]Art Gallaher, Jr., "The Role of the Advocate and Directed Change," in *Media and Educational Innovations*, W. C. Meierhenry, ed. (Lincoln: University of Nebraska Press, 1964), pp. 33–40.

siastically, a likely result is the creation of expectations beyond the bounds of possibility. The situation can become particularly explosive when there is a combination of rising expectations and the tactic for the acceptance of change is a sanction involving relative deprivation.

The implications to be drawn from what we have been suggesting range from the dramatic to the subtle. There are dramatic examples aplenty, when frustrations born of economic expectations not met, political promises unfilled, and civil liberties subverted suddenly exploded into ghetto riots. Equally significant, though not as sensational, and much more common, is the subtle emergence of dependency and expectations as norms in the social system. For an example, we can draw again upon the example of Plainville.

It was determined that, during the fifteen years covered in the analysis of Plainville, local units representing the centralized authority of government had successfully intervened to solve many complex problems for the community. The activities of these units converged in many areas of behavior, one of which was to convince Plainvillers of new living standards based mainly on modern technology. As Plainvillers were sold on the notion of technology as the solution to their problems, the government units sold themselves also as especially competent to facilitate the needed innovations. The result was that Plainvillers surrendered many areas of decision-making autonomy to the interventionists, came to depend upon them for innovative direction, and at the same time developed strong expectations of change in their technology. The big problem came when Plainvillers extended the notion of American technology as undergoing constant modification to mean that the solutions to their problems would be continually improved upon. Improvements in their standard of living were assumed, and government units upon whose authority they had come to depend for the ways and means of innovation were under fire constantly for not coming up with something new.

We turn our attention now to the consequences for the social system of the acceptance of an innovation. At issue here is the matter of the integration of the system, that is, the relationships among the institutions and other patterns which comprise the social system being modified. For the interventionist, this means careful attention to how innovations are to be incorporated into an existing situation. For example, are they to enter a social system as alternatives to patterns already present, in which case acceptance or rejection becomes a function of competitive worth? Or should the innovation be taken into the system as a replacement for that which is already there? This makes sharper demands on people, and forces the basic processes of learning and forgetting to a level of consciousness not otherwise demanded. One is more apt to find this integrative process at work in crises. On the other hand, should the innovation be integrated into a system by fusing it with the prior condition? There is evidence that, left to their own ends, people frequently employ this means of integration.

One point not to be ignored is that different qualities of an innovation may become integrated in different ways. The form of an innovation, for example, may be integrated as a replacement for a preexistent form, but the meaning and functions attaching to that form will be integrated as an alternative, or perhaps be fused with a prior pattern.

It is to be remembered, too, that societies vary in the extent to which they are loosely or tightly integrated, and this bears on how innovations are incorporated into them. At one end of a continuum are societies such as the Yir Yoront in Australia, which are tightly integrated. For those who live in such folklike societies there are few alternatives; except for the differences that accrue to age and sex, the patterns by which they relate to physical, social, and supernatural environments tend to be very much the same for all. In this kind of society, the slightest change may precipitate profound modification and lead to near or complete collapse. On the other hand, in a community such as Plainville, where there are a maximum number of alternatives, massive changes can be integrated into the social system more successfully over a short period of time. This does not mean, of course, that people in less tightly integrated communities are indiscriminate acceptors, nor that their communities are any less susceptible to ultimate dissolution.

This brings us to one final point regarding intervention and the responsibilities, ethical and otherwise, of interventionists. Any human community can fail to maintain its integration through too little intervention, or none at all, or through too much intervention, or the wrong kind. The world abounds with examples of interventionists who have charted courses that destroyed the very friends they sought to help.

Index

Abortion, 206, 418, 421–422, 425, 427
Academic colonialism, 154–156, 171, 174–177
Accommodation, 126, 382, 476–477
Acculturation, 104–105, 115, 227, 310; of Canadian Indians, 290–294; differential, 122–123; of Ojibwa, 246, 249, 252
Achievement: of goals by anthropologists, 467–470; level of, 255, 292–293
Action anthropology model, 438–441, 477
Action research, and change, 455–456
Adams, John, 398
Adams, Richard N., 128
Adaptation: and evolution, 187, 198; to new culture, 104–105, 382; of populations, 225, 226; to urban life, 400–406
Ad Hoc Committee on Afro-American Issues, 167, 169–170
Adolescents: and Alianza, 100; and education, 81, 285–290, 312, 329; and Gusii life, 339, 340–341, 343, 379; and Houma, 87–88; and rioting, 368, 399
Adrenal stress, 396–397
Affluence, and pollution, 408, 410, 411, 413–414, 415, 416
Afghanistan, 159, 160
Africa, 111, 112, 117, 131, 139, 148, 159, 161, 163, 164, 178, 235, 236, 300, 309, 381; and ASA, 165–174; Gusii tribe of, 336–345; Hausa of, 451; populations of, 196, 198
African. See Blacks.
African District Council, 345
African Heritage Studies Association (AHSA), 167, 169, 170, 171
African Studies Association (ASA), 9, 165–174
Aggression: and animal experiments, 396–398, 431–432; of blacks, 76–78, 82, 83, 362, 367, 369; and discrimination, 76–78, 82, 83; and the environment, 386, 398; in Gusii sexual practices, 336–345; and Netsilik, 370–378; origin in, 388–389, 430, 431; and population, 425; research on, 431–432; and XYY prisoners, 432. See also Violence
Agnew, Spiro, 233
Ahmad, Imtiaz, 176
Aid to Families with Dependent Children (AFDC), 232, 247, 250
Aivilik, 373, 374
Akuri, 32–33
Alaska, 45, 292, 293, 370
Alberta, Canada, 291, 292–293, 294, 328
Albuquerque, N. M., 98, 99, 101, 102
Alcohol usage, 82; among Indians, 25, 249, 251–252, 471; Mayan and homicides, 335, 347, 348, 350, 352–353
Aleuts, 45, 292
Algeria, 159, 238–239
Alianza movement, 96–103, 106–107
Alliance for Progress, 320
Almolonga Indians, 318
Amanas, 439
Amatenango del Valle, Mexico, 316–318
American Anthropological Association, 3, 8, 9, 170, 327; Committee on Ethics, 8, 19; Committee on Potentially Harmful Research, 8; principles of professional responsibility of, 46–51; resolutions of, 19, 43–48, 52, 59, 138, 149, 157; statement on Problems of Research and Ethics, 153, 164, 165; Thailand, statements concerning, 54–55
American Association for the Advancement of Science (AAAS), 44, 398, 409
American Civil Liberties Union, 49–50
"American dream," 103, 107

Amerindian race, 191
Amish, 67
Amyloidosis in ducks, 397
Angola, 160
Annual energy unit (AEU), 392–393
Anonymity, and urban life, 404–405
Anthropologists: responsibilities of, 3, 8–61, 157–159, 160–161, 162, 179, 208; and values, 10–18, 59–61, 162, 464–466
Anthropology: applied vs. scientific, 1–2, 128, 132, 465; conservatism in, 116, 118–119, 121–123, 126–130; feedback in, 467–468; relevancy of, 1–4
Anthropotherapy, 327
Anxiety, 77, 78, 83, 250–252, 440, 441, 471
Apache tribes, 133
Apartheid, 173, 174, 236
Apathy, 77, 83, 368, 396, 464, 471
Applied anthropology: conservatism in, 126–130, 131; vs. scientific, 128, 132, 465
Arapaho Indians, 68–70, 71, 73
Ardrey, Robert, 388
Argentina, 139, 159, 160
Arroyos, 451
Arviligjuarmiut, 372
Aryans, 188–189, 210
Asia, 112, 119, 139, 152–157, 159–160, 161, 165, 178
Asian race, 191
Asimov, Isaac, 389–395, 429
Aspiration level: and disorganization, 470–471; and poverty, 235, 239, 253–259, 265, 268, 269–270, 273, 319
Aspirational culture, 268–270, 273
Assimilation, cultural, 66–67, 104, 105, 113, 131, 249, 250, 251, 439
Assistance programs: effects of, 113–126, 129, 130; technical, 315, 320–321, 323
Association for Asian Studies, 9, 154, 175
Atomic energy, use of, 43, 56, 58, 179. See also Nuclear testing
Attitudes. See Values
Australia, 159, 334, 397, 457–464, 478
Australian aborigines, 4, 457–464, 478
Australoid or Australian race, 191
Authority, attitude toward, 447, 477

Bajema, Carl Jay, 423–429
Baker, Paul T., 200
Balikci, Asen, 370–378
Balinese, 123, 125
Baltimore study, 219, 221
Bantu, 197, 336–345
Baratz, Stephen S. and Joan C., 299–310, 327, 328
Barr, Stringfellow, 120
Basque race, 191
Batalla, Guillermo Bonfil, 126–130, 131
Bayou Dularge, 87, 90
Bayou Pointe au Chênes, 85, 87, 88, 89, 90
Bayou Terrebonne, 85, 87, 90
Beals, Alan R., 355–360, 379, 380
Beals, Ralph L., 122, 164, 165
"Beautiful Ones," 396
Becker, E., 7
Behavior: and crowding, 395–400; and culture, 265–270; and poverty, 240–253, 260–270, 273; and race, 187–188, 192, 206, 217, 224–227, 300–301, 307, 308–309 (See also Intelligence); and urban life, 400–406
Behaviorism, 210, 267–268
Benedict, Ruth, 64–65
Bensman, Joseph, 39, 40, 42–43
Berkeley, California, 175, 178
Berreman, Gerald D., 3, 4, 8–10, 55, 58–62,

112–113, 178–179
Berry, Brewton, 84
Bestiality, 339–340
Biobehavioral monism, 201–203, 206
Biosphere, 423
Birth control. See Population control.
Birth order and assimilation, 88
Black Caucus of African Studies Association, 165–173
"Blackfish Village" Kwakiutl study, 293
Blackfoot Indians, 291, 292–293
Black Melanism, 170
Black Muslims, 382
Black power groups, 101, 105, 106, 369, 382, 473
Blacks, 43–44, 101–102, 112, 201; alleged inferiority of, 212, 218, 221–223, 224, 226, 227; black caucus at ASA, 165–174; discrimination against, 56–57, 76–83, 105, 156; in Hunters Point, 361–369; language differences of, 299, 300, 301–307, 309, 311, 313, 314; male roles among, 81–82, 260–264, 362, 364; and melting pot myth, 66, 67, 105, 184, 185; middle-class, 82–83, 365, 366; and Moynihan Report, 232–234; lower-class, 78–82; and poverty, 136, 158, 239, 240, 253–259; and schooling, 279, 280, 281, 282, 299–310, 310–315, 329, 362
Bleibtreu, Hermann K., 3, 184–188, 224–227
Blood Indians, 293–294
Blood types, 189–190, 191, 213, 224–225, 417–418
Boas, Franz, 51–52, 59, 64–65
Body-buffer zones, 398
Bolivia, 26–31, 139, 160
Bolsa system, 453
Boothia Peninsula, 374
Boston schools, 281
Boulding, Kenneth, 428
Boyd, W. C., 189–190, 191, 196, 197, 198
Brain damaged children, 220, 221
"Brain-washing," 475
Brazil, 139, 160, 323, 325, 334, 385, 417, 418, 419, 420
Brecher, Michael, 177
Bridewealth, 338, 343, 344–345
British Columbia, 293
Bronfenbrenner, Urie, 40, 41
Brues, Alice M., 50–51
Bureau of Indian Affairs, 25, 43, 85, 106, 119, 133, 297, 451, 453
Burke, Edmund, 61
Burke, Fred G., 111
Burma, 159
Burnett, Jacquetta Hill, 285–290
Burundi, 196
Bushmen, 196, 198
Bystander intervention, 402–403

Calhoun, John B., 396, 431
California, 99, 106, 361–369
Cambodia, 159
Cameroon, 159, 160
Campbell, Donald, 222
Canada, 139, 174; ASA meeting in Montreal, 165–174; Indian education in, 290–294, 328
Canjilon, N. M., 97, 100
Cantel, Guatemala, 318–320
Canyon de San Diego, 99
Cape York Peninsula, 457
Carbon dioxide emissions, 388, 393
Caribbean Islands, 385
Carson National Forest, 100

Casanova, González, 129
Casarabe, 27
Caste, and conflict, 78, 357, 358, 359, 360, 380
Castro, Fidel, 238, 325
Catawbe Indians, 85
Catholic Church, 247, 248, 271, 445, 446
Caucasoid, 191
Caudillo, 443
Censorship, 165, 178
Central Intelligence Agency (CIA): and ethics, 22,
    60, 148–149, 150, 164, 173, 176; in India,
    152, 175; in Latin America, 148–149, 150
Centralization, lack of, in Latin America, 447
Ceremony, in American schools, 285–290
Ceylon, 159, 160
Challenor, Herchelle Sullivan, 131, 165–170
Chama Canyon Grant. See San Joaquin Grant
Chamberlain, Stewart, 200, 210
Chance, Norman A., 55
Change: 26–33, 105, 114, 435–478; avoidance
    of, 116, 118–119, 121–123, 127–128,
    129–130; cultural view of, 267–268; and
    internal conflict, 355–360, 470–473;
    through intervention, 23–39, 113–126,
    435–478; research and development
    approach to, 453–455, 464–470; and
    revitalization processes, 452, 470–475;
    resistance to, 115–116, 117, 118, 122,
    123–125, 452, 453; and schools, 315–326;
    selective acceptance of, 115, 122–123;
    strategies for, 436, 450–457; and violence,
    379–382. See also Intervention
Charles, Ray, 292, 293
Chavez, Cesar, 101
Che Guevara, 325, 473
Cheyenne Indians, 68–70, 71, 73, 137
Chiapas, 316, 317, 318
Chicago, Ill., 251, 406
Chicanos, 67, 106–107, 112, 178; and pecan
    shellers' strike, 91–96; and schooling, 279,
    328
Childhood, and personality development, 78–83,
    235, 237
Chile, 138, 139, 140, 143, 159, 320, 385
Chinese Communists, 475
Chippewa River, 246
Chitimacha Indians, 85
Choctaw Indians, 84, 85
Chomsky, Noam, 59–60
Churches. See Religions
Cincinnati, Ohio, 399
Civilian Conservation Corp, 451,
    453
Civilities, and urban life, 404
Civil Rights movement and legislation, 90, 91,
    184, 233, 237
Class differences. See Middle-class values
Class lines, in Latin America, 446–447
Cleveland, Ohio, 399
"Client states," 159, 160
Cloak, F. T., Jr., 45
Cluster analysis of race, 192, 195–196, 198, 201,
    204–205
Code, for revitalization, 471, 472, 473, 474
Coercion, and ethics, 22, 24
Cofradia system, 452
Cohen, Rosalie, 328–329
Cold War, 158–159
Cole, La Monte, 385
Coleman River, 457
College: Brooklyn, 139; Hunter, 167
Colonialism, 112–114, 115, 116, 124, 125, 130,
    158–159, 160, 178, 235; academic, 175;
    and ASA, 166, 168, 169, 171; and change,
    451, 456; and Gusii tribe, 337, 345, 381;
    internal, 112–113, 154, 158
Colorado, 99, 106–107
Columbia, 139, 159, 160, 325
Columbus study, 219
Comitan, 316
Commission on Human Rights, 250
Committee for Industrial Organization (CIO),
    94–95
Committee of Nine, 282
Committee of South Asia, 154
Committee for African Studies in Canada, 168,
    169
Committee on Environmental Alterations, 409

Committee on Research and Ethics, 153, 164
Commoner, Barry, 388, 407–416
Common lands, 98–99
"Common man," belief in, 446–447
Communications, 13, 239, 382, 437, 440, 456,
    472, 473, 475
Communist countries, 158–159, 163, 164
Communist party, 473
Community: attitudes in Philadelphia study,
    254–259; and conflict, 355–360, 374; and
    education, 279, 288, 289, 290, 295–296,
    312, 313, 314–315, 316, 317, 318–319,
    328, 329–330; Mayan, 346–348; sense of,
    368, 381, 382; slum, 235, 236, 237, 238,
    361, 365
Community Action Programs (CAP), 295, 297,
    298
Community development programs, 452, 453–
    454, 456, 457
Community ethic, 100–101
Compadrazgo, 237
Competition, 444
Conant, James, 282
Conceptual style, 328
Concerned Asian Scholars, 9
Concubinage, 445–446
Confederation of Free City States. See Alianza
    movement
Conference of Indian Sociologists, 176
Confidentiality, and ethics, 23, 24–25
Conflict: among Netsilik, 370–378; and change
    in India, 355–360. See also Aggression and
    Violence
Congo, Republic of the, 139, 159, 160
Congress of World Federalists, 432
Congress on Racial Equality (CORE), 101
Consensual union, 236, 237, 247, 446
Consent, and ethics, 20–22, 23–26
Conservatism, 116, 118–119, 121–123,
    126–130
Consumption, increased, 391–393, 407,
    408–410, 412–416
Corona, Bert, 101
Corr, Michael, 407–416
Correlation of characteristics, 203–204, 224
Costa Rica, 455
Council on Anthropology and Education, 327
Counterinsurgency, study of, 138–152
Cowan, Daniel, 397
Crawford, Michael H., 4, 386–389, 429–432
Creativity, 396, 424
Creek Indians, 85
Crime, 25, 77, 400, 403, 404
Crowding: animal studies on, 395–400,
    431–432; effects of, 386, 394, 395–400,
    431
Crusade for Justice, 101, 105
Cuba, 139, 141, 159, 163, 238
Cultural anomie, 115, 122
Cultural change. See Change
Cultural distortion, 472
Cultural integration, 115–116, 117–118,
    122–125
Cultural pluralism, 107, 113, 131, 245, 439
Cultural relativism, 3, 121, 122, 128
"Cultural shock," 125
"Cultural therapy," 327
Cultural transmission, 278, 279–280, 330
Culture: aboriginal, 457–464; aspirational,
    268–270, 273; and behavior, 55–56,
    199–200, 201, 225–226; of blacks,
    300–301, 307–308, 309, 312–313;
    concepts of, 265–270; effect of, on
    population, 187–188, 200, 206, 207;
    ghetto-specific, 260–264; ideal and real,
    104; and personality, 76–83, 105;
    pluristic, 107–121; of poverty, 3–4,
    232–245, 253–270, 271, 272, 273,
    280, 309; and schooling, 278–280,
    312–313; subcultures of, 107; transfer,
    472, 473, 474
"Culture engineering," 422
Culture vacuum, 260, 262
Curers, in Mayan community, 346, 347, 348,
    349, 350, 352–354

Dakar, 168, 169
Damas, Léon, 169

d'Arboussier, Gabriel, 168
Darley, J. M., 403
Darwin, Charles, 206, 210, 426
DDT, 388, 430, 431
Deceit, and ethics, 22–23, 26
Decker, Clarence R., 115, 120
Deerpoint Community, 246–253
de Gobineau, Joseph Arthur, 210
Deloria, Vine, Jr., 130–137
Democracy, and the social scientist, 15–18,
    59, 61
Density, 391–392, 395–400. See also Crowding
"Density syndrome," 396–397
Depression, from discrimination, 78, 83
Deprivation and deprivation studies, 213, 220,
    281, 303–306, 313, 396
Detergents, 409, 410, 411, 412, 413, 430
Detroit, Michigan, riots, 399
Developing nations. See Third World
Dichotomy-Dismissal Approach, 199–200,
    218–223
Differential acculturation, 115, 122–123
Discrimination, 44, 47, 56–57, 76–83, 399;
    against blacks, 76–83, 300–315; against
    Chicanos, 91–96; against Hispanos, 100;
    against Houmas, 84–91; against Indians,
    118–119, 291, 297; and education, 279,
    280, 291, 297, 300–315, 321, 328, 330;
    and personality formation, 76–83
Disease. See Health
Disintegration, of culture, 115, 118
Disorganization, cultural, 115–116, 117, 118,
    128, 130; and revitalization, 470–475; and
    Yir Yoront, 457–464
Dobzhansky, T., 190, 194, 197, 200, 206
Dominican Republic, 138, 139, 160
Dorsey, George A., 182–183
Double standard, 445, 446
Dowd, Douglas, 59, 60
Downs, John Langdon Haydon, 210–211, 217
"Drop-outs," 282, 293–294
Du Bois, Cora, 31–32, 113
Du Bois, William E. B., 166
Dubos, René, 389, 425–426, 432
Ducks, density and disease among, 397
Dumont, René, 385
Dungan, Ralph, 138
Dunn, Stephen P., 50–51
Durkheim, E., 284, 346

Eastern Pueblo Indians, 20
East Pakistan, 385
Ecology. See Environment
Economic aid programs. See Assistance programs
Ecosystem, 407, 411–412, 420, 423
Ecuador, 122–123, 139, 159, 160, 239
Education, 4, 280–325; adult, 319, 325, 440,
    469, 470; anthropological study of, 326–
    330; and Fox Indians, 439, 440, 441; and
    Hispanos, 100, 102; and Houmas, 86–87,
    89–90, 91; as intervention, 299–310, 322–
    323, 453–454, 464–470; and social
    change, 315–320; strategy of, 452, 453–
    454, 464–470; technical assistance to, 315,
    320–321; in Vicos, 466. See also Schooling
Educationist, 315, 321
Egypt, 139, 385
Ehrlich, Paul, 182–183, 386, 389, 395–396,
    400, 430
Ehrlich, Robert W., 50, 51
Einstein, Albert, 276–277
Ejido lands, 98–99, 316
El Nogal, 93
El Salvador, 139, 400
Empiricism, strategy of, 455, 456
Employment: and Indians, 293–294; and poverty,
    235, 236, 240–245, 248, 256, 257, 259,
    270
England. See Great Britain
English Poor Laws, 272
The Enlightenment, 13, 158, 162
Environment, 4, 386–432; crowding of, 396–
    400, 429–430; and intelligence, 218–223,
    224; pollution of, 393–394, 407–416,
    430–431; and race, 186–187, 188,
    189–190, 192, 193, 195, 198, 199–200,
    201–203, 204, 206–208, 211, 213,

214–215, 217, 226; urban living and, 400–406
Enyangi, 337
Erasmus, Charles J., 122
Eskimos, 45, 292, 370–378
Esquirol, J. E. D., 210
Esser, A. H., 395
Ethics, 19–43, 128, 162; AAA committee report on, 46–48, 49–50; in population research, 208; and Project Camelot, 142, 146–148
Ethiopia, 159
Ethnic groups and ethnic awareness, 66–67, 105, 107, 184, 282, 283, 284, 403
Ethnicization, 184
Ethnocentrism, 178, 263, 273, 299, 300, 301–302, 326, 442
Eugenic tests and programs, 308, 428
Europe, 139, 159, 160, 163, 238, 323, 334
European race, 191
Evolution: Latin American study of, 416–423; theory of, 185, 186–187, 189, 197, 224, 227, 416–423
Exploitation, 58, 162; of Chicanos, 91–96; of Hispanos, 99; of Houmas, 84–88, 90–91; of Sioux, 73–74
Export-Import Bank, 120

Failure: and fatalism, 449–450; fear of, 438, 440, 441
Fair Labor Standards Act, 95–96
The family: among blacks, 79, 80–81; and education, 279, 310–311, 313–314, 315; in Latin America, 444–446; limiting size of, 425, 426–427, 430; matrifocal, 81, 236, 240, 260, 262–263, 362, 445–446; nuclear, 313, 444; and poverty, 79, 232–233, 234, 235, 236, 237, 240, 260–264, 299, 301, 302–303; role of black males in, 80–82, 260–264; social pathology model and, 299, 301, 302–303; and urban renewal, 399
Family planning, 420–422, 425, 430. See also Population control
Famine. See Starvation
Fatalism, in Latin America, 449–450
Fear, and discrimination, 77, 82
Federal Bureau of Investigation (FBI), 100
Federal Housing Act of 1964, 399
Federated Alliance of Land Grants, 98
Feedback: in anthropology, 467; from environment, 206
Ferguson, Adam, 158
Fertilizers, 408, 409, 411, 430
Firth, Louis, 118
Fischer, Ann, 84–91, 106
Fisher, A. D., 290–294, 327, 328
Fishman, Joshua, 67
Folk people, Indians as, 132–133
Food production, and population growth, 389, 390, 391, 392, 410, 411
Fore group, 334
Foreign Aid. See Assistance programs
Foreign relations, 158–160, 161; assistance programs, 113–126, 129, 130, 315, 320–321, 323; and ASA, 167, 169; and political intervention, 138–148, 148–152, 476, 478; and Project Camelot, 138–152; and research projects, 175–176, 177, 178–179
Foster, George, 44, 127, 128
Foster, John S., Jr., 153
Fox Indians, 4, 438–441; "laziness" of, 438, 440, 441
France, 130, 139, 158, 159
Frazier, E. Franklin, 260
Freedman, Jonathan, 395–396, 400
Freedom: human, 11, 12–14, 17, 18; and melting pot myth, 66–67, 103–107; in research, 39–41, 42–43, 137, 138, 141, 147–148
Freire, Paolo, 325
French Guiana, 169
Freud, Sigmund, 202
Friedenberg, Edgar, 281
Frump, Alfred, 132
Fuenzalida, Eduardo, 140
Fulbright, J. William, 138, 141, 151, 154
Fulbright scholarships, 164

Gabon, 160

Gadsden Purchase territory, 451, 453
Gallaher, Art, Jr., 4, 436–437, 475–478
Gallin, Bernard, 33–39, 113
Galton, Francis, 211, 216, 222
Galtung, Johan, 140
Gambling, and self-esteem, 82
Gangs, neighborhood, 237
Gans, Herbert J., 231, 265–270, 272, 273, 283
Gardiner, Robert, 168
Garn, S. M., 189, 191, 193, 194, 196, 197
Garry Lake, 374
Gearing, Fred, 438–441
Gene frequencies, 188–190, 191, 195, 198, 200, 201, 205–206, 214, 224, 226
Gene pool, 193–196, 207, 212, 213, 216, 225, 420, 421, 429, 430
Genetic counseling and testing, 206–207, 421–422, 424, 428–429
Genetic defects, 421–422, 424, 427, 429. See also Mutations.
Genetic inferiority model, 299, 301, 308, 309. See also Racial hierarchy
Genetics: and population control, 423–429; and race, 184, 185–187, 188–197, 200–208, 212–215, 221–222, 225–227, 299, 301, 307–308; and racial hierarchy, 210–212, 217
Genotype: developing potential of, 422, 426; and race, 203, 204, 206, 207–208, 212, 214–215, 217, 218, 429
Genovese, Catherine, 402–403
Gerlach, Luther, 473
Germany, 67, 473, 474–475
Gestalt, 470, 475
Ghana, 159
Ghetto: and crowding, 398–399; and rioting, 361–369, 398
Ghetto mother, 79, 80–81, 299, 303–306, 308, 313. See also Matrifocal families
Ghetto-specific culture, 260–264. See also Culture, of blacks
Ghost-dance religion, 71–76, 105, 475
Gila River Prima, 134
Ginsburg, Benson E., 199–209, 218
Gleason, Philip J., 103
Gluckman, Max, 114, 118, 126, 285
Goal achievement, by anthropologists, 454, 467–470
"Goal culture," 472, 473
Goal striving. See Aspiration level
Gonzales, Rodolfo "Corky," 101
Gough, Kathleen, 60, 156–165
Gouldner, A., 7, 61
Government: and anthropological studies, 138–152, 163–164, 165; anthropologists' responsibility to, 48, 51–52, 53, 165; and intervention, 138–152, 476, 478
Grande Caillou, 87, 90
Grayson, Donald K., 32–33, 113
Great Britain, 130, 158, 159, 211–212, 217, 222, 335
Greece, 67, 139, 334
Gross National Product (GNP), 408, 410–411, 414, 416
Group ties, 91, 100, 237
Guatemala, 139, 160, 315–320, 351, 452, 456
Gulbarge District in India, 357–360
Gullahs, 301
Gusii tribe, 336–345, 370, 379, 381, 382
Guyana, 160, 175

Haldane, J. B. S., 215
Hall, Edward T., 398
Hannerz, Ulf, 4, 260–264, 265, 309
Hardin, Garrett, 426–427, 430
Harrington, Michael, 234, 272
Hausa tribe, 451
Havana, Cuba, 238
Havighurst, Robert, 292
Headstart projects: among blacks, 299–310, 311–312; among Indians, 294–298
Health, among poverty groups, 249, 419–420, 439, 451, 456, 467
Hedonism, and discrimination, 77, 82
Henry, Jules, 279, 281, 284, 310–311
Heritability, 209, 213–215, 217, 222, 224. See also Gene and genetic headings
Herskovits, Melville, 260, 300, 308–309

Heterogeneity of urban population, 401
Hiernaux, Jean, 192–198, 199
Himalayan Border Countries Project, 152–154, 178
Hippler, Arthur E., 361–369
Hirsch, Jerry, 209–218
Hispanos, 96–103, 106–107
History-making, and human freedom, 12–14, 16–17
Hitler, Adolf, 188, 210, 474
Ho Chi Minh, 175
Hofstader, R., 282
Holistic synthesis, 199, 201–203, 206
Hollander, P., 402–403
Holm, Richard W., 182–183
Holmberg, Allan R., 26–31, 113, 442–450, 454, 464–470
Holt, John, 281
Homicide, 4: among Mayans, 346–354, 379; among Netsilik, 370–378
Homosexuality, 83, 339–340, 405
Honduras, 160, 400
Hong Kong, 395
Hopelessness, feelings of, 233, 235, 236, 237, 245, 256, 270
Hopi Indians, 66, 67
Hopper, Rex, 139, 140
Horowitz, Irving Louis, 138–148
Horowitz, Mardi J., 398
Hostility, between blacks and whites, 77, 82, 83, 361–369
Houma Indians, 67, 84–91, 106
Housing: and aggression, 398–399; and pollution, 410; and poverty, 237, 259, 361
Howe, Irving, 59
Howells, W., 194
Hsin Hsing, 33–38
Hughes, Everett C., 282
Hughes, Thomas L., 164
Hulse, F. S., 186
"Human adaptability studies," 225
Human Relations Area File (HRAF), 175
Human Rights Commission, 97
Hunters Point, 361–369, 380, 382
Huxley, Aldous, 214, 430, 465
Hymes, Dell, 9, 44
Hysterical conversion, 474–475

Ibo tribe, 22
Ideal culture, 104
Idealization, 80, 82, 83
Identity, search for, 100, 239, 284, 329
Illegitimacy, in Latin America, 446
Illich, Ivan, 279, 280, 320–326, 327
Imperialism: academic, 174–177; anthropologists and, 158, 159, 160, 161, 162; ASA and, 171; U.S. and, 112–113, 124
Inadequate mothering. See Ghetto mother
Income: distribution of, 129; poverty and, 236, 240–245, 254–257, 258, 268
India, 131, 152–156, 159, 160, 161, 163, 176, 177, 178, 238, 419; conflict within, 355–360, 379, 380; population in, 385
Indian Institute of Advanced Study, 154
Indian Reorganization Act, 439
Indians, American, 25, 26, 158, 184, 196, 223, 471; AAA resolution for, 43, 45; and anthropologists, 130–137, 178; and culture change, 26–31, 111, 118–119, 124–125, 134–135, 137, 451–452; Fox, 438–441; Ghost-dance doctrine, 68–75, 475; Houma, 84–91; Mayan, 315–320, 346–354, 370, 379, 380, 382, 452; Navajo, 66, 67, 351, 465; Oijibwa, 245–253; Picuris, 335; and population genetics, 416–423; and population growth, 425; poverty among, 239, 245–253; as a race, 191; and schooling, 4, 279, 280, 290–298, 328; Seneca, 471; Sioux, 66, 68, 71–76, 105, 134–135, 137, 292–293, 294; Xanante, Yamomama, and Makiritare, 416–423. See also other specific tribes
Indians, Asian. See India
Individualism, 14–15, 17, 442–443, 444–445, 471
Indochina, 64–65, 398
Indonesia and Indonesian race, 139, 159, 160
Indo-Dravidian race, 191

Industry, proposed role for, 324–325
Infancy and intelligence, 218–220
Infanticide, 370, 418, 421
Inferiority of races. See Racial hierarchy
Institute of Indigenous Affairs of Peru, 453, 466, 467
Institute of International Studies, 178
Instituto Nacional Indigenista of Mexico (INI), 316
"Insurgency prophylaxis," 139, 151, 163
Integration, of Houmas, 84–85, 86–88, 98–91
Intelligence and intelligence quotient (IQ): and Headstart, 306, 307, 308; and population control, 424, 425; and race, 182–183, 209, 217, 218–222, 223, 224, 226–227; testing for, 203, 209, 212, 218–221, 282, 314
Internal colonialism, 112, 113, 154, 158
International Bank for Reconstruction and Development, 120
International Conference of Africanists, 168
Interrelations in culture, 115, 117, 121
Intervention; 33–39, 464–470; bystander, 402–403; and culture change, 4, 26–33, 435–478; education as, 322–323; Headstart as, 299–310; military, 138–152, 163, 175–176, 178–179; political aspects of, 113–126, 138–148, 148–152, 476, 478; strategies of, 450–457, 477; and Vicosinos, 453–455, 456, 464–470
Involvement, 436–437. See also Intervention
Iowa, Fox Indians in, 438–441
Iran, 139, 159
Iraq, 159
Irish, 67, 184, 260, 281, 283
Iroquois, 471
Isle de Jean Charles, 85, 87, 88, 90
Israel, 171, 177, 217–218
Italians, 67, 184, 283
Ixtapa, saint of, 349, 354

James, Bernard J., 4, 245–253, 273
Japan, 2, 159, 279, 329, 334, 419
Jatra in India, 358
Java, 385
Jensen, Arthur R., 209, 214, 215, 217, 218, 308
Jews, 67, 184, 185, 211–212, 216, 217–218, 223, 238, 278, 329
Jicarilla Apaches, 133
Johnson, Lyndon B., 138, 141, 148, 164
Johnson, Matthew, 361, 365
Johnson, William C., 397
Jones, Garth N., 450–457
Jorgensen, Joseph G., 19–26, 53, 54, 55
Jourdain, Roger, 136

Kagor tribe, 456
Kalabahi, 32
Kampf, Louis, 9
Kansas City, 399
Kardiner, Abram, 76–83
Kechskemeti, Paul, 17
Keil, Charles, 260–261, 262
Kenya, 159, 160, 336–345, 379, 381
Khleif, Bud B., 280–284
Kidding pattern, in U.S., 448
Kinball, Solon, 281
King, Martin Luther, 101, 102
King William Island, 370
Kin ties: among aborigines, 459, 461, 462; among Netsilik, 374, 375, 377, 378; among Gusii, 337–339, 343, 345, 379; among Hispanos, 98; among Indians, 349, 350, 391, 471; between Indian villages, 357, 359, 360; in Latin America, 349, 350, 444–445, 446; and poverty, 237; and violence, 349, 357, 359, 360, 374, 375, 377, 387, 391
Kinzel, Augustus F., 398
Kiowa Indians, 71
Kipsigis, 336, 340
Kleiner, Robert J., 4, 253, 259
Kluckhohn, Clyde, 351
Korea, 139, 143, 159, 436, 476
Kupferer, Harriet J., 3, 66–67, 103–107

Lac Court Oreilles, 246, 248, 250, 251
Lac La Birche region, 293–294
Ladinos, 316, 317, 318, 319, 346, 452

La Fourche, 87, 90
Lake Erie, 408
Lake Willerstedt, 377
Land disputes: of Hispanos, 97, 98–101; of Houmas, 85–86, 88, 89, 90–91; of Sioux, 73–74
Land redistribution, 123, 124
Language differences, and education, 278, 279, 299, 301–307, 309, 310, 311, 313, 314, 328–329
Laos, 160
Lapp race, 191
"La Raza," 100
Lasswell, Harold, 465–566
Las Vegas, Nevada, 408
Latané, B., 403
Latin America, 126, 129, 236, 334; applied anthropology in, 126–130, 131; culture of, contrasted, 4, 442–450, 475; education of Indians in, 280, 320–326; population genetics study in, 416–423; and Project Camelot, 138–152, 163, 178; and U.S. military aid, 45, 46, 112, 119
Latin American Faculty of Social Science (FLACSO), 140
Laughlin, William S., 199–209, 218
Law of Ancestral Heredity, 216
Law of Regression, 216
"Law of the saints," 452
Leader dogs, and genetics, 207
Leadership training programs, 132–133
League of United Latin-American Citizens (Lulac), 94
Leakey, L. S. B., 431
Learning, in man, 187–188, 199, 208, 217. See also Education
Leckachman, Robert, 47
Leeds, Anthony, 49–50
Levi, Werner, 119–120
Lévi-Strauss, Claude, 111
Le Vine, Robert A., 336–345, 379
Lewis, Gordon K., 121
Lewis, Hylan, 231, 268
Lewis, Oscar, 4, 233, 234–240, 270, 272–273
"Liberal myth," 321, 326
Liebow, Elliot, 4, 240–245, 261, 262, 265, 273, 315
Life style in U.S., 424–425, 442–450
Lindzey, Gardner, 188–192
Linguistic competency. See Languages differences
Linton, Ralph, 105, 123–125
Literacy, 235, 239, 317, 318–319
Local action in Latin America, 443, 447
London, pollution in, 432
Lorenz, Konrad, 388, 430
Los Angeles, California, 166, 400, 408
Los Angeles Mexican-American Political Association (MAPA), 101
Louisiana, Houmas in, 84–91
Lower class, 79–83, 302, 304, 305–306, 311. See also Education and Poverty
Lynd, Robert, 60
Lynd, Staughton, 9

Macho, 445
Madronal, 317
Maghreb, 385
Makiritare group, 416, 417, 419
Malaysia, 139, 159
Malinowski, B., 27, 114, 117, 118, 123, 130, 283
Malnutrition, effects of, 219, 220, 221
Malthus, Thomas, 386
Manhattan, 392, 393, 401, 404
Manhattan Project, 145
Manners, Robert A., 113–126, 130
"Mano Negra," 99
Mao Tse Tung, 325, 473
Marginality, and change, 106, 129, 456
Maricopa tribe, 134
Marriage: among blacks, 82, 83, 236, 240, 260, 262–263; ceremonies among Gusii, 336–339; and culture of poverty, 236, 240, 260, 262–263; "Indian custom," 247; in Latin America, 445–446; among Netsilik, 371, 373, 375
Marx, Karl, 12, 16, 238

Mass media. See Communications
Mass transit systems, 414–415
Masturbation, 339–340
Maternal deprivation. See Ghetto mothers
Matrifocal families, 81, 236, 237, 240, 260, 262–263, 362, 445–446
Mayan Indians: and revitalization, 452; and schooling, 315–320; and violence, 346–354, 370, 379, 380, 382
Mayer, P., 337, 339
Mayr, E., 190–191, 418
McClellan, John, 399
McIlhenny Island, 86
McLaughlin, James, 71, 75
McNamara, Robert, 138, 141, 143
Mead, George Herbert, 250, 252
Mead, Margaret, 8, 44, 114, 199, 276–277, 279, 333, 380
Meaney, John, 3, 184–188, 224–227
Mediterranean race, 191
Melanesia, 475
Melanesian and Melanesian-Papuan race, 191
Melena del Sur, 238
Men, role of: among blacks, 81–82, 83, 260–264, 311, 362, 364; in Latin America, 445–446
Mencher, Joan, 45
Mendel, Gregor, 214, 216–217
Mentally ill, in Philadelphia study, 254–259
Mercury contamination, 388, 410, 411, 415–416, 430
Mescalero Apaches, 133
Meso-America, 316
Messiah Letter, 69
Metis Indians, 293–294
Mexico, 130, 139, 159, 237, 239, 270, 320, 385, 443; Mayan Indians of, 315–320, 346–354; schools in, 315–319. See also Latin America
Mexico City, 237
Michigan, riots in, 399
Micronesian race, 191, 279
Middle-class values, 236, 239–240; blacks and, 82–83, 300–301, 304, 305, 306, 311, 313–315; in education, 282–283, 292, 300–301, 304, 305, 306, 311, 313–315; in Latin America, 442; and research, 265–267, 273, 304, 311
Middle East, 112, 119, 139, 177, 385
Miles, Rufous, 427
Milgram, Stanley, 400–406
Military intervention: and Project Camelot, 138–152; and research, 163, 175–176, 178–179
Miller, Walter, 266, 267–268
Mills, C. Wright, 10–18, 59, 60, 61, 128
Milwaukee, Wisc., 399
Minimum wage law, effect of, 95–96
Minneapolis, Minn., 399
Minnesota, 136, 399
Minority groups. See Discrimination and specific groups
Mitchell River, 464
Model: for black child, 80–81, 262–263; social pathology, 299, 301, 308, 309, 310
Mongolia, 159
Mongolism, 210–211, 217
Mongoloid race, 191
Montagu, A., 188
Montreal, ASA meeting in, 165–174
Mooney, James, 68–76, 105, 107
Morgan City, 85
Morocco, 159
Mothers. See Ghetto mothers and Matrifocal families
Movies, and change, 469–470
Moynihan, Patrick J., and Moynihan Report, 232, 233, 234, 253, 259, 260, 271, 301
Mozambique, 160
Multiple causation theory, 128
Muskogian Indians, 85
Mutations, 387, 421, 424, 427, 428, 431
Myers, Kenneth, 397
Myrdal, Gunnar, 223
Myrdal, Jan, 159
Myths: of education, 321, 326, 330; to maintain culture, 460, 462–464, 474; of the melting

pot, 3, 63–67, 103–107; of Yir Yoront, 460, 462–464

"Nader's Raiders," 436
Narcotics usage, and self-esteem, 82
Nash, June, 346–354, 379
Nash, Manning, 315–320, 327
National Academy of Sciences, 57, 175, 218, 222–223
National Association for the Advancement of Colored People (NAACP), 106, 366
National Indian Youth Council, 105
National Industrial Recovery Act (NIRA), 93
National Institute of Mental Health, 148, 164, 396
National Labor Relations Board, 94, 95
National Recovery Administration (NRA), 92, 93
National Science Foundation, 148, 164
Nativistic cult, 103
Natural resources, depletion of, 389, 391, 392–393
Navajo Indians, 66, 67, 351, 456
Nayon, Ecuador, 122–123
Nazi party, 473, 474
Needs, 118–119, 126, 128, 130, 455
Neel, James V., 416–423
"Negotiated order," 281
Negroes. See Blacks
Negroid, 191
Negro-ideal formation, 77, 80–81, 83
Neighborhood Youth Corps, 296
Nelson, John P., 89, 90–91
Nepal, 159
Netsilik Eskimos, 370–378, 382
Neuhauser, Charles, 175
Neutral nations, 159–160
Newark, N.J., 401
New City, N.Y., 404
New Delhi Parliament, 152
New Guinea, 148, 334, 475
New Haven study, 219, 220, 221
New Left, 473
New Mexico, 96–103, 106–107, 335
New Mexico Civil Liberties Union, 97
New Orleans, La., 85, 87, 89
New York City, N.Y., 400, 401, 402–403, 404, 405, 406, 408
New Zealand, 159
Nicaragua, 160
Nigeria, 139, 159, 176, 381, 451, 456
Nixon, Richard M., 385
Nobel Prize, 57
Noninvolvement, and urban life, 402–406
Norm-of-reaction concept, 212–215, 217–218
North Africa, 385
North America, 159, 163, 175, 176, 177; culture of, contrasted, 442–450; and education, 291, 292
Nuclear energy. See Atomic energy
Nuclear testing, 387, 430, 431
Nuniurut, 371–372
Nyack, N.Y., 404

Oakland area, 361
Oceania, 112
Office of Economic Opportunity (OEO), 295, 296
Office of Education, 148
Ogalala Sioux, 73, 134–135
Ogosonia, 339
Ojibwa Indians, 245–253
Oppenheimer, Robert, 57, 179, 435, 436
Oppression. See Repression
Optimism, in U.S., 449–450
Organization of American States (OAS), 400
Orwell, George, 430
Oslo, 140
Overcrowding. See Crowding
Overload, and urban behavior, 400–406
Overpopulation, 4, 386, 387, 390–395, 407
Ovesey, Lionel, 76–83

Paiute Indians, 70–71, 134
Pakistan, 159
Palo Alto, Calif., 405
Panama, 160
Papago Indians, 451, 453
Paraguay, 139, 146, 160
Parker, Seymour, 3–4, 232–234, 253–259, 271–273, 292, 293

Participation, strategy of, 452–453
"Parties" in India, 357, 358, 359, 360, 380
Pasamanick, Benjamin, 218–223
Passivity. See Apathy
Patrón and peón relations, 443, 465, 466, 467, 468
Pauling, Linus, 57
Pawnee, 70
Peace Corps, 294
Pearson, Karl, 211, 216–217
Pecan shellers' strike, 91–96
Pecan Shelling Workers' Union, 93
Peer groups, 263, 279
Pelly Bay, 371, 373, 374, 377
Penrose Research Laboratory, 397
Pentecostalism, 473
People's Republic of China, 159
Personal dignity, 443–444
Personalism, 442–444
Personality formation: and discrimination, 76–83; and Ojibwa, 245–253; and poverty, 259, 271
Personal space, 394, 398, 431
Peru, 4, 139, 159, 160, 239, 323, 443, 453–455, 464–470
Pesticides, build up of, 388, 407, 408, 410, 411, 412, 413
Phenocopies, 215
Phenotype, 193, 201, 202, 203, 204, 207, 208, 212, 214–216, 224, 422
Philadelphia study, 253–259, 406
Philippine Islands, 159, 160
Phoenix, Ariz., 408
Phylogeny, 197–198
Piaget, J., 314
Picuris, New Mexico, 335
Pine Ridge, 72–73, 74, 75, 135, 137, 294
Placement, strategy of, 454–455
Plains Cree Indians, 292
Plains Indians, 134
"Pliancy factor," 468
Pointe au Chênes, 85, 87, 88, 89, 90
Point Four Program, 114–115, 119, 120
Pokoman dialect, 452
Poland and Poles, 211, 283
Police, in black community, 362–364, 365–366, 368
Police Community Relations Unit, 367, 368
Pollution, 4, 386, 387, 393–394, 407–416, 430–431; air, 388, 393, 407, 408, 411, 412–413, 414; and aluminum, 409, 410, 413, 414; and automobile usage, 409, 414–415, 430–431; and energy usage, 392–394, 409, 412, 413, 415, 431; legislation against, 430–431; in London, 432; mercury, 388, 410, 411, 415–416; pesticides, 388, 407, 408, 410, 411, 412, 413, 430; and respiratory diseases, 388; sensory, 388, 430, 431; and stress, 407; thermal, 407–408, 411, 412
Polygyny, and genetics, 418–419, 420
Polynesian race, 191
Poor People's March, 102
Population: increase in U.S., 408, 416; in Latin America, 320, 400; race as, 190, 192, 193, 194, 196, 197–198, 202–204, 224, 225; statistics of, 215–216
Population control, 323, 390, 392, 394, 395, 407, 420–429, 429–430; compulsory, 426–429; voluntary, 392, 426, 429; among Yanomama, 417, 418
Population genetics, 184, 185–187, 225, 416–423
Population reticulum, 198, 201
"Populist" character of new nations, 159
Portuguese, 445, 475
Portuguese Guinea, 160
Postman, Neil, 326
Poverty: anthropology of, 129; and black males, 81–82, 83, 240–245, 259–264; and culture, 3–4, 229–273, 476; culture of, 232–240, 253–259, 476; and education 278, 297, 299–315, 318–319, 330; and Indians, 84–91, 245–253, 294, 295–296; and intelligence, 218, 219, 220–221, 223; and marriage, 236, 446; and middle-class researchers, 239–240, 265–270; and rioting in Hunters Point, 361–369

Power diplomacy, 114–115, 119–121, 125
Prejudice, racial, 182–183, 222. See also Discrimination
Prenatal environment, and intelligence, 219, 220, 221
"Present-time orientation," 82, 237, 239, 244, 245, 273
Pressure, strategy of, 450–451, 477
Privacy: right to, 19–20, 23, 24, 42, 46–47, 208; and urban life, 403, 405, 425
Production, increased, 408–416, 466–467
Proefstation Oost Java (POJ), 455
Project Agile, 165
Project Camelot, 3, 46, 60, 138–152, 163, 164, 178
Project Follow-Through, 306
Project Revolt, 139
Protestantism, 271–272, 273, 449, 474
Publics, and self-knowledge, 15, 17
Public welfare, 232–233, 247, 248, 250, 251, 262, 266, 291, 362
Pueblo Indians, 20, 99, 335
Puerto Ricans, and schooling, 279, 329
Puerto Rico, 238, 239, 260, 270
Pyramid Lake Paiutes, 134

Quetelet, Adolphe, 216
Quezaltenango Indians, 318
Quiche language, 318

Rabinowitch, Eugene, 182–183
Race, 3, 181–227; and behavior, 187–188, 192, 224–227; concepts of, 188–209, 224; dichotomy-dismissal approach, 200; and evolution, 186–187; holistic synthesis approach, 201–202; and intelligence, 182–183, 209, 217, 218–222, 223, 224, 226–227; unlike-but-equal approach, 200–201
Racial hierarchy, 199–200, 209, 210–212, 216, 217, 218, 221, 227, 299, 301, 308–309. See also Genetic inferiority model
Racism, 3, 57, 58, 173, 179, 182–227, 233, 234, 314; advocates of, 210–212; at ASA meeting, 171–172; in Hunters Point, 363, 367, 368; institutional, 299–310; positive, 184; scientific, 185. See also Race
Radiation and radioactivity, 207, 387, 394, 395, 407, 408, 421
Radical Caucus, 8, 436
Rage, caused by discrimination, 77–78, 82
Rainwater, Lee, 231, 259, 265, 266
Ramapo, N.Y., 404
Rand Corporation (RAND), 141, 142, 175–176
Rasmussen, Knud, 371, 374, 375–376, 377
Real culture, 104
Realpolitik, 113, 115, 120
Reason, and social scientist, 10–18
Red Cloud, 134, 135
Redfield, Robert, 7, 437, 466
Red Lake Chippewa tribe, 136
Regional Plan Association, 401
Relevance, and anthropology, 1–4
Religions, 123, 271–272, 334, 358; current role of, 281, 284; in Latin America, 443, 445, 446, 448, 449–450, 452; as new codes, 472, 474, 475; among Ojibwa, 247, 248–249; and population control, 392, 420, 421; Sioux Ghost dance, 68–75, 105; and Yir Yoront, 460, 462–464. See also Witch-craft
Repression, and personality development, 76–83, 105–106
Research: clandestine, 47, 48, 53, 165; problems of, 163–165
Research and development approach, 464–470
Reservation, life on the, 130–137, 245–253, 273, 294–298
Responsibility of anthropologists, 3, 8–61, 157–159, 160–161, 162, 179, 208; to popularize concepts, 55–57; principles of, 46–48
Resynthesis, 474–475
Revenge, among Netsilik, 373–375, 378
Revitalization processes, 452, 470–475
Revolutionary organizations, and change, 101, 105, 106, 473–474
Rhodesia, 159, 160

Riesman, David, 282, 284
Rio Arriba County, 102
Rioting: and crowding, 398–399; at Hunters
    Point, 361–369, 380, 382
Rites of passage, 286–287, 289, 291–292, 293,
    322, 329
Ritual in schools: American, 285–290, 322–323,
    326, 330; Canadian, 290–294
RNA, 221
Roles: of black males, 81, 260–264, 362, 364,
    365, 368; conflicts of, in Ojibwa life,
    247–249; of mice in overcrowding study,
    396; modeling of, 80–81, 262–263, 292;
    in urban life, 405–406. See also Sex roles
Rosebud reservation, 74, 75
Rosier, Bernard, 385
Roszak, Theodore, 9
Rubel, Arthur J., 3, 66–67, 103–107
Rural vs. urban behavior, 400–406
Rusk, Dean, 141
Russia, 122, 211, 323, 475
Rwanda, 196

Saberwal, Satish, 131, 152, 174–177
Sabines, 84
Sacks, Karen, 45
Sahel, 385
Sahlins, Marshall, 148–152
Saigon, 175
St. Louis, 399
San Antonio, Texas, strike in, 91–96
San Carlos Apaches, 133
San Francisco, 361–369, 382
San Francisco Housing Authority, 361, 362, 363,
    364, 365
San Francisco Human Rights Commission, 365
San Joaquin Corporation, 100–101
San Joaquin del Rio de Chama Grant, 100–101
San Juan, 237
San Juan Norte, 455
Sanchez, Alfonso, 97, 99, 102
Santa Cruz Chinautla, 452
Santa Fe, N. M., 99, 100
Santiago, Chile, 139–140
Santo Domingo, 138
"Sardine Syndrome," 388–389
Sartre, Jean-Paul, 111, 157
Saudi Arabia, 159
Sawyer County, 250
Scandinavian, 67
Schizophrenics, and space, 398
Schooling, 275–330; "cult of," 320–326, 327;
    in Latin America, 315–326; patterns of,
    329–330; and social equality, 321. See also
    Education
Schools, 4; American secondary, 285–290; inter-
    vention by, 299–310; role of village,
    315–320; as societies, 280–284
Scotland, 158
Scots-English, 66, 67
Sédar, Leópold, 169
Self-confidence, 440, 441
Self-esteem: and culture of poverty, 244, 254,
    258, 259, 272; and discrimination, 76–79,
    80, 82, 83, 106, 156; and resynthesis, 474
"Self-fulfilling prophecy," 361
Self-hatred, 77, 83, 254, 362, 364
Self-ideal, 258
Self-identity, 100, 284, 329
Self-image, 67, 106, 238, 321; of blacks, 79–83,
    258, 362, 364, 365, 367, 368, 369;
    of Indian, 246, 249, 250–252
Seminole Indians, 85
Seneca Indians, 471
Separatism in U.S., 369
Serological classification, 189–190, 191,
    417–418
Sertao, 385
Sex differences: and crowding, 400; infanticide,
    418; and trust, 404
Sex discrimination, resolutions against, 45, 47
Sex roles: among blacks, 81–82, 83; in Latin
    America, 445–446; among Yir Yoront,
    459–460, 461, 462. See also Roles
Sexual activities: and crowding studies, 396, 397;
    among blacks, 81, 83, 262–264; among
    Houmas, 84–85; among Ojibwa, 248–249,
    250

Sexual practices and offenses among Gusii, 4,
    335, 336–345, 379
Shaman, 373, 377
Shapiro, Harold Arthur, 91–96, 107
Sharp, Lauriston, 457–464
Shelley, John, 365–366
Shockley, William, 218, 222, 223
Shoshoni Indians, 71
Sicily and Sardinia, 334
Siegel, Bernard J., 4, 334–336, 379–382
Simmel, George, 284, 401
Simpson, G. G., 190, 206
Singleton, John, 4, 278–280, 326–330
Sioux Indians, 66, 68, 71–76; outbreak of 1890,
    71–76, 105; current problems of, 134–135,
    137; and schooling, 292–293, 294
Sirioni Indians, 26–31
Skinner, B. F., 214
Skinner, Elliott, P., 168
Sleeping sickness among Hausa, 451
Smith, Edwin, 128
Smog, 407, 408
Sociability, and discrimination, 78–81, 82
Social change, and village schools, 315–320.
    See also Change, Revitalization, and
    Violence
Social controls: among Mayans, 352–354; and
    the police, 362–363; and public opinion,
    364–365
Social integration, and education, 315–320,
    320–326
Social mobility, 239, 278–279, 283, 284, 442,
    444, 446–447, 448
Social pathology model, 299, 301, 308, 309, 310
Social responsibility in urban life, 402–406
Social Security Administration, 323
Socialism, and poverty, 238–239
Socialization: education as, 327; and poverty,
    233, 234, 262–264; and schooling,
    278–279, 281, 283, 290, 291
"Sociological imagination," 10–18
Song duels, 371, 375–376
Sonoran, Mexico, 453
South Africa, 159, 160, 173, 176, 236, 237,
    334, 475
South America. See Latin America
South Dakota Indians, 292
Southeast Asia, 53, 54–55, 148, 152, 153, 154,
    157, 161, 178–179
Southern Arabia, 160
South Nyanza Luo, 336, 337, 340
South-West Africa, 159, 160
Southwestern Anthropological Association, 58
Spain, 443, 445, 449, 450, 475
Spalding, Douglas, 213, 217
SPEARPOINT, 142
Special Operations Research Organization (SORO),
    138, 141, 142–143, 144
Species reticulum, 202, 207–208
Speck, F. G., 85, 89
Spillius, James, 33
Spindler, George, 293, 327, 328
Springdale, N.Y., 41–42
Spring Valley, N.Y., 404
Spuhler, James N., 188–192
Srinivas, M. N., 176–177
"Stage of exhaustion," 474
Stamler, Paul J., 407–416
Standard of living, 67; of chicano workers, 91–93,
    96; and cost of education in Latin America,
    321–324; at poverty level, 234–240
Standing Man Community, 295–296, 297
Standing Rock reservation, 75
Stanford-Binet test, 221
Starvation, 385, 386, 392, 429
State Industrial Commission, 95
State of the Union Message of 1968, 221
Statistics, and racial comparisons, 215–216
Status: of blacks, 82–83, 312, 362; of Indians,
    84–91, 249–250, 251, 252, 297; in Latin
    America, 318, 323–324, 442, 443,
    446–447; and poverty, 256–258, 272, 398;
    and schooling, 4, 278–279, 283, 289, 290,
    292, 318, 323–324
"Status politics," 281, 284
Status strivings, 82
Steenhoven, Geert van den, 372, 373, 375, 377,
    378

Stereotypes, 185, 222, 241, 249–250, 251, 252,
    314, 364, 367, 369, 471
Sterilization, 421, 427
Sternglass, Ernst, 387
Steward, Omer C., 55–57
Stoll, Estie, 395–400
Stonequist, Everett, 106
Stony Point, N.Y., 404
Strain, in Indian villages, 355–358, 360, 380
Strategic Social Science, 148, 150
Strategies and tactics for change, 450–457, 477
Streetcorner men, 240–245, 260, 261, 262,
    263–264
Street life, 81
Stress: and animal studies, 396–397; and change,
    462, 464, 471–472, 474; and pollution,
    407; and violence, 335, 379, 381, 388–389,
    394, 398–399, 430
Stress induction, strategy of, 451–452, 454
Strike, by chicano pecan shellers, 91–96
Strontium-90, 387
Student Mobilization Committee, 9, 53, 54
Student Nonviolent Coordinating Committee
    (SNCC), 60, 101
Subcultures or subsystems, 4, 107, 268; among
    blacks, 240–245, 253–259, 260–264; of
    Ojibwa, 245–253; of poverty, 232–273; and
    schooling, 279, 280, 307
Subgroups, and conflict, 356–357
Success, 471; and individualism, 444–445;
    -phobia, 83; poverty and, 257–258, 262,
    270, 272; and schooling, 278–279, 292,
    328
Sudan, 159
Sudzal, 129
Suicide, 335, 346, 370, 380, 395
Sumeria, 334
Sunlit Cloud Iguana Clan, 459, 460, 463
Survival, rules for, among Mayans, 350
Swandesh, Frances L., 96–103, 106
Symbols in our culture, 103–104, 105, 107
Synthetic organic chemical usage, 409, 410–413,
    415
Syria, 159

Taiwan, 33–38, 159
Talbert, Carol, 310–315, 327, 328
Tanzania, 159
Taos Pueblo, 99
Taxonomy of mankind, 192–198, 200, 205, 224
Technical assistance programs. See Assistance
    programs
Technology; and change, 239, 423, 424, 455,
    456, 457, 463, 478; and pollution, 387,
    389, 392, 407–416, 430
Teklum Mayans, 346–354, 370, 380, 382
Terrebonne Parish, 86–87
Terre sans mal, 475
Texas, 91–96, 99
Thailand, 53, 54, 64–65, 139, 148, 159, 160,
    165, 178
Third world, 3, 109–179, 381, 385; academic
    colonialism in, 154–156, 171, 174–177;
    African studies and ASA, 165–174; assistance
    programs to, 113–126, 129, 130; Indian
    reservations as, 130–137; and Project
    Camelot, 138–152, 163, 164, 178;
    responsibilities of anthropologists to,
    126–130, 157–159, 160–161, 162, 179;
    and schooling, 280, 320–326; and U.S.
    intervention, 118–121, 138–152, 163,
    175–176, 178–179. See also specific
    countries
Tibaera, Bolivia, 27, 29, 30
Tierra Amarilla Grant and uprising, 97, 98, 99,
    100, 102
Tijerina, Cristobal, 101, 102
Tijerian, Reies, 97, 98, 100, 101, 102
Tiyospaye, 297–298
Tlingit, 292
Tobago, 160
Togo, 160
Torres, Camilo, 325
Totemic clans, 459, 460, 462–463
Totonicipan Indians, 318
Trading partner relationships, 458–459, 461–462
Traits. See Phenotype
Transfer culture, 472, 473, 474

Transportation, 407, 414–415, 473
Treaty of Guadalupe Hidalgo, 97
Tribal Council, 296, 297
Tribalism, 132–133
Trinidad, 160
Truman, Harry S., 114, 115, 120
Trust of strangers, and urban life, 403–404
Turkey, 139, 159, 385
Turner, Terence S., 55
Tutsi, 196
Tuxtla area, 316
Twelfth Annual African Studies Association
    Meeting at Montreal, 165–174
Typological thinking, 185, 192, 208, 216
Tzeltal language, 317, 346

Udall, Stewart, 387
Uganda, 159
Ulcers, and crowding, 397
Underdeveloped nations. See Third world
Unemployment, 232, 235, 236, 240–245,
    272, 291, 361, 368
United Arab Republic, 159
United Cannery, Agricultural, Packing and
    Allied Workers Union (Ucapawa), 94, 95
United Nations, 57, 114, 120, 432; Economic
    Commission for Africa, 168; Children's Fund
    (UNESCO), 114, 119, 120, 200
United States: AAA resolutions concerning govern-
    ment of, 43–44, 45, 59; and academic
    colonialism, 154–156, 171, 174–177;
    assistance programs of, 113–126, 129, 130,
    175; democracy in, 13, 15–17; and Indians,
    71–76, 439, 440, 441; intervention by,
    113–126, 129, 138–152; orbit of
    power of, 159–161; population control in,
    423–429; production and pollution in,
    407–416; urban life in, 400–406. See also
    Government.
U.S. Air Force, 141, 142
U.S. Army, 138, 139, 140, 141, 142, 143, 145,
    146, 147, 149, 150, 151, 164, 175
U.S. Bureau of the Census, 408
U.S. Congress, 115, 120, 136, 137, 138,
    140–141, 143–144, 145
U.S. Department of Commerce, 2
U.S. Department of Defense (DOD), 163, 175;
    and India, 152, 153, 154, 178; and Latin
    America, 138, 139, 141, 142
U.S. Department of Health, Education, and
    Welfare (HEW), 164
U.S. Department of Labor, 95–96, 232
U.S. Department of State, 138, 140, 142, 143,
    144, 147–148, 149, 163, 164, 175, 238
U.S. House Foreign Affairs Committee, 141
U.S. Immigration and Naturalization Service, 163
U.S. Medical Center for Federal Prisoners, 398
U.S. Senate Committee on Foreign Relations, 138,
    141, 153
U.S. Supreme Court, 300
Universities, and government grants, 144–145
University: American, 139, 144–145, 168;

Boston, 167; City University of New York,
    403, 405, 406; Columbia, 168, 396; Cornell,
    40, 41, 42, 453, 456, 464, 467; George
    Washington, 175; Harvard, 175; Indiana,
    175; McGill, 177; Michigan State, 175, 176,
    397; New York, 405; Northwestern, 175,
    398; Pennsylvania State, 398; Stanford, 167,
    175, 405; Temple, 167; of California, 111,
    152, 154, 175, 398; Yale, 175; of Chicago,
    438; of Chile, 139–140; of Michigan, 416;
    of Minnesota, 398; of Oslo, 139–140; of
    Pittsburgh, 139–140; of Washington, 167,
    314
Unlike-but-Equal approach, 199, 200–201
Urban League, 106
Urban life: and crowding, 394, 395–400; and
    human behavior, 400–406; and ghetto
    education, 310–315; in Latin America,
    320–321; and pollution, 387–388
Urban renewal programs, 398, 399
Utah, 99
Ute Indians, 70
U Thant, 432
Utilitarian strategies, 454
Utopic strategy, 450–451, 477

Valentine, Charles, 233, 315, 328
Value-freedom, myth of, 1–2, 3, 60, 162
Values: anthropologist and, 10–18, 59–61, 162,
    464–466; blacks and, 300–301, 313;
    change and, 122–123, 128, 333, 355–360,
    380, 453; of diverse cultures, 128,
    178–179; in Latin America, 448–450; of
    Ojibwa, 249–250, 252; and poverty,
    232–236, 240, 253–259, 260, 262, 266,
    267, 272; and schooling, 279, 283, 284,
    292–294; secondary, 233, 236, 244–245,
    253, 260, 273; and value judgments,
    160–161, 464–466. See also Middle-class
    values
Vandalism, and urban life, 405
Van den Berghe, Pierre L., 171–172
Van Gennep, A., 285
Venezuela, 139, 159, 160, 417, 419
Vicious cycle, of Fox-White relations, 438, 439,
    440, 441
Vicos, hacienda of, 453–455, 464–470
Vicosinos, 4, 453–455, 456, 464–470
Vidich, Arthur, 39–41, 42–43
Vietnam, 44, 58, 60, 136, 139, 143, 156–158,
    159, 160, 161, 175, 436
Viner, Jacob, 120
Violence, 4, 239, 251, 331–382, 430, 473; black
    rioting, 361–369, 398–399; and crowding,
    395, 425; in India, 355–360; among
    Mayans, 346–354; schooling and, 325–326;
    and stress, 335, 379, 381, 388–389, 430,
    472
VISTA, 294, 296, 297
von Frankenberg, G., 193
Vulnerability, and social responsibility, 403, 404,
    406

Wallace, Anthony F., 103, 105, 470–475
Waller, Willard, 281, 284, 327
Wallerstein, Immanuel, 161, 173–174
War, 44, 55–56, 59, 61, 223, 379–380, 386,
    389, 395, 429, 476
Washburn, S. L., 197, 206
Washington, D.C., 138, 139, 140
WASPS, 279
Water pollution, 407, 408, 411, 412, 430
Watts riot, 364, 365
Wax, Murray, 281, 284, 294–298, 327
Wax, Rosalie H., 294–298, 327
Wealth, redistribution of, 129, 454, 465–467
Weaver, Thomas, 1–4
Welfare. See Public welfare
Welfare state, U.S. as, 425, 426
Wenner-Gren Foundation, 56
West Africa, 279
West Clarkstown, N.Y., 404
Western Sahara, 385
West Indians, 166, 169, 170, 171
White Mountain Apaches, 133
White Reform Caucus, 169, 172
Whyte, William Foote, 39–41, 442–450, 454
Wife-swapping, among Eskimos, 371, 373, 375
Wirth, Louis, 401, 405
Wisconsin, 245–253
Witchcraft: and Gusii, 337; and Mayan homicides,
    347, 348, 349, 350, 351, 352, 353, 354;
    among Netsilik, 371, 372, 373–374, 377,
    378; and Seneca, 471
Wolf, Eric R., 53, 54, 55, 59
Women: 100, 281, 400, 404; discrimination
    against, 45, 47; and education, 281, 282,
    304–306; role among blacks, 81–82, 83,
    236, 240 (See also Ghetto mothers and
    Matrifocal families); role among Tekum
    Mayan, 348–349; role among Yir Yoront,
    458, 459, 460, 461, 462
Work, and Puritan ethic, 448–449, 474
World Health Organization (WHO), 120, 388
Worsley, Peter, 159, 161
Wounded Knee, 72, 75
"Write Your Own Book" program, 314

Xavante, 416, 417, 419

Yanomama, 416, 417, 418, 419, 420
Yemen, 139, 159, 160
Yir Yoront, 457–464, 478
Youth. See Adolescents
Youth for Service, 365
Youth Opportunity Center, 368
Yule, 216

Zero population growth, 423, 426, 427, 429
Zimbardo, P. G., 405
Zionist movement, 171, 177
Zulu tribe, 334
Zunil Indians, 318

1 2 3 4 5 6 7 8 9 10 11 12 13 14 15 16 17 18 19 20 21 22 23 24 25   78 77 76 75 74 73